# *A Gardener's Guide to Native Plants*

# *of Northeastern Pennsylvania*

**ISBN: 978-0615450988**

Published by Pennystone Books, Henryville, Pennsylvania

# A Gardener's Guide
## to Native Plants
### of Northeastern Pennsylvania

Geoffrey Mehl
The Pennystone Project
www.pennystone.com

*For Judy*

# Table of Contents

## *Introduction*

*Continued next page*

## Table of Contents, continued

# Preface

Some years ago, we had the opportunity to ask "the soil guy" at a major public garden a question about a problem with a soil that might be too rich. Patiently looking for a solution, he turned to an enormous three-ring binder. When asked about it, he shrugged. It was simply the soil research they had developed and gathered for every species on the site.

We could only wonder how many gardeners would covet such valuable material. But of course, it's the proprietary data that makes a thriving horticultural institution competitive and will never find its way onto anyone's bookshelf.

Our own investigation into native plants, their habitats and how to grow them, how they fit into ecological communities, and the soils upon which they grow has, over time, created a mound of notes, snippets of data from here and there, and a sagging bookshelf of reference books

There are more than 2,100 species of plants native to the North American continent that include Pennsylvania in their natural range. There are nearly 400 different cataloged ecological communities in the several dozen major forest systems identified in the commonwealth, probably just the tip of the iceberg in the relatively recent science of vegetation mapping.

Our focus is on a smaller region — the four northeastern counties of Carbon, Monroe, Pike and Wayne. It is here that three major ecological regions intersect (the actual map point is in the vicinity of the intersection of Routes 715 and 314 in Monroe County). And it is also here that two vast groups of plants — those extending northward into Canada and those extending south into the southern Appalachians — really overlap.

So just within the neighborhood, there are 1,300 species of native plants, 130 ecological communities and nearly 100 different kinds of soils.

The Pennystone Project (www.pennystone. com) is an effort to encourage the use of native plants in landscape designs by gathering and sharing information as freely as possible. While our focus is on the four northeastern counties of Pennsylvania, some of the material may be useful to a wider audience, especially the information about various species of plants.

Unlike the public garden's collection, this is not proprietary material; any enthusiast willing to rummage around and follow some occasionally challenging trails can find it. Our objective with this book was to save duplication of effort, leave some trail markers for individual investigation and perhaps some ideas to inspire landscape design.

# *Rendezvous*

We come from many paths but gather at a common point: landscaping with native plants promises solutions, opportunities and enlightenment.

Some carry a nagging anxiety about the health of the planet, some bring gardening experience and search for new challenges, and still others may be simply frustrated with the neighborhood deer herd or an exasperating patch of shade.

The trail to a native plant landscape is littered with obstacles and rich with opportunities.

Our travels will take us to craggy peaks, mucky swamps, embattled floodplains, rolling meadows and miles and miles of forests of all kinds. We shall visit more than 130 ecological communities in three major geologic regions on 100 different kinds of soils, within which more than 1,200 species of plants thrive.

And yet all of this is found in the very northeastern corner of Pennsylvania, loosely described as the Poconos: Carbon, Monroe, Pike and Wayne counties.

The more we explore, the more we discover that landscaping with natives is riddled with interesting side trails and diversions. For every answer, there are only more questions, and for every conclusion only new concepts to consider. It is not an all-or-nothing proposition, but it can be. It is not uncomplicated, but it can be simple. It is not care-free, but it can be easy.

It is, ultimately, what we choose to make it. Our only limits are our resources — time, interest, investment — but even the most modest involvement brings satisfaction.

On this journey, we discover that we are not so much in control of the habitat as we are a participant in the ecosystem. This can be an exhilarating experience in the smallest garden.

## A sense of perspective

We stroll through vast public gardens or trek through dramatic wilderness parks to harvest inspiration. When we thumb through periodicals and books, we discover motivation. When we become uneasy about environmental matters, we capture resolve.

But when we transplant dreams to our own limited resources, we can encounter discouragement. To regain our footing, we simply must recognize:

- A garden with few plants in a small space can be more challenging than a huge horticultural display.

- A stunning wilderness ecosystem cannot be replicated, or even modeled, in a home garden, but merely suggested.

- With a bit of careful planning, success with native plants is virtually assured.

- Any installation of appropriate native species makes a positive contribution to the health of the planet.

- It's entirely possible to spend less money and less time on a stunning landscape than with conventional design ... and protect natural resources as well.

Those with limited landscaping experience will find greater confidence with some preliminary planning and education. Quality reference materials offer better answers and direction than impulse shopping at a garden center.

Those with more expertise know that with expanding horizons comes the excitement of the challenge of applying research to existing landscape themes.

But for all, size is less important than perspective. A garden is as much amusement and recreation as it is artistic expression; when it becomes a chore, it is too big, too complicated and should be reduced to a level of pleasure and satisfaction.

## Nature drives design

Landscaping is often coupled with the adjectives *natural* and *sustainable*, and they are not necessarily synonymous.

*Natural* suggests an evolving landscape that might appear to be self-driven. We often speak of plant species that are used to "naturalize" an area — i.e., spread without constraint to cover the ground, methodically developing a landscape that we observe but not overtly manage. Or it can suggest using a combination of wildflowers in some rough pattern to imply that it all grew there by itself — i.e., it is naturally occurring.

Natural smacks of marketing. We all like natural in our food, lifestyle and gardens because it is the opposite of artificial (phony, pretentious, fake, synthetic). We are attracted to natural landscapes because they are often portrayed as easy to care for, minimal effort, simple.

*Sustainable* is a relatively new expression, slippery with connotations, sometimes depending on who's pitching what. It generally implies ecologically-friendly development and activities, often with a good measure of social justice and economic premises thrown in. The criteria can become quite exotic. But the noted architect and environmentalist William McDonough summed it up brilliantly with a simple, profound question: "How can we design in a way that loves *all* the children of *all* species for *all* time?"

Theoreticians continually develop sustainability models and debate policies to encourage it. Gardeners, meanwhile, are left with two options:

- control an artistic concept with whatever means are necessary (chemical fertilizers, watering, use of any species of plant that supports the design, etc.), or

- adapt to localized microhabitats and circumstances, and design to support the potential for a self-sustaining landscape.

The first approach is traditional and literally off the shelf. The commercial nursery industry is well-prepared with standardized ideas, plans, solutions, suggestions, materials and supplies. We need only to pick from an appealing array of landscape kits, spend the money, and decorate our property. With any luck, it might actually work and even be *natural.*

The sustainable alternative is a bit more involved. Because of habitat requirements, varied ranges and subtle character, many native species are difficult to mass market and so we must ferret them out. Many landscaping conventions do not apply, and nature — the real natural — ultimately drives design. Much of the published research is oriented to botanists and ecologists, not home landscapers. The learning curve is thus a bit steeper, but not insurmountable.

In traditional landscaping, someone has done the thinking; we need only spend the money and be comfortable with conformity. In native plant landscaping, we must do the thinking, but the upfront cost can be substantially lower and the adventure and satisfaction level much higher.

## Natives in conventional landscapes

Native plants, simply on the basis of visual merit, can support and enhance conventional landscapes in a variety of ways, including solving problems.

An impressive array of ferns of all sizes and textures balance exotic ornamentals in shade gardens, but *Actaea racemosa* (black cohosh) and *Actaea podocarpa* (mountain bugbane) contribute major drama with their summertime spikes of white flowers. *Rudbeckia, Echinacea, Heliopsis* and *Helianthus* species contribute relatively low-maintenance zest to meadow beds.

Interesting and well-behaved low-growing species offer a range of edge plants and accents. We might opt for the color and bloom character of *Chrysogonum virginianum* (goldenstar), the fluffy early spring display of *Tiarella cordifolia* (foam-flower) or the lush texture of Asarum canadense (wild ginger)

Difficult circumstances might be spots with complex drainage concerns, steep dry banks, or shallow, weak soils found at the base of many maples. This may require an open-minded approach, like choosing the finer texture of *Deschampsia flexuosa* (wavy hairgrass) in xeric shade rather than the firm form of a decorative sedge that insists on more moisture. Outlying garden areas, beyond the reasonable ability for close management, may beg for exuberant spreaders that need only lots of space to roam, such as *Anemone canadensis* (Canada anemone), *Polemonium reptans* (spreading Jacob's ladder) or *Geranium maculatum* (wild geranium).

Browsing plant lists sometimes offers unexpected delights. For example, hosta enthusiasts wait patiently for spikes to appear in mid-spring, but can celebrate the season much earlier by interplanting with *Mertensia virginiana* (Virginia bluebells). Mertensia is up very early, blooms exuberantly and retreats to full dormancy just as hostas unfurl for the season. As autumn wanes, wood asters, particularly *Symphyotrichum cordifolium* (blue wood aster) give a late burst of color just as leaves form the falling curtain on the season.

Of the 2,150 species of native plants in Pennsylvania, nearly 1,200 are commercially available, and of those 760 include the northeastern counties as home. There is just no shortage of opportunities.

## The myth of moisture requirements

A popular generalization asserts that landscaping with native plants is ecologically shrewd because natives require much less water than popular introduced species.

Just as many hybrids are developed specifically to withstand periods of drought, there are native plants that can handle prolonged dry periods, and we tend to find them in habitats where drainage is fast, microclimate is warmer, and rainfall erratic.

However, these are relatively few in number. In nature, as in any artificial environment, plant populations tend to congregate around reliable sources of water, and the vast majority prefer moist, well-drained, soils.

Northeastern Pennsylvania typically sees an average of 50 inches of precipitation annually, and data suggest an average distribution of about

4 inches per month year round — about the moisture requirements for most garden plants.

Botanists suggest plant moisture requirements have less to do with the ongoing supply but more toward how long a given species can do without it. Hence, xeric species are less sensitive to dry spells than wetland dwellers and ecosystems are often driven by how water is either discarded or hoarded. It is here that native plant enthusiasts pay most attention.

Helpful direction comes from the U.S. Fish and Wildlife Service, which has researched many native species of trees, shrubs and herbaceous plants for probability of occurrence in wetlands. A coded scale, ranging from 1 to 99 percent probability of occurrence, suggests the ongoing moisture requirements for many species and gives us the familiar designations of UPL, FACU, FAC, FACW and OBL (dry to wet), with shades in between. *(See page 305 for details; these designations help us to determine correct habitat for plants)*

Summit soils tend to be dry, while bottomland features — especially swamps, lake edges, and primary floodplains — tend to be saturated most of the time. The varied habitats found in between provide clues on moisture requirements for many species that must be met if we are to enjoy success in the landscape.

While silts, clays and peats are materials favored by wetland plants and coarse sands for xeric species, the context and nature of humus and compost layers play critical roles in stabilizing water supplies for an enormous range of plants. The lessons they offer suggest strategies all gardeners may find helpful for wise resource use.

## The myth of easy care

Native species are often touted as being rugged, durable, easy-care, grow-anywhere plants, thus the perfect landscape solution for the time-harried gardener.

Like any generalization in landscaping this is best met with skepticism. Some species have the reputation as "good do-ers" but many more can be amazingly fussy. And so to the assertion, the caveat is, "it depends."

Self-sustaining ecosystems in nature may be the basis the "easy-care" argument. After all, no one tends the day-to-day needs of a group of plants in the middle of a national park or preserve. They clearly appear to fend for themselves *when in the correct habitat and when they can compete for space.*

A shrewd designer evaluates habitat and adapts to it. Localized climate, soil character, moisture (both long-term averages and short term variables), and subtle patterns in nutrition — such as specifically what kind of leaf litter arrives on an annual basis — together can form very specific habitats. The interactions of various species may also have a dramatic impact on the success of the entire community.

In ideal circumstances, virtually any species of plant will grow to a genetic maximum, reproduce, and colonize to the limit of the situation. But nature is rarely ideal — hence the "balance" that we heard of as school children. Each species has a range of adaptation, a sometimes demonstrable survival minimum as well as a perfect circumstance.

There are, happily for some and to the consternation of others, native species that have adapted to very wide ranges of habitats and perform well in varied circumstances. *Acer rubrum* (red maple) ranks as the most common tree in the region as a result, with some species of *Quercus* (oaks) right behind. Aggressive species of ferns such as *Dennstaedtia punctilobula* (hayscented fern) and *Pteridium aquilinum* (northern bracken fern) race through leaf litter to form enormous colonies when deer have browsed away all competition.

However, legions of plant species are so limited in range that inclusion into our landscape depends on whether we populate a carefully appraised habitat or are willing to do the work to create one in miniature. These species often hover on the edges of survival and, of course, are what prompts us to conservation of special wild places.

To adapt our landscape design to include them, especially when we come to possess an appropriate microhabitat, is a positive environmental action. To demolish the habitat to create something more convenient is an expedient but negative environmental action.

And so we are left to *think*, to evaluate, search and perhaps modify our design. A lush and healthy landscape signals our success.

## Size matters ... but only sometimes

A nearby, impressive and popular native plant display, open to the public, offers us a wide array of examples to model in our back yard. Easily accessible, no admission and open year-round, it exhibits many hundreds of plant species in stunning, self-sustaining ecological communities. It has a understandably substantial full-time staff and attracts serious students of ecology.

The total size of this wildscape is 68,714 acres. Most of us are familiar with it as the Delaware Water Gap National Recreation Area.

This is not an exceptionally large national park, but it protects of a variety of important ecosystems along an important eastern river system, including the durable upland forests that occupy the Delaware River Valley. So total size matters: ecological communities must be completely encompassed to function freely.

While public parks inspire our designs, they can also overwhelm us. How it is possible for individuals to conserve or even model ecosystems of this magnitude? Our own back yard project seems puny; time, energy, funding, and skills conspire to whittle ambitions to practical size.

To avoid discouragement, *garden well in a small space.* Masters of bonsai tend gardens of just a square foot or so to levels of artistic perfection, sometimes for many generations in a culture of design that *suggests*, not replicates or models, the beauty of the natural world. Stunning beauty in miniscule courtyards and shallow pots holds the attention of the gardener and provides endless interest.

Rather than attempting manor-scale landscapes, we concentrate on perhaps a small sitting area, to which we retreat in free moments to unwind, relax, and tinker with a manageable garden. As our time and interest allows, we expand with restraint.

When we compare our exquisitely developed, perfectly groomed and visually attractive "wildscape" to the vastness of a park, we may also recognize the park has limitations, too. There are weeds everywhere, design is chaotic and disorganized, paths need grooming and many of the naturally-occurring species are just not very attractive.

Perhaps size indeed matters, but not as we might initially believe.

## Compressions of nature

Native plant landscaping often becomes equated with wildland conservation. Perhaps we dwell in a meadow, a woodland or for whatever odd reason a swamp, active floodplain or bog. We might believe that if we remove all introduced species and install a prescribed set of natives, our reward will be a classic, fully-functioning ecosystem.

As much as we might yearn to "put it back the way it was," replicating or restoring a functioning ecosystem can be an insurmountable challenge.

Environmental restoration comes with substantial hurdles:

- Soil structure on residential lots has been substantially altered. Simple excavation impacts subtle divisions in soil layers, especially humus layers, permanently changing the habitat.

- More than a third of the native species are commercially unavailable. Sometimes this is not a major concern, especially with families of plants such as Carex; but in many cases, important species are simply not on the market. Poaching is frowned upon, if not illegal.

- Even commercially available species may not adapt well. In ecosystem restoration, *provenance* is crucial; oftentimes, reintroduction of a species implies that it must come from within 50 miles of the site. Shopping for natives can be a national search, and while the species may be correct, localized evolution may lead to failure on a site hundreds of miles distant.

- Many species are simply not desirable landscape plants. Some are weedy in appearance, others are extremely aggressive, and more are problematic for other reasons — for example, *Toxicodendron radicans* is a significant component of some ecological communities, but few of us consider eastern poison ivy as attractive landscape specimen.

- Herbivores, or the lack of them, may have substantial impact. Many gardeners are continually frustrated with deer browsing, which will almost certainly be an issue with most native species. Exclusionary fencing creates a different set of problems, most of it centering around the consequences of a patch of land without predators. The usual difficulty are thousands of seedling trees that almost instantly take root.

Functioning ecosystems are *groups* of communities that interact with each other and perform as a larger unit. Segmentation lacks the supporting neighborhood structures, and simply may not have enough square footage (or acreage) to manage on its own.

Instead, consider gardens as compressions of nature, organized in an artistic manner for visual appeal. Draw upon nature for inspiration, but respond with horticultural standards. It may be impossible to get it prefect, but getting close is an admirable and achievable goal.

## Progressive planning

The most common patterns in home landscaping are often summarized in one of two approaches:

- A comprehensive plan, often prepared by a design professional, that includes all hardscaping and most of the plant installations in a single construction event. The advantage of having a completed landscape is countered by the initial cost and reliance on typically off-the-shelf design. Because most landscape designers and contractors do not build with native plants, the end solution will likely be almost entirely introduced species.

- An evolving plan, often resulting from springtime inspiration and browsing a favorite garden center. Native plant sales, often to benefit environmentally-oriented organizations, are commonly spring events and feature a relatively limited range of popular species.

We replace plants that no longer appeal or extend planting areas. Driven by affordability of the moment, this approach can lead to design decisions organized on impulse and patchwork, disorganized results.

A more organized approach, especially when landscaping with natives is a disciplined process that begins with site analysis, research, market exploration, plan development and eventually purchase decisions. Our garden evolves in progressive stages toward a resolved design.

Crucial to any landscape development, but especially so with natives, *site analysis* considers light, soil, hydrology, herbivore issues, and use planning for adjacent areas. This is the time to consider garden themes (purely local or larger regional plant palettes, for example) and physical size that can be realistically managed.

*Research plants to build a list* of appropriate species. This may include far more than will actually be installed, but also provides options. Some species are difficult to propagate, others may be acceptably aggressive. The latter may lead to progressive expansion, which may impact long-term planning and purchase decisions.

*Identify plant sources.* This may involve internet or catalog browsing, telephone calls, and perhaps even preliminary visits to nurseries to determine actual availability, cost, and ask those final questions. From this step, actual purchase plans are resolved.

Following completed site preparation, revisit sources, obtain stock, and *install the initial set of plants*, recognizing that judgmental errors may occur and adjustments may be required either in habitat or species mix.

Shopping adventures may also lead to discoveries of species we might have overlooked, but if the initial investigation was thorough, last-minute surprises will be minimal.

## Start small, plan big

The key to an affordable and sustainable landscape is neither unlimited budget or high expertise in horticulture. Our success lies in the plan sketched on a scrap of paper at the kitchen table *plus* the grander vision we hold in the back of our mind.

Because no garden is too small, begin with the affordable and manageable, especially if inexperienced in gardening. This allows us to measure compatibility and interest, become familiar with the vagaries of stewardship, and make the expected mistakes.

Consider two landscapes. One decorates the front of our home and is often called "curb appeal." The second is where we retreat for our private time, typically in the back of the house.

A logical long-term development of the public side of the home is from adjacent to the front door toward building corners and then progressively forward, sometimes along recognized pathways such as driveways or sidewalks.

The private space often begins around patios or decks and then gradually expands toward side and rear property lines. It is here that we must make the most crucial choices in design: a pathway *through* a landscape design or a *negative space* (frequently lawn) bordered by a sweep of interesting objects to view from the outdoor living space. Neither is right or wrong, good or bad, but it's not easy to mix the two.

If appearances are important, we can call upon relatively simple materials for undeveloped space, and there are substantial options for this other than popular turf grasses.

House-to-curb development or elaborate back yard stroll gardens may never be built. That's all right. Any expansion phase may certainly may be honed before actual construction. That's okay, too.

A solid vision keeps an overall landscape design on track to a conclusion to be constrained only by time and interest. Focus on the pleasure and satisfaction with the current garden, knowing that growth doesn't imply back tracking and starting fresh a second time.

## Simple, must-have tools

We're all familiar with the basic arsenal of gardening tools: shovels, rakes, trowels, hoes and cultivators. When purchasing new tools, we're willing to spend a bit more for quality, especially where the handle meets the business end of equipment.

The well-stocked shed might also include any

or all of these, too:

**A six foot, heavy steel pry bar** with a well-rounded top and a wide flat end for separating and lifting rocks. Frost-churned materials in most soils tend to angle downward, and when a shovel meets a rock it can be one of two things: a collection of interlocked *channers* — typically flat chunks of sedimentary rock about six inches long — or boulders about the size of Massachusetts. A hefty pry bar with stone acting as a fulcrum can lift enormous rocks from a planned path or planting bed, even a few inches at a time (carefully use smaller rocks to shore up the rising stone, which will eventually flop onto the surface). Really big rocks make outstanding landscape features and the annoying channers form good stone retaining wall material.

**A two to five pound mallet** is essential for encouraging the pry bar or (see below) for setting marking stakes.

**A pair of tent stakes and at least 8 feet of clothesline** becomes a rudimentary compass for laying out nice curves in paths. Adjust the line length for the desired radius, secure one stake in the ground and use the second one to draw the line in fresh soil. An 8-foot radius curve is about the minimum for a lawn tractor pulling a cart.

**A convenient length of 4-inch ABS plastic pipe** serves as both a guide for path width but also a leveling/smoothing device while building paths. The pipe is cheap and comes in 10-foot lengths; cut to the narrowest width a path will be. Because the pipe is light weight, it can be used easily while on hands and knees. Because it is rigid, it can be used in conjunction with an inexpensive carpenter's level to keep grades even side to side and even steady along path length. It can be used as a rolling pin, light plow, and even a tamper on freshly prepared path material.

**Various lengths of (used) water well pipe** are better for laying out path and bed curves than garden hose because they bend just enough to create smooth lines. Discarded pipe from well pump repair is the best because it's free; otherwise, it's modestly priced in large rolls at most home centers and plumbing supply houses. The downside is storage of pipe when not in use.

**A few bundles of grade surveying stakes,** found at most home centers, are helpful when marking out path or bed lines. Short stakes work nicely with well pipe used for path marking (just stagger them on opposite sides of the pipe); taller stakes are good in conjunction with string and a simple line level to keep stone retaining walls level. Medium sized stakes are helpful in laying out fence lines; start with the two ends and a long length of light rope to set a straight line, then use stakes at locations for fence posts along the path. Tall stakes are good when considering routes of paths and whether equipment can easily and safely navigate the route.

**Long-handled loppers and a simple bow saw** are essential for pruning shrubs and lower limbs on trees, and certainly safer than a chain saw.

**Worn out or ruined garden hose,** cut into short lengths as needed, can be threaded with braided galvanized wire to form support lines for trees and shrubs; the hose will prevent the wire from damaging the bark.

**Construction marking flags**, typically fluorescent orange, sometimes pink, usually in bundles of 25 for a few pennies each at major home centers. When we plant in the fall, it's easy to forget where to expect the plant to show up in the spring, and plant labels are always casualties of frost heaving. The long thin wire gets well into the soil and the plastic flag can be labeled with a indelible permanent marker. Expect only a season or two from these, because the wire rusts.

**A decent pair of bypass shears with a leather holster**. Models that clip onto the belt are convenient, but those where the belt threads through it won't fall off into a huge pile of compost at inconvenient moments. Useful for heavy-duty snipping, shears more significantly give you the proper look of a landscape professional on gardening television shows (those folks *never* wear a cell phone holster).

# On the trail

## Latin spoken here

Few species illustrate the precision of Latin (or scientific) plant names more than *Hydrastis canadensis* (goldenseal), which also variously identified by these common names: Eye balm, Eye root, Ground raspberry, Indian dye, Indian paint, Indian plant, Jaundice root, Orange root, Turmeric root, Wild curcuma, Yellow puccoon and Yellow root. The species, like many, also owns common names in a variety of other languages.

While botanists pursue taxonomy — the seemingly endless endeavor to properly classify species in a genetically correct order — the gardener is gifted with an internationally-agreed identification for discussion purposes in a neutral language with consistent pronunciation rules.

For some, this common ground launches strenuous resistance, frequently that identifying a species by a scientific name implies haughtiness and arrogance, traits out of place when digging in the dirt on hands and knees. So the discussion goes:

> "I don't know how to pronounce (or spell) *Chrysogonum virginianum,* so, too bad, it's green-and-gold and that's that."

> "Actually, it's goldenstar."

> "No, green-and-gold."

> "Well, some people call it golden-knees."

> "They're from Ohio and they don't know any better."

The secure haven of Latin is occasionally ruffled when botanists gather to review research, debate and abruptly make dramatic changes. Those who had barely achieved comfort with *Cimicifuga* — notably *C. racemosa* and *C. americana* — quite literally awoke one day to learn it had become *Actaea racemosa* and *Actaea podocarpa.*

Even more frustrating for some was the complete rearrangement of the genus *Aster* in the new groups *Eurybia* and *Symphyotrichum*. What we knew as white wood aster *(Aster divaricatus)* became *Eurybia divaricata* and the sturdy blue wood aster *(Aster cordifolius)* turned into *Symphyotrichum cordifolium.*

Blue wood aster has at one time or another had 20 synonymous Latin names, particularly in varieties and subspecies. All were consolidated when a single name was settled, reminding us that science continually marches toward greater precision.

Many in the media tolerate our penchant for the comfort of an easy name, so the correct Latin identification is often sometimes in parentheses after the common name. However, a distinct advantage of learning about new plants is that any name is fresh, so the Latin version is as good as any. The proper formatting is Latin first and the courtesy of a common name afterward.

## Interpreting "native"

Most authorities define "native plant" as a species that was discovered to be indigenous in North America at the time of European settlement. This has less to do with cultural arrogance and more to do with wholesale importation of seeds and plants from countries of origin, primarily for agricultural purposes.

Fortunately, colonial botanists were encouraged to investigate native species, and many were named almost right away.

Matters become murky when landscapers attempt to carry the term to narrower political subdivisions. Is a species native to Pennsylvania? Is it native to northeastern Pennsylvania? Is it native to Carbon, Monroe, Pike or Wayne counties?

Ecologists prefer to map the *range* of a species and recognize that many circumstances, large and small, impact range. Glaciers caused everything to shift south; a warming climate permits migration northward. Periodic variations in climate drive some species to higher elevations, or encourage evolution to adapt to new circumstances.

Northeastern Pennsylvania is at a crossroads of many species that range from here northward into Canada and another block that range southward into the southern Appalachians. This results in enormous diversity and gardening options.

Even if the precise range of a particular species in the early eighteenth century were known, land use practices of settlers for the last 300 years have substantially altered the map. For the purposes of modern decorative horticulture, the original map doesn't matter very much. The usefulness of a species is measured only by its success in our garden.

Contemporary vegetation mapping, which really blossomed in just the past 50 years, concerns itself with *distribution* of species — that is, specifically where in a general range a particular plant has been observed. For example, many species are *native* to the continent, have a *range* that includes Pennsylvania as well as varied adjacent states, and a *distribution* that includes the northeastern counties.

Confounding the issue further is the casual expression "wildflower," a plant, most commonly herbaceous, that can survive and reproduce without human support. All natives are wildflowers, but "wildflowers" include many introduced — and some invasive — species as well.

In Pennsylvania, the generally recognized authority for statewide distribution and whether a species is native or introduced (even from elsewhere in the United States and Canada) is the Morris Arboretum of the University of Pennsylvania, summarized in *The Plants of Pennsylvania* (Rhoads and Block), an online database (http://www.paflora.org), and citation by the U.S. Department of Agriculture (http://plants.usda.gov).

For our purposes, wildflower and native are synonymous because introduced species aren't included in the discussion except when useful,

e.g., when invasive presence is of concern.

As a matter of rhetorical convenience, we discuss "natives" of northeastern Pennsylvania in the context that they are continentally native, the range includes Pennsylvania, and distribution includes the northeastern counties.

## Casting a wide native net

In the initial stages of planning native plant gardens, our first decision of somewhat lasting consequence will be defining a thematic palette of species from which we will populate the landscape.

No firm standards exist, nor should they. Each garden is an individual expression of botanical interest and artistic design. To unify a landscape design, establish the theme early on and stay with it.

For a purely conservation or restoration design, sift through ecological communities for an exact or closest match. The nature of existing tree canopy, soil and general site characteristics identifies a researched community or two, from which a plant list will be evident.

In an artistically-defined or specimen garden, an existing site could be modified to create suitable microhabitats for out-of-habitat species. This can be complicated for some plans, or simple for those that are fairly close to the existing situation.

Conservation/restoration gardens — often leaning toward "wildscapes" — will represent the least work, cost and ongoing effort. To counter potential monotony of a limited number of species, design in masses and appreciate the characteristic that a native plant in the right habitat colonizes as far as it can.

Obstacles can include obtaining essential plants for a limited species list, especially when plants may be commercially uncommon, or perhaps undoing environmental damage, most especially with invasives or recent agricultural practices. Commitment to restoration might mean favorite introduced garden plants must go.

Landscapes oriented to artistic design and botanical collection may result in landscapes that could never logically occur in nature, but nonetheless support environmental responsibility. We may garden in the shade, but our collection might include species native to the driest ridgetops to the wettest bogs, perhaps grouped by habitat similarities but generally creating a visually stimulating display.

An illustration is the combination of *Actaea racemosa* (black cohosh) and *Actaea podocarpa* (mountain bugbane) as background or specimen plantings in a pattern to create design rhythm. *A. podocarpa's* Pennsylvania distribution limited to a few southwestern counties and both species rarely overlap. Neither are appropriate for a dry upland site, but localized habitat can be easily created by enriching surface soil with humus. Technically inappropriate for northeastern Pennsylvania, *A. podocarpa* is listed as rare in the state, so it might be argued that including it in a garden is a positive step. Between them, they offer interesting floral displays, one following the other, for sustained midsummer interest.

A strict conservation/restoration garden on a xeric site would exclude both; a more relaxed standard would welcome them if the effort was worthwhile. Either way, set the rules before the first shovelful of soil is turned.

## Vegetation mapping

Native plant enthusiasts are the benefactors of a progressive science called "vegetation mapping." The process searches for relationship patterns between plant species and their environment.

Each new generation of field research and evaluation clarifies and gives more detail to the last. Very broadly defined systems — typically focusing on tree canopy — are subdivided into more specific associations, then communities. The advantage of knowing what species of trees, shrubs and herbaceous plants are found together is the obvious creation of lists of species that could grow well together in our gardens.

More recently, researchers define site characteristics. This might be as general as "cool, north-facing slopes" or as specific as "isolated basins or kettles, lacking inlet or outlet streams, in glaciated regions with nutrient-poor acidic peat soils."

Debate arises among investigators when disturbed lands gradually revert (perhaps) to their original state. At what point is a former farm pasture sufficiently successional to classify as a legitimate ecological community? The cataloging, nonetheless, continues.

The limitations of this process are clear. Only so much research can be funded, only so much land is accessible to measure, and much of Pennsylvania has been developmentally modified, if only by timbering. We are left with a quandary: the number of species with local distribution substantially exceeds the composite list of recognized ecosystems.

If obsessed with pure conservation/restoration, we might be distressed that an accurate prescription is unavailable. But if we are open-minded, we recognize that even if the frontiers of natural science are right in front of us, a hefty stack of useful information is much better than none. Besides, it can be rather exhilarating to be skating along the cutting edge of science and our modest efforts may even make a contribution.

We can also draw good inferences. If two species are in the same community on one list, and a third species is found in similar habitat on a second list, our likelihood of success with all three in the same bed is high.

Few things satisfy gardeners more than a good list of plants; someone has saved us considerable trial and error. The introduction of the Internet, and the use of databases to pool information brings almost all the currently known data to ordinary gardeners such as ourselves.

## The cultivar controversy

One of the more controversial facets of native plant landscaping swirls around the arrival of named varieties known as *cultivars*.

In species taxonomy, subsets are relatively common. An illustration would be *Tiarella cordifolia var. collina*. For reasons differentiated only by botanists, *var.* and *ssp.*, or subspecies, are nearly interchangeable, and connote that a recognized species like foamflower has in nature some aberrations. Very often when taxonomy is tidied up, many of the varieties vanish into footnotes.

In the nursery industry, cultivars are nearly as exciting as hybrids, especially when a named variety is so good that it merits trademarking, for all the obvious rewards of owning the name.

The difference is that while hybrids are crosses between species, a *cultivated variety* concentrates on genetic modification of a singe species, sometimes building on a spontaneous mutation (size, color, variegation, etc.), sometimes enhancing a specific trait (disease or pest resistance, flower size, bloom period, etc.)

We know the curious plant Doll's Eyes by its proper name of *Actaea pachypoda*. We also find a cultivar, "Misty Blue," a product of selective breeding. Is "Misty Blue" really a native? Genetically, yes. If not, we would consider it a hybrid. Is it off limits for a restoration project? Probably so, if only because of local provenance requirements. Is it off limits for a garden? Not really.

Detractors decry deliberate manipulation of plants to create marketing opportunities, while nurseries assert that nature responds to mutations all the time.

*Actaea pachypoda* that grows in Florida is very likely different than the same species found in Quebec, and possibly not interchangeable in the same habitats. Each has adapted local climate conditions — which is why good counsel for mail-order shopping would be to buy from the nearest reliable vendor.

The nursery industry also strives for plants that excel in the widest range of circumstances and field tests new ideas thoroughly and constantly. This is simply of a fact of life when developing products for a fickle public. "Misty Blue" may well be superior in many ways that run-of-the-mill Doll's Eyes.

This reasoning dismays purists who firmly believe that plants should evolve naturally and not for the amusement of landscapers, for many more reasons than convenience. It is rare to see anyone acknowledge it by inserting a complimentary *var.* before such names.

This is one of those fuzzy areas separating conservation/restoration enthusiasts from landscape design enthusiasts.

It is also up to the individual landscaper to decide whether to determine whether a cultivar is acceptable in the larger garden theme.

## Shades of shade

Native plant species can be fussy about the precise nature of light received on a daily basis, but descriptive adjectives can often be fuzzy. For example, "light" shade and "high shade" can mean the same thing — a considerable amount of sunlight filtered by a high, thin tree canopy — or be different, when a full-sun plant gets a little bit of shade from time to time.

For our purposes, only a few kinds of shade describe plant habitats, and tolerances are listed secondarily, e.g., "sun to part shade, prefers part sun."

Species that lean toward preference for sun may grow in part shade as described, but won't perform as well in such circumstances. Typically, flower/fruit production is lower and plants may be more spindly to the point of sometimes requiring support. Conversely, part shade to shade plants can endure sunshine, but only if moisture is plentiful and intensity is not strong; the penalty to the landscape are plants that wilt and droop during such exposure.

As with any habitat issue, deviation from preference often leads to unsatisfactory results; better, if only for the sake of appearance, to be honest and appropriate about selections for a quality design.

- *Sun* — unobstructed sunshine for a least eight hours daily. Full sun suggests constant sunshine from sunrise to sunset.

- *Part sun* — unobstructed sunshine for several hours daily, especially at midday or afternoon, when the sun's rays are strongest. Glade-loving species and some westward-facing woods edge plants congregate in these situations.

- *Part shade* — unobstructed sunshine for several hours daily, but most often in the mornings, when the sun's rays are gentle. These are species likely to be found on the east side of thickets and edges. An important secondary definition implies *dappled shade*, that is, somewhat rapidly moving pools of sunshine that penetrate the canopy. If it persists for an hour or more, it starts to become part sun.

• *Shade* — light that is shrouded often by high or thin deciduous canopies, sometimes with very rapidly moving pools of sunlight. Many deciduous woodland ephemerals are part shade to shade, escaping dormancy early when full sun warms the forest floor and blooming before leaves are fully open. A variant is "full shade," which implies much lower light levels, such as those found in conifer stands. Because most plants need some good light to thrive, full-shade options are the most limited, but not impossible.

When we consider options, it is typically better to lean toward the sunnier side of the scale. A plant labeled "full sun to part shade" probably isn't the best choice for what we perceive as part shade; it may really prefer full sun, and part shade could be something of a stretch. A "part-shade to shade species" would be a wiser alternative because it will probably perform best in part shade.

## A few notes about rocks

Few obstacles to gardening in northeastern Pennsylvania elicit more growls than rocks. Some even sigh and confess that about the only thing they can grow are rocks, which seem to continually sprout from already discouraging soils.

Among the most exasperating are *channers*, which are generally flat stones about six inches long and most typically bits of gray shale and siltstone. Also high on the list of frustrating lurkers in the dirt are fractured sandstone rocks that are well along to becoming gravels. Both of these give the person at the end of a shovel the idea that they've turned up a huge boulder — only to eventually discover that it's nothing more than tightly packed fractured small stone.

In the area generally north of Interstate 80, which was covered by glaciers on several occasions, much of the rock was piled up as till and is sharp edged. To the south and in valleys, these same kinds of rock are worn and rounded, reflecting the action of the enormous volume of water that flowed from the glacier as it melted and washed it down into the southern half of the area.

Yet another source of rock in soils is fractured bedrock, a result of 5,000 years of permafrost following glaciation.

With the exception of the bases of steep slopes (where rocks accumulate as a result of gravity and are called *colluvium*) and riparian areas (where rocks become river stone enroute to Philadelphia and the Chesapeake Bay as *alluvium*), rock often migrates to the surface as a result of *frost churning*. Because it is a soft sedimentary rock, once it makes its way to the top it's doomed to erosion and will become a coarse gravel, then a sand, then a silt and finally a clay.

In the meantime, of course, it waits for our shovel and lawnmower to find it.

The plus side of rock in soil, however, has to do with plant roots, which slither through it and can even fracture it. Tree roots have been measured to exert more than 3,000 pounds of pressure per square inch, which can crack almost any rock. When water seeps in and freezes, the boulder doesn't stand a chance.

Plant roots can feed almost directly off the stone in the soil (which, of course, is nothing more than ground up rock) as minerals are released in solution with water. But they also serve as a means to drain away excess moisture, stabilize soil temperatures and confound burrowing animals like moles and voles, who otherwise would enjoy the roots of our landscape plants as a convenient source of food.

In regional ecosystems, rocks are simply another helpful participant in the overall scheme.

# The stuff under foot

An entire field of geology concentrates on soil science. Because of historic agrarian and civil engineering interest, American soil maps are accurate to within fractions of an acre. All the data and its implications for a variety of uses — including landscaping — are available to us from the National Resource Conservation Service of the U.S. Department of Agriculture.

Soil types are crucial to many ecosystems, and hence of importance to native plant landscapes.

Pennsylvania gardeners also enjoy free online soil mapping services from The Pennsylvania State University, with options including satellite images and conventional mapping symbols to allow us to identify soil type on a specific lot.

Geologists speak of soils as some combination of minerals subdivided into sand, silt and clay on the basis of particle size.

- *Clay particles* are less than 0.002 millimeter in diameter. How much and what kind of clay effects fertility and physical condition of the soil, including the ability to react chemically and retain water. Clays are responsible for shrink-swell potential and therefore drainage, as well as plasticity, ease of soil dispersion and saturated hydraulic conductivity.

- *Silt particles* range from 0.002 to 0.05 millimeter in diameter, and are the most efficient source of minerals for plants. It is easily and most commonly transported in water (as well as ocean currents) and is fine enough to be moved great distances by wind as dust.

- *Sand particles* are 0.05 millimeter to 2 millimeters in diameter; larger particles are considered gravels. We find sandy soils to

be easily worked, well drained and quick to warm up in the spring. Because they keep the soil from compaction, water easily passes to improve drainage and counter clay and organic matter, which impedes flow and retains water, respectively.

All soils began as rock — mostly sedimentary rock in Pennsylvania. Diverse parent materials formed in shallow sea beds and were uplifted in continental collisions. More recent disturbance, especially glaciation, has created more than 100 soil types in northeastern Pennsylvania alone.

Geologists describe layers of soil as *horizons*, which are meticulously described in texture, minerals and color. Beginning at the surface, horizons include:

- O — organic material with undecomposed litter at the surface and well-decomposed material at the bottom.

- A — commonly called topsoil, composed of minerals containing the most organic matter from the O horizon and soil life. In older soils, this may lay directly above a horizon in which mineral compounds have been leached, called the E Horizon.

- B — typically called subsoil, where iron, clay, aluminum and organic compounds are accumulated.

- C — a layer often containing big chunks of broken bedrock and substantial amounts of minerals.

- R — the bedrock itself; in glaciated areas, thousand of years of permafrost following ice retreat fractured this rock, which permits vast amounts of water to move through it, hence both our home wells and much of the supply for streams and rivers. Water leaking from bedrock outcrops creates seeps.

## Soil categories

Common soil descriptors, especially in the context of horticulture, attempt to describe the combination of soil particles in relatively simple terms, such as "sandy loam" or "silt loam" but recognize that the precise combination is more of a range of clay, sand and silt.

This model permits gardeners to easily define a soil mix to evaluate habitat potential or deter-

mine what adjustments might be needed to create a microhabitat.

We need to know at least two of the three percentages of sand, silt and clay, all of which are available for every *soil series*, or family of soils.

Starting with the percentage segments on the respective sides of the triangle, follow the *diagonal lines* of any two values to the point of intersect. For example, Oquaga-Lackawanna Channery Loam is 17 percent clay, 43.3 percent sand and 39.7 percent silt. An approximate 43 percent sand line and 40 percent silt line intersects on the word "loam" and identifies the soil as "loam."

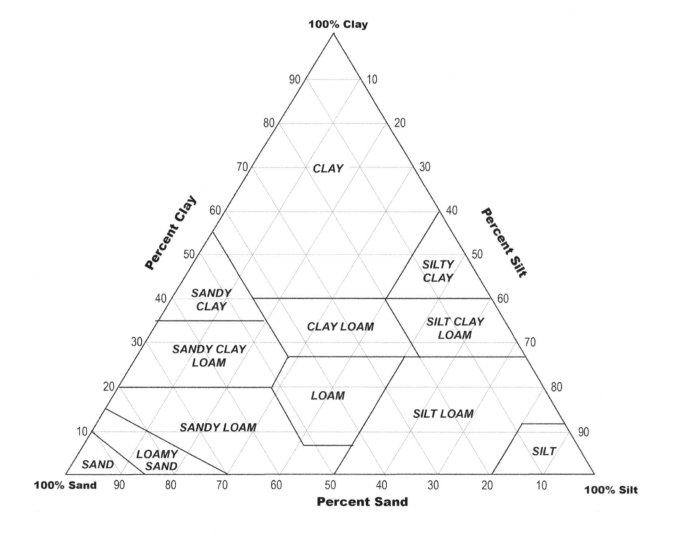

## The organic soil component

Soil organic matter is plant and animal residue at various stages of decomposition.

The standard for measuring organic content is a percentage by weight of soil material less than 2 millimeters in diameter. Many forest soils are surprisingly lean in organic matter, with just one to two percent being relatively common.

In a normal forest ecosystem, a series of layers of decomposing organic materials — generally leaf litter, twigs and branches, last season's herbaceous plant matter and the remains of a variety of animal life create layers. At the top is fresh material, and at the bottom is a thin veneer of completely decomposed matter that provides nutrition to plant roots below as chemicals leached into the soil by water.

In agricultural practice, organic soil content is maintained, perhaps enhanced, by returning crop residue to the soil; decorative landscapes are routinely amended with the addition of imported humus and surfacing with rapidly decomposing mulches.

It is reported that soil with more than six percent organic matter will likely have virtually no stormwater runoff, but high organic content is not always a good thing. An overload of nutrients can cause excessive growth and ultimate weakness in some herbaceous species and can be toxic to others. Soils very high in organic content also subside upon drying and cause destabilized root systems, and because of high porosity will need larger volumes of water on a sustained basis to recover.

Humus improves porosity of fine textured soils and binds together particles in coarse-textured soils. These properties enhance internal drainage and aeration and increase field capacity of the soil.

A correct balance creates an efficient soil, primarily because of water-retention capacity, the promotion of soil organism activity, and as a nutrient source. Nature regulates this process with thick layers of forest litter in varying stages of decomposition. Fresh material on top acts as an insulation to stabilize soil temperature and reduce transpiration rates. It also captures and holds passing water supplies for sustained support of the active system below.

Older material is modified by microbial and fungal activity, which breaks materials down into workable humus. Water passing though often forms mild acids to transport mineral content toward roots and also breaks down the mineral content in the soil — all providing a complex chain of organic compounds to sustain the plant.

Trees in particular are exceptional models of recycling, drawing a specific blend of compounds from the soil, using them temporarily in the active phase of growth, both for structure and to assist in phytochemical processes that produce flowers, seed and new growth. When leaves are discarded in the fall, the mineral content of the leaf has changed and returns the materials to the soil surface for use in future years.

## Mull, mor and beyond

The chemistry and biology are exotic, the variations many and the implications profound when it comes to the scraps and leftovers of plant and animal life on the soil surface and just beneath it.

Some of the conclusions illuminate how highly specialized ecosystems evolve and point us in helpful directions for our own garden endeavors. Not all organic matter is the same, or even appropriate, for many species.

Mineral content of leaves, twigs and branches varies from species to species and from month to month in the growing season. When they fall to the ground, they provide an important mulch, block competition and provide the proper nutrient balance for that particular species.

There are, in fact, three major kinds of organic layers atop mineral soil: *mull, mor and moder* (sometimes called *duff mull*) and the distinctions can be very important for the plant life dwelling within it.

The organic layer that we might call "mulch" includes the fresh forest litter (L horizon) which covers a layer of partly decomposed materials (F horizon). And it is here that things become variable.

*Mulls* lack the well-decomposed matter (H horizon) that is unrecognizable as to origin, and instead shifts directly to the surface mineral soil horizon (A horizon), into which organic matter has filtered or infiltrated — or in the case of agriculture, has been tilled in.

*Mor* has a substantial H horizon, but very little, if any, A horizon. Subsoil lies directly beneath the decomposed material.

*Moder* is something of a compromise. It has both the H and A horizons, although the A horizon may be thinner than that of a mull humus.

Among conifers, mor is highly acidic, has a high carbon-nitrogen ratio (always above 20, sometimes as high as 40), and very low biological activity. This results in very slow decomposition, often creates thick layers of organic matter and creates a habitat inhospitable to most deciduous trees and — coupled with denser shade — not attractive to most herbaceous plants.

*Moder*, a transitional form of humus between mor and mull, is often found in mountain grassland soils and *loesses* (silty soils transported by wind). Litter can be substantially thinner. Carbon-nitrogen ratio is 15 to 25, and the mineral organic product moves freely into the soil.

Not surprisingly, there are even finer subdivisions: firm mull, sand mull, coarse mull, medium mull, fine mull, twin mull, thick (or moder) and thin duff mull, granular mor, felty mor, greasy mor, thin mor and even imperfect mor, each of which carry specific definitions.

More common is *mull*, which is biologically very active, tends to have higher soil pH, sometimes approaching neutral, a carbon-nitrogen ratio near 10 and an ability to create stable mineral-organic complexes. It is often found in soils under cultivation. Because of high nitrogen availability, it creates a habitat preferred by hardwood tress and is not very attractive to conifers.

Specific species or combinations of trees form and perpetuate distinct soil chemistry; the chemical composition of leaves, twigs, and fallen branches is widely varied. While mull decomposition is primarily caused by bacteria, mor decomposition is a process of fungi, and this along with the effect of rainwater passing through leads to subtle shifts in soil chemistry and varying impact on dissolving minerals in the underlying soil — all of which affect the species growing above.

All of this results in organized ecological communities. When we alter the arrangement, usually to discard leaves, maintain a lawn or install humusy topsoil for a garden, we dramatically impair the natural soil, especially for trees.

## An overview of soil variability

Like its counterpart in botany, soil taxonomy is a field of geology that seeks to analyze and classify the many different types of soils found throughout the natural world. Sand, for example, is rock weathered to a particle size, but what kind of rock is crucial.

As with plant taxonomy, similar items are organized into groups and families, and approximate equivalent to a "species" is a soil *series*. Names can be mysterious, descriptive or even charming — not much Latin lurks here. This effort would be a relatively straightforward process that dirt doesn't always stay in the same place and soils can be mixed into many exotic blends.

Few forces can form and rearrange earth as dramatically as glaciers, which crush bedrock, pulverize the stone, grind it into fine particles and move it sometimes hundreds of miles. Where the glacier ends, deposition begins and very often secondary forces — particularly water running from the glacier but also wind — continue the migratory process of soil. *Till* becomes a soup of different minerals that coats everything in the wake of a glacier.

When the ice runs parallel to ridges, the deposits are relatively thin — sometimes measured in inches. When it traverses ridges, whole valleys can be filled with glacial trash many feet deep and entire river systems are altered. Variances in depth, drainage and precise mineral composition of the soil can have a substantial impact on the species most likely to be accommodated.

Where bedrock crops out from steep hillsides, ordinary weathering often leads to distinct habitats surrounding *colluvium* — soils moved by gravity. Erosion often drives soil materials into floodplains, where it becomes *alluvial* — soils moved by running water. Even the most solid-looking ridgetops are methodically ground by wind and the fine dust becomes *eolian* when it takes flight. Airborne dust settles in raindrops and provides nutrition for mosses.

On outwash plains, rounded and smooth rocks and soil fan out to form some of the region's better plant habitats. Where materials were simply dropped, the fractured rock is sharper, grittier and unpleasant to dig. Soils that gardeners find to be delightful are, to nature, not much different than soils that prompt dismay. The natural world has an appropriate species for every circumstance, hence the diversity of plant life in northeastern Pennsylvania.

Field geologists have identified it all and have even organized patterns of associations, very much like plant communities. But as with botanists, they have for the most part only theories about how it all interacts and interrelates.

But gardeners know subtle variances in soils can have profound impact on landscape planning, and, if nothing else, soils can be very difficult to substantially alter more than a foot or so deep.

Not much virgin soil is left in our region, mostly because farmers turned much of the top layers of soil with plows to forever blur *horizons* (layers). Every house involves excavation, and all that dirt is never put back exactly as it was. So we are left with at least 12 inches of modified soil, fairly well defined and certainly well mapped.

## Soils and too much water

Engineering and agriculture professionals have understandable interest when too much water is predicted in any given soil.

As a result, soil series descriptions assembled by the National Resource Conservation Service of the U.S. Department of Agriculture pay careful attention to how well drained a soil might be, how easily water flows through it well below the surface, and issues of ponding and flooding.

These last two possibilities interest ecologists and conservationists because these are zones where wetland species often concentrate. Native plant landscapers designing water features ranging from artificial ponds to rain gardens will also find such zones to be helpful models.

*Flooding* is a temporary inundation of an area caused by overflowing streams, from stormwater running off adjacent slopes, or by ocean tides. Water that stands for a short period after rainfall or snow melt is not typically considered flooding. Sites that grow in flood-prone areas are useful for landscape rills and rain gardens because they can withstand inundation for varying periods of time.

*Ponding* is standing water in a closed depression and includes swamps and marshes. Water exits by deep percolation, transpiration, evaporation or some combination of all three. Swales, bioretention basin and rain gardens are built specifically for the potential of ponding.

Frequency of occurrences in the context of soil science relates to the number of events anticipated in an average year.

Flooding values include:

- "None" — not probable; the chance of flooding is nearly 0 percent in any year. Flooding occurs less than once in 500 years.

- "Very rare" — very unlikely but possible under extremely unusual weather conditions, less than 1 percent chance in any year.

- "Rare" — unlikely but possible under unusual weather conditions, with a 1 to 5 percent chance in any year.

- "Occasional" — occurs infrequently under normal weather conditions, with a 5 to 50 percent chance in any year.

- "Frequent" — likely to occur often under normal weather conditions, with a more than 50 percent chance in any year but less than a 50 percent chance in all months in any year.

- "Very frequent" — likely to occur very often under normal weather conditions, with a chance of more than 50 percent in all months of any year.

Ponding values include:

- "None" — not probable; the chance of ponding is nearly 0 percent in any year.

- "Rare" — unlikely but possible under unusual weather conditions, with a nearly 0 percent to 5 percent chance in any year.

- "Occasional" — occurs, on average, once or less in 2 years, with a 5 to 50 percent chance in any year.

- "Frequent" — occurs, on average, more than once in 2 years, with a more than 50 percent chance in any year.

## A steady supply of moisture

Few mulch products are more effective but less appreciated than the routine blanket of leaves, twigs and rotting branches that gather on a forest floor.

In the best of circumstances, they are left in place; in the worst, they are stuffed in plastic bags and sent to landfills. Although the practice is considered dangerous on several levels, burning leaves releases potash to revive soils — like a good, cleansing brush fire periodically improves the overall health of a forest. Some municipalities collect unwanted leaves from curbside, grind them in specialized machines, and quickly turn it over as exceptional compost.

Because trees aren't in much of a hurry, leaf litter accumulates in stages, with large unbroken pieces over material coarsely shredded by microbes and fungi, over a thin blanket of humus that gradually feeds nutrition into the soil. This veneer of brown crumbs is often the most stubborn to remove when clearing a forest floor to install a proper lawn.

Besides plant nutrients about to be recycled, leaves accomplish two worthy mulch goals: they insulate the topsoil from the passing whims of climate and they retain an enormous amount of water that slowly oozes downward to feed the plant roots, or drifts upward to regulate the surrounding air temperature.

A simple experiment reveals the value of leaves. In one area, bare soil is kept weed-free and with regular precipitation needs no other protection. An adjacent plot is blanketed with a few inches of conventional wood mulch. A third area is untouched leaf litter. In normal periods of rain, all do equally well. After several weeks of drought, the highly organic open soil shrinks to expose much of the plant's roots and is so porous that it is impossible to keep moist. The wood mulch becomes hard and brittle, the underlying soil abruptly dries and is also difficult to rejuvenate. The base of the leaf layer is still saturated,

the soil underneath moist and the ground temperature cool.

One of the purposes is to block any competition — that is, our garden — from the nutrients desired by trees. Some leaves are toxic when they hit the ground, specifically to poison seedlings. Leaves are fine in the wild, but will quickly smother many landscape plants.

A solution takes advantage of the principle that the more a leaf is shredded, the more quickly it decomposes. Many herbaceous species prefer a winter mulch, just as long as it doesn't get out of hand. With most species already in dormancy, we can harvest leaves from planting beds and shred them. Some go back for winter protection and will decompose rapidly in spring. That's when the remaining leaf litter is lightly scattered around the plants to provide nutrients and shelter in the summer months.

A variety of shredders are available, but a simple lawnmower works well. Mow in a constant pattern to chew up the leaves and blow them into orderly piles or rows. Repeat the action for an even finer shred if desired. Use an ordinary hayfork to move them to application sites or a compost pile for later use.

## The finer points of pH

Much of soil activity is governed by *reaction* defined as acidity or alkalinity, a numeric scale called pH, developed by a Danish chemist in 1909. Exactly what "pH" stands for is a matter of some debate, but the value of it in many fields is well established.

The most common soil laboratory measurement of soil pH is the 1:1 water method. A crushed soil sample is mixed with an equal amount of water, and a measurement is made of the suspension. Neutral — that is, neither acidic or alkaline, is 7.0.

The scale of acid to alkaline is *logarithmic*, not *linear,* which means that soil with a pH of 6.0 is *ten times* more acidic than pH 7.0, and a pH of 5.0 would be 100 times more acidic than the neutral point.

Soils in northeastern Pennsylvania commonly range from about pH 5.5 to 6.2, but can drop very low in bogs and slightly alkaline in areas with high concentrations of limestone. When soil pH nears the 7.0 mark, it is said to be *circumneutral.*

Valuable nutrients for plants are affected by soil acidity. The solubility of iron, manganese, zinc, boron and phosphorus declines as pH values go up and improve in more acidic circumstances. Calcium, magnesium and molybdenum are more available at higher pH values. The familiar nitrogen, phosphorus and potash are most efficiently available at pH ranges from about 6.3 to 7.5.

Plant species differ in their ability to take up nutrients at a given pH level. Most are concentrated between pH 6.0 and 7.0, but many prefer pH ranges of 5.0 to 6.0 or less.

Typical lawns do best at about pH 6.8 in full sun. But in shady areas, when pH drops because lime has been withheld, mosses thrive and can overrun turf grass within a couple of years. If leaf litter is untouched, pH drops a bit further and several species of ferns will explode into substantial colonies.

Excessive supplies of some nutrients because pH levels are too high can be toxic to many species, a factor to consider when installing an acid-lover in a circumneutral setting. Inadequate nutrition typically leads to slow decline and death, sometimes foreshadowed by chlorosis — a sign of insufficient iron.

Because adaptability is a useful trait in natural survival, many species of plants operate within two ranges of pH — a broader band in which an individual can grow, flower and seed, and a narrower band in which it will genuinely thrive.

Among native plant pioneers on the subject of pH preferences was Clarence Birdseye, who made a fortune in fast-freezing food technology and devoted his later years to native landscaping and research in New England. He and his wife, Eleanor, wrote *Growing Woodland Plants* in 1951, an essential reference book for those who garden with natives and one of the very few references of detailed pH preferences.

## Further investigation

What we often dismiss as "really crummy dirt" is, in fact, a very busy, fully-functioning ecosystem all by itself and the subject of very serious research called soil science.

A fascinating exploration of the geology, chemistry and biology of forest soils can be found in *Forest Soils,* by Harold Lutz and Robert F. Chandler Jr., published in 1946 and painstakingly referenced to a great many international research going back many years before that.

The work discusses in detail soil-forming minerals, soil-forming rocks, disintegration and decomposition of minerals and rocks, forest soil organics and organic matter, the nature and properties of soil colloids, general physical properties of forest soils, the relationship of water to soil, classification and erosion/deterioration.

Along the way we are introduced to many varied soil residents, ranging from burrowing mammals to fungi and microbes, as well as detailed experiments on the chemical composition of leaves, twigs and branches and what happens when they fall to earth.

Another helpful text, but of a more general nature, is *The Nature and Properties of Soils* by Nyle C. Brady, published in 1990. It includes a general review of what soils are and discusses origin, nature and classification of parent materials; soil formation; physical properties; characteristics and behavior of soil water; impact of air and temperature; colloids and reaction; organisms; organic matter; major and minor nutrients and how to manage them and erosion and pollution.

A highly detailed discussion, *The Geology of Pennsylvania,* published by the Pennsylvania Geological Survey and the Pittsburgh Geological Society and edited by Charles. H. Schultz, takes us step by step and region by region on how all those soils and landforms can to be. Major topics include stratigraphy and sedimentary tectonics, structural geology and tectonics, regional geophysics, physiography, geologic history, mineral and water resources, environmental and engineering applications, and landforms from an aesthetic point of view.

# *Uplands and lowlands*

## Elemental orogeny

Should we desire to create an entire mountain range, we must first decide precisely how we might set the Earth's tectonic plates in motion. If an oceanic plate is *subducted*, or pushed downward under an existing plate, we create ranges like the Andes of South America, often with many volcanoes. If a continental plate collides and uplifts another one, we create ranges like the Appalachians or, more recently, the Alps in Europe and the Himalayas in Asia.

To illustrate how this occurs with Pennsylvania as the model, we require a kitchen table, tablecloth and an assistant or two — perhaps a dubious child or tolerant spouse. Station the assistants at the corners identified as Erie and Pittsburgh, then take up a position at about Philadelphia. The assistants hold the tablecloth firmly to prevent it from drifting away. The mountain-builder spreads both hands at a reasonable distance on the tablecloth and then slowly pushes toward the center of the table.

In geology, this action is called *orogeny*, or mountain building.

As the force methodically and slowly moves inward, a line of ridges magically appears, running generally from southwest to northeast. The more the tablecloth, which represents a former shallow seabed, is compressed, the more *ridges and valleys* form and the higher they get. Ultimately, some may fold over on themselves and continue development — these will likely become anthracite coal fields.

When we are satisfied with the size and scale of our tabletop mountain range, the tectonic pressure eases and erosion processes begin. To the east a *coastal plain* and the continental shelf will form. To the west is the Allegheny Plateau.

This not-so-gentle pressure continued for 200 million years and formed the supercontinent Pangea. When deep rifts severed the landmass, the Atlantic Ocean resulted, and part of the Appalachians wound up in Morocco.

When we step back to survey our miniature landscape, we might also consider that in the beginning, Philadelphia would have been on the southwestern corner of the state, below the equator and naturally quite tropical, and Pittsburgh in the northwest. The entire state rotated 90 degrees and rose from a string of early islands into a substantial landmass.

But just as importantly, the present northwestern and northeastern corners were shrouded with glaciers thousands of feet thick on several occasions, curiously ignoring the Wyoming Valley in the area of Scranton and Wilkes-Barre. Entire ridge tops were sheared off and shoved into valleys to a *high plateau*. In our region, the limit of glaciation follows a line generally defined by Interstate 80.

Not only did these give the terrain its present shape, they also created vast rivers to deliver enormous volumes of material to, among other things, develop the Chesapeake Bay and the land upon which Philadelphia is built. Ridges and valleys, a coastal plain and an upland plateau create the widely varied geography upon which habitats in northeastern Pennsylvania occur.

*(Learn more: an interesting and richly detailed presentation about how continents, particularly ours, evolved can be found in* Annals of the Ancient World *by John McPhee.)*

## Slope dynamics and modeling

Dramatic and varying changes in elevation offer tantalizing landscaping options. Slopes can suggest the experience of a remote mountain trail, both a means of isolation from the day's routine and escape into a visual adventure.

A rising slope brings low-growing plants closer to our visual line and creates interesting perspectives; the downslope offers a vista that gives us a sense of power over domain.

Slopes enhance the illusion of height when planting in low-to-high patterns, or reduce perspective and foreshorten scale when planting taller species at the path edge and shorter specimens partway up a steep hill — or stretch scale when the shorter specimen is partway up a long, gradual rise.

In nature, slopes are rarely evenly graded banks and never a unified ecological structure. As we investigate ecological communities further on, we'll encounter all sorts of slope expressions and we can certainly use knowledge of slopes to improve (or even theme) our garden designs.

More often, the top of a slope, or *creep slope,* is convex and consequently stormwater runs off quickly. Hence upper segments of slopes tend to be both drier and sandier, characteristics even more pronounced on slopes with south and west *aspects* — the direction a slope faces. South and west aspect slopes are subjected to more sun and heat than identical slopes with north and east aspects, which not surprisingly are comparatively cooler and more moist.

Toward the base of a slope, terrain takes on a concave profile, because this is where water flow tends to slow and soil deposition accumulates. Here we find richer, deeper soils, well sheltered from the harsher elements above. If the slope is steep, the base, or *wash slope,* may include substantial amounts of *talus*, or loose rock that has broken away from summits. Material moved by gravity is *colluvium* and it hosts many unique ecological opportunities.

The base of a slope often concludes with wetlands. Depending on the terrain, we may find meadows, fens, bogs, swamps or river systems. In stream and river courses, various forms of flooding may result in alluvial *terraces*. These may be simple low banks or the foundation for a wide array of *riparian* native plant landscaping models.

Slopes define a conservation/restoration plan. Some may prefer to landscape an element of a larger dynamic. If we enhance terrain by creating slopes, we can suggest a series of interrelated geologic features to develop a clever design.

## Noses, feet, toes and hollows

Bases of ridgelines may run fairly straight or form meandering patterns, easily discerned on topographical maps and with significant implications for slope habitats.

Where sections of a ridge extend from the average baseline, the slope element is called a *nose*. Where it retreats from the average line, it becomes a *hollow*. These may be large or small, but share a common drainage characteristic. The center line of a *nose slope* is drier because water runs away from it in three directions: directly downslope and toward the adjacent hollows.

Because hollows represent an indentation in the general line of a slope, water from the adjacent side slopes runs into it, supplementing the normal volume coming down from above. This makes a hollow more moist and often cooler than the nearby nose slopes, but slightly different than a *cove* — defined as a walled, rounded head end of a narrow, steep valley.

Sometimes a straight stretch divides the end of a nose and the beginning of a hollow, often identified as a *side slope* and it, too, can lead to specific habitats.

Ecological implications of sheltered versus exposed sites, moisture concentrations and erosional opportunities are profound and lead to distinct community development.

Secondary slope activity can also occur toward the bottom of a hillslope. A large, gently inclined section of the washslope is identified as a *footslope* because of its resemblance to the profile of a human foot.

A smaller convex slope just above bottomland can be called a *toeslope* because it is the final extension of a footslope. These regions also imply unique ecological community development and because the feature is common they are studied for ecological patterns.

Footslopes and toeslopes are distinct from *alluvial terraces*, which tend to resemble plateaus

# Slope elements

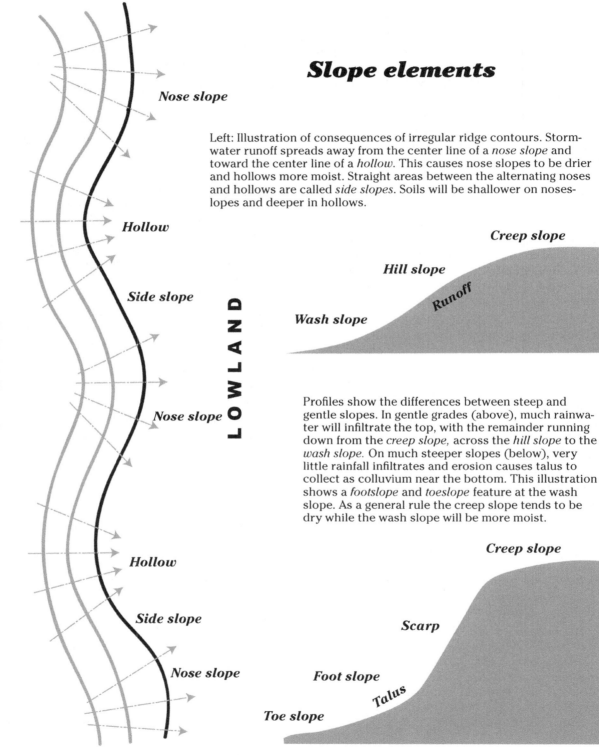

Left: Illustration of consequences of irregular ridge contours. Storm-water runoff spreads away from the center line of a *nose slope* and toward the center line of a *hollow*. This causes nose slopes to be drier and hollows more moist. Straight areas between the alternating noses and hollows are called *side slopes*. Soils will be shallower on nose-slopes and deeper in hollows.

Profiles show the differences between steep and gentle slopes. In gentle grades (above), much rainwater will infiltrate the top, with the remainder running down from the *creep slope,* across the *hill slope* to the *wash slope.* On much steeper slopes (below), very little rainfall infiltrates and erosion causes talus to collect as colluvium near the bottom. This illustration shows a *footslope* and *toeslope* feature at the wash slope. As a general rule the creep slope tends to be dry while the wash slope will be more moist.

Nose slope

Hollow

Side slope

Nose slope

Hollow

Side slope

Nose slope

UPLAND

LOWLAND

Creep slope

Hill slope

Wash slope

Runoff

Creep slope

Scarp

Foot slope

Talus

Toe slope

margined by a fairly evenly-graded bank or riparian cut. As elements of a washslope, they receive generous supplies of water from both stormwater runoff above and from seeping groundwater below and are often lush with vegetation — either forested or the upper edges of meadows and seeps.

In native plant landscaping, we might consider development of a footslope by building a gentle, somewhat concave landform on an upgrade from the path, and perhaps conclude it with the acute but thin dropoff to fashion the toe. Soils will tend to be sandy to silty loams with substantial organic material and sites should be mesic to moist.

## An overview of wetlands

About half of the researched ecological communities in the region are classified as wetlands, a distinction with serious ramifications for permitted land use and responsibilities — so much so that precisely what defines a wetland is as much a legal issue as an environmental one.

We often think of wetlands in the context of open swamps and marshes, lake and pond edges, bogs and the active channel of rivers and streams. But geologic anomalies create a number of other habitats that lead to distinct ecological communities. These include woodland swamps, seeps, fens, and even some wet meadows.

The common thread is that significant amounts of water are very close by, either laying on, just at or right under the surface and very often mucky soils are hosts to plant species that like it much more than damp.

*Swamps* can be any area of low, saturated ground — usually because of poor drainage or high water tables — and sometimes covered with water, with or without the accumulation of peat. They are similar to *marshes*, which can be periodically wet to continually flooded with shallow water and are often dominated by sedges, cattails, rushes and hydrophytic plants.

Stagnant water left in poor drainage areas behind natural floodplain levees and the adjacent slopes are called *backswamps*.

*Bogs* are waterlogged, spongy ground that attract sedges, heaths and especially mosses such as sphagnum. These are usually highly acidic,

---

> ### *The full, exact definition*
> *A wetland* is an ecosystem that depends on constant or recurrent, shallow inundation or saturation at or near the surface of the substrate. The minimum essential characteristics of a wetland are recurrent, sustained inundation or saturation at or near the surface and the presence of physical, chemical, and biological features reflective of the recurrent, sustained inundation or saturation. Common diagnostic features of wetlands are hydric soils and hydrophytic vegetation. These features will be present except where specific physicochemical, biotic, or anthropogenic factors have removed them or prevented their development. — (National Research Council, 1995 p. 55)

---

low-nutrient sites with strong potential to develop into peat. *Fens*, on the other hand, are waterlogged but often circumneutral to slightly alkaline, and often considered closely related to very wet meadows. Reeds and rushes are more common.

When moisture is substantial under the surface but somewhat more dry than fens, *meadows* are the common result. To remain as open ground and not become forested, substantial water flow often demolishes trees and shrubs trying to get started.

Meadows are often found on the floodplains of high volume rivers, where seasonal flooding and ice scour cleanses the surface. When clogged by unexpected occurrences or the activity of creatures like beavers even small stream blockages cause meadows to develop because the ground becomes too saturated for trees to grow.

Where aquifers leak in small areas, we find springs or the lesser-flow *seeps,* where reflow or lateral subsurface flow keeps the surface saturated during dry periods. A substantial seep may be less than an acre in size, but a unique ecological community nonetheless.

*For more discussion on this topic, see page 188 for information concerning prairies, meadows, fens, swamps, marshes and bogs.*

# *Problems on four legs*

## Defeating deer

Among the most common questions about any plant material is, "do deer eat it?"

With very few exceptions, the answer is "perhaps," "probably" or "certainly." None of these answers seem acceptable when the plant under consideration has a $14.99 price tag dangling from the pot.

Among the sought-after plant lists are those revealing "deer-proof" or "deer-resistant" species. Many of the plants on those lists are cheerfully consumed by deer within 24 hours of being planted, perhaps because deer are illiterate and can't read them. Commercial chemical sprays, along with exotic homemade formulas work for only short periods and require continual effort and expense. Miss one application, and the landscape is reduced to zero.

Experience teaches us three things are true about deer.

- Deer *browse*, not graze, from the ground up to about five feet. Browsing herbivores do not eat graminoids — grasses, sedges and rushes.

- Deer are effectively excluded by fencing a minimum of seven feet high.

- Native herbaceous plants unpalatable to deer often form vast colonies in regions where deer pressure is high.

We might easily reject fencing in the front of a home. It is unattractive and can be impractical because of driveway entries and the corresponding need for always secure gates.

In smaller applications, however, a combination of traditional pickets strung between tall posts that support an upper level of relatively fine mesh may diminish the visual problem and establish the design of a cottage garden. The entry might be a lightly-gated arbor straddling a footpath.

Grasses, particularly tall clumping specimens, can be arranged in the same manner as shrubs, large perennials or hedges. Native prairie grasses have the additional advantage of adaptability to poor soils and drought.

To protect new shrubs and sapling trees, surround the specimen with a temporary fence, constructed from plastic-coated welded wire. Shape a 4-foot long segment into a circle, and secure with tent stakes to the ground or use a lightweight post. Once the plant is well above 60 inches, remove the temporary protection and recycle for the next specimen. Deer will obligingly manage any sucker growth from the base of trees and shrubs.

In the wild, vast colonies of hayscented, bracken and New York ferns, as well as mayapples and the shrub sweetfern (*Comptonia peregrina*), are aggressive spreaders, unpalatable to deer. They also require virtually no care, not even leaf removal in the fall. Shrewd gardeners create "pools" of ferns in problem landscapes, surrounded by the negative space of lawns (or, better still, mosses or low sedges) for dramatic effect.

## Deer fencing options

Exclusionary fencing options include an array of varied materials, each with qualities and drawbacks.

The most common are two forms of polypropylene mesh, most often in black, sold in rolls of 50 to 100 feet and 84 inches in height. These are lightweight, easy to install and offer good durability in normal weather conditions. It is relatively inexpensive and forms an effective deer barrier.

Plastic fencing is readily penetrated by rabbits and even squirrels, which chew strands to create larger spaces. Bears can easily rip through plastic mesh, and deer can expand small herbivore openings to slip through the fence. Slight variances in ground surface grade can lead to sagging along the top of the fence. To solve this, weave light twisted galvanized (better) or plastic-coated single strand (no rust, but weaker) wire through the uppermost mesh and secure it to the fence posts.

- *Deer mesh* is approximately 1x1 inches and because of the tight pattern is more visible from a distance. It forms a very effective barrier and is ideal for temporary fencing, such as annually installed (often saved over winter) for vegetable gardens.

- *Deer fence*, often sold by mail order, is typically a 2x3 inch mesh in 100 and larger rolls, and is nearly invisible from a distance — so much so that vendors encourage installers to hang temporary white ribbons on it to help deer learn that it's there.

Welded wire fencing is more expensive and cumbersome to install. Plastic coated wire fence — typically dark green — is barely visible and easily available at major home centers. It is virtually permanent. Ordinary galvanized fencing is less expensive, has a lifespan of 10 to 30 years, depending on quality and is available from many farm supply outlets. The silvery metallic finish reflects light, which makes it more visible, but it eventually develops a rusty veneer.

The mesh is typically 2x3 inches. It usually comes in 50-foot rolls, but only in 48 and 60 inch height. However, fencing can be installed in two tiers, with 4 over 4 feet resulting in a 7 foot fence *with an extra foot folded outward on the ground.* This last barrier gives us a preventive measure for animals attempting entry by nosing under the wire. "Stitch" welded wire together at 12 to18 inch intervals with aluminum twist ties or hog clips made for chain link fence.

The 60-inch version can be cut and wrapped around concrete forms, then slid off as fencing tubes to protect shrubs and sapling trees until they grow tall enough to be above the browse range of deer.

Although it cannot be chewed by rabbits, groundhogs or penetrated by bears, very young rabbits can slip through the mesh.

An alternative is to use a narrow band of chicken wire (or poultry netting), either galvanized or plastic coated for permanency, in place of the bottom tier of welded wire. Three-foot chicken wire, with one foot folded out along the ground, plus 60 inch welded wire totals the requisite 7 feet.

A third option, wild game fencing, is high-tensile, flexible galvanized wire specifically made to contain (or exclude) large game animals. The mesh varies from very open at the top to relatively tight at the bottom (although not small enough to exclude rabbits). The most cost effective of all the fencing (about half of polypropylenes and a third of plastic-coated welded wire), it comes in 96 inch rolls 330 feet long that weigh 350 pounds.

## Other annoying little problems

The soft cushion of mulches, especially shredded leaves, are an open invitation for some of the smallest, but most damaging, herbivores, especially voles. Pennsylvania is home to four species:

*Microtus pennsylvanicus* (meadow vole)
*Clethrionomys gapperi* (red-backed vole)
*Microtus chrotorrhinus* (rock vole)
*Microtus pinetorum* (woodland or pine vole)

Woodland voles are reported to be more common in southeastern Pennsylvania, but the remaining three can play havoc with plants because they feed primarily on roots, especially rhizomes, just under the surface, or just at the base of stems. When enough of the root system is consumed, the plant immediately wilts and can be easily hoisted to survey the damage. Stems are found laying next to the plant site, and very few species are exempt from the assault.

They are rapid breeders, often producing several litters of typically three to six offspring each year

A sure sign that voles are present will be runways across open ground (especially in lawns) where the surface inch is fluffed up. Look also for small holes, about three-quarters of an inch in diameter, anywhere in the vicinity of plants, but recognize that tunnel entries in loose litter, such as leaves, are almost impossible to see. The energetic voles create vast networks of tunnels, just below the surface.

A variety of chemicals are on the market to discourage and kill voles, but as with larger mammals who show up to simply make a living, it may prove to be an uphill battle. When a plant succumbs to voles, the case for negative space in the landscape is clear: simply step into the bed, use the toe of the shoe to detect soft spots that occur along tunnel routes, and step down hard to demolish the excavation.

If the stomp-and-squish technique doesn't appeal, consider predators. Voles are relatively easy prey for semi-feral cats and foxes, but especially raptors. A pole 10 to 15 feet tall with a one to two inch diameter perch on top makes a perfect observation post for hawks and owls and simple do-it-yourself plans are available for owl houses that invite screech owls in wooded areas or barn owls in meadow regions.

Experts suggest that all it takes is one for every five acres. As voles reproduce, the raptors have an ongoing supply of food.

Meanwhile losses on the ground can be minimized. Sometimes the best defense is right under foot: rocks. Picking up on a hint of installing hardware cloth rings at the bases of prized specimen sapling trees, clever gardeners plant with soil in one adjacent pile and heavy gravel in another. Line the hole with loosely organized channers, then freely mix the stone with soil going back into the hole around the base of the plant. As they do in nature, the roots develop into the broken rock, most of it beyond the reach of even the most dedicated vole.

---

## Fence line strategies

When planning a fence line to exclude deer and other herbivores, some steps can reduce cost and prevent rework.

*Extend the perimeter.* While being attentive to zoning or homeowner association restrictions and certain of property boundaries, an attractive plan may involve running fence through existing woody materials (trees and shrubs) beyond the planned scope of the garden itself.

The added cost becomes a reward when the fence is not a distraction from the garden or when the garden expands toward the fence. Light patterns in wooded areas help camouflage deer fencing of any type, but especially galvanized wire.

*Survey stakes* inexpensively identify post locations and, with a long rope as a guide, establish very straight lines.

*Use structures as fence.* Houses, garages and other outbuilding sides along the fence line reduce the amount of materials and also help "square up" a garden plan.

*Make generous gates.* For a fence to work, all gates must routinely be securely closed. This is a principle all farmers, but few children, fully grasp. An open gate on a farm lets the cows out; in a garden, it lets the deer in. The easier it is to keep a gate closed, the less chance one will remain open.

*Utility gates* — to move materials and equipment in and out of the garden — should be as tall as the fence, but as wide as possible. A minimum width is 60 inches if equipment such as lawn tractors has straight access to the gate. Consider 96 to 120 inches for maximum flexibility. Because gate locations imply heavy traffic, keep space on either side clear of obstructions, especially if egress to maintain unfenced property is important.

*People gates* — limited to human traffic and typically installed at the entry point, they can be lower if part of an arbor. While technically able to jump over the gate, the surrounding arbor becomes a visual confusion and, if well located, will not be challenged by deer.

Use sturdy fence posts, properly anchored, never trees. Metal fence posts rust; pressure treated lumber should be in concrete.

# *Some thoughts on design*

From the charming formality of European traditions to the gentle mystery of Japanese retreats, we discover that the many native plants found in Pennsylvania are as design-suitable for many design themes.

Used in combination with introduced species, natives extend decorative range and solve problems. Natives must meet the same criteria as any other species in making a positive contribution to a design. Blending natives with exotics permits transition from purely introduced species to purely native in comfortable stages.

Native plants offer an entirely distinct design option: wildscapes. We can suggest all the drama of wilderness within the practicalities of our little back yard. If we feel hobbled because about a third of the species are not commercially available, we find solace in knowing that the most attractive two-thirds are.

*Wildscape* and restoration enthusiasts may cringe at the notion of restraining native plants with a design leash. Yet those who design with natives rather than introduced species still support the larger environment. Butterflies, bees and hummingbirds are indifferent to how plants are organized; they are only interested in having them available.

And so there is really no reason why natives can't be used in the formal traditions that began in Italy, were relaxed a bit in France, evolved even more in England and strongly influenced American design from the earliest colonization. The only drawback would be more modest bloom sizes and shorter bloom duration.

European lineage gives us *Early American design*, the familiar and often symmetrical display that softens the lines of houses, anchors the negative space typically used for lawn, and gains perspective from finishing plantings at curb or sidewalk edges, which sometimes border walkways and driveways.

The transition from traditional vegetable garden space behind homes into outdoor living areas created familiar *casual American design* with its relaxed and flowing lines, its recognition of unobtrusive edges and recreational space.

For both of these, natives again can be substituted freely, primarily because developed beds will probably be fairly well drained, fairly rich in humus and fairly mesic. Soil management means habitats for more xeric or more wetland species are feasible.

Design theorists continually urge gardeners to research first and buy with discipline; it applies equally well to using native species.

The rising popularity of retreat gardens, with lineage that traces to Japanese styles, creates an interesting variant on wildscapes. *Stroll and courtyard gardens* are clearly celebrations of nature, but grooming is fastidious and design a high art form.

With just a handful of plants and spaces smaller than most back yards, landscapes that hold gardening interest for a lifetime are feasible, and ideal opportunities for landscaping with natives.

## The welcome mat

A garden style instantly recognized by any homeowner, Early American softens the rigid lines of the front of a house with a combination of larger perennials, often shrubs. Originally intended to hide foundation lines and symmetrically organized, these gardens are straightforward decoration — the proverbial "curb appeal."

A lawn typically extends from street to garden; the negative space frames the long, narrow garden and building to provide a welcome mat. Landscapers sometimes edge the sidewalk to beef up a visual line to the entry, and occasionally use shrubs, fences or other front-edge planting to create depth. Graceful shade trees complete a bucolic scene that dates all the way back to the first grand colonial homes on the continent.

With less symmetrical house fronts, opportunities for more asymmetrical landscape design have become popular — but the purpose is the same: visually enhance the building.

Native species easily substitute for popular introduced plants for this relatively uncomplicated garden. Nature offers us a substantial range of attractive spring-flowering shrubs, well-behaved groundcovers and edge materials and dramatic mass-forming perennials, all of which are relatively easy care.

Just as with conventional planning and idea gathering, we research natives with library books and periodicals, the Internet and trusted garden centers

Some native plant enthusiasts have recently pushed the limits by asserting lawns are evil and the entire space ought to be given a nice "wild" (some read that as "weedy") look as a sort of green manifesto. This can cause concern in more urban circumstances because it understandably interferes with the general look of the neighborhood. Some private communities ban this activity outright.

To keep the neighborhood peace, restraint is exercised in this very public area of the garden. A lawn is simply a fact of life and a garden should appear well kept and compliment the building.

Focus on the general design principle of creating a visual line that leads right to the front door, obey the rules of scale, keep it all well groomed, and save the eclectic for the back yard.

In more rural settings, where the driveway seems to vanish into the woods, the whole concept reverses. Here we can wildscape right to the pavement and build the illusion of remote privacy, or create a grand manor look with masses of herbaceous material like ferns, mayapples and sedges, in an open woodland style.

## Wildscaping theory and practice

Most often a restoration effort, but sometimes a plan arising from installing a home on a lot with minimal disturbance to a working ecosystem, *wildscapes* are growing in popularity as we increasingly turn to "sustainable" or "green" landscaping. Nature rules, and we are relegated to the role of admiring bystanders.

Native species used for such projects are expected to organize themselves as efficiently as habitats permit. Our only intrusion might be a trail or small sitting area to enjoy unfettered nature, much as we do when visiting public wilderness areas. Our garden, in fact, may be a model of vast scenery tucked deep in our memory.

Unfortunately, nature isn't always what we'd like it to be. Some ecosystems can be quite boring, with relatively few species of plants comprising canopy, subcanopy, shrub and herbaceous layers. This can be enhanced with some artistic management — i.e., a pleasant mulch path meandering through a vast colony of ferns or sensitive pruning to remove dead branches. For some landscapers, the limited palette is an expression of simplicity and gentle elegance; for others it means rejecting attractive species that would be out of place.

The allure of "easy, no-care" is something of a mirage. Wildscape managers must always be on guard to remove invasives and sometimes referee species that are unusually successful in a given microhabitat.

Relatively little is known about the exact composition of habitats we might use as a guide. Useful summaries of sample plots may point us in the right direction, but aren't necessarily complete or precise. Additionally, more than a third of the natives identified for the northeastern Pennsylvania counties are unavailable in the commercial marketplace. Unless they are already present in the planned wildscape, the design product can only be a reasonable representation and not the genuine thing.

Functioning ecosystems can occupy huge spaces and often interact with neighboring systems in many ways not yet completely understood. When developing small plots out of context, we must bear in mind that we are compressing nature into a microhabitat. But the upside of these limitations is a liberation from concern about "getting it right." We need only to "get it reasonable."

Our wildscape might not be a precise microcosm, and might more closely resemble a decently groomed state or national park than a true wilderness, but with some care and attention, we can get a dramatic and interesting result. Such parks represent an escape from urbanity. To design new landscapes or develop existing features as wildscapes, our guiding principles are the same as the National Park Service: "stimulation of the senses, a place for learning, a feeling of safety, re-creation for the soul, exercise for the body and overwhelming satisfaction."

To that end, our focus should be on a trail, rather than a path, that takes us from one distinct point of interest or experience to another in an evenly paced and engaging journey of discovery. Clever designers will complement wildscape plant beds with accessory features right out of the NPS handbook and model trails to the standard specifications found in parks.

A feasible goal for wildscaping might be not so much hoping to ignite a functioning ecosystem as comfortable authenticity. It is, after all, a garden.

## The challenge of Japanese design

As an art form with a thousand-year legacy, Japanese landscape design celebrates nature and therefore becomes a design style attractive to native plant enthusiasts.

While some try to exactly *mimic* this Asian cultural icon with everything from stone lanterns to half-moon bridges, leading Japanese designers patiently free us from cliché. They gently remind us that Japanese gardens are found in Japan; American gardens might be Japanese in style, but can never be truly Japanese. One designer suggests that rather than portraying icons of Japanese culture, Americans might wish to suggest their own regional ecosystems — with the emphasis being on "suggest" rather than "replicate."

Instead, we can draw upon some of the principles of an interesting design and apply our own cultural values to it.

The upside of this style are neatly groomed, tightly controlled natural designs of great beauty, where native species can be exceptionally useful. By extending the design range to multiple ecosystems, we are freed from the natural site limitations and opportunities expand. For example, we might begin with a dry, upland site but can modify it freely to include something of a wetland, or a midslope, or an alpine display. Or perhaps we can have all of them in an arranged display. In either event, we are liberated when shopping for plants.

What makes Japanese design appealing is the emphasis on contemplative experience rather than striking display. Flowers are nice, but incidental. We build serenity with green, and apply subtlety to the visual interest range.

Stroll gardens take us on a journey of reflection and discovery, and were originally used for warlords to recall and celebrate their adventures. More recently, whispered suggestions of cultural icons, even poetry, are in vogue. They may be very small or quite large; individual resources are the only guide. An exceptional example, measuring just 55 by 65 feet, is found at the Japanese bonsai pavilion at the National Arboretum near Washington, D.C. and well worth a pilgrimage to study.

Any good stroll garden is a journey of transcendence, departing the mundane through gates or across bridges, for personal retreat, spiritual refreshment and introspective discovery. Through meticulous grooming, the ordinary is made special and the garden speaks in whispers.

The challenge of this style is the complexity of three dimensional design, intense grooming and infusions of subtle imagery to be discovered and appreciated by the visitor. Masters strive to ensure each visitor has the same positive experience, even down to the effect of the sound of the path under foot and the pace of how each point of interest is unveiled. The garden design must be cohesive in all four seasons, for a garden is to be enjoyed year round.

Because of its nature, this may be the most labor-intensive and intellectually taxing of all the designs, but therein lies the appeal. Gardening itself is a journey of discovery and participation, not just decoration from a kit.

## A folklore theme idea

Design themes for native plant landscapes don't necessarily have to faithfully model ecosystems or well-established styles.. As gardens, they can follow any number of different and unusual directions, too.

One of the more interesting ideas relates to two facets of North American folklore. Not surprisingly, Native Americans relied on a wide array of regional plants for foods, medicines, spiritual aids and a number of superstitions, i.e., rubbing a weapon with certain plants would result in a successful hunt.

Settlers from Europe brought their own ideas and pursued traditions of Native Americans, making Appalachia rich with herbal traditions, some of which are recognized pharmaceuticals today; indeed, several local species are agricultural cash crops (black cohosh, goldenseal, ginseng to name a few).

Good sources of information are *A Guide to Medicinal Plants of Appalachia*, published by the U.S. Department of Agriculture in 1969 and reprinted in 2005, and *Native American Ethnobotany* by Daniel E. Moerman.

## Natives in a relaxed landscape

Developing the traditional back yard into garden-oriented landscapes most typically calls upon what many call "casual American design," a highly flexible concept defined more by use than a singular artistic objective.

Begin with the notion of an outdoor room — an extension of the home and often anchored by a patio or deck. The extent of lawn as an open activity space depends on homeowner preference, but the accenting flower beds are where gardening enthusiasts practice their craft and find native plants helpful from both a design and conservation standpoint.

In open areas, we define property edges with border beds rich with low-to-tall meadow and prairie wildflowers, and find clumps of tall native grasses as supportive complements. Or create "pools" of wildflowers in gently curving shapes to soften corner lines, break up masses of lawn, or surround our sunny sitting space.

Woodland lots invite borders of species often found at forest or thicket borders to ease the visual transition from blank space to the woods beyond, especially when home site excavation has left us with a flat cut into a hillside. Extend the theme with the vast array of part-sun/part-shade species to bring a visual line to the sitting area or perhaps develop an inviting, even mysterious pathway to a refuge tucked into the thicket just out of view from the house.

All the conventional concepts of landscaping apply: site analysis, planning, hardscaping, walkways, establishment of line, rhythm, texture, scale and perspective. The plant selection is merely from an alternative list.

The upside of using natives is choosing species with a high probability of success as well as supporting important habitats for pollinators, birds and small mammals, a practice encouraged by the entomologist Doug Tallamy in his book *Bringing Nature Home*, and intriguing and sobering call for back yard ecology.

The challenge comes in either locating a designer committed to native plants (*see a list of several on page 311*) or self-designing with species that are rarely found in convenient garden centers. Turn to libraries, used book vendors, and websites to construct a mosaic on kitchentable notepads. There are no shortage of good visual ideas. All that is required is identifying comparable and appropriate native plants and substituting them for the pictured exotics.

Instead of wandering the aisles of a conventional garden center hoping to find something to fit or simply accepting a plant someone needs to sell, we understand the habitat we have and then develop a broad shopping list. Then we consult a native plant nursery or order online from many reputable vendors.

The reward for this approach is a more organized plan and a sense of being in control of the design, as well as the satisfaction that comes from growing with a garden.

# *Paths, mysteries, retreats*

Although the obvious purpose is to get from here to there, foot traffic routes in landscapes serve much more important functions, summarized by the old adage, "it's the journey, not the destination."

Simple and often desirable landscapes are a single line of view or single garden "room," which we can enjoy from a static position. More complex designs involve walkways that take us *into* and *through* the landscape. For that, plan with care.

In wildscaping, examine design theory of state and national parks, which construct *trails* to allow us to immerse ourselves in nature and move from one point of interest to another. While these can be primitive primarily for ardent hikers, they are most often rustic but sedate for the general public and especially for persons with disabilities.

A trail might take us into mysterious or serene woodlands, cheerful meadows and prairies, along dramatic wetlands and streams, sometimes seamlessly because the trail construction standard is relatively uniform. Along the way we might encounter bridges, turnpikes, and resting places, all designed to reinforce the sense of wild place.

Much more formality is suggested by a garden *path*, which is most often a strip of well-groomed lawn but may be made from stone or brick pavers, occasionally crushed gravel.

- Lawn paths offer the advantage of widening and narrowing to create the illusion of rooms bordered in often sweeping curves by bedding plants, but also require ongoing care as a garden element.

- Paved paths may be punctuated by tiny sitting areas to enjoy a point of interest, and

give the garden a sense of elegance and permanence. The downside, of course, is the installation cost, which often keeps them narrower in width and rarely opened into plazas.

Trail builders have standards for grade — how a pathway rises and falls, for what distance and steepness and with how much flat ground in between. The more accessibility is required, the more gentle the route.

Path builders enjoy the most success when the walkway is on as close to level a line as possible, an astonishing example of which is found in the Alpine Garden at Jardin des Plantes in Paris. The section of a city park recreates high mountain habitats of France with landscape rising and falling dramatically along what is a nearly level gravel path — a native plant collection in the heart of one of the world's major cities for all to freely enjoy.

As a trail becomes a metaphor for wilderness adventure, a path suggests an extended courtyard when paved or a lazy, meandering river when grassed (or better still, mossed). In either event, they draw us into the native plant landscape and allow us to immerse ourselves in the pleasure of participation.

## NPS Trail specifications

The National Park Service manuals for designing and building trails includes an array of terms related to precise construction specifications. Here's a summary of the major ones that landscapers can use in their own backyard designs.

**Tread width** — the actual walking surface of the trail, and should be initially constructed or smoothed to standard. In less used areas, the bare tread may eventually evolve into one that requires mowing, but should nonetheless be on a smooth underlying structure. Four feet is a recognized standard for two persons walking side by side. (Garden tractors should have a minimum of five feet of space.)

**Clearing width** — the area "kept free of brush, limbs, briars, tall grass, weeds and other obstructions that would slap against the hiker or their pack or soak them following a rain or heavy dew." Clearing width is defined as the space on *each side* of the tread. NPS also recognizes the value of varying the clearing width, widening it at points of interest and narrowing it when aesthetics or control issues dictate. For example, a path can narrow to save a couple of large trees that somewhat crowd the tread. Narrow points are used to discourage horses or ATV traffic.

**Clearing height** — NPS picks eight to 10 feet to prevent backpack snags, with consideration for winter hikers on heavy snow. Anything below eight feet becomes a doorway, through which tools and implements must safely pass.

# Some key NPS Trail Specifications

| Desired Standard | Urban | Rural/Roaded | Semiprimitive |
|---|---|---|---|
| **Tread width** | | | |
| Hiking segment | 48 inches | 24 inches | 18 inches |
| Accessible segments | 60 inches | 36 inches | 28 inches |
| Clearing width | 24 inches | 12 inches | 12 inches |
| Clearing height (minimum) | 10 feet | 8 feet | 8 feet |
| **Sustained slope** | | | |
| Hiking segments | 10 percent | 10 percent | 15 percent |
| Accessible segments | 3 percent | 8 percent | 12 percent |
| **Maximum slope** | | | |
| Hiking segments | 15% for 100 feet | 20% for 100 feet | 30% for 100 feet |
| Accessible segments | 8% for 30 feet | 10% for 50 feet | 10% for 50 feet |
| Cross slope | 3 percent | 5 percent | 8 percent |
| Passing spot (maximum interval) | n/a | 600 feet | 1200 feet |
| Rest area interval- maximum | 1200 feet | 1200 feet | 1/2 mile |
| **Surfaces** | | | |
| Urban | Asphalt, aggregate, woodchip, sod | | |
| Rural/roaded | Native wood chip, aggregate | | |
| Semiprimitive | Native material | | |
| **Accessible surfaces** | | | |
| Urban | Asphalt, aggregate | | |
| Rural/roaded | Asphalt, aggregate | | |
| Semiprimitive | Native material, stabilized aggregate | | |

**Slope, sustained** — goes to trail stability and erosion prevention. Calculated in degrees, slope is determined by dividing the vertical distance by the horizontal distance. For example, a rise of five feet along 100 feet of path is a 5 percent slope.

**Slope, maximum** — brief, steep grades are sometimes essential, but reasonable limits for both erosion and comfort remain.

**Cross slope** — If a path is cut into the side of the hill, water flowing downhill must be encouraged to cross the path and keep going. Radical departures from level, however, are both uncomfortable and can erode in heavy runoff situations. A 5 percent cross slope on a 48-inch tread is a drop of 2.4 inches. Ankles will notice it.

**Rest areas and passing places** — Although not a safety issue in back yard gardens, consider it from an aesthetic standpoint. Widen the trail clearing at regular intervals or points of interest to encourage the visitor to pause and admire the view.

**Trail surfaces** — Hard paving such as asphalt is not essential except in extraordinarily heavily-trafficked gardens, and pavers tend to formalize it. Stabilized aggregate — the kind of gravel often used in driveways — is a firm surface that, when packed with a tamper, becomes very sturdy. Septic sand, graded and tamped, is a bit softer and easier to weed, but prone to erosion. Turf grasses are reasonably traffic-friendly, but of limited value in densely wooded areas. Wood chips create a softer feel, but must be refreshed on a regular basis because of decomposition — incidentally creating useful humus.

### Steps and stairs

When we cannot avoid stairways tread-to-rise ratios should be comfortable for walking. Common materials for risers are rocks, logs, overlapping rocks, plank-style retaining stairways and crib-ladder stairways. Standards for steps are:

| Rise | Tread width |
|------|-------------|
| 4 inches | 19 inches |
| 5 inches | 15 inches |
| 6 inches | 12.5 inches |
| 7 inches | 10.75 inches |

(*"Accessible" refers to Americans With Disability Act-required accessibility for persons with disabilities, particularly those who use wheelchairs.*

For garden purposes, the primitive specifications have been discarded — grades are steep, tread is very narrow, and in general it is not conducive to gardens other than perhaps simple access routes to the rear of deep beds.

## Concepts for rain gardens

A certain amount of mystique surrounds *rain gardens*, which are nothing more than *swales,* commonly found in nature, that briefly pond in response to bursts of precipitation.

Swales are low areas in the terrain, created by a variety of forces and widely varied in depth, size and drainage characteristics. They pond easily from stormwater runoff and drain relatively fast. Low areas that drain poorly may become *bogs*, *swamps* or *marshes*, which are all characterized by standing water.

Swales are sometimes constructed to alleviate acute runoff problems in residential and commercial developments. When used to collect stormwater from large parking lots that includes pollutants that should not be in streams, they can be *bioretention basins* populated with specific species of native plants, especially shrubs and trees, recognized for their ability to pull pollution from the water.

Swales are also an element of *permaculture* strategies, especially in developing countries, to harvest unexpected excesses of stormwater and then disperse it slowly into agricultural fields.

In our own landscapes, rain gardens take advantage of runoff making its way down a steep slope or emitting from a gutter downspout, hold it in a decoratively planted area, and then slowly ease it into the ground. From impermeable surfaces such as driveways or inefficient areas such as lawns, runoff can be cleverly directed into swales and gradually dispersed into the groundwater supply rather than into storm drains.

Swales can be anything from barely a dent in the surface to considerably deep, but should always be on the *downhill side* of buildings, *never* over septic fields, *a minimum* of 15 feet from foundations and designed to drain within 72 hours — the length of time it takes for mosquitoes to get into action.

Many models in nature offer tantalizing opportunities for rain gardens. Attentive to the principle that the land is inundated, perhaps for only a short time, perhaps for a day or more, perhaps in varying degree, we need only to look at floodplain communities for inspiration.

Stream and river flooding ranges from very infrequent to great regularity, and the exact amounts very often result in *terraces* that support distinct ecological communities. Some are sunny, some are shaded. Some are mauled with high velocity scouring of all but very specific types of plants, while others are stuck in ooze for extended periods behind natural levees as *backswamps*.

If enough water is available, we may construct dikes and terraces on a broad area to suggest several different kinds of floodplains, or we may opt for concentrated pits to develop into *thickets*. If we spend a bit of time learning about alluvial possibilities, we may find clues on how to resolve a runoff dilemma or simply create an interesting landscape feature just as an amusement.

## Rills as landscape features

Beginning with the first decorative landscapes in Persia, Babylonia and other middle eastern cultures, rills have been strategically used not only to move water around but as a significant design element.

In nature, a rill is the first hint a gulley will soon develop. It is a thin, ephemeral water course following a natural contour, eventually to be shaped and expanded by erosion.

In sustainable urban design, especially in Europe, artificial shallow rills feed stormwater runoff into *rain gardens* along city streets, then out into parks (where they provide endless entertainment for children) and into *swales* that serve as bioretention basins. It's a practice that began in Roman times and continues in an ever more sophisticated way today.

Moving water in nature always attracts the interest of various species of plants and rills that evolve into short-term brooks are often margined with natives that enjoy periodic doses of heavy watering, but don't require the constant moisture of wetlands.

If we install a garden pond and route water from the top of a slope down to it, we have created a rill that can be decorated with an interesting array of native plants that thrive along small streams.

But more likely the water surging from our downspouts after a rainstorm will make its way somewhere, and it is here that our creativity can bloom.

In stormwater management, one type of rill might be a curved ditch, a foot or less wide and several inches deep, lined with all those *channers*, or flat bits of rock six inches or so in size, that we harvest from our lawn. Some of the water will slip through the spaces and ease into the soil; the remainder will flow until it dissipates.

Another type is more tightly sealed to prevent adjacent groundwater saturation and move more water to a specific location, such as a rain garden.

The first example will support a plant community along the edges, which are saturated; the second has very little groundwater impact.

When we design paths, it may be useful to consider the routing of rills as well, because they make exceptional features on the side of a path — quite literally a drainage ditch that feeds attractive groundcovers like *Asarum canadense* (wild ginger) and *Tiarella cordifolia* (foamflower), or a host of interesting grasses and sedges. If the supply is regular and the circumstances sufficiently acidic, ideal habitats for many mosses will result as well.

## Tiny, intimate retreats

The expression "garden" typically conjures images of vast, sweeping landscapes of artfully designed form and complementary species arrangements pleasing to the eye.

Those intrigued by landscaping with native species but with limited resources and excessive responsibilities discard the impractical "vast, sweeping," and landscape on a much tighter and often more challenging scale.

Small personal retreats appear to have evolved from two directions. The cottage garden of English culture is often a very small area, usually on the street side of the home, very tightly packed

## Ideas: landforms as garden models

Many regional geologic features provide interesting themes for gardens where a landform is actually created. Some varying ideas might include:

*Backswamp* — Extensive, marshy or swampy, depressed areas of flood plains between natural levees and valley sides or terraces.

*Barrens* — Woodland or shrubland communities where tree growth is limited by environmental conditions or disturbance. Most often associated with thin or excessively drained soils.

*Bog* — Waterlogged, spongy ground, primarily mosses, containing acidic, decaying vegetation such as sphagnum, sedges, and heaths that may develop into peat.

*Drumlin* — Low, smooth, elongated oval hill, mound, or ridge of compact till with a core of bedrock or drift. It usually has a blunt nose facing the direction approached by glacial ice and a gentler slope tapering in the other direction. The longest axis is parallel to the general direction of glacier flow. Drumlins are products of streamline flow of glaciers, which molded the subglacial floor through a combination of erosion and deposition.

*Ephemeral stream* – A small stream, or upper reach of a stream, that flows only in direct response to precipitation. It receives no protracted water supply from melting snow or other sources and its channel is above the water table at all times. An simple example is the water running away from a gutter downspout.

*Fen* — Waterlogged, open-canopy spongy ground containing decaying alkaline vegetation, characterized by reeds, that eventually develops into peat.

*Flood plain* — A nearly level plain bordering a stream and is subject to inundation under flood-stage conditions; usually an evolving landform built of sediment deposited during overflow and lateral migration of the streams. In high energy rivers, flood and ice scour are common.

*Glade* – a grassy, open depression or small valley, such as a high meadow; sometimes marshy and forming the headwaters of a stream, or a low, grassy marsh that is periodically inundated.

*Hummock* — A rounded or conical mound or other small elevation; a slight rise of ground above a level surface.

*Marsh* — Periodically wet or continually flooded areas with the surface not deeply submerged. Covered dominantly with sedges, cattails, rushes, or other hydrophytic plants and usually having little or no peat accumulation.

*Plain* — a flat, lowland area, large or small, at a low elevation of comparatively smooth and level gently undulating land. A plain has few or no prominent hills or valleys but sometimes has considerable slope, and usually occurs at low elevation relative to surrounding areas. A plain may be forested or bare of trees and may be formed by deposition or erosion.

*Seep* — a usually small area, where water slowly flows from the land surface. Flow rates for seeps are too small to be considered springs, but reflow sometimes lateral subsurface flow keeps the surface or soil just under the surface saturated during dry periods.

*Swale* — A shallow, open depression in unconsolidated materials which lacks a defined channel but can funnel overland or subsurface flow into a drainageway. Soils in swales tend to be moister and thicker compared to surrounding soils. *Swell and swale* topography is composed of small, well-rounded hillocks and shallow, closed depressions irregularly spaced across low-relief ground moraine; the effect is a subdued, irregularly undulating surface that is common on *ground moraines*. We commonly model them as rain gardens.

*Swamp* — a wooded wetland, intermittently or permanently flooded.

with a wide variety of plants. The courtyard garden from Japanese culture is similarly compact, typically immediately adjacent to an exit (or very large window), and strives for a pleasing artistic arrangement with relatively few plants.

Full sun and perhaps a picket fence define the native plant opportunity for the former toward jolly wildflowers to attract butterflies in a mesic but well-drained habitat, which may be a decorative extension of an entry arbor blanketed by *Lonicera sempervirens* (honeysuckle) to enchant hummingbirds.

The far more subtle courtyard garden may be bounded on at least one side by a screening wall, often include an open-habitat shrub or two, and include artificially-created banks of mosses, ferns, and deep-shade groundcovers. A considerable amount of stone hints at remote craggy peaks. The isolation of the miniature landscape focuses attention and exudes serenity.

The challenge of small space gardening is keeping a composition in balance without physical size to rescue us from the still appropriate concepts of line, repetition, texture, scale and perspective. The joy of these little gardens is the ability to keep them well cared for and highly groomed without huge investments of time.

Some native plant enthusiasts garden with no exterior space at all.

Colonial Americans harvested clumps of *Mitchella repens* (Partridgeberry) for the Christmas holiday, attracted by the perennial dark green leaves and bright red, long-lasting berries. These were planted in glasses, then bowls, as table decorations. By the 1840s, the fad of miniature landscapes became something of a national mania. Bowls and plant materials became ever more elaborate, giving birth to *terrariums*.

Today a fish tank of almost any size can be populated with a wide variety of native plants, which model very tiny segments of nature. Mosses and lichens are obvious choices, but miniscapes can include an array of small ferns, delicate ephemerals such as *Thalictrum thalictroides* (rue anemone), *Tridentalis borealis* (starflower), or *subshrubs* like *Linnaea borealis* (twinflower), *Gaultheria procumbens* (wintergreen) and, of course, partridgeberry for that proper holiday spirit. Even carniv-

orous bog plants or a wide variety of miniature orchids are fair game for these well-managed and charming habitats.

## Hide and reveal design elements

The practice of hide-and-reveal (sometimes called mystery-and-reward) strengthens the total presentation by creating evenly-spaced points of interest for visitors to enjoy. The concept dominates trail planning in state and national parks and is a fundamental in Japanese stroll and tea gardens.

We delight in it because it underscores the concept of a trail or path taking us on a journey of discovery, reflection, and higher consciousness.

In wilderness areas, trail designers guide the trail to identified points of interest, sometimes placing them at the end of brief side trails if very fragile, but more often along the main route. In Japanese design, as well as American designs influenced by the concept, specific dramatic points are most often deliberately placed in locations along a predetermined path, unless a naturally occurring feature (perhaps a giant moss-covered boulder or unusual tree) impacts the routing of the path.

In both situations, we round a bend, pass a visual obstacle, or enter a defined area and there it is: a visual treat emphasized with a more open area and perhaps a bench that invites us to linger and admire it.

Hide and reveal also has roots in the more formal gardens of Europe, where features, often types of doorways, shroud the next area on the walk. These traditions are fond of mystery, even a hint of danger, which might cause us to queue up a bit of courage. As we enter a room, the discovery forms a prize, or reward, for our bravery. (This style is a constant theme in the children's garden at Longwood Gardens in Kennett Square, Pa. Although not a native plant garden, it is stuffed with design inspiration.)

Similar emotional triggers can be applied to native plant designs, especially those in denser woodlands. The path might be narrowed with ever encroaching, ever more looming dense shrubs, with only a minimal portal beyond. When we scamper through and enter a small *glade*, we pause to catch our breath and take in an artfully presented display of species found on woodland edges. The visual line directs us back to the path to continue our journey.

Some designers suggest that especially longer paths include overlook points for the sake of emotional security; we can look out and get a sense of where the path will eventually take us. Others encourage garden developers to build the discoveries to either a logical sequence of events or to a climax with one final rest area to savor not only the moment, but the entire journey, before we depart.

Either way, the strategy of hide and reveal creates powerful and exciting native plant design that cannot be found in stock patterns from any publication. We are obligated to walk the imaginary path many times to find the garden that lies hidden within a unique bit of terrain.

## A brief discussion about moss

The enthusiastic new homeowner had at the top of his landscaping agenda the matter of developing a fine, well-manicured lawn. The property was covered by very mature oak trees, which could be dealt with by hiring a tree service to improve the canopy. But the real problem, he sighed, was an utterly awful infestation of moss.

He would have friends at The Pennsylvania Turfgrass Council, which is dedicated to the proposition of eradicating moss from proper lawns, especially targeting those found on the putting greens of golf courses. Chemical possibilities abound.

At the opposite end of the spectrum are environmentally-anxious landscape enthusiasts who see moss as the green alternative to the evil lawn, which comes with such side effects as fertilizers that damage groundwater supplies and poison streams along with the pollution related to mowing equipment.

Turf buffs see moss as something akin to algae (which, in its defense, contributes substantially to the oxygen supply we breathe). While moss grows pretty much on its own, grooming is another matter and is not as easy as a lawn. Moss is usually hand cleaned because most species are too fragile to rake.

Mosses are *bryophytes*, reproducing by spores and generally drawing nutrition from dust in the air, which means they can leisurely grow on sterile soil, rocks, anywhere circumstances are convenient. They are rarely discussed in the context of native plants, but there are more than 300 species of them (along with more than 100 species of liverworts) in Pennsylvania.

Mosses can be quite particular about where they set up shop, how they compete with other bryophytes as climate fluctuates during the season, and have a variety of growth habits. Most make poor substitutes for lawn because they are fragile, require constant moisture in cool and acidic habitats, and even the smallest bit of litter creates an overwhelming obstacle.

Perhaps the most convenient of the mosses are *mniums* and *polytrichums*, both of which can withstand raking and if well cultivated create smooth carpets that withstand light foot traffic. *Polytrichums* in particular are prized species in Japanese temple gardens, appearing in many stunning images of well-groomed ground cover and accents.

Most mosses require patient hand grooming to look their best, and about the easiest way to get started is to clear a patch of poor ground and keep it free of any herbaceous material. Mosses can be transplanted with varied results, depending mostly on how different the new site is from the old.

An exceptional guide for the region is *Outstanding Mosses and Liverworts of Pennsylvania and Nearby States* by Susan Munch of Albright College (susanm@alb.edu).

# Soils of Northeastern Pennsylvania

The National Resource Conservation Service of the USDA has over the years amassed a wealth of data about soils, oriented primarily for commercial agriculture, civil engineering and even military purposes. Free, highly detailed maps are available from two online services, permitting home landscapers to identify soil to areas less than an acre in size.

We all know that nearly all soils in the region are a long way from the silky black loams that we often associate with ideal garden sites, and soil testing services from our local extension service offices will typically suggest a variety of amendments to bring it up to par for decorative, vegetable and turf-oriented landscaping.

However, when we consider landscaping with native plants, unamended soils are essential — hence the suggestion that native plant landscaping saves money because soil preparation investment is virtually zero.

For conservation/restoration styles of landscaping, knowing specifically what sort of soil lies under our feet brings us first to the soil mapping services and then to the very useful data we need for proper plant choices.

The data in this section, all from NRCS, includes a series of tables for all of the 92 soil groups in Carbon, Monroe, Pike and Wayne counties. These identify a soil from the mapping code composition in terms of sand, silt and clay, the amount of organic matter found in the top 12 inches, and the soil's reactivity, or pH.

Soil composition is shown as percentages in dry weight. Organic matter (Org.) is also a percentage by dry weight.

A secondary list of all soils by group names indicates the origin of the soil, where it is likely found, potential depth, flooding, ponding or saturation issues and a brief discussion about potential challenges landscapers may face.

Plant cultivation information almost always discusses a general soil type, i.e., "sandy loam," and sometimes pH preferences. Our plant lists also describe the general type of habitat where a species might be found, and ecological community lists include brief descriptions of habitats and other species that might be associated. Together, these data form a mosaic to help guide the landscaper toward choices appropriate for local conditions or an indication of what microhabitat alterations may be fruitful when planting species that may not be an ideal natural fit.

## How to identify local soils

A useful service of The Pennsylvania State University permits landscapers to identify soil groups to individual lots. The National Resource Conservation Service of the USDA offers a similar service, which is a bit more complicated but in the end leads directly to soil data reports.

Both services tend to be oriented to soil scientists and civil engineers, so a bit of patience helps when using these sites.

Procedures for Penn State begin with the university's soil map service (http://soilmap.psu.edu/code/mapindex.asp)
- Click on "Find Place"
- Choose county, then municipality.
- On the focused map, select "Map Layers" in the left column
- Select roads (both boxes), and hit refresh.

In the layers options list, users can also select the aerial photo feature to help pinpoint a specific area of interest, such as a residence or other nearby landmark.

Other layers on the map show flood plains,

creeks and rivers, topographical maps, and a shaded texture representation to easily grasp landforms.

Select the hand icon at the top of the map and use the cursor to center the map on a desired location, then zoom in. When sufficiently close, boundaries of the soil groups and soil codes appear.

Residents of Carbon, Monroe, Pike and Wayne Counties can make use of soil data published here, simply by locating the symbol on the summary tables and learning more detail from the soil series list following the table section.

Others can go to the datamart at NRCS (http://soildatamart.nrcs.usda.gov/):

- Select state (Pennsylvania), then County
- Locate the soil symbol in the list; then choose the type of report desired; note the formal name for the soil group in your area of interest is provided.
- Select "generate reports" to produce and email a customized pdf-format document for personal use.

For more detailed information, go to the soil database (http://ortho.ftw.nrcs.usda.gov/cgi-bin/osd/osdnamequery.cgi) and enter the name (not the code) of the soil group.

***Other states***

Those outside of Pennsylvania begin at the NRCS map site (http://soildatamart.nrcs.usda.gov/).

Click on "Start WSS" and first define an area of interest by manipulating the map to a reasonable center point, zooming in and using the "area of interest" (AOI) tool to get within 10,000 acres. These maps include roads and aerial photos as a base. When an area is identified, click the "Soil Map" tab on the top and a map will be generated. The legend will appear on the left and show a soil series name that can be used to obtain detailed information from the datamart.

With the soil abbreviation in hand, now go to the datamart at NRCS:

- Select state, then county
- Locate the soil symbol in the list; then choose the type of report desired; make a note of the formal name for the soil group.
- Select "generate reports" for a customized pdf-format document for personal use.

For more detailed information, go to the soil database (http://ortho.ftw.nrcs.usda.gov/cgi-bin/osd/osdnamequery.cgi) and enter the name (not the code) of the soil group.

## Three common geology expressions relating to soils

***Loam soils*** are composed of relatively even concentrations of clay, silt and sand. They feel gritty to plastic when moist, easily retain water, but will drain well where topography permits. They tend to be higher in nutrients than sandy soils and are often described as feeling "mellow" and easy to work in a wide range of moisture conditions.

Soils dominated by one or two of the particle size groups can behave like a loam when it has a strong granular structure resulting from high content of organic matter.

A soil that is technically a loam might become unlike loamy earth when it is depleted of organic matter, compacted or has dispersive clay in its fine-earth fraction.

Common expressions describe variables in composition: sandy loam, silty loam, clay loam, sandy clay loam, silty clay loam. (*See chart on page 16.*)

***Fragipans*** are naturally-occurring dense layers of hard soil found in some soils at varying depths. Because of the compaction or extreme density rather than high clay content, there is relatively slow permeability to water and their presence can greatly impact plants growing above.

***Channers*** are pieces of limestone, sandstone or schist that are relatively thin and flat and up to about 6 inches in length on their longest side. "Channery" is an expression that describes their presence in a number of loams found in the region.

# Key physical properties of regional soils

## Soils of Carbon County

| Code | Soil name | Clay | Sand | Silt | Org. | pH |
|------|-----------|------|------|------|------|-----|
| AaA | Albrights channery loam, 0 to 3 percent slopes | 17.6 | 42.8 | 39.6 | 1.98 | 4.7 |
| AaB2 | Albrights channery loam, 3 to 8 percent slopes moderately eroded | 17.6 | 42.8 | 39.6 | 1.98 | 4.7 |
| AbA | Albrights silt loam, 0 to 3 percent slopes | 22.2 | 29.0 | 48.8 | 1.98 | 5.5 |
| AbB2 | Albrights silt loam 3 to 8 percent slopes moderately eroded | 22.2 | 29.0 | 48.8 | 1.98 | 5.5 |
| AcB | Albrights very stony loam, 0 to 8 percent slopes | 17.6 | 42.8 | 39.6 | 1.98 | 4.7 |
| AcD | Albrights very stony loam, 8 to 25 percent slopes | 17.6 | 42.8 | 39.6 | 1.98 | 4.7 |
| AdA | Allenwood gravelly loam and silt loam, 0 to 3 percent slopes | 18.6 | 41.3 | 40.1 | 2.35 | 4.6 |
| AdB2 | Allenwood gravelly loam and silt loam, 3 to 8 percent slopes, moderately eroded | 18.6 | 41.3 | 40.1 | 2.35 | 4.6 |
| AdC2 | Allenwood gravelly loam and silt loam, 8 to 15 percent slopes, moderately eroded | 18.6 | 41.3 | 40.1 | 2.35 | 4.6 |
| AgA | Allenwood gravelly silt loam, 0 to 3 percent slopes | 18.6 | 28.3 | 53.1 | 2.35 | 4.6 |
| AgB2 | Allenwood gravelly silt loam, 3 to 8 percent slopes, moderately eroded | 18.6 | 28.3 | 53.1 | 2.35 | 4.6 |
| AgC2 | Allenwood gravelly silt loam, 8 to 15 percent slopes, moderately eroded | 18.6 | 28.3 | 53.1 | 2.35 | 4.6 |
| AgD2 | Allenwood gravelly silt loam, 15 to 25 percent slopes, moderately eroded | 18.6 | 28.3 | 53.1 | 2.35 | 4.6 |
| AmC3 | Allenwood gravelly silty clay loam, 8 to 15 percent slopes, severely eroded | 18.6 | 28.3 | 53.1 | 2.35 | 4.6 |
| AmD3 | Allenwood gravelly silty clay loam, 15 to 25 percent slopes, severely eroded | 18.6 | 28.3 | 53.1 | 2.35 | 4.6 |

# Soils of Carbon County

| Code | Soil name | Clay | Sand | Silt | Org. | pH |
|------|-----------|------|------|------|------|-----|
| AnB | Alvira gravelly silt loam, 0 to 8 percent slopes | 17.7 | 27.6 | 54.8 | 1.22 | 4.6 |
| ArB | Alvira very stony silt loam, 0 to 8 percent slopes | 17.7 | 27.6 | 54.8 | 1.22 | 4.6 |
| AsA | Alvira and Shelmadine silt loams, 0 to 3 percent slopes | 18.5 | 27.6 | 55.3 | 1.40 | 4.6 |
| AsB2 | Alvira and Shelmadine silt loams, 3 to 8 percent slopes, moderately eroded | 18.5 | 27.6 | 55.3 | 1.40 | 4.6 |
| AtB | Alvira and Shelmadine very stony silt loams, 0 to 8 percent slopes | 18.5 | 27.6 | 55.3 | 1.40 | 4.6 |
| AvA | Andover very stony loam, 0 to 3 percent slopes | 23.8 | 39.6 | 36.6 | 1.23 | 5.0 |
| BcB2 | Buchanan gravelly loam, 3 to 10 percent slopes, moderately eroded | 21.6 | 40.8 | 37.6 | 1.01 | 4.6 |
| BhB | Buchanan very stony loam, 0 to 8 percent slopes | 21.6 | 40.8 | 37.6 | 1.44 | 4.6 |
| BhD | Buchanan very stony loam, 8 to 25 percent slopes | 21.6 | 40.8 | 37.6 | 1.44 | 4.6 |
| CmA | Comly silt loam, 0 to 3 percent slopes | 19.3 | 26.5 | 54.3 | 1.88 | 5.0 |
| CmB2 | Comly silt loam, 3 to 8 percent slopes, moderately eroded | 19.3 | 26.5 | 54.3 | 1.88 | 5.0 |
| CmC | Comly silt loam, 8 to 15 percent slopes | 19.3 | 26.5 | 54.3 | 1.88 | 5.0 |
| CnC3 | Comly silty clay loam, 8 to 15 percent slopes, severely eroded | 28.1 | 17.8 | 54.1 | 1.88 | 5.0 |
| CoB | Comly very stony silt loam, 0 to 8 percent slopes | 19.3 | 26.5 | 54.3 | 3.28 | 5.0 |
| CoD | Comly very stony silt loam, 8 to 25 percent slopes | 19.3 | 26.5 | 54.3 | 3.28 | 5.0 |
| CtA | Conotton gravelly loam, 0 to 3 percent slopes | 14.3 | 52.0 | 33.7 | 1.28 | 5.6 |
| CtB | Conotton gravelly loam, 3 to 8 percent slopes | 14.3 | 52.0 | 33.7 | 1.28 | 5.6 |
| CtD | Conotton gravelly loam, 15 to 25 percent slopes | 14.3 | 52.0 | 33.7 | 1.28 | 5.6 |
| DeB | Dekalb very stony loam, 0 to 8 percent slopes | 15.0 | 44.8 | 40.2 | 2.96 | 4.1 |
| DeD | Dekalb very stony loam, 8 to 25 percent slopes | 15.0 | 44.8 | 40.2 | 2.96 | 4.1 |
| DeF | Dekalb very stony loam, 25 to 100 percent slopes | 15.0 | 44.8 | 40.2 | 2.96 | 4.1 |

# Soils of Carbon County

| Code | Soil name | Clay | Sand | Silt | Org. | pH |
|------|-----------|------|------|------|------|-----|
| DrA | Drifton loam, 0 to 3 percent slopes | 20.3 | 41.7 | 38.0 | 1.42 | 4.6 |
| DrB2 | Drifton loam, 3 to 8 percent slopes, moderately eroded | 20.3 | 41.7 | 38.0 | 1.42 | 4.6 |
| DsB | Drifton very stony loam, 0 to 8 percent slopes | 20.3 | 41.7 | 38.0 | 1.75 | 4.6 |
| FtA | Fleetwood sandy loam, 0 to 3 percent slopes | 21.0 | 62.5 | 16.5 | 1.42 | 4.6 |
| FtB2 | Fleetwood sandy loam, 3 to 8 percent slopes, moderately eroded | 21.0 | 62.5 | 16.5 | 1.42 | 4.6 |
| FtC2 | Fleetwood sandy loam, 8 to 15 percent slopes, moderately eroded | 21.0 | 62.5 | 16.5 | 1.42 | 4.6 |
| FvB | Fleetwood very stony loam, shallow, 0 to 8 percent slopes | 19.5 | 51.2 | 29.2 | 1.92 | 4.3 |
| FvD | Fleetwood very stony loam, shallow, 8 to 25 percent slopes | 19.5 | 51.2 | 29.2 | 1.92 | 4.3 |
| FvF | Fleetwood very stony loam, shallow, 25 to 100 percent slopes | 19.5 | 51.2 | 29.2 | 1.92 | 4.3 |
| FwB | Fleetwood very stony sandy loam, 0 to 8 percent slopes | 19.5 | 62.0 | 18.4 | 1.92 | 4.3 |
| FwD | Fleetwood very stony sandy loam, 8 to 25 percent slopes | 19.5 | 62.0 | 18.4 | 1.92 | 4.3 |
| HaA | Hartleton channery silt loam, 0 to 3 percent slopes | 19.2 | 32.7 | 48.2 | 1.42 | 5.0 |
| HaB2 | Hartleton channery silt loam, 3 to 8 percent slopes, moderately eroded | 19.2 | 32.7 | 48.2 | 1.42 | 5.0 |
| HaC2 | Hartleton channery silt loam, 8 to 15 percent slopes, moderately eroded | 19.2 | 32.7 | 48.2 | 1.42 | 5.0 |
| HaC3 | Hartleton channery silt loam, 8 to 15 percent slopes, severely eroded | 19.2 | 32.7 | 48.2 | 1.42 | 5.0 |
| HaD2 | Hartleton channery silt loam, 15 to 25 percent slopes, moderately eroded | 19.2 | 32.7 | 48.2 | 1.42 | 5.0 |
| HaD3 | Hartleton channery silt loam, 15 to 25 percent slopes, severely eroded | 19.2 | 32.7 | 48.2 | 1.42 | 5.0 |
| HsB | Hartleton very stony loam, 0 to 8 percent slopes | 19.2 | 41.9 | 38.9 | 1.42 | 5.0 |
| HsD | Hartleton very stony loam, 8 to 25 percent slopes | 19.2 | 41.9 | 38.9 | 1.42 | 5.0 |
| HtA | Hazleton loam, 0 to 3 percent slopes | 14.3 | 39.1 | 46.6 | 1.90 | 4.6 |
| HtB | Hazleton loam, 3 to 8 percent slopes | 14.3 | 39.1 | 46.6 | 1.90 | 4.6 |

# Soils of Carbon County

| Code | Soil name | Clay | Sand | Silt | Org. | pH |
|------|-----------|------|------|------|------|-----|
| HtB2 | Hazleton loam, 3 to 8 percent slopes, moderately eroded | 14.3 | 39.1 | 46.6 | 1.90 | 4.6 |
| HtC2 | Hazleton loam, 8 to 15 percent slopes, moderately eroded | 14.3 | 39.1 | 46.6 | 1.90 | 4.6 |
| HvB | Hazleton very stony loam, 0 to 8 percent slopes | 14.3 | 39.1 | 46.6 | 1.90 | 4.6 |
| HvD | Hazleton very stony loam, 8 to 25 percent slopes | 14.3 | 39.1 | 46.6 | 1.90 | 4.6 |
| Hy | Holly silt loam | 22.0 | 24.6 | 53.4 | 2.45 | 6.4 |
| KcB2 | Klinesville channery silt loam, 3 to 8 percent slopes, moderately eroded | 16.1 | 29.7 | 54.2 | 0.71 | 5.3 |
| KcC2 | Klinesville channery silt loam, 8 to 15 percent slopes, moderately eroded | 16.1 | 29.7 | 54.2 | 0.71 | 5.3 |
| KcC3 | Klinesville channery silt loam, 8 to 15 percent slopes, severely eroded | 16.1 | 29.7 | 54.2 | 0.71 | 5.3 |
| KcD2 | Klinesville channery silt loam, 15 to 25 percent slopes, moderately eroded | 16.1 | 29.7 | 54.2 | 0.71 | 5.3 |
| KcD3 | Klinesville channery silt loam, 15 to 25 percent slopes, severely eroded | 16.1 | 29.7 | 54.2 | 0.71 | 5.3 |
| KcE2 | Klinesville channery silt loam, 25 to 35 percent slopes, moderately eroded | 16.1 | 29.7 | 54.2 | 0.71 | 5.3 |
| KcE3 | Klinesville channery silt loam, 25 to 35 percent slopes, severely eroded | 16.1 | 29.7 | 54.2 | 0.71 | 5.3 |
| KcF | Klinesville channery silt loam, 35 to 80 percent slopes | 16.1 | 29.7 | 54.2 | 0.71 | 5.3 |
| KcF3 | Klinesville channery silt loam, 35 to 80 percent slopes, severely eroded | 16.1 | 29.7 | 54.2 | 0.71 | 5.3 |
| KvD | Klinesville very stony silt loam, 8 to 25 percent slopes | 16.1 | 29.7 | 54.2 | 1.47 | 5.3 |
| KvF | Klinesville very stony silt loam, 25 to 80 percent slopes | 16.1 | 29.7 | 54.2 | 1.47 | 5.3 |
| LaB2 | Laidig gravelly loam, 3 to 8 percent slopes, moderately eroded | 23.8 | 51.5 | 24.6 | 1.17 | 4.6 |
| LaC2 | Laidig gravelly loam, 8 to 15 percent slopes, moderately eroded | 23.8 | 51.5 | 24.6 | 1.17 | 4.6 |
| LaD3 | Laidig gravelly loam, 15 to 25 percent slopes, severely eroded | 23.8 | 51.5 | 24.6 | 1.17 | 4.6 |

# Soils of Carbon County

| Code | Soil name | Clay | Sand | Silt | Org. | pH |
|------|-----------|------|------|------|------|-----|
| LdB | Laidig very stony loam, 3 to 8 percent slopes | 23.3 | 51.6 | 25.0 | 1.17 | 4.6 |
| LdD | Laidig very stony loam, 8 to 25 percent slopes | 23.3 | 51.6 | 25.0 | 1.17 | 4.6 |
| LeA | Leck kill channery silt loam, 0 to 3 percent slopes | 18.3 | 28.2 | 53.4 | 1.42 | 5.3 |
| LeB2 | Leck kill channery silt loam, 3 to 8 percent slopes, moderately eroded | 18.3 | 28.2 | 53.4 | 1.42 | 5.3 |
| LeC2 | Leck kill channery silt loam, 8 to 15 percent slopes, moderately eroded | 18.3 | 28.2 | 53.4 | 1.42 | 5.3 |
| LeC3 | Leck kill channery silt loam, 8 to 15 percent slopes, severely eroded | 18.3 | 28.2 | 53.4 | 1.42 | 5.3 |
| LeD2 | Leck kill channery silt loam, 15 to 25 percent slopes, moderately eroded | 18.3 | 28.2 | 53.4 | 1.42 | 5.3 |
| LeD3 | Leck kill channery silt loam, 15 to 25 percent slopes, severely eroded | 18.3 | 28.2 | 53.4 | 1.42 | 5.3 |
| LkB | Leck kill very stony loam, 0 to 8 percent slopes | 18.3 | 37.5 | 44.2 | 2.75 | 5.3 |
| LkD | Leck kill very stony loam, 8 to 25 percent slopes | 18.3 | 37.5 | 44.2 | 2.75 | 5.3 |
| LkF | Leck kill very stony loam, 25 to 100 percent slopes | 18.3 | 37.5 | 44.2 | 2.75 | 5.3 |
| LsA | Lickdale and Tughill loams and silt loams, 0 to 3 percent slopes | 22.5 | 32.3 | 56.2 | 12.00 | 4.8 |
| LtA | Lickdale and Tughill very stony loams, 0 to 8 percent slopes | 22.2 | 45.3 | 46.7 | 12.00 | 4.8 |
| LvB | Lordstown very stony silt loam, 0 to 8 percent slopes | 13.0 | 30.7 | 56.3 | 1.70 | 5.4 |
| LvD | Lordstown very stony silt loam, 8 to 25 percent slopes | 13.0 | 30.7 | 56.3 | 1.70 | 5.4 |
| LvF | Lordstown very stony silt loam, 25 to 80 percent slopes | 14.7 | 30.1 | 55.2 | 1.53 | 5.4 |
| MbA | Meckesville channery loam, 0 to 3 percent slopes | 18.8 | 42.8 | 38.4 | 1.98 | 4.6 |
| MbB2 | Meckesville channery loam, 3 to 8 percent slopes, moderately eroded | 18.8 | 42.8 | 38.4 | 1.98 | 4.6 |
| MbC2 | Meckesville channery loam, 8 to 15 percent slopes, moderately eroded | 18.8 | 42.8 | 38.4 | 1.98 | 4.6 |

# Soils of Carbon County

| Code | Soil name | Clay | Sand | Silt | Org. | pH |
|------|-----------|------|------|------|------|-----|
| McB | Meckesville very stony loam, 0 to 8 percent slopes | 18.8 | 42.8 | 38.4 | 1.98 | 4.6 |
| McD | Meckesville very stony loam, 8 to 25 percent slopes | 18.8 | 42.8 | 38.4 | 1.98 | 4.6 |
| MdA | Middlebury silt loam, 0 to 3 percent slopes | 11.9 | 32.0 | 56.1 | 4.69 | 5.8 |
| MdB | Middlebury silt loam, 3 to 8 percent slopes | 11.9 | 32.0 | 56.1 | 4.69 | 5.8 |
| MeA3 | Middlebury and Tioga silt loams, 0 to 3 percent slopes, severely eroded | 11.9 | 32.3 | 56.2 | 4.69 | 6.2 |
| MoA | Montevallo channery silt loam, 0 to 3 percent slopes | 18.0 | 26.9 | 55.1 | 1.23 | 5.3 |
| MoB2 | Montevallo channery silt loam, 3 to 8 percent slopes, moderately eroded | 18.0 | 26.9 | 55.1 | 1.23 | 5.3 |
| MoB3 | Montevallo channery silt loam, 3 to 8 percent slopes, severely eroded | 18.0 | 26.9 | 55.1 | 1.23 | 5.3 |
| MoC2 | Montevallo channery silt loam, 8 to 15 percent slopes, moderately eroded | 18.0 | 26.9 | 55.1 | 1.23 | 5.3 |
| MoC3 | Montevallo channery silt loam, 8 to 15 percent slopes, severely eroded | 18.0 | 26.9 | 55.1 | 1.23 | 5.3 |
| MoD2 | Montevallo channery silt loam, 15 to 25 percent slopes, moderately eroded | 18.0 | 26.9 | 55.1 | 1.23 | 5.3 |
| MoD3 | Montevallo channery silt loam, 15 to 25 percent slopes, severely eroded | 18.0 | 26.9 | 55.1 | 1.23 | 5.3 |
| MoE2 | Montevallo channery silt loam, 25 to 35 percent slopes, moderately eroded | 18.0 | 26.9 | 55.1 | 1.23 | 5.3 |
| MoE3 | Montevallo channery silt loam, 25 to 35 percent slopes, severely eroded | 18.0 | 26.9 | 55.1 | 1.23 | 5.3 |
| MoF2 | Montevallo channery silt loam, 35 to 100 percent slopes, eroded | 18.0 | 26.9 | 55.1 | 1.23 | 5.3 |
| MrB | Morris very stony silt loam, 0 to 8 percent slopes | 20.0 | 26.5 | 53.5 | 3.00 | 5.3 |
| Mu | Muck and Peat | 0 | 0 | 0 | 84.50 | |
| NaB | Natalie very stony loam, 0 to 8 percent slopes | 21.2 | 41.0 | 37.7 | 1.62 | 4.6 |
| NoA | Norwich silt loam, 0 to 3 percent slopes | 19.8 | 31.3 | 48.8 | 4.33 | 5.8 |
| NoB | Norwich silt loam, 3 to 8 percent slopes | 18.5 | 27.1 | 54.4 | 6.50 | 5.8 |
| NvB | Norwich very stony loam, 0 to 8 percent slopes | 18.5 | 43.0 | 38.5 | 6.50 | 5.8 |

# Soils of Carbon County

| Code | Soil name | Clay | Sand | Silt | Org. | pH |
|------|-----------|------|------|------|------|-----|
| Pa | Papakating silty clay loam | 28.3 | 17.8 | 53.8 | 2.42 | 6.4 |
| PkA | Pekin silt loam, 0 to 3 percent slopes | 22.3 | 9.9 | 67.8 | 1.42 | 6.2 |
| RsB | Rushtown shaly silt loam, 3 to 8 percent slopes | 22.2 | 23.4 | 54.4 | 0.68 | 5.3 |
| RsC | Rushtown shaly silt loam, 8 to 15 percent slopes | 22.2 | 23.4 | 54.4 | 0.68 | 5.3 |
| RsD | Rushtown shaly silt loam, 15 to 25 percent slopes | 22.2 | 23.4 | 54.4 | 0.68 | 5.3 |
| RsE | Rushtown shaly silt loam, 25 to 35 percent slopes | 22.2 | 23.4 | 54.4 | 0.68 | 5.3 |
| ShA | Shelmadine silt loam, 0 to 3 percent slopes | 18.5 | 26.2 | 55.3 | 1.40 | 4.6 |
| ShB2 | Shelmadine silt loam, 3 to 8 percent slopes, moderately eroded | 18.5 | 26.2 | 55.3 | 1.40 | 4.6 |
| SmB | Shelmadine very stony silt loam, 0 to 8 percent slopes | 18.5 | 26.2 | 55.3 | 1.40 | 4.6 |
| SsB | Swartswood channery silt loam, 0 to 8 percent slopes | 15.4 | 44.1 | 40.5 | 1.04 | 4.6 |
| SsC2 | Swartswood channery silt loam, 8 to 15 percent slopes, moderately eroded | 15.4 | 44.1 | 40.5 | 1.04 | 4.6 |
| SwB | Swartswood very stony loam, 0 to 8 percent slopes | 15.4 | 44.1 | 40.5 | 1.04 | 4.6 |
| SwD | Swartswood very stony loam, 8 to 25 percent slopes | 15.4 | 44.1 | 40.5 | 1.04 | 4.6 |
| Tf | Tioga fine sandy loam | 11.5 | 44.0 | 44.5 | 1.67 | 6.2 |
| Tg | Tioga silt loam | 11.5 | 32.3 | 56.2 | 3.14 | 6.2 |
| TmB | Tioga and Middlebury very stony loams, 0 to 8 percent slopes | 11.5 | 42.3 | 46.2 | 3.14 | 6.2 |
| TuA | Tunkhannock gravelly loam, 0 to 3 percent slopes | 15.0 | 51.5 | 33.5 | 2.08 | 4.8 |
| TuB | Tunkhannock gravelly loam, 3 to 8 percent slopes | 15.0 | 51.5 | 33.5 | 2.08 | 4.8 |
| TuC | Tunkhannock gravelly loam, 8 to 15 percent slopes | 15.0 | 51.5 | 33.5 | 2.08 | 4.8 |
| TuD | Tunkhannock gravelly loam, 15 to 25 percent slopes | 15.0 | 51.5 | 33.5 | 2.08 | 4.8 |
| VeB | Very stony land, 0 to 8 percent slopes | 12.5 | 43.2 | 44.3 | 0.71 | 4.6 |

# Soils of Carbon County

| Code | Soil name | Clay | Sand | Silt | Org. | pH |
|------|-----------|------|------|------|------|-----|
| VeD | Very stony land, 8 to 25 percent slopes | 12.5 | 43.2 | 44.3 | 0.71 | 4.6 |
| VeF | Very stony land, 25 to 120 percent slopes | 12.5 | 43.2 | 44.3 | 0.71 | 4.6 |
| VoB | Volusia silt loam, 0 to 8 percent slopes | 18.0 | 32.8 | 49.2 | 3.52 | 5.5 |
| VsB | Volusia very stony loam, 0 to 8 percent slopes | 21.4 | 46.1 | 32.4 | 3.52 | 5.5 |
| WaB2 | Watson gravelly silt loam, 0 to 8 percent slopes, moderately eroded | 22.3 | 23.7 | 53.9 | 1.43 | 5.0 |
| WsA | Watson silt loam, 0 to 3 percent slopes | 22.3 | 23.7 | 53.9 | 1.43 | 5.0 |
| WsB2 | Watson silt loam, 3 to 8 percent slopes, moderately eroded | 22.3 | 23.7 | 53.9 | 1.43 | 5.0 |
| WsC2 | Watson silt loam, 8 to 15 percent slopes, moderately eroded | 22.3 | 23.7 | 53.9 | 1.43 | 5.0 |
| WtC3 | Watson silty clay loam, 8 to 15 percent slopes, severely eroded | 22.3 | 23.7 | 53.9 | 1.43 | 5.0 |
| WuA | Wurtsboro channery loam, 0 to 3 percent slopes | 15.0 | 44.3 | 40.7 | 1.72 | 4.6 |
| WuB2 | Wurtsboro channery loam, 3 to 8 percent slopes, moderately eroded | 15.0 | 44.3 | 40.7 | 1.42 | 4.6 |
| WvB | Wurtsboro very stony loam, 0 to 8 percent slopes | 15.0 | 44.3 | 40.7 | 1.72 | 4.6 |
| WvD | Wurtsboro very stony loam, 8 to 25 percent slopes | 15.0 | 44.3 | 40.7 | 1.72 | 4.6 |

## All about alluvium

Alluvium is soil or sediments deposited by a river or other running water. Alluvium is composed of a variety of materials, such as fine particles of silt and clay and larger particles of sand and gravel.

Water flowing from glaciers may also deposit alluvium, but deposits directly from ice are *till*.

A river continually picks up and drops solid particles of rock and soil from its bed along its entire length. Where the river flows fast, more particles are picked up than dropped. Where the river slows, more particles are dropped than are picked up. We call areas where more particles are dropped *alluvial* or *flood plains*, and the dropped particles are called *alluvium*.

Even small streams make alluvial deposits, but it is in flood plains and deltas of large rivers that substantial and geologically-significant alluvial deposits are most often found.

# Soils of Monroe County

| Code | Soil Name | Clay | Sand | Silt | Org. | pH |
|------|-----------|------|------|------|------|-----|
| 7B | Shohola-Edgemere complex, 0 to 8 percent slopes, very rubbly | 11.5 | 45.3 | 43.2 | 0.98 | 4.7 |
| 7C | Shohola-Edgemere complex, 8 to 15 percent slopes, very rubbly | 11.5 | 45.3 | 43.2 | 0.98 | 4.7 |
| 9B | Craigsville-Wyoming complex, 0 to 8 percent slopes, extremely stony | 10.0 | 57.8 | 32.2 | 1.66 | 5.0 |
| 11A | Edgemere extremely stony loam, 0 to 3 percent slopes, very rubbly | 9.6 | 45.3 | 43.2 | 3.62 | 4.8 |
| 18 | Paupack mucky peat | 0.0 | 0.0 | 0.0 | 40.00 | n/a |
| 20 | Freetown mucky peat | 0.0 | 0.0 | 0.0 | 72.25 | n/a |
| 30B | Wurtsboro stony fine sandy loam, 0 to 8 percent slopes, extremely stony | 14.0 | 69.6 | 16.4 | 1.33 | 4.6 |
| 30C | Wurtsboro stony fine sandy loam, 8 to 15 percent slopes, extremely stony | 11.5 | 67.5 | 21.0 | 1.33 | 4.6 |
| 111B | Edgemere-Shohola complex, 3 to 15 percent slopes, very rubbly | 11.5 | 45.3 | 43.2 | 3.62 | 4.8 |
| 239B | Oquaga very stony loam, 0 to 8 percent slopes, extremely bouldery | 17.0 | 31.6 | 51.4 | 1.67 | 4.8 |
| 239C | Oquaga very stony loam, 8 to 15 percent slopes, extremely bouldery | 17.0 | 43.3 | 39.7 | 1.67 | 4.8 |
| 239D | Oquaga very stony loam, 15 to 30 percent slopes, extremely bouldery | 17.0 | 43.3 | 39.7 | 1.67 | 4.8 |
| 240F | Oquaga-Arnot-Rock outcrop complex, 20 to 60 percent slopes, very rubbly | 17.0 | 43.3 | 39.7 | 1.67 | 4.8 |
| 321D | Lackawanna channery loam, 15 to 30 percent slopes, extremely stony | 15.7 | 52.8 | 31.5 | 2.80 | 5.3 |
| Ad | Alden mucky silt loam | 22.6 | 24.3 | 53.0 | 13.64 | 6.3 |
| AnA | Allenwood gravelly silt loam, 0 to 3 percent slopes | 21.2 | 26.4 | 52.4 | 1.94 | 4.6 |
| AnB | Allenwood gravelly silt loam, 3 to 8 percent slopes | 21.2 | 26.4 | 52.4 | 1.94 | 4.6 |
| AnC | Allenwood gravelly silt loam, 8 to 20 percent slopes | 21.2 | 26.4 | 52.4 | 1.94 | 4.6 |
| As | Alluvial land | 11.2 | 67.4 | 21.4 | 0.70 | 5.5 |
| AvB | Alvira gravelly silt loam, 3 to 8 percent slopes | 16.9 | 28.3 | 54.8 | 1.29 | 4.6 |
| AwB | Alvira and Watson very stony loams, 0 to 12 percent slopes | 16.9 | 40.1 | 43.0 | 1.29 | 4.6 |

# Soils of Monroe County

| Code | Soil Name | Clay | Sand | Silt | Org. | pH |
|------|-----------|------|------|------|------|-----|
| BaB | Bath channery silt loam, 3 to 8 percent slopes | 11.5 | 32.3 | 56.2 | 3.07 | 5.3 |
| BaC | Bath channery silt loam, 8 to 15 percent slopes | 11.5 | 32.3 | 56.2 | 3.07 - | 5.3 |
| BaD | Bath channery silt loam, 15 to 25 percent slopes | 11.5 | 32.3 | 56.2 | 3.07 | 5.3 |
| BbB | Bath very stony silt loam, 0 to 8 percent slopes | 11.5 | 36.6 | 51.9 | 1.83 | 5.3 |
| BbC | Bath very stony silt loam, 8 to 25 percent slopes | 11.5 | 36.6 | 51.9 | 1.83 | 5.3 |
| BeB | Benson-Rock outcrop complex, 0 to 8 percent slopes | 20.0 | 26.5 | 53.5 | 2.72 | 6.8 |
| BeC | Benson-Rock outcrop complex, 8 to 25 percent slopes | 20.0 | 26.5 | 53.5 | 2.72 | 6.8 |
| BeF | Benson-Rock outcrop complex, 25 to 70 percent slopes | 20.0 | 26.5 | 53.5 | 2.72 | 6.8 |
| BrA | Braceville gravelly loam, 0 to 3 percent slopes | 17.5 | 32.8 | 49.7 | 0.72 | 5.3 |
| BrB | Braceville gravelly loam, 3 to 8 percent slopes | 17.5 | 32.8 | 49.7 | 0.72 | 5.3 |
| BuB | Buchanan loam, 3 to 8 percent slopes | 19.4 | 42.4 | 38.2 | 1.70 | 4.6 |
| BxB | Buchanan extremely stony loam, 0 to 8 percent slopes | 22.2 | 40.4 | 37.4 | 1.47 | 4.6 |
| BxC | Buchanan extremely stony loam, 8 to 25 percent slopes | 21.2 | 41.0 | 37.7 | 0.72 | 4.6 |
| ChA | Chenango gravelly loam, 0 to 3 percent slopes | 12.0 | 53.8 | 34.2 | 2.92 | 5.3 |
| ChB | Chenango gravelly loam, 3 to 8 percent slopes | 12.0 | 53.8 | 34.2 | 2.92 | 5.3 |
| ChC | Chenango gravelly loam, 8 to 15 percent slopes | 12.0 | 53.8 | 34.2 | 2.92 | 5.3 |
| CmA | Chippewa and Norwich silt loams, 0 to 5 percent slopes | 21.2 | 25.5 | 54.6 | 4.33 | 5.8 |
| CnB | Chippewa and Norwich extremely stony soils, 0 to 8 percent slopes | 21.2 | 25.5 | 54.6 | 4.33 | 5.8 |
| CpA | Clymer loam, 0 to 3 percent slopes | 21.7 | 41.0 | 37.3 | 2.03 | 4.6 |
| CpB | Clymer loam, 3 to 8 percent slopes | 21.7 | 41.0 | 37.3 | 2.03 | 4.6 |
| CpC | Clymer loam, 8 to 15 percent slopes | 21.7 | 41.0 | 37.3 | 2.03 | 4.6 |
| CxB | Clymer extremely stony loam, 0 to 8 percent slopes | 21.7 | 41.0 | 37.3 | 2.03 | 4.6 |

# Soils of Monroe County

| Code | Soil Name | Clay | Sand | Silt | Org. | pH |
|------|-----------|------|------|------|------|-----|
| CxC | Clymer extremely stony loam, 8 to 25 percent slopes | 21.7 | 41.0 | 37.3 | 2.03 | 4.6 |
| DxB | Dekalb extremely stony loam, 0 to 8 percent slopes | 14.0 | 53.7 | 32.3 | 2.01 | 4.9 |
| DxC | Dekalb extremely stony loam, 8 to 25 percent slopes | 14.0 | 53.7 | 32.3 | 2.00 | 4.9 |
| DxE | Dekalb extremely stony loam, 25 to 80 percent slopes | 14.0 | 53.7 | 32.3 | 2.01 | 4.9 |
| ExB | Empeyville extremely stony sandy loam, 0 to 8 percent slopes | 9.5 | 77.2 | 13.3 | 2.05 | 5.5 |
| HaB | Hartleton channery silt loam, 2 to 8 percent slopes | 18.7 | 28.2 | 53.2 | 1.43 | 5.0 |
| HaC | Hartleton channery silt loam, 8 to 20 percent slopes | 18.7 | 28.2 | 53.2 | 1.43 | 5.0 |
| HxB | Hazleton extremely stony sandy loam, 0 to 8 percent slopes | 12.5 | 67.9 | 19.6 | 1.41 | 4.6 |
| HxC | Hazleton extremely stony sandy loam, 8 to 25 percent slopes | 12.5 | 67.9 | 19.6 | 1.41 | 4.6 |
| Hy | Holly silt loam | 20.2 | 37.1 | 42.8 | 2.50 | 6.4 |
| KaB | Kedron silt loam, 2 to 8 percent slopes | 23.2 | 21.9 | 55.0 | 1.69 | 4.6 |
| KaC | Kedron silt loam, 8 to 15 percent slopes | 23.2 | 21.9 | 55.0 | 1.69 | 4.6 |
| KdB | Kedron very stony loam, 0 to 8 percent slopes | 23.2 | 21.9 | 55.0 | 2.94 | 4.6 |
| KvB | Klinesville channery silt loam, 3 to 8 percent slopes | 16.2 | 29.6 | 54.2 | 0.96 | 5.3 |
| KvC | Klinesville channery silt loam, 8 to 15 percent slopes | 16.2 | 29.6 | 54.2 | 0.96 | 5.3 |
| KvD | Klinesville channery silt loam, 15 to 25 percent slopes | 16.2 | 29.6 | 54.2 | 0.96 | 5.3 |
| LaB | Lackawanna channery loam, 2 to 8 percent slopes | 16.2 | 43.8 | 40.1 | 1.42 | 5.0 |
| LaC | Lackawanna channery loam, 8 to 15 percent slopes | 16.2 | 43.8 | 40.1 | 1.42 | 5.0 |
| LaD | Lackawanna channery loam, 15 to 25 percent slopes | 16.2 | 43.8 | 40.1 | 1.42 | 5.0 |
| LbB | Lackawanna extremely stony loam, 0 to 8 percent slopes | 16.2 | 43.8 | 40.1 | 1.42 | 5.0 |

# Soils of Monroe County

| Code | Soil Name | Clay | Sand | Silt | Org. | pH |
|---|---|---|---|---|---|---|
| LbC | Lackawanna extremely stony loam, 8 to 25 percent slopes | 16.2 | 43.8 | 40.1 | 1.42 | 5.0 |
| LBE | Lackawanna and Bath extremely stony soils, steep | 16.2 | 43.8 | 40.1 | 1.42 | 5.0 |
| LgB | Laidig extremely stony loam, 0 to 8 percent slopes | 21.8 | 40.6 | 37.6 | 1.64 | 4.6 |
| LgC | Laidig extremely stony loam, 8 to 25 percent slopes | 21.8 | 40.6 | 37.6 | 1.64 | 4.6 |
| Lh | Lawrenceville silt loam | 19.2 | 12.5 | 68.2 | 2.62 | 5.3 |
| LkB | Leck kill channery silt loam, 2 to 8 percent slopes | 18.8 | 26.4 | 54.8 | 1.26 | 5.9 |
| LkC | Leck kill channery silt loam, 8 to 15 percent slopes | 18.8 | 26.4 | 54.8 | 1.26 | 5.9 |
| LkD | Leck kill channery silt loam, 15 to 25 percent slopes | 18.8 | 26.4 | 54.8 | 1.26 | 5.9 |
| LsB | Lordstown channery silt loam, 3 to 8 percent slopes | 13.0 | 30.7 | 56.3 | 1.70 | 5.4 |
| LsC | Lordstown channery silt loam, 8 to 15 percent slopes | 13.0 | 30.7 | 56.3 | 1.70 | 5.4 |
| LsD | Lordstown channery silt loam, 15 to 25 percent slopes | 13.0 | 30.7 | 56.3 | 1.70 | 5.4 |
| LxB | Lordstown extremely stony silt loam, 0 to 8 percent slopes | 13.0 | 30.7 | 56.3 | 1.70 | 5.4 |
| LxC | Lordstown extremely stony silt loam, 8 to 25 percent slopes | 13.0 | 30.7 | 56.3 | 1.70 | 5.4 |
| LyE | Lordstown and Oquaga extremely stony soils, 25 to 70 percent slopes | 14.0 | 36.0 | 50.0 | 1.70 | 5.4 |
| MaB | Mardin channery silt loam, 2 to 8 percent slopes | 12.3 | 31.7 | 56.0 | 2.07 | 5.2 |
| MaC | Mardin channery silt loam, 8 to 15 percent slopes | 12.3 | 31.7 | 56.0 | 2.07 | 5.2 |
| MbB | Mardin very stony silt loam, 0 to 8 percent slopes | 12.7 | 34.8 | 52.5 | 2.17 | 5.0 |
| MbC | Mardin very stony silt loam, 8 to 25 percent slopes | 12.7 | 34.8 | 52.5 | 2.17 | 5.0 |
| MeA | Meckesville gravelly loam, 0 to 3 percent slopes | 20.4 | 41.8 | 37.8 | 1.99 | 4.6 |

# Soils of Monroe County

| Code | Soil Name | Clay | Sand | Silt | Org. | pH |
|---|---|---|---|---|---|---|
| MeB | Meckesville gravelly loam, 3 to 8 percent slopes | 20.4 | 41.8 | 37.8 | 1.99 | 4.6 |
| MeC | Meckesville gravelly loam, 8 to 15 percent slopes | 20.4 | 41.8 | 37.8 | 1.99 | 4.6 |
| MfB | Meckesville very stony loam, 0 to 8 percent slopes | 20.4 | 41.8 | 37.8 | 1.98 | 4.6 |
| MfC | Meckesville very stony loam, 8 to 25 percent slopes | 20.4 | 41.8 | 37.8 | 1.98 | 4.6 |
| MgB | Morris channery silt loam, 2 to 10 percent slopes | 19.0 | 27.4 | 53.6 | 3.00 | 5.4 |
| MoB | Morris extremely stony silt loam, 0 to 8 percent slopes | 20.0 | 26.5 | 53.5 | 3.00 | 5.3 |
| MoC | Morris extremely stony silt loam, 8 to 20 percent slopes | 20.0 | 26.5 | 53.5 | 3.00 | 5.3 |
| Mp | Mucky peat, deep | 0.0 | 0.0 | 0.0 | 72.25 | n/a |
| Ms | Mucky peat, shallow | 0.0 | 0.0 | 0.0 | 40.00 | n/a |
| OkB | Oquaga-Lackawanna channery loams, 3 to 8 percent slopes | 17.0 | 43.3 | 39.7 | 1.70 | 4.8 |
| OkC | Oquaga-Lackawanna channery loams, 8 to 15 percent slopes | 17.0 | 43.3 | 39.7 | 1.70 | 4.8 |
| OkD | Oquaga-Lackawanna channery loams, 15 to 25 percent slopes | 17.0 | 43.3 | 39.7 | 1.70 | 4.8 |
| OxB | Oquaga-Lackawanna extremely stony loams, 0 to 8 percent slopes | 17.0 | 43.3 | 39.7 | 1.70 | 4.8 |
| OxC | Oquaga-Lackawanna extremely stony loams, 8 to 25 percent slopes | 17.0 | 43.3 | 39.7 | 1.70 | 4.8 |
| Ph | Philo silt loam | 14.0 | 36.9 | 49.1 | 2.70 | 5.3 |
| Po | Pope silt loam | 10.2 | 32.8 | 57.0 | 2.12 | 4.6 |
| Pp | Pope silt loam, high bottom | 10.2 | 32.8 | 57.0 | 2.12 | 4.6 |
| ReA | Rexford gravelly silt loam, 0 to 3 percent slopes | 14.7 | 30.2 | 55.1 | 3.00 | 5.5 |
| ReB | Rexford gravelly silt loam, 3 to 8 percent slopes | 14.7 | 30.2 | 55.1 | 3.00 | 5.5 |
| RuC | Rushtown shaly silt loam, 5 to 15 percent slopes | 21.7 | 25.2 | 53.0 | 1.57 | 5.3 |
| RuD | Rushtown shaly silt loam, 15 to 30 percent slopes | 21.7 | 25.2 | 53.0 | 1.57 | 5.3 |

# Soils of Monroe County

| Code | Soil Name | Clay | Sand | Silt | Org. | pH |
|------|-----------|------|------|------|------|-----|
| Sh | Sheffield silt loam | 25.5 | 7.0 | 67.5 | 2.65 | 5.2 |
| SmA | Shelmadine silt loam, 0 to 3 percent slopes | 18.7 | 26.0 | 55.3 | 1.34 | 4.6 |
| SpB | Shelmadine very stony silt loam, 0 to 8 percent slopes | 18.7 | 26.0 | 55.3 | 1.34 | 4.6 |
| SwB | Swartswood channery sandy loam, 3 to 8 percent slopes | 16.0 | 65.1 | 18.9 | 2.00 | 4.6 |
| SwC | Swartswood channery sandy loam, 8 to 15 percent slopes | 16.0 | 65.1 | 18.9 | 2.00 | 4.6 |
| SxB | Swartswood extremely stony sandy loam, 0 to 8 percent slopes | 16.0 | 65.1 | 18.9 | 2.00 | 4.6 |
| SxC | Swartswood extremely stony sandy loam, 8 to 25 percent slopes | 16.0 | 65.1 | 18.9 | 2.00 | 4.6 |
| VaC | Very stony land and Rock outcrops, sloping | 12.8 | 42.2 | 45.0 | 1.60 | 4.6 |
| VaE | Very stony land and Rock outcrops, steep | 12.8 | 42.2 | 45.0 | 1.60 | 4.6 |
| VoA | Volusia gravelly silt loam, 0 to 3 percent slopes | 22.5 | 28.2 | 49.3 | 2.80 | 5.5 |
| VoB | Volusia gravelly silt loam, 3 to 8 percent slopes | 22.5 | 28.2 | 49.3 | 2.83 | 5.5 |
| VxB | Volusia extremely stony silt loam, 0 to 8 percent slopes | 22.5 | 24.8 | 52.7 | 2.73 | 5.5 |
| WaB | Watson silt loam, 2 to 8 percent slopes | 21.0 | 25.2 | 53.8 | 1.69 | 5.0 |
| Wb | Wayland silty clay loam | 28.5 | 7.0 | 64.5 | 4.71 | 6.6 |
| WeB3 | Weikert channery silt loam, 3 to 8 percent slopes, eroded | 21.0 | 26.3 | 52.7 | 1.23 | 5.3 |
| WeC3 | Weikert channery silt loam, 8 to 15 percent slopes, eroded | 21.0 | 26.3 | 52.7 | 1.23 | 5.3 |
| WeD3 | Weikert channery silt loam, 15 to 25 percent slopes, eroded | 21.0 | 26.3 | 52.7 | 1.23 | 5.3 |
| WhB | Weikert-Hartleton channery silt loams, 3 to 8 percent slopes | 21.0 | 26.3 | 52.7 | 1.23 | 5.3 |
| WhC | Weikert-Hartleton channery silt loams, 8 to 15 percent slopes | 21.0 | 26.3 | 52.7 | 1.23 | 5.3 |
| WhD | Weikert-Hartleton channery silt loams, 15 to 25 percent slopes | 21.0 | 26.3 | 52.7 | 1.23 | 5.3 |
| WKE | Weikert and Klinesville soils, steep | 21.0 | 26.3 | 52.7 | 1.23 | 5.3 |
| WmB | Wellsboro channery loam, 3 to 8 percent slopes | 18.0 | 43.1 | 38.9 | 2.07 | 5.1 |

## Soils of Monroe County

| Code | Soil Name | Clay | Sand | Silt | Org. | pH |
|------|-----------|------|------|------|------|----|
| WmC | Wellsboro channery loam, 8 to 15 percent slopes | 18.0 | 43.1 | 38.9 | 2.07 | 5.1 |
| WpB | Wellsboro extremely stony loam, 0 to 8 percent slopes | 18.0 | 43.1 | 38.9 | 2.07 | 5.1 |
| WpC | Wellsboro extremely stony loam, 8 to 25 percent slopes | 18.0 | 43.1 | 38.9 | 2.07 | 5.1 |
| WrB | Worth extremely stony sandy loam, 0 to 8 percent slopes | 10.5 | 68.1 | 21.4 | 3.36 | 5.1 |
| WrC | Worth extremely stony sandy loam, 8 to 25 percent slopes | 10.5 | 68.1 | 21.4 | 3.36 | 5.1 |
| WsB | Wurtsboro channery loam, 2 to 12 percent slopes | 15.0 | 50.0 | 35.0 | 1.71 | 4.6 |
| WxB | Wurtsboro extremely stony loam, 0 to 8 percent slopes | 15.0 | 44.3 | 40.7 | 1.42 | 4.6 |
| WxC | Wurtsboro extremely stony loam, 8 to 25 percent slopes | 15.0 | 44.3 | 40.7 | 1.42 | 4.6 |
| WyA | Wyoming gravelly sandy loam, 0 to 3 percent slopes | 11.8 | 67.1 | 21.1 | 1.88 | 4.8 |
| WyB | Wyoming gravelly sandy loam, 3 to 8 percent slopes | 11.8 | 67.1 | 21.1 | 1.88 | 4.8 |
| WyC | Wyoming gravelly sandy loam, 8 to 15 percent slopes | 11.8 | 67.1 | 21.1 | 1.88 | 4.8 |
| WyD | Wyoming gravelly sandy loam, 15 to 25 percent slopes | 11.8 | 67.1 | 21.1 | 1.88 | 4.8 |
| WyE | Wyoming gravelly sandy loam, 25 to 70 percent slopes | 12.0 | 67.2 | 20.8 | 2.05 | 4.8 |

### Describing soils by reaction

"Soil reaction" — which describes how acidic or alkaline a soil might be — is usually expressed as a pH value.

Some common terms associated with specific ranges of pH include:

Extremely acid: less than 4.5
Very strongly acid: 4.5 to 5.0
Strongly acid: 5.1 to 5.5
Moderately acid: 5.6 to 6.0
Slightly acid: 6.1 to 6.5;
Neutral or circumneutral: 6.6 to 7.3
Slightly alkaline: 7.4 to 7.8
Moderately alkaline: 7.9 to 8.4
Strongly alkaline: 8.5 to 9.0
Very strongly alkaline: over 9.1

*Calcareous soils* are high in calcium carbonate, often as a result of subsurface materials and have a pH above 7.0 in the topsoil and subsoil horizons, impacting plants.

# Soils of Pike County

| Code | Soil Name | Clay | Sand | Silt | Org. | pH |
|------|-----------|------|------|------|------|-----|
| 5B | Suncook loamy sand, 0 to 8 percent slopes | 1.9 | 83.6 | 14.5 | 2.94 | 5.5 |
| 7B | Shohola-Edgemere complex, 0 to 8 percent slopes, very rubbly | 11.5 | 45.3 | 43.2 | 0.98 | 4.7 |
| 7C | Shohola-Edgemere complex, 8 to 15 percent slopes, very rubbly | 11.5 | 45.3 | 43.2 | 0.98 | 4.7 |
| 9B | Craigsville-Wyoming complex, 0 to 8 percent slopes, extremely stony | 10.0 | 57.8 | 32.2 | 1.66 | 5.0 |
| 11A | Edgemere extremely stony loam, 0 to 3 percent slopes, very rubbly | 9.6 | 45.3 | 43.2 | 3.62 | 4.8 |
| 12 | Gleneyre-Kimbles complex, 0 to 2 percent slopes | 10.0 | 5.8 | 84.2 | 10.70 | 5.9 |
| 14 | Braceville fine sandy loam | 9.8 | 68.6 | 21.5 | 4.27 | 5.3 |
| 15 | Pope fine sandy loam | 10.8 | 68.0 | 21.2 | 1.42 | 4.6 |
| 18 | Paupack mucky peat | 0.0 | 0.0 | 0.0 | 40.00 | n/a |
| 19B | Morris very channery loam, 0 to 8 percent slopes, very stony | 20.0 | 42.1 | 37.9 | 3.00 | 5.3 |
| 19C | Morris very channery loam, 8 to 15 percent slopes, very stony | 20.0 | 42.1 | 37.9 | 3.00 | 5.3 |
| 20 | Freetown mucky peat | 0.0 | 0.0 | 0.0 | 72.25 | n/a |
| 21B | Manlius very channery silt loam, 3 to 8 percent slopes, very bouldery | 12.0 | 39.4 | 48.6 | 2.45 | 4.8 |
| 21C | Manlius very channery silt loam, 8 to 15 percent slopes, very bouldery | 12.0 | 39.4 | 48.6 | 2.45 | 4.8 |
| 24A | Delaware fine sandy loam, 0 to 3 percent slopes | 6.0 | 63.5 | 30.5 | 3.00 | 6.2 |
| 24B | Delaware fine sandy loam, 3 to 8 percent slopes | 6.0 | 63.5 | 30.5 | 3.00 | 6.2 |
| 24C | Delaware fine sandy loam, 8 to 20 percent slopes | 6.0 | 63.5 | 30.5 | 3.00 | 6.2 |
| 25B | Wurtsboro channery fine sandy loam, 0 to 8 percent slopes, stony | 12.5 | 70.9 | 16.6 | 1.40 | 4.6 |
| 25C | Wurtsboro channery fine sandy loam, 8 to 15 percent slopes, stony | 12.5 | 70.9 | 16.6 | 1.40 | 4.6 |
| 26 | Philo loam | 14.0 | 57.2 | 28.8 | 1.62 | 5.3 |
| 27 | Barbour fine sandy loam | 12.0 | 71.3 | 16.7 | 2.54 | 5.3 |
| 28B | Wellsboro stony loam, 0 to 8 percent slopes, extremely stony | 16.3 | 43.7 | 39.9 | 3.42 | 5.2 |

# Soils of Pike County

| Code | Soil Name | Clay | Sand | Silt | Org. | pH |
|------|-----------|------|------|------|------|-----|
| 28C | Wellsboro stony loam, 8 to 15 percent slopes, extremely stony | 16.3 | 43.7 | 39.9 | 3.42 | 5.2 |
| 28D | Wellsboro stony loam, 15 to 25 percent slopes, extremely stony | 16.3 | 43.7 | 39.9 | 3.42 | 5.2 |
| 29B | Wellsboro channery loam, 0 to 8 percent slopes, stony | 19.3 | 42.5 | 38.1 | 2.75 | 5.3 |
| 29C | Wellsboro channery loam, 8 to 15 percent slopes, stony | 19.3 | 42.5 | 38.1 | 2.75 | 5.3 |
| 30B | Wurtsboro stony fine sandy loam, 0 to 8 percent slopes, extremely stony | 14.0 | 69.6 | 16.4 | 1.33 | 4.6 |
| 30C | Wurtsboro stony fine sandy loam, 8 to 15 percent slopes, extremely stony | 11.5 | 67.5 | 21.0 | 1.33 | 4.6 |
| 30D | Wurtsboro stony fine sandy loam, 15 to 25 percent slopes, extremely stony | 11.5 | 67.5 | 21.0 | 1.33 | 4.6 |
| 38B | Swartswood stony fine sandy loam, 0 to 8 percent slopes, extremely stony | 15.3 | 68.5 | 16.1 | 2.83 | 4.6 |
| 38C | Swartswood stony fine sandy loam, 8 to 15 percent slopes, extremely stony | 15.3 | 68.5 | 16.1 | 2.83 | 4.6 |
| 38D | Swartswood stony fine sandy loam, 15 to 30 percent slopes, extremely stony | 15.3 | 68.5 | 16.1 | 2.83 | 4.6 |
| 50C | Wasnot very flaggy sandy loam, 3 to 15 percent slopes, very rocky | 4.0 | 66.6 | 29.4 | 3.27 | 4.8 |
| 50E | Wasnot very flaggy sandy loam, 15 to 35 percent slopes, very rocky | 4.0 | 66.6 | 29.4 | 3.27 | 4.8 |
| 58C | Skytop very flaggy sandy loam, 8 to 15 percent slopes, extremely stony | 4.2 | 66.5 | 29.4 | 1.83 | 4.7 |
| 58E | Skytop very flaggy sandy loam, 15 to 35 percent slopes, extremely stony | 4.2 | 66.5 | 29.4 | 1.83 | 4.7 |
| 60B | Mardin channery silt loam, 0 to 8 percent slopes, stony | 14.0 | 35.2 | 50.8 | 3.50 | 5.1 |
| 60C | Mardin channery silt loam, 8 to 15 percent slopes, stony | 14.0 | 35.2 | 50.8 | 3.50 | 5.1 |
| 61B | Mardin stony loam, 0 to 8 percent slopes, extremely stony | 14.0 | 44.8 | 41.2 | 3.50 | 5.1 |
| 61C | Mardin stony loam, 8 to 15 percent slopes, extremely stony | 14.0 | 44.8 | 41.2 | 3.50 | 5.1 |
| 75 | Unadilla silt loam | 10.0 | 21.2 | 68.8 | 5.00 | 5.3 |

# Soils of Pike County

| Code | Soil Name | Clay | Sand | Silt | Org. | pH |
|------|-----------|------|------|------|------|-----|
| 89B | Chenango gravelly fine sandy loam, 0 to 8 percent slopes | 8.5 | 69.7 | 21.8 | 3.42 | 5.3 |
| 89C | Chenango gravelly fine sandy loam, 8 to 15 percent slopes | 8.5 | 69.7 | 21.8 | 3.42 | 5.3 |
| 89D | Chenango gravelly fine sandy loam, 15 to 25 percent slopes | 8.5 | 69.7 | 21.8 | 3.42 | 5.3 |
| 97B | Lordstown very channery loam, 3 to 8 percent slopes, very stony | 14.8 | 62.3 | 22.9 | 1.83 | 5.4 |
| 97C | Lordstown very channery loam, 8 to 15 percent slopes, very stony | 14.8 | 62.3 | 22.9 | 1.83 | 5.4 |
| 108B | Wyoming and Chenango soils, 0 to 8 percent slopes | 10.8 | 69.7 | 22.2 | 3.42 | 5.3 |
| 108C | Wyoming and Chenango soils, 8 to 15 percent slopes | 10.8 | 69.7 | 22.2 | 3.42 | 5.3 |
| 111B | Edgemere-Shohola complex, 3 to 15 percent slopes, very rubbly | 11.5 | 45.3 | 43.2 | 3.62 | 4.8 |
| 121D | Manlius-Arnot-Rock outcrop complex, 15 to 30 percent slopes, rubbly | 12.0 | 39.4 | 48.6 | 2.45 | 4.8 |
| 121F | Manlius-Arnot-Rock outcrop complex, 30 to 80 percent slopes, rubbly | 12.0 | 39.4 | 48.6 | 2.45 | 4.8 |
| 143 | Wyalusing fine sandy loam | 17.0 | 67.9 | 15.2 | 2.15 | 5.8 |
| 239B | Oquaga very stony loam, 0 to 8 percent slopes, extremely bouldery | 17.0 | 31.6 | 51.4 | 1.67 | 4.8 |
| 239C | Oquaga very stony loam, 8 to 15 percent slopes, extremely bouldery | 17.0 | 43.3 | 39.7 | 1.67 | 4.8 |
| 239D | Oquaga very stony loam, 15 to 30 percent slopes, extremely bouldery | 17.0 | 43.3 | 39.7 | 1.67 | 4.8 |
| 240F | Oquaga-Arnot-Rock outcrop complex, 20 to 60 percent slopes, very rubbly | 17.0 | 43.3 | 39.7 | 1.67 | 4.8 |
| 258F | Skytop-Wasnot-Rock outcrop complex, 15 to 60 percent slopes, very rubbly | 4.2 | 66.5 | 29.4 | 1.83 | 4.7 |
| 320B | Lackawanna channery loam, 3 to 8 percent slopes, stony | 15.7 | 52.8 | 31.5 | 2.50 | 5.3 |
| 320C | Lackawanna channery loam, 8 to 15 percent slopes, stony | 15.7 | 52.8 | 31.5 | 2.50 | 5.3 |
| 321B | Lackawanna channery loam, 3 to 8 percent slopes, extremely stony | 15.7 | 52.8 | 31.5 | 2.80 | 5.3 |

## Soils of Pike County

| Code | Soil Name | Clay | Sand | Silt | Org. | pH |
|------|-----------|------|------|------|------|-----|
| 321C | Lackawanna channery loam, 8 to 15 percent slopes, extremely stony | 15.7 | 52.8 | 31.5 | 2.80 | 5.3 |
| 321D | Lackawanna channery loam, 15 to 30 percent slopes, extremely stony | 15.7 | 52.8 | 31.5 | 2.80 | 5.3 |
| 402C | Arnot very channery loam, 3 to 15 percent slopes, very rocky | 13.0 | 45.4 | 41.6 | 1.63 | 4.8 |
| 402E | Arnot very channery loam, 15 to 35 percent slopes, very rocky | 13.0 | 45.4 | 41.6 | 1.63 | 4.8 |
| 442B | Wyoming very cobbly sandy loam, 3 to 8 percent slopes | 10.8 | 68.2 | 21.0 | 0.98 | 4.8 |
| 442C | Wyoming very cobbly sandy loam, 8 to 15 percent slopes | 10.8 | 68.2 | 21.0 | 0.98 | 4.8 |
| 442D | Wyoming very cobbly sandy loam, 15 to 30 percent slopes | 10.8 | 68.2 | 21.0 | 0.98 | 4.8 |
| 897B | Lordstown-Swartswood complex, 0 to 8 percent slopes, extremely stony | 14.8 | 62.3 | 22.9 | 1.83 | 5.4 |
| 897C | Lordstown-Swartswood complex, 8 to 15 percent slopes, extremely stony | 14.8 | 62.3 | 22.9 | 1.83 | 5.4 |
| 897D | Lordstown-Swartswood complex, 15 to 30 percent slopes, extremely stony | 14.8 | 62.3 | 22.9 | 1.83 | 5.4 |

### Notes on colluvium

Loose bodies of sediment deposited or built up at the bottom of a low-grade slope or against a barrier on that slope, transported by gravity are called *colluvium*.

Rock deposits found at the foot of a steep slope or cliff are also called colluvium.

Colluvium often *interfingers* with alluvium (deposits moved downslope by water).

Coarse deposits from avalanches, mudslides and landslides at a cliff base are called *talus* (*scree*), and the building process is called *colluviation*.

Humps at the bases of mountains or fan-shaped deposits covering old ground, similar to the shape of alluvial fans, are common results of colluviation, an important phenomenon in the fields of archaeology and soil science.

Many colluvial soils have a *fragipan* associated with them that are a brittle subsoil layer typically high in clay. One fragipan formation theory is the soil smearing during the colluvial process causes clays to seal the surface between the moving portion of soil and the stationary soil on which it slides.

Fragipans created barriers for both roots and water, impacting the plants on the surface soil.

## Soils of Wayne County

| Code | Soil Name | Clay | Sand | Silt | Org. | pH |
|------|-----------|------|------|------|------|-----|
| 7B | Shohola-Edgemere complex, 0 to 8 percent slopes, very rubbly | 11.5 | 45.3 | 43.2 | 0.98 | 4.7 |
| 7C | Shohola-Edgemere complex, 8 to 15 percent slopes, very rubbly | 11.5 | 45.3 | 43.2 | 0.98 | 4.7 |
| 9B | Craigsville-Wyoming complex, 0 to 8 percent slopes, extremely stony | 10.0 | 57.8 | 32.2 | 1.66 | 5.0 |
| 11A | Edgemere extremely stony loam, 0 to 3 percent slopes, very rubbly | 9.6 | 45.3 | 43.2 | 3.62 | 4.8 |
| 12 | Gleneyre-Kimbles complex, 0 to 2 percent slopes | 10.0 | 5.8 | 84.2 | 10.70 | 5.9 |
| 18 | Paupack mucky peat | 0.0 | 0.0 | 0.0 | 40.00 | |
| 20 | Freetown mucky peat | 0.0 | 0.0 | 0.0 | 72.25 | |
| 26 | Philo loam | 14.0 | 57.2 | 28.8 | 1.62 | 5.3 |
| 28B | Wellsboro stony loam, 0 to 8 percent slopes, extremely stony | 16.3 | 43.7 | 39.9 | 3.42 | 5.2 |
| 30B | Wurtsboro stony fine sandy loam, 0 to 8 percent slopes, extremely stony | 14.0 | 69.6 | 16.4 | 1.33 | 4.6 |
| 30C | Wurtsboro stony fine sandy loam, 8 to 15 percent slopes, extremely stony | 11.5 | 67.5 | 21.0 | 1.33 | 4.6 |
| 111B | Edgemere-Shohola complex, 3 to 15 percent slopes, very rubbly | 11.5 | 45.3 | 43.2 | 3.62 | 4.8 |
| 143 | Wyalusing fine sandy loam | 17.0 | 67.9 | 15.2 | 2.15 | 5.8 |
| 239B | Oquaga very stony loam, 0 to 8 percent slopes, extremely bouldery | 17.0 | 31.6 | 51.4 | 1.67 | 4.8 |
| 239D | Oquaga very stony loam, 15 to 30 percent slopes, extremely bouldery | 17.0 | 43.3 | 39.7 | 1.67 | 4.8 |
| 240F | Oquaga-Arnot-Rock outcrop complex, 20 to 60 percent slopes, very rubbly | 17.0 | 43.3 | 39.7 | 1.67 | 4.8 |
| 320C | Lackawanna channery loam, 8 to 15 percent slopes, stony | 15.7 | 52.8 | 31.5 | 2.50 | 5.3 |
| 321B | Lackawanna channery loam, 3 to 8 percent slopes, extremely stony | 15.7 | 52.8 | 31.5 | 2.80 | 5.3 |
| 321C | Lackawanna channery loam, 8 to 15 percent slopes, extremely stony | 15.7 | 52.8 | 31.5 | 2.80 | 5.3 |
| 321D | Lackawanna channery loam, 15 to 30 percent slopes, extremely stony | 15.7 | 52.8 | 31.5 | 2.80 | 5.3 |

# Soils of Wayne County

| Code | Soil Name | Clay | Sand | Silt | Org. | pH |
|------|-----------|------|------|------|------|-----|
| ArB | Arnot channery loam, very rocky, 3 to 8 percent slopes | 13.0 | 45.4 | 41.6 | 1.80 | 4.8 |
| ArC | Arnot channery loam, very rocky, 8 to 15 percent slopes | 13.0 | 45.4 | 41.6 | 1.80 | 4.8 |
| ArD | Arnot channery loam, very rocky, 15 to 25 percent slopes | 13.0 | 45.4 | 41.6 | 1.80 | 4.8 |
| Ba | Barbour loam | 12.0 | 45.0 | 43.0 | 3.00 | 5.3 |
| Bh | Basher silt loam | 12.0 | 32.1 | 55.9 | 3.00 | 4.8 |
| FF | Fluvents and Fluvaquents, cobbly | 11.2 | 67.4 | 21.4 | 0.72 | 5.4 |
| Ho | Holly silt loam | 20.0 | 26.3 | 53.7 | 3.50 | 6.5 |
| La | Linden fine sandy loam, rarely flooded | 14.0 | 69.6 | 16.4 | 2.35 | 4.8 |
| LaB | Lackawanna channery loam, 3 to 8 percent slopes | 16.2 | 43.8 | 40.1 | 1.42 | 5.0 |
| LaD | Lackawanna channery loam, 15 to 25 percent slopes | 16.2 | 43.8 | 40.1 | 1.42 | 5.0 |
| LbB | Lackawanna extremely stony loam, 3 to 8 percent slopes | 16.2 | 43.8 | 40.1 | 1.42 | 5.0 |
| LbD | Lackawanna extremely stony loam, 8 to 25 percent slopes | 16.2 | 43.8 | 40.1 | 1.42 | 5.0 |
| LdB | Lordstown channery loam, 3 to 8 percent slopes | 13.0 | 45.4 | 41.6 | 1.70 | 5.4 |
| LdC | Lordstown channery loam, 8 to 15 percent slopes | 13.0 | 45.4 | 41.6 | 1.70 | 5.4 |
| LdD | Lordstown channery loam, 15 to 25 percent slopes | 13.0 | 45.4 | 41.6 | 1.70 | 5.4 |
| LxB | Lordstown extremely stony loam, 3 to 8 percent slopes | 14.0 | 44.8 | 41.2 | 1.70 | 5.4 |
| LxC | Lordstown extremely stony loam, 8 to 25 percent slopes | 14.0 | 44.8 | 41.2 | 1.70 | 5.4 |
| MaB | Mardin channery loam, 3 to 8 percent slopes | 17.0 | 43.6 | 39.4 | 2.17 | 5.0 |
| MaC | Mardin channery loam, 8 to 15 percent slopes | 17.0 | 43.6 | 39.4 | 2.17 | 5.0 |
| MaD | Mardin channery loam, 15 to 25 percent slopes | 17.0 | 43.6 | 39.4 | 2.17 | 5.0 |
| MdB | Mardin extremely stony loam, 3 to 8 percent slopes | 17.0 | 43.6 | 39.4 | 2.17 | 5.0 |
| MdD | Mardin extremely stony loam, 8 to 25 percent slopes | 17.0 | 43.6 | 39.4 | 2.17 | 5.0 |

# Soils of Wayne County

| Code | Soil Name | Clay | Sand | Silt | Org. | pH |
|------|-----------|------|------|------|------|-----|
| ME | Medihemists and Medifibrists | 0.0 | 0.0 | 0.0 | 75.00 | - |
| MoA | Morris channery loam, 0 to 3 percent slopes | 15.0 | 44.3 | 40.7 | 3.00 | 5.3 |
| MoB | Morris channery loam, 3 to 8 percent slopes | 15.0 | 44.3 | 40.7 | 3.00 | 5.3 |
| MoC | Morris channery loam, 8 to 15 percent slopes | 15.0 | 44.3 | 40.7 | 3.00 | 5.3 |
| MxB | Morris extremely stony loam, 0 to 8 percent slopes | 15.0 | 44.3 | 40.7 | 3.00 | 5.3 |
| MxC | Morris extremely stony loam, 8 to 15 percent slopes | 20.0 | 42.1 | 37.9 | 3.00 | 5.3 |
| NcA | Norwich and Chippewa channery silt loams, 0 to 3 percent slopes | 21.2 | 24.5 | 54.4 | 4.33 | 5.7 |
| NxA | Norwich and Chippewa extremely stony silt loams, 0 to 3 percent slopes | 19.8 | 31.3 | 48.8 | 4.33 | 5.8 |
| OaB | Oquaga channery loam, 3 to 8 percent slopes | 17.0 | 37.7 | 45.3 | 1.70 | 4.8 |
| OaC | Oquaga channery loam, 8 to 15 percent slopes | 17.0 | 37.7 | 45.3 | 1.70 | 4.8 |
| OaD | Oquaga channery loam, 15 to 25 percent slopes | 17.0 | 37.7 | 45.3 | 1.70 | 4.8 |
| OxB | Oquaga extremely stony loam, 3 to 8 percent slopes | 17.0 | 37.7 | 45.3 | 1.70 | 4.8 |
| OxD | Oquaga extremely stony loam, 8 to 25 percent slopes | 17.0 | 37.7 | 45.3 | 1.70 | 4.8 |
| OyF | Oquaga and Lordstown extremely stony loams, 25 to 70 percent slopes | 17.0 | 37.7 | 45.3 | 1.70 | 4.8 |
| Re | Rexford loam | 14.7 | 30.2 | 55.1 | 3.00 | 5.5 |
| RoD | Rock outcrop-Arnot complex, 3 to 25 percent slopes | - | - | - | - | - |
| SwB | Swartswood channery sandy loam, 3 to 8 percent slopes | 16.0 | 65.1 | 18.9 | 2.00 | 4.6 |
| SwC | Swartswood channery sandy loam, 8 to 15 percent slopes | 16.0 | 65.1 | 18.9 | 2.00 | 4.6 |
| SwD | Swartswood channery sandy loam, 15 to 25 percent slopes | 16.0 | 65.1 | 18.9 | 2.00 | 4.6 |
| SxB | Swartswood extremely stony sandy loam, 3 to 8 percent slopes | 16.0 | 65.1 | 18.9 | 2.00 | 4.6 |
| SxD | Swartswood extremely stony sandy loam, 8 to 25 percent slopes | 16.0 | 65.1 | 18.9 | 2.00 | 4.6 |

# Soils of Wayne County

| Code | Soil Name | Clay | Sand | Silt | Org. | pH |
|------|-----------|------|------|------|------|-----|
| VoA | Volusia channery silt loam, 0 to 3 percent slopes | 22.5 | 24.8 | 52.7 | 2.73 | 5.5 |
| VoB | Volusia channery silt loam, 3 to 8 percent slopes | 22.5 | 24.8 | 52.7 | 2.73 | 5.5 |
| VoC | Volusia channery silt loam, 8 to 15 percent slopes | 22.5 | 24.8 | 52.7 | 2.73 | 5.5 |
| VxB | Volusia extremely stony silt loam, 0 to 8 percent slopes | 22.5 | 24.8 | 52.7 | 2.73 | 5.5 |
| VxC | Volusia extremely stony silt loam, 8 to 15 percent slopes | 22.5 | 22.4 | 55.1 | 2.83 | 5.5 |
| WeB | Wellsboro channery loam, 3 to 8 percent slopes | 18.0 | 43.1 | 38.9 | 2.07 | 5.1 |
| WeC | Wellsboro channery loam, 8 to 15 percent slopes | 18.0 | 43.1 | 38.9 | 2.07 | 5.1 |
| WeD | Wellsboro channery loam, 15 to 25 percent slopes | 18.0 | 43.1 | 38.9 | 2.07 | 5.1 |
| WkB | Wurtsboro channery loam, 3 to 8 percent slopes | 15.0 | 44.3 | 40.7 | 1.42 | 4.6 |
| WkC | Wurtsboro channery loam, 8 to 15 percent slopes | 15.0 | 44.3 | 40.7 | 1.42 | 4.6 |
| WoB | Wellsboro extremely stony loam, 3 to 8 percent slopes | 18.0 | 43.1 | 38.9 | 2.07 | 5.1 |
| WoD | Wellsboro extremely stony loam, 8 to 25 percent slopes | 18.0 | 43.1 | 38.9 | 2.07 | 5.1 |
| WxF | Wellsboro and Mardin extremely stony loams, 25 to 50 percent slopes | 19.3 | 42.5 | 38.1 | 2.08 | 5.1 |
| Wy | Wyalusing silt loam | 13.4 | 42.4 | 44.2 | 3.53 | 5.8 |
| WyB | Wyoming gravelly sandy loam, 3 to 8 percent slopes | 11.8 | 67.1 | 21.1 | 1.88 | 4.8 |
| WyC | Wyoming gravelly sandy loam, 8 to 15 percent slopes | 11.8 | 67.1 | 21.1 | 1.88 | 4.8 |
| WyD | Wyoming gravelly sandy loam, 15 to 25 percent slopes | 11.8 | 67.1 | 21.1 | 1.88 | 4.8 |
| WyE | Wyoming gravelly sandy loam, 25 to 45 percent slopes | 11.8 | 67.1 | 21.1 | 1.88 | 4.8 |

# Soil series: profiles and landscape challenges

### Albrights loams

Found on ridges in Carbon County, Albrights loams consist of colluvium derived from acid red sandstone, siltstone, and shale. While there is no flooding or ponding and the soils are moderately well drained, depth to a root restrictive fragipan is 18 to 32 inches. A seasonal zone of water saturation is at about 22 inches during winter months

The series includes two channery loams, 0 to 3 percent slopes (AaA) and 3 to 8 percent slopes (AaB2) and two silt loams, 0 to 3 percent slopes (AbA) and 8 to 8 percent slopes (AbB2). All four are at risk of erosion without moderate conservation practices.

Two very stony loams, 0 to 8 percent slopes (AcB) and 8 to 25 percent slopes (AcD) have severe limitations and are considered unsuitable for typical agricultural cultivation.

Landscape challenges include the shallow depth to saturation, gravel content in the channery loams and large stones in the silt loams and very stony loams.

### Alden loam

Alden mucky silt loam (Ad) is found in till plain depressions in Monroe County and consists of glacial till with 0 to 3 percent slopes. Although depth to a root restrictive layer is more than 60 inches, the soil is very poorly drained. Because it is frequently ponded with water saturation at the surface in winter and spring, the soil is considered hydric. This severely limits choice of plants and requires careful management. Ponding and depth to water saturation are the primary challenges for landscapers.

### Allenwood loams

Found on valley sides and uplands in Carbon and Monroe Counties, Allenwood loams are com-posed of old till derived from sedimentary rock. Soils tend to be deep, well drained and never flooded or ponded.

In Carbon County, the Allenwoods are in three types:

- A gravelly *and* silt loam combination, including 0 to 3 percent slopes (AdA), 3 to 8 percent slopes (AdB2), and 8 to 15 percent slopes (AdC2). Gravel and large stone content can create landscape challenges.

- A gravelly silt loam, ranging from 0 to 3 percent slopes (AgA), 3 to 8 percent slopes (AgB2), 8 to 15 percent slopes (AgC2) and 15 to 25 percent slopes (AgD2). Steeper slopes can impact landscape plans.

- A gravelly silty clay loam, including 8 to 15 percent slopes (AmC3) and 15 to 25 percent slopes (AmD3), both of which are typically severely eroded. Slope is a potential landscape concern.

In Monroe County, series are limited to Allenwood gravelly silt loam, 0 to 3 percent slopes (AnA), 3 to 8 percent slopes (AnB), and 8 to 20 percent slopes (AnC).

The most level of all these are good for agricultural purposes and have few limitations restricting its use. As the slopes become steeper, the risk of erosion is higher and limitations rise from moderate to severe, requiring moderate up to special conservation practices. Gravel and stone content are relatively minor issues for landscapers, but on steeper grades, slope becomes a factor.

### Alluvial land

Found on flood plains in Monroe County with slopes of 0 to 3 percent, alluvial land (As) parent material is alluvium deposited and often stratified by repeated river and stream flooding. Composition is about 70 percent fluvents, i.e., freely drained Entisols that form in water-deposited sediments on floodplains.

The soils are moderately well drained and fairly deep (as much as 60 inches) but frequently flooded from October through April. Although fluvents can be used for forest, pasture or wildlife habitat and sometimes cropland, the regular flooding precludes commercial agriculture and in Monroe County restricts use to recreational purposes, wildlife habitat, watershed or aesthetic purposes. Flooding and depth to saturation are the primary challenges for any landscape effort.

### Alvira loams

Till forms the parent material of Alvira soils on flanks of valleys and margins of eroding uplands in Carbon and Monroe Counties. With depth to a fragipan at just 15 to 28 inches, natural drainage can be somewhat poor even though Alvira loams are neither flooded or ponded; water saturation can be at 12 inches from October through May.

In Carbon County, both variations are found on less than 8 percent slopes. A gravelly silt loam (AnB) and a very stony silt loam (ArB) both have severe use limitations because of water and stone and require special conservation practices. Depth to saturation, gravel and large stone content create landscape challenges.

In Monroe county, a silt loam on a 3 to 8 percent slope (AvB) requires similar special care, with depth to saturation a primary challenge and gravel content a secondary one. A complex of Alvira and Watson very stony loams (55 and 35 percent, respectively) is found on 0 to 12 percent slopes (AwB) and best uses are pasture, forestland or wildlife habitat. In this series, depth to saturation is of concern for landscapers, followed by large stone content.

### Alvira — Shelmadine silt loams

A 50-50 mix of Alvira and Shelmadine soils in Carbon county creates a complex found on depressions along the flanks of valleys and in the margins of eroding uplands. The parent material consists of till; in the case of Shelmadine it is usually a loamy till. Shelmadine soils can contain wetlands and be classified as hydric.

The complex is poorly drained, with a fragipan between 15 and 30 inches. Neither flooded or ponded, water saturation can be at 12 inches from October through May.

The two silt loams, less than 3 percent slope (AsA) and 3 to 8 percent slopes (AsB2) are have significant landscape challenges because of the water issue and require special conservation practices. A very stony silt loam with less than 8 percent slope (AtB) has a compounding landscape issue of large stone in the soil.

### Andover loam

Found on depressions in Carbon County, Andover loam parent material consists of mountain slope colluvium derived from sedimentary rock. Although depth to a root restrictive layer is greater than 60 inches, Andover is poorly drained with water saturation is at 3 inches during October through June.

As a very stony loam on slopes of less than 3 percent (AvA), Andover therefore meets criteria to be classified as hydric carries substantial landscape challenges because of it.

### Arnot loams

Found on valley sides in Pike and Wayne Counties, Arnot channery loam parent material consists of till derived from sandstone, siltstone and shale. Despite the shallow depth of lithic bedrock — just 10 to 20 inches — natural drainage is considered excessively drained and the soils are neither flooded or ponded, with no zone of water saturation within a depth of 72 inches.

In Pike County, Arnot very channery loam is found on very rocky 3 to 15 percent slopes (402C) and 15 to 35 percent slopes (402E). Landscape issues center around droughty character, depth to bedrock, gravel content and secondarily large stone content.

In Wayne County, Arnot channery loam is found on very rocky 3 to 8 percent slopes (ArB), 8 to 15 percent slopes (ArC) and 15 to 25 percent slopes (ArD). Depth to bedrock and droughty character are the primary challenges for landscapers, as well as slope on the steeper grades.

### Barbour loams

Found on slopes less than 3 percent on flood plains in Pike and Wayne Counties, Barbour parent material consists of reddish coarse-loamy alluvium derived from sedimentary rock. The soils are deep and well-drained, with saturation at 54 inches from January to April. Barbour soils are occasionally flooded, but not ponded.

In Pike County, fine sandy loam (27) is more than 70 percent sand, while in Wayne County, Barbour loam (Ba) is much lower in sand and higher in silt. Neither has any use restrictions. Potential for flooding is the paramount challenge for landscapers.

### Basher silt loam

Found on Wayne County floodplains with slopes less than 3 percent, Basher silt loam (Bh) parent material consists of reddish alluvium derived from sedimentary rock. The soils are deep, moderately well drained and occasionally flooded but not ponded. A seasonal zone of water saturation is at 21 inches from January to May. These factors create some limitations that require moderate conservation efforts and may impact plant choices. Flooding potential and depth to saturation are the primary concerns for landscapers.

### Bath loams

Found on mountains in Monroe County, Bath parent material consists of coarse-loamy till derived mainly from gray and brown siltstone, sandstone, and shale. Although the soils a shallow with a fragipan between 21 and 38 inches, the soils are well drained and is not flooded or ponded. A seasonal zone of water saturation is at 25 inches in early spring.

Erosion may be a factor for Bath channery silt loams in 3 to 8 percent (BaB), 8 to 15 percent (BaC) and 15 to 25 percent (BaD) slopes; the steeper the slope, the more caution is needed in management. In the most level areas, gravel content, depth to saturation and large stone content are relatively minor issues; on steeper areas, slope factors become the dominant challenge.

Very stony silt loam, 0 to 8 percent (BdB) and 8 to 25 percent (BbC), have challenges in large stone content and, to a lesser extent, depth to saturation and gravel content. On steeper grades, slope becomes a major issue.

### Benson-Rock outcrop complex

Found on uplands and flanks of valleys and the margins of eroding uplands in Monroe County, Benson parent material consists of loamy till. Between outcrops, depth to lithic bedrock, is 12 to 20 inches. Soils are well drained and neither flooded or ponded.

All three in the complex, 0 to 8 percent slopes (BeB), 8 to 25 percent slopes (BeC) and 25 to 70 percent slopes (BeF) have major challenges with slope, depth to bedrock and large stone content.

### Braceville loams

Found on terraces in Monroe and Pike Counties, Braceville loam parent material consists of coarse-loamy glacial outwash. The soils are relatively shallow, with a depth to fragipan of 18 to 30 inches, but well drained and neither flooded or ponded.

In Monroe County, water saturation can range from 6 to 27 inches in November through March on two gravelly loams: 0 to 3 percent slopes (BrA) and 3 to 8 percent slopes (BrB). Because of the water, the soils have moderate limitations reducing plant choices and requiring some conservation practices. Gravel content and droughty character are relatively minor issues for landscapers.

In Pike County, water saturation is at 21 inches from November to April and the fine sandy loam on 0 to 3 percent slopes (14) has similar limitations. Depth to saturation is a landscaping challenge

### Buchanan loams

Buchanan soils are found on mountain slopes and valley sides in Carbon and Monroe Counties. Parent material is mountain slope colluvium derived from sedimentary rock. A fragipan ranges from 20 to 36 inches, but soils are moderately well drained and neither flooded or ponded.

In Carbon County, a gravelly loam on 3 to 10 percent slopes with moderate erosion (BcB2) requires moderate conservation practices because of erosion threat. Very stony loams, 0 to 8 percent slopes (BhB) and 8 to 25 percent slopes (BhD) are unsuitable for cultivation and limited to pasture, forestland or wildlife habitat. Water saturation is at 20 inches from December to March. Water saturation, gravel content, stone content and, on the steeper grades, slope represent the major landscape challenges.

In Monroe County, Buchanan loam on 3 to 8 percent slopes (BuB) requires moderate conservation practices because of erosion threat. Extremely stony loam on 0 to 8 percent slopes (BxB) and 8 to 25 percent slopes (BxC) has severe limitations with depth to saturation (BuB and BxC), large stone content (BxB and BxC) and slope (BxC).

### Chenango loams

Chenango parent material consists of gravelly outwash that formed the outwash terraces on which it is found in Monroe and Pike Counties. The soils are deep, with a root-restrictive layer more than 60 inches, and well drained. They are neither flooded or ponded, and there is no water saturation within 72 inches.

In Monroe County, Chenango gravelly loam on 0 to 3 percent (ChA), 3 to 8 percent (ChB) and 8 to 15 percent (ChC) slopes have moderate to severe limitations and require moderate to special conservation practices, primarily because of stony nature and potential erosion.

The same limitations apply to gravelly fine sandy loams in Pike County on 0 to 8 percent slopes (89B), 8 to 15 percent slopes (89C), and 15 to 25 percent slopes (89D).

Minor concerns for landscapers are large stone and gravel content and droughty character, but slope can be a factor on steeper grades.

### Chippewa-Norwich loams

An evenly divided mix of Chippewa and Norwich soils form a complex found in depressions in Monroe County. Parent material consists of fine loamy till derived from sandstone and siltstone. A fragipan is at 10 to 24 inches, and the soil is poorly drained. Although the soil is not flooded or ponded, seasonal water saturation at the surface in March and April and high organic content helps qualify it as hydric.

A silt loam with a 0 to 5 percent slope (CmA) carries severe limitations requiring specialized plant selection and very careful management. An extremely stony soil with 0 to 8 percent slope (CnB) is unsuitable for cultivation and best uses are pasture, forestland or wildlife habitat.

The primary challenge for landscapers is depth to saturation and to a lesser extent droughty character in late summer.

### Clymer loams

Found on mountains in Monroe County, Clymer soil parent material consists of loose material left behind from sandstone weathering. A deep soil, it is well drained, not flooded or ponded and no water saturation within a depth of 72 inches.

Among the straight loams, 0 to 3 percent slope material (CpA) has few limitations that restrict its use. On 3 to 8 percent slopes (CpB), erosion becomes a factor and suggests moderate conservation practices; these soils pose no other serious challenges to landscapers. On 8 to 15 percent slopes (CpC), the risk is higher and practices become special; slope becomes a landscaping challenge. Among extremely stony loams, 0 to 8 percent (CxB) and 8 to 25 percent slopes (CxC), large stone content and, on steeper grades, slope become issues for landscapers.

### Comly loams

Found on hills and valleys in Carbon County, Comly series parent material consists of colluvium derived from shale and siltstone. Soils are deep, high in silt content and moderately well drained; although not flooded or ponded, a seasonal zone of saturation is at 20 inches from November to March.

This results in silt loam on less than 3 percent slopes (CmA) having limitations on plant selection and requiring moderate conservation practices. Erosion becomes a restrictive factor on 3 to 8 percent slopes (CmB2) and 8 to 15 percent slopes (CmC). Water saturation levels can pose a landscape challenge.

A silty clay loam, 8 to 15 percent slope and severely eroded (CnC3), requires special conservation practices in addition to saturation levels, slope may be a landscape challenge.

Very stony silt loams, 0 to 8 percent slope (CoB) and 8 to 25 percent slopes (CoD) are unsuitable for conventional cultivation and best uses are pasture, forestland or wildlife habitat. Large stone content in soil and slope on the steeper grades, as well as depth to water saturation pose the most significant landscape challenges.

### Conotton loams

Gravelly glacial outwash is the parent material of Conotton soils on outwash terraces in Carbon County. These deep soils are well drained, not flooded or ponded, and with no water saturation within a depth of 72 inches. The stony nature of the soils on 0 to 3 percent slopes (CtA), 3 to 8 percent slopes (CtB) and 15 to 25 percent slopes (CtD) leads to limitations on plant selection and special conservation practices. Droughty characteristics and high gravel content form landscape challenges.

### Craigsville-Wyoming complex

Composed primarily of Craigsville and slightly less amounts of Wyoming, this complex appears on flood plains and mountain terraces in Monroe, Pike and Wayne Counties. Craigsville comes from acid, gravelly alluvium derived from sandstone and siltstone, while Wyoming is from water-sorted gravelly outwash derived from sedimentary rock.

The soils are deep, well drained and occasionally flooded, with water saturation highest at 72 inches in December to March. In the area, they are also extremely stony on slopes of less than 8 percent (9B), with large stone content, some flooding and droughty character representing the most common challenges to landscapers.

### Dekalb loams

Material left behind from weathering of sandstone and shale in the mountains of Carbon and Monroe counties are the parent materials of Dekalb loams. Shallow, with lithic bedrock at 20 to 40 inches, the loams are well drained, neither flooded or ponded, and with no water saturation.

Carbon County very stony loams on 0 to 8 percent slopes (DeB), 8 to 25 percent slopes (DeD) and 25 to 100 percent slopes (DeF) are unsuitable for conventional cultivation and best uses are pasture, forestland or wildlife habitat. The most significant landscape challenges are large stone content and droughty character of more level soils, while slope becomes an additional factor on the steeper grades.

The same limitations apply to extremely stony loams found in Monroe County on 0 to 8 percent (DxB), 8 to 25 percent (DxC) and 25 to 80 percent (DxE) slopes. Large stone content, droughty character, depth to bedrock and slope on steeper grades become issues for landscapers.

### Delaware sandy loam

Found on terraces and in river valleys in Pike County, Delaware loam parent material consists of postglacial alluvium from sandstone and shale. Soils are deep, well drained and without water saturation above 72 inches.

On 0 to 3 percent slopes (24A), there are few limitations on use, but on 3 to 8 percent slopes (24B), erosion becomes a factor for moderate conservation practices. On 8 to 20 percent slopes (24C), the limitations become severe and require very careful management. There are no substantial challenges for landscapers except for slope on steeper greades.

### Drifton loams

Drifton loams are found on hills and uplands in Carbon County. Parent material consists of loamy till, which is deep, well drained, and not flooded or ponded. Seasonal water saturation is at 26 inches from November through March, leading to moderate limitations on slopes of less than 3 percent (DrA). Erosion becomes a concern when slopes are 3 to 8 percent (DrB2). A very stony loam with less than 8 percent slope (DsB) is considered unsuitable for conventional cultivation.

Depth to saturation is a minor landscaping factor in all three, but large stone content in DsB is potentially a major challenge.

### Edgemere loams

Found in depressions in Monroe, Pike and Wayne Counties, Edgemere loams come from coarse-loamy till derived from sandstone and siltstone. A fragipan is found at 15 to 25 inches, the soil is poorly drained and while not flooded it is occasionally ponded. Water saturation is at surface from November through May and the soil meets the criteria to be classified as hydric.

Locally, extremely stony loam has a less than 3 percent slope (11A), is very rubbly and because of depth to saturation and ponding as well as large stone content, a challenge for landscapers.

### Empeyville loam

Found on till plains in Monroe County, Empeyville soils developed from loamy till derived from acid sandstone. Soils are shallow, with a fragipan at 14 to 22 inches, but well drained and not flooded or ponded. Water saturation peaks at 21 inches from February through May. The extremely stony sandy loam with less than 8 percent slope (ExB) has substantial challenge for landscapers because of large stone content and, secondarily, depth to saturation.

### Fleetwood loams

A variety of Fleetwood loams are found on ridges in Carbon County, all from remaining material of weathered sandstone. Lithic bedrock is at 20 to 40 inches, but the soil is well drained, not flooded or ponded, or with any water saturation. bedrock is classified as lithic. The natural drainage class is well drained and water movement in the most restrictive layer is moderately high.

Among the sandy loams, only those on slopes less than 3 percent (FtA) are unrestricted in use. Erosion becomes an increasing issue from 3 to 8 percent slopes (FtB2) toward 8 to 15 percent slopes (FtC2) and conservation practices tighten accordingly. Neither poses substantial landscape challenges other than slope on the steeper grades.

Very stony loams include less than 8 percent slopes (FvB), 8 to 25 percent slopes (FvD), and 25 to 100 percent slopes (FvF), all of which are unsuitable for conventional cultivation and have substantial landscape challenges in terms of slope, large stone content, droughty character and depth to bedrock. The same limitations apply to very stony sandy loams, including less than 8 percent slopes (FwB) and 8 to 25 percent slopes (FwD). Stone and gravel content may be a landscape challenge, along with slope on steeper grades.

### Fluvents and Fluvaquents

This floodplain complex is composed of 70 percent Fluvents and 20 percent Fluvaquents, both of which are sandy and silty alluvium derived from sandstone and siltstone. Fluvents appear on flood plain steps and river valleys, while Fluvaquents are found in depressions. Slopes are 0 to 3 percent (FF).

Fluvents excessively drained, while Fluvaquents are poorly drained. Both soils are frequently flooded, but not ponded. In fluvents areas, water saturation peaks at 36 inches, while the level rises to 6 inches for Fluvaquents between November and April, supporting classification as hydric. Potential for flooding, ponding and depth to saturation are the primary concerns for landscapers.

### Gleneyre-Kimbles complex

The complex is composed primarily of Gleneyre soils (50 percent) and Kimbles soils (30 percent). Found on the remnants of ancient lakebeds in Pike and Wayne Counties, Gleneyre parent material consists of coarse-silty over sandy and gravelly lake deposits. The complex is deep, but very poorly drained. Gleneyre soils are frequently flooded and ponded, while Kimbles soils are neither. Water saturation is at the surface throughout the year, so the soils are considered hydric.

The consequence is that the complex with less than 2 percent slope (12), surface-level water and the impracticality to correct it interferes with conventional cultivation. Challenges for landscapers are flooding, ponding and depth to saturation.

### Hartleton loams

Hartleton loams are found on deep, well-drained uplands and mountain slopes in Carbon and Monroe counties. They form from glacial till or frost-churned material weathered from sandstone and shale, are not flooded or ponded, and there is no water saturation above 72 inches. Lithic bedrock is 48 to 96 inches in Carbon County and 40 to 80 inches in Monroe.

In Carbon County, loams laced with *channers* (flat rock fragments about six inches long), the channery silt loams on 0 to 3 percent slopes (HaA) have moderate limitations on plant choices. As grades increase, so do limitations, mostly because of erosion concerns. Loam on 3 to 8 percent slopes (HaB2) have moderate limitations. Large stone content and droughty character may pose landscape challenges.

Erosion factors on channery silt loam slopes of 8 to 15 percent may be moderate (HaC2) or severe (HaC3) and pose severe limitations requiring special to very careful management. Limitations increase on 15 to 25 percent slopes that are moderately (HaD2) or severely eroded (HaD3), and landscape challenges include droughty character, large stone content and slope issues.

Carbon County also includes a very stony loam in this series on 0 to 8 percent slopes (HsB) and 8 to 25 percent slopes (HsD), both of which are unsuitable for conventional cultivation pose challenges because of large stone content and droughty character.

In Monroe County, Hartleton channery silt loam on 2 to 8 percent slopes (HaB) and 8 to 20 percent slopes (HaC) have similar erosion challenges and require moderate to special conservation practices. Large stone content, droughty character and, on steeper grades, slope issues challenge landscapers.

### Hazleton loams

Found on mountain slopes, Hazleton soils come from materials remaining after sandstone weathering. They are fairly deep, ranging from 40 to 96 inches over lithic bedrock, well drained, neither flooded or ponded and without water saturation in the top 72 inches.

In Carbon County, only the loams on less than 3 percent slopes (HtA) have few limitations on use. Those on 3 to 8 percent slopes (HtB), moderate eroded 3 to 8 percent slopes (HtB2) and moderately eroded 8 to 15 percent slopes (HtC2) have increasing limitations that require moderate to special conservation practices. The very stony loams on both 0 to 8 percent slopes (HvB) and 8 to 25 percent slopes (HvD) are considered unsuitable for conventional cultivation and best used for pasture, forestland or wildlife habitats.

In Monroe County, Hazleton extremely stony sandy loam on 0 to 8 percent slopes (HxB) and 8 to 25 percent slopes (HxC) are challenging for landscaper primarily because of large stone content and slopes on steeper grades.

### Holly silt loam

Holly loams are found depressions on flood plains and sections of floodplains where deposits of fine silts and clays settle after a flood, usually behind a stream's natural levees. Parent material consists of loamy alluvium derived from sandstone and shale.

Although soils are deep, drainage is poor and the soil is considered hydric. This soil is frequently flooded, but not usually ponded in Carbon or Monroe Counties; it is reported as frequently ponded in Wayne County. Water is usually near or at the surface from December through May.

In all three counties, Holly silt loam (Hy) requires special conservation practices because water is in or near the soil surface, and flooding plus depth to saturation present the greatest landscape challenge.

### Kedron loams

Kedron loams come from colluvium, till or both derived from sandstone, siltstone and shale and are found in drainageways and basins between mountains in Monroe County. They are shallow, with depth to a fragipan of 20 to 32 inches, but moderately well drained and neither flooded or ponded.

Water saturation can rise to six inches between November and the end of May, which causes silt loam on 2 to 8 percent slopes (KaB) to be somewhat limited in plant selection and require moderate conservation practices. On 8 to 15 percent slopes (KaC), the risk of erosion calls for close-growing plant cover and special conservation practices. Depth to saturation and slope on steeper grades are landscape challenges

A very stony loam, on slopes less than 8 percent (KdB) is challenging because of depth to saturation and large stone content.

### Klinesville loams

Klinesville soils are found on ridges and valleys in Carbon and Monroe Counties, range from relatively shallow (20 inches) to deep over lithic bedrock. Drainage is somewhat excessive, with no flooding or ponding and no water saturation. The soils formed from frost-churned residual material weathered from siltstone.

In Carbon County, channery silt loams present a variety of circumstances and limitations. These include:

- Moderately eroded 3 to 8 percent slopes (KcB2), erosion requiring special conservation practices

- Moderately eroded 8 to 15 percent slopes (KcC2) , erosion requiring very careful management

- Considered best used for forestland or wildlife habitat:

  Severely eroded 8 to 15 percent slopes (KcC3)
  Moderately eroded 15 to 25 percent slopes (KcD2) and severely eroded 15 to 25 percent slopes (KcD3)
  Moderately eroded 25 to 35 percent slopes (KcE2) and severely eroded 25 to 35 percent slopes (KcE3)
  Loams on 35 to 80 percent slopes (KcF) and severely eroded 35 to 80 percent slopes (KcF3)
  Very stony silt loams on 8 to 25 percent slopes (KvD) and 25 to 80 percent slopes (KvF)

Gravel content, droughty character, large stone content, and slope on the steeper grades present landscape challenges to varying degrees.

In Monroe County, channery silt loams on 3 to 8 percent slopes (KvB) and 8 to 15 percent slopes (KvC) require careful conservation practices because of erosion potential, with landscaping challenges concentrated mostly on droughty character and gravel content. Loams on 15 to 25 percent slopes (KvD) have the additional challenge of slope.

### Lackawanna loams

Lackawanna loams are found on ridges, flanks of valleys and margins of eroding uplands and ridges in Monroe, Pike and Wayne Counties. They form from a coarse-loamy till derived from sandstone and siltstone. Although they are shallow, with a fragipan at 17 to 36 inches, the loams are well drained with no flooding or ponding. Water saturation can be found at 25 inches during March and April.

Because of erosion threats in Monroe County and Wayne County, close plant cover and varying conservation practices are important for the channery loams, ranging from moderate on 2 to 8 percent slopes (LaB), special on 8 to 15 percent slopes (LaC) and very careful management on 15 to 25 percent slopes (LaD). Large stone content is the primary challenge for landscapers, with depth to saturation a secondary concern. Slope becomes an issue on steeper grades.

An extremely stony variant in Monroe and Wayne, with 15 to 30 percent slopes (321D), is challenging because of slope and large stone content. The same issues are found with extremely stony loams on 0 to 8 percent slopes (LbB) and 8 to 25 percent slopes (LbC).

In Pike County, stony channery loams require moderate conservation practices on 3 to 8 percent slopes (320B) and special practices on 8 to 15 percent slopes (320C). Gravel content is a primary issue for landscapers, as well as slope on steeper grades.

In both Pike and Wayne Counties, extremely stony loams on 3 to 8 percent slopes (321B), 8 to 15 percent slopes (321C) and 15 to 30 percent slopes (321D) have landscape issues with large stone content, occasionally slope and sometimes depth to saturation.

### Lackawanna-Bath complex

Lackawanna soils comprise 40 percent and Bath soils 30 percent of the complex, with the remainder in minor soils. The complex is found on ridges, flanks of valleys and margins of eroding uplands in Monroe County. Coarse-loamy till derived from sandstone and siltstone is the parent material

While a fragipan is found between 21 and 38 inches, the soil is well drained, neither flooded or ponded, and seasonal water saturation can reach 25 inches during March and April. Extremely steep and stony, the complex (LBE) is challenging for slope, large stone and, to a lesser extent, depth to saturation.

### Laidig loams

Colluvium derived from sandstone and siltstone is the parent material of Laidig loams, found along mountain slopes in Carbon and Monroe counties. Moderately deep with a fragipan at 30 to 50 inches, the soils are well drained, neither flooded or ponded, and seasonal water saturation can reach 30 inches from January through March.

Moderately eroded slopes of gravelly loams in Carbon County, 3 to 8 percent (LaB2) and 8 to 15 percent (LaC2) require moderate to special conservation practices and close-growing plant cover. On 15 to 25 percent slopes (LaD3), erosion is more severe and very careful management is required. Gravel content is the most significant landscape factor on lesser grades.

Two very stony loams on 3 to 8 percent slopes (LdB) and 8 to 25 percent slopes (LdD) are the most limited because of slope and large stone content issues. Two extremely stony loams of this series are found in Monroe County on 0 to 8 percent slopes (LgB) and 8 to 25 percent slopes (LgC), with large stone content and slope on steeper grades being the primary landscape concerns.

### Lawrenceville loam

Found on upland slopes of 0 to 3 percent (Lh) in Monroe County, Lawrenceville loam consists of silty deposits from wind. With a fragipan ranging from 24 to 36 inches, the soil is moderately well drained with no flooding or ponding, but water saturation is at 18 inches from November through March. Because of that, the soil has modest limitations that reduce plant selection and suggest moderate conservation practices; the primary challenge for landscapers is depth to saturation.

### Leck kill loams

A moderately deep soil parented by reddish materials left behind by weathering of shale and siltstone, Leck kill loams are found on ridges in Carbon and Monroe Counties and valleys in Carbon County. Depth to lithic bedrock is 20 to 40 inches, and the soils are well drained without flooding or ponding. There is no zone of water saturation.

In Carbon County channery silt loams on 0 to 3 percent slopes (LeA) and 3 to 8 percent slopes (LeB2) are shallow, droughty and stony, with severe limitations suggesting special conservation practices. These increase to very careful management requirements on 8 to 15 percent slopes (LeC2) and in a severely eroded variant on 8 to 15 percent slopes (LeC3). Depth to bedrock, droughty character, and large stone content pose challenges to the landscaper. On 15 to 25 percent slopes that are moderately eroded (LeD2) and severely eroded (LeD3), slope joins the list of landscape concerns.

Very stony loams, including 0 to 8 percent slopes (LkB), 8 to 25 percent slopes (LkD) and 25 to 100 percent slopes (LkF) have the same issues.

Similar identification codes in Monroe County have slightly different meanings,. These are channery silt loams on 2 to 8 percent slopes (LkB), 8 to 15 percent slopes (LkC) and 15 to 25 percent slopes (LkD). Erosion issues intensify with slopes, resulting in moderate to very careful conservation and management requirements. Gravel content is a minor issue on shallow grades, but slope becomes a landscaping factor on steeper grades.

### Lickdale and Tughill loams

Comprised of 50 percent Lickdale and 50 percent Tughill loams, this complex is found in Carbon County depressions with very poor drainage. The soils are not ponded or flooded, but organic matter in the surface horizon is about 12 percent. The soils meet criteria to be classified as hydric.

Lickdale parent material consists of colluvium derived from sandstone and shale, while Tughill comes from till. Depth to bedrock is between 40 and 60 inches, but water saturation is between 3 inches and the surface from November through June.

Consequently, loam and silt loams (LsA) and very stony loams (LtA) with less than 8 percent slope have very severe limitations requiring careful management, with depth to saturation, droughty character, ponding and large stone content posing the most significant landscape challenges.

### Linden loam

Found on flood plains with slopes of less than 3 percent in Wayne County, Linden fine sandy loam (La) comes from alluvium derived from sedimentary rock. Soils are very deep, well drained, rarely flooded and never ponded. Water saturation is at 54 inches during from November through March. It is considered prime farmland and has few use limitations.

### Lordstown loams

An extensive series of soils found on hills in Carbon, Monroe, Pike and Wayne counties, Lordstown soil comes from reddish coarse-loamy till derived from sandstone and siltstone.

The loams are relatively shallow, with depth to bedrock being 20 to 40 inches, but are well drained, not flooded or ponded, and with no water saturation.

In Carbon County very stony silt loams on 0 to 8 percent slopes (LvB), 8 to 25 percent slopes (LvD) and 25 to 80 percent slopes (LvF) pose substantial challenges to the landscaper primarily because of depth to bedrock and stone and gravel content on the lesser grades, but with slope and droughty character issues becoming the most predominant concern on steeper grades.

In Monroe County, channery silt loams on 3 to 8 percent slopes (LsB), 8 to 15 percent slopes (LsC) and 15 to 25 percent slopes (LsD) all have erosion issues and require increasingly attentive conservation practices. Depth to bedrock and large stone content are challenges for landscapers, with slope entering the picture as grades become steeper.

Extremely stony silt loam on 0 to 8 percent slopes (LxB) and 8 to 25 percent slopes (LxC) challenges because of large stone content, depth to bedrock and slope on steeper grades.

Also in Monroe, an extremely stony soil complex of primarily Lordstown (40 percent) and Oquaga (35 percent) loams form 25 to 70 percent slopes (LyE) and are best used for forest or wildlife habitats. Large stone content, slope and depth to bedrock are the primary challenges for landscapers.

In Pike County, very channery and very stony loams on 3 to 8 percent slopes (97B) and 8 to 15 percent slopes (97C), have similar use limitations.

In Wayne County, erosion is a primary concern with channery loam on 3 to 8 percent slopes (LdB), 8 to 15 percent slopes (LdC) and 15 to 25 percent slopes (LdD), requiring increasing levels of conservation practices. Depth to bedrock, large stone and gravel content and as grades steepen, slope issues confront landscapers. Extremely stony silt loam on 3 to 8 percent slopes (LxB) and 8 to 25 percent slopes (LxC) challenge landscapers with large stones content, depth to bedrock and slope on steeper grades.

### Lordstown-Swartswood complex

Comprised of 40 percent Lordstown soil and 35 percent Swartswood soil, this complex is found on hills and uplands in Pike County. Parent material is coarse-loam till derived from sandstone and siltstone. Somewhat shallow, with a depth to lithic bedrock of 20 to 40 inches, the soil is well drained, neither flooded or ponded, but has a water saturation level of 30 inches during March and April.

The shallow, stony nature of the soils means the extremely stony complex material on 0 to 8 percent (897B), 8 to 15 percent (897C) and 15 to 30 percent (897D) slopes is unsuitable for conventional cultivation primarily because of large stone content and depth to bedrock. Slope becomes an increasingly important factor as grades become steeper.

### Manlius silt loam

Manlius soils are found on valley sides in Pike County, with parent material coming from channery till derived from shale. The soils are somewhat shallow, with depth to lithic bedrock between 20 and 40 inches, and well drained, with no flooding, ponding or water saturation.

However, because the very channery silt loams are also very bouldery, those on 3 to 8 percent slopes (21B) and 8 to 15 percent slopes (21C) are considered unsuitable for conventional cultivation. Large stone content, droughty character and depth to bedrock are the primary issues for landscapers.

### Manlius-Arnot-Rock outcrop complex

Found on valley sides in Pike County, the complex is comprised of 40 percent Manlius and 35 percent Arnot soils. The parent material consists of channery till derived from shale (Manlius) and loamy till derived from sedimentary rock (Arnot).

Depth to lithic bedrock is 10 to 40 inches, and soils are well to excessively drained with no flooding, ponding or water saturation. Found on 15 to 30 percent slopes (121D) and 30 to 80 percent slopes (121F), slope, gravel content, droughty character, large stone content and depth to bedrock are the primary landscape issues.

### Mardin loams

Mardin loams are found on hills in Monroe, Pike and Wayne Counties, with parent material consisting of coarse-loamy till derived from sandstone and siltstone. Soils are shallow, with depth to a fragipan at 14 to 26 inches, moderately well drained, and not subject to flooding or ponding. In March and April, water saturation can reach 15 inches.

In Monroe County and Wayne counties, channery silt loam on 2 to 8 percent slopes (MaB) requires moderate conservation practices because of water saturation. Loams on 8 to 15 percent slopes (MaC) and 15 to 25 percent slopes (MaD) have erosion issues requiring special conservation practices. Depth to saturation, droughty character, gravel content and in some areas slope are the primary challenges for landscapers.

Very stony silt loam on 0 to 8 percent slopes in Monroe and extremely stony loam on 3 to 8 percent slopes in Wayne (both MbB) and very stony/extremely stony loams on 8 to 25 percent slopes (MbC) are challenging because of depth to saturation, large stone content, droughty character and on slope on steeper grades.

In Pike County, channery silt loam on 0 to 8 percent slopes (60B) requires moderate conservation practices because of water, while soils on 8 to 15 percent slopes (60C) have erosion issues requiring special conservation practices. Extremely stony loam on 0 to 8 percent slopes (61B) and 8 to 15 percent slopes (61C) complete the series, all of which include landscaping challenges of depth to saturation, large stone content, droughty nature and in some circumstances, slope.

### Meckesville loams

Found in mountain valleys in Carbon and Monroe Counties, Meckesville loams come from sandstone, siltstone and shale colluvium derived from sedimentary rock. Although the soils are somewhat shallow with a fragipan at 25 to 48 inches, they are well drained, not subject to flooding or ponding and have no water saturation issues.

In Carbon County, Meckesville channery loam on up to 3 percent slopes (MbA) has few limitations for use, while those at 3 to 8 percent (MbB2) and 8 to 15 percent (MbC2) slopes have erosion issues that require increasing levels of conservation practices and close-growing plant cover. Gravel and large stone content pose landscape challenges.

Very stony loams on 0 to 8 percent slopes (McB) and 8 to 25 percent slopes (McD) are considered unsuitable for conventional cultivation. Large stone content and slope, respectively, become the dominant landscape issues.

In Monroe County, gravelly loams on up to 3 percent slopes have few use limitations, but erosion is a concern on 3 to 8 percent slopes (MeB) and 8 to 15 percent slopes (MeC), both requiring attention to conservation practices. Gravel and large stone content are relatively minor concerns for landscapers.

Very stony loams in Monroe on 0 to 8 percent slopes (MfB) and 8 to 25 percent slopes (MfD) have some issues with large stone content and slope on steeper grades.

### Medihemists and Medifibrists

Medihemists are of layers of black, well-decomposed organic material, while Medifibrists are composed of slightly decomposed organic matter that appears as thick, continuous fibric materials with little or no impedance to water movement. Organic content is at least 75 percent. Together in about a 2 to 1 ratio, they form the stuff of bogs and meet the criteria to be classified as hydric.

Not surprisingly, these are poorly drained soils that are not flooded but frequently ponded, with water saturation at the surface throughout the year and slopes are less than 3 percent (ME). Consequently, commercial plant production is precluded and use is limited to wildlife habitat, watershed or aesthetic purposes.

### Middlebury and Tioga silt loams

Divided equally between Middlebury and Tioga components at about 45 percent each, this group is found on floodplains in Carbon County. The soils (MeA3) are deep, moderately well drained, occasionally flooded, but is not ponded. This soil does not meet hydric criteria. Water saturation can be as high as 25 inches from December through May. Because of flooding potential, the soil has moderate limitations on plant selection and may require conservation practices; flooding potential is the issue for landscapers.

### Middlebury silt loams

Found on flood plains and in valleys in Carbon County, Middlebury soils are from post glacial alluvium derived from sandstone and shale. Soils are deep and moderately well drained, occasionally flooded, but not ponded. It does not meet hydric criteria. A seasonal zone of water saturation is at 25 inches from December through May.

On 0 to 3 percent slopes (MdA) and 3 to 8 percent slopes (MdB), these silt loams may require moderate conservation practices and careful plant selection, with flooding and high saturation levels being the primary concern of landscapers.

### Montevallo loams

Montevallo soils are found on valley sides in Carbon County, with parent material consisting of material left by weathering shale and siltstone. The soils are shallow, with paralithic bedrock at 10 to 20 inches, somewhat excessively drained, and neither flooded or ponded. There water saturation within a depth of 72 inches.

Channery silt loams on less than 3 percent slopes (MoA) has limitations because it is shallow, droughty and stony, which requires special conservation practices. The risk of erosion grows on 3 to 8 percent slopes that are moderately eroded (MoB2) or severely eroded (MoB3), and on 8 to 15 percent moderately eroded (MoC2) or severely eroded (MoC3).

Primary landscaping challenges are the droughty nature, depth to bedrock, gravel and to a much lesser extent large stone content in the soil and slope.

Commercial cultivation is considered unsuitable on even steeper slopes including moderately eroded 15 to 25 percent (MoD2) and severely eroded (MoD3); 25 to 35 percent moderately eroded (MoE2) and severely eroded (MoE3) and 35 to 100 percent slopes (MoF2). Slope and droughty character, closely followed by gravel content, are the primary landscape concerns.

### Morris loams

Found on uplands and till plains in Carbon, Monroe, Pike and Wayne Counties, Morris soils are reddish glacial melt till derived from sandstone and siltstone. The soils are shallow, with depth to a fragipan of just 11 to 22 inches, and drainage is somewhat poor. Although the soil is neither flooded or ponded, water saturation can be as high as six inches during March and April.

These include:

- In Carbon County, very stony silt loam on up to 8 percent sloes (MrB) where saturation depth and large stone content are the primary landscape challenges;

- In Monroe County, extremely stony silt loam on 0 to 8 percent (MoB) and 8 to 20 percent (MoC) slopes, with depth to saturation, droughty character and gravel content being of greatest concern to landscapers;

- In Pike County, very channery loam on 0 to 8 percent slopes (19B) and 8 to 15 percent slopes (19C), with depth to saturation, large stone content and some slope issues to challenge landscapers;

- In Wayne County, extremely stony loam on 0 to 8 percent slopes (MxB) and 8 to 15 percent slopes (MxC), with depth to saturation and large stone content are issues for landscapers.

Exceptions that require special conservation practices and offer limited opportunities in plant selection include:

- In Monroe County, channery silt loam on 2 to 10 percent slopes (MgB) with depth to saturation, droughty character and gravel content being the primary challenges for landscapers; and

- In Wayne County, channery loams on 0 to 3 percent slopes (MoA), 3 to 8 percent slopes (MoB) and 8 to 15 percent slopes (MoC), where depth to saturation, gravel content and slope on steeper grades pose challenges for landscapers.

### Mucky peat soils

Found in depressions in Carbon County, Muck and Peat soil (MU) is almost entirely organic material. Although it can 5 feet thick, it is very poorly drained and while it is not flooded or ponded, water saturation is at or near the surface throughout the year.

Organic matter content in the surface horizon and in the top 12 inches is about 84 percent, and it the criteria to be classified as hydric. It is consequently not suitable for commercial plant production and best used for wildlife habitat, watershed or aesthetic purposes.

Within swamps in Monroe, Pike and Wayne counties, Paupack mucky peat (18 in Pike and Ms in Monroe) consists of woody organic material over gravelly alluvium. It, too, too can be more than 5 feet deep and very poorly drained with water saturation at the surface throughout the year.

Sometimes ponded, the soil has about 40 percent organic matter in the top 12 inches and is classified as hydric. Because the water interferes with cultivation and is impractical to change, use is limited to watershed, forestland and wildlife habitat.

Freetown mucky peat (Mp in Monroe and 20 in Wayne and Pike) is found in swamps in Monroe, Pike and Wayne Counties and consists of highly decomposed organic material that can be more than 5 feet deep. Again, drainage is very poor, the soil is often ponded and water saturation is at the surface from November through May.

Organic material in the surface horizon is about 75 percent and the soil is classified as hydric.

All these are challenging to landscape because of ponding and depth to saturation.

### Natalie loams

Found on ridges in Carbon County, Natalie soils are derived from sandstone and siltstone, with parent material consisting of reddish glacial melt till. Deep and well drained, the soils are neither flooded or ponded but saturation can be at 20 inches from November through March.

Very stony loams are on slopes up to 8 percent (NaB) and large stone content, followed by depth to saturation and, to a much lesser extent, gravel content create the primary landscape challenges.

### Norwich loams

Norwich loams are found in depressions in Carbon County and consist of fine-loamy till derived from sandstone and siltstone. With a fragipan at 10 to 24 inches, the soils are very poorly drained and water saturation can reach the surface during March and April. Hence it meets criteria to be classified as hydric.

Silt loam on less than 3 percent slopes (NoA)

can sometimes be ponded and changing that can be impractical. On 3 to 8 percent slopes (NoB), there is no ponding, but the water saturation remains a concern. The depth to saturation and potential for ponding are major landscape challenges, followed by droughty character in summer.

Very stony loam on less than 8 percent slopes (NvB) has its own limitation and is similarly best used for pasture, forestland or wildlife habitat. Depth to saturation and large stone content form the primary landscape issues.

### Norwich-Chippewa loams

About 50 percent Norwich and 33 percent Chippewa soils, both fine loamy till derived from sandstone and siltstone, are the foundation for this Wayne County complex. With a fragipan at 10 to 24 inches, the shallow soil is poorly to very poorly drained and while not flooded is occasionally ponded. Water saturation can be at the surface during March and April, and the soils meet criteria to be classified as hydric.

Channery silt loam on less than 3 percent slope (NcA) requires very careful management and has a limited option in plant selection because of the water issue. Extremely stony silt loam on less than 3 percent slope is considered unsuitable for conventional cultivation with depth to saturation, ponding, and droughty character serving as the most significant challenges to landscapers.

### Oquaga loams

Found on uplands, flanks of valleys and margins of eroded uplands in Monroe, Pike and Wayne Counties, Oquaga comes from reddish glacial-melt till derived from sandstone and siltstone. Relatively shallow, with lithic bedrock at 20 to 40 inches, loams are well drained, not flooded or ponded and without any water saturation.

In Monroe, Wane and Pike Counties, very stony loams on less than 8 percent slopes (239B), 8 to 15 percent slopes (239C) and 15 to 30 percent slopes (239D) are limited because they are shallow, droughty and stony. Droughty character, large stone content, depth to bedrock and on some sites slope become the challenges to landscapers. Gravel content may be a minor issue.

In Wayne County erosion concerns are a management factor for channery loams on 3 to 8 percent slopes (OaB), 8 to 15 percent slopes (OaC), and 15 to 25 percent slopes (OaD), and the intensity of conservation practices increases with the slope. Droughty characteristics, gravel content and depth to bedrock are major landscaping issues, with large stone content an important factor. Extremely stony loams on 3 to 8 percent slopes (OxB) and 8 to 25 percent slopes (OxD) have large stone content, droughty character and occasionally slope issues as landscape concerns.

### Oquaga-Arnot-Rock outcrop

Oquaga comprises 40 percent and Arnot 30 percent of the complex, with the balance in rock outcrop, throughout Monroe, Pike and Wayne Counties.

Oquaga soils are found on uplands and hillslopes, while Arnot soils are generally on valley sides. While Oquaga parent material is derived from reddish glacial-melt deposits from sandstone and siltstone, Arnot material consists of till derived from sandstone, siltstone and shale. Depth to lithic bedrock ranges from 10 to 40 inches.

The complex is well drained, not flooded or ponded and without water saturation issues. Found on 20 to 60 percent slopes (240F), the complex challenges landscapers with slope, droughty character, large stone content and depth to bedrock issues.

### Oquaga — Lackawanna loams

Found on ridges, uplands, flanks of valleys and margins of eroding uplands in Monroe County, the parent material of Oquaga-Lackawanna soils consists of reddish glacial melt till derived from sandstone and siltstone. The mix of the two soils varies with slope. Depth is 20 to 40 inches to lithic bedrock, and/or 21 to 36 inches to fragipan.

Soils are well drained, neither flooded or ponded, but potential for water saturation up to 25 inches during March and April. Erosion is the greatest concern for most soils in the series, with conservation practice intensity increasing with the slope.

Channery loams include:

- 3 to 8 percent slopes (OkB) — 50 percent Oquaga, 35 percent Lackawanna

- 8 to 15 percent slopes (OkC) — 55 percent Oquaga, 30 percent Lackawanna

- 15 to 25 percent slopes (OkD) — 60 percent Oquaga, 25 percent Lackawanna

Droughty character, gravel content, depth to bedrock and large stone content are issues for landscapers.

Extremely stony loams, best used for pasture, forestland or wildlife habitat, include:

- 0 to 8 percent slopes (OxB) — 50 percent Oquaga, 35 percent Lackawanna

- 8 to 25 percent slopes (OxC) — 60 percent Oquaga, 30 percent Lackawanna

Large stone content, droughty character, depth to bedrock and slope on steeper grades represent the major landscaping challenges.

### Oquaga-Lordstown stony loam

Composed of 45 percent Oquaga and 25 percent Lordstown soils, this complex is found uplands, flanks of valleys and margins of uplands in Wayne County. Parent material is coarse-loamy till derived from sandstone and siltstone.

Somewhat shallow with depth to lithic bedrock at 20 to 40 inches, the complex is well drained, not flooded or ponded, and with no water saturation issues. Extremely stony loams on 25 to 70 percent slopes (OyF) have challenges in slope, large stone content and depth to bedrock as major landscape concerns.

### Papakating silty clay loam

Papakating silty clay loam (Pa) is found on Carbon County flood plains, coming from recent alluvium. Soils are deep but very poorly drained, often flooded and sometimes ponded, with water saturation at or near the surface throughout the year.

The soil meets criteria to be classified as hydric and as such results in severe limitations on plant choices and requires careful conservation management. Ponding, flooding and depth to saturation are the chief issues for landscaping.

### Pekin silt loam

Found on stream terraces in Carbon County, Pekin silt loam (PkA) comes from acidic alluvium derived from sedimentary rock. Soils are deep, moderately well drained, rarely flooded and never ponded, with water saturation reaching 20 inches during March and April.

Slopes are less than 3 percent but because it can be stony has moderate limitations on plaint choices and requires moderate conservation practices. Depth to saturation represents the primary landscaping issue.

### Philo loams

Found is on nearly level flood plains, Philo loams are coarse-loamy alluvium derived from sandstone and siltstone. Very deep and moderately well drained, the soil is frequently flooded but is not ponded. Water saturation is at 27 inches From December through April.

Philo silt loam (Ph) in Monroe County and Philo loam (26) in Pike and Wayne counties have moderate limitations that impact plant selection and require moderate conservation practices. Flooding potential is the primary challenge for landscaping.

### Pope loams

Found is on flood plains with slopes of less than 3 percent, Pope loams consist of coarse-loamy alluvium derived from sandstone and siltstone. Soils are deep, well drained, with no saturation issues.

In Monroe County, silt loam (Po) is occasionally flooded, while high bottom silt loam (Pp) is rarely flooded. Neither are ponded and both have few limitations restricting use. In Pike County, fine sandy loam (15) can have moderate limitations impacting plant selection and require moderate conservation practices. Flooding potential is the primary landscape challenge.

### Rexford loams

Rexford loams occur in depressions in Monroe and Wayne Counties, and consist of coarse-loamy outwash derived from sandstone and shale. Fairly shallow at 15 to 24 inches, they are somewhat poorly drained, but not flooded or ponded. However, water saturation can reach 6 inches during March and April, so it meets the criteria to be classified as hydric.

In Monroe County, gravelly silt loam on less than 3 percent slopes (ReA) and 3 to 8 percent

slopes (ReB), have severe limitations affecting plant options and requiring special conservation practices. The same limitations affect Rexford loam (Re) in Wayne County. Depth to saturation and droughty character represent the primary challenges for landscapers.

### Rock outcrop-Arnot complex

Composed of 70 percent rock outcrop and 20 percent Arnot soils, this complex is found on valley sides in Wayne County, with parent material consisting of till derived from sandstone, siltstone and shale. Depth to lithic bedrock is 10 to 20 inches.

Well drained and neither flooded or ponded, there is no water saturation concern. Erosion issues on 3 to 25 percent slopes (RoD) are coupled with landscaping issues that include depth to bedrock, droughty character and slope.

### Rushtown loams

Rushtown soils are found on mountains and ridges in Carbon and Monroe counties and come from colluvium derived from shale and siltstone. Fairly deep with depth to bedrock ranging from 40 to 144 inches, they are excessively drained and there is no flooding, ponding or water saturation.

In Carbon County, erosion is a concern on shaly silt loams that include 3 to 8 percent slopes (RsB), and 8 to 15 percent slopes (RsC), both of which require special conservation practices. On 15 to 25 percent slopes (RsD) and 25 to 35 percent slopes (RsE), the soils are considered unsuitable for conventional cultivation and best used for pasture, forestland or wildlife habitat. Gravel content and to a much lesser extent droughty character are the primary landscape challenges, with slope becoming a factor on steeper grades.

In Monroe County, shaly silt loam on 5 to 15 percent slopes (RuC) require very careful management because of erosion potential, while 15 to 30 percent slopes (RuD) are best used for pasture, forestland or wildlife habitat. Gravel content and slope on steeper grades represent the primary issues for landscapers.

### Sheffield loams

Found in depressions on Monroe County till plains with slopes less than 3 percent, Sheffield loams (Sh) come from till. With depth to a fragipan of just 15 to 26 inches, the soil is poorly drained and while not flooded is often ponded. Water saturation is at the surface from December through May, and it meets the criteria to be classified as a hydric soil. The consequence is that the soil has limitations impacting plant selection and requiring special conservation practices. Depth to saturation and potential for ponding represent challenges for landscapers.

### Shelmadine loams

Found in depressions in Carbon and Monroe Counties, Shelmadine soil comes from loamy till. The soil is poorly drained and shallow, with a fragipan at 18 to 30 inches. Not flooded or ponded, it nonetheless meets hydric criteria because water saturation rises to 3 inches from November through June.

In Carbon County, silt loams on up to 3 percent slopes (ShA) and 3 to 8 percent moderately eroded slopes (ShB2) require very careful management including plant selection; depth to saturation is the primary landscaping issue. Very stony silt loam on up to 8 percent slopes (SmB) are considered unsuitable for cultivation because of depth to saturation and large stone content. In Monroe County, the comparable silt loam is identified as SmA and the very stony silt loam as SpB.

### Shohola-Edgemere complex

A combination of Shohola and Edgemere soils forms two complexes found in depressions in Monroe, Pike and Wayne counties. Parent material for both is coarse loamy till derived from sandstone and siltstone; Edgemere soils meet the criteria to be classified as hydric.

The complexes are shallow, with a fragipan at 15 to 30 inches, poorly drained, flooded but occasionally ponded, and water saturation can reach 12 inches from November through May. Because of the shallow depth and stony nature, all are best used for pasture, forestland or wildlife habitat.

One complex, about a 2 to 1 ratio of Shohola to Edgemere, occurs on soils of less than 8 percent slopes (7B) and 8 to 15 percent slopes (7C). The second, comprised of 42 percent each of the two major soils is found on very rubbly 3 to 15 percent slopes (111B). All represent challenges to landscapers because of depth to saturation, large stone content and to a lesser extent either ponding or slope.

### Skytop loams

Found on ridges and mountains in Pike County, Skytop consists of channery till derived from sandstone. Relatively shallow, with depth to lithic bedrock at 20 to 40 inches, the soil is well drained, neither flooded or ponded, and without water saturation issues.

Extremely stony very flaggy sandy loam on 8 to 15 percent slopes (58C) and 15 to 35 percent slopes (58E) are challenging for landscapers because of large stone content, slope, gravel content, droughty character and depth to bedrock.

### Skytop-Wasnot-Rock outcrop complex

Skytop soils comprise 45 percent and Wasnot soils 25 percent of a complex found on ridges and mountain slopes in Pike County. Parent material consists of channery till derived from sandstone (Skytop) and sandstone, quartzite and conglomerate (Wasnot).

Although depth to lithic bedrock is 10 to 40 inches, the soils are well to excessively drained, not flooded or ponded, and with no saturation issues. Occurring on very rubbly 15 to 60 percent slopes (285F), the soil is best used for forestland or wildlife habitat.

### Suncook loamy sand

Suncook loamy sand is found on floodplains in Pike County, with parent material consisting of sandy glaciofluvial deposits derived from sandstone. Soils are deep and well drained, occasionally flooded but not ponded. There is water saturation within a depth of 72 inches.

Found on slopes of less than 8 percent (5B), the soil may have limitations on plant selection or require special conservation practices. Primary challenges for landscapers are the droughty character of the soil and the potential for flooding.

### Swartswood loams

Swartswood soils are found on hills and uplands throughout the region. Parent material consists of coarse-loamy till derived from sandstone.

Depth to a fragipan is greater than 60 inches in Carbon, Monroe and Wayne counties and 28 to 36 inches in Pike County. The soil is moderately well drained, and not flooded or ponded.

Water saturation varies slightly: 28 inches from January through March in Carbon, 28 inches from November through April in Monroe and Wayne, and 30 inches in March and April in Pike.

In Carbon County, channery loam on less than 8 percent (SsB) and 8 to 15 percent slopes (SsC2) have erosion potential and require moderate to special conservation practices. Gravel content and slope on steeper grades represent modest landscape challenges, with droughty character and depth to saturation minor issues.

Very stony loams of less than 8 percent (SwB) and 8 to 25 percent (SwD) are unsuitable for conventional cultivation with landscape challenges concentrated on large stone content, droughty character and slope on the steeper grades.

In Monroe County and Wayne County, channery sandy loam on 3 to 8 percent slopes (SwB) and 8 to 15 percent slopes (SwC) have erosion potential and require moderate to special conservation practices. Gravel content and slope on steeper grades are the primary challenge for landscapers.

Extremely stony sandy loams on less than 8 percent slopes (SxB) and 8 to 25 percent slopes (SxC in Monroe and SxD in Wayne) are challenging because of large stone content, with lesser issue of droughty character and depth to saturation, and slope a factor on steeper grades.

In Pike County, extremely stony fine sandy loam on less than 8 percent slopes (38B), 8 to 15 percent slopes (38C) and 15 to 30 percent slopes (38D) are unsuitable for conventional cultivation and best used for pasture, forestland or wildlife habitats. Large stone content and droughty character are the primary landscaping concerns.

### Tioga and Middlebury loams

Found on flood plains in Carbon County, Tioga soils are from acidic alluvium derived from sedimentary rock, while parentage of Middlebury soils is post-glacial alluvium derived from sandstone and shale.

Deep and moderately well-drained to well drained, the soil is occasionally flooded but not ponded. Water saturation is at 25 to 54 inches from February through April. Very stony loams on less than 8 percent slopes (TmB) can range from very few limitations to some requiring moderate conservation practices. Flooding potential is less a concern than large stone content for landscapers, with gravel content and depth to saturation minor issues.

### Tioga loams

Found on flood plains in Carbon County, Tioga soils are from acidic alluvium derived from sedimentary rock. Deep and well drained the soil is occasionally flooded but not ponded and water saturation is at 54 inches from February through April. Both fine sandy loam (Tf) and silt loam (Tg) have few limitations restricting use. Flooding potential is a significant concern for landscapers.

### Tunkhannock loams

Found on outwash terraces in mountains in Carbon County, Tunkhannock material consists of water sorted gravelly outwash derived from sandstone and siltstone and/or shale. Deep, well drained and not flooded, ponded, there are no water saturation issues.

Gravelly loams on less than 3 percent (TuA) and 3 to 8 percent slopes (TuB) may require moderate conservation practices, while those on 8 to 15 percent slopes (TuC) and 15 to 25 percent slopes (TuD), have erosion potential and may require more rigorous conservation efforts. Gravel content represents a major challenge for landscapers, along with slope on steeper grades. Large stone content and droughty character can be minor issues.

### Unadilla silt loam

Unadilla loam is found on Pike County outwash terraces with less than 3 percent slopes (75). With parent material consisting of glacial outwash, the soils are deep, well drained, neither flooded or ponded and without water saturation issues. It has few limitations that restrict its use.

### Very Stony Land and Rock outcrops

Found on mountain slopes in Carbon and Monroe counties, the parent material of Very Stony Land and Rock Outcrops generally consists of coarse-loamy till derived from sandstone and siltstone. Somewhat shallow with lithic bedrock at 40 inches, the soils are well drained not flooded or ponded and without water saturation issues.

In Carbon County, very stony land on 0 to 8 percent slopes (VeB), 8 to 25 percent slopes (VeD) and 25 to 120 percent slopes (VeF) is listed only as a miscellaneous area by soil surveyors. Large stone content, depth to bedrock and slope represent substantial landscape challenges.

In Monroe County sloping stony land and outcrops with 2 to 15 percent slopes (VaC) and steep land and outcrops with 25 to 99 percent slopes (VaE) are best used for forestland or wildlife habitat.

### Volusia loams

Volusia loams are found on plateaus and valley sides in Carbon, Monroe and Wayne counties. Parent material is fine-loamy basal till derived from sandstone and siltstone. Deep but somewhat poorly drained, it is neither flooded or ponded, but water saturation can reach 12 inches in Carbon from November through May and 6 inches in Monroe and Wayne during March and April.

In Carbon County, silt loam on 0 to 8 percent slopes (VoB) requires special conservation practices because of saturation issues, a major concern for landscapers. Very stony loam on less than 8 percent slopes (VsB) is challenging because of depth to saturation, large stone content and droughty character.

In Monroe County, *gravelly* silt loam on less than 3 percent slopes (VoA) and 3 to 8 percent sloes (VoB) is limited because of water saturation and may require special conservation practices. Depth to saturation and droughty character are the primary challenges for landscapers.

In Wayne County, *channery* silt loam on less than 3 percent slopes (VoA), 3 to 8 percent slopes (VoB) and 8 to 15 percent slopes (VoC) is limited because of water saturation and may require special conservation practices. The major landscape issues are depth to saturation and droughty character, with large stone content a minor factor.

In both Monroe and Wayne counties, extremely stony silt loam on less than 8 percent slopes (VxB) and 8 to 15 percent slopes (VxC) is challenging because of depth to saturation, large stone content, and droughty character.

### Wasnot loams

Found on ridges and mountains in Pike County, Wasnot parent material consists of channery till derived from sandstone, quartzite and conglomerate. The soils are shallow, with depth to bedrock at just 10 to 20 inches, excessively drained, neither flooded or ponded and with no water saturation.

Very flaggy sandy loam on 3 to 15 percent slopes (50C) and 15 to 35 percent slopes (50E) are best used for pasture, forestland or wildlife habitat. Primary landscaping challenges are depth to bedrock, droughty character, large stone and gravel content, as well as slope on steeper grades.

### Watson loams

Watson loams occur on valley sides in Carbon and Monroe counties, with parent material consisting of old till derived from sedimentary rock. Deep and moderately well drained , it is neither flooded or ponded, but water saturation can reach 18 to 26 inches from November through March.

In Carbon County, saturation issues impact a number of soils in the series. Moderately eroded gravelly silt loam on less than 8 percent slopes (WaB2), silt loam on less than 3 percent slopes (WsA), moderately eroded 3 to 8 percent slopes (WsB2), moderately eroded silt loam on 8 to 15 percent slopes (WsC2) and severely eroded silt loam on 8 to 15 percent slopes all require moderate to special conservation practices. Depth to saturation is a minor challenge for landscapers, but on steeper grades, slope becomes an important factor.

In Monroe County, similar limitations apply to silt loam on 2 to 8 percent slopes (WaB). The primary landscape challenge is depth to a saturated zone.

### Wayland loams

Found on flood plains in Monroe County, Wayland loams come from recent alluvium. Soils are deep but very poorly drained, frequently flooded and often ponded. Water saturation is at the surface from December through June, an the soil meets the criteria to be classified as hydric.

Consequently, silty clay loam on less than 3

percent slopes requires very careful management and plant options are limited. Flooding, ponding and depth to saturation are the major issues for landscapers.

### Weikert loams

Found on hills in Monroe County, Weikert loams come from materials left by weathering shale and siltstone. Soils are somewhat shallow, with depth to lithic bedrock at 40 to 60 inches, excessively drained, neither flooded or ponded, and with no saturation concerns.

Erosion is the primary concern, requiring special to very careful management on eroded channery silt loams on 3 to 8 percent sloes (WeB3) and 8 to 15 percent slopes (WeC3). Droughty character and gravel content are challenges for landscapers. Soils on eroded 15 to 25 percent slopes (WeD3) are also challenging because of slope issues.

### Weikert-Hartleton soil complex

Comprised of 50 percent Weikert and 40 percent Hartleton soils, the complex is found on hills and uplands in Monroe County. Parent material consists of glacial till or frost-churned materials weathered from shale and sandstone.

The complex can be shallow to deep, is excessively to well drained, neither flooded or ponded, with no saturation issues. Erosion potential impacts the entire series, calling for special to very careful management of silt loams on 3 to 8 percent slopes (WhB), 8 to 15 percent slopes (WhC), and 15 to 25 percent slopes (WhD). Droughty character, gravel content and slope on steeper grades are the primary challenges for landscapers.

### Weikert — Klinesville complex

Weikert loams make up 50 percent and Klinesville 30 percent of the complex, with slopes ranging from 25 to 80 percent (WKE) on hills, ridges and in valleys in Monroe County. Parent material is remaining material from weathered shale (Weikert) and siltstone (both). Lithic bedrock is at a depth 40 to 60 inches, the soils are somewhat excessively drained and neither flooded or ponded and without saturation issues. Erosion potential is high, and landscape challenges include slope, droughty character and gravel content.

### Wellsboro loams

Found on valley sides in Monroe, Pike and Wayne counties, Wellsboro parent material consists of coarse-loamy till derived from sandstone and siltstone. The soils are shallow, with a fragipan at 14 to 26 inches, moderately well drained not flooded or ponded. Water saturation can reach 15 inches during March and April.

In Monroe County channery loam on 3 to 8 percent slopes (WmB) is limited by potential saturation plant choices are limited, while erosion potential impacts 8 to 15 percent slopes (WmC). Extremely stony loam on less than 8 percent slopes (WpB) and 8 to 25 percent slopes (WpC) round out the series, all of which pose challenges because of large stone content, depth to saturation and, on steeper grades, slope.

In Pike County extremely stony loam on less than 8 percent slopes (28B), 8 to 15 percent slopes (28C) and 15 to 25 percent sloes (28D) are challenging for depth to saturation, large stone content and on steeper grades increasing issues of slope. Channery loam on less than 8 percent slopes (29B) is limited because of saturation issues while erosion is a concern on 8 to 15 percent slopes (29C), with both requiring moderate to special conservation practices. Depth to saturation, gravel content and slope are landscape issues.

In Wayne County, extremely stony loam on less than 8 percent slopes (28B) challenges landscapers with depth to saturation and large stone content issues. Channery loams on 3 to 8 percent slopes (WeB) has saturation issues while 8 to 15 percent (WeC) and 15 to 25 percent slopes (WeD) are impacted by erosion potential, all requiring conservation management efforts. The primary challenges for landscapers are large stone content, depth to saturation and slope as grades become steeper. Extremely stony loams on 3 to 8 percent slopes (WoB) and 8 to 25 percent slopes (WoD), as well as a Wellsboro-Mardin extremely stony loam on 25 to 50 percent slopes pose challenges of large stone content, depth to saturation, slope and droughty character.

### Worth loams

Worth soils are found on Monroe County till plains, where parent material consists of loamy till derived from acid sandstone and siltstone. Although the soil is shallow, with a fragipan at 18 to 36 inches, it is not flooded or ponded, but water saturation is at 27 inches from February through May.

Extremely stony sandy loam on up to 8 percent slopes (WrB) and 8 to 25 percent slopes (WrC) are challenging to landscapers for large stone content and slope on steeper grades..

### Wurtsboro loams

Wurtsboro soils, found on hills and uplands throughout the region, are from coarse-loamy till derived from sandstone. Deep and moderately well drained, it is not flooded or ponded, but water saturation can reach 18 inches from November through March.

In Carbon county, saturation issues impact channery loams on 0 to 3 percent slopes (WuA) and moderately eroded 3 to 8 percent slopes (WuB2), limiting plant options and calling for moderate conservation practices. Of some concern for landscapers is depth to saturation and, to a much lesser extent, gravel content. Very stony loams on up to 8 percent slopes (WvB) and 8 to 25 percent slopes (WvD) are very challenging because of large stone content and depth to water saturation.

In Monroe County stony fine sandy loam on 0 to 8 percent slopes (30B) and 8 to 15 percent slopes (30C), as well as extremely stony loam on up to 8 percent slopes (WxB) and 8 to 25 percent slopes (WxC) are best suited for pasture, forestland or wildlife habitats. A channery loam on 2 to 12 percent slopes (WsB) has limitations on plant options and requires moderate conservation practices. Large stone content and depth to saturation are the primary challenges for landscapers, as well as slope on the steeper grades.

In Pike County, channery fine sandy loam on 0 to 8 percent slopes (25B) and 8 to 15 percent slopes (25C) is limited because of water saturation and requires moderate to special conservation practices. Depth to saturation and slope on steeper grades are the primary landscape challenges.

In Pike and Wayne counties, Stony fine sandy loam on 0 to 8 percent slopes (30B), 8 to 15 percent slopes (30C) and 15 to 25 percent slopes

(30D) is best uses for pasture, forestland or wildlife habitat. Depth to saturation and large stone content head the list of landscaping challenges, but slope becomes a major factor on steeper grades.

In Wayne County, channery loams on 3 to 8 percent slopes (WkB) and 8 to 15 percent slopes (WkC) are impacted by water saturation and erosion potential, respectively, and require moderate to special conservation practices.

### Wyalusing sandy loam

Found with less than 3 percent slopes on flood plains in Pike and Wayne counties, Wyalusing sandy loams come from coarse-loamy alluvium over sandy and gravelly alluvium. Deep but poorly drained, it is frequently flooded, but not ponded. Water saturation is at 3 inches from September through June, and it meets criteria to be classified as hydric.

In Pike and Wayne counties, fine sandy loam (143) has severe limitations on plant choices and requires very careful management. In Wayne County, a silt loam (Wy) has identical limitations. Flooding and depth to saturation are the primary landscape concerns.

### Wyoming loams

Wyoming sandy loams are found on terraces in Monroe, Pike and Wayne counties, and comes from water-sorted gravelly outwash derived from sedimentary rock. Deep and excessively drained, the soil is not flooded, ponded or saturated.

In Monroe County and Wayne counties, gravelly sandy loams on 0 to 3 percent slopes (WyA), 3 to 8 percent slopes (WyB) and 8 to 15 percent slopes (WyC) have limitations because of soil composition reducing plant choice options and sometimes calling for special conservation practices. On 15 to 25 percent slopes (WyD) and 25 to 70 percent slopes (WyE), erosion potential is high. Droughty character and gravel content are the primary challenges for landscapers, but as grades increase, the issues of slope become paramount.

In Pike County, very cobbly sandy loams on 3 to 8 percent slopes (442B) and 8 to 15 percent slopes (442C) have limitations because of soil composition suggesting reduced plant options and special conservation practices. Erosion potential on 15 to 30 percent slopes (442D) imply very careful management as well. Primary landscaping issues are large stone content and droughty conditions.

### Wyoming-Chenango complex

Chenango and Wyoming soils each make up 40 percent of a complex found on Pike County outwash terraces. Parent material consists of water-sorted glacial outwash derived from sedimentary rock and the soil is well drained to somewhat excessively drained with no flooding, ponding or water saturation.

On slopes up to 8 percent (108B) and 8 to 15 percent (108C), the stony nature of the soil reduces plant options and requires special conservation practices. Large stone content and, in some circumstances, slope are the primary landscape issues, with some concern about gravel content.

## Evolving vegetation maps

Vegetation mapping is a relatively young science that earnestly struggles to put nature into a tidy organization chart. Instead of boxes connected by lines, scholars look for patterns and draw lines on continental maps.

Notable pioneers in the field are E. Lucy Braun, who researched ecology for years before producing *Deciduous Forests of Eastern North America* in 1950 and A.W. Küchler, who pondered standards for classifying ecological communities before authoring *Vegetation Mapping* in 1967 as the support for a stunning map that took vegetation mapping to an entirely new level.

Since then, the lines and color coding on maps have oscillated, wiggled, and been rearranged any number of times by ecologists striving to understand a fundamental question: what herbaceous plants and shrubs are found under the canopies of certain groups of trees. Even major federal agencies use different maps, and different names, to describe the same general areas.

Scholarly research is almost always a new layer expanding over an old one. A solid 87-page book, *Terrestrial and Palustrine Communities of Pennsylvania* by Jean Fike for the Pennsylvania Natural Diversity Inventory in 1999 expanded on *Natural Ecological Communities of Pennsylvania,* written by Tom Smith eight years earlier. Fike's work is no longer printed because of budget cuts in Pennsylvania, but is available from the Department of Conservation and Natural Resources as a downloadable pdf.

The work of these pioneers set the stage for the National Park Service and the U.S. Geological Survey, collaborating with a group of ecologists in a coalition called NatureServe. This newest and very ambitious project is an evolving mound of field data continually being sifted to form some of the most detailed vegetation maps yet.

# *Discovering models in nature*

The more we understand habitat preferences for any plant, the more success and satisfaction we will have when we garden with it. The more we know what plants grow together in the wild, the better we define our landscape options.

And so we come to the most current research into *ecological communities*, which investigates plant associations and characteristics of habitat. Much of this thicket of data challenges patience, because each group of investigators create their own descriptive names, draw their own lines on maps, and reaches its own inferences based upon extensions of sampling.

Sample plots, typically on public land and especially in national parks, are usually less than an acre and hopefully representative.

While this process may diminish the joy scientists find in absolute precision, it points gardeners in the correct direction for planning natural landscapes. We have already discarded the gardening paradigm of *control* by installing appropriate exotics, no matter where in the world they come from, to create an artistic design. Instead we rely on patterns that might be found in a defined habitat and *collaborate* with nature.

These patterns, called *associations*, are composed of species that manage to grow in a given set of circumstances but sometimes also support each other in ways that aren't yet fully understood. For example, a specific type of soil lines a stream bank partially covered by a canopy of silver maple that blocks harsh afternoon sun; the stream might occasionally flood, but not with much force. Thus, a group of plants finds the habitat amenable.

However, the leaf litter from the silver maple and the decaying vegetation from last season's growth impacts the chemical composition of the soil itself, which may be altered even further during the occasional floods. Insects, birds, reptiles and mammals — even vast armies of microbial life — all reside here and all the pieces impact each other in sometimes very subtle ways. This, of course, is the magic of an ecosystem and the anxiety over unwitting damage to it is what drives our interest in landscaping with natives.

Now the label on the pot at the nursery becomes hopelessly inadequate. "Sun to part shade in moist soil" has little meaning. We require *ecological* information, i.e., a good description of native habitat, and the more detail, the better. Field guides are faint improvement as we step beyond "grows in woods" and hunt for such detail as "well-drained upland forest sites, open hillsides and ridges, especially on dry, fresh, sandy and coarse loamy soils" (*Apocynum androsaemifolium*).

Associations yield clues that offer one of two options, sometimes both. Sifting two or more associations for what is common to all expands a species list to create a larger landscape palette. For those whose orientation is toward conservation and restoration, a match closest to our own property might become a single, complete plant list.

The hybrid option is a specific list for one bed in the garden that models a single community and an altogether different list for a second bed that models something else. We achieve these combinations by altering the structure of the beds to closely match a specific habitat, i.e., a moist stream bank as a theme for one bed and a woodland glade as the model for another.

When we study a natural habitat, we find varying degrees of chaos and monotony. A meadow is a jumble of weeds or a woodland is a canopy with sparse shrubs, a lot of leaf litter and a few scattered herbaceous species. The difference between a restoration-conservation garden and one that more closely replicates conventional landscape design is the extent to which we thin, prune, weed and groom as well as the extend that we rely on broad brush strokes of a single species for a dramatic sweeping effect.

More than 130 ecological communities have been catalogued in the three eco-regions that intersect in northeastern Pennsylvania. Although they might be used as a resolved landscape model, it's helpful to consider them as tools, too. When we compare the lists of native plants whose range includes Pennsylvania and observed distribution includes the northeastern counties, the ecological communities are clearly limited. But when we apply habitat and soil descriptions of plants to the general themes of the ecological communities, our individual research broadens landscaping opportunities in a substantial way.

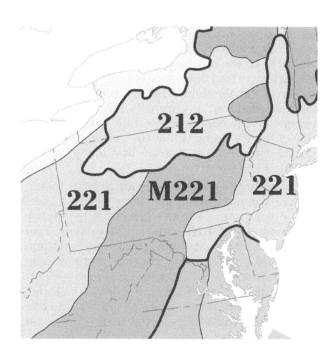

## Subdivisions of nature

For the benefit of those new to ecosystem mapping, the U.S. Forest Service first divided the North American continent into broad *domains,* then distinct *divisions,* then *provinces*, and finally the neighborhood *sections.*

Pennsylvania is found within the Humid Temperate Domain (coded as "200"), but at this juncture the very unique circumstances of northeastern Pennsylvania diverge into the Hot Continental Division (220), the Hot Continental Regime Mountains (M220) and the Warm Continental Division (210).

Within the Hot Continental Division we find the Eastern Broadleaf Forest (Oceanic) Province (221), which is further subdivided into the local Hudson Valley Section (221B).

Within the Hot Continental Regime Mountains lies the Central Appalachian Broadleaf Forest-Coniferous Forest-Meadow Province (M221), which is localized as the Northern Ridge and Valley Province (M221A).

The Warm Continental Division includes the Laurentian Mixed Forest Province (212), and within that we find the Northern Glaciated Allegheny Plateau Section (212F).

Ecological communities in the region may be found within any combination of these three sections, but have been identified in at least one. Because one of the field studies was done in the Delaware Water Gap National Recreation Area by the National Park Service, an extraordinary amount of material is available on wetlands and riparian habitats, but common woodlands and forests, meadows and high-elevation sparse vegetation zones are very well represented.

First we get a sense of the character of each of the three eco-regions found in the area: Northern Ridge and Valley, Hudson Valley, and Northern Glaciated Allegheny Plateau:

### *Northern Ridge and Valley (Section M221A)*

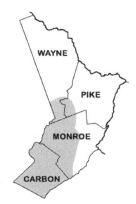

Parallel, relatively narrow valleys and mountain ridges on a generally southwest to northeast line from eastern Tennessee, along western Virginia and eastern West Virginia, central Pennsylvania and ending in northern Lackawanna County. They are the result of varying rates of erosion on intensely faulted and folded bedrock. To the east is the Great Valley lowland, while the western boundary is a high, steep ridge known as the Allegheny Front (locally often called the "Pocono Front"). Curiously, the front broadly sweeps up the center of the state to the western side of the Wyoming Valley, then abruptly reverses direction to form a prong that many call the Pocono Plateau.

A variety of erosion forces are at play, including gravity and stream and river forces, as well as water movement under ground. The result is a veneer of assorted materials overlaying bedrock, typically shale, sandstone and siltstone, but also some limestone. We thus find *residuum*, or the leftovers of weathering, on generally flat to sloping uplands; *colluvium*, or piles of materials carried to the bases of slopes by gravity, and *alluvium,* or materials transported by flowing water, in valley bottoms. Elevations can range from 300 to 4,000 feet, but local relief is more typically 500 to 1,500 feet.

Because most of the section lies in a rain shadow created by the Allegheny Mountains section to the west, vegetation commonly reflects somewhat dry conditions. Whereas annual rainfall in the Alleghenies can reach 60 inches a year, Ridge and Valley is more typically 35 to 45, with 20 percent of that as snow. In northeastern Pennsylvania counties, the average annual precipitation is about 48 to 50 inches.

In her pioneering work, Lucy Braun referred to much of the region as oak-chestnut; it was one of the areas dominated by *Castanea dentata* (American chestnut) before the blight of the early 20th century, which left oaks to become dominant. In his vegetation mapping work, A.M. Küchler described the region as Appalachian oak forest, oak-hickory-pine forest, and some northern hardwoods forest.

Generally speaking, *Quercus rubra* (northern red oak) and *Quercus alba* (white oak) tend to prefer productive, mesic sites, while *Quercus coccinea* (scarlet oak), *Quercus prinus* (chestnut oak) and *Quercus velutina* (black oak) lean toward the drier sites. And while *Pinus strobus* (Eastern white pine) is most often found on the lower portions of slopes, *Pinus rigida* (pitch pine) and *Pinus*

*virginiana* (Virginia pine) are staples of the driest upland sites.

### Hudson Valley (Section 221B)

Described as a linear lowland, part of which is an ancient glacial lake plain, bounded on either side by high escarpments, the region was created by a combination of faulting, weathering of soft bedrock and glacial scour. The band extends from central Berks County northeasterly across eastern Monroe and Pike Counties, then up the Hudson River Valley in New York.

Erosion of riverbeds, transport and deposition of soils by flowing water, and the impact of gravity on adjacent slopes account for most of the activity in the region, which are mostly gentle slopes ranging from elevations of 500 to 1,000 feet, and more than half the area would be considered uplands. The northern half of the central lowland is covered by former lake bed sediments, while the rest is materials deposited by flowering water (alluvium). Upland areas feature a thin, stony till over bedrock, mostly conglomerates and limestone.

Vegetation is generally northern hardwood and Appalachian oak forest, but can include central hardwoods, transition hardwoods and northern hardwoods along the south-to-north line; remaining forests are primarily limited to steep, shallow or other land considered unsuitable for agriculture or development. Average annual precipitation is 40 inches.

### Northern Glaciated Allegheny Plateau (Section 212F)

Considered a maturely dissected plateau of moderate relief this region covers most of northeastern Pennsylvania and much of southern New York State from the Hudson River nearly all the way to the Great Lakes. Moraine, drumlin, kettle, scour and other glacial features are common on an irregular topography that can include broad, rolling high hills and steep valleys typified by the Finger Lakes.

Escarpments — north facing along Lake Ontario and east-facing along the Hudson River, define boundaries to the north, while the familiar Pocono Front marks the line in northeastern Pennsylvania. Geomorphic processes include the mass wasting of slopes by gravitational force, ongoing erosion of river beds, transport and deposition of alluvium and the erosional forces of water moving underground.

More than 75 percent of the area is considered upland, with gentle slopes on about a third of the landscape; elevation ranges from 650 to nearly 2,000 feet, with local relief typically varying from about 600 feet.

A thin, stony till and stratified drift covers most of the region, under which sandstone, siltstone and shale are the common bedrocks. The escarpments themselves can include limestone and sandstone, with a conglomerate forming the most prominent scarp in the southeastern area of the range.

Streams and small lakes are common and provide abundant water. Upland streams are often high gradient and bedrock controlled, with low to moderate gradient streams in valleys. Swamps and marshes are found on poorly drained sites in both uplands and valleys, and waterfalls and rapids are frequent where streams traverse beds of resistant rock. Runoff in the east and west are highest, especially in spring; lowest runoff occurs in summer and fall, when occasional drought can be an issue. Precipitation ranges from 30 to 50 inches.

Vegetation generally involves northern hardwoods and Appalachian oak forest, especially Appalachian oak-hickory and oak-pine forests, beech-maple mesic forest and hemlock-northern hardwood forest, but most of the land has been modified for agricultural use and only about a third remains as forest.

### Notes on using this section

In an effort to help the reader, this large block of material is subdivided into smaller sections, including:

Deciduous Forests
Deciduous Woodlands
Evergreen Forests
Evergreen Woodlands
Mixed Deciduous and Evergreen Forests
Mixed Deciduous and Evergreen Woodlands
Shrublands
Perennial Graminoid Vegetation
Perennial Forb Vegetation
Rocky Sparse Vegetation
Hydromorphic Vegetation

*Forests* are regions in which the tree canopy is between 60 and 100 percent closed, while *woodlands* are between 25 and 60 percent closed. The obvious difference is the amount of light penetrating the canopy to reach the forest floor below, which impacts herbaceous vegetation.

*Shrublands* consist of terrain with little to no trees, but rather a sparse to occasionally dense cover by shrubs.

*Graminoid* (grasses, sedges and rushes) vegetation is distinct from *forb* vegetation because these areas, typically meadows, are overwhelmingly dominated by graminoids.

*Hydromorphic* vegetation includes plants that grow in water either as submergents or emergents. Some are critical indicators of the relative health of a lake or stream, but all are helpful as materials for standing water features like back yard ponds.

# *Deciduous forests*

## Green Ash - Maple Bottomland Forest

**Formal name**: *Acer (rubrum, saccharinum) - Fraxinus pennsylvanica - Ulmus americana / Boehmeria cylindrica Forest*

### *Environmental summary*

**Where it is found:** poor drainage backswamps, sloughs, abandoned oxbows, and depressions of large-stream and river floodplains, from New Jersey and Pennsylvania south to West Virginia and Kentucky.

**Soil information:** sticky clay or silty-clay loams with gleyed or mottled upper horizons. Chemical analysis indicates moderate acidity (about pH 5.1) and moderately high calcium, magnesium, and total base saturation levels.

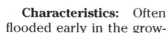

**Characteristics:** Often flooded early in the growing season, and some water may be ponded in shallow hollows for much of the year, so species are predominantly those with high tolerance for relatively deep and prolonged inundation.

### *Vegetation*

Canopy dominants are varying combinations of *Fraxinus pennsylvanica* (green ash), *Acer rubrum* (red maple) and *Acer saccharinum* (silver maple). Where *A. rubrum* dominates, *A. saccharinum* may be nearly absent, and vice versa. *Ulmus americana* (American elm) is a common associate. Other associates may include:

*Acer negundo* (box elder)
*Betula nigra* (river birch)
*Platanus occidentalis* (American sycamore)

*Quercus bicolor* (swamp white oak)
*Quercus palustris* (pin oak)

The shrub layer is generally sparse to absent, but can include tree saplings of *Carpinus caroliniana* (American hornbeam), *Cephalanthus occidentalis* (common buttonbush), *Cornus amomum* (silky dogwood) and *Lindera benzoin* (northern spicebush). Meanwhile, vines - especially *Toxicodendron radicans* (poison ivy), *Parthenocissus quinquefolia* (Virginia creeper), and *Vitis spp.* (grape) - are common.

The herb layer is usually dense except for sites in deeper hollows. Typical species include:

*Boehmeria cylindrica* (smallspike false nettle)
*Carex crinita* (fringed sedge)
*Carex grayi* (Gray's sedge)
*Carex lupulina* (hop sedge)
*Carex stipata* (awlfruit sedge)
*Carex tribuloides* (blunt broom sedge)
*Cinna arundinacea* (sweet woodreed)
*Geum canadense* (white avens)
*Glyceria striata* (fowl mannagrass)
*Impatiens capensis* (jewelweed)
*Leersia virginica* (whitegrass)
*Lobelia cardinalis* (cardinal flower)
*Pilea pumila* (Canadian clearweed)
*Polygonum arifolium* (halbardleaf tearthumb)
*Polygonum punctatum* (dotted smartweed)
*Symplocarpus foetidus* (skunk cabbage)

## Maple - Ash - Elm Swamp Forest

**Formal name:** *Acer (rubrum, saccharinum) - Fraxinus spp. - Ulmus americana Forest*

### *Environmental summary*

**Where it is found:** east-central United States and adjacent Canada in wetland depressions on level plains and flood-plain backswamps.

**Soil information:** silt loam, silty clay loam or clay loam usually deeper than 20 inches, with the water table near or at the surface for at least several months. Although ponding is common, soils can become dry in summer.

**Characteristics:** broad-leaved deciduous tree-dominated forests on level to nearly level soils formed by alluvial sediments along major rivers. Ponding is common for most of the year in shallow depressions, while winter and spring flooding, which can extend into much of the growing season, can be more than three feet.

Because of soil moisture and seasonal inundation, the dominance structure is fairly constant, and soil saturation reduces density of vegetation. Slight ridges and swales within the forest from flooding events and soil deposition create patchiness. The range of the forest has been significantly reduced because of land clearing for agricultural use.

### Vegetation

*Acer rubrum* (red maple) and/or *Acer saccharinum* (silver maple), along with *Fraxinus pennsylvanica* (green ash) and *Ulmus americana* (American elm) dominate a closed canopy. *U. americana* might have been the dominant before the introduction of Dutch elm disease. Associates may include *Quercus palustris* (pin oak) and *Nyssa sylvatica* (black gum).

Shrubs - including *Toxicodendron radicans* (poison ivy) - typically include a mix of:
> *Alnus incana* (gray alder)
> *Carpinus caroliniana* (American hornbeam)
> *Ilex verticillata* (winterberry)
> *Lindera benzoin* (northern spicebush)
> *Sambucus canadensis* (American black elderberry)
> *Viburnum recognitum* (southern arrow wood)

Herbaceous layer species vary considerably because of depth and duration of flooding and the amount of light penetrating the canopy. High vegetative mortality results from prolonged saturation, but pioneer species quickly colonize openings when conditions improve. Among the most commonly reported species are:
> *Arisaema triphyllum* (Jack-in-the-pulpit)
> *Carex spp.* (sedges)
> *Glyceria striata* (fowl mannagrass)
> *Impatiens capensis* (jewelweed)
> *Juncus* spp. (rushes)

## Box-elder Floodplain Forest

**Formal name:** *Acer negundo Forest*

### Environmental summary

**Where it is found:** active floodplains along large rivers and on sandbars, possibly some distance from the riverfront following disturbance; throughout the southern, eastern and midwestern United States.

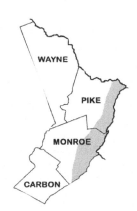

**Soil information:** open alluvial deposits that are often sandy, especially on higher floodplain terraces where soil is less rocky and often used for agriculture or habitation. They are often temporarily flooded in the spring.

**Characteristics:** an early successional community evolving from natural and cultural disturbances on floodplains with a semi-open to closed canopy.

### Vegetation

The canopy is dominated by *Acer negundo* (box elder). Other characteristic species include:
> *Acer rubrum* (red maple)
> *Acer saccharinum* (silver maple)
> *Carpinus caroliniana* (American hornbeam)
> *Carya cordiformis* (bitternut hickory)
> *Fraxinus pennsylvanica* (green ash)
> *Juglans nigra* (black walnut)
> *Liriodendron tulipifera* (tuliptree)

*Platanus occidentalis* (American sycamore)
*Robinia pseudoacacia* (black locust)
*Ulmus rubra* (slippery elm)

The shrub and herb layers range from sparse to relatively lush, and the vine component often is dense. *Lindera benzoin* (northern spicebush) often dominates the shrub layer.

The herb layer consists of a mixture of weedy exotics and native floodplain species. Natives often listed include:

*Ageratina altissima* (white snakeroot)
*Boehmeria cylindrica* (smallspike false nettle)
*Carex grayi* (Gray's sedge)
*Cryptotaenia canadensis* (Canadian honewort)
*Mertensia virginica* (Virginia bluebells)
*Polygonum virginianum* (jumpseed)
*Prunella vulgaris* (common selfheal)
*Urtica dioica ssp. dioica* (stinging nettle)

# Red Maple Seepage Swamp

**Formal name:** *Acer rubrum - Fraxinus (pennsylvanica, americana) / Lindera benzoin / Symplocarpus foetidus Forest*

### Environmental summary

**Where it is found:** a variety of palustrine settings, including small upland depressions, impounded drainages, poorly drained floodplains of small creeks, in depressions at the edges of floodplains subjected to overland flooding in addition to groundwater inputs, or as part of a larger wetland complex. Found from southern New England to the Piedmont of Virginia.

**Soil information:** shallow to moderately acidic and somewhat poorly to very poorly drained soil such as shallow mucky peat, Alden mucky silt loam, or the Fredon-Halsey complex; also described as deep mucks over mineral soils.

**Characteristics:** seepage swamps that are not very species rich, with saturated soils. This as-

sociation can be temporarily to permanently flooded and can be associated with impounded drainages.

### Vegetation

*Acer rubrum* dominates a closed (more than 60 percent cover) canopy, with 25 to 95 percent coverage and a height of 60 to 80 feet. Associates include *Ulmus americana* (American elm), *Fraxinus pennsylvanica* (green ash), and *Fraxinus americana* (white ash). *Fraxinus nigra* (black ash) is not generally associated with this type and, if present, occurs only as scattered individuals. Conifers such as *Tsuga canadensis* (eastern hemlock) or *Pinus strobus* (eastern white pine) are generally absent or very infrequent.

Other canopy or subcanopy associates may include:

*Betula lenta* (sweet birch)
*Carpinus caroliniana* (American hornbeam)
*Carya ovata* (shagbark hickory)
*Fagus grandifolia* (American beech)
*Liriodendron tulipifera* (tuliptree)
*Platanus occidentalis* (sycamore)
*Prunus serotina* (black cherry)
*Quercus bicolor* (swamp white oak)
*Quercus palustris* (pin oak)
*Ulmus rubra* (slippery elm)

A sparse subcanopy extends from 30 to 50 feet in height and contains red maple and other species from the canopy.

The tall-shrub layer can be sparse to dense (5 to 60 percent cover) and varied. Common tall shrubs are:

*Alnus serrulata* (smooth alder)
*Clethra alnifolia* (summersweet)
*Cornus amomum* (silky dogwood)
*Ilex montana* (mountain holly)
*Ilex verticillata* (common winterberry)
*Lindera benzoin* (northern spicebush)
*Rhododendron viscosum* (swamp azalea)
*Vaccinium corymbosum* (highbush blueberry)
*Viburnum dentatum var lucidum* (southern arrowwood)

Typical short shrubs (20 to 40 percent cover) include Rubus hispidus (bristly dewberry) and the species found in the tall-shrub layer.

The herbaceous layer covers from 30 to 70

percent of the forest floor and can include:

> *Arisaema triphyllum* (Jack-in-the-pulpit)
> *Boehmeria cylindrica* (smallspike false nettle)
> *Carex intumescens* (greater bladder sedge)
> *Carex lacustris* (hairy sedge)
> *Carex radiata* (eastern star sedge)
> *Chrysoplenium americanum* (American golden saxifrage)
> *Galium aparine* (cleavers)
> *Geum canadense* (white avens)
> *Glycera striata* (fowl mannagrass)
> *Onoclea sensibilis* (sensitive fern)
> *Osmunda cinnamomea* (cinnamon fern)
> *Osmunda regalis* (royal fern)
> *Symplocarpus foetidus* (skunk-cabbage)
> *Thelypteris noveboracensis* (New York fern)
> *Theylteris palustris* (eastern marsh fern)

Vines such as *Vitis labrusca* (fox grape) can also be abundant, while *Parthenocissus quinquefolia* (Virginia creeper) and *Toxicodendron radicans* (eastern poison ivy) are relatively common but sparsely distributed.

Pronounced microtopography results from tip-ups. Tree seedlings and Sphagnum mosses are common on hummocks generally do not in form extensive carpets. Additional nonvascular species can include *Plagiomnium cuspidatum* (*Mnium cuspidatum*) and *Calliergon spp.*

## Red Maple - Blackgum Basin Swamp

**Formal name:** *Acer rubrum - Nyssa sylvatica - Betula alleghaniensis / Sphagnum spp. Forest*

### Environmental summary

**Where it is found:** saturated to seasonally wet perched basins in small watersheds located in upland forests; from the central Appalachians to central New England (the northern edge of *Nyssa sylvatica* range).

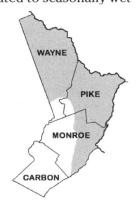

**Soil information:** mineral soil under a deep, highly acidic and nutrient-poor muck or peat layer. Alden mucky silt loam is typical.

**Characteristics:** Isolated pockets in small upland depressions that are parts of larger wetland complexes, or in basins near small headwater drainages. A varied tree canopy ranging from open woodland to nearly closed, with shrubs that can be locally dense and a patchy herbaceous layer dominated by only a few species. Variable bryophytes can carpet extensive hummock-and-hollow microtopography, especially in hollows where standing water is brief.

The presence of *Nyssa sylvatica* distinguishes these swamps from other basin swamps in the northern Appalachians. The absence of *Rhododendron maximum* and *Rhododendron viscosum* are characteristic of Southern black gum swamps.

### Vegetation

An open canopy covers 25 to 60 percent of the wetland, dominated by *Acer rubrum* (red maple) and *Nyssa sylvatica* (black gum) and ranging from 15 to 65 feet in height. Common associates are *Betula alleghaniensis* (yellow birch), *Tsuga canadensis* (eastern hemlock), *Pinus rigida* (pitch pine) and *Picea mariana* (black spruce).

*Vaccinium corymbosum* (highbush blueberry) or *Rhododendron maximum* (great laurel) are characteristic dominants of the dense tall shrub layer, with 30 to 90 percent cover. In addition to all the species in the canopy, the layer also includes:

> *Alder spp.* (alders)
> *Cephalanthus occidentalis* (common buttonbush)
> *Ilex verticillata* (winterberry)
> *Lyonia ligustrina* (maleberry)
> *Nemopanthus mucronatus* (catberry)
> *Rhododendron viscosum* (swamp azalea)
> *Viburnum spp.* (viburnums)

Comprising a somewhat dense short-shrub layer are:

> *Chamaedaphne calyculata* (leatherleaf)
> *Gaultheria procumbens* (wintergreen)
> *Gaylussacia baccata* (black huckleberry)
> *Kalmia angustifolia* (sheep laurel)
> *Spiraea alba var. latifolia* (white meadowsweet)

*Osmunda cinnamomea* (cinnamon fern) usually dominates the herb layer, which is found primarily on hummocks surrounding the base of woody plants and in standing water. Associates may include:

> *Calla palustris* (water arum)
> *Carex atlantica ssp. capillacea* (prickly bog sedge)
> *Carex folliculata* (northern long sedge)
> *Carex intumescens* (great bladder sedge)
> *Carex trisperma* (threeseeded sedge)
> *Coptis trifolia* (threeleaf goldthread)
> *Drosera rotundifolia* (roundleaf sundew)
> *Dulichium arundinaceum* (threeway sedge)
> *Eleocharis spp.* (spikerushes)
> *Glyceria canadensis* (rattlesnake manna-grass)
> *Juncus canadensis* (Canada rush)
> *Maianthemum canadense* (Canada mayflower)
> *Osmunda regalis* (royal fern)
> *Scirpus cyperinus* (woolgrass)
> *Symplocarpus foetidus* (skunk cabbage)
> *Thelypteris palustris* (eastern marsh fern)
> *Triadenum virginicum* (Virginia marsh St. John's wort)
> *Woodwardia virginica* (Virginia chain fern)

A sphagnum moss layer, including *Sphagnum palustre* and *Sphagnum magellanicum*, is common and covers 25 to 50 percent.

## Acidic Seepage Swamp

**Formal name:** *Acer rubrum - Nyssa sylvatica / Ilex verticillata - Vaccinium fuscatum / Osmunda cinnamomea Forest*

### Environmental summary

**Where it is found:** groundwater-saturated flats and low slopes along streams in the Ridge and Valley, northern Blue Ridge, and western Piedmont provinces, at elevations of 700 to 2,900 feet.

**Soil information:** underlain by acidic sedimentary and metamorphic rocks, substrates are poorly drained mineral soils with many hydric indicators, such as low

chroma, gley, mottles and saturated horizons. Local areas of organic muck sometimes accumulate in depressions. Soils are reported to be very strongly acidic with moderately low to very low base status.

**Characteristics:** A slightly sloping ground surface, with drainage commonly via small and intricately braided channels, interspersed by hummocks. Plant habitats are often narrow and elongated. Moss mats, predominantly Sphagnum, are common and provide a rooting medium for herbaceous species. Community patches are generally shaded by overhanging trees, but sunny spots may be created by canopy gaps and bigger patches can have small open centers.

This association has a small geographic range and is limited to groundwater-saturated, nutrient-poor habitats large enough to support forest vegetation.

### Vegetation

The usually-closed canopy consists of *Acer rubrum* (red maple), *Nyssa sylvatica* (black gum), and *Liriodendron tulipifera* (tuliptree). *Pinus rigida* (pitch pine) is a frequent overstory associate in some local stands, but its numbers have recently declined because of southern pine beetle outbreaks. Other tree species, especially at higher elevations, include *Quercus alba* (white oak), *Betula lenta* (sweet birch), and *Pinus strobus* (white pine).

The shrub may be dense and can include:

> *Alnus serrulata* (hazel alder)
> *Carpinus caroliniana* (American hornbeam)
> *Gaylussacia baccata* (black huckleberry)
> *Gaylussacia frondosa* (blue huckleberry)
> *Ilex verticillata* (common winterberry)
> *Kalmia latifolia* (mountain laurel)
> *Lindera benzoin* (northern spicebush)
> *Rhododendron viscosum* (swamp azalea)
> *Smilax spp.*, (greenbrier)
> *Toxicodendron vernix* (poison sumac)
> *Vaccinium corymbosum* (highbush blueberry)
> *Viburnum dentatum* (southern arrow-wood)
> *Viburnum nudum var. cassinoides* (witherod)

*Rubus hispidus* (bristly dewberry) is an abundant creeping vine in many stands.

Commonly reported herbaceous plants are:
*Carex gynandra* (nodding sedge)
*Lycopodium obscurum* (tree groundpine)
*Medeola virginiana* (Indian cucumber)
*Osmunda cinnamomea* (cinnamon fern)
*Osmunda regalis var. spectabilis* (royal fern)
*Symplocarpus foetidus* (skunk cabbage)
*Thelypteris noveboracensis* (New York fern)
*Veratrum viride* (green false hellebore)
*Viola cucullata* (marsh blue violet)

The bryophyte layer may also be diverse; species of mosses and liverworts identified include:
*Atrichum undulatum* (atrichum moss)
*Aulacomnium palustre* (aulacomnium moss)
*Bryhnia novae-angliae* (New England bryhnia moss)
*Callicladium haldanianum* (callicladium moss)
*Campylium radicale* (campylium moss)
*Dicranum scoparium* (dicranum moss)
*Hypnum imponens* (hypnum moss)
*Jungermannia gracillima* (liverwort)
*Leucobryum albidum* (leucobryum moss)
*Mnium hornum* (horn calcareous moss)
*Pellia epiphylla* (liverwort)
*Plagiomnium ciliare* (plagiomnium moss)
*Platygyrium repens* (platygyrium moss)
*Steerecleus serrulatus* (steerecleus moss)
*Thuidium delicatulum* (delicate thuidium moss)

## Forested Acidic Seep

**Formal name:** *Acer rubrum - Nyssa sylvatica High Allegheny Plateau, Central Appalachian Forest*

### Environmental summary

**Where it is found:** substrates saturated for extended periods during the growing season but rarely have standing water, including forested seeps, hillsides, stream heads, floodplain edges, and poorly-drained depressions. Occurrences are usually small. Found in the central Appalachian Mountains and High Allegheny regions.

**Soil information:** acidic humus over poorly drained mineral substrates.

**Characteristics:** Continually moist, acidic areas typically covered primarily by *Acer rubrum* (red maple) and *Nyssa sylvatica* (black gum).

### Vegetation

The canopy is dominated by *Acer rubrum* (red maple) and *Nyssa sylvatica* (black gum), and associates include *Tsuga canadensis* (eastern hemlock) and *Betula alleghaniensis* (yellow birch).

The shrub layer often includes:
*Alnus serrulata* (hazel alder)
*Ilex verticillata* (common winterberry)
*Photinia pyrifolia* (red chokeberry)
*Rhododendron maximum* (great rhododendron)
*Rubus hispidus* (bristly dewberry)
*Vaccinium corymbosum* (highbush blueberry)

Comprising the herbaceous layer are:
*Carex folliculata* (northern long sedge)
*Carex intumescens* (great bladder sedge)
*Carex stricta* (upright sedge)
*Carex trisperma* (three seeded sedge)
*Osmunda cinnamomea* (cinnamon fern)
*Osmunda regalis* (royal fern)

Sphagnum mosses are common.

## Red Maple Swamp

**Formal name:** *Acer rubrum / Nemopanthus mucronatus - Vaccinium corymbosum Forest*

### Environmental summary

**Where it is found:** small upland depressions, impounded or braided drainages, wetland borders or as part of a larger wetland complex.

**Soil information:** vary, and can range from acidic to circumneutral, but almost always very poorly drained mineral soil, often with a layer of muck, as in Alden mucky silt loam.

**Characteristics:** often semi-permanently or permanently flooded and can be associated with past impoundments, sometimes beaver-influenced. Generally an open woodland to closed canopy of *Acer rubrum* (red maple) over a thick tall-shrub layer of *Vaccinium corymbosum* (highbush blueberry).

### Vegetation

The canopy typically more than 60 percent of the wetland, but can be as low as 25 percent, and is usually 30 to 50 feet in height. A sparse subcanopy covers 10 to 40 percent, reaching 15 to 30 feet. *Acer rubrum* (red maple) is the dominant tree in the canopy and subcanopy. Other associated canopy and subcanopy trees include:

> *Abies balsamea* (balsam fir)
> *Betula alleghaniensis* (yellow birch)
> *Fraxinus nigra* (black ash)
> *Fraxinus pennsylvanica* (green ash)
> *Nyssa sylvatica* (black gum)
> *Picea rubens* (red spruce)
> *Populus deltoides* (eastern cottonwood)
> *Quercus palustris* (pin oak)
> *Tsuga canadensis* (eastern hemlock)
> *Ulmus americana* (American elm)

A tall shrub layer covers 15 to 15 percent of the area and short shrubs cover 20 to 30 percent. The shrub layer is often dominated by *Vaccinium corymbosum* (highbush blueberry). Other shrubs reported in the wetland include:

> *Alnus incana* (gray alder)
> *Alnus serrulata* (hazel alder)
> *Cornus amomum* (silky dogwood)
> *Ilex verticillata* (common winterberry)
> *Lindera benzoin* (northern spicebush)
> *Lyonia ligustrina* (maleberry)
> *Nemopanthus mucronatus* (mountain holly)
> *Physocarpus opulifolius* (common ninebark)
> *Rhododendron maximum* (great rhododendron)
> *Rhododendron viscosum* (swamp azalea)
> *Rosa palustris* (swamp rose)
> *Spiraea alba var. latifolia* (white meadowsweet)
> *Viburnum nudum var. cassinoides* (witherod viburnum)
> *Viburnum recognitum* (southern arrowwood)

The herbaceous layer ranges from sparse to dense and is usually dominated by Carex stricta (tussock sedge) and a mixture of ferns. Most often reported are:

> *Dryopteris cristata* (crested woodfern)
> *Onoclea sensibilis* (sensitive fern)
> *Osmunda cinnamomea* (cinnamon fern)
> *Osmunda claytoniana* (interrupted fern)
> *Osmunda regalis* (royal fern)
> *Thelypteris palustris* (eastern marsh fern)

Other typical herbaceous species include:

> *Arisaema triphyllum* (Jack-in-the-pulpit)
> *Calamagrostis canadensis* (bluejoint)
> *Caltha palustris* (marsh marigold)
> *Carex intumescens* (great bladder sedge)
> *Carex trisperma* (three-seeded sedge)
> *Chrysosplenium americanum* (American golden saxifrage)
> *Galium palustre* (common marsh bedstraw)
> *Impatiens spp* (touch me not)
> *Ludwigia palustris* (marsh seedbox)
> *Symplocarpus foetidus* (skunk cabbage)

*Sphagnum spp.* and *Mnium spp.* are common among bryophyte flora and cover approximately 10 to 30 percent of the wetland.

Vines such as *Parthenocissus quinquefolia* (Virginia creeper), *Toxicodendron radicans* (eastern poison ivy), and *Smilax rotundiflora* (roundleaf greenbrier) are present, but sparse.

## Silver Maple Floodplain Levee Forest

**Formal name:** *Acer saccharinum - (Populus deltoides) / Matteuccia struthiopteris - Laportea canadensis Forest*

### Environmental summary

**Where it is found:** point bars, levees and adjacent terraces of medium to large, moderate gradient and high-energy rivers with substantial sedimentation and erosion, commonly flooded in the spring. Found throughout the northeastern United States.

**Soil information:** silty to moderately coarse, deep alluvium.

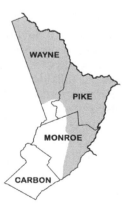

**Characteristics:** River banks and bars subjected to substantial erosion and sedimentation, with silver maple dominating a high, arching closed canopy and ferns dominating the herbaceous layer.

### Vegetation

*Acer saccharinum* (silver maple) dominates the nearly closed to closed canopy. Associates may be scattered or locally common. These include:

*Acer negundo* (box elder)
*Fraxinus americana* (white ash)
*Fraxinus pennsylvanica* (green ash)
*Juglans nigra* (black walnut)
*Populus deltoides* (eastern cottonwood)
*Quercus rubra* (red oak)
*Ulmus rubra* (slippery elm)

*P. deltoides* indicates siltier soils and levees within these forests.

The shrub cover tends to be low and scattered. Often reported are:

*Cornus amomum* (silky dogwood)
*Lindera benzoin* (northern spicebush)
*Sambucus canadensis* (black elderberry)

Also observed are potentially invasive nonnative *Lonicera spp., Rosa multiflora* (multiflora rose), or *Ligustrum vulgare* (common privet)

Vines such as *Vitis riparia* (river grape) are common at some sites.

*Matteuccia struthiopteris* (ostrich fern) and Laportea canadensis (Canadian wood nettle) dominate a generally lush herbaceous layer. Associates include:

*Ageratina altissima* (white snakeroot)
*Amphicarpaea bracteata* (American hog peanut)
*Arisaema triphyllum* (Jack-in-the-pulpit)
*Boehmeria cylindrica* (smallspike false nettle)
*Cinna arundinacea* (sweet woodreed)
*Circaea lutetiana* (enchanter's nightshade)
*Elymus riparius* (riverbank wild rye)
*Elymus virginicus* (Virginia rye grass)
*Leersia virginica* (whitegrass)
*Onoclea sensibilis* (sensitive fern)
*Polygonum virginianum* (jumpseed)
*Thalictrum pubescens* (king of the meadow)

Two variations in the herbaceous layer have been reported. In the ostrich fern variant, *Mat-teuccia struthiopteris* is more frequent than *Laportea canadensis; Ageratina altissima*, and *Impatiens spp.* are often prevalent, while *Toxicodendron radicans* (poison ivy) and *Boehmeria cylindrica* are scarce. In the wood nettle variant, *Laportea canadensis* is much more common than *Matteuccia struthiopteris*, and *Toxicodendron radicans, Leersia virginica, Boehmeria cylindrica,* and *Cinna arundinacea* are common.

Bryoids are relatively minor.

## Silver Maple Forest

**Formal name:** *Acer saccharinum - Acer negundo / Ageratina altissima - Laportea canadensis - (Elymus virginicus) Forest*

### Environmental summary

**Where it is found:** banks and first bottoms of major river floodplains in the Mid-Atlantic states.

**Soil information:** Briefly innundated nutrient-rich silt loams, sand loams, and sands. Flooding is annually to less often.

**Characteristics:** closed canopy forests immediately adjacent to major rivers and dominated by silver maple and box elder.

### Vegetation

Closed canopies are dominated by *Acer saccharinum* (silver maple), with *Acer negundo* (box elder) dominating a subcanopy layer. Other minor associates include:

*Celtis occidentalis* (common hackberry)
*Fraxinus pennsylvanica* (green ash)
*Juglans nigra* (black walnut)
*Populus deltoides* (eastern cottonwood)
*Ulmus americana* (American elm)

*Lindera benzoin* (northern spicebush) frequently dominates the shrub layer, which ranges from sparse in low elevations to dense in higher areas.

Commonly reported in the herbaceous layer are:

*Ageratina altissima* (white snakeroot)

*Cryptotaenia canadensis* (Canadian honewort)
*Elymus riparius* (river rye)
*Elymus virginicus* (Virginia rye)
*Geum canadense* (white avens)
*Impatiens pallida* (pale touch-me-not)
*Laportea canadensis* (Canadian wood-nettle)
*Leersia virginica* (whitegrass)
*Pilea pumila* (Canadian clearweed)
*Rudbeckia laciniata* (cutleaf coneflower)
*Viola sororia* (common blue violet)

Vines of *Toxicodendron radicans* (poison ivy) and *Parthenocissus quinquefolia* are common.

## Silver Maple - American Elm Forest

**Formal name:** *Acer saccharinum - Ulmus americana / Physocarpus opulifolius Forest*

### Environmental summary

**Where it is found:** floodplains of smaller rivers throughout the region.

**Soil information:** mineral soils, often saturated.

**Characteristics:** freely drained floodplains with diverse tree, shrub and herb layers, often with closed canopies.

### Vegetation

A nearly-closed canopy is dominated by *Acer rubrum* (red maple), *Acer saccharinum* (silver maple), and *Ulmus americana* (American elm). Associates include:
    *Carpinus caroliniana* (American hornbeam)
    *Carya cordiformis* (bitternut hickory)
    *Fraxinus americana* (white ash)
    *Juglans cinerea* (butternut)
    *Juglans nigra* (black walnut)
    *Platanus occidentalis* (American sycamore)
    *Populus deltoides* (eastern cottonwood)
    *Quercus rubra* (red oak)
    *Tilia americana* (American basswood)

Often abundant shrubs, vines and herbs can include:
    *Boehmeria cylindrica* (smallspike false nettle)
    *Cornus amomum* (silky dogwood)
    *Lindera benzoin* (northern spicebush)
    *Onoclea sensibilis* (sensitive fern)
    *Toxicodendron radicans* (poison ivy)
    *Urtica spp.* (nettle)

## Silver Maple Floodplain Forest

**Formal name:** *Acer saccharinum - Ulmus americana Forest*

### Environmental summary

**Where it is found:** generally on large, regularly and temporarily flooded floodplains of major rivers and smaller perennial streams, throughout the midwestern and parts of the eastern United States. Locally, this floodplain forest is likely at downstream ends of islands and on high terraces along the shoreline of the Delaware River.

**Soil information:** well-drained and sandy, tending toward loamy on less frequently flooded levees and bottomlands and deep silts on stabilized sites along major rivers. Low energy floodwaters often leave deep, sandy sediments. The substrate is typically silt loam or sandy loam, as in Delaware fine sandy loam or Pope fine sandy loam.

**Characteristics:** governed by the flooding regime, it can include river-deposited debris on the forest floor, ice scars on trees, and abandoned channels that retain water above or at the level of the main river channel. Flooding is typically annual but brief, may be absent in dry years or extensive during flash-flood years. The forest floor along the Delaware River frequently has numerous parallel swales created by flood scour, and these forests are inundated only during larger flood events.

### Vegetation

The canopy cover is generally closed, about 60 to 100 feet high, and dominated by *Acer sac-*

*charinum* (silver maple) with between 40 and 75 percent of the cover. Codominants may include *Platanus occidentalis* (sycamore), *Betula nigra* (river birch), and rarely *Acer saccharum* (sugar maple). Associated species may include:

> *Acer negundo* (box elder)
> *Carya cordiformis* (bitternut hickory)
> *Celtis occidentalis* (hackberry)
> *Fraxinus pennsylvanica* (green ash)
> *Juglans nigra* (black walnut)
> *Ostrya virginiana* (eastern hop-hornbeam)
> *Prunus serotina* (black cherry)
> *Salix nigra* (black willow)
> *Ulmus americana* (American elm)
> *Ulmus rubra* (slippery elm)

The sapling and shrub and sapling layer is generally open (less than 25 percent cover). Species that have been reported include *Sambucus canadensis* (American elder), *Rubus occidentalis* (black raspberry) and *Lindera benzoin* (northern spicebush).

Woody and herbaceous vines can be prominent, including among the woody vines *Parthenocissus quinquefolia* (Virginia creeper), *Toxicodendron radicans* (poison ivy), and *Vitis riparia* (riverbank grape). Herbaceous vine species include *Apios americana* (ground nut), *Amphicarpaea bracteata* (American hog peanut), and *Echinocystis lobata* (wild cucumber).

Grasses, forbs, and ferns dominate the herbaceous layer, including:

> *Arisaema triphyllum* (Jack-in-the-pulpit)
> *Boehmeria cylindrica* (smallspike false nettle)
> *Cinna arundinacea* (sweet woodreed)
> *Elymus virginicus* (Virginia wild rye)
> *Erythronium americanum* (dogtooth violet)
> *Glechoma hederacea* (ground ivy)
> *Impatiens pallida* (touch-me-not)
> *Laportea canadensis* (Canadian woodnettle)
> *Leersia virginica* (whitegrass)
> *Matteuccia struthiopteris* (ostrich fern)
> *Onoclea sensibilis* (sensitive fern)
> *Phalaris arundinacea* (reed canarygrass)
> *Pilea pumila* (Canadian clearweed)
> *Polygonum persicaria* (spotted ladysthumb)
> *Solidago gigantea* (giant goldenrod)
> *Symphyotrichum lateriflorum* (calico aster)
> *Urtica dioica* (stinging nettle)

## Silver Maple Floodplain Bottom Forest

**Formal name:** *Acer saccharinum / Onoclea sensibilis - Boehmeria cylindrica Forest*

### Environmental summary

**Where it is found:** river bottoms, lake plains, and the inner floodplain of medium to large rivers, mostly at less than 800 feet elevation, throughout the northeastern United States.

**Soil information:** generally associated with calcareous or sedimentary bedrock and with fine-grained surficial deposits, but may occur in coarser soils or tills.

**Characteristics:** Most typical of rivers that have been fed by a number of streams or smaller rivers, are subjected to spring flooding of high frequency and duration, and with soils that are poorly drained and deep. The canopy ranges from closed to somewhat open and is usually high and arching. There are few shrubs, and the herb layer is very well-developed. Bryoids are minor. The overall effect is of tall, well-spaced trees over a lush carpet of herbaceous plants.

This association is different than Silver Maple Floodplain Levee Forest because of more poorly drained soils, longer flood duration, and the reduced importance of *Matteuccia struthiopteris* (ostrich fern) relative to *Onoclea sensibilis* (sensitive fern). Also, the herb layer is generally richer, and the canopy lacks *Populus deltoides* (Eastern cottonwood) and *Salix nigra* (black willow). It can be bordered the upland edge by terrace forests that are dominated by *Acer saccharum* (sugar maple).

### Vegetation

*Acer saccharinum* (silver maple) strongly dominates the canopy. Associated trees include *Fraxinus pennsylvanica* (green ash), *Ulmus americana* (American elm), and occasionally *Quercus bicolor* (swamp white oak). *Prunus serotina* (black cherry), and *Acer rubrum* (red maple) have been occasionally observed in the Poconos.

The herb layer is seasonally variable, with spring ephemerals, including *Erythronium americanum* (dogtooth violet), *Sanguinaria canadensis* (bloodroot), and *Arisaema triphyllum* (Jack-in-the-pulpit), succeeded by dense cover of mixed ferns, forbs and graminoids. These almost always include *Onoclea sensibilis* (sensitive fern) and *Boehmeria cylindrica* (smallspike false nettle). *Matteuccia struthiopteris* (ostrich fern) and *Laportea canadensis* (Canadian woodnettle) may be present but are not abundant; other typical species include:

> *Bidens tripartita* (three-lobe beggarticks)
> *Calamagrostis canadensis* (bluejoint)
> *Cinna spp.* (woodreeds)
> *Ludwigia palustris* (marsh seedbox)
> *Lycopus uniflorus* (northern bugleweed)
> *Osmunda regalis* (royal fern)
> *Pilea pumila* (Canadian clearweed)
> *Scutellaria lateriflora* (blue skullcap)
> *Thalictrum pubescens* (king of the meadow)
> *Thelypteris palustris* (marsh fern)

## Sugar Maple - Ash Hardwood Forest

Formal name: *Acer saccharum - (Fraxinus americana) / Arisaema triphyllum Forest*

### Environmental Summary

**Where it is found:** ridgetops and slight concavities on slopes between 800 and 2,000 feet.

**Soil information:** slightly enriched soils, especially silt loams derived from sedimentary rock made of clays or other subacidic bedrock.

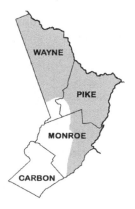

**Characteristics:** Sometimes small sections within typical northern hardwood forests, they can occur over larger areas and be the locally dominant northern hardwood forest. Unlike most systems, which occur north and south sides of Pennsylvania, this one extends only northward into Quebec.

### Vegetation

The closed-canopy forest has sparse to moderate shrub cover, a substantial herb cover, and may have local carpets of *Acer saccharum* seedlings in the ground vegetation. Mosses are a minor component of the forest floor. The association appears to be less fertile than other communities of Laurentian-Arcadian Northern Hardwood and Appalachian Northern Hardwood forests; rich-soil indicators such as *Adiantum pedatum*, *Caulophyllum thalictroides*, and *Tilia americana* are lacking.

*Acer saccharum* (sugar maple) dominates the canopy, often with *Fraxinus americana* (white ash) as an associate or even canopy codominant. Other associates include *Betula alleghaniensis* (yellow birch) and *Betula lenta* (sweet birch). *Fagus grandifolia* (American beech) is common but less abundant than in similar northern hardwood forests. Conifers are sparse.

Typical shrubs include:

> *Acer pensylvanicum* (striped maple)
> *Cornus alternifolia* (alternate leaf or pagoda dogwood)
> *Lindera benzoin* (northern spicebush)
> *Ostrya virginiana* (hop hornbeam)
> *Sambucus racemosa* (red elderberry)

Typical herbs of this semi-rich type, which are scarce or absent from standard beech-birch-maple forests, include:

> *Actaea pachypoda* (doll's eyes)
> *Arisaema triphyllum* (jack-in-the-pulpit)
> *Botrychium spp.* (ferns)
> *Carex laxiculmis* (spreading sedge)
> *Carex pedunculata* (longstalk sedge)
> *Carex platyphylla* (broadleaf sedge)
> *Eurybia divaricata* (white wood aster)
> *Osmunda cinnamomea* (cinnamon fern)
> *Osmunda claytoniana* (interrupted fern)
> *Solidago flexicaulis* (zig-zag goldenrod)
> *Tiarella cordifolia* (foamflower)
> *Viola rotundifolia* (roundleaf yellow violet)

## Sugar Maple - Beech Hardwood Forest

**Formal name:** *Acer saccharum - Betula alleghaniensis - Fagus grandifolia / Viburnum lantanoides Forest*

## Environmental Summary

**Where it is found:** usually on the middle of gentle to moderately steep slopes - 5 to 30 percent - with a northern or sometimes eastern aspect. Most are at low to mid elevations, typically under 1700 feet.

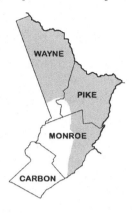

**Soil information:** most often on shallow, moderate to well-drained tills with a pH of 5.0. Channery silt loams to gravelly sand loams with rock outcrops are common (e.g., Benson-Rock Outcrop complex soil series, Lordstown-Wallpack complex - Very Rocky). Some stands occur on deep tills and can range from mildly acid to alkaline, reflecting the calcareous nature of the underlying substrate - typically limestone, or calcareous sandstones, siltstones and shale.

**Characteristics:** The deciduous-to-mixed canopy is mostly closed with variable lower cover. Tall shrubs are common but scattered, with occasional denser patches. Herbs are sparse and bryoids are nearly absent. Ericads and other dwarf-shrubs are also scarce, a characteristic that distinguishes this association from most other red oak forests in the northeast. On some rocky, higher-elevation sites, dense ferns and other herbs may form a lush understory, known as the "fern-glade variant."

## Vegetation

The canopy is dominated by *Acer saccharum* (sugar maple) mixed with variable amounts of *Fagus grandifolia* (American beech) and/or *Betula alleghaniensis* (yellow birch). Canopy height is 65 to 120 feet, depending on local site conditions. Conifers make up less than 20 percent of the canopy. Subcanopy can range from 15 to 70 feet and sparse (5 percent) to moderately dense (30 percent) Sugar maple can comprise more than 75 percent of both canopy and subcanopy. Associated hardwood species include:

> *Acer rubrum* (red maple)
> *Betula lenta* (sweet birch)
> *Betula papyrifera* (paper birch)
> *Carya glabra* (pignut hickory)
> *Fraxinus americana* (white ash)
> *Juglans cinerea* (butternut)
> *Tilia americana* (American basswood)
> *Ulmus americana* (American elm)

In mid-successional stands, low abundance species include:

> *Picea rubens* (red spruce) (northern range)
> *Pinus strobus* (eastern white pine)
> *Quercus alba* (white oak) (southern range)
> *Quercus rubra* (northern red oak) (southern range)
> *Tsuga canadensis* (eastern hemlock)

Small trees reported include *Acer pensylvanicum* (striped maple) and, especially in the southern range, *Cornus florida* (flowering dogwood) and *Prunus serotina* (black cherry).

Understory shrubs or subcanopy trees vary from nearly absent to 30 percent of total cover and range from 5 to 15 feet. Saplings of canopy tree species, especially sugar maple, American beech and sweet birch, also include shrub/small-tree species such as *Ostrya virginiana* (eastern hop-hornbeam) and *Carpinus caroliniana* (American hornbeam).

Reported tall shrubs include:

> *Acer pensylvanicum* (striped maple)
> *Acer spicatum* (mountain maple) (northern end of the range)
> *Amelanchier arborea* (serviceberry)
> *Hamamelis virginiana* (witch hazel)
> *Kalmia latifolia* (mountain laurel) (southern end of the range)
> *Lindera benzoin* (spicebush) (southern end of the range)
> *Rhododendron maximum* (great rhododendron)
> *Viburnum lantanoides* (hobblebush)

The short-shrub layer is generally under 5 feet with sparse to moderate total cover, 5 to 30 percent and occasionally higher. Typical short shrubs include seedlings and saplings of canopy species, especially sugar maple and American beech, as well as northern spicebush, and occasionally *Vaccinium pallidum* (Blue Ridge blueberry).

High in nitrogen relative to lignin, sugar maple

leaf litter quickly decomposes and increases the nutrient pool in the soil organic layer. Structure and composition of the forest are maintained primarily by single small tree-fall gaps. Yellow birch grows in mineral soils on "tip-up mounds."

The patchy herbaceous layer (20 to 60 percent cover) is a mix of ferns, rhizomatous herbs and club mosses, generally less than 3 feet in height. Characteristic species include:

>*Clintonia borealis* (bluebead lily)
>*Dennstaedtia punctilobula* (hayscented fern)
>*Dryopteris carthusiana* (spinulose woodfern
>*Dryopteris intermedia* (intermediate woodfern)
>*Maianthemum canadense* (Canada mayflower)
>*Oclemena acuminata* (whorled wood aster)
>*Polystichum acrostichoides* (Christmas fern)
>*Thelypteris noveboracensis* (New York fern)
>*Trientalis borealis* (starflower)
>*Uvularia sessilifolia* (sessileleaf bellwort)

Occasional species include

>*Aralia nudicaulis* (wild sarsaparilla)
>*Brachyelytrum erectum* (northern shorthusk)
>*Carex pensylvanica* (Pennsylvania sedge)
>*Cinna latifolia* (drooping woodreed)
>*Dryopteris campyloptera* (mountain woodfern)
>*Gaultheria procumbens* (teaberry)
>*Medeola virginiana* (Indian cucumber)
>*Mitchella repens* (partridgeberry)
>*Pteridium aquilinum* (northern bracken fern)
>*Solidago macrophylla* (largeleaf goldenrod)
>*Streptopus lanceolatus* (twisted stalk)
>*Trillium erectum* (red trillium)
>*Trillium undulatum* (painted trillium)

On more nutrient-rich soils, the herb layer may contain

>*Caulophyllum thalictroides* (blue cohosh)
>*Dryopteris marginalis* (marginal woodfern)
>*Eurybia divaricata* (white wood aster)
>*Solidago caesia* (wreath goldenrod)

The bryophyte layer may include *Dicranum spp.* and *Leucobryum glaucum*.

## Sugar Maple-Cherry Hardwood Forest

**Formal Name:** *Acer saccharum - Betula alleghaniensis - Prunus serotina Forest*

### Environmental Summary

**Where it is found:** flat to moderate mesic slopes of any aspect, although north-facing cool sites are the most common.

**Soil information:** moderate to deep and acidic (less than pH 5.0) to circumneutral loams or loamy sands, mesic to wet-mesic and nutrient-rich soils. A thick layer of leaf litter is usually found on the forest floor. In the glaciated portion of the range, this vegetation occurs on glacial tills, and in the unglaciated portion on sandstone or shale of northern slopes and high elevations.

**Characteristics:** Mixed hardwoods where logging was commonly practiced.

### Vegetation

The canopy tends to be dominated by *Prunus serotina* (black cherry), *Acer saccharum* (sugar maple), *Betula alleghaniensis* (yellow birch), and *Fagus grandifolia* (American beech). Conifers typically comprise less than 25 percent cover. *Acer rubrum* may be the most abundant tree in stands with recent harvests.

Other associates include:

>*Acer rubrum* (red maple)
>*Betula lenta* (sweet birch)
>*Fraxinus americana* (white ash)
>*Fraxinus pennsylvanica* (green ash)
>*Liriodendron tulipifera* (tuliptree)
>*Ostrya virginiana* (hop hornbeam)
>*Pinus strobus* (eastern white pine)
>*Quercus rubra* (northern red oak)
>*Tsuga canadensis* (eastern hemlock)

The shrub layer consists of

>*Acer pensylvanicum* (striped maple)
>*Amelanchier arborea* (serviceberry)

*Corylus cornuta* (beaked hazelnut)
*Hamamelis virginiana* (witch hazel)
*Ilex montana* (mountain holly) in the unglaciated portion of the range
*Lonicera canadensis* (American fly honeysuckle)
*Viburnum acerifolium* (maple-leaf viburnum)

Within a rich herbaceous layer may be found:
*Aralia nudicaulis* (wild sarsaparilla)
*Arisaema triphyllum* (jack-in-the-pulpit)
*Carex appalachica* (Appalachian sedge)
*Carex blanda* (eastern woodland sedge)
*Carex debilis* (white edge sedge)
*Carex digitalis* (slender woodland sedge)
*Chimaphila maculata* (striped prince's pine)
*Clintonia borealis* (bluebead lily)
*Dennstaedtia punctilobula* (hayscented fern)
*Dryopteris intermedia* (intermediate woodfern)
*Lycopodium spp.* (clubmosses)
*Maianthemum canadense* (Canada mayflower)
*Milium effusum* (American millet grass)
*Oxalis montana* (mountain wood sorrel)
*Polystichum acrostichoides* (Christmas fern)
*Pteridium aquilinum* (northern bracken fern)
*Streptopus lanceolatus var. roseus* (twisted stalk)
*Thelypteris noveboracensis* (New York fern)
*Viola blanda* (sweet white violet)
*Viola rotundifolia* (roundleaf yellow violet)

# Calcareous Talus Slope Forest

**Formal name:** *Acer saccharum - Fraxinus americana - Juglans cinerea / Staphylea trifolia / Adlumia fungosa Forest*

### Environmental Summary

**Where it is found:** talus slopes or shallow rocky soils overlying calcareous or circumneutral bedrock, usually facing north to east.

**Soil information:** very steep, bouldery to gravelly mesic, shallow, rocky soils. Soils can be very fertile.

**Characteristics:** Exposed rock (boulder and outcrop) cover can be up to 50 percent, which reduces both species richness and herbaceous cover.

### Vegetation

Because of relatively rapid weathering of carbonate materials and very fertile soils, these habitats are often thickly populated with herbaceous plants. High cover of mosses provides a foothold, as do many organic mats and soil pockets. Although invasive exotic weeds do not appear to be a major problem, wind throw, slumping or landslides of unstable rock and other erosion disturbances are common.

Cited as diagnostic features are the infrequency of *Quercus spp.*, the presence of *Juglans cinerea* (butternut), and the abundance of *Staphylea trifolia* (American bladdernut) and *Adlumia fungosa* (Allegheny vine). It combines both dry, open forests and other moderately moist forests along margins that are by bedrock, mineral soil development and slope position.

Canopy dominants are *Acer saccharum* (sugar maple) and *Fraxinus americana* (white ash). Canopy associates include:
*Betula alleghaniensis* (yellow birch)
*Juglans cinerea* (butternut)
*Ostrya virginiana* (hop hornbeam)
*Quercus rubra* (northern red oak)
*Tilia americana* (American basswood)

The open shrub layer is characterized by *Staphylea trifolia* (American bladdernut), *Rubus odoratus* (purple flowering raspberry) , and *Cornus rugosa* (roundleaf dogwood). *Adlumia fungosa* (Allegheny vine) is a common vine in the northern portion of the range.

Often reported in a diverse herbaceous layer:
*Adiantum pedatum* (northern maidenhair fern)
*Allium tricoccum* (ramp)
*Anemone quinquefolia* (wood anemone)
*Aralia racemosa* (American spikenard)
*Asarum canadense* (wild ginger)

*Caulophyllum thalictroides* (blue cohosh)
*Cystopteris bulbifera* (bulblet bladderfern)
*Dicentra cucullaria* (squirrel corn)
*Dryopteris goldiana* (Goldie's woodfern)
*Sanguinaria canadensis* (bloodroot)

Characteristic graminoids include *Carex platyphylla* (broadleaf sedge), *Carex sprengelii* (Sprengel's sedge), *Elymus hystrix* (bottlebrush grass), and *Piptatherum racemosum* (blackseed ricegrass).

## Sugar Maple - Tuliptree Forest

**Formal name:** *Acer saccharum - Fraxinus americana - Tilia americana - Liriodendron tulipifera / Actaea racemosa Forest*

### Environmental summary

**Where it is found:** northwest to east-facing coves, lower slopes, slope bases and on moderate slopes in the Central Appalachians, High Alleghenies and Western Allegheny Plateau. Located at elevations from about 1,500 to 3,000 feet, often on steep, concave slopes.

**Soil information:** sands, loams and silt loams that are generally fertile, deep and moderately to well-drained, often from calcareous parent materials. Found on over a variety of bedrock, including limestone, dolomite, metabasalt, granitic rocks and sandstone, with pH ranging from 4.2 to 6.8. Soils have high calcium and moderately high magnesium levels. Soil moisture-holding and cation-exchange capabilities are high.

**Characteristics:** Often known as "rich," "mixed mesophytic" and "rich northern hardwood" forests, many stands are on flat to rolling surfaces with some on steep slopes.

The tree canopy of these forests varies, but *Acer saccharum*, *Fraxinus americana*, and *Tilia americana* are almost always present. Because of excellent site conditions for tree growth, stands are very vulnerable to logging and are further threatened by shade-tolerant exotic weeds.

### Vegetation

*Acer saccharum* (sugar maple) dominates the canopy, and *Fraxinus americana* (white ash), *Liriodendron tulipifera* (tulip-tree) and *Tilia americana* (American basswood) are characteristic primary associates. Other associated canopy trees include:

*Acer rubrum* (red maple)
*Betula alleghaniensis* (yellow birch)
*Betula lenta* (sweet birch)
*Carya cordiformis* (bitternut hickory)
*Fagus grandifolia* (American beech)
*Juglans nigra* (black walnut)
*Ostrya virginiana* (hop-hornbeam)
*Prunus serotina* (black cherry)
*Quercus rubra* (red oak)
*Ulmus rubra* (slippery elm)

A variable shrub layer is generally characterized by:

*Cornus alternifolia* (alternate-leaf dogwood)
*Hamamelis virginiana* (witch-hazel)
*Lindera benzoin* (northern spicebush)
*Lonicera canadensis* (American fly honeysuckle)
*Rhododendron periclymenoides* (pink azalea)
*Viburnum acerifolium* (maple-leaf viburnum)

Frequently reported in a diverse herb layer are:

*Actaea racemosa* (black cohosh)
*Adiantum pedatum* (northern maidenhair fern)
*Allium tricoccum* (ramp)
*Anemone quinquefolia* (wood anemone)
*Arisaema triphyllum* (Jack-in-the-pulpit)
*Asarum canadense* (wild ginger)
*Botrychium virginianum* (rattlesnake fern)
*Cardamine concatenata* (cutleaf toothwort)
*Cardamine spp.* (bittercress)
*Caulophyllum thalictroides* (blue cohosh)
*Claytonia virginica* (Virginia spring beauty)
*Deparia acrostichoides* (silver false spleenwort)
*Dicentra spp.* (bleeding heart)
*Dryopteris marginalis* (marginal woodfern)
*Elymus hystrix* (bottlebrush grass)
*Galearis spectabilis* (showy orchid)

*Geranium maculatum* (wild geranium)
*Hepatica nobilis var. obtusa* (roundlobe hepatica)
*Hydrophyllum virginianum* (eastern waterleaf)
*Impatiens pallida* (touch-me-not)
*Laportea canadensis* (Canadian woodnettle)
*Maianthemum racemosum* (false lily of the valley)
*Osmorhiza spp.* (sweetroot)
*Sanguinaria canadensis* (bloodroot)
*Trillium grandiflorum* (white trillium)
*Uvularia grandiflora* (merrybells)
*Viola spp.* (violets)

# Sugar Maple - Basswood Forest

**Formal name:** *Acer saccharum - Fraxinus americana - Tilia americana / Acer spicatum / Caulophyllum thalictroides Forest*

### *Environmental summary*

**Where it is found:** Nutrient-rich, mesic to wet-mesic sloping to rolling terrain, especially colluvial sites at slope bottoms. Sites range from the northeastern United States and Ontario, Canada, to the central Great Lakes area, and south along the High Alleghenies of Virginia and West Virginia. In the northern Appalachians, sites are often found in concave slopes and enriched coves between 400 and 2,700 feet where ground cover is mostly nitrogen-rich sugar maple leaf litter.

**Soil information:** Deep sand, loamy sand, or loam, sometimes over sandy clay loam to clay loam. Sites can range from poorly drained to well-drained, with a water table 18 to 72 inches below the surface. Within these forests, soils in small seep areas are typically saturated. Soils can range from moderately acidic to moderately alkaline, tend to be very fertile and are usually from calcareous parent materials. Soil moisture-holding and cation-exchange capacities are usually quite high.

**Characteristics:** A well-developed canopy of deciduous trees with scattered shrubs and an extensive herbaceous layer. Ferns are common, while bryoids are minor components of the nitrogen-rich sugar maple leaf litter. Although the community is widely distributed, local sites are limited because mesic sites with fertile soils in more topographically gentle locations have been destroyed for agriculture, while others have been altered by past logging. The result is remaining acreage is variable in quality.

These forests are different than less-rich northern hardwood forests because of the rich and varied herbaceous layer and the importance of sugar maple and ash in the canopy instead of beech.

### *Vegetation*

*Acer saccharum* (sugar maple) and *Fraxinus americana* (white ash) dominate the tree canopy. *Tilia americana* (American basswood) is common but not usually abundant. Ostrya virginiana (hophornbeam) is very common in the subcanopy. Associates, ranging from limited to occasional, include:

   *Acer rubrum* (red maple)
   *Betula alleghaniensis* (yellow birch)
   *Fagus grandifolia* (American beech)
   *Juglans cinerea* (butternut)
   *Prunus serotina* (black cherry)
   *Ulmus rubra* (slippery elm)

The scattered shrub layer may include:
   *Cornus alternifolia* (alternate-leaf dogwood)
   *Dirca palustris* (eastern leatherwood)
   *Hamamelis virginiana* (witch-hazel)
   *Lonicera canadensis* (American fly honeysuckle)
   *Viburnum lantanoides* (hobblebush)

A diverse herbaceous layer consists primarily of nutrient- and light-requiring species, many of which are spring ephemerals. Ferns are common, and a variety of sedges are reported, especially the *Laxiflorae*.

Ephemerals may include:
   *Actaea pachypoda* (doll's eyes)
   *Asarum canadense* (wild ginger)
   *Caulophyllum thalictroides* (blue cohosh)
   *Dicentra canadensis* (squirrel corn)
   *Dicentra cucullaria* (Dutchman's breeches)

*Erythronium americanum* (dogtooth violet)
*Hepatica spp.* (hepatica species)
*Osmorhiza claytonii* (Clayton's sweetroot)
*Panax quinquefolius* (American ginsing)
*Sanguinaria canadensis* (bloodroot)
*Viola canadensis* (Canadian white violet)
*Viola rotundifolia* (roundleaf yellow violet)

Among the fern population, *Matteuccia stru-thiopteris* (Ostrich fern) is often found in seepy spots. Other species in the forest can include:

*Adiantum pedatum* (northern maidenhair fern)
*Cystopteris bulbifera* (bulblet bladderfern)
*Deparia acrostichoides* (silver false spleen-wort)
*Dryopteris goldiana* (Goldie's woodfern)
*Dryopteris filix-mas* (male fern)
*Dryopteris marginalis* (marginal wood fern)
*Botrychium virginianum* (rattlesnake fern)
*Athyrium filix-femina* (common ladyfern)
*Phegopteris hexagonoptera* (broad beech-fern)

Among sedges reported for the forest are

*Carex laxiflora* (broad looseflower sedge)
*Carex platyphylla* (broadleaf sedge)
*Carex plantaginea* (plantainleaf sedge)
*Carex leptonervia* (nerveless woodland sedge)
*Carex hitchcockiana* (Hitchcock's sedge)
*Carex aestivalis* (summer sedge)
*Carex davisii* (Davis' sedge)
*Carex bebbii* (Bebb's sedge)

The herbaceous flora in seeps frequently includes:

*Calamagrostis canadensis* (bluejoint)
*Carex scabrata* (eastern rough sedge)
*Ageratina altissima* (white snakeroot)
*Glyceria melicaria* (mellic mannagrass)
*Impatiens capensis* (jewelweed)
*Impatiens pallida* (pale touch-me-not)
*Solidago flexicaulis* (zig-zag goldenrod)

## Sugar Maple - Ash Floodplain Forest

Formal name: *Acer saccharum - Fraxinus ameri-cana / Carpinus caroliniana / Podophyllum pelta-tum Forest*

### *Environmental summary*

**Where it is found:** low to mid terraces of the Delaware River and its tributaries, as well as slightly elevated alluvial terraces and active flood-plains of larger rivers throughout the Mid-Atlan-tic States from the inte-rior to the coastal plain. System may occur very close to riverbanks if the water channel is well-en-trenched.

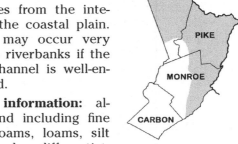

**Soil information:** al-luvial and including fine sandy loams, loams, silt loams and undifferentiat-ed alluvium, ranging from slightly acidic to alkaline. Underlying bedrock is a variety of dolomite, limestone, calcareous shale and siltstone.

**Characteristics:** stands on lower terraces may sometimes flood, but inundation is brief and less regular than soils supporting floodplain forests dominated by silver maple or sycamore.

### *Vegetation*

Canopy height ranges from 60 to 100 feet, with total cover ranging from 70 to 90 percent, and is dominated by *Acer saccharum* (sugar maple). *Fraxinus americana* (white ash) is a common as-sociate and may co-dominate in some stands. Mi-nor associates include:

*Carya glabra* (pignut hickory)
*Fagus grandifolia* (American beech)
*Prunus serotina* (black cherry)
*Quercus velutina* (black oak)
*Ulmus Americana* (American elm)

Sugar maple may be the only species in a sub-canopy that varies from 15 to 75 feet and ranges from 5 to 30 percent cover. *Carpinus caroliniana* (American hornbeam) is a minor associate.

A sparse to absent shrub layer, ranging from 6 to 25 feet, is comprised of *Lindera benzoin* (north-ern spicebush) and sugar maple saplings.

The herbaceous layer is variable in cover and diverse, often featuring a variety of spring ephem-erals such as *Claytonia virginica* (Virginica spring beauty), *Dicentra canadensis* (squirrel corn) and

*Erythronium americanum* (trout lily).

Other native species reported include:
*Arisaema triphyllum* (Jack-in-the-pulpit)
*Caulophyllum thalictroides* (blue cohosh)
*Deparia acrostichoides* (silver false spleen-wort)
*Elymus riparius* (riverbank wild rye)
*Elymus virginicus* (Virginia wild rye)
*Galium aparine* (cleavers)
*Leersia virginica* (whitegrass)
*Onoclea sensibilis* (sensitive fern)
*Podophyllum peltatum* (mayapple)
*Polystichum acrostichoides* (Christmas fern)
*Carex spp.* (sedges)

## Ridge and Valley Calcareous Forest

**Formal name:** *Acer saccharum - Liriodendron tulipifera - Fraxinus americana / Staphylea trifolia Forest*

### Environmental summary

**Where it is found:** steep east- and north-facing, rocky-bottomed upland draws with ephemeral and intermittent creeks.

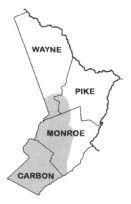

**Soil information:** mineral soil weathered from calcareous shales and sandstones, with much colluvium that has over time washed downslope. Soils can be slightly to very acidic and generally well drained.

**Characteristics**: a rich, mesic forest dominated by some combination of *Acer saccharum, Liriodendron tulipifera* and *Fraxinus americana*, the site slopes are steep and concave near creek headwaters and susceptible to mudslides.

### Vegetation

Varying combinations of *Acer saccharum* (sugar maple), *Liriodendron tulipifera* (tulip-tree) and *Fraxinus americana* (white ash) dominate the canopy. Among reported local associates are:

*Carya glabra* (pignut hickory)

*Carya ovata* (shagbark hickory)
*Celtis occidentalis* (common hackberry)
*Fagus grandifolia* (American beech)
*Juglans nigra* (black walnut)
*Quercus alba* (white oak)
*Quercus muhlenbergii* (chinkapin oak)
*Quercus prinus* (chestnut oak)
*Quercus rubra* (red oak)
*Quercus velutina* (black oak)
*Tilia americana var. heterophylla* (American basswood)
*Ulmus rubra* (slippery elm)

The shrub layer tends to be dense and dominated by taller species, including:
*Carpinus caroliniana* (American hornbeam)
*Cercis canadensis* (eastern redbud)
*Hamamelis virginiana* (witch-hazel)
*Lindera benzoin* (northern spicebush)

The sparse to moderately dense herbaceous layer may include:
*Actaea racemosa* (black cohosh)
*Adiantum pedatum* (northern maidenhair fern)
*Arisaema triphyllum* (Jack-in-the-pulpit)
*Asarum canadense* (wild ginger)
*Claytonia virginica* (Virginia spring beauty)
*Dicentra canadensis* (squirrel corn)
*Dryopteris intermedia* (intermediate woodfern)
*Impatiens capensis* (jewelweed)
*Impatiens pallida* (pale touch me not)
*Maianthemum canadense* (Canada mayflower)
*Maianthemum racemosum* (false lily of the valley)
*Menispermum canadense* (common moonseed)
*Osmorhiza claytonii* (Clayton's sweetroot)
*Parthenocissus quinquefolia* (Virginia creeper)
*Podophyllum peltatum* (mayapple)
*Polygonatum biflorum* (Solomon's seal)
*Polystichum acrostichoides* (Christmas fern)
*Sanguinaria canadensis* (bloodroot)
*Trillium grandiflorum* (white trillium)
*Viola spp.* (violets)

## Sugar Maple - Chinkapin Oak Forest

**Formal name:** *Acer saccharum - Quercus muehlenbergii / Cercis canadensis Forest*

### Environmental summary

**Where it is found:** Low hills and knobs in small, occasionally linear patches, except where carbonate substrates are more continuously exposed.

**Soil information:** dry to dry-mesic rich but thin soils over calcareous substrates, occasionally associated with limestone glades.

**Characteristics:** typically closed-canopy, but in some stands the canopy may vary from closed to somewhat open, especially at the northern edge of the range in Pennsylvania

### Vegetation

The stands are primarily composed of *Acer saccharum* (sugar maple), *Quercus muhlenbergii* (chinkapin oak), *Fraxinus americana* (white ash), and *Ostrya virginiana* (hop hornbeam).

Associates include:
*Carya ovalis* (red hickory)
*Carya ovata* (shagbark hickory)
*Celtis occidentalis* (common hackberry)
*Quercus alba* (white oak)
*Quercus prinus* (chestnut oak)
*Tilia americana* (American basswood)
*Ulmus rubra* (slippery elm)

A variable subcanopy and shrub layer contains:
*Cercis canadensis* (eastern redbud)
*Cornus florida* (flowering dogwood)
*Hamamelis virginiana* (witch hazel)
*Rosa carolina* (Carolina rose)
*Viburnum prunifolium* (black haw)
*Viburnum rafinesquianum* (downy arrowwood)

The sparse to well-developed herb layer may contain:
*Ageratina altissima* (white snakeroot)
*Anemone virginiana var. virginiana* (Virginia anemone)
*Antennaria plantaginifolia* (plantain pussytoes)
*Aquilegia canadensis* (wild columbine)
*Arabis laevigata* (smooth rockcress)
*Asclepias quadrifolia* (whorled milkweed)
*Bromus pubescens* (hairy woodland brome)
*Clematis occidentalis* (blue virgins bower),
*Danthonia spicata* (poverty oatgrass)
*Dichanthelium boscii* (Bosc's panicgrass)
*Elymus hystrix* (bottlebrush grass)
*Erigeron pulchellus var. pulchellus* (robin's plantain)
*Galium circaezans* (licorice bedstraw)
*Packera obovata* (roundleaf ragwort)
*Polygonum scandens* (climbing false buckwheat)
*Sanicula canadensis* (black rattlesnakeroot)
*Saxifraga virginiensis* (Virginia saxifrage)
*Scutellaria elliptica* (hairy skullcap)
*Solidago ulmifolia var. ulmifolia* (elmleaf goldenrod)
*Symphyotrichum patens var. patens* (late purple aster)

## Rich Boulderfield Forest

**Formal name:** *Acer saccharum - Tilia americana / Staphylea trifolia / Dryopteris marginalis - (Impatiens pallida) Forest*

### Environmental summary

**Where it is found:** steep slopes, usually along streams or rivers, that are covered with rocky colluvium originating from calcium-bearing sedimentary, metasedimentary and igneous bedrock. Sources include calcareous shale, limestone and dolomite. Most face toward north and east in the Central Appalachians of Pennsylvania, Maryland, northern Virginia and northeastern West Virginia, extending eastward into sections of the Piedmont.

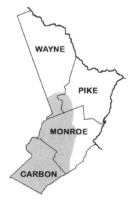

**Soil information:** highly calcareous soils among

dense rock and boulder coverage - average of 15 percent exposed bedrock and 42 percent boulders and large rocks. If local topography allows, colluvial soils may form deeper deposits. Substrates vary from stable, large-block boulder fields to fine talus and unstable loose scree. Samples are reported to range from strongly acidic to circumneutral, but with high to very high calcium levels, high magnesium, and moderately low iron and aluminum.

**Characteristics:** a rich, mesophytic forest subject to frequent blowdowns in unstable substrates resulting in many canopy gaps and remaining somewhat open, dominated primarily by *Tilia americana* (American basswood). The habitats usually include sections of outcrops that are often extensive above the talus deposits. Often found in small patches, it occurs in rugged habitats that are less prone to anthropogenic disturbances than many others.

### Vegetation

The canopy is primarily *Tilia americana* (American basswood) - usually *var. americana* but sometimes *var. heterophylla*, *Fraxinus americana* (white ash), and *Acer saccharum* (sugar maple). *Acer nigrum* (black) may also co-dominate in a few western localities. Minor canopy associates include:

> *Carya cordiformis* (bitternut hickory)
> *Celtis occidentalis* (common hackberry)
> *Liriodendron tulipifera* (tuliptree)
> *Quercus muehlenbergii* (chinkapin oak)
> *Quercus prinus* (chestnut oak)
> *Quercus rubra* (red oak)
> *Ulmus rubra* (slippery elm)

The shrub layer is generally dominated by *Staphylea trifolia* (American bladdernut), but can also locally include:

> *Hydrangea arborescens* (wild hydrangea)
> *Ostrya virginiana* (hop hornbeam)
> *Parthenocissus quinquefolia* (Virginia creeper)
> *Toxicodendron radicans* (poison ivy)

The herb layer is affected by the season, nature of rock cover, colonizing opportunities after blowdowns and available microhabitats. Spring ephemerals are common in some stands, especially *Cardamine concatenata* (cutleaf toothwort)

and *Dicentra canadensis* (squirrel corn) while dense colonies of *Impatiens pallida* (pale touch-me-not) can overwhelm the late-season cover of some stands. Other herbs that frequently reported are:

> *Actaea racemosa* (black cohosh)
> *Arisaema triphyllum* (Jack-in-the-pulpit)
> *Asarum canadense* (wild ginger)
> *Dryopteris marginalis* (marginal woodfern)
> *Eurybia divaricata* (white wood aster)
> *Hydrophyllum virginianum* (eastern waterleaf)
> *Maianthemum racemosum ssp. racemosum* (Canada mayflower)
> *Polystichum acrostichoides* (Christmas fern)
> *Solidago flexicaulis* (zig-zag goldenrod)

Less frequently reported local herbs that may be important include:

> *Arabis laevigata* (smooth rockcress)
> *Cystopteris bulbifera* (bulblet bladderfern)
> *Pilea pumila* (Canadian clearweed)
> *Sanguinaria canadensis* (bloodroot)
> *Symphyotrichum cordifolium* (blue wood aster)
> *Thalictrum dioicum* (early meadow-rue)

## Sugar Maple - Hophornbeam Forest

**Formal name:** *Acer saccharum / Ostrya virginiana / Brachyelytrum erectum Forest*

### Environmental summary

**Where it is found:** level to gently sloping natural levees, low ridges, and terraces bordering river floodplains or high-gradient streams, northward into New England.

**Soil information:** Moist, well-drained sandy loams or alluvial sands, generally above coarser substrates and sometimes layered with organic materials. Soils are most often derived from sandstone and shales; while mesic conditions remain through most of the growing season, there is

occasional flooding.

**Characteristics:** Dominated by sugar maple, sites are subject to brief, intense flooding that can dramatically alter the composition. Seasonal flood stress creates canopy openings that are immediately colonized by early and mid-successional species.

### Vegetation

*Acer saccharum* (sugar maple) dominates the canopy; associates can include *Quercus rubra* (red oak) and *Betula alleghaniensis* (yellow birch). A common smaller tree is *Ostrya virginiana* (hop hornbeam). Also reported are *Corylus americana* (American hazelnut), *Prunus serotina* (black cherry) and *Cornus florida* (flowering dogwood).

Shrubs are minor, but may include *Lindera benzoin* (northern spicebush) and *Aralia spinosa* (devil's walking-stick)

Unlike other floodplain forests, ferns are limited in an otherwise lush herbaceous layer that often features:

> *Brachyelytrum erectum* (bearded short-husk)
> *Campanulastrum americanum* (American bellflower)
> *Carex intumescens* (great bladder sedge)
> *Danthonia spicata* (poverty oat grass)
> *Solidago caesia* (wreath goldenrod)

## Yellow Birch-Red Oak Forest

**Formal name:** *Betula alleghaniensis - Quercus rubra / Acer (pensylvanicum, spicatum) / Dryopteris intermedia - Oclemena acuminata Forest*

### Environmental summary

**Where it is found:** high elevation areas of the Central Appalachians in Pennsylvania, Maryland, West Virginia and Virginia on rocky, cool, northeast to northwest-facing slopes.

**Soil information:** Very to extremely acidic (about 4.2 pH) thin, sterile, sandy soils over sandstone, greenstone, and granite, with bedrock and boulders covering more than a third of the ground surface.

**Characteristics:** Mesic to submesic sites are often exposed to severe winter temperatures, wind and ice; lichen and bryophyte coverage is more

than 10 percent, with *Betula alleghaniensis* and *Quercus rubra* the dominants in the canopy.

### Vegetation

*Betula alleghaniensis* (yellow birch) and *Quercus rubra* (red maple) are the constant, high-cover, generally codominant canopy. Minor canopy associates may include:

> *Acer saccharum* (sugar maple)
> *Betula lenta* (sweet birch)
> *Fraxinus americana* (white ash)
> *Tilia americana* (American basswood)
> *Tsuga canadensis* (eastern hemlock)

Among the most common and characteristic understory trees are *Acer pensylvanicum* (striped maple) and *Acer spicatum* (mountain maple). *Ilex montana* (mountain holly) may be locally abundant.

Typical shrubs reported include:

> *Hamamelis virginiana* (witch hazel)
> *Hydrangea arborescens* (wild hydrangea)
> *Rhododendron maximum* (great laurel)
> *Sambucus racemosa* (red elderberry)

Herb layer species can range from somewhat sparse to dense and may include:

> *Ageratina altissima* (white snakeroot)
> *Arisaema triphyllum* (Jack-in-the-pulpit)
> *Athyrium filix-femina* (common lady fern)
> *Carex aestivalis* (summer sedge)
> *Carex debilis var. rudgei* (wet edge sedge)
> *Circaea alpina* (small enchanter's nightshade)
> *Clintonia borealis* (bluebead)
> *Dennstaedtia punctilobula* (hayscented fern)
> *Dryopteris intermedia* (intermediate woodfern)
> *Dryopteris marginalis* (marginal woodfern)
> *Eurybia divaricata* (white wood aster)
> *Impatiens pallida* (pale touch-me-not)
> *Maianthemum canadense* (Canada mayflower)
> *Oclemena acuminata* (whorled wood aster)

*Trillium undulatum* (painted trillium)
*Viola blanda* (sweet white violet)

## River Birch Low Floodplain Forest

**Formal name:** *Betula nigra - Platanus occidentalis / Impatiens capensis Forest*

### Environmental summary

**Where it is found:** levees, gravel bars, braided channels and other areas of frequent flooding along large and moderately large rivers, throughout the Mid-Atlantic states.

**Soil information:** sandy, gravelly, well drained alluvial soils.

**Characteristics:** Floodplains under substantial tree canopy comprised of *Betula nigra* and *Platanus occidentalis.*

### Vegetation

*Betula nigra* (river birch) and *Platanus occidentalis* (American sycamore) dominate a well-developed tree canopy. Associates include *Acer negundo* (box elder) and sometimes Acer saccharinum (silver maple) and *Fraxinus pennsylvanica* (green ash).

Reported in the shrub layer are *Cornus amomum* (silky dogwood), *Cornus sericea* (red osier dogwood), and *Lindera benzoin* (northern spicebush).

Vine and herb layers are rich and varied. They may include

*Boehmeria cylindrica* (smallspike false nettle)
*Elymus hystrix* (bottlebrush grass)
*Impatiens capensis* (jewelweed)
*Impatiens pallida* (pale touch-me-not)
*Laportea canadensis* (Canadian wood nettle)
*Pilea pumila* (Canada clearweed)
*Toxicodendron radicans* (poison ivy)
*Parthenocissus quinquefolia* (Virginia creeper)
*Vitis riparia* (river grape)

*Chasmanthium latifolium* (northern sea oats)
*Podophyllum peltatum* (mayapple)
*Polygonum virginianum* (jumpseed)
*Apocynum cannabinum* (Indian hemp)
*Urtica sp.* (woodnettle)

## Bitternut Hickory-Black Cherry Forest

**Formal name:** *Carya cordiformis - Prunus serotina / Ageratina altissima Forest*

### Environmental summary

**Where it is found:** mid to high floodplain terraces of medium to large rivers. It is currently documented from the Delaware, Upper Delaware and Cheat Rivers and may occur on other regional river systems. Known sites are in formerly cleared and settled floodplain areas.

**Soil information:** Soils on these stabilized terraces are derived from alluvial deposits and consist of fine sandy loams and loamy fine sand.

**Characteristics:** Dominated by *Carya cordiformis* (Bitternut hickory), flood frequency is unknown, but it is likely flooded less often than *Platanus occidentalis* and *Acer saccharinum* forests found on lower floodplain terraces.

### Vegetation

The canopy ranges from somewhat open to closed - i.e., 70 to 90 percent - and between 60 and 80 feet in height. *Carya cordiformis* (bitternut hickory) dominates, although associates have the potential for co-dominance. These include

*Acer saccharinum* (silver maple)
*Fraxinus americana* (white ash)
*Juglans cinerea* (butternut)
*Prunus serotina* (black cherry)
*Quercus rubra* (northern red oak)
*Ulmus americana* (American elm)

With cover ranging from 20 to 30 percent, the composition of the subcanopy is similar to the canopy layer and ranges from 15 to 60 feet. This layer may also include *Acer rubrum* (red maple) and *Acer saccharum* (sugar maple)

Tall- and short-shrub layers are generally sparse and may sometimes include saplings of canopy and subcanopy species as well as scattered individuals of *Rubus occidentalis* (black raspberry), and *Rubus flagellaris* (northern dewberry).

Common herbaceous layer species include *Ageratina altissima var. altissima* (white snakeroot), *Hydrophyllum virginianum* (Shawnee salad), *Matteuccia struthiopteris* (ostrich fern), *Polygonum virginianum* (jumpseed), *Claytonia virginica* (Virginia spring beauty) and sedges (*Carex spp.*).

## Tuliptree - Beech - Maple Forest

**Formal name:** *Fagus grandifolia - Betula lenta - Liriodendron tulipifera - Acer saccharum Forest*

### Environmental Summary

**Where it is found:** gentle to slightly steep low and midslopes, often on mesic toeslopes, in coves, or along small drainages, where near-surface groundwater creates mesic conditions, or where past disturbance has opened up the forest canopy (e.g., logging, abandoned farmland).

**Soil information:** sandy loam on higher floodplain terraces to gravelly and channery loams and silt loams on midslopes of ridges. Typical bedrock types include shale, siltstone, and sandstone and soils are moderately deep and not extremely acidic.

**Characteristics:** disturbed land where evidence of past agriculture (e.g., stone walls, drainage ditches) or timbering is visible and *Liriodendron tulipifera* (tuliptree) dominates the canopy.

### Vegetation

The tree canopy is characterized by dominance of *Liriodendron tulipifera* (tuliptree). The canopy ranges from 80 to 120 feet and usually more than 70 per cent cover. Typical associates include:

> *Acer saccharum* (sugar maple)
> *Betula alleghaniensis* (yellow birch)
> *Betula lenta* (sweet birch)
> *Fagus grandifolia* (American beech)
> *Fraxinus americana* (white ash)

Early successional trees such as *Populus tremuloides* (quaking aspen) and *Robinia pseudoacacia* (black locust) can be found, especially in stands with recent disturbance. Oaks are few to absent.

The subcanopy is typically 50 to 65 feet in height with total cover of 10 to 30 per cent. Typical subcanopy trees are *Acer rubrum* (red maple), *Carpinus caroliniana* (American hornbeam), *Ostrya virginiana* (hop hornbeam), *Cornus florida* (flowering dogwood), as well as sugar maple, sweet birch, and white ash.

Typical species of the tall shrub layer, ranging from 5 to 15 feet, include *Hamamelis virginiana* (witch hazel) and *Lindera benzoin* (northern spicebush) as well as saplings of the canopy layer. It covers 15 to 60 per cent.

The short-shrub layer is less than 5 feet in height and may vary from 10 to 80 percent cover. The native dominant may be *Viburnum acerifolium* (mapleleaf viburnum).

The herbaceous layer is typically less than 3 feet in height with 30 to 50 percent total cover. Typical herbaceous species include:

> *Ageratina altissima var. altissima* (white snakeroot)
> *Allium tricoccum* (ramp)
> *Arisaema triphyllum* (jack-in-the-pulpit)
> *Botrychium virginianum* (rattlesnake fern)
> *Claytonia virginiana* (Virginia spring beauty)
> *Dennstaedtia punctilobula* (hayscented fern)
> *Dicentra canadensis* (squirrel corn)
> *Dicentra cucullaria* (Dutchman's breeches)
> *Maianthemum canadense* (Canada mayflower)
> *Podophyllum peltatum* (mayapple)
> *Polystichum acrostichoides* (Christmas fern)
> *Potentilla canadensis* (dwarf cinquefoil)
> *Sanguinaria canadensis* (bloodroot)

Vines may be present, usually as creeping plants in the herb or short-shrub layer, but may occasionally reach the lower portion of the canopy (usually summer grape, *Vitis aestivalis*). Typical vines include *Parthenocissus quinquefolia* (Virginia creeper), and *Smilax rotundifolia* (greenbrier).

## Red Maple - Black Ash Forest

Formal name: *Fraxinus nigra - Acer rubrum - (Larix laricina) / Rhamnus alnifolia Forest*

### Environmental summary

**Where it is found:** Along streams or at headwaters where bedrock is calcareous, throughout the northeastern United States.

**Soil information:** saturated organic muck or peat (but rarely sphagnum) that can be very deep, influenced by calcium-rich groundwater seepage.

**Characteristics:** calcareous to circumneutral seepage swamps having moderate to closed canopies; *Larix laricina* (tamarack) indicates maintained canopy gaps within the swamps.

### Vegetation

*Acer rubrum* (red maple) and *Larix laricina* (tamarack) dominate the canopy; *Fraxinus nigra* (black ash) is occasionally prominent. *Picea rubens* (red spruce) can be an associate at northern sites or higher elevations. Other canopy associates include:

> *Betula alleghaniensis* (yellow birch)
> *Carpinus caroliniana* (American hornbeam)
> *Pinus strobus* (eastern white pine)
> *Tsuga canadensis* (eastern hemlock)

The extent of canopy cover inversely impacts the density of the shrub layer, typical species of which may include:

> *Cornus sericea* (red osier dogwood)
> *Ilex verticillata* (winterberry)
> *Rhamnus alnifolia* (alderleaf buckthorn)
> *Salix candida* (sageleaf willow)
> *Toxicodendron vernix* (poison sumac)
> *Vaccinium corymbosum* (highbush blueberry)

Characteristic of a diverse herb layer are:

> *Caltha palustris* (yellow marsh marigold)
> *Cardamine bulbosa* (bulbous bittercress)
> *Carex flava* (yellow sedge)
> *Carex interior* (inland sedge)
> *Carex lacustris* (hairy sedge)
> *Carex leptalea* (bristlystalked sedge)
> *Carex stricta* (upright sedge)
> *Cypripedium parviflorum* (lesser yellow ladys slipper)
> *Dryopteris cristata* (crested woodfern)
> *Geum rivale* (purple avens)
> *Iris versicolor* (harlequin blueflag)
> *Osmunda cinnamomea* (cinnamon fern)
> *Packera aurea* (goldenragwort)
> *Saxifraga pensylvanica* (eastern swamp saxifrage)
> *Solidago patula* (roundleaf goldenrod)
> *Symplocarpus foetidus* (skunk cabbage)
> *Thelypteris palustris* (eastern marsh fern)
> *Trollius laxus* (American globeflower)

## Red Maple - Black Ash Swamp

**Formal name:** *Fraxinus nigra - Acer rubrum / Rhamnus alnifolia / Carex leptalea Saturated Forest*

### Environmental summary

**Where it is found:** poorly drained depressions or seepage zones or as portions of larger swamps in the High Allegheny Plateau, the Central Appalachians and unglaciated portions of Lower New England/Northern Piedmont, from New York to Maryland and West Virginia.

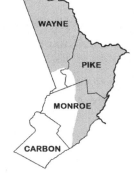

**Soil information:** typically muck without substantial peat development over calcareous bedrock.

**Characteristics:** a closed canopy deciduous swamp with a pH level somewhat higher than typical *Acer rubrum* sites and a lack of peat development in the mucky soil. A patchy understory may range from shrub-dominated to sedge-dominated.

### Vegetation

*Acer rubrum* (red maple) and *Fraxinus nigra* (black ash) dominate a closed canopy. Associates can include:
  *Betula alleghaniensis* (yellow birch)
  *Pinus strobus* (eastern white pine)
  *Ulmus americana* (American elm)
  *Ulmus rubra* (slippery elm)

Locally observed shrubs include:
  *Alnus incana* (gray alder)
  *Lindera benzoin* (northern spicebush)
  *Rhamnus alnifolia* (alderleaf buckthorn)
  *Salix spp.* (willow)
  *Toxicodendron vernix* (poison sumac)

Among the species reported in a diverse herb layer are:
  *Caltha palustris* (yellow marsh marigold)
  *Cardamine bulbosa* (bulbous bittercress)
  *Carex bromoides* (brome-like sedge)
  *Carex lacustris* (hairy sedge)
  *Carex leptalea* (bristlystalked sedge)
  *Dryopteris cristata* (crested woodfern)
  *Geum rivale* (purple avens)
  *Impatiens capensis* (jewelweed)
  *Osmunda cinnamomea* (cinnamon fern)
  *Platanthera grandiflora* (greater purple fringed orchid)
  *Saxifraga pensylvanica* (eastern swamp saxifrage)
  *Symplocarpus foetidus* (skunk cabbage)
  *Trollius laxus* (American globeflower)
  *Veratrum viride* (green false hellebore)

## Green Ash Floodplain Forest

**Formal name:** *Fraxinus pennsylvanica - (Juglans nigra, Platanus occidentalis) Forest*

### Environmental summary

**Where it is found:** behind levees and on low terraces that are briefly flooded annually, usually less than one week annually. It can also be found on islands, bars, and mid-terrace shorelines in the northern piedmont region of Pennsylvania, New Jersey, Delaware and Maryland.

**Soil information:** silts or clay loams, but may have coarser substrates where flood water velocity is higher.

**Characteristics:** Water table is high for the majority of the growing season. Diagnostic features of this floodplain forest include the presence of Juglans nigra and rich herbs.

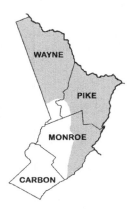

### Vegetation

The canopy is co-dominated by *Fraxinus pennsylvanica* (green ash) with *Juglans nigra* (black walnut) and/or *Platanus occidentalis* (American sycamore), although in some areas *Fraxinus americana* (white ash) may replace *F. pennsylvanica*. Additional associates include *Ulmus americana* (American elm), *Celtis occidentalis* (common hackberry), *Acer rubrum* (red maple), *Acer saccharinum* (silver maple), and *Quercus palustris* (pin oak).

Subcanopy and shrub layers are sparse and generally comprised of canopy species saplings as well as:
  *Carpinus caroliniana* (American hornbeam)
  *Carya cordiformis* (bitternut hickory)
  *Lindera benzoin* (northern spice bush)
  *Cornus amomum* (silky dogwood)
  *Viburnum prunifolium* (black haw)
  *Viburnum dentatum* (southern arrow wood)

The lush herbaceous layer can include:
  *Arisaema triphyllum* (Jack-in-the-pulpit)
  *Boehmeria cylindrica* (smallspike false nettle)
  *Circaea lutetiana* (enchanter's nightshade)
  *Hydrophyllum canadense* (bluntleaf waterleaf)
  *Impatiens capensis* (jewel weed)
  *Impatiens pallida* (pale touch-me-not)
  *Laportea canadensis* (Canadian wood nettle)
  *Onoclea sensibilis* (sensitive fern)
  *Podophyllum peltatum* (mayapple)
  *Symplocarpus foetidus* (skunk cabbage)
  *Thalictrum pubescens* (king of the meadow)
  *Viola spp.* (violets)

Woody vines include *Toxicodendron radicans* (poison ivy) and *Parthenocissus quinquefolia* (Virginia creeper).

## Inland Pitch Pine - Oak Forest

**Formal name:** *Pinus rigida - Quercus (velutina, prinus) Forest*

### Environmental Summary

**Where it is found:** ridges and south facing slopes, throughout the northeast.

**Soil information:** well-drained to droughty, acidic, sandy to rocky loams in glacial outwash or till.

**Characteristics:** dominated by *Pinus rigida* and oaks, although with lack of fire *Pinus strobus* and other deciduous species gain more prominence.

### Vegetation

The tree canopy is co-dominated by *Pinus rigida* (pitch pine) and several oak species, including *Quercus velutina* (black oak), *Quercus alba* (white oak), and *Quercus prinus* (chestnut oak), and an understory of ericaceous species.

Canopy associates include *Pinus strobus* (eastern white pine) and, less frequently, *Quercus rubra* (northern red oak), and *Pinus resinosa* (red pine) to the north or *Pinus virginiana* (Virginia pine) to the south. With the lack of fire, Pinus strobus and other deciduous species gain greater prominence.

The shrub layer tends to be fairly open. Reported are:

> *Comptonia peregrina* (sweetfern)
> *Gaylussacia baccata* (huckleberry)
> *Kalmia latifolia* (mountain laurel)
> *Vaccinium angustifolium* (lowbush blueberry)
> *Vaccinium pallidum* (Blue Ridge blueberry)

*Quercus ilicifolia* (bear oak) is occasionally reported, but usually absent in the Western Allegheny Plateau where *Vaccinium stamineum* (deerberry) is more common.

Typical herbs include

> *Aralia nudicaulis* (wild sarsaparilla)
> *Carex communis* (fibrousroot sedge)

> *Carex pensylvanica* (Pennsylvania sedge)
> *Desmodium spp.*
> *Gaultheria procumbens* (teaberry)
> *Lespedeza capitata* (roundhead lespedeza)
> *Pteridium aquilinum* (northern bracken fern)
> *Solidago odora* (on the High Allegheny Plateau)

## Sycamore - Hickory Floodplain Forest

**Formal name:** *Platanus occidentalis - Acer negundo - Juglans nigra / Asimina triloba / Mertensia virginica Forest*

### Environmental summary

**Where it is found:** higher elevations of floodplains, low terraces and floodplain berms of major rivers, or as the main floodplain of smaller rivers that drain areas of nutrient-rich substrates.

**Soil information:** texture varies from silty-clay loams to loams, tending toward pH above 6.0, with high calcium content.

**Characteristics:** closed, mixed overstory forest covering rich large-stream floodplain forests of the Mid-Atlantic Piedmont and Central Appalachians; not rare, but limited in geographic range to the larger rivers.

### Vegetation

The canopy may be co-dominated by *Acer saccharinum* (silver maple) in a few stands, but is primarily a mix of several other major species:

> *Carya cordiformis* (bitternut hickory)
> *Celtis occidentalis* (common hackberry)
> *Fraxinus pennsylvanica* (green ash)
> *Juglans nigra* (black walnut)
> *Liriodendron tulipifera* (tulip-tree)
> *Platanus occidentalis* (American sycamore)
> *Ulmus americana* (American elm)

*Acer negundo* (box elder) strongly dominates the subcanopy.

*Lindera benzoin* (northern spicebush) dominates a moderately dense to dense shrub layer.

Spring ephemerals and other nutrient-demanding species form a rich her layer. Among the locally reported species are:

>Mertensia virginica (Virginia bluebells)
>Asarum canadense (wild ginger)
>Hydrophyllum canadense (bluntleaf waterleaf)
>Viola striata (striped cream violet)
>Phlox divaricata (wild blue phlox)
>Podophyllum peltatum (mayapple)
>Erythronium americanum (dogtooth violet)
>Dicentra canadensis (squirrel corn)
>Sanicula odorata (clustered black snakeroot)
>Packera aurea (golden ragwort)
>Claytonia virginica (Virginia springbeauty)
>Festuca subverticillata (nodding fescue)
>Carex grisea (inflated narrow-leaf sedge)
>Osmorhiza longistylis (longstyle sweetroot)
>Ranunculus abortivus (littleleaf buttercup)

## Sycamore - Green Ash Forest

**Formal name:** *Platanus occidentalis - Fraxinus pennsylvanica Forest*

### Environmental summary

**Where it is found:** floodplain mid terraces of major tributaries to the Delaware River, such as Bushkill Creek and Flat Brook. It also occurs on islands, bars, and mid terrace shorelines of the Delaware River. These mid terraces are often slightly elevated above the water's channel and consequently flood less frequently than the main channel flood plain.

**Soil information:** Moderately well-drained sandy loam and cobble or sand alluvial substrates of floodplain islands or cobble shores.

**Characteristics:** an early- to-mid successional forest on the floodplains of high energy rivers.

### Vegetation

A closed to somewhat open canopy at 60 to 80 feet is usually dominated by *Platanus occidentalis* (sycamore), comprising 25 to 50 percent of the canopy, with the balance from a variety of deciduous species.

Present but not common are:

>*Acer saccharinum* (sugar maple)
>*Populus deltoides* (eastern cottonwood)
>*Ulmus americana* (American elm)

Occasional associates may include

>*Acer negundo* (box elder)
>*Acer rubrum* (red maple)
>*Acer saccharum* (silver maple)
>*Betula nigra* (river birch)
>*Carya cordiformis* (bitternut hickory)
>*Celtis occidentalis* (common hackberry)
>*Fraxinus americana* (white ash)
>*Fraxinus pennsylvanica* (green ash)
>*Juglans cinerea* (butternut)
>*Liriodendron tulipifera* (tuliptree)
>*Robinia pseudoacacia* (black locust)

Shrubs - generally sparse - or subcanopy trees, about 20 to 50 feet, are variable depending on geography and can include:

>*Alnus serrulata* (hazel alder)
>*Betula nigra* (river birch)
>*Carpinus caroliniana* (American hornbeam)
>*Cornus amomum* (silky dogwood)
>*Ilex verticillata* (common winterberry)
>*Lindera benzoin* (spicebush)
>*Salix nigra* (black willow)

The herbaceous layer can range from sparse to locally abundant; commonly found are:

>*Ageratina altissima var. altissima* (white snakeroot)
>*Athryium filix-femina* (ladyfern)
>*Carex bromoides* (brome-like sedge)
>*Geum canadense* (white avens)
>*Hydrophyllum virginianum* (Virginia waterleaf)
>*Matteuccia struthiopteris* (ostrich fern)
>*Onoclea sensibilis* (sensitive fern)
>*Osmunda cinnamomea* (cinnamon fern)
>*Podophyllum peltatum* (mayapple)
>*Polygonum amphibium* (water knotweed)
>*Solidago canadensis* (Canada goldenrod)
>*Solidago rugosa* (wrinkle-leaf goldenrod)
>*Symplocarpus foetidus* (skunk cabbage)

*Urtica dioica* (great nettle)

Locally reported vines include *Toxicodendron radicans* (poison ivy) and *Parthenocissus quinquefolia* (Virginia creeper)

## Dry Oak-Hickory Forest

**Formal name:** *Quercus (alba, rubra, velutina) / Cornus florida / Viburnum acerifolium Forest*

### Environmental Summary

**Where it is found:** high to midslopes, steps-in-slope and other dry-mesic sites, predominantly on southern or eastern exposures, often downslope from dry oak-heath forests on slightly less xeric sites and upslope of the more mesic northern red oak-mixed hardwood forest. More sparse stands occur on slopes of broken rock and stone below weathering siltstone and shale outcrops. Slopes can be gentle to steep and may contain scattered boulders and rocks.

**Soil information:** well-drained loam sand over sandstone, shale or siltstone bedrock, varying from extremely stony xeric soils to less rocky and more mesic soils..

**Characteristics:** Canopy cover of 70 to 80 percent, dominated by *Quercus rubra* (northern red oak), *Quercus alba* (white oak) and *Quercus velutina* (black oak). Small scattered seeps or drainages influence the herbaceous layer immediately around them

These forests have likely been harvested numerous times in the past several centuries and are ecologically transitional between dry-rich oak-hickory forests of relatively high diversity and dry, acidic oak species-poor forests.

### Vegetation

Tree canopy dominants include *Quercus rubra* (northern red oak), *Quercus alba* (white oak) and *Quercus velutina* (black oak). Toward the southern end of the range, *Quercus prinus* (chestnut oak) and *Quercus coccinea* (scarlet oak) are iden-tified as canopy associates. Canopy cover is between 70 and 80 percent, with tree height ranging from 50 to 100 feet.

Other associates include:
*Acer rubrum* (red maple)
*Acer saccharinum* (sugar maple)
*Amelanchier arborea* (serviceberry)
*Carya alba* (mockernut hickory)
*Carya glabra* (pignut hickory)
*Carya ovalis* (red hickory)
*Carya ovata* (shagbark hickory)
*Juniperus virginiana* (eastern red cedar)
*Nyssa sylvatica* (black gum)
*Sassafras albidum* (sassafras)
*Tsuga canadensis* (eastern hemlock)

At the northern end of its range, *Pinus strobus* (eastern white pine) and *Betula lenta* (sweet birch) may also occur as minor associates.

Subcanopy trees range from 15 to 60 feet and provide 10 to 50 percent cover and consists of red maple, black gum, sugar maple, common serviceberry, eastern red cedar (*Juniperus virginiana*), and the oaks and hickories found in the canopy. Stands with a dense white pine regeneration suggest the site may succeed to Dry White Pine - Oak Forest in the future.

Tall shrubs are sparse, covering up to only 30 percent. The shrub layer is characterized by *Viburnum acerifolium* (maple-leaf viburnum). Frequent associates include:
*Cornus florida* (flowering dogwood)
*Corylus americana* (American hazelnut)
*Corylus cornuta* (beaked hazelnut)
*Hamamelis virginiana* (witch hazel)
*Vaccinium corymbosum* (highbush blueberry)

On north-facing slopes, this forest may contain dense stands of *Rhododendron maximum* (great rhododendron).

A dwarf-shrub layer is often found, but not usually abundant - less than 40 percent coverage of the forest floor - and is characterized by *Vaccinium pallidum* (Blue Ridge blueberry) and *Gaylussacia baccata* (black huckleberry), with *Vaccinium angustifolium* (lowbush blueberry) reported more frequently to the north. Heath patches are often punctuated with dense stands of *Dennstaedtia punctilobula* (hayscented fern).

The herbaceous layer varies widely due to site-specific conditions and land use history; coverage can range from 5 to 70 percent. In stands with open woodland canopies, the herbaceous layer may be well-developed and dominated by graminoids. These include:

*Agrostis perennans* (upland bentgrass)

*Carex pensylvanica* (Pennsylvania sedge)

*Carex rosea* (rosy sedge)

*Carex swanii* (Swann's sedge)

*Danthonia spicata* (poverty oat grass)

*Deschampsia flexuosa* (wavy hairgrass)

*Dichanthelium acuminatum var. acuminatum* (tapered rosette grass)

In addition to hayscented fern and reported in herbaceous layers are:

*Aralia nudicaulis* (wild sarsaparilla)

*Aureolaria spp.*

*Chimaphila maculata* (striped prince's pine)

*Desmodium glutinosum* (pointedleaf ticktrefoil)

*Desmodium paniculatum* (panicledleaf ticktrefoil)

*Dryopteris marginalis* (marginal wood fern)

*Eurybia divaricata* (white wood aster)

*Helianthemum canadense* (longbranch frostweed)

*Hieracium venosum* (rattlesnake weed)

*Maianthemum canadense* (Canada mayflower)

*Maianthemum racemosum* (false Solomon's seal)

*Medeola virginiana* (Indian cucumber)

*Melampyrum lineare* (narrowleaf cowwheat)

*Mitchella repens* (partridgeberry)

*Polygonatum biflorum* (Solomon's seal)

*Pteridium aquilinum* (northern bracken fern)

*Solidago bicolor* (white goldenrod)

*Trientalis borealis* (starflower)

*Uvularia sessilifolia* (sessileleaf bellwort)

# Allegheny Oak Forest

**Formal name:** *Quercus (velutina, alba) / Vaccinium pallidum High Allegheny Plateau, Western Allegheny Plateau Forest*

## *Environmental Summary*

**Where it is found:** dry upper slopes and terraces of sandstone or shale in unglaciated portions of the Central Appalachians, High Allegheny Plateau and Western Allegheny Plateau.

**Soil information:** sandy or rocky, well drained.

**Characteristics:** common closed canopy dry deciduous upland, dominated by several species of oaks.

## *Vegetation*

The tree canopy is dominated by a mixture of *Quercus velutina* (black oak), *Quercus alba* (white oak), *Quercus rubra* (northern red oak), *Quercus coccinea* (scarlet oak), *Acer rubrum* (red maple), and *Quercus prinus* (chestnut oak).

Associates include:

*Betula lenta* (sweet birch)

*Carya glabra* (pignut hickory)

*Carya ovata* (shagbark hickory)

*Nyssa sylvatica* (black gum)

*Prunus serotina* (black cherry)

*Sassafras albidum* (sassafras)

*Castanea dentata* (American chestnut) was formerly common in this forest - and likely dominant - but wiped out in the 20th century by chestnut blight. Stump sprouts may remain in the understory.

Disturbance, such as wind throw and logging, favor *Quercus velutina* and *Betula lenta*.

The understory is characterized by *Nyssa sylvatica* (black gum) in the east, and in the western portion of the range by *Oxydendrum arboreum* (sourwood).

The low-shrub layer is characterized by a sparse to moderate coverage of ericaceous shrubs, depending on canopy density. Reported are:

  *Gaylussacia baccata* (huckleberry)
  *Kalmia latifolia* (mountain laurel)
  *Rhododendron periclymenoides* (pink aza-lea, pinxter flower)
  *Vaccinium angustifolium* (lowbush blue-berry)
  *Vaccinium pallidum* (Blue Ridge blueberry)
  *Vaccinium stamineum* (deerberry)
  *Viburnum acerifolium* (maple-leaf vibur-num)

Typical species of the herbaceous layer include:

  *Carex pensylvanica* (Pennsylvania sedge)
  *Cypripedium acaule* (pink lady's slipper)
  *Hieracium venosum* (rattlesnake weed)
  *Krigia biflora* (dwarf dandelion)
  *Oryzopsis asperifolia* (rough-leaved rice-grass)
  *Polygala paucifolia* (gaywings)
  *Pteridium aquilinum* (northern bracken fern)
  *Trientalis borealis* (starflower)
  *Waldsteinia fragarioides* (barren straw-berry)

## Low-Elevation Mixed Oak Forest

**Formal name:** *Quercus alba - Quercus (coccinea, velutina, prinus) / Gaylussacia baccata Forest*

### Environmental summary

**Where it is found:** mountain valleys and lower mountain slope benches, generally in nutrient-poor soils of the Central Appalachians, Piedmont and Coastal Plain uplands, typically on ancient alluvial fan deposits.

**Soil information:** Deep, nutrient poor, gravelly loams with low pH. Exposed rocks of any nature are generally sparse to absent. Bedrock can be sandstone, siltstone, chert or shale.

**Characteristics:** Elevations range from 100 to 2,300 feet on rolling to

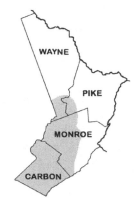

nearly level sites, with generally flat to westerly aspects. Because habitats are drought-prone and a considerable amount of flammable shrubs are found on these sites, periodic fires often result. This leads to a rapid invasion of mesophytic, fire-intolerant species when fire has been excluded for many decades.

### Vegetation

A variable canopy, ranging from very open to closed, is dominated by *Quercus alba* (white oak), *Quercus velutina* (black oak), *Quercus coccinea* (scarlet oak) and *Quercus prinus* (chestnut oak). A variety of pine species, including *Pinus virginiana* (Virginia pine), *Pinus strobus* (eastern white pine) and *Pinus rigida* (pitch pine) are common associates, especially after logging or fire disturbances.

Less common associates include *Quercus stellata* (post oak), *Carya glabra* (pignut hickory), and *Carya alba* (mockernut hickory). Meanwhile, *Nyssa sylvatica* (black gum) and *Amelanchier arborea* (common serviceberry) can be very successful in these forests by dominating subcanopy sometimes reaching the overstory. *Acer rubrum* (red maple) and *Sassafras albidum* (sassafras) are reported as common understory trees.

In typical stands, the shrub layer is dominated by deciduous ericaceous species. Often reported locally are:

  *Cornus florida* (flowering dogwood)
  *Gaylussacia baccata* (black huckleberry)
  *Kalmia latifolia* (mountain laurel)
  *Lyonia ligustrina* (maleberry)
  *Quercus ilicifolia* (bear oak)
  *Rhododendron periclymenoides* (pink aza-lea)
  *Smilax glauca* (cat greenbrier)
  *Smilax rotundifolia* (roundleaf greenbrier)
  *Vaccinium pallidum* (Blue Ridge blueberry)
  *Vaccinium stamineum* (upland highbush blueberry)

The herbaceous layer ranges from moderate to low in richness and tends to be sparse. Comprising the layer may be combinations of:

  *Amphicarpaea bracteata* (American hogpea-nut)
  *Angelica venenosa* (hairy angelica)
  *Antennaria plantaginifolia* (woman's to-

bacco)
*Botrychium virginianum* (rattlesnake fern)
*Carex blanda* (eastern woodland sedge)
*Chimaphila maculata* (striped prince's pine)
*Comandra umbellata* (bastard toadflax)
*Conopholis americana* (American cancer root)
*Cypripedium acaule* (pink lady's slipper)
*Danthonia spicata* (poverty oat grass)
*Desmodium nudiflorum* (naked flower ticktrefoil)
*Dioscorea villosa* (wild yam)
*Epigaea repens* (trailing arbutus)
*Galium spp.* (bedstraw)
*Iris verna* (dwarf violet iris)
*Isotria verticillata* (large whorled pogonia)
*Maianthemum racemosum* (false lily of the valley)
*Medeola virginiana* (Indian cucumber)
*Polygonatum biflorum* (Solomon's seal)
*Prenanthes altissima* (tall rattlesnake root)
*Pteridium aquilinum var. latiusculum* (northern bracken fern)
*Thelypteris noveboracensis* (New York fern)

## Swamp White Oak Floodplain Forest

**Formal name:** *Quercus bicolor - Acer rubrum / Carpinus caroliniana Forest*

### Environmental summary

**Where it is found:** lower floodplains and terraces of major rivers in the northeastern United States and Canada, often near the coast.

**Soil information:** silty and somewhat enriched.

**Characteristics:** poorly drained, especially of marine origin soil, with *Quercus bicolor* (swamp white oak) as a codominant canopy species.

### Vegetation

*Quercus bicolor* (swamp white oak) dominates the canopy, with *Acer rubrum* (red maple) or *Acer saccharinum* (silver maple) as frequent associates.

Additional associates may include *Ulmus americana* (American elm), *Fraxinus pennsylvanica* (green ash), *Betula nigra* (river birch), and sometimes *Carya ovata* (shagbark hickory). An understory of *Carpinus caroliniana* (American hornbeam) sometimes occurs.

The shrub layer typically a combination of *Cornus amomum* (silky dogwood), *Cephalanthus occidentalis* (common buttonbush), *Viburnum dentatum* (southern arrowwood), *Ilex verticillata* (winterberry), and *Viburnum lentago* (nannyberry).

Vines are frequently present and may include *Toxicodendron radicans* (poison ivy), *Menispermum canadense* (common moonseed), and *Parthenocissus quinquefolia* (Virginia creeper).

More poorly drained the lower portions of the flood plain are characterized by
*Boehmeria cylindrica* (smallspike false nettle),
*Carex crinita* (fringed sedge),
*Carex stricta* (upright sedge),
*Cinna arundinacea* (sweet woodreed)
*Iris versicolor* (blue flag iris)
*Lysimachia terrestris* (earth loosestrife)
*Onoclea sensibilis* (sensitive fern)
*Osmunda regalis* (royal fern)
*Thelypteris palustris* (marsh fern)

The drier terrace is often composed of:
*Athyrium filix-femina* (lady fern)
*Carex debilis* (white edge sedge)
*Elymus riparius* (riverbank rye)
*Solidago rugosa* (wrinkleleaf goldenrod)
*Thelypteris noveboracensis* (New York fern)

## Pin Oak - Swamp White Oak Forest

**Formal name:** *Quercus palustris - (Quercus bicolor) - Acer rubrum / Vaccinium corymbosum / Osmunda cinnamomea Forest*

### Environmental summary

**Where it is found:** seasonally wet (usually winter and early spring) hardwood basin areas with a shallow, perched water table that tend to be dry in late summer and early fall; throughout the northeastern United States from Virginia to New Hampshire.

**Soil information:** generally acidic sandy loams or clayey soils from glacial lake plains, or on soils with impermeable fragipans in unglaciated regions. While substrates can vary, all often have a layer that impedes drainage and can get groundwater seepage. Parent soil material consists of sand, gravelly or sandy alluvium, muck or peat, usually with a pH below 5.5

**Characteristics:** These are closed to partially open, deciduous, seasonally flooded forests dominated by *Quercus palustris, Quercus bicolor* and *Acer rubrum.* Hummock-and-hollow microtopography tends to be common.

The pattern of flooding in winter-spring and drying in late summer-early fall leads to a condition commonly called "flatwoods." During the wet season, water slowly penetrates soils with impermeable clays or fragipans developed from glacial periods; later in the season, the soil dries rapidly and causes vegetation wilts. Because of the hardpan, tree species may look stunted. Where stands receive groundwater seepage, soils can remain most during dry periods.

### Vegetation

*Quercus palustris* (pin oak) and/or *Quercus bicolor* (swamp white oak) and *Acer rubrum* (red maple) dominate the canopy. Common associates include *Nyssa sylvatica* (black gum) and sometimes *Tsuga canadensis* (eastern hemlock) or *Carya spp.* (hickories).

A sparse to dense shrub layer is often composed of:

> *Cephalanthus occidentalis* (common buttonbush)
> *Ilex verticillata* (winterberry)
> *Kalmia angustifolia* (sheep laurel)
> *Vaccinium corymbosum* (highbush blueberry)
> *Viburnum dentatum* (southern arrow-wood)

Comprising a usually sparse herb layer are:

> *Carex crinita* (fringed sedge)
> *Glyceria striata* (fowl mannagrass)
> *Isoetes spp.* (quillworts)

> *Onoclea sensibilis* (sensitive fern)
> *Osmunda cinnamomea* (cinnamon fern)
> *Osmunda regalis* (royal fern)
> *Scirpus cyperinus* (woolgrass)
> *Thelypteris palustris* (eastern marsh fern)
> *Thelypteris simulata* (bog fern)

## Pin Oak Small River Floodplain Forest

**Formal name:** *Quercus palustris - Acer rubrum / Carex grayi - Geum canadense Forest*

### Environmental summary

**Where it is found:** high terraces above major rivers (such as the Delaware) and on low-terrace floodplains of smaller creeks and streams, as well as on any broad, flat area with braided or diffuse drainage. Found in Pennsylvania, New York and southern New England.

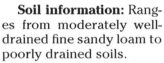

**Soil information:** Ranges from moderately well-drained fine sandy loam to poorly drained soils.

**Characteristics:** Can be seasonally, temporarily, or intermittently flooded, often with networks of small drainages and pools throughout. Many of these areas were previously used as pasture.

### Vegetation

The canopy, generally ranging from 60 to 100 feet, is dominated by *Quercus palustris* (pin oak) and *Quercus bicolor* (swamp oak), which comprise between 25 and 50 percent of the cover. Subcanopy trees, in the 30 to 60 foot range, form between 20 and 50 percent of cover and include younger canopy trees. Among the canopy associates are

> *Acer rubrum* (red maple)
> *Carya cordiformis* (bitternut hickory)
> *Fraxinus americana* (white ash)
> *Fraxinus pennsylvanica* (green ash)
> *Nyssa sylvatica* (black gum)
> *Ulmus americana* (American elm)

More typically upland trees sometimes found on terraces include:

*Acer saccharinum* (silver maple)
*Acer saccharum* (sugar maple)
*Betula alleghaniensis* (yellow birch)
*Betula nigra* (river birch)
*Liriodendron tulipifera* (tuliptree)
*Pinus strobus* (eastern white pine)
*Quercus alba* (white oak)

The tall shrub layer, which ranges from 15 to 60 percent cover, often includes:

*Amelanchier arborea* (common service-berry)
*Carpinus caroliniana* (American horn-beam),
*Hamamelis virginiana* (American witch-ha-zel)
*Ilex verticillata* (common winterberry)
*Lindera benzoin* (northern spicebush)
*Vaccinium corymbosum* (highbush blue-berry)
*Viburnum dentatum var. lucidum* (southern arrow-wood)
*Viburnum prunifolium* (blackhaw)

The short-shrub layer, with 25 to 50 percent cover, contains *Rubus occidentalis* (black rasp-berry), *Rubus flagellaris* (northern dewberry), *Rubus alleghiensis*, (Allegheny blackberry), *Vaccinium angustifolium* (lowbush blueberry), and species from the tall-shrub, canopy and sub-canopy layers.

The herbaceous layer is typically variable and dense with diverse flora. Common reported spe-cies are:

*Arisaema triphyllum* (Jack-in-the-pulpit)
*Carex intumescens* (greater bladder sedge)
*Carex prasina* (drooping sedge)
*Carex rosea* (rosy sedge)
*Dennstaedtia punctilobula* (eastern hay-scented fern)
*Duchesnea indica* (Indian strawberry)
*Epilobium leptophyllum* (bog willowherb)
*Galium asprellum* (rough bedstraw)
*Impatiens spp* (touch-me-not)
*Leersia virginica* (whitegrass)
*Maianthemum canadense* (Canada may-flower)
*Matteuccia struthiopteris* (ostrich fern)
*Mitchella repens* (partridgeberry)
*Onoclea sensibilis* (sensitive fern)
*Osmunda cinnamomea* (cinnamon fern)

*Panax trifolius* (dwarf ginseng)
*Polygonum persicaria* (spotted ladysthumb)
*Potentilla simplex* (common cinquefoil)
*Solidago rugosa* (wrinkleleaf goldenrod)
*Symplocarpus foetidus* (skunk-cabbage)
*Viola cucullata* (marsh blue violet)

Vines such as *Parthenocissus quinquefolia* (Virginia creeper) and *Toxicodendron radicans* (eastern poison ivy) can be abundant, while *Smilax rotundifolia* (roundleaf greenbrier) is usually sparsely distributed.

## Chestnut - Scarlet - Red Oak Forest

**Formal name:** *Quercus prinus - (Quercus coc-cinea, Quercus rubra) / Kalmia latifolia / Vaccini-um pallidum Forest*

### Environmental Summary

**Where it is found:** Dry middle and upper slopes, especially exposed convex slopes in the central Appalachians.

**Soil information:** infer-tile, acidic sandy loam, of-ten stony, and so thin that bedrock may be exposed. As a result, moisture po-tential is often subxeric to xeric.

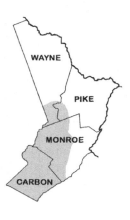

**Site characteristics:** a combination of canopy dominance by *Quercus prinus* (chestnut oak), a tall-shrub layer thick with *Kalmia latifolia* (mountain laurel), and a low shrub layer dominated by either *Vaccinium pallidum* (low bush blueberry), *Vaccinium stamineum* (deerberry) or *Gaylussacia baccata* (black huckleberry). Wind throw and ice storms are common environmental issues.

### Vegetation

Once dominated by *Castanea dentata* (Ameri-can chestnut), the canopy is overwhelmingly *Quercus prinus* (chestnut oak). *C. dentata*, pres-ent as a low subcanopy species from root spouts, was wiped out by the chestnut blight in the first half of the 20th century.

Most common canopy associates are *Quercus*

*coccinea* (scarlet oak) and *Quercus rubra* (northern red oak). Research suggests that *Q. rubra* is more frequent in sheltered slopes facing north while *Q. coccinea* is more prevalent on open or exposed sites, especially those which have been heavily timbered or subjected to fire in the past 100 years.

Minor associates include *Quercus alba* (white oak), *Quercus velutina* (black oak), *Nyssa sylvatica* (black gum), *Sassafras albidum* (sassafras) or *Robinia pseudoacacia* (black locust). *Acer rubrum* (red maple) and *N. sylvatica* are listed as abundant in understory tree layers.

By far the most dominant in the tall shrub layer is *Kalmia latifolia* (mountain laurel), but *Viburnum acerifolium* (maple-leaved viburnum) and *Rhododendron periclymenoides* (pinxter-flower) may be present.

Any of three species can locally dominate the low-shrub layer: *Vaccinium angustifolium* (low bush blueberry), *Vaccinium stamineum* (deerberry) or *Gaylussacia baccata* (black huckleberry).

A sparse herbaecous layer may include:
*Aureolaria virginica* (downy false-foxglove)
*Chimaphila maculata* (pipsisswea)
*Cypripedium acaule* (pink lady's slipper)
*Danthonia spicata* (poverty oat grass)
*Dennstaedtia punctilobula* (hay scented fern)
*Epigaea repens* (trailing arbutus)
*Gaultheria procumbens* (teaberry)
*Hieracium venosum* (rattlesnake weed)
*Medeola virginiana* (Indian cucumber root)
*Monotropa uniflora* (Indian pipe)
*Pteridium aquilinum* (northern bracken fern)

# Chestnut - Red - Black Oak Forest

**Formal name:** *Quercus prinus - Quercus (rubra, velutina) / Vaccinium angustifolium Forest*

### Environmental Summary

**Where it is found:** common on dry ridgetops, high plateaus, high slopes, steep side slopes, especially in the glaciated low plateau in Pennsylvania. Range is central and southern New England south to the northern Piedmont and central Appalachian Mountains.

**Soil information:** shallow, acidic, rocky and in-

fertile soils such as found in the Manlius, Mardin, Arnot, Oquaga, Lackawanna, Lordstown, Hazelton, and Dekalb series. Rock outcrops, boulders and large rocks are frequent on the forest floor. This association occurs on shale, siltstone and sandstone.

**Characteristics:** ericaceous species form substantial heath layers under a closed canopy (90 percent cover) or occasionally an open canopy (30 percent cover) in disturbed stands primarily composed of *Quercus prinus* (chestnut oak), ranging from 90 percent (closed) to 30 percent (open).

Wind throw, fire, and ice storms are common natural disturbances in these habitats. In areas that have experienced significant tree mortality, this association may resemble a woodland.

### Vegetation

Dominant in the canopy is *Quercus prinus* (chestnut oak), sometimes with *Quercus rubra* or *Quercus alba* as a codominant. Canopy trees range from 50 to 100 feet.

Typical canopy associates include:
*Acer rubrum* (red maple)
*Betula lenta* (sweet birch)
*Carya glabra* (pignut hickory)
*Nyssa sylvatica* (black gum)
*Pinus rigida* (pitch pine)
*Pinus strobus* (eastern white pine)
*Quercus coccinea* (scarlet oak)
*Quercus velutina* (black oak)
*Sassafras albidum* (sassafras)
*Tsuga canadensis* (eastern hemlock)

Subcanopy cover, from 10 to 60 percent and ranging from 15 to 65 feet, is generally dominated by the canopy trees as well as *Amelanchier arborea* (serviceberry) and *Photinia melanocarpa* (black chokeberry).

A primary characteristic is an ericaceous shrub layer usually dominated in the tall-shrubs by *Kalmia latifolia* (mountain laurel), although others may be present:

*Acer pensylvanicum* (striped maple)
*Castanea dentata* (chestnut oak) - once perhaps a dominant and now limited to sprouts that range to 25 feet.
*Hamamelis virginiana* (witch hazel)
*Ilex montana* (mountain holly)
*Quercus ilicifolia* (bear oak)
*Rhododendron prinophyllum* (early or roseshell azalea)
*Viburnum acerifolium* (maple-leaf viburnum)
*Viburnum prunifolium* (black-haw)

In addition to seedlings of canopy and subcanopy trees, ericads also dominate the short-shrub layer, primarily

*Epigaea repens* (trailing arbutus)
*Gaultheria procumbens* (teaberry)
*Gaylussacia baccata* (black huckleberry)
*Kalmia angustifolia* (sheep laurel)
*Vaccinium angustifolium* (lowbush blueberry)
*Vaccinium pallidum* (Blue Ridge blueberry)
*Vaccinium stamineum* (deerberry)

Density of the herbaceous layer varies with the shrub cover. While scattered graminoid or herbaceous species persist underneath dense shrubs, better opportunities are found in open patches between shrub clumps. Among the most common herbaceous representatives are:

*Deschampsia flexuosa* (wavy hairgrass)
*Dennstaedtia punctilobula* (eastern hay-scented fern)

Throughout the range, the following are also reported:

*Ageratina altissima var. altissima* (white snakeroot, or *Eupatorium rugosum*)
*Antennaria plantaginifolia* (pussytoes, woman's tobacco)
*Aralia nudicalis* (wild sarsaparilla)
*Aureolaria laevigata* (yellow false foxglove)
*Carex pensylvanica* (Pennsylvania sedge)
*Carex rosea* (rosy sedge)
*Carex swanii* (Swann's sedge)
*Chimaphila maculata* (princes' pine)
*Comandra umbellata* (bastard toadflax)
*Corydalis sempervirens* (rock harlequin)
*Cypripedium acaule* (pink lady's slipper)

*Danthonia spicata* (poverty oatgrass)
*Dryopteris marginalis* (marginal woodfern)
*Goodyera pubescens* (downy rattlesnake plantain)
*Hieracium venosum* (rattlesnake weed)
*Lycopodium clavatum* (running clubmoss)
*Medeola virginiana* (Indian cucumber)
*Melampyrum lineare* (narrowleaf cow-wheat)
*Monotropa uniflora* (Indian pipe)
*Polygonatum biflorum* (Solomon's seal)
*Potentilla canadensis* (dwarf cinquefoil)
*Pteridium aquilinum* (northern bracken fern)
*Trientalis borealis* (starflower)
*Uvularia sessilifolia* (sessile bellwort)

If vines are present, they may include *Parthenocissus quinquefolia* (Virginia creeper) and *Smilax rotundifolia* (roundleaf greenbrier).

## Dry-Mesic Chestnut - Red Oak Forest

**Formal name:** *Quercus prinus - Quercus rubra / Hamamelis virginiana Forest*

### Environmental Summary

**Where it is found:** primarily protected, rocky, mountain slopes, especially in lower to middle slope areas. Can also be found on steep and generally concave slopes, as well as relatively high surface cover of outcrops, boulders and stones. Slopes typically face north to southeast.

**Soil information:** Strongly to very strongly acidic, but with moderately high levels of calcium, suggesting occurrence on moderately base-rich substrates.

**Characteristics:** Dominated by *Quercus prinus* (chestnut oak) and *Quercus rubra* (northern red oak). Intermediate in site conditions and composition between oak / heath forests of exposed, xeric, infertile sites and richer cove or mountain oak-hickory forests of sheltered, fertile sites.

### Vegetation

Dominating the canopy are *Quercus prinus* (chestnut oak) and *Quercus rubra* (northern red oak). Associates are reported to include:

*Acer rubrum* (red maple)
*Acer saccharum* (sugar maple)
*Amelanchier arborea* (serviceberry)
*Betula lenta* (sweet birch)
*Carya alba* (mockernut hickory)
*Carya glabra* (pignut hickory)
*Carya ovalis* (red hickory)
*Fagus grandifolia* (American beech)
*Fraxinus americana* (white ash)
*Liriodendron tulipifera* (tuliptree)
*Nyssa sylvatica* (black gum)
*Ostrya virginiana* (hop hornbeam)
*Robinia pseudoacacia* (black locust)
*Tilia americana* (American basswood)
*Tsuga canadensis* (eastern hemlock)

A tall-shrub layer, sometimes absent, can be characterized by *Hamamelis virginiana* (witch hazel) and, less often by *Cornus florida* (flowering dogwood) and at higher elevations, *Acer pensylvanicum* (striped maple).

The lower shrub layer is described as patchy and contains a mixture of scrambling vines, ericads, and non-ericaceous species. In general, ericaceous species are patchy to sparse in this community. Reported are:

*Hydrangea arborescens* (wild hydrangea)
*Parthenocissus quinquefolia* (Virginia creeper)
*Toxicodendron radicans* (poison ivy)
*Vaccinium pallidum* (Blue Ridge blueberry)
*Vaccinium stamineum* (deerberry)
*Viburnum acerifolium* (maple leaf viburnum)
*Vitis aestivalis* (summer grape)

The herbaceous layer is usually sparse but may include:

*Dryopteris marginalis* (marginal wood fern)
*Eurybia divaricata* (white wood aster)
*Ageratina altissima* (white snakeroot)
*Polygonatum biflorum* (Solomon's seal)
*Solidago caesia* (wreath goldenrod)
*Festuca subverticillata* (nodding fescue)
*Thelypteris noveboracensis* (New York fern)
*Sanicula trifoliata* (black snakeroot)
*Prenanthes altissima* (tall rattlesnakeroot)

*Polystichum acrostichoides* (Christmas fern)
*Desmodium nudiflorum* (naked flower tick-trefoil)
*Houstonia purpurea* (Venus' pride)
*Maianthemum racemosum* (false Solomon's seal)

Although not one of the more constant herbs, *Aralia nudicaulis* (wild sarsaparilla) can sometimes dominate the herb layer in large clonal patches.

## Oak - Red Maple Successional Forest

**Formal name:** *Quercus rubra - Acer rubrum - Betula spp. - Pinus strobus Forest*

### Environmental summary

**Where it is found:** northern and eastern-facing coves and midslopes, following severe disturbance, such as clearing, fires, hurricanes, pasturing, logging and fragmented residential development.

**Soil information:** deep, moist to well-drained silt loams and loams, often on northern and eastern coves and midslopes. Some are reported on dry-mesic fine loamy sands and sandy loams.

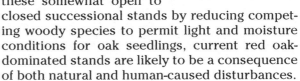

**Characteristics:** Although fire helps maintain these somewhat open to closed successional stands by reducing competing woody species to permit light and moisture conditions for oak seedlings, current red oak-dominated stands are likely to be a consequence of both natural and human-caused disturbances.

It may also persist where soils are limited, such as ridgelines.

Canopy trees typically range in age from 40 to 100 years and total community composition varies with site history.

A thin canopy that includes early successional species such as red maple, low populations of hardwoods other than red oak, and the absence of a well-developed heath shrub layer - typical in oak pine woodlands - differentiates this association from similar forests and woodlands. Red oak is the only oak species of any abundance.

### Vegetation

The canopy trees, ranging from 40 to 100 years old, ranges from somewhat open to closed and is typically dominated by a mix of *Quercus rubra* (red oak), *Acer rubrum* (red maple), *Pinus strobus* (white pine) and *Fagus grandifolia* (American beech).

Associates are often wind-dispersed, light-requiring trees such as:

> *Acer saccharum* (sugar maple)
> *Betula papyrifera* (paper birch)
> *Betula populifolia* (gray birch)
> *Fraxinus americana* (white ash)
> *Picea rubens* (red spruce)
> *Populus grandidentata* (bigtooth aspen)
> *Populus tremuloides* (quaking aspen)
> *Prunus serotina* (black cherry)

Often indicating predisturbance conditions, understory species may include:

> *Acer pensylvanicum* (striped maple)
> *Corylus cornuta* (beaked hazelnut)
> *Hamamelis virginiana* (witch hazel)
> *Vaccinium angustifolium* (low-bush blueberry)
> *Viburnum acerifolium* (mapleleaf viburnum)

A characteristic of this association is *Pteridium aquilinum* (northern bracken fern) and is likely dominant in the herbaceous layer. Other common species include:

> *Aralia nudicaulis* (wild sarsaparilla)
> *Deschampsia flexuosa* (wavy hairgrass)
> *Geranium maculatum* (wild geranium)
> *Maianthemum canadense* (Canada mayflower)
> *Medeola virginiana* (Indian cucumber)
> *Polystichum acrostichoides* (Christmas fern)
> *Trientalis borealis* (starflower)

Coverage of bryophytes varies and typically includes *Dicranum polysetum* (dichranum moss) and *Polytrichum commune* (polytrichum moss).

## Red Oak - Northern Hardwood Forest

**Formal name:** *Quercus rubra - Acer saccharum - Fagus grandifolia / Viburnum acerifolium Forest*

### Environmental Summary

**Where it is found:** Midslopes and coves, commonly at low to mid elevations under 1,700 feet.

**Soil information:** slightly acidic, well-drained loamy and often rocky soils of intermediate fertility; depth is often shallow, but some stands occur on deep tills.

**Characteristics:** Glaciated areas between temperate and boreal regions, these mesic forests comprised of oak and other hardwoods only occasionally include hemlock or pine.

Keys reported as differences with other hardwood forests include:

> More oak than other hardwood forests
> More hardwoods than other oak forests
> Much less hemlock than hemlock-hardwood forests
> Absence of dwarf-shrub ericads
> Conifers comprise less than 20 percent of the canopy cover

### Vegetation

The deciduous-to-mixed canopy is mostly closed, and the lower layers are variable in extent. Tall shrubs are well-represented, although scattered, with occasional denser patches. Herbs are sparse and mosses are nearly absent.

Canopy composition is a variable mixture of *Quercus rubra* (northern red oak), *Fagus grandifolia* (American beech), *Acer saccharum* (sugar maple), *Acer rubrum* (red maple), and in some stands *Pinus strobus* (eastern white pine) or *Tsuga canadensis* (eastern hemlock). *Q. rubra* is usually at least 30 percent of the canopy.

Minor canopy associates include:

> *Betula lenta* (sweet birch)
> *Fraxinus americana* (white ash)
> *Juglans cinerea* (butternut)
> *Tilia americana* (American basswood)
> *Ulmus americana* (American elm)

Reported as common small trees in the subcanopy are:

    *Acer pensylvanicum* (striped maple)
    *Cornus florida* (flowering dogwood)
    *Prunus serotina* (black cherry)

The shrub layer tends to be comprised of *Corylus cornuta* (beaked hazelnut), *Viburnum acerifolium* (mapleleaf viburnum), and *Hamamelis virginiana* (witch hazel). *Kalmia latifolia* (mountain laurel) and *Lindera benzoin* (northern spicebush) are reported as occasional.

Typical species in the herb layer include:

    *Aralia nudicaulis* (wild sarsaparilla)
    *Brachyelytrum erectum* (bearded short-husk)
    *Dennstaedtia punctilobula* (hayscented fern)
    *Dryopteris intermedia* (intermediate woodfern)
    *Gaultheria procumbens* (teaberry)
    *Maianthemum canadense* (Canada mayflower)
    *Medeola virginiana* (Indian cucumber)
    *Polystichum acrostichoides* (Christmas fern)
    *Pteridium aquilinum* (northern bracken fern)
    *Thelypteris noveboracensis* (New York fern)
    *Trientalis borealis* (starflower)
    *Uvularia sessilifolia* (sessileleaf bellwort)

On more nutrient-rich soils, the herb layer may contain:

    *Caulophyllum thalictroides* (blue cohosh)
    *Dryopteris marginalis* (marginal woodfern)
    *Eurybia divaricata* (white wood aster)
    *Solidago caesia* (wreath goldenrod)

## Rich Red Oak - Sugar Maple Forest

**Formal name:** *Quercus rubra - Acer saccharum - Liriodendron tulipifera Forest*

### Environmental Summary

**Where it is found:** Coves, moist north and east-facing, sometimes steep, midslopes and well-drained flats, primarily in the Allegheny Plateau and Appalachian Mountain regions.

**Soil information:** slightly acidic, of intermediate fertility and may be rocky. Soils vary from loamy sand and fine sandy loam to extremely stony silt loams. Soil pH varies from pH 5.6 to pH 7.3 in most stands, with some stands being

much more acidic (pH less than 5.5). Soils are typically well-drained but not droughty. Bedrock tends to be siltstone, sandstone, conglomerate, limestone and limy shales.

**Characteristics:** *Quercus rubra* (northern red oak) dominates in association with varied hardwoods.

### Vegetation

The tree canopy, ranging from 80 to over 100 feet, is typically nearly to completely closed, with cover in excess of 80 per cent. *Quercus rubra* (northern red oak) may be dominant share dominance with:

    *Acer rubrum* (red maple)
    *Betula lenta* (sweet birch)
    *Carya cordiformis* (bitternut hickory)
    *Carya glabra* (pignut hickory)
    *Quercus velutina* (black oak)

Occasional associates may include:

    *Acer saccharum* (sugar maple)
    *Fagus grandifolia* (American beech)
    *Fraxinus americana* (white ash)
    *Liriodendron tulipifera* (tuliptree)
    *Nyssa sylvatica* (black gum)
    *Quercus alba* (white oak)
    *Quercus coccinea* (scarlet oak)
    *Tilia americana* (American basswood)

A subcanopy, with 20 to 40 per cent total cover, ranges from 15 to 65 feet in height, depending on the stand. The dominant subcanopy tree is *Carpinus caroliniana* (American hornbeam), often with *Cornus florida* (flowering dogwood), sweet birch and red maple as associates or co-dominants.

The tall-shrub layer varies from 5 to 30 per cent total cover, usually 5 to 15 feet and often contains one or more of the following reported as a dominant or codominant:

    *Hamamelis virginiana* (witch hazel)
    *Lindera benzoin* (northern spicebush)
    *Ostrya virginiana* (eastern hop-hornbeam)
    *Tsuga canadensis* (eastern hemlock) saplings

The short-shrub layer varies in total cover from 10 to 30 per cent and is less than 5 feet in height. Composition is variable with one or more of the following typically present and/or abundant:

*Lindera benzoin* (northern spicebush)
*Vaccinium pallidum* (Blue Ridge blueberry)
*Viburnum acerifolium* (mapleleaf viburnum)
Seedlings of canopy trees

Occasionally reported in the shrub layer, but never dominant, are:

*Amelanchier arborea* (serviceberry)
*Amelanchier laevis* (Allegheny service-berry)
*Cornus spp.* (dogwoods)
*Kalmia latifolia* (mountain laurel)
*Vaccinium angustifolium* (lowbush blue-berry)
*Viburnum recognitum* (southern arrow-wood)
*Vitis riparia* (frost grape)

The herbaceous layer is highly variable, usually less than 3 feet in height and ranges from 10 to 50 per cent cover.

Characteristic species may include:

*Actaea pachypoda* (doll's eyes)
*Actaea racemosa* (black cohosh)
*Actaea rubra* (red baneberry)
*Ageratina altissima* (white snakeroot)
*Arisaema triphyllum* (jack-in-the-pulpit)
*Brachyelytrum erectum* (bearded short-husk)
*Carex digitalis* (slender woodland sedge)
*Caulophyllum thalictroides* (blue cohosh)
*Chimaphila maculata* (striped prince's pine)
*Dennstaedtia punctilobula* (hayscented fern)
*Dryopteris intermedia* (intermediate wood-fern)
*Dryopteris marginalis* (marginal woodfern)
*Erythronium americanum* (dogtooth violet)
*Eurybia divaricata* (white wood aster)
*Galium triflorum* (fragile bedstraw)
*Gaultheria procumbens* (teaberry)
*Lycopodium spp.* (club mosses)
*Maianthemum canadense* (Canada may-flower)
*Maianthemum racemosum* (false Solomon's seal)

*Medeola virginiana* (Indian cucumber)
*Mitchella repens* (partridgeberry)
*Pilea pumila* (Canada clearweed)
*Podophyllum peltatum* (mayapple)
*Polystichum acrostichoides* (Christmas fern)
*Thalictrum thalictroides* (rue anemone)
*Thelypteris noveboracensis* (New York fern)
*Uvularia sessilifolia* (sessileleaf bellwort)
*Viola pubescens* (downy yellow violet)
*Viola sororia* (common blue violet)

## Oak - Hickory Sedge Lawn Forest

**Formal name**: *Quercus rubra - Carya (glabra, ovata) / Ostrya virginiana / Carex lucorum Forest*

### Environmental Summary

**Where it is found:** low-elevation ridgetops, upper slopes, south- or west-facing side slopes but most commonly southeast.

**Soil information:** Well-drained loams or sandy loams and often circum-neutral, derived from alkaline bedrock. Soils range from stony to extremely rocky, often from Benson, Manlius, Arnot, Oquaga and Lackawanna series. Exposed bedrock, boulders and cobbles is sparse in some areas, while in others, boulders and large rocks are frequent on the forest floor where soils are more acidic and shallow.

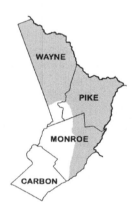

**Characteristics:** generally described as a dry, rich hickory forest dominated by a mixture of hickories and oaks over a hop-hornbeam subcanopy and a park-like sedge lawn.

### Vegetation

The forest canopy is dominated by hickories more than oaks and ranges from partially open (40 percent cover) to nearly closed (75 percent cover). Canopy trees range from 30 to 80 feet and primarily include:

*Carya alba* (mockernut hickory)
*Carya glabra* (pignut hickory)
*Carya ovalis* (red hickory)

*Quercus alba* (white oak)
*Quercus prinus* (chestnut oak)
*Quercus rubra* (northern red oak)
*Quercus velutina* (black oak)

Occasional canopy associates include *Fraxinus americana* (white ash), *Pinus strobus* (eastern white pine), *Quercus coccinea* (scarlet oak) and *Acer rubrum* (red maple).

*Ostrya virginiana* (hop hornbeam) is common in the subcanopy, which ranges from 3 to 50 feet. Subcanopy can be absent to moderately dense and include saplings of the canopy trees as well as:

*Acer pensylvanicum* (striped maple)
*Amelanchier arborea* (serviceberry)
*Cornus florida* (flowering dogwood)
*Hamamelis virginiana* (witch hazel)
*Juniperus virginiana* (eastern red cedar)
*Viburnum acerifolium* (maple-leaf viburnum)

Low shrubs are reported to include
*Gaylussacia baccata* (black huckleberry)
*Rubus allegheniensis* (Allegheny blackberry)
*Rubus flagellaris* (northern dewberry)
*Rubus idaeus* (American red raspberry)
*Vaccinium angustifolium* (lowbush blueberry)
*Vaccinium pallidum* (Blue Ridge blueberry)
*Vaccinium stamineum* (deerberry)
*Viburnum dentatum* (southern arrowwood)
*Viburnum prunifolium* (black haw)
*Viburnum rafinesquianum* (downy arrowwood)

Especially when canopy is more open, graminoids dominate the herbaceous layer, and form what is described as a sedge lawn. The herbaceous layer is typically moderately dense to dense (50 to 95 percent cover) and can be fairly diverse compared to other xeric forest types.

Common species represented include:
*Agrostis perennans* (upland bentgrass)
*Anthoxanthum odoratum* (vernal sweetgrass)
*Bromus pubescens* (hairy woodland brome)
*Carex appalachica* (Appalachian sedge)

*Carex lucorum* (Blue Ridge sedge)
*Carex pensylvanica* (Pennsylvania sedge)
*Carex rosea* (rosy sedge)
*Carex swanii* (Swann's sedge)
*Carex woodii* (pretty sedge)
*Danthonia spicata* (poverty oatgrass)
*Deschampsia flexuosa* (wavy hairgrass)
*Dichanthelium acuminatum var. acuminatum* (tapered rosette grass)
*Dichanthelium boscii* (Bosc's panicgrass)
*Elymus hystrix* (eastern bottlebrush grass)
*Festuca subverticillata* (nodding fescue)

Other herbaceous species include:
*Ageratina altissima* (white snakeroot)
*Aralia nudicalis* (wild sarsaparilla)
*Claytonia virginica* (Virginia springbeauty)
*Desmodium glutinosum* (pointedleaf ticktrefoil)
*Desmodium paniculatum* (panicleafed ticktrefoil)
*Erythronium americanum* (yellow trout lily)
*Hepatica nobilis var. obtusa* (roundlobed hepatica)
*Lycopodium clavatum* (running clubmoss)
*Maianthemum racemosum* (false solomon's seal)
*Packera obovata* (roundleaf ragwort)
*Packera paupercula* (balsam groundsel)
*Paronychia canadensis* (smooth forked nailwort)
*Polystichum acrostichoides* (Christmas fern)
*Potentilla canadensis* (dwarf cinquefoil)
*Prenanthes alba* (white rattlesnakeroot)
*Saxifraga virginiensis* (early saxifrage)
*Solidago arguta* (Atlantic goldenrod)
*Solidago bicolor* (white goldenrod)
*Solidago juncea* (early goldenrod)
*Symphyotrichum patens* (late purple aster)
*Symphyotrichum undulatum* (wavy-leaved aster)
*Uvularia perfoliata* (perfoliate bellwort)
*Veronica officinalis* (common gypsyweed)

# *Deciduous woodlands*

## Red Maple - Tussock Sedge Marsh

**Formal name:** *Acer rubrum / Carex stricta - Onoclea sensibilis Woodland*

### *Environmental summary*

**Where it is found:** poorly drained depressions influenced by groundwater, especially in basin settings near streams and lakes.

**Soil information:** Muck soils or mineral soils with a surface organic layer

**Characteristics**: Typically flooded in spring, pools and small streams may persist throughout much of the growing season and soils may remain saturated or dry on the surface during the season. Hummock and hollow topography is not uncommon.

### *Vegetation*

Scattered trees, usually with less than 25 percent cover, form a sparse canopy, dominated by *Acer rubrum* (red maple). Associates can include *Fraxinus nigra* (black ash), *Ulmus americana* (American elm), *Pinus strobus* (eastern white pine), *Tsuga canadensis* (eastern hemlock) or *Picea rubens* (red spruce). Standing dead trees are frequent.

The shrub layer is varies from patchy to extensive and is often characterized by *Vaccinium corymbosum* (highbush blueberry), *Spirea alba var. latifolia* (white meadowsweet) and/or *Ilex verticillata* (common winterberry)

The herbaceous layer is typically dominated by the graminoids *Carex stricta* (upright sedge), *Carex lacustris* (hairy sedge), or *Calamagrostis canadensis* (bluejoint) or the ferns *Onoclea sensibilis* (sensitive fern), *Osmunda cinnamomea* (cinnamon fern) or *Osmunda claytoniana* (interrupted fern).

Less abundant herbs include
> *Caltha palustris* (yellow marsh marigold)
> *Carex canescens* (silvery sedge)
> *Carex folliculata* (northern long sedge)
> *Carex intumescens* (greater bladder sedge)
> *Carex trisperma* (three-seeded sedge)
> *Cicuta bulbifera* (bulblet-bearing water hemlock)
> *Dryopteris cristata* (crested woodfern)
> *Galium palustre* (common marsh bedstraw)
> *Glyceria striata* (fowl mannagrass)
> *Impatiens capensis* (jewelweed)
> *Lycopus uniflorus* (northern bugleweed)
> *Osmunda regalis* (royal fern)
> *Symplocarpus foetidus* (skunk cabbage)
> *Thelypteris palustris* (marsh fern)

The bryophyte cover is variable, but generally dominated by *Sphagnum spp.*

## Hardwood - Oak Talus Slope Woodland

**Formal name:** *Betula alleghaniensis - Quercus rubra / Polypodium virginianum Woodland*

### *Environmental summary*

**Where it is found:** talus slopes at low to mid-level (to 1,700 feet) elevations in the northern Appalachians extending to New England and New Brunswick, Canada, in the north and the northern Piedmont in the south

**Soil information:** thin and patchy, nutrient poor coarse-textured mineral materials, generally in crevices of talus.

**Characteristics:** an acidic-large boulder talus slope woodland with less than 50 percent canopy closure, dominated by a variety of oak and birch species. A patchy shrub layer may form thickets in openings and a sparse herb layer may include dense patches where soil is available. Bryophytes are scarce and ground cover tends to be exposed talus, moss-covered boulders and deciduous litter. Rich-site indicator herbs are absent.

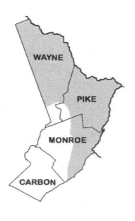

### Vegetation

The tree canopy is dominated by a variable mixture of oak and birch species, including *Quercus rubra* and *Betula alleghaniensis*. In the northern portion of this community's range, Quercus rubra may drop out entirely, with *Betula* spp. and *Acer* spp. dominant. Other canopy associates may include:

> *Acer rubrum* (red maple)
> *Acer saccharum* (sugar maple)
> *Betula papyrifera* (paper birch)
> *Betula populifolia* (gray birch)
> *Fagus grandifolia* (American beech)
> *Pinus strobus* (eastern white pine)
> *Populus grandidentata* (bigtooth aspen)
> *Prunus pensylvanica* (pin cherry)
> *Quercus alba* (white oak)
> *Quercus prinus* (chestnut oak)
> *Tsuga canadensis* (eastern hemlock)

Ericaceous shrubs are atypical, but if present may include *Vaccinium angustifolium* (lowbush blueberry), *Gaylussacia baccata* (black huckleberry) and or *Kalmia angustifolia* (sheep laurel). The understory is generally composed of clumped, scattered small trees and tall shrubs, reported to include:

> *Acer pensylvanicum* (striped maple)
> *Acer spicatum* (mountain maple)
> *Ribes spp.* (currants)
> *Rubus spp.* (blackberries)
> *Viburnum acerifolium* (mapleleaf viburnum)

Especially characteristic are vines, which may locally include:

> *Parthenocissus quinquefolia* (Virginia creeper)
> *Toxicodendron radicans* (poison ivy)
> *Toxicodendron rydbergii* (giant poison ivy)
> *Celastrus scandens* (American bittersweet)
> *Polygonum cilinode* (fringed black bindweed)

Scattered ferns and herbs are:

> *Aralia nudicaulis* (wild sarsaparilla)
> *Carex lucorum* (Blue Ridge sedge)
> *Carex pensylvanica* (Pennsylvania sedge)
> *Corydalis sempervirens* (rock harlequin)
> *Deschampsia flexuosa* (wavy hairgrass)
> *Dryopteris marginalis* (marginal woodfern)
> *Eurybia macrophylla* (bigleaf aster)
> *Maianthemum racemosum* (false lily of the valley)
> *Polypodium virginianum* (rock polypody)
> *Pteridium aquilinum* (northern bracken fern)
> *Solidago bicolor* (white goldenrod)
> *Solidago caesia* (wreath goldenrod)

Bryophytes include *Polytrichum commune* (polytrichum moss), *Leucobryum glaucum* (leucobryum moss), *Umbilicaria spp.* (navel lichen), and *Cladina spp.* (reindeer lichen).

## Sweet Birch - Oak Talus Woodland

**Formal name:** *Betula alleghaniensis - Quercus rubra / Polypodium virginianum Woodland*

### Environmental summary

**Where it is found:** edges of large, barely weathered block fields covered mostly by lichens as well as more weathered boulder fields and slopes that are covered by coarse to fine, bouldery colluvium, throughout the Blue Ridge and Ridge and Valley sections of Pennsylvania, Virginia, West Virginia, and Maryland, extending northeast to the Pennsylvania-New Jersey border.

A very good example is a rocky, steep southeast-facing slope of the Kittatinny Ridge along Interstate 80

and on occasional boulderfields in other sections of the Delaware Water Gap National Recreation area. The parent material is sandstone and sandstone conglomerate of the Silurian Shawangunk Formation.

**Soil information:** local, shallow, infertile, acidic, organic and root-rich duff deposits between rocks, where air spaces may be more than 3 feet below the surface, or to moss pads on thin, organic to sandy material developed on wide and flat boulder surfaces.

**Characteristics:** Usually steeply sloping talus sites, but also found on gentler benches and ridge crests, extending through the central Appalachians to the western Allegheny Plateau in Pennsylvania. Cover varies, but is typically open with gnarled and widely spaced trees. In addition to stresses caused by soil materials, trees taking root in these habitats are subject to frequent wind and ice storm damage. Weathered sandstone caprock is the usual source of rubble. Sites may include incised hollow bottoms, concave hollow heads, slide masses and landslide scarps, all of which are generally xeric. However, evidence of subsurface drainage is reduced because of higher elevations and north aspects that often slow evaporation and increase moisture-holding capabilities of the bouldery substrate.

These boulder fields are examples landscapes that evolve from one that cannot support vegetative communities to fully forested mountain slopes with well developed mineral soils. Mosses and lichens often lead the way.

### Vegetation

Locally, *Quercus prinus* (chestnut oak) and *Betula lenta* (sweet birch) dominate an open forest canopy that is 50 to 80 percent cover, but other associations see the role of *Q. prinus* diminish to an associate while other birch species rise to dominance. Canopy trees are typically 30 to 50 feet in height. Associates include:
*Acer rubrum* (red maple)
*Carya glabra* (pignut hickory)
*Nyssa sylvatica* (black gum)
*Pinus rigida* (pitch pine)
*Pinus strobus* (eastern white pine)
*Quercus alba* (white oak)
*Quercus coccinea* (scarlet oak)

*Quercus velutina* (black oak)
*Tsuga canadensis* (eastern hemlock)

A sparse subcanopy - 10 to 30 percent cover - is locally dominated by sweet birch and black gum, and includes other canopy associates.

Comprising a tall shrub layer that covers from 10 to 40 percent are:
*Acer pensylvanicum* (striped maple)
*Amelanchier arborea* (common serviceberry)
*Castanea dentata* (American chestnut)
*Hamamelis virginiana* (witch-hazel)
*Kalmia latifolia* (mountain laurel)
*Rhus glabra* (smooth sumac)

The short-shrub layer, which ranges from zero to 30 percent cover, may contain:
*Gaylussacia baccata* (black huckleberry)
*Rubus allegheniensis* (Allegheny blackberry)
*Rubus flagellaris* (northern dewberrry)
*Vaccinium angustifolium* (lowbush blueberry)
*Vaccinium pallidum* (Blue Ridge blueberry)

Because of the bouldery surface, the herbaceous layer is often very sparse but illustrative of species that can manage in xeric habitats:
*Aralia nudicaulis* (wild sarsaparilla)
*Asplenium platyneuron* (ebony spleenwort)
*Carex swanii* (Swann's sedge)
*Danthonia spicata* (poverty oatgrass)
*Deschampsia flexuosa* (wavy hairgrass)
*Dryopteris marginalis* (marginal woodfern)
*Eurybia divaricata* (white wood aster)
*Heuchera americana* (American alumnroot)
*Polypodium virginianum* (rock polypody)
*Woodsia obtusa* (bluntlobe cliff fern)

Potentially common are the vines *Toxicodendron radicans* (poison ivy) and *Parthenocissus quinquefolia* (Virginia creeper).

The nonvascular layer covers up to 65 percent of some microhabitats, primarily with lichens such as *Lasallia papulosa* (blistered naval lichen), *Umbilicaria mammulata* (navel lichen) and *Flavoparmelia baltimorensis* (Baltimore flavoparmelia lichen).

## Sycamore - Birch Scour Woodland

**Formal name:** *Platanus occidentalis - Betula nigra - Salix (caroliniana, nigra) Woodland*

### Environmental summary

**Where it is found:** typically on cobble bars and sand/gravel bars adjacent to or contiguous with the shoreline of the Delaware River; also on the upstream ends of islands.

**Soil information:** coarse (cobbly to bouldery) to fine-textured (silty or muddy). Along high-gradient river stretches subject to frequent and high-energy flooding and ice scouring, soils are usually sandy in a tight mix of cobbles and boulders, and droughty when periodically exposed. In low-gradient, frequently flooded depositional bars and shorelines, soils are reported to have a substantial silt component and are poorly drained even after long periods of exposure. Both soils tested as circumneutral with high calcium levels and 100 percent total base saturation.

**Characteristics:** The association is subject to frequent floods, high stream velocity and ice scour, and while highly variable in appearance is generally dominated by stunted and often battered and flood-trained trees up to 30 feet tall.

### Vegetation

Most common trees are *Platanus occidentalis* (sycamore) and *Betula nigra* (river birch). *Salix caroliniana* (coastal plain willow) and *Salix nigra* (black willow) can be dominants or co-dominants in some stands. Other floodplain trees, especially *Acer saccharinum* (silver maple) and *Fraxinus pennsylvanica* (green ash), may occur as minor associates.

Shrubs include *Cornus amomum* (silky dogwood), *Salix sericea* (silky willow), *Alnus serrulata* (hazel alder), and occasionally Cephalanthus occidentalis (buttonbush) or Physocarpus opulifolius (ninebark).

The herbaceous layer ranges from sparse to moderately dense and can contain a wide variety of typical wetland and prairie species. Common species include:

> *Agrostis perennans* (upland bentgrass)
> *Asclepias incarnata* (swamp milkweed)
> *Boehmeria cylindrica* (smallspike false nettle)
> *Dichanthelium clandestinum* (deertongue)
> *Leersia virginica* (whitegrass)
> *Onoclea sensibilis* (sensitive fern)
> *Panicum virgatum* (switchgrass)
> *Phalaris aruninacea* (reed canarygrass)
> *Pilea pumila* (Canadian clearweed)
> *Polygonum hydropiper* (marshpepper knotweed)
> *Polygonum hydropiperoides* (swamp smartweed)
> *Polygonum pensylvanicum* (Pennsylvania smartweed)

Vines such as *Vitis riparia* (riparian grape) and *Toxicodendron radicans* (poison ivy) are often found throughout this association.

## Limestone Chinquapin Oak Woodland

**Formal name:** *Quercus muehlenbergii - Cercis canadensis / Packera obovata - Lithospermum canescens Woodland*

### Environmental summary

**Where it is found:** south to southwest-facing steep limestone and dolmitic slopes — from 20 to 30 degrees to much steeper — at elevations ranging from 1,000 to 2,600 feet in the central Appalachians from central Pennsylvania through northeastern Virginia and western Virginia.

**Soil information:** shallow, stony, dry calcareous loams derived from limestone or dolomite bedrock, from circumneutral to moderately alkaline, with very high calcium and magnesium levels. Many loose stones and exposed bedrock occupy about half the surface.

**Characteristics:** Slopes are predominantly and

sometimes dramatically convex, with rugged, complex, and variable microtopography, sometimes exposed xeric cliffs and large outcrops of carbonate rock that has been undercut by rivers or large streams. Plants are rooted in crevices and thin-soil ledges. Periodic drought results in occasional mortality of shrubs and trees.

### Vegetation

The dominant tree in the open calcareous glade is *Quercus muehlenbergii* (chinkapin oak), with associates including:

> *Celtis tenuifolia* (dwarf hackberry)
> *Cercis canadensis* (eastern redbud)
> *Fraxinus americana* (white ash)
> *Juniperus virginiana* (eastern red cedar)
> *Ostrya virginiana* (hophornbeam)

Sparse shrubs may include *Rhus aromatica* (fragrant sumac), possibly *Rosa spp.* and occasionally *Cornus florida* (flowering dogwood)

The herbaceous layer is patchy but may be quite diverse. Local graminoids include *Carex pensylvanica* (Pennsylvania sedge), *Danthonia spicata* (poverty oatgrass), *Elymus hystrix* (bottlebrush grass) and *Poa compressa* (Canada bluegrass)

Among local associated forbs may be:

> *Anemone virginiana* (Virginia anemone)
> *Antennaria plantaginifolia* (woman's tobacco)
> *Aquilegia canadensis* (red columbine)
> *Arabis lyrata* (lyrate rockcress)
> *Asclepias verticillata* (whorled milkweed)
> *Cynoglossum officinale* (gypsyflower)
> *Euphorbia corollata* (flowering spurge)
> *Galium pilosum* (hairy bedstraw)
> *Helianthus divaricatus* (woodland sunflower)
> *Heuchera americana* (American alumnroot)
> *Houstonia longifolia* (longleaf summer bluet)
> *Minuartia michauxii* (Michaux's stitchwort)
> *Packera obovata* (roundleaf ragwort)
> *Paronychia montana* (mountain nailwort)
> *Penstemon hirsutus* (hairy beardtongue)
> *Phlox subulata* (moss phlox)
> *Pycnanthemum incanum* (hoary mountainmint)
> *Scutellaria ovata* (heartleaf skullcap)
> *Silene caroliniana ssp. pensylvanica* (Pennsylvania catchfly)
> *Sisyrinchium mucronatum* (needletip blue-eyed grass)
> *Solidago ulmifolia* (elmleaf goldenrod)
> *Symphyotrichum undulatum* (wavyleaf aster)
> *Viola spp.* (violets)

## Xeric Oak Shale Woodland

**Formal name:** *Quercus prinus / Quercus ilicifolia / Danthonia spicata Woodland*

### Environmental summary

**Where it is found:** Low elevations of the central Appalachians, from Pennsylvania south into Maryland, West Virginia and Virginia, on usually steep, west- to south-facing middle to upper slopes, typically with exposed mineral soils, loose stones and many shale outcrops. Often found on the borders of shale barrens, with slopes generally convex in at least one direction and very low soil moisture.

**Soil information:** extremely acidic — typically pH 4.4 — and shallow, with low calcium and magnesium levels, but high levels of aluminum and iron. Common bedrock may include Devonian and Ordovician shales or Cambrian metashale. The nature of the soil is regarded as a major ecological factor in maintaining the woodland, but some stands may also have been impacted by periodic fire.

**Characteristics:** an open to very open woodland on steep shale slopes, dominated by *Quercus prinus* (chestnut oak), where canopy trees are often gnarled and stunted.

### Vegetation

Joining *Quercus prinus* (chestnut oak) in the overstory are generally minor associates *Quercus rubra* (Northern red oak) and *Carya glabra* (Pignut hickory). *Pinus virginiana* (Virginia pine) may appear in some stands and be entirely absent from others.

Found in a patchy shrub layer are:
*Amelanchier arborea* (common service-
berry)
*Quercus ilicifolia* (bear oak)
*Rosa carolina* (Carolina rose)
*Vaccinium pallidum* (Blue Ridge blueberry)
*Vaccinium stamineum* (deerberry)
*Viburnum rafinesqueanum* (downy arrow-
wood)

A patchy, sparse herb layer includes a variety
of graminoids and forbs adapted to dry, arid hab-
itats. Locally observed are:
*Carex pensylvanica* (Pennsylvania sedge)
*Cunila origanoides* (common dittany)
*Danthonia spicata* (poverty oatgrass)
*Helianthus laevigatus* (smooth sunflower)
*Houstonia longifolia* (longleaf summer
bluet)
*Paronychia montana* (mountain nailwort)
*Polygonatum biflorum* (Solomon's seal)
*Potentilla canadensis* (dwarf cinquefoil)
*Silene caroliniana ssp. pensylvanica* (Penn-
sylvania catchfly)
*Solidago bicolor* (white goldenrod)
*Symphyotrichum undulatum* (wavyleaf as-
ter)

## Red Oak - Heath Woodland

**Formal name:** *Quercus rubra - (Quercus prinus)
/ Vaccinium spp. / Deschampsia flexuosa* Woodland

### Environmental Summary

**Where it is found:** Dry low- to mid-elevation
summits and south-facing upper slopes with
prominent, exposed bed-
rock.

**Soil information:** shallow, well-drained, acidic,
nutrient-poor gravels and
coarse sands.

**Characteristics:**
droughty soils and in-
creased light on the forest
floor allow drier species
to predominate. To main-
tain *Quercus rubra* at more
dry-mesic sites, fire may

be required. Canopy cover ranges from open and
patchy to closed depending on site conditions. It
covers a usually extensive dwarf-shrub layer and
a sparse tall-shrub layer. Herb cover is scattered
and variable while bryoid cover is limited to small
scattered patches on the rocky substrate.

### Vegetation

Scattered and often stunted *Quercus rubra*
(northern red oak) dominates the canopy. De-
pending on geography, minor and scattered as-
sociates may include:
*Acer rubrum* (red maple)
*Betula lenta* (sweet birch)
*Betula papyrifera* (paper birch)
*Betula populifolia* (silver birch)
*Pinus rigida* (pitch pine)
*Pinus strobus* (eastern white pine)
*Quercus coccinea* (scarlet oak)
*Quercus prinus* (chestnut oak)
*Quercus velutina* (black oak)

Tall shrubs may include *Quercus ilicifolia* (bear
oak), *Hamamelis virginiana* (witch hazel), *Amelanchier spp.* (serviceberry), and *Prunus pensylvanica* (pin cherry).

Heaths heavily dominate the dwarf-shrub lay-
er. Reported are:
*Comptonia peregrina* (sweetfern)
*Gaylussacia baccata* (black huckleberry)
*Gaylussacia frondosa* (blue huckleberry)
*Kalmia angustifolia* (sheep laurel)
*Vaccinium angustifolium* (lowbush blue-
berry)
*Vaccinium myrtilloides* (velvetleaf huckle-
berry)
*Vaccinium pallidum* (Blue Ridge blueberry)

The herbaceous layer is composed of:
*Aralia nudicaulis* (wild sarsaparilla)
*Carex lucorum* (Blue Ridge sedge)
*Comandra umbellata* (bastard toadflax)
*Danthonia spicata* (poverty oatgrass)
*Deschampsia flexuosa* (wavy hairgrass)
*Epigaea repens* (trailing arbutus)
*Gaultheria procumbens* (teaberry)
*Melampyrum lineare* (narrowleaf cow-
wheat)
*Polygala paucifolia* (gaywings)
*Pteridium aquilinum* (northern bracken
fern)

The bryophyte layer includes *Polytrichum commune* (common haircap moss), *Leucobryum glaucum* (leucobryum moss) and others.

## Basswood - Ash - Dogwood Woodland

**Formal name:** *Tilia americana - Fraxinus americana / Cornus florida Woodland*

### Environmental summary

**Where it is found:** mountainous sections of the central Appalachians, primarily in Maryland and West Virginia, as well as Pennsylvania.

**Soil information:** pockets within calcareous to circumneutral talus comprised of large boulders, or on rock outcrops.

**Characteristics:** open, generally bouldery, calcareous to circumneutral woodlands with a canopy of *Acer saccharum, Fraxinus americana, Tilia americana*, and *Quercus rubra*.

### Vegetation

The canopy is dominated by a combination of *Tilia americana* (American basswood), *Fraxinus americana* (white ash) and *Cornus florida* (flowering dogwood), with *Acer saccharum* (sugar maple) and *Quercus rubra* (red oak) as occasional associates.

A scattered, viney shrub layer includes *Acer spicatum* (mountain maple), *Acer pensylvanicum* (striped maple) and *Parthenocissus quinquefolia* (Virginia creeper).

Herbs are reported to include:
*Adlumia fungosa* (Allegheny vine)
*Antennaria plantaginifolia* (pussy-toes)
*Carex umbellata* (parasol sedge)
*Clematis occidentalis* (western blue virgins-bower)
*Cystopteris bulbifera* (bulblet bladderfern)
*Geranium robertianum* (Robert geranium)

## Dry Oak - Hickory Woodland

**Formal name:** *Carya (glabra, ovata) - Fraxinus americana - Quercus spp. Forest*

### Environmental Summary

**Where it is found:** Mid to upper level dry to mesic slopes, coves and ridgetops, predominantly on southern or eastern exposures. Found throughout the Lower New England - Northern Piedmont, Central Appalachians, Western Allegheny Plateau, and High Allegheny Plateau

**Soil information:** slightly acidic to circumneutral, rich well-drained loams or sandy loams and occasionally rocky soils.

**Characteristics:** A relatively open canopy, sparse shrub layer, and dense herbaceous layer impart a park-like appearance to many of these forests. Because total canopy can exceed 60 percent, it is technically a forest rather than a woodland. Also, much of the herbaceous layer are shade species, with those preferring high light levels typically found only in small openings.

### Vegetation

The tree canopy ranges from closed to partially open and co-dominated by *Quercus* and *Carya* species, with *Fraxinus americana* common but not abundant. Cover is typically about 20 percent hickory. Dominant species include:
*Carya cordiformis* (bitternut hickory)
*Carya glabra* (pignut hickory)
*Carya ovalis* (red hickory)
*Quercus alba* (white oak)
*Quercus rubra* (northern red oak)
*Quercus velutina* (black oak)

Common associates include *Acer saccharum* (sugar maple), *Tilia americana* (American basswood), and *Celtis occidentalis* (common hackberry).

Ericaceous species are present in a variable shrub layer, but not especially prominent. Commonly reported shrubs include:
*Carpinus caroliniana* (American hornbeam)
*Corylus spp.*
*Ostrya virginiana* (hop hornbeam)
*Vaccinium spp.*

*Viburnum acerifolium* (maple leaf viburnum)
*Viburnum rafinesquianum* (downy arrowwood)

Reported in a diverse herbaceous layer are:
*Actaea rubra* (red baneberry)
*Ageratina altissima* (white snakeroot)
*Antennaria plantaginifolia* (plantain-leaved pussytoes)
*Arabis canadensis* (sicklepod)
*Asclepias quadrifolia* (fourleaf milkweed)
*Asplenium platyneuron* (ebony spleenwort)
*Aureolaria pedicularia* (fernleaf false foxglove)
*Carex blanda* (eastern woodland sedge)
*Carex laxiculmis* (spreading sedge)
*Carex laxiflora* (broad looseflower sedge)

*Carex pensylvanica* (Pennsylvania sedge)
*Carex retroflexa* (reflexed sedge)
*Carex siccata* (dryspike sedge)
*Desmodium glutinosum* (pointedleaf ticktrefoil)
*Desmodium paniculatum* (panicledleaf ticktrefoil)
*Desmodium rotundifolium* (prostrate ticktrefoil)
*Hepatica nobilis var. obtusa* (round-lobed hepatica)
*Hieracium venosum* (rattlesnakeweed)
*Polygonatum pubescens* (hairy Solomon's seal)
*Schizachryium scoparium* (little bluestem)
*Solidago odora* (anisescented goldenrod)
*Viola pedata* (birdfoot violet)
*Viola rotundifolia* (roundleaf yellow violet)

---

## Black Walnut Bottomland Forest

Formal name: *Juglans nigra — Fraxinus americana / Lindera benzoin Forest*

### Environmental summary

**Where it is found:** drainage swales and floodplains of smaller streams in the Delaware River valley, as well as mid to high floodplain terraces. A somewhat unique community found on island terraces in the Delaware Water Gap National Recreation Area.

**Soil information:** ranges from silt loam to gravelly sandy loams, with Venango silt loam, Hoosic-Otisville complex and Delaware fine sandy loam being frequently reported.

**Characteristics:** strongly dominated by *Juglans nigra* (black walnut), with a sparse shrub and subcanopy layer.

### Vegetation

Canopy is more than 50 percent *Juglans nigra* (black walnut) and usually 60 to 100 feet. Associates can include *Fraxinus americana* (white ash), *Ulmus americana* (American elm) and *Acer saccharum* (sugar maple).

Subcanopy is generally open, 30 to 45 feet and may include scattered individuals of canopy trees as well as *Celtis occidentalis* (common hackberry), *Carpinus caroliniana* (American hornbeam) and *Carya cordiformis* (bitternut hickory).

Tall shrubs, ranging from 6 to 15 feet, are often sparse and can include *Viburnum prunifolium* (blackhaw), *Lindera benzoin* (northern spicebush) and *F. americana* saplings.

The short shrub layer is less than 6 feet and can vary in density, but is most often sparse, with *L. benzoin* and *V. prunifolium*, along with the invasive exotic *Rosa multiflora* (multiflora rose) reported.

Within the herb layer, one or a few species dominate variable patches. Characteristic are *Podophyllum peltatum* (mayapple), *Impatiens capensis* (jewelweed), *Circaea lutetiana ssp canadensis* (broadleaf enchanter's nightshade) and *Ageratina altissima var. altissima* (white snakeroot). Vines are occasional but rarely abundant; *Parthenocissus quinquefolia* (Virginia creeper) is a typical vine species.

# *Coniferous forests*

## Spruce Swamp Forest - Bog Complex

**Formal name:** *Picea rubens - (Tsuga canadensis) / Rhododendron maximum Saturated Forest*

### *Environmental summary*

**Where it is found:** generally flat terrain in poorly drained bottomlands of small streams at high elevations in the central to southern Appalachians and isolated upland depressions on ridgetops in the Allegheny Plateau of Pennsylvania and New York.

**Soil information:** Acidic organic matter over thin rocky soils with poor drainage.

**Characteristics:** Flooding is rare and soils are reported to be seasonally to semi-permanently saturated because of high water tables or seepage from adjacent slopes. Some theories suggest it is the late successional stage of primary succession from originally extensive and open bog areas, and will remain a forest unless the canopy loses to tree blowdown or logging.

### *Vegetation*

The canopy is dominated by *Picea rubens* (red spruce) or mixtures of *P. rubens* and *Tsuga canadensis* (eastern hemlock). Associates found in the canopy or subcanopy include *Betula alleghaniensis* (yellow birch), *Acer rubrum var. rubrum* (red maple), *Taxus canadensis* (Canada yew), and *Amelanchier arborea* (common serviceberry).

An often dense shrub layer is dominated by

*Rhododendron maximum* (great rhododendron). Other local associates may include:

> *Ilex verticillata* (common winterberry)
> *Kalmia latifolia* (mountain laurel)
> *Photinia melanocarpa* (black chokeberry)
> *Vaccinium spp.* (blueberries)
> *Viburnum nudum var. cassinoides* (witherod)

The herbaceous layer is sparse, with the majority of herbaceous species restricted to openings, and includes:

> *Carex folliculata* (northern long sedge)
> *Carex trisperma* (three-seeded sedge)
> *Dryopteris campyloptera* (mountain woodfern)
> *Glyceria melicaria* (melic mannagrass)
> *Huperzia lucidula* (shining clubmoss)
> *Maianthemum canadense* (Canada mayflower)
> *Oclemena acuminata* (whorled wood aster)
> *Osmunda cinnamomea* (cinnamon fern)
> *Osmunda regalis* (royal fern)

The bryophyte layer is of variable cover but is dominated by sphagnum, especially in small depressions. Other nonvascular plants include *Bazzania trilobata* and *Leucobryum glaucum*.

## Appalachian Spruce - Fir Swamp

**Formal name:** *Picea rubens - Abies balsamea / Gaultheria hispidula / Osmunda cinnamomea / Sphagnum spp. Forest*

### *Environmental summary*

**Where it is found:** wetland flats and basins on the glaciated plateau and across the northern Appalachians, typically in small basins or along the margins of larger drainage basins or lowland slopes, usually in areas with some surface seepage.

**Soil information:** Saturated mineral soils, sometimes with a shallow peat layer.

**Characteristics:** Boreal-type trees and shrubs reflect the cool environmental conditions.

*Vegetation*

A canopy dominated by *Picea rubens* (red spruce) and *Abies balsamea* (balsam fir) can range from partial (50 percent) to dense, and the shrub and herbaceous layers vary from sparse to dense depending on available light. Canopy associates include *Picea mariana* (black spruce) or *Larix laricina* (tamarack).

Frequent gaps in the canopy result in locally dense shrub cover, which often includes:

> *Gaultheria hispidula* (creeping snowberry)
>
> *Kalmia angustifolia* (sheep laurel)
>
> *Nemopanthus mucronatus* (catberry)
>
> *Sorbus americana* (American mountain ash)
>
> *Vaccinium angustifolium* (lowbush blueberry)
>
> *Viburnum nudum var. cassinoides* (witherod)

Most common in the herbaceous layer are *Osmunda cinnamomea* (cinnamon fern) and *Carex trisperma* (three-seeded carex). Common associates reported locally include *Dalibarda repens* (robin runaway), *Coptis trifolia* (three-leaf goldthread), and *Clintonia borealis* (bluebead). *Symplocarpus foetidus* (skunk cabbage) may be locally abundant in coastal settings.

Sphagnum mosses dominate the bryophyte layer, especially *Sphagnum girgensohnii*. Also observed are *Bazzania trilobata*, *Pleurozium schreberi*, and *Aulacomnium palustre*.

## Red Spruce Swamp

**Formal name:** *Picea rubens / Rhododendron maximum - Kalmia latifolia / Eriophorum virginicum / Sphagnum spp. Forest*

*Environmental summary*

**Where it is found:** headwater basins at higher elevations. Only six occurrences within the Allegheny Mountains region of West Virginia and to the Pocono Plateau and northeastern Pennsylvania are known and it is ranked as imperiled. It is limited by its requirement for saturated peat conditions along flat or very gently sloping headwater basins at higher elevation. The Pennsylvania state rank for this type is Imperiled - Vulnerable.

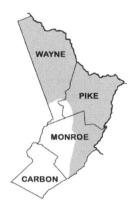

**Soil information:** Soils are moderately to very poorly drained peat over rich clay.

**Characteristics:** Microtopography is characterized by a mix of rounded peat hummocks and irregular moss-covered hummocks formed over tree roots, woody stem clusters, and decaying wood. The community is characterized by an open canopy of stunted, inundation-stressed trees with a diverse shrub and herb layer growing on hummock-forming bryophytes.

*Vegetation*

The canopy is dominated by *Tsuga canadensis* (eastern hemlock) and *Picea rubens* (red spruce), occasionally including low cover of *Acer rubrum* (red maple) or *Betula alleghaniensis var. alleghaniensis* (yellow birch). Canopy height is less than 50 feet and sometimes as low as 15 feet.

The shrub layer includes the canopy species and *Rhododendron maximum* (great rhododendron), *Kalmia latifolia* (mountain laurel), *Nemopanthus mucronatus* (catberry), and *Ilex verticillata* (common winterberry). Other species that occasionally occur with low cover in the tall-shrub layer include:

> *Amelanchier laevis* (Allegheny serviceberry)
>
> *Hamamelis virginiana* (witch hazel)
>
> *Ilex montana* (mountain holly)
>
> *Photinia pyrifolia* (red chokeberry)
>
> *Sorbus americana* (American mountain ash)
>
> *Vaccinium corymbosum* (highbush blue-

berry)

*Viburnum nudum var. cassinoides* (withe-rod)

The herbaceous layer typically includes

*Carex gynandra* (nodding sedge)

*Carex trisperma var. trisperma* (three-seed sedge)

*Dennstaedtia punctilobula* (hayscented fern)

*Drosera rotundifolia var. rotundifolia* (roundleaf sundew)

*Eriophorum virginicum* (tawny cottongrass)

*Glyceria melicaria* (melic mannagrass)

*Juncus effusus* (common rush)

*Maianthemum trifolium* (three-leaf false lily-of-the-valley)

*Oclemena acuminata* (whorled wood aster)

*Osmunda cinnamomea var. cinnamomea* (cinnamon fern)

*Rubus hispidus* (bristly dewberry)

*Solidago uliginosa* (bog goldenrod)

Nonvascular plants are dominated by *Sphagnum spp.* and *Polytrichum commune.*

## Red Pine Forest

**Formal name:** *Pinus resinosa / Menziesia pilosa / Polypodium appalachianum Forest*

### Environmental summary

**Where it is found:** steep, north to northwest-facing slopes, usually near summits, on sandy acidic soils over sandstone. Ranges from the Mid-Atlantic states to the western Great Lakes and north-central Minnesota and adjacent Ontario.

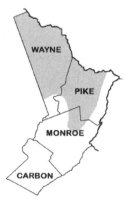

**Soil information:** dry to fresh, deep mineral soil - usually coarse sand or coarse loam soils, as well as some fine sands and silts - over Precambrian Shield bedrock, commonly 20 to 25 inches deep. Soil deposition can be both morainal and glaciofluvial.

**Characteristics:** dry to mesic pine forests with a pine overstory and a poorly developed under-story. This ecosystem is likely to be fire-dependent, with studies suggesting presettlement *Pinus resinosa* communities were maintained by a combination of ground fires every 20 to 30 years and severe crown fires every 100 to 150 years.

### Vegetation

*Pinus resinosa* (red pine) strongly dominates the canopy, and frequent associates include *Betula lenta* (sweet birch), *Pinus rigida* (pitch pine), and *Quercus rubra* (red oak). Occasionally reported locally are *Pinus strobus* (eastern white pine), *Sorbus americana* (American mountain ash), and *Pinus virginiana* (Virginia pine).

Subcanopy species may include:

*Acer pensylvanicum* (striped maple)

*Acer rubrum* (red maple)

*Amelanchier arborea* (serviceberry)

*Betula lenta* (sweet birch)

*Hamamelis virginiana* (witch hazel)

Reported in shrub layers are:

*Gaultheria procumbens* (wintergreen)

*Gaylussacia baccata* (black huckleberry)

*Kalmia latifolia* (mountain laurel)

*Linnaea borealis* (twinflower)

*Rhododendron prinophyllum* (early azalea)

*Ribes spp.* (current)

*Smilax herbacea* (smooth carrionflower)

*Vaccinium angustifolium* (lowbush blueberry)

*Vaccinium myrtilloides* (velvetleaf huckleberry)

The sparse herbaceous layer, which may be less than 10 percent depending on canopy cover and moisture, can locally include:

*Actaea racemosa* (black cohosh)

*Ageratina altissima var. altissima* (white snakeroot)

*Agrostis spp.* (bentgrass)

*Aralia nudicaulis* (wild sarsaparilla)

*Asteraceae spp.* (asters)

*Carex argyrantha* (hay sedge)

*Carex brunnescens* (brownish sedge)

*Danthonia spicata* (poverty oat grass)

*Deschampsia flexuosa* (wavy hairgrass)

*Dryopteris intermedia* (intermediate wood-fern)

*Dryopteris marginalis* (marginal woodfern)

*Epigaea repens* (trailing arbutus)

*Galium spp.* (bedstraw)
*Maianthemum stellatum* (starry false lily of the valley)
*Milium effusum* (American milletgrass)
*Polygala paucifolia* (gaywings)
*Polypodium appalachianum* (Appalachian polypody)
*Potentilla canadensis* (dwarf cinquefoil)
*Pteridium aquilinum* (northern bracken fern)

Mosses are often extensive, up to 35 percent coverage. Often reported are *Dicranum* spp. and *Pleurozium schreberi* (Schreber's big red stem moss).

## White Pine - Eastern Hemlock Forest

**Formal name:** *Pinus strobus - Tsuga canadensis / Acer pensylvanicum / Polystichum acrostichoides Forest*

### Environmental Summary

**Where it is found:** mid-slopes in the northern part of the Central Appalachians and in ravines along the Susquehanna river; uncommon but not rare.

**Soil information:** dry-mesic, well-drained, nutrient-poor sandy acidic soils

**Characteristics:** Dominated by *Pinus strobus* and/or *Tsuga canadensis* of varying amounts on dry-mesic sites with infertile, sandy soils.

### Vegetation

The vegetation is a closed-canopy conifer forest dominated by *Pinus strobus* and/or *Tsuga canadensis.*

Canopy associates include:
*Acer rubrum* (red maple)
*Betula alleghaniensis* (yellow birch)
*Betula lenta* (sweet birch)
*Fagus grandifolia* (American beech)
*Liriodendron tulipifera* (tuliptree)
*Quercus rubra* (northern red oak)

The sparse shrub layer contains:
*Acer pensylvanicum* (striped maple)
*Acer spicatum* (mountain maple)
*Hamamelis virginiana* (witch hazel)
*Rhododendron maximum* (great rhododendron)
*Viburnum acerifolium* (mapleleaf viburnum)

The sparse herb layer includes:
*Cypripedium acaule* (pink lady's slipper)
*Gaultheria procumbens* (teaberry)
*Lycopodium spp.* (club mosses)
*Maianthemum canadense* (Canada mayflower)
*Medeola virginiana* (Indian cucumber)
*Mitchella repens* (partridgeberry)
*Polystichum acrostichoides* (Christmas fern)
*Trientalis borealis* (starflower)

## Eastern White Pine Forest

**Formal name:** *Pinus strobus - Tsuga canadensis Lower New England / Northern Piedmont Forest*

### Environmental Summary

**Where it is found:** moderately to steeply sloping sites or in sheltered ravines.

**Soil information:** moderately to extremely well-drained, dry-mesic to mesic loamy sands, silt loam and sandy loams, often stony or bouldery and over shales.

**Characteristics:** dominated by *Pinus strobus*, often in association with White Pine - Oak Forest. The major natural disturbance in this forest type is generally single-tree blow downs. Fire is not a significant feature of this forest type.

### Vegetation

The characteristic canopy for this forest association is dominated by *Pinus strobus* (eastern white pine) with cover exceeding 50 per cent. However, in somewhat sheltered ravines on south-facing slopes, *Tsuga canadensis* (eastern hemlock) dominates all layers and can exceed 50 per cent coverage.

Canopy trees range in height from 60 to 130 feet and usually cover 80 to 90 percent of the stand. Occasional associates may include:

*Acer rubrum* (red maple)
*Acer saccharum* (sugar maple)
*Betula lenta* (sweet birch)
*Carya alba* (mockernut hickory)
*Pinus rigida* (pitch pine)
*Quercus rubra* (northern red oak)
*Quercus velutina* (black oak)
*Tsuga canadensis* (eastern hemlock)

Depending on geography, other associates may include:

*Acer pensylvanicum* (striped maple)
*Betula alleghaniensis* (yellow birch)
*Betula papyrifera* (paper birch)
*Betula populifolia* (gray birch)
*Fraxinus americana* (white ash)
*Prunus serotina* (black cherry)

Subcanopy trees cover 10 to 40 percent of the area, range from 15 to 100 feet and are generally eastern white pine and the same associates as the canopy.

The tall- and short-shrub layers are absent to sparse to absent (0 to 20 per cent cover). Common species include:

*Hamamelis virginiana* (witch-hazel)
*Kalmia latifolia* (mountain laurel)
*Rhododendron maximum* (great rhododendron)
*Vaccinium angustifolium* (lowbush blueberry)
*Viburnum acerifolium* (mapleleaf viburnum)
Seedlings of canopy trees

The herb layer is also characteristically sparse, with 5 per cent or less cover. Scattered common species are reported to include:

*Aralia nudicalis* (wild sarsaparilla)
*Dryopteris carthusiana* (spinulose woodfern)
*Dryopteris intermedia* (intermediate woodfern)
*Dryopteris marginalis* (marginal woodfern),
*Gaultheria procumbens* (teaberry)
*Maianthemum canadense* (Canada mayflower)
*Medeola virginiana* (Indian cucumber)
*Mitchella repens* (partridgeberry)

*Monotropa uniflora* (Indian pipe)
*Polypodium virginianum* (rock polypody)
*Polystichum acrostichoides* (Christmas fern)
*Thelypteris noveboracensis* (New York fern)
*Trientalis borealis* (starflower)
*Uvularia sessilifolia* (sessileleaf bellwort)

*Deschampsia flexuosa* (wavy hairgrass) and other grasses may be present in small openings and gaps.

Nonvascular plants tend to be sparse but can include *Leucobryum albidum* and *Polytrichum* and *Dicranum* species.

## Mixed Pine - Hillside Blueberry Forest

**Formal name:** *Pinus virginiana - Pinus (rigida, echinata) - (Quercus prinus) / Vaccinium pallidum Forest*

### Environmental summary

**Where it is found:** narrow ridges and knobs, steep upper slopes, bluff and cliff tops, and other exposed sites, usually facing the south, southeast or southwest.

**Soil information:** excessively drained, infertile, shallow sandy and rocky.

**Characteristics:** often low stature, with a somewhat open to closed canopy, sparse to very dense shrub cover dominated by ericaceous species, and a thin herb layer.

### Vegetation

*Pinus virginiana* (Virginia pine) is the canopy dominant throughout the range of the type. Carbon County is locally the extent of *P. virginiana's* northward range, although it appears further north elsewhere in Pennsylvania. In some parts of the range, other pine species, notably *Pinus rigida* (pitch pine) and *Pinus strobus* (eastern white pine) may be significant canopy associates, as well as dry-site oak species such as *Quercus prinus* (chestnut oak) and *Quercus coccinea* (scarlet oak). Some *Acer rubrum* (red maple) and *Nyssa sylvatica* (black gum) are reported.

Canopy height is relatively short, usually under 65 feet and tending to more open than closed. It decreases as the immediate habitat becomes less hospitable. Deciduous species may form a subcanopy or sapling layer, especially in areas where fire has been prevented.

Common dominants in the shrub layer include *Vaccinium pallidum* (Blue Ridge blueberry), *Vaccinium stamineum* (upland highbush blueberry), *Gaylussacia baccata* (black huckleberry), and *Kalmia latifolia* (mountain laurel).

Herbs vary with geography but are typical of infertile, xeric habitats. Leaf litter often dominates the ground layer. Some typical herbs in this forest are:

> *Antennaria plantaginifolia* (plantain pussytoes)
> *Baptisia tinctoria* (wild indigo)
> *Carex albicans var. albicans* (white-tinged sedge)
> *Chimaphila maculata* (striped prince's pine)
> *Danthonia spicata* (poverty oatgrass)
> *Dichanthelium commutatum* (variable panicgrass)
> *Dichanthelium dichotomum* (cypress panicgrass)
> *Epigaea repens* (trailing arbutus)
> *Euphorbia corollata* (flowering spurge)
> *Gaultheria procumbens* (teaberry)
> *Hieracium gronovii* (queendevil)
> *Hieracium venosum* (rattlesnakeweed)
> *Hypoxis hirsuta* (common goldstar)
> *Krigia biflora* (two-flower dwarf dandelion)
> *Lespedeza violacea* (violet lespedeza)
> *Opuntia humifusa* (eastern prickly pear cactus)
> *Pteridium aquilinum* (northern bracken fern)
> *Schizachyrium scoparium* (little bluestem)
> *Solidago squarrosa* (stout goldenrod)
> *Tephrosia virginiana* (Virginia tephrosia)

## Hemlock - Hardwood Swamp

**Formal name:** *Tsuga canadensis - Betula alleghaniensis / Ilex verticillata / Sphagnum spp. Forest*

### Environmental Summary

**Where it is found:** throughout and common much of Pennsylvania, New York and New England in glaciated areas south of spruce-fir regions, in poorly drained basins over bedrock or compacted till.

**Soil information:** Usually acidic, ranging from saturated muck to imperfectly drained mineral soils and are often acidic. These organic soils remain saturated for most or all of the growing season, but may partially dry in smaller basins.

**Characteristics:** "Pocket swamps" are found in upland valleys in bedrock depressions, on lower slopes, or adjacent to streams and lakes, often transitional between upland and wetland communities. The canopy is generally nearly complete; shrubs are sparse, and while the herbaceous layer may be well developed, it is often dominated by ferns. Bryophytes are extensive.

### Vegetation

*Tsuga canadensis* (northern hemlock) may dominate the canopy or be mixed with other trees, such as:

> *Acer rubrum* (red maple)
> *Betula alleghaniensis* (yellow birch)
> *Fraxinus nigra* (black ash)
> *Nyssa sylvatica* (black gum)
> *Pinus strobus* (eastern white pine)

The shrub layer is thin and scattered. Often reported are

> *Ilex verticillata* (winterberry)
> *Lyonia ligustrina* (maleberry)
> *Nemopanthus mucronatus* (catberry)
> *Vaccinium corymbosum* (blueberry)
> *Viburnum nudum var. cassinoides* (witherod)

In the herbaceous layer, the most prominent reported ferns include *Osmunda cinnamomea* (cinnamon fern), *Osmunda regalis* (royal fern), and *Onoclea sensibilis* (sensitive fern). Associates may include

> *Carex disperma* (softleaf sedge)
> *Carex folliculata* (northern long sedge)
> *Carex trisperma* (threeseeded sedge)

*Coptis trifolia* (threeleaf goldthread)
*Dryopteris cristata* (crested woodfern)
*Maianthemum canadense* (Canada mayflower)
*Mitchella repens* (partridgeberry)
*Rubus pubescens* (dwarf red blackberry)

Bryophytes include *Sphagnum girgensohnii* (Girgensohn's sphagnum), *Sphagnum palustre* (prairie sphagnum) other Sphagnum species, as well as *Pleurozium schreberi* (Schreber's big red stem moss ) and *Bazzania trilobata*.

## Hemlock - Great Laurel Swamp

**Formal name:** *Tsuga canadensis / Rhododendron maximum / Sphagnum spp. Forest*

### Environmental summary

**Where it is found:** upland bedrock depressions, low slopes, around small streams, lakes and drainages in the central Appalachians, southeastern New York and northern New Jersey.

**Soil information:** acidic mucky peat or Alden mucky silt loam over a poorly drained substrate.

**Characteristics:** *Tsuga canadensis* forests that are semipermanently to permanently flooded, usually with vegetation on hummocks surrounded by standing water. These wetlands commonly flood from beaver or man-made impoundments. Hemlocks in many stands can decline due to the hemlock wooly adelgid and/or recent flooding resulting from beaver activity.

### Vegetation

The canopy is dominated by *Tsuga canadensis* (eastern hemlock), which covers at least 25 percent of the area. Co-dominants may include:
*Acer rubrum* (red maple)
*Betula alleghaniensis* (yellow birch)
*Nyssa sylvatica* (black gum)

The canopy trees range from 50 to 75 feet and cover between 50 and 90 percent of the surface. Subcanopy trees - typically *T. canadensis* and *A. rubrum* - are 15 to 40 feet and cover 10 to 30 per-

cent of the area.

A dense thicket of *Rhododendron maximum* (great laurel) or saplings of the canopy trees comprises the shrub layer, representing 30 to 70 percent coverage. Reported as common associates are:
*Hamamelis virginiana* (American witch-hazel)
*Ilex verticillata* (winterberry)
*Lindera benzoin* (northern spicebush)
*Nemopanthus mucronatus* (catberry)
*Rhododendron viscosum* (swamp azalea)
*Vaccinium corymbosum* (highbush blueberry)

A herbaceous layer can range from sparse to dense and include:
*Bidens connata* (purple stem beggerticks)
*Boehmeria cylindrica* (smallspike false nettle)
*Calla palustris* (water arum)
*Carex comosa* (longhair sedge)
*Carex disperma* (softleaf sedge)
*Carex folliculata* (northern long sedge)
*Carex intumescens* (greater bladder sedge)
*Carex lurida* (shallow sedge)
*Carex stricta* (tussock sedge)
*Carex trisperma* (threeseeded sedge)
*Carex vulpinoidea* (fox sedge)
*Coptis trifolia* (threeleaf goldthread)
*Cornus canadensis* (bunchberry)
*Impatiens capensis* (jewelweed)
*Iris versicolor* (harlequin blueflag)
*Leersia oryzoides* (rice cutgrass)
*Lycopus uniflorus* (northern bugleweed)
*Maianthemum canadense* (Canada mayflower)
*Onoclea sensibilis* (sensitive fern)
*Osmunda cinnamomea* (cinnamon fern)
*Osmunda regalis* (royal fern)
*Symplocarpus foetidus* (skunk cabbage)
*Thelypteris palustris* (eastern marsh fern)
*Trientalis borealis* (starflower)
*Viola spp.* (violets)

Sphagnum mosses strongly dominate a well-developed bryophyte layer. Other mosses may include: *Aulacomnium palustre* (aulacomnium moss), *Hypnum imponens* (hypnum moss), and *Leucobryum glaucum* (leucobryum moss) on drier hummocks.

# *Coniferous woodlands*

## Red Spruce Woodland

Formal name: Picea rubens / Vaccinium angustifolium High Allegheny Plateau Woodland

### *Environmental summary*

**Where it is found:** acidic bedrock outcrops, talus or summits on the High Allegheny Plateau and the Allegheny Front of the Central Appalachians.

**Soil information:** soil is sparse and shallow, with often only a thin layer of duff over and generally occurring in cracks and pore spaces between rocks, and characterized by very high organic matter and low macro- and micronutrients.

**Characteristics:** a stunted and open canopy of Picea rubens (red spruce) over many heath shrubs and lichens. Seasonal temperatures range from very cold winter days to hot summer days, with precipitation toward the lower range for red spruce in the Appalachians.

### *Vegetation*

With about 40 percent cover, the canopy is strongly dominated by *Picea rubens* (red spruce). Associates can include:

*Acer rubrum* (red maple)
*Amelanchier laevis* (Allegheny serviceberry)
*Betula alleghaniensis var. alleghaniensis* (yellow birch)
*Pinus rigida* (pitch pine)
*Sorbus americana* (American mountain ash)
*Tsuga canadensis* (eastern hemlock)

*Kalmia latifolia* (mountain laurel), *Nemopanthus mucronatus* (catberry) and *Rhododendron maximum* (great laurel), along with regenerating tree saplings, dominate the tall-shrub layer. A diverse short-shrub layer frequently includes:

*Gaylussacia baccata* (black huckleberry)
*Menziesia pilosa* (minniebush)
*Photinia melanocarpa* (black chokeberry)
*Vaccinium angustifolium* (lowbush blueberry)

Occasional shrubs may include:

*Acer pensylvanicum* (striped maple)
*Acer spicatum* (mountain maple)
*Gaultheria procumbens* (wintergreen)
*Hamamelis virginiana* (witch hazel)
*Ilex montana* (mountain holly)
*Prunus pensylvanica var. pensylvanica* (pin cherry)
*Rhododendron prinophyllum* (early azalea)
*Ribes glandulosum* (skunk currant)
*Ribes rotundifolium* (Appalachian gooseberry)
*Vaccinium myrtilloides* (velvetleaf huckleberry)
*Viburnum nudum var. cassinoides* (witherod)

A sparse herbaceous layer may often include:

*Aralia nudicaulis* (wild sarsaparilla)
*Carex brunnescens* (brownish sedge)
*Deschampsia flexuosa var. flexuosa* (wavy hairgrass)
*Epigaea repens* (trailing arbutus)
*Maianthemum canadense* (Canada mayflower)
*Polypodium appalachianum* (Appalachian polypody)
*Pteridium aquilinum* (northern bracken fern)

Crutose lichens are very common in the nonvascular stratum, along with:

>*Cladina rangiferina* (greygreen reindeer lichen)
>*Umbilicaria muehlenbergii* (Muehlenberg's navel lichen)
>*Hypnum imponens* (hypnum moss)
>*Leucobryum glaucum* (leucobryum moss)
>*Pleurozium schreberi* (Schreber's big red stem moss)
>*Lasallia papulosa* (blistered naval lichen)

## Mesic Pine Barrens

**Formal name:** *Pinus rigida - Quercus ilicifolia - Rhododendron canadense Woodland*

### Environmental Summary

**Where it is found:** the Long Pond Barrens in Pennsylvania and the Shawangunk Ridge in New York. Some acreage in this rare community has been lost to development and road construction.

**Soil information:** The Monroe County area is relatively fine-textured, compact till, less permeable than the typical "pine barren" sands. The Poconos soils are seasonally wet in spots but subject to drought in summer.

**Characteristics:** Unlike all other dry pine barrens, this association occurs on deep, fine-loamy Illinoisan till. The origin of this association is uncertain, but there evidence suggests this community persists as a result of frequent fire. Shallow depressions within the barrens tend to form permanent closed basins and frost pockets that influence community composition.

The presence of *Rhododendron canadense* and some species of grasses and sedges is an important factor; the community is closely related to the ridgetop pitch pine-scrub oak associations and is considered to be critically imperiled.

The barrens occurs locally as part of a larger complex of *Pinus rigida - Quercus ilicifolia* vegetation locally known as the Long Pond Barrens system or Poconos Till Barrens.

### Vegetation

This community is essentially shrub-dominated with *Quercus ilicifolia* forming a dense tall-shrub layer of up to 10 feet and *Rhododendron canadense* and *Kalmia angustifolia* occurring in a lower shrub layer, often less than 3 feet. Taken as a group, they create an "interlocking shrub canopy" with greater than 60 percent cover.

Scattered *Pinus rigida* (pitch pine) and sometimes *Acer rubrum* (red maple) is usually present and a few other ericaceous shrubs, including *Vaccinium angustifolium* (lowbush blueberrry), *Gaultheria procumbens* (wintergreen), and *Gaylussacia baccata* (black huckleberry) are typical.

The herbaceous layer is characterized by:

>*Calamagrostis coarctata* (Arctic reedgrass)
>*Carex pensylvanica* (Pennsylvania sedge)
>*Deschampsia flexuosa* (wavy hairgrass)
>*Piptatherum racemosum* (blackseed ricegrass)
>*Pteridium aquilinum* (northern bracken fern)
>*Rubus hispidus* (bristly dewberry)

Other associates include:

>*Amianthium muscitoxicum* (flypoison)
>*Carex polymorpha* (variable sedge)
>*Doellingeria umbellata* (parasol whitetop)
>*Lygodium palmatum* (American climbing fern)
>*Melampyrum lineare* (narrowleaf cowwheat)

## Pitch Pine Rocky Summit

**Formal name:** *Pinus rigida / (Quercus ilicifolia) / Photinia melanocarpa / Deschampsia flexuosa Woodland*

### Environmental Summary

**Where it is found:** dry rocky ridges and summits of low to moderate elevations, anywhere from near sea level to about 1,700 feet.

**Soil information:** derived from acidic bedrock and are typically shallow, well to excessively drained, coarse sands or gravels that develop in pockets of the exposed bedrock expanses.

**Characteristics:** an element the Central Appalachian Pine-Oak Rocky Woodland, the open canopy features trees that are often stunted, usually less than 50 feet and sometimes less than 30 feet. Tall shrubs are scattered and not abundant, while the dwarf-shrub layer is moderately to well-developed — typically more than 20 percent cover and often even more dense. Herbs are sparse. The bryoid layer is of variable cover, with lichens prominent. The ground cover is bare rock and deciduous and coniferous litter. Fire is an important element in preservation.

### *Vegetation*

The canopy is dominated by *Pinus rigida* with a variable mixture of associates, including:

> *Acer rubrum* (red maple)
> *Betula lenta* (sweet birch)
> *Betula papyrifera* (paper birch)
> *Betula populifolia* (gray birch)
> *Carya glabra* (pignut hickory)
> *Picea rubens* (red spruce)
> *Pinus resinosa* (pitch pine)
> *Pinus strobus* (eastern white pine)
> *Prunus serotina* (black cherry)
> *Quercus prinus* (chestnut oak)
> *Quercus rubra* (northern red oak)

The tall-shrub layer is composed of scattered *Quercus ilicifolia* (bear oak), *Quercus prinoides* (dwarf chinkapin oak) and sometimes *Ilex mucronata* (catberry). The remaining shrub layer is dominated by:

> *Comptonia peregrina* (sweetfern)
> *Gaylussacia baccata* (black huckleberry),
> *Kalmia angustifolia* (sheep laurel)
> *Photinia melanocarpa* (black chokeberry)
> *Rhododendron canadense* (rhodora)
> *Vaccinium angustifolium* (lowbush blueberry)
> *Vaccinium myrtilloides* (velvetleaf huckleberry)
> *Vaccinium pallidum* (Blue Ridge blueberry)
> *Viburnum nudum* (possumhaw)

The herbaceous layer typically includes:

> *Aralia nudicaulis* (wild sarsaparilla)
> *Carex lucorum* (Blue Ridge sedge)

> *Carex pensylvanica* (Pennsylvania sedge)
> *Corydalis sempervirens* (rock harlequin)
> *Cypripedium acaule* (pink lady's slipper)
> *Danthonia spicata* (poverty oat grass)
> *Deschampsia flexuosa* (wavy hairgrass)
> *Erechtites hieraciifolia* (American burnweed)
> *Fragaria virginiana* (Virginia strawberry)
> *Maianthemum canadense* (false Solomon's seal)
> *Melampyrum lineare* (narrowleaf cowwheat)
> *Pteridium aquilinum* (northern bracken fern)
> *Schizachyrium scoparium* (little bluestem)
> *Trientalis borealis* (starflower)

## Pitch Pine Bog

**Formal name:** *Pinus rigida / Chamaedaphne calyculata / Sphagnum spp. Woodland*

### *Environmental summary*

**Where it is found:** shallow, poorly drained depressions or basins with a deep accumulation of peat, sometimes near upland sand plain pine barrens.

**Soil information:** acidic, deep peat or shallow peat over sandy mineral soil.

**Characteristics:** an open canopy of *Pinus rigida* with an understory of ericaceous shrubs such as *Chamaedaphne calyculata.* Sphagnum mosses form a dense mat.

### *Vegetation*

*Pinus rigida* (pitch pine) dominates the open canopy; associates may include *Acer rubrum* (red maple), *Betula populifolia* (gray birch), and *Nyssa sylvatica* (black gum).

Comprising the shrub layer are:

> *Gaylussacia baccata* (black huckleberry)
> *Kalmia angustifolia* (sheep laurel)
> *Photinia pyrifolia* (red chokeberry)
> *Vaccinium corymbosum* (high bush blueberry)

*Vaccinium myrtilloides* (velvetleaf huckle-berry)

Typical herbs reported include:
*Calopogon tuberosus* (tuberous grasspink)
*Carex trisperma* (three seeded sedge)
*Drosera intermedia* (spoonleaf sundew)
*Drosera rotundifolia* (roundleaf sundew)
*Eriophorum spp.* (cottongrass)
*Rhynchospora alba* (white beaksedge)
*Scirpus spp.* (rushes)
*Vaccinium macrocarpon* (cranberrry)

Other herbs that may be found include:
*Cornus canadensis* (bunchberry)
*Gaultheria procumbens* (wintergreen)
*Maianthemum canadense* (Canada may-flower)
*Osmunda cinnamomea* (cinnamon fern)
*Pteridium aquilinum* (northern bracken fern)
*Trientalis borealis* (starflower)

## Pitch Pine - Scrub Oak Barrens

**Formal name:** *Pinus rigida / Quercus ilicifolia / Lespedeza capitata Woodland*

### Environmental summary

**Where it is found:** northeastern sand plains, outwash plains, sand dunes and glacial till.

**Soil information:** typi-cally sandy, well drained and nutrient poor.

**Characteristics:** an open canopy of *Pinus rigida* (pitch pine) and scrubby oaks appear over fewer than 20 occurrences of this community, many of which are severely de-graded small remnants. This community is depen-dent on a regular and frequent fire regime. Many occurrences are fire-suppressed, and unlikely to persist without an active fire management pro-gram.

Very few occurrences are sufficiently large to support a full set of native fauna (in particular the characteristic lepidoptera). An estimated 10 percent of the original pre-settlement acreage remains because of development pressure, frag-mentation, and fire suppression.

### Vegetation

Pinus rigida forms an open canopy with 30 to 70 percent cover. The canopy may also contain scattered:
*Betula populifolia* (gray birch)
*Populus tremuloides* (quaking aspen)
*Prunus pensylvanica* (pin cherry)
*Prunus serotina* (black cherry)

The characteristic structure of the community is a tall shrub layer, varying from 25 to 95 per-cent, of *Quercus ilicifolia* (bear oak) or *Quercus prinoides* (dwarf chinkapin oak).

Sometimes present is a short-shrub layer that can include:
*Comptonia peregrina* (sweetfern)
*Gaylussacia baccata* (black huckleberry)
*Vaccinium angustifolium* (lowbush blue-berry)
*Vaccinium pallidum* (Blue Ridge blueberry)

Small grassy openings are usually dominated by *Schizachyrium scoparium* (little bluestem), but are rich in herbaceous species that create impor-tant habitat for several rare invertebrates. Spe-cies reported are:
*Andropogon gerardii* (big bluestem)
*Helianthemum canadense* (longbranch frostweed)
*Lechea mucronata* (hairy pinweed)
*Lespedeza capitata* (roundhead lespedeza)
*Lupinus perennis* (sundial lupine)
*Lysimachia quadrifolia* (whorled yellow loosestrife)
*Polygala nuttallii* (Nutall's milkwort)
*Pteridium aquilinum* (northern bracken fern)
*Sorghastrum nutans* (Indian grass)

## White-cedar Cliff Woodland

**Formal name:** *Thuja occidentalis / Carex ebur-nea - Pellaea atropurpurea Woodland*

### Environmental summary

**Where it is found:** north-facing, steep calcare-ous cliffs and uplands above the cliffs, with usu-ally limestone or dolomite bedrock in the Appalachian and Allegheny Plateau regions of the United States.

**Soil information:** shallow, dry, calcareous, with plants often rooted in crevices or on narrow ledges. Where soils are deeper, hardwoods generally do better.

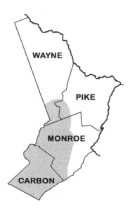

**Characteristics:** woodlands, usually dominated by coniferous trees, are associated with steep, rocky, limestone, mostly north- and east-facing slopes along permanent streams. Some stands are associated with cold-air drainages. Dip slopes provide light seepages and keep humidity higher than the local average to provide a cooler-than-normal microclimate. Closed-canopy stands have very few vascular species in the lower strata, while stands with broken canopies contain scattered shrubs and a substantial number of herbaceous species.

Rugged, complex microtopography includes sheer faces, ledges, and crevices of variable configuration. Slopes range from 40 to 90 degrees and exposed bedrock constitutes more than 90 percent of the surface. Sites are typically sub-xeric, eased with frequent zones of ephemeral seepage and by sheltered north aspects, which slow evaporation.

Estimates suggest fewer than 50 occurrences of this community range wide, and it is considered a critically imperiled ecosystem. Because they are on small ledges of steep cliffs, communities are difficult to survey and little field work has been done.

### Vegetation

Varying with geography, the association structure can range from a very open but stunted canopy of *Thuja occidentalis* (white cedar) to a mixed conifer-deciduous woodland can resemble a forest structure. In addition to *T. occidentalis*, the most common canopy species might be:

*Acer saccharum* (sugar maple)
*Celtis occidentalis* (common hackberry)

*Juniperus virginiana* (eastern red cedar)
*Quercus alba* (white oak)
*Quercus muehlenbergii* (chinkapin oak)
*Quercus rubra* (red oak)
*Tsuga canadensis* (eastern hemlock)
*Ulmus rubra* (slippery elm)

Shrub and small tree species include

*Cercis canadensis* (eastern redbud)
*Cornus florida* (flowering dogwood)
*Hydrangea arborescens* (wild hydrangea)
*Ostrya virginiana* (hop hornbeam)
*Rhus aromatica* (fragrant sumac)
*Hamamelis virginiana* (witch hazel)

Primarily because of extend of canopy cover and potential seepage influence, the structure of the herbaceous layer can very widely.

Composition of the herbaceous and shrub strata can also vary due to seepage influence. Among species reported for this habitat are:

*Aquilegia canadensis* (red columbine)
*Arabis hirsuta* (hairy rockcress)
*Arabis laevigata* (smooth rockcress)
*Asarum canadense* (wild ginger)
*Asplenium rhizophyllum* (walking fern)
*Asplenium trichomanes* (maidenhair spleenwort)
*Carex eburnea* (bristleleaf sedge)
*Cystopteris bulbifera* (bulblet bladderfern)
*Eurybia divaricata* (white wood aster)
*Hepatica nobilis var. acuta* (sharplobe hepatica)
*Heuchera americana* (American alumroot)
*Pachysandra procumbens* (Allegheny spurge)
*Parthenocissus quinquefolia* (Virginia creeper)
*Pellaea atropurpurea* (purple cliffbrake)
*Pilea pumila* (Canadian clearweed)
*Sedum ternatum* (woodland stonecrop)
*Solidago caesia* (wreath goldenrod)
*Solidago flexicaulis* (zigzag goldenrod)
*Symphyotrichum cordifolium* (blue wood aster)
*Toxicodendron radicans* (poison ivy)

## Spruce - Fir Rocky Ridge

**Formal name:** *Picea rubens / Vaccinium angustifolium / Sibbaldiopsis tridentata Woodland*

### Environmental summary

**Where it is found:** acid bedrock outcrops or summits in the northern Appalachians.

**Soil information:** shallow, well-drained to excessively-drained coarse, acidic sands in crevices or sheltered areas.

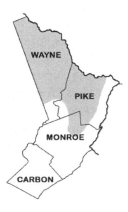

**Characteristics:** red spruce patchy and open canopy with areas of moderate cover interspersed with sparse vegetation and open rock, with sparse tall shrubs and herbs, and variable dwarf-shrub layer and bryoids layers that range from sparse to extensive. Ground cover is sparse needle litter and exposed bedrock.

### Vegetation

*Picea rubens* (red spruce) and *Abies balsama* (balsam fir) dominate the canopy, with Pinus strobus as an occasional co-dominant. Associated species are reported to include

> *Betula papyrifera var. cordifolia* (mountain paper birch)
> *Betula papyrifera var. papyrifera* (paper birch)
> *Picea mariana* (black spruce)
> *Pinus rigida* (pitch pine)
> *Thuja occidentalis* (white cedar)

*Morella pensylvanica* (northern bayberry) and *Picea glauca* (white spruce) may be present in this community near the seacoast, but generally found among tall shrubs are:

> *Amelanchier spp.* (serviceberry)
> *Nemopanthus mucronatus* (catberry)
> *Photinia melanocarpa* (black chokeberry)
> *Sorbus americana* (American mountain ash)
> *Sorbus decora* (northern mountain ash)
> *Viburnum nudum var. cassinoides* (witherod)

The low heath layer is often composed of:
> *Gaylussacia baccata* (black huckleberry)
> *Kalmia angustifolia* (sheep laurel)
> *Vaccinium angustifolium* (lowbush blueberry)
> *Vaccinium myrtilloides* (velvetleaf huckleberry)

Forbs and graminoids may include:
> *Danthonia spicata* (poverty oat grass)
> *Deschampsia flexuosa* (wavy hairgrass)
> *Maianthemum canadense* (Canada mayflower)
> *Piptatherum pungens* (mountain ricegrass)
> *Sibbaldiopsis tridentata* (shrubby five fingers)
> *Solidago simplex ssp. randii* (Rand's goldenrod)

Bryoids will typically include:
> *Cladina spp.* (reindeer lichen)
> *Pleurozium schreberi* (Schreber's big red stem moss)
> *Dicranum polysetum* (dicranum moss)
> *Polytrichum juniperinum* (juniper polytrichum moss)
> *Polytrichum piliferum* (polytrichum moss)
> *Polytrichum commune* (polytrichum moss)

# Deciduous-coniferous forest

## Hardwood - White Pine Forest

**Formal name:** *Acer saccharum - Pinus strobus / Acer pensylvanicum Forest*

### Environmental Summary

**Where it is found:** on sandy-gravelly soils, often on eskers and in narrow bands along lakeshores. This forest generally occupies a less mesic setting than northern hardwoods lacking white pine. It occurs widely throughout the upper Midwestern and northeastern United States and eastern Canada.

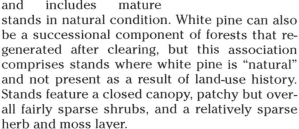

**Soil information:** well-drained, acidic, sandy or gravelly soil over glacial till.

**Characteristics:** white pine suggests relatively dry, nutrient-poor sites and includes mature stands in natural condition. White pine can also be a successional component of forests that regenerated after clearing, but this association comprises stands where white pine is "natural" and not present as a result of land-use history. Stands feature a closed canopy, patchy but overall fairly sparse shrubs, and a relatively sparse herb and moss layer.

### Vegetation

*Pinus strobus* (eastern white pine) often occurs as a "supercanopy" over such dominants as *Acer saccharum* (sugar maple), *Betula alleghaniensis* (yellow birch), and *Fagus grandifolia* (American beech). Minor canopy associates may include *Quercus rubra* (northern red oak) and *Tsuga canadensis* (eastern hemlock). In the northern end of the range, sparse *Abies balsama* (balsam fir), *Picea rubens* (red spruce) and *Thuja occidentalis* (northern white cedar) may occur.

The subcanopy is almost always dominated by *Acer pensylvanicum* (striped maple).

Shrubs are scattered and generally small: *Vaccinium angustifolium* (lowbush blueberry), *Gaylussacia baccata* (black huckleberry) and *Gaultheria procumbens* (teaberry) are reported. Equally sparse is a herbaceous layer characterized by *Pteridium aquilinum* (northern bracken fern), *Trientalis borealis* (starflower), *Maianthemum canadense* (Canada mayflower) and *Oryzopsis asperifolia* (rough leaved rice grass).

Bryophytes include *Polytrichum commune*, *Pleurozium schreberi*, *Bazzania trilobata*, or *Hypnum imponens*.

## Conifer - Red Maple Acidic Swamp

**Formal name:** *Picea rubens — Acer rubrum / Nemopanthus mucronatus Forest*

### Environmental summary

**Where it is found:** basins or low flats with poor drainage in glaciated areas of the Northeastern United States

**Soil information:** organic muck or shallow peat over clay loam

**Characteristics:** Pronounced hummock-and-hollow microtopography covered by slowly decomposing leaf/needle litter.

### Vegetation

The tree canopy is closed to partly open and co-dominated by *Picea rubens* (red spruce) and *Acer rubrum* (red maple). Regional associates often include:

> *Abies balsamea (balsam fir)*
> *Betula alleghaniensis (yellow birch)*
> *Betula populifolia (gray birch)*
> *Tsuga canadensis (eastern hemlock)*

The most abundant of a well-developed tall shrub layer are:

> *Alnus incana* (gray alder)
> *Ilex verticillata* (common winterberry)
> *Nemopanthus mucronatus* (catberry)
> *Spiraea alba* (meadowsweet)
> *Vaccinium corymbosum* (highbush blueberry)

Four ferns usually dominate the herbaceous layer:

> *Onoclea sensibilis* (sensitive fern)
> *Osmunda cinnamomea* (cinnamon fern)
> *Osmunda regalis* (royal fern)
> *Thelypteris palustris* (marsh fern)

Herbaceous associates often include:

> *Carex intumescens* (great bladder sedge)
> *Carex trisperma* (three-seeded sedge)
> *Cornus canadensis* (bunchberry)
> *Doellingeria umbellata* (parasol whitetop)
> *Oclemena acuminata* (whorled wood aster)
> *Trientalis borealis* (starflower)

The bryophyte layer is dominated by *Sphagnum spp.* including *Sphagnum girgensohnii* and *Sphagnum magellanicum*.

## White Pine - Oak Forest

**Formal name:** *Pinus strobus - Quercus (rubra, velutina) - Fagus grandifolia Forest*

### Environmental Summary

**Where it is found:** Mid and lower slopes. In the glaciated portion: outwash plains or moraines, within protected ravines, on protected ridges of shale, sandstone or other sedimentary rock, sometimes underlain by metamorphic or igneous rock. In unglaciated plateaus: on rolling topography underlain by sandstone. Low elevation sites are flat to gently sloping.

**Soil information:** dry-mesic to mesic, acidic, nutrient-poor, sandy loam to sandy soils, locally including extremely stony, xeric soils of the Arnot series and on lower elevations Wyoming very cobbly sandy loam. This association occurs over shale and siltstone bedrock and alluvial deposits.

**Characteristics**: Dominant species are pines and oaks, with much Pinus strobus in the tall-shrub canopy.

### Vegetation

The canopy is dominated — 50 to 70 percent — by pines and oaks and a tall-shrub layer of regenerating *Pinus strobus* is common. Canopy trees are generally 65 to 130 feet. Dominant species include:

> *Pinus rigida* (pitch pine)
> *Pinus strobus* (Eastern white pine)
> *Quercus prinus* (chestnut oak)
> *Quercus rubra* (red oak)

Associates include:

> *Juniperus virginiana* (eastern red cedar)
> *Quercus coccinea* (scarlet oak)
> *Quercus velutina* (black oak)
> *Tsuga canadensis* (eastern hemlock, in decline)

Subcanopy species, which range from 15 to 60 feet and 15 to 40 percent cover, include:

> *Acer rubrum* (red maple)
> *Juniperus virginiana* (eastern red cedar)
> *Pinus strobus* (eastern white pine)
> Oaks found in the canopy

In addition, the same forest type can also support:

> *Carpinus caroliniana* (hop hornbeam)
> *Cornus florida* (flowering dogwood)
> *Corylus americana* (American hazelnut)
> *Hamamelis virginiana* (witch hazel)
> *Nyssa sylvatica* (black gum)
> *Sassafras albidum* (sassafras)

The tall-shrub layer can range from dense (about 80 percent) to sparse (about 5 percent) depending how many sapling eastern white pines are present. Saplings of other canopy trees may be scattered in this layer, as well as *Quercus ilicifolia* (bear oak) and an occasional *Kalmia latifolia* (mountain laurel) or *Viburnum prunifolium* (black-haw)

The short-shrub layer, with 20 to 60 percent cover typically contains scattered patches of low heath. Common ericaceous species include:

> *Gaultheria procumbens* (teaberry)
> *Gaylussacia baccata* (black huckleberry)
> *Vaccinium angustifolium* (lowbush blueberry)
> *Vaccinium pallidum* (Blue Ridge blueberry)
> *Vaccinium stamineum* (deerberry)

The herbaceous layer is typically very sparse, with less than 5 percent cover, to sometimes moderately dense. Very common are:

> *Carex pensylvanica* (Pennsylvania sedge)
> *Chimaphila maculata* (striped prince's pine)
> *Deschampsia flexuosa* (wavy hairgrass)
> *Mitchella repens* (partridgeberry)
> *Trientalis borealis* (starflower)

Across the range, however, the following have also been reported as part of the herbaceous layer:

> *Ageratina altissima* (white snakeroot, or Eupatorum rugosum)
> *Amphicarpaea bracteata* (American hog peanut)
> *Aralia nudicaulis* (wild sarsaparilla)
> *Brachyelytrum erectum* (Bearded shorthusk grass)
> *Carex communis* (fibrousroot sedge)
> *Carex debilis* (white edge sedge)
> *Carex lucorum* (Blue ridge sedge)
> *Carex woodii* (pretty sedge)
> *Desmodium nudiflorum* (nakedflower tick-trefoil)
> *Galium latifolium* (purple bedstraw)
> *Goodyera pubescens* (downy rattlesnake plantain)
> *Hieracium venosum* (rattlesnake weed)
> *Houstonia purpurea* (Venus' pride)
> *Maianthemum canadense* (Canada mayflower)
> *Maianthemum racemosum* (false Solomon's seal)
> *Medeola virginiana* (Indian cucumber)
> *Melampyrum lineare* (narrow leaf cowwheat)
> *Monotropa uniflora* (Indian pipe)
> *Poa cuspidata* (early bluegrass)
> *Polygonatum biflorum* (Solomon's seal)
> *Polystichum acrostichoides* (Christmas fern)
> *Pteridium aquilinum* (northern bracken fern)
> *Viola hastata* (halberdleaf yellow violet)

Mosses, where they occur, are likely to be *Leucobryum glaucum* (cushion moss) and *Polytrichum commune* (common haircap moss).

## Oak-Pine Successional Forest

**Formal name:** *Quercus (rubra, velutina, alba) — Betula lenta — (Pinus strobus) Forest*

### *Environmental Summary*

**Where it is found:** former agricultural land and old fields no longer intensively mowed, plowed or managed. Sites are typically flat to gently sloping and sometimes bounded by stone walls or fence rows.

**Soil description:** Moderately well-drained to well-drained sandy loams, sometimes covered by a thick layer of pine needle duff. Fertility varies; more organic sites may have supported crops, but more likely weak fertility results in pasture land.

**Characteristics:** Depending on successional status, varying amounts of *Pinus strobus* (eastern white pine) colonizes open fields, typically from the outer edges of the field into the center or as scattered clumps throughout the field. Without disturbance, the sites evolve into Eastern White Pine Forest or Northeastern Modified Successional Forest. Associated woody and herbaceous species vary with geography.

### *Vegetation*

In young forests, scattered trees, usually *Pinus strobus* (eastern white pine), but sometimes *Picea abies* (Norway or red spruce) or *Picea glauca* (white spruce) may be the "signature tree" or part of the composition. Heights range from 15 to 30 feet. If the site is close to northern hardwood forests, *Quercus rubra* (northern red oak), *Quercus velutina* (black oak), *Fraxinus americana* (white ash) and *Acer saccharum* (sugar maple) may be present.

On more developed sites, saplings of many other species are likely to be found, inlcuding: *Acer rubrum* (red maple), *Betula lenta* (sweet birch), and mesic oaks, including *Quercus rubra* (northern red oak) and *Quercus palustris* (pin oak). *Juniperus virginiana* (eastern red cedar) and *Tsuga canadensis* (eastern hemlock) may be common in the canopy or subcanopy. Other common associates include

> *Acer saccharum* (sugar maple)
> *Betula alleghaniensis* (yellow birch)
> *Carya cordiformis* (bitternut hickory)
> *Fagus grandifolia* (American beech)
> *Fraxinus americana* (white ash)
> *Populus grandidentata* (bigtooth aspen)
> *Prunus serotina* (black cherry)
> *Quercus alba* (white oak)
> *Quercus velutina* (black oak)

The subcanopy may contain *Carpinus caroliniana* (American hornbeam) and/or *Ostrya virginiana* (hop hornbeam)

Found in a scattered shrub layer are:
> *Cornus racemosa* (gray dogwood)
> *Juniperus virginiana* (Eastern red cedar)
> *Rhus glabra* (smooth sumac)
> *Rubus allegheniensis* (Allegheny blackberry)
> *Rubus occidentalis* (black raspberry)
> *Rubus phoenicolasius* (wine raspberry)
> *Viburnum prunifolium* (black-haw)

As successions evolve, a sparse to moderately dense tall-shrub layer develops consisting of *Lindera benzoin* (spicebush), *Ilex verticillata* (winterberry), *Viburnum prunifolium* (black-haw), *Viburnum recognitum* (southern arrow-wood), and increasing numbers of saplings of canopy tree species. Ericaceous shrubs may be scattered in this type, however, they usually cover less than 25 percent of the forest floor.

The herbaceous layer is variable depending on the density of tree and shrub cover. Typical species are those associated with old fields, little

bluestem grasslands, and agricultural sites. Common species include:
> *Anthoxanthum odoratum* (sweet vernalgrass)
> *Euthamia graminifolia* (flat-top goldentop)
> *Monarda fistulosa* (wild bergamot)
> *Potentilla simplex* (common cinquefoil)
> *Pycnanthemum virginianum* (Virginia mountain mint)
> *Schizachyrium scoparium* (little bluestem)
> *Solidago gigantea* (giant goldenrod)
> *Solidago rugosa* (wrinkleleaf goldenrod)
> *Toxicodendron radicans* (eastern poison ivy)

In stands that are more heavily forested, herbs may include:
> *Aralia nudicaulis* (wild sarsaparilla)
> *Dennstaedtia punctilobula* (hayscented fern)
> *Lycopodium spp.*
> *Maianthemum canadense* (Canada mayflower)
> *Mitchella repens* (partridgeberry)
> *Trientalis borealis* (starflower)

## Hemlock-Maple Swamp-Bog Complex

**Formal name:** *Tsuga canadensis - Acer rubrum - (Liriodendron tulipifera, Nyssa sylvatica) / Rhododendron maximum / Sphagnum spp. Forest*

### *Environmental Summary*

**Where it is found:** often near occasionally flooded streams, in poorly drained bottomlands, especially along small, braided headwaters of streams that drain visible groundwater discharge. Microtopography often takes the form of ridges and sloughs or depressions.

**Soil information:** rich, alluvial materials that are strongly acidic — about pH 4.8.

**Characteristics:** a palustrine forest with open to closed canopy and an open to dense shrub layer that is interspersed with small sphagnum and herb dominated depressions.

Development, conversion to pasture and agriculture and hydrologic alterations in the flat areas along streams have permanently altered many of these systems, most of which are less than five acres in size.

### Vegetation

A mixture of evergreen and deciduous species, often *Tsuga canadensis* (eastern hemlock) and *Acer rubrum* (red maple), less often *Liriodendron tulipifera* (tuliptree), *Nyssa sylvatica* (black gum), *Pinus strobus* (eastern white pine) or *Pinus rigida* (pitch pine), compose a canopy that can range from open to closed.

*Rhododendron maximum* (great laurel) and *Kalmia latifolia* (mountain laurel) are often the dominant shrubs; others in the layer may include:

   *Alnus serrulata* (hazel alder)
   *Cornus amomum* (silky dogwood)
   *Ilex montana* (mountain holly)
   *Salix nigra* (black willow)
   *Toxicodendron vernix* (poison sumac)
   *Viburnum nudum var. cassinoides* (witherod)

Herbs in sphagnum-herb dominated openings include:

   *Carex folliculata* (northern long sedge)
   *Carex gynandra* (nodding sedge)
   *Carex leptalea* (bristly-stalked sedge)
   *Carex scabrata* (eastern rough sedge)
   *Carex stricta* (upright sedge)
   *Dalibarda repens* (robin runaway)
   *Leersia virginica* (whitegrass)
   *Osmunda cinnamomea* (cinnamon fern)
   *Sagittaria latifolia* (broadleaf arrowhead)
   *Sarracenia purpurea* (purple pitcherplant)
   *Solidago patula var. patula* (roundleaf goldenrod)
   *Symphyotrichum puniceum* (purplestem aster)

Herbs in the more forested communities include:

   *Dalibarda repens* (robin runaway)
   *Glyceria melicaria* (melic mannagrass)
   *Lycopodium obscurum* (rare clubmoss)
   *Maianthemum canadense* (Canada mayflower)
   *Onoclea sensibilis* (sensitive fern)
   *Osmunda cinnamomea* (cinnamon fern)

   *Osmunda regalis var. spectabilis* (royal fern)
   *Solidago patula* (roundleaf goldenrod)
   *Symphyotrichum puniceum* (purplestem aster)
   *Thelypteris noveboracensis* (New York fern)

## Hemlock - Sugar Maple - Birch Forest

**Formal name:** *Tsuga canadensis - Betula alleghaniensis - Acer saccharum / Dryopteris intermedia Forest*

### Environmental Summary

**Where it is found:** Often north-facing rocky flat to moderately steep (14 to 25 percent) slopes throughout the northeastern U.S. In unglaciated areas, sites include deep, sheltered ravines and along high-gradient mountain streams.

**Soil information:** dry-mesic to mesic loam and sand soils, sometimes acidic. Parent material is glacial till in the north and sandstone in the unglaciated south. Soils may have a thick, poorly decomposed duff layer. The bedrock varies from shale to calcareous shale and limestone. Soils are typically channery to very stony silt loams (for example, Lordstown-Wallpack complex, Hoosic-Otisville complex and Edgemere-Shohola complex soil series).

**Characteristics:** *Tsuga canadensis* dominates a coniferous to mixed canopy.

### Vegetation

*Tsuga canadensis* (eastern hemlock) is characteristic and usually dominant in the coniferous to mixed canopy. While hemlock generally forms at least 50 per cent of the canopy, in some cases it may be as low as 25 percent relative dominance. The canopy is typically 65 to 100 feet, with cover usually greater than 70 per cent.

Co-dominants are either *Betula lenta* (sweet birch) or *Betula alleghaniensis* (yellow birch) and *Acer saccharum* (sugar maple). The presence of *Betula alleghaniensis* or *Betula lenta* and *Acer sac-*

*charum* and a lack of abundant *Quercus spp.* or *Pinus strobus* are diagnostic characteristics.

Hemlock woolly adelgid (*Adelges tsugae*) is decimating hemlock stands in the eastern United States. *Betula lenta* (sweet birch) is a common colonizer following the death of hemlocks. Minor associates, which range from absent to scattered, include:

> *Fagus grandifolia* (American beech)
> *Pinus strobus* (eastern white pine)
> *Acer rubrum* (red maple)
> *Quercus rubra* (northern red oak)
> *Quercus alba* (white oak)
> *Quercus prinus* (chestnut oak)
> *Ostrya virginiana* (hop hornbeam)

Subcanopy ranges from 30 to 50 feet and may include minor associates species. It varies from 10 to 50 percent cover.

The tall-shrub layer is typically sparse and often absent, consisting of scattered saplings of canopy tree species and occasionally *Acer pensylvanicum* (striped maple). The short-shrub layer is sparse and generally less than 10 feet, with total cover generally under 15 percent. Short shrubs include tree saplings and occasionally some ericad shrubs at very low cover, such as *Vaccinium pallidum* (Blue Ridge blueberry) and *Viburnum acerifolium* (maple-leaf viburnum).

The herbaceous layer is usually sparse (less than 10 percent total cover) but may reach 50 percent cover where the canopy is more open. Characteristic herbs include:

> *Chimaphila maculata* (striped prince's pine)
> *Coptis trifolia* (threeleaf goldthread)
> *Dennstaedtia punctilobula* (hayscented fern)
> *Dryopteris intermedia* (intermediate wood-fern)
> *Eurybia divaricata* (white wood aster)
> *Huperzia lucidula* (shining clubmoss)
> *Maianthemum canadense* (Canada mayflower)
> *Medeola virginiana* (Indian cucumber)
> *Mitchella repens* (partridgeberry)
> *Oclemena acuminata* (whorled wood aster)
> *Oxalis montana* (mountain wood sorrel)
> *Polystichum acrostichoides* (Christmas fern)
> *Thelypteris noveboracensis* (New York fern)
> *Trientalis borealis* (starflower)
> *Uvularia sessilifolia* (sessileleaf bellwort)

Vines are usually absent, with *Parthenocissus quinquefolia* (Virginia creeper) sometimes present at low cover. Bryophyte cover is usually less than 5 percent but may be as high as 20 percent where the canopy is more open.

## Hemlock - Black Cherry Forest

**Formal name:** *Tsuga canadensis - Betula alleghaniensis - Prunus serotina / Rhododendron maximum Forest*

### Environmental summary

**Where it is found:** rocky ravines or moderately steep slopes of any aspect, on stream terraces, or occasionally on flats throughout the Central Appalachian Mountains and High Allegheny Plateau

**Soil information:** acidic, dry-mesic to mesic sandy loams and sands of glacial till or sandstone

**Characteristics:** closed-canopy, late-successional, mixed forest, widespread and common type over much of its range, but potentially threatened by the hemlock woolly adelgid. In areas of severe infestation, dead hemlock litters the forest floor with downed wood and stimulates massive increases in understory growth, particularly of *Betula spp.* and *Acer pensylvanicum*. *Rhododendron maximum*, *Sambucus racemosa*, and the abundance of *Prunus serotina* in the canopy differentiate this from other associations of this alliance.

### Vegetation

The forest is dominated by *Tsuga canadensis* (eastern hemlock) with associated deciduous canopy species, including:

> *Acer saccharum* (sugar maple)
> *Betula alleghaniensis* (yellow birch)
> *Fagus grandifolia* (American beech)
> *Liriodendron tulipifera* (tuliptree)
> *Prunus serotina* (black cherry)

Other associates include:

*Acer rubrum* (red maple)
*Betula lenta* (sweet birch)
*Carya spp.* (hickories)
*Pinus strobus* (eastern white pine)
*Quercus alba* (white oak)
*Quercus rubra* (northern red oak)
*Ulmus americana* (American elm)
*Ostrya virginiana* (hop hornbeam)

The shrub layer is often patchy, but may have locally dense cover of *Rhododendron maximum* (great rhododendron). It varies in cover and composition but may also consist of some mixture of

*Corylus cornuta* (beaked hazelnut)
*Diervilla lonicera* (northern bush honey-suckle)
*Hamamelis virginiana* (witch hazel)
*Kalmia latifolia* (mountain laurel)
*Lindera benzoin* (northern spicebush)
*Sambucus racemosa* (red elderberry)
*Vaccinium pallidum* (Blue Ridge blueberry)
*Viburnum lantanoides* (hobblebush)

Commonly reported ferns in the herbaceous layer include:

*Dennstaedtia punctilobula* (hayscented fern)
*Dryopteris carthusiana* (spinulose wood-fern)
*Dryopteris intermedia* (intermediate wood-fern)
*Thelypteris noveboracensis* (New York fern)

Forb composition varies, but can include:

*Anemone quinquefolia* (wood anemone)
*Cardamine diphylla* (crinkleroot)
*Cornus canadensis* (bunchberry)
*Eurybia divaricata* (white wood aster)
*Maianthemum canadense* (Canada may-flower)
*Medeola virginiana* (Indian cucumber)
*Mitchella repens* (partridgeberry)
*Oxalis montana* (mountain wood sorrel)
*Trientalis borealis* (starflower)
*Trillium erectum* (red trillium)
*Trillium grandiflorum* (white trillium)
*Viola spp.* (violets)

A bryophyte layer may be well-developed, often characterized by the liverwort *Bazzania trilobata* (liverwort)

# Hemlock - Birch Seepage Swamp

**Formal name:** *Tsuga canadensis - Betula alleghaniensis / Veratrum viride - Carex scabrata - Oclemena acuminata Forest*

## Environmental summary

**Where it is found:** high-elevation valleys or slope concavities, in diffuse stream headwaters and lateral, groundwater-saturated flats along larger streams. Occasionally, stands occupy gentle depressions or basins influenced by seasonally perched groundwater but without flowing streams.

**Soil information:** rich and moist but with shallow organic horizons that very strongly to extremely acidic.

**Characteristics:** usually flat to moderately sloping sites with more than 20 percent surface cover of boulders and stones weathered from metabasalt, granitic rocks, or sandstone. Stream-bottom areas feature moss-covered mounds and intertwining roots of *Betula alleghaniensis* (Yellow birch), mucky pools, and braided drainage channels.

## Vegetation

*Tsuga canadensis* (eastern hemlock) and *Betula alleghaniensis* (yellow birch) in varying proportions dominate the canopy. Minor canopy associates include:

*Acer rubrum* (red maple)
*Fraxinus americana* (white ash)
*Pinus strobus* (eastern white pine)
*Quercus alba* (white oak)
*Quercus rubra* (northern red oak)

Small-tree and shrub layers range from sparse to open and most frequently include

*Acer pensylvanicum* (striped maple)
*Hamamelis virginiana* (witch hazel)
*Ilex verticillata* (common winterberry)
*Kalmia latifolia* (mountain laurel)
*Alnus incana ssp. rugosa* (speckled alder)
*Rhododendron catawbiense* (Catawba rho-

dodendron)

The herb layer is generally lush and well-developed. Abundant species may include:

*Anemone quinquefolia* (wood anemone)
*Athyrium felix-femina ssp. asplenioides* (lady fern)
*Carex scabrata* (eastern rough sedge)
*Chelone glabra* (white turtlehead)
*Chrysosplenium americanum* (American golden saxifrage)
*Circaea alpina* (small enchanter's nightshade)
*Dryopteris cristata* (crested woodfern)
*Glyceria melicaria* (melic mannagrass)
*Impatiens capensis* (jewelweed)
*Maianthemum canadense* (Canada mayflower)
*Oclemena acuminata* (whorled wood aster)
*Osmunda cinnamomea* (cinnamon fern)
*Oxypolis rigidior* (stiff cowbane)
*Thalictrum pubescens* (king-of-the-meadow)
*Thelypteris noveboracensis* (New York fern)
*Veratrum viride* (green false hellebore)
*Viola cucullata* (marsh blue violet)
*Viola macloskeyi ssp. pallens* (smooth white violet)

## Hemlock - Beech - Oak Forest

**Formal name:** *Tsuga canadensis - Fagus grandifolia - Quercus rubra Forest*

### Environmental Summary

**Where it is found:** mesic to sub-mesic valley side slopes and broad, convex ridges, from New England to Virginia.

**Soil information**: dry to dry-mesic, nutrient-poor, well-drained, often stony sandy loams or loamy sands. Underlying bedrock is acidic.

**Characteristics:** Varies with precise site and disturbance characteristics; a common type of forest on dry-mesic acidic soils with various settings.

### Vegetation

Composition of stands of this forest association vary with precise site and disturbance characteristics. At the drier end, *Fagus grandifolia* (American beech) and/or *Quercus rubra* (northern red oak) tend to be more prevalent. Cooler sites, where soils may freeze for longer durations, have

especially abundant *Tsuga canadensis* (eastern hemlock). Disturbance affects composition, as *Fagus grandifolia* can regenerate profusely through root-suckering.

Associated tree species include *Betula lenta* (sweet birch), which is sometimes replaced by *Betula papyrifera* (paper birch) at the northern end of this type's range. Also reported are *Pinus strobus* (eastern white pine) and *Acer rubrum* (red maple).

Shrubs are often sparse but locally abundant. Heaths are rarely prominent. In addition to saplings of canopy species, shrubs include:

*Acer pensylvanicum* (striped maple)
*Hamamelis virginiana* (witch hazel)
*Ilex montana* (mountain holly) — southern end of range
*Kalmia latifolia* (mountain laurel)
*Viburnum acerifolium* (mapleleaf viburnum)

The herbaceous layer is generally sparse but usually includes several of the following:

*Aralia nudicaulis* (wild sarsaparilla)
*Coptis trifolia* (threeleaf goldthread)
*Dennstaedtia punctilobula* (hayscented fern)
*Dryopteris intermedia* (intermediate woodfern)
*Epifagus virginiana* (beechdrops)
*Gaultheria procumbens* (teaberry)
*Lycopodium annotinum* (stiff clubmoss)
*Lycopodium dendroideum* (tree groundpine)
*Lycopodium digitatum* (fan clubmoss)
*Lycopodium obscurum* (rare clubmoss)
*Maianthemum canadense* (Canada mayflower)
*Medeola virginiana* (Indian cucumber)
*Mitchella repens* (partridgeberry)
*Monotropa uniflora* (Indian pipe)
*Pteridium aquilinum* (northern bracken fern)
*Trientalis borealis* (starflower)
*Uvularia sessilifolia* (sessileleaf bellwort)

# Dry Hemlock - Chestnut Oak Forest

**Formal name:** *Tsuga canadensis - Quercus prinus - Betula lenta Forest*

### Environmental Summary

**Where it is found:** moderate to very steep sheltered slopes, usually middle slope sites facing northeast to northwest with elevations ranging from 500 to 2500 feet, from New Jersey to Virginia. Some sites are boulder fields, with up to 60 percent cover by large rocks.

**Soil description:** very stony to extremely stony sandy loams, consistently low in plant nutrients, with very low pH, typically over shale, sandstone, siltstone and limestone bedrock. In the Poconos, Oquaga, Lackawanna, Benson and Lordstown series soils — all extremely stony — are reported here.

**Characteristics:** dry-site species, notably *Tsuga canadensis* and *Quercus prinus*, dominate the canopy on north-facing slopes. Because of the xeric setting, the hemlocks in these forests are at the greatest risk of mortality once infested with hemlock wooly adelgid. The future composition and structure of these forests are uncertain.

### Vegetation

Canopy trees range in height from 65 to 100 feet and typically cover 75 to 90 percent of the stand. Dominant species in the tree canopy are *Quercus prinus* (chestnut oak) and *Tsuga canadensis* (eastern hemlock).

Major associates, which can co-dominate the canopy, and are indicative of dry, infertile soils, include:

*Betula lenta* (sweet birch)
*Quercus coccinea* (scarlet oak)
*Quercus rubra* (northern red oak)
*Quercus velutina* (black oak)

Secondary canopy associates include:

*Acer rubrum* (red maple)
*Carya alba* (mockernut hickory)

*Carya glabra* (pignut hickory)
*Fagus grandifolia* (American beech)
*Liriodendron tulipifera* (tuliptree)
*Nyssa sylvatica* (black gum)
*Pinus strobus* (eastern white pine)
*Quercus alba* (white oak)
*Sassafras albidum* (sassafras)

Because of the density of the hemlock cover, small trees from 15 to 60 feet and shrubs may be sparse to absent. Subcanopy trees cover 10 to 60 percent of the area and typically include eastern hemlock, red maple, sweet birch, common serviceberry (*Amelanchier arborea*), and oaks and hickories from the canopy. *Acer saccharum* (sugar maple) may be sometimes be present in the subcanopy

In the tall-shrub layer, the most consistently present is *Hamamelis virginiana* (witch hazel), with *Kalmia latifolia* (mountain laurel), *Rhododendron maximum* (great rhododendron) and *Viburnum acerifolium* (maple-leaf viburnum) less common.

Common among lower shrubs are *Gaylussacia baccata* (huckleberry) and *Vaccinium pallidum* (Blue Ridge blueberry)

The herb layer of this community is typically very sparse or absent; typical scattered species include:

*Aralia nudicaulis* (wild sarsaparilla)
*Carex swanii* (Swan's sedge)
*Chimaphila maculata* (striped prince's pine)
*Dennstaedtia punctilobula* (hay scented fern)
*Deschampsia flexuosa* (wavy hairgrass)
*Eurybia divaricata* (white wood aster)
*Gaultheria procumbens* (teaberry)
*Goodyera pubescens* (downy rattlesnake plantain)
*Maianthemum canadense* (Canada mayflower)
*Mitchella repens* (partridgeberry)
*Monotropa hypopithys* (pinesap)
*Monotropa uniflora* (Indian pipe)
*Parthenocissus quinquefolia* (Virginia creeper)

# *Deciduous-coniferous woodlands*

## Acidic Shale Woodland

**Formal name:** *Pinus virginiana - Juniperus virginiana - Quercus rubra / Solidago arguta var. harrisii - Opuntia humifusa Woodland*

### *Environmental summary*

**Where it is found:** unstable, steep shale slopes, often with areas of exposed bedrock, in the central Appalachians from Pennsylvania to southwestern Virginia, typically at elevations ranging from 1,000 to 3,000 feet. Most are convex slopes, ridge spurs or clifftops, with southeast to west aspects.

**Soil information:** Very strongly acidic and derived from shale, but sandstone is an occasional component. Moderately high calcium and magnesium levels and relatively low levels of organic matter. Available moisture is scarce.

**Characteristics:** Extensive stretches of exposed bedrock — as high as 80 percent — are common and coverage ranges from sparse enough to be described as a sparse shrubland to locally dense enough to occur as a closed forest. Where a canopy occurs, a mix of oak and conifers co-dominate. An herb layer is usually less than 25 percent coverage. There are fewer than 100 examples in the range.

### *Vegetation*

Canopy dominants are *Juniperus virginiana* (eastern red cedar), *Pinus virginiana* (Virginia pine), *Quercus rubra* (red oak), and *Quercus prinus* (chestnut oak). Associates vary and include:

*Carya alba* (mockernut hickory)
*Carya glabra* (pignut hickory)
*Celtis tenuifolia* (dwarf hackberry)
*Fraxinus americana* (white ash)
*Quercus alba* (white oak)
*Quercus stellata* (post oak)

Scattered and usually sparse shrubs may include:

*Amelanchier arborea* (common serviceberry)
*Quercus ilicifolia* (bear oak)
*Rhus aromatica* (fragrant sumac)
*Rhus copallinum* (winged sumac)
*Rosa carolina* (Carolina rose)
*Vaccinium pallidum* (Blue Ridge blueberry)
*Vaccinium stamineum* (upland highbush blueberry)

Typical graminoids reported are:

*Carex pensylvanica* (Pennsylvania sedge)
*Danthonia spicata* (poverty oatgrass)
*Deschampsia flexuosa* (wavy hairgrass)
*Schizachyrium scoparium* (little bluestem)

Typical forbs include:

*Antennaria plantaginifolia* (pussy-toes)
*Cheilanthes lanosa* (hairy lipfern)
*Cunila origanoides* (common dittany)
*Hedeoma pulegioides* (American false pennyroyal)
*Houstonia longifolia* (longleaf summer bluet)
*Opuntia humifusa* (prickly pear cactus)
*Paronychia montana* (mountain nailwort)
*Pellaea atropurpurea* (purple cliffbrake)
*Polygonum scandens var. cristatum* (climbing false buckwheat)
*Scutellaria ovata* (heartleaf skullcap)
*Selaginella rupestris* (northern selaginella)

## Pine - Oak / Heath Woodland

**Formal name:** (*Table Mountain Pine, Pitch Pine) - Chestnut Oak / (Bear Oak) / Black Huckleberry Woodland*

### Environmental summary

**Where it is found:** convex, xeric, rocky and generally south to west facing slopes, crests, clifftops and ridge spurs in the Central Appalachians, typically above 900 feet.

**Soil information:** shallow and droughty infertile soils with a thick and poorly decomposed duff layer, commonly over acidic sedimentary substrates.

**Characteristics:** Two variances are often found: a) with *Pinus rigida* (pitch pine) dominance and typically on mid to high-level elevations on moderately steep upper slopes and crests with little rock cover but very dense duff and, more to the south, b) abundant *Pinus pungens* (table mountain pine) at low to middle elevations and usually on cliffs and steep sideslopes with substantial rock cover

Because of the duff layer, dead wood and ericaceous shrub cover, these are strongly fire-prone habitats; soil circumstances perpetuate the vegetation.

Periodic fire is an important ecological process, providing chances for regeneration of canopy pines and less competitive herbaceous species, while reducing successional encroachment of xeric oaks.

### Vegetation

Locally, dominance by Pinus rigida; scattered canopy and subcanopy associates may include:

*Acer rubrum* (red maple)
*Amelanchier arborea* (serviceberry)
*Castanea dentata* (American chestnut)
*Nyssa sylvatica* (black gum)
*Pinus virginiana* (Virginia pine)
*Quercus coccinea* (scarlet oak)
*Quercus rubra* (red oak)
*Sassafras albidum* (sassafras)

*Quercus ilicifolia* (bear oak) typically dominates a moderately open to very dense tall-shrub layer, while varying mixes form a dense lower shrub layer. These may locally include:

*Gaylussacia baccata* (black huckleberry)
*Kalmia latifolia* (mountain laurel)
*Vaccinium angustifolium* (lowbush blueberry)
*Vaccinium pallidum* (Blue Ridge Blueberry)
*Vaccinium stamineum* (deerberry)
and other ericads

*Smilax rotundifolia* (roundleaf greenbrier) and *Smilax glauca* (cat greenbrier) may be notable climbers among shrubs.

Herbaceous species are generally very sparse and rooted in small openings among shrubs, rocks, and in disturbed areas where mineral soil is exposed. Typical herbs and subshrubs include:

*Aralia hispida* (bristly sarsaparilla)
*Carex tonsa* (shaved sedge)
*Epigaea repens* (trailing arbutus)
*Gaultheria procumbens* (wintergreen)
*Lycopodium tristachyum* (deeproot clubmoss)
*Melampyrum lineare var. latifolium* (narrowleaf cowwheat)
*Pteridium aquilinum var. latiusculum* (northern bracken fern)

# *Shrublands*

## Gray Alder Swamp

**Formal name:** *Alnus incana Swamp Shrubland*

### *Environmental summary*

**Where it is found:** on shores, along edges of beaver meadows in stream floodplains, upland forests, and swales associated with small peatland streams, throughout the midwestern and northeastern United States and southern Canada.

**Soil information:** muck, well-decomposed peat, saturated or mineral soils.

**Characteristics:** Generally level to very slight slopes, with conditions ranging from temporarily flooded to more commonly seasonally flooded.

Water is typically not stagnant, nutrient rich and slightly calcareous, but can be somewhat stagnant and nutrient poor when over acidic bedrock or glacial till.

### *Vegetation*

A moderately open to dense shrub canopy is typical, ranging from 6 to 25 feet in height, with an understory of shorter shrubs and herbaceous species. The understory density varies inversely with the tall-shrub canopy.

*Acer rubrum* (red maple), *Fraxinus nigra* (black ash), and *Thuja occidentalis* (arborvitae) may be scattered in some stands.

*Alnus incana* (gray alder) overwhelmingly dominates the canopy. In areas where it is less dense, other shrub species may include:

*Cornus sericea* (red osier dogwood)
*Ilex verticillata* (common winterberry)
*Rubus idaeus* (American red raspberry)
*Salix spp.* (willows)
*Spiraea alba* (white meadowsweet)
*Spiraea tomentosa* (steeplebush)
*Viburnum spp.* (viburnum)

If the tall-shrub canopy is open, graminoids can become dense. The herbaceous layer contains species such as:

*Calamagrostis canadensis* (bluejoint)
*Caltha palustris* (swamp marigold)
*Carex lacustris* (hairy sedge)
*Carex prairea* (prairie sedge)
*Carex trisperma* (three-seeded sedge)
*Doellingeria umbellata* (parasol whitetop)
*Eupatorium maculatum* (spotted trumpet-weed)
*Glyceria melicaria* (melic mannagrass)
*Glyceria striata* (fowl mannagrass)
*Impatiens capensis* (jewelweed)
*Lycopus uniflorus* (northern bugleweed)
*Onoclea sensibilis* (sensitive fern)
*Osmunda cinnamomea* (cinnamon fern)
*Rubus pubescens* (dwarf red blackberry)
*Scirpus atrovirens* (green bulrush)
*Symphyotrichum lanceolatum var. lanceolatum* (white panicle aster)
*Symphyotrichum puniceum* (purple-stem aster)
*Symplocarpus foetidus* (skunk cabbage)
*Thelypteris palustris* (eastern marsh fern)
*Typha spp.* (cattails)
*Viola spp.* (violets)

Observed mosses include *Climacium dendroides* and *Sphagnum spp.*

## Floodplain Alder Thicket

**Formal name:** *Alnus serrulata - Physocarpus opulifolius Shrubland*

### Environmental summary

**Where it is found:** along rivers and streams on rocky shoals and gravel bars in the Central Appalachians, High Alleghenies and Western Allegheny Plateau regions.

**Soil information:** generally mineral with a thin organic layer.

**Characteristics:** a variety of environmental settings, including upland edge of marshes, adjacent to red maple wetlands, small upland depressions, and at the base of slopes, usually dominated by *Alnus serrulata* (hazel alder).

### Vegetation

*Alnus serrulata* and *Physocarpus opulifolius* (Ninebark) dominate the canopy, with, the latter generally contributing less cover in relation to Alnus. Woody associates include:

> *Cephalanthus occidentalis* (buttonbush)
> *Cornus amomum* (silky dogwood)
> *Decodon verticillatus* (swamp loosestrife)
> *Ilex verticillata* (common winterberry)
> *Rhododendron viscosum* (swamp azalea)
> *Salix spp.* (willows)
> *Sambucus canadensis* (black elderberry)

Herbaceous species may include
> *Carex stricta* (upright sedge)
> *Osmunda regalis* (royal fern)
> *Peltandra virginica* (green arrow arum)
> *Thelypteris palustris* (marsh fern)
> *Typha latifolia* (common cattail)

## Smooth Alder Swamp

**Formal name:** *Alnus serrulata Swamp Shrubland*

### Environmental summary

**Where it is found:** upland marsh borders, small upland depressions, at the edges of red maple swamps or other ponded drainages (often influenced by beavers), or in colluvium at the bases of slopes. Occurs throughout the northeastern United States south of near-boreal regions

**Soil information:** muck overlying mineral soils; peat deposits are atypical.

**Characteristics:** shrubby, circumneutral to slightly calcareous muck usually dominated by *Alnus serrulata* (smooth or hazel alder). Many of these wetlands may have been influenced by beaver or other impoundments.

This type can overlap with *Alnus incana* Swamp Shrubland where ranges abut in Pennsylvania. Where both alder species are present, this type is distinguished from the Alnus incana nominal type by the presence of species with more Central Appalachian / Alleghenian characteristics, such as *Physocarpus opulifolius*, *Rhododendron viscosum* and *Peltandra virginica*. More northern species like *Nemopanthus mucronatus* and *Myrica gale* are characteristic of *A. incana* Swamp Shrubland. Where communities blend, the two Alnus species vary in dominance; however if *Alnus serrulata* is present in more limited quantity, ecologists consider it to be a Smooth Alder Swamp.

### Vegetation

Tall shrubs, especially *Alnus serrulata* (hazel or smooth alder), sometimes in a mixture with (or rarely replaced by) *Alnus incana* (gray or speckled alder), dominate the vegetation. Saplings of *Acer rubrum* (red maple) are typical. Associate shrubs vary somewhat with geography and include:

> *Cornus sericea* (red osier dogwood)
> *Physocarpus opulifolius* (common ninebark)
> *Rosa palustris* (swamp rose)
> *Salix spp.* (willow)
> *Viburnum dentatum* (southern arrow-wood)

Short shrubs include *Spiraea alba var. latifolia* (meadowsweet) and *Lindera benzoin* (northern spicebush). Less frequent shrubs include:

*Cephalanthus occidentalis* (common buttonbush)
*Ilex verticillata* (common winterberry)
*Rhododendron viscosum* (swamp azalea)
*Sambucus canadensis* (elderberry)

Herbaceous species often reported are:
*Bidens cernua* (nodding beggartick)
*Calamagrostis canadensis* (bluejoint)
*Carex stricta* (upright sedge)
*Cicuta maculata* (spotted water hemlock)
*Galium spp.* (bedstraw)
*Galium tinctorium* (stiff marsh bedstraw)
*Glyceria striata* (fowl mannagrass)
*Osmunda regalis* (royal fern)
*Peltandra virginica* (green arrow arum)
*Thelypteris palustris* (eastern marsh fern)
*Typha latifolia* (broadleaf cattail)

## Buttonbush Shrub Swamp

**Formal name:** *Cephalanthus occidentalis - Decodon verticillatus Shrubland*

### Environmental summary

**Where it is found:** backwater sloughs or oxbow ponds, wet swales in floodplains, pond and lake borders, and small, isolated upland depressions where water levels recede very slowly, such as those with perched water tables. Found throughout the northeastern United States.

**Soil information:** loose organic muck or silt loams. The substrate may be organic or mineral soil.

**Characteristics:** swamps that experience prolonged or semi-permanent flooding throughout the growing season.

Water tables recede below the soil surface only during drought or very late in the growing season.

Fairly common in small-patch settings, this type of swamp is vulnerable to groundwater disruption, agricultural runoff, and adjacent forest clearing.

### Vegetation

*Cephalanthus occidentalis* (buttonbush) is so dominant, with coverage in excess of 50 percent as a tall or short shrub, that it is often monotypic. Occasional associates usually found in drier areas vary with precise environmental setting. These include:
*Cornus amomum* (silky dogwood)
*Rhododendron viscosum* (swamp azalea)
*Salix sericea* (silky willow)
*Sambucus nigra ssp. canadensis* (common elderberry)
*Vaccinium corymbosum* (highbush blueberry)

*Acer rubrum* (red maple) trees may be scattered in the wetland but are more likely along with *Fraxinus pennsylvanica* (white ash), *Acer saccharinum* (silver maple) and *Viburnum dentatum* (southern arrow wood) near upland borders and adjacent to floodplains.

The herbaceous layer is typically sparse to moderately dense and contains:
*Bidens connata* (purplestem beggarticks)
*Boehmeria cylindrica* (smallspike false nettle)
*Carex comosa* (longhair sedge)
*Dulichium arundinaceum* (threeway sedge)
*Galium trifidum* (threepetal bedstraw)
*Osmunda regalis* (royal fern)
*Scutellaria lateriflora* (blue skullcap)
*Sium suave* (hemlock water parsnip)
*Sparganium americanum* (American burreed)

Floating or submerged aquatic species such as *Lemna minor* (lesser duckweed), *Potamogeton natans* (broadleaf pondweed) and *Nuphar variegata* (variegated yellow pond lily) may be present. Bryophytes, if present, cling to shrub bases.

## Calcareous Shrub Fen

**Formal name:** *Cornus amomum - Salix candida / Dasiphora fruticosa ssp. floribunda / Carex stricta Shrubland*

### Environmental summary

**Where it is found:** small areas in Pennsylvania and New Jersey where calcareous groundwater seeps up to the surface, frequently at the base of such glacial features as gravelly moraines, on gently to moderately sloping surfaces.

**Soil information:** woody peat that gets most of its water supply from mineral-rich seepage, where seepage interaction with rock has increased alkalinity of the soil and raised nutrient levels. Areas of calcium carbonate or lime-rich mud or mudstone are typical.

**Characteristics:** hummocky microtopography covered by dense patches of shrubs and occasional graminoid openings. A portion of the water budget is comprised of strongly minerotrophic seepage water.

### Vegetation

Characteristic and dominant shrubs include *Cornus amomum* (silky dogwood), *Cornus sericea* (red osier dogwood), and *Salix* spp. (willows — especially *Salix candida, Salix petiolaris, Salix serissima,* and *Salix discolor*). *Juniperus virginiana* (eastern red cedar) is reported as scattered individuals at sites in New Jersey. Other shrubs include:

> *Alnus incana* (gray alder)
> *Myrica gale* (sweet gale)
> *Toxicodendron vernix* (poison sumac)
> *Viburnum dentatum* (southern arrow-wood)

In addition to the characteristic *Carex stricta* (upright sedge), common herbaceous species are

> *Carex lacustris* (hairy sedge)
> *Deschampsia caespitosa* (tufted hairgrass)
> *Drosera rotundifolia* (roundleaf sundew)
> *Equisetum fluviatile* (water horsetail)
> *Eupatorium maculatum* (spotted joe pye weed)
> *Ludwigia palustris* (marsh seedbox)
> *Muhlenbergia glomerata* (spiked muhly)
> *Parnassia glauca* (fen grass of Parnassus)
> *Solidago patula* (roundleaf goldenrod)
> *Solidago uliginosa* (bog goldenrod)
> *Spiranthes cernua* (nodding lady's tresses)
> *Thelypteris palustris* (marsh fern)
> *Trollius laxus* (American globeflower)

## Ridgetop Scrub Oak Barrens

**Formal name:** *Quercus ilicifolia — Prunus pumila Shrubland*

### Environmental summary

**Where it is found:** Open or sparsely wooded high-elevation ridges, hilltops and outcrops or rocky slopes.

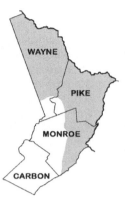

**Soil information:** excessively well-drained, extremely thin and shallow soils over acidic sandstone and shale bedrock.

**Characteristics:** patchy vegetation with occasional *Quercus ilicifolia* (bear oak) and stunted Pinus spp. Some areas have a fairly well-developed heath shrub layer, others a graminoid layer. Conditions are dry and nutrient-poor, and many sites have a history of fire.

### Vegetation

This shrubland is dominated by *Quercus ilicifolia* (bear oak), which occurs with variable cover depending on site conditions. Scattered and stunted trees, less than 30 feet, are common and include species from the surrounding ridgetop forests, such as:

> *Betula populifolia* (gray birch)
> *Carya glabra* (pignut hickory)
> *Pinus rigida* (pitch pine)
> *Populus tremuloides* (quaking aspen)
> *Quercus alba* (white oak)
> *Quercus prinus* (chestnut oak)
> *Quercus rubra* (northern red oak)

Associated shrubs, with cover of greater than 25 percent, include:

> *Amelanchier arborea* (serviceberry)
> *Comptonia peregrina* (sweetfern)
> *Gaylussacia baccata* (black huckleberry)
> *Kalmia angustifolia* (sheep laurel)
> *Photinia melanocarpa* (black chokeberry)
> *Prunus pumila* (sand cherry)
> *Quercus prinoides* (dwarf chinkapin oak)
> *Vaccinium angustifolium* (lowbush blueberry)

*Vaccinium pallidum* (Blue Ridge blueberry)

The herbaceous layer varies from 40 to 70 percent, depending on the density of shrub cover; about 50 percent is typical. Typical herbs reported include:

*Andropogon gerardii* (big bluestem)
*Carex pensylvanica* (Pennsylvania sedge)
*Comandra umbellata* (bastard toadflax)
*Corydalis sempervirens* (rock harlequin)
*Danthonia spicata* (poverty oatgrass)
*Deschampsia flexuosa* (wavy hairgrass)
*Gaultheria procumbens* (teaberry)
*Hypericum gentianoides* (orangegrass)
*Melampyrum lineare* (narrowleaf cowwheat)
*Polygonatum biflorum* (Solomon's seal)
*Pteridium aquilinum* (northern bracken fern)
*Schizachyrium scoparium* (little bluestem)
*Sibbaldiopsis tridentata* (shrubby fivefingers)

Mosses may be present with low total cover, especially polytrichum mosses (*Polytrichum* spp.).

## Willow River-Bar Shrubland

**Formal name:** *Salix nigra / Phalaris arundinacea - Apocynum cannabinum Temporarily Flooded Shrubland*

### Environmental summary

**Where it is found:** along moderate- to high-energy rivers in the northeastern United States and the high Allegheny plateau.

**Soil information:** cobble substrates within a sand or gravel matrix

**Characteristics:** occurs in areas that are flooded only during high-water events, but are also subjected to winter ice-scour. On a disturbance gradient, it is in between herbaceous cobble shores and higher floodplain forests.

### Vegetation

Salix nigra is often dominant or co-dominant with

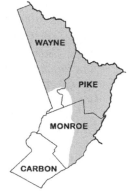

other willows or dogwoods that form a dense shrub layer. Less frequent shrubs and tree saplings are reported to include:

*Acer rubrum* (red maple)
*Acer saccharinum* (silver maple)
*Alnus incana* (gray alder)
*Alnus serrulata* (hazel alder)
*Cornus amomum* (silky dogwood)
*Cornus sericea* (red osier dogwood)
*Platanus occidentalis* (American sycamore)
*Populus deltoides* (eastern cottonwood)
*Salix eriocephala* (Missouri river willow)
*Salix lucida* (shining willow)
*Salix sericea* (silky willow)
*Spiraea alba var. latifolia* (white meadowsweet)

A typically sparse herbaceous later is of variable composition. It may include:

*Agrostis spp.* (bentgrass)
*Apocynum cannabinum* (Indian hemp)
*Bidens spp.* (beggarticks)
*Calamagrostis canadensis* (bluejoint)
*Carex torta* (twisted sedge)
*Dichanthelium clandestinum* (deertongue)
*Elymus virginicus* (Virginia wild rye)
*Eupatorium maculatum* (spotted trumpetweed)
*Lysimachia terrestris* (earth loosestrife)
*Panicum dichotomiflorum* (fall panicgrass)
*Panicum virgatum* (switchgrass)
*Phalaris arundinacea* (reed canarygrass)
*Polygonum spp.* (smartweed)
*Solidago gigantea* (giant goldenrod)
*Solidago rugosa* (winkleleaf goldenrod)

## Blueberry Wetland Thicket

**Formal name:** *Vaccinium corymbosum - Rhododendron viscosum - Clethra alnifolia Shrubland*

### Environmental summary

**Where it is found:** seasonally flooded zones within larger wetlands, the margins of coastal plain ponds, closed sandplain basins and small open basins throughout the eastern United States.

**Soil information:** typically a thin organic layer over mineral soil, often sand.

**Characteristics:** A tall-shrub swamp fluctuating water table floods the area in spring and early summer, then drops below the soil surface by late summer.

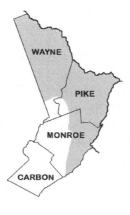

### Vegetation

While scattered *Acer rubrum* (red maple) is common, the habitat is composed primarily of tall shrubs dominated by *Vaccinium corymbosum* (highbush blueberry), *Ilex verticillata* (winterberry) and *Rhododendron viscosum* (swamp azalea).

Characteristic, but not usually dominant, are *Lyonia ligustrina* (maleberry) and *Cephalanthus occidentalis* (buttonbush).

Associates in the shrub layer include:
    *Alnus serrulata* (hazel alder)
    *Chamaedaphne calyculata* (leatherleaf)
    *Clethra alnifolia* (sweet pepperbush)
    *Decodon verticillatus* (swamp loosestrife)
    *Ilex glabra* (inkberry)
    *Kalmia angustifolia* (sheep laurel)
    *Leucothoe racemosa* (swamp doghobble)
    *Myrica gale* (sweet gale)
    *Photinia spp.* (chokeberry)
    *Spiraea tomentosa* (steeplebush)

The herbaceous layer typically includes:
    *Calla palustris* (water arum)
    *Dulichium arundinaceum* (threeway sedge)
    *Glyceria striata* (fowl mannagrass)
    *Juncus effusus* (common rush)
    *Leersia oryzoides* (rice cutgrass)
    *Lycopus uniflorus* (northern bugleweed)
    *Onoclea sensibilis* (sensitive fern)
    *Osmunda cinnamomea* (cinnamon fern)
    *Osmunda regalis* (royal fern)
    *Thelypteris palustris* (marshfern)
    *Triadenum virginicum* (Virginia marsh St. Johnswort)
    *Woodwardia virginica* (Virginia chainfern)

A layer of peat moss is typical and often includes *Sphagnum fimbriatum, Sphagnum rubellum, Sphagnum magellanicum, Sphagnum fallax,* and *Sphagnum viridum.*

## Steeplebush Successional Meadow

**Formal name:** *Spiraea tomentosa - Rubus spp. / Phalaris arundinacea Shrubland*

### Environmental summary

**Where it is found:** low areas of old fields or pastures, headwater basins and beaver-impacted wetlands, throughout the Poconos. It is known from the Central Appalachian ecoregion, the High Alleghany Plateau, Western Alleghany Plateau, North Atlantic Coast, and the Lower New England / Northern Piedmont ecoregions, and is likely in others.

**Soil information:** a layer of surface muck over a substrate of usually mineral soil.

**Characteristics**: a wetland that typically floods early in the growing season and may remain saturated for some of the growing season, but generally dry for much of the year.

### Vegetation

Varies from shrub thickets to herbaceous meadows with scattered shrubs. Commonly reported are:
    *Cornus amomum* (silky dogwood)
    *Rubus allegheniensis* (Allegheny blackberry)
    *Rubus hispidus* (bristly dewberry)
    *Salix spp.* (willow)
    *Spiraea alba var. alba* (white meadowsweet)
    *Spiraea tomentosa* (steeplebush)

Depending on land-use history, herbaceous species are variable in composition. Widely reported are:
    *Calamagrostis canadensis* (bluejoint)
    *Carex folliculata* (northern long sedge)
    *Carex lupulina* (hop sedge)
    *Carex lurida* (shallow sedge)
    *Carex scoparia* (broom sedge)
    *Carex trichocarpa* (hairyfruit sedge)
    *Carex vulpinoidea* (fox sedge)

*Eleocharis spp.* (spikerush)
*Eupatorium maculatum* (Joe-pye weed)
*Impatiens capensis* (jewelweed)
*Juncus effusus* (corkscrew rush)
*Leersia oryzoides* (rice cutgrass)
*Lycopus uniflorus* (northern bugleweed)
*Onoclea sensibilis* (sensitive fern)
*Phalaris arundinacea* (reed canary-grass)
*Polygonum sagittatum* (arrowleaf tear-thumb)
*Scirpus cyperinus* (woolgrass)
*Scirpus expansus* (woodland bulrush)
*Solidago canadensis* (Canada goldenrod)
*Solidago gigantea* (giant goldenrod)
*Solidago rugosa* (wrinkleleaf goldenrod)
*Thelypteris palustris* (eastern marsh fern)
*Triadenum virginicum* (Virginia marsh saint johnswort)
*Vernonia noveboracensis* (New York iron-weed)

## Highbush Blueberry Bog Thicket

**Formal name:** *Vaccinium corymbosum / Sphagnum spp. Shrubland*

### *Environmental summary*

**Where it is found**: typically as a border thicket around more open dwarf heath shrub peatlands or within small, isolated basins or kettles, lacking inlet or outlet streams, in glaciated regions of the northeastern United States.

**Soil information:** typically deep, acidic peat, ranging from nutrient poor to weak.

**Characteristics:** a tall-shrub bog thicket with substantial fluctuation in seasonal water levels, usually wetter than dwarf heath shrub bogs.

### *Vegetation*

Some sparse and scattered trees may occur, depending on the environmental setting, including:

*Acer rubrum* (red maple)

*Betula populifolia* (gray birch)
*Larix laricina* (tamarack)
*Nyssa sylvatica* (black gum)
*Picea mariana* (black spruce)
*Pinus rigida* (pitch pine)
*Pinus strobus* (eastern white pine)

The characteristic tall shrub layer features significant Vaccinium corymbosum (highbush blueberry). Locations result in variable mixes.

In more northern or cooler microclimates:
*Chamaedaphne calyculata* (leatherleaf)
*Gaylussacia baccata* (black huckleberry)
*Kalmia angustifolia* (sheep laurel)
*Lyonia ligustrina* (maleberry)
*Nemopanthus mucronatus* (catberry)
*Rhododendron canadense* (rhodora)

In locally wetter areas:
*Cephalanthus occidentalis* (common buttonbush)
*Decodon verticillatus* (swamp loosestrife)

More coastal areas:
*Clethra alnifolia* (sweet pepperbush)
*Gaylussacia dumosa* (dwarf huckleberry)
*Leucothoe racemosa* (swamp doghobble)

Although patches can be locally abundant, the herbaceous layer is usually somewhat sparse. Reported locally are:
*Carex trisperma* (threeseeded sedge)
*Maianthemum trifolium* (threeleaf false lily of the valley)
*Osmunda cinnamomea* (cinnamon fern)
*Sarracenia purpurea* (purple pitcher plant)
*Thelypteris palustris* (marsh fern)
*Triadenum virginicum* (Virginia marsh St. Johns wort)
*Woodwardia virginica* (Virginia chainfern)

Hummock-and-hollow microtypography is typically covered by Sphagnum mosses, including: *Sphagnum magellanicum, Sphagnum centrale, Sphagnum rubellum, Sphagnum capillifolium, Sphagnum fimbriatum,* and *Sphagnum fuscum.*

## Appalachian Blueberry Shrubland

**Formal name:** *Vaccinium (angustifolium, myrtilloides, pallidum) Central Appalachian Dwarf-shrubland*

## Environmental summary

**Where it is found:** mid- to high-elevation acidic rock outcrops or summits, ledges, summits of igneous or metamorphic rock; sometimes found in depressions on level outwash plains or valley floor frost pockets.

**Soil structure:** shallow accumulations of organic material on bedrock habitats, or rapidly drained and nutrient-poor sands on outwash plains.

**Characteristics:** abundant dwarf Vaccinium spp. in areas with frequent fire and/or droughty soils.

## Vegetation

Commonly referred to as "heath barrens," the community is dominated by heaths or heath-like shrubs, typically blueberries:

>*Vaccinium angustifolium* (lowbush blueberry)
>*Vaccinium myrtilloides* (velvetleaf huckleberry)
>*Vaccinium pallidum* (Blue Ridge blueberry)
>*Vaccinium stamineum* (upland highbush blueberry)

Small trees may be present but are infrequent. In addition to Vaccinium, the shrub layer typically contains other low shrubs such as

>*Comptonia peregrina* (sweetfern)
>*Gaylussacia baccata* (black huckleberry)
>*Kalmia angustifolia* (sheep laurel)
>*Kalmia latifolia* (mountain laurel)
>*Lyonia ligustrina* (maleberry)
>*Quercus ilicifolia* (bear oak)

The herbaceous layer is usually sparse with low diversity. Herbaceous plants scattered among the shrubs include:

>*Carex argyrantha* (hay sedge)
>*Carex pensylvanica* (Pennsylvania sedge)
>*Danthonia spicata* (poverty oatgrass)
>*Deschampsia flexuosa* (wavy hairgrass)
>*Lycopodium dendroideum* (tree groundpine)
>*Lycopodium digitatum* (fan clubmoss)
>*Lysimachia quadrifolia* (whorled yellow loosestrife)
>*Melampyrum lineare* (narrowleaf cowwheat)
>*Piptatherum pungens* (mountain ricegrass)
>*Rubus hispidus* (bristly dewberry)
>*Schizachyrium scoparium* (little bluestem)
>*Solidago canadensis* (Canada goldenrod)

Mosses (including *Polytrichum* spp.) and lichens usually are present.

# Blueberry Granite Barrens

**Formal name:** *Vaccinium angustifolium - Sorbus americana / Sibbaldiopsis tridentata Dwarf-shrubland*

## Environmental Summary

**Where it is found:** northern or high-elevation rocky ridges, summits and outcrops in the glaciated northeastern states.

**Soil information:** shallow, well-drained, dry, acidic coarse sands that accumulate in sheltered areas or crevices within exposed bedrock, often granite.

**Characteristics:** the combination of boreal species like *Sorbus americana* and *Sibbaldiopsis tridentata* combined with temperate species such as *Quercus rubra, Quercus prinus, Carex pensylvanica, Carex lucorum,* and *Betula populifolia*. If trees are present, they are stunted and provide less than 10 percent cover. Scattered tall shrubs are limited to protected areas; dwarf shrubs cover as much as 75 percent. Sparse herbs can be found in rock crevices and depressions, and a bryoid layer that includes both lichens and mosses can range from sparse to well developed.

## Vegetation

Patchy and variable the community character can be woodland, shrubland or sparsely vegetated rock.

Tree species reported for this association include:

*Abies balsamea* (balsam fir)
*Acer rubrum* (red maple)
*Betula papyrifera* (paper birch)
*Betula populifolia* (gray birch)
*Picea rubens* (red spruce)
*Pinus strobus* (eastern white pine)
*Quercus rubra* (northern red oak)

Scattered tall shrubs include:
*Amelanchier spp.* (serviceberry)
*Comptonia peregrina* (sweetfern)
*Nemopanthus mucronatus* (mountain holly)
*Photinia melanocarpa* (black chokeberry)
*Sorbus americana* (American mountain ash)
*Viburnum nudum var. cassinoides* (witherrod viburnum)

Prominent dwarf heath shrubs include
*Arctostaphylos uva-ursi* (kinnikinnick)
*Gaylussacia baccata* (black huckleberry)
*Kalmia angustifolia* (sheep laurel)
*Vaccinium angustifolium* (lowbush blueberry)
*Vaccinium myrtilloides* (velvet-leaf huckleberry)
*Vaccinium pallidum* (Blue Ridge blueberry)

The sparse herb layer includes:
*Carex lucorum* (Blue Ridge sedge)
*Danthonia spicata* (poverty oatgrass)
*Deschampsia flexuosa* (wavy hairgrass)
*Gaultheria procumbens* (teaberry)
*Maianthemum canadense* (Canada mayflower)
*Minuartia glabra* (Appalachian stitchwort)
*Piptatherum pungens* (mountain ricegrass)
*Pteridium aquilinum* (northern bracken fern)
*Schizachyrium scoparium* (little bluestem)
*Sibbaldiopsis tridentata* (shrubby fivefingers)
*Trientalis borealis* (starflower)

Abundant mosses and lichens are reported to form a bryophyte layer that include:
*Cladonia* and *Cladina* lichens (reindeer lichens)
*Dicranum polysetum* (dicranum moss)
*Polytrichum commune* (polytrichum moss)
*Polytrichum juniperinum* (juniper polytrichum moss)
*Polytrichum piliferum* (polytrichum moss)

## Leatherleaf Bog

**Formal name:** *Chamaedaphne calyculata - (Gaylussacia dumosa) - Decodon verticillatus / Woodwardia virginica Dwarf-shrubland*

### Environmental summary

**Where it is found:** peat-accumulating basins that offer little to support life, generally in areas of black spruce bogs that become too wet to support Picea mariana, in the glaciated northeast, westward to the western Allegheny Plateau, and Ontario, Canada.

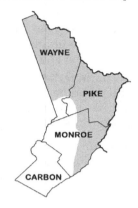

**Soil information:** ombrotrophic — that is, a mat of wet, spongy peat forming ground that gets water and nutrients directly from rainfall, usually with a pH of less than 4.2 and dominated by sphagnum moss.

**Characteristics:** a quaking or floating bog dominated by Sphagnum mosses and ericaceous shrubs.

### Vegetation

*Chamaedaphne calyculata* (leatherleaf) dominates. Local associate species generally occur with low cover, although they may be locally common and include:
*Gaylussacia baccata* (black huckleberry)
*Kalmia angustifolia* (sheep laurel)
*Kalmia polifolia* (bog laurel)
*Vaccinium macrocarpon* (cranberry)
*Vaccinium oxycoccos* (small cranberry)

Scattered tall shrubs may occur, but always with low cover. These include:
*Acer rubrum* (red maple)
*Larix laricina* (tamarack)
*Picea mariana* (black spruce)
*Rhododendron viscosum* (swamp azalea)
*Vaccinium corymbosum* (highbush blueberry)

A low herbaceous cover may include scattered:
*Calopogon tuberosus* (tuberous grasspink)
*Carex trisperma* (three seeded sedge)

*Drosera intermedia* (spoonleaf sundew)
*Drosera rotundifolia* (roundleaf sundew)
*Eriophorum virginicum* (tawny cottongrass)
*Pogonia ophioglossoides* (snakemouth orchid)
*Sarracenia purpurea* (purple pitcherplant)
*Woodwardia virginica* (Virginia chainfern)

Wetter fen meadows may include:
*Carex canescens* (silvery sedge)
*Carex limosa* (mud sedge)
*Glyceria canadensis* (rattlesnake mannagrass)
*Triadenum virginicum* (Virginia marsh St. John's wort)
*Utricularia cornuta* (horned bladderwort)
*Rhynchospora alba* (white beaksedge)
*Scheuchzeria palustris* (rannoch-rush)

Edges of floating mats tend to receive more nutrient enrichment and support such species as *Peltandra virginica* (green arrow arum), *Decodon verticillatus* (swamp loosestrife), and *Dulichium arundinaceum* (three-way sedge)

A well-developed bryophyte layer is generally dominated by *Sphagnum capillifolium*, *Sphagnum magellanicum*, *Sphagnum rubellum*, and *Sphagnum fuscum* with *Sphagnum bartlettianum*, *Sphagnum cuspidatum*, *Sphagnum fallax*, and *Sphagnum recurvum* also possible in some areas.

## Silky Willow Shrub Swamp

**Formal name:** *Salix sericea Shrubland*

### Environmental summary

**Where it is found**: topographic basins, floodplain backswamps, along slow-moving streams and on lake shores.

**Soil information:** Bedrock may be shale, limestone, or sandstone. Soil texture varies and is composed of moderately to very poorly drained silty clay, silt, muck, or peat

**Characteristics:** commonly a successional shrub swamp on temporarily or semi-permanently flooded or saturated soils

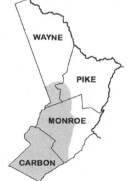

in the Allegheny Mountains. Reported as a small patch on gently sloping land along seepage zones in open wetlands and headwater drainages with intermittent overland flow.

### Vegetation

*Salix sericea* (silky willow) forms a dominant tall-shrub canopy six to 10 feet in height. Associated shrubs in the Central Appalachian region and *Alnus incana ssp. rugosa* (speckled alder). Sometimes reported are:
*Ilex verticillata* (common winterberry)
*Photinia melanocarpa* (black chokeberry)
*Photinia pyrifolia* (red chokeberry)
*Picea rubens* (red spruce)
*Populus tremuloides* (quaking aspen)
*Sambucus canadensis* (black elderberry)
*Vaccinium myrtilloides* (velvetleaf huckleberry)

A dense and varied herbaceous layer often includes:
*Carex gynandra* (nodding sedge)
*Carex leptalea ssp. leptalea* (bristly-stalked sedge)
*Carex lurida* (shallow sedge)
*Carex scoparia var. scoparia* (broom sedge)
*Carex stipata* (awlfruit sedge)
*Dryopteris cristata* (crested woodfern)
*Euthamia graminifolia* (flat-topped goldentop)
*Galium tinctorium* (stiff marsh bedstraw)
*Glyceria canadensis* (rattlesnake mannagrass)
*Glyceria laxa* (limp mannagrass)
*Glyceria striata* (fowl mannagrass)
*Juncus effusus* (common rush)
*Leersia oryzoides* (rice cutgrass)
*Osmunda cinnamomea var. cinnamomea* (cinnamon fern)
*Polygonum sagittatum* (arrowleaf tearthumb)
*Rubus hispidus* (bristly dewberry)
*Solidago uliginosa* (bog goldenrod)
*Symphyotrichum puniceum var. puniceum* (purplestem aster)
*Typha latifolia* (common cattail)

Hummocks are often covered by *Sphagnum spp.*

# *Perennial graminoid vegetation*

## Fall-line Riverwash Bedrock Prairie

**Formal name**: *Andropogon gerardii - Panicum virgatum - Baptisia australis Herbaceous Vegetation*

### Environmental summary

**Where it is found:** along high-gradient sections of major rivers, especially gorges and along the fall-line.

It is usually found in rocky areas within the active channel shelf at an intermediate level, between low-water and bank-full levels, throughout the east-central United States.

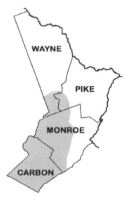

**Soil information:** rapidly-drained unconsolidated course and fine sand deposits, with soil material restricted to spaces of tightly-packed boulders or small crevices in bedrock exposures. Neutral to high pH is typical.

**Characteristics:** Flood scouring and ice floods represent significant abrasive forces that shape the physiognomy and composition of an association dominated by robust, luxuriant grasses.

Although coarse-textured substrates have the potential to be well drained, fluvial topography and high water tables can result in a mix of well-drained and poorly drained microsites.

Scoured out potholes on flat bedrock often hold flood and rain water, and vegetation tends to be confined to cracks and sediment accumulations.

Frequent flash flooding dramatically alters the association and keeps vegetation open.

### Vegetation

Scattered and flood-battered shrubs and tree saplings can occur, but the surface is primarily dominated by a variety of grasses and resembles prairie vegetation.

If trees and shrubs are present, they tend to be short and display the consequences of flood battering. Observed trees and shrubs include:

*Alnus serrulata* (hazel alder)
*Betula nigra* (river birch)
*Cephalanthus occidentalis* (common buttonbush)
*Chionanthus virginicus* (white fringe-tree)
*Cornus amomum* (silky dogwood)
*Diospyros virginiana* (common persimmon)
*Fraxinus americana* (white ash)
*Fraxinus pennsylvanica* (green ash)
*Hypericum prolificum* (shrubby St. John-swort)
*Platanus occidentalis* (American sycamore)
*Salix caroliniana* (coastal plain willow)
*Ulmus americana* (American elm)
*Ulmus rubra* (slippery elm)

Graminoids, however, dominate the scene. These primarily include:

*Andropogon gerardii* (big bluestem)
*Panicum virgatum* (switchgrass)
*Sorghastrum nutans* (Indiangrass)
*Spartina pectinata* (prairie cordgrass)

Many of the locally observed forbs are prairie-typical, including:

*Allium cernuum* (nodding onion)
*Apocynum cannabinum* (Indian hemp)
*Baptisia australis* (wild blue indigo)
*Bidens frondosa* (devil's beggar tick)
*Chasmanthium latifolium* (northern sea oats)
*Cyperus strigosus* (false nutsedge)

*Eupatorium coelestinum* (blue mistflower)
*Eupatorium fistulosum* (Joe Pye weed)
*Lespedeza violacea* (slender bush clover)
*Lobelia cardinalis* (cardinal flower)
*Ludwigia alternifolia* (false loosestrife)
*Packera aurea* (golden ragwort)
*Physostegia virginiana* (false dragonhead)
*Potentilla simplex* (old field cinquefoil)
*Pycnanthemum virginianum* (mountain-mint)
*Rhynchospora capitellata* (beak rush)
*Solidago juncea* (early goldenrod)
*Symphyotrichum laeve* (smooth blue aster)
*Teucrium canadense* (wild germander)
*Toxicodendron radicans* (poison ivy)
*Veronicastrum virginicum* (Culver's root)
*Viola cucullata* (blue marsh violet)
*Zizia aurea* (golden Alexander)

## Bluejoint Wet Meadow

**Formal name:** *Calamagrostis canadensis - Eupatorium maculatum Herbaceous Vegetation*

### Environmental summary

**Where it is found:** small stream floodplains, poorly drained depressions, levees, lakeshores and beaver meadows, throughout the northeastern and midwestern U.S. and central and eastern Canada.

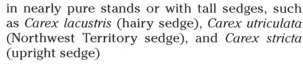

**Soil information:** mineral soil, peat silt loam, or well-decomposed peat usually with a thick root mat.

**Characteristics:** can be temporarily or seasonally flooded, with a dense graminoid cover dominated by *Calamagrostis canadensis* (Canada blue joint). This type of meadow is reported to be drier than sedge meadows and less peaty than shore fens; it is usually less than 50 percent sedge cover.

### Vegetation

Graminoid cover is often very dense, leading to a hummocky microtopography. *Calamagrostis canadensis* is so dominant that it sometimes occurs in nearly pure stands or with tall sedges, such as *Carex lacustris* (hairy sedge), *Carex utriculata* (Northwest Territory sedge), and *Carex stricta* (upright sedge)

*Carex lasiocarpa* (woolyfruit sedge) is reported in fen transitions, and sometimes abundant are *Agrostis gigantea* (redtop), *Glyceria grandis* (American mannagrass), *Poa palustris* (fowl bluegrass), *Poa compressa* (Canada bluegrass), *Scirpus cyperinus* (woolgrass), and *Typha latifolia* (broadleaf cattail).

Examples of typical forbs are:
*Campanula aparinoides* (marsh bellflower)
*Comarum palustre* (purple marshlocks)
*Epilobium leptophyllum* (bog willowherb)
*Eupatorium maculatum* (spotted trumpet weed)
*Eupatorium perfoliatum* (common boneset)
*Impatiens capensis* (jewel weed)
*Iris versicolor* (blue flag iris)
*Polygonum amphibium* (water knotweed)

Some scattered shrubs may obtain a foothold, and would commonly include:
*Alnus incana* (gray alder)
*Alnus serrulata* (hazel alder)
*Cornus amomum* (silky dogwood)
*Spiraea alba* (white meadowsweet)
*Viburnum dentatum* (southern arrow-wood)
*Viburnum nudum* (possum-haw)

## Mixed Graminoid Meadow

**Formal name:** *Calamagrostis canadensis - Scirpus spp. - Dulichium arundinaceum Herbaceous Vegetation*

### Environmental summary

**Where it is found:** flats, floodplains of small streams, lakeshores and beaver meadows in the northeastern United States.

**Soil information:** slightly acidic (pH 5.0 to 6.0) well-decomposed peat or muck over mineral soil.

**Characteristics:** generally flooded in spring,

most sites dry to exposed soil during the summer while some remain very saturated, with vegetation dominated by strong graminoids or graminoid-shrub mixes. Shrub cover ranges from zero to 50 percent, but graminoids usually exceeds woody cover and can range from 40 to nearly 100 percent cover.

Similar to other wet meadow types, these sites are different because they are not dominated by *Carex stricta*, *Calamagrostis canadensis*, or *Phalaris arundinacea*.

### Vegetation

Reported shrub species most commonly include *Spiraea alba* (white meadowsweet) and *Salix spp.* (willow). Others vary with the site and may include:

> *Alnus incana* (gray alder)
> *Alnus serrulata* (hazel alder)
> *Cephalanthus occidentalis* (common buttonbush)
> *Cornus sericea* (red osier dogwood)
> *Ilex verticillata* (winterberry)
> *Myrica gale* (sweetgale)
> *Salix pedicellaris* (bog willow)
> *Spiraea tomentosa* (steeplebush)
> *Vaccinium corymbosum* (highbush blueberry)
> *Viburnum dentatum* (southern arrow-wood)

Dominating the herbaceous layer is a combination of *Calamagrostis canadensis* (bluejoint), *Scirpus* spp. (including *Scirpus cyperinus*, *Scirpus expansus*, and *Scirpus atrovirens*) (bulrush), and *Dulichium arundinaceum* (threeway sedge)

> Other locally common species may include
> *Acorus calamus* (calamus)
> *Carex lacustris* (hairy sedge)
> *Carex lupulina* (hop sedge)
> *Carex lupuliformis* (false hop sedge)
> *Carex lurida* (shallow sedge)
> *Carex stricta* (upright sedge)
> *Carex utriculata* (Northwest Territory sedge)
> *Glyceria canadensis* (rattlesnake mannagrass)
> *Glyceria grandis* (American mannagrass)
> *Iris versicolor* (harlequin blueflag)
> *Hypericum ellipticum* (pale St. Johnswort)
> *Juncus canadensis* (Canada rush)

> *Leersia oryzoides* (rice cutgrass)
> *Leersia virginica* (whitegrass)
> *Lysimachia terrestris* (earth loosestrife)
> *Onoclea sensibilis* (sensitive fern)
> *Osmunda regalis* (royal fern)
> *Phalaris arundinacea* (reed canarygrass)
> *Poa palustris* (fowl bluegrass)
> *Triadenum fraseri* (Fraser's marsh St. Johnswort)

*Typha latifolia* (common cattail) is occasionally observed, but these sites are usually higher in relation to the water table than typical cattail marshes.

## Prairie Sedge - Tussock Sedge Fen

**Formal name:** *Carex prairea - Carex stricta - Pycnanthemum virginianum Herbaceous Vegetation*

### Environmental summary

**Where it is found:** saturated peat-accumulating, wet, sedge-dominated glaciated areas of Pennsylvania near calcareous seeps and springs.

**Soil information**: peaty, organic soil over coarse-textured glacial materials, saturated by base-rich groundwater.

**Characteristics:** open to dense graminoids shorter than 36 inches form most of the vegetation.

### Vegetation

*Carex prairea* (prairie sedge) and *Carex stricta* (upright sedge) usually dominate the site. Associated sedges are reported to include:

> *Carex aquatilis* (water sedge)
> *Carex lacustris* (hairy sedge)
> *Carex lasiocarpa* (woolyfruit sedge)
> *Carex leptalea* (bristlystalked sedge)
> *Carex sterilis* (dioecious sedge)

Associated herbs may include:

> *Cirsium muticum* (swamp thistle)
> *Epilobium leptophyllum* (bog willow herb)
> *Eupatorium maculatum* (spotted joe pye weed)
> *Galium tinctorium* (stiff marsh bedstraw)

*Impatiens capensis* (jewelweed)
*Juncus balticus* (mountain rush)
*Maianthemum stellatum* (starry false lily of the valley)
*Onoclea sensibilis* (sensitive fern)
*Pycnanthemum virginianum* (Virginia mountainmint)
*Typha latifolia* (common cattail)
*Verbena hastata* (swamp verbena)

Bryophytes typically include: *Campylium stellatum* (star campylium moss), *Thuidium delicatulum* (delicate thuidium moss), *Sphagnum teres* (sphagnum).

## Tussock Sedge Meadow

**Formal name:** *Carex stricta - Carex vesicaria Herbaceous Vegetation*

### Environmental summary

**Where it is found:** seasonally flooded basins or on lake or stream edges, throughout the northeastern United States.

**Soil information:** muck or peat or muck of varied depth over mineral soil.

**Characteristics:** Depending on precipitation and local conditions, standing water can be present at the beginning of or throughout the growing season.

Soils remain saturated even when water levels drop, and microtopography is characterized by large tussocks, especially when the community remains quite wet.

### Vegetation

Shrub cover is less than 25 percent and trees are absent. When present, they may include:
*Alnus incana* (gray alder)
*Chamaedaphne calyculata* (leatherleaf)
*Ilex verticillata* (common winterberry)
*Myrica gale* (sweetgale)
*Spiraea alba* (meadowsweet)

The strong and varied herbaceous layer is primarily graminoids and *Carex stricta* (tussock sedge) in tussock form is typically dominant. *Carex vesicaria* (blister sedge), *Carex utriculata* (Northwest territory sedge), and *Calamagrostis canadensis* (bluejoint) may be locally abundant.

Associated graminoids include:
*Carex atlantica* (prickly bog sedge)
*Carex canescens* (silvery sedge)
*Carex comosa* (longhair sedge)
*Carex folliculata* (northern long sedge)
*Carex scoparia* (broom sedge)
*Carex stipata* (awlfruit sedge)
*Carex vulpinoidea* (fox sedge)
*Dulichium arundinaceum* (three-way sedge)
*Glyceria canadensis* (rattlesnake mannagrass)
*Juncus effusus* (common rush)
*Leersia oryzoides* (rice cutgrass)
*Scirpus cyperinus* (woolgrass)

Forbs and ferns include:
*Angelica atropurpurea* (purplestem angelica)
*Asclepias incarnata* (swamp milkweed)
*Campanula aparinoides* (marsh bellflower)
*Comarum palustre* (purple marshlocks)
*Eupatorium maculatum* (spotted trumpetweed)
*Eupatorium perfoliatum* (common boneset)
*Galium obtusum* (bluntleaf bedstraw)
*Galium tinctorium* (stiff marsh bedstraw)
*Lycopus americanus* (American water horehound)
*Lysimachia terrestris* (earth loosestrife)
*Osmunda regalis* (royal fern)
*Polygonum hydropiperoides* (swamp smartweed)
*Polygonum sagittatum* (arrowleaf tearthumb)
*Thelypteris palustris* (eastern marsh fern)

Bryophytes, where present, include:
*Sphagnum magellanicum*
*Sphagnum girgensohnii*
*Sphagnum palustre*
*Drepanocladus aduncus*

Bryophyte cover is usually sparse but may occasionally reach over 50 percent.

## Cobble Scour Rivershore

**Formal name:** *Carex torta - Apocynum cannabinum - Cyperus spp. Herbaceous Vegetation*

### Environmental summary

**Where it is found:** cobble, gravel, and sand bars or banks along medium to high energy river channels and, less often, on exposed lakeshores with heavy wave activity from Pennsylvania through New England.

**Soil information:** large coarse substrates that are alluvial deposits.

**Characteristics:** Seasonal flooding and ice-scour keep these communities open. They develop in areas of active channels that are exposed at low water levels or during drought years. Vegetative cover is often inversely proportional to scour and inundation.

### Vegetation

Density varies with the degree of flooding and length of exposure, with the most characteristic perennial species being *Carex torta* (twisted sedge) and low *Salix spp.* (willow) both of which can tolerate the environment.

Associated species are sparse, highly variable and diverse. Often reported are:

> *Apocynum cannabinum* (Indian hemp)
> *Verbena hastata* (swamp verbena)
> *Symphyotrichum puniceum* (purplestem aster)
> *Doellingeria umbellata* (parasol flattop)
> *Solidago rugosa* (wrinkleleaf goldenrod)
> *Solidago canadensis* (Canada goldenrod)
> *Solidago gigantea* (giant goldenrod)
> *Calamagrostis canadensis* (bluejoint)
> *Phalaris arundinacea* (reed canarygrass)
> *Scirpus expansus* (woodland bulrush)
> *Scirpus cyperinus* (woolgrass)
> *Thelypteris palustris* (eastern marsh fern)
> *Scutellaria lateriflora* (blue skullcap)
> *Dichanthelium clandestinum* (deertongue)
> *Eupatorium maculatum* (spotted joe pye

weed)
> *Eupatorium perfoliatum* (common boneset)
> *Elymus riparius* (riverbank rye)
> *Cyperus strigosus* (straw-colored flat sedge)
> *Eleocharis spp.* (spikerush)
> *Lobelia cardinalis* (cardinal flower)
> *Onoclea sensibilis* (sensitive fern)
> *Viola spp.* (violets)
> *Clematis virginiana* (virgins bower)
> *Polygonum amphibium* (water knotweed)
> *Polygonum hydropiper* (marshpepper knotweed)
> *Polygonum pensylvanicum* (Pennsylvania smartweed)
> *Polygonum sagittatum* (arrowleaf tearthumb)
> *Polygonum punctatum* (dotted smartweed)
> *Polygonum lapathifolium* (curly-top knotweed)
> *Schizachyrium scoparium* (little bluestem)
> *Andropogon gerardii* (big bluestem)
> *Sanguisorba canadensis* (Canadian burnet)

Battered and stunted shrubs and trees may include *Salix sericea* (silky willow), *Salix eriocephala* (Missouri River willow), *Cornus amomum* (silky dogwood), *Betula nigra* (river birch), *Populus deltoides* (eastern cottonwood), and *Platanus occidentalis* (American sycamore). Nonvascular plants can be sparse, but where present can include *Bryum spp.*

## Twisted Sedge Rocky Bar and Shore

**Formal name:** *Carex torta Herbaceous Vegetation*

### Environmental summary

**Where it is found:** rock, gravel and sand bars along frequently flooded, active channel shelves of high-gradient streams and small rivers in valleys and gorges. Found throughout the Central Appalachians, Allegheny Mountains, Piedmont, Southern Appalachians and Cumberland Plateau.

**Soil information:** moderately to poorly drained sand with pH averaging 6.5. No organic soils are present.

**Characteristics:** Small, discontinuous linear patches of alluvial wetlands featuring light-requiring, tough-rooted herbaceous perennials, especially *Carex torta* (twisted sedge) tolerant of frequent inundation and flood-scouring, which can occur at any time of year.

Periodic major flooding transports and deposits many cobbles, stones and even boulders to form bars within the channel as islands and along the stream banks. The bars become depositories for finer alluvium and habitats for sturdy herbaceous plants that can adapt to flood battering and colonize it with huge networks of perennial rootstocks. Regular high-energy flooding batters and often removes woody plants that take root, which in turn maintains an open canopy. When herbaceous perennials establish colonies on the bars, they serve to stabilize it until severe floods reshape it or add new deposits.

### Vegetation

The features of these associations can vary from purely herbaceous to shrubby, depending on localized conditions, including the frequency and energy of flooding.

Overhanging canopy may include *Platanus occidentalis* (American sycamore), *Betula alleghaniensis* (yellow birch) or *Acer rubrum* (red maple), and overhanging shrubs may include *Rhododendron maximum* (great rhododendron).

Observed in some stands within the association are scattered shrubs and small, battered specimens of *P. occidentalis*, *Betula nigra* (river birch), *Cornus amomum* (silky dogwood), *Alnus serrulata* (hazel alder) and *Carpinus caroliniana* (American hornbeam).

The dominant herbaceous layer features *Carex torta* (twisted sedge) in dense and extensive colonies. Locally associated species vary, but may include:

> *Acalypha rhomboidea* (common three-seed mercury)
> *Amphicarpaea bracteata* (American hogpeanut)
> *Boehmeria cylindrica* (smallspike false nettle)
> *Dichanthelium clandestinum* (deertongue)

> *Equisetum arvense* (field horsetail)
> *Eupatorium fistulosum* (trumpetweed)
> *Hypericum mutilum* (dwarf St. Johnswort)
> *Impatiens capensis* (jewelweed)
> *Juncus effusus* (common rush)
> *Leersia oryzoides* (rice cutgrass)
> *Lobelia cardinalis* (cardinal flower)
> *Lycopus virginicus* (Virginia water horehound)
> *Onoclea sensibilis* (sensitive fern)
> *Osmunda regalis* (royal fern)
> *Polygonum sagittatum* (arrowleaf tear thumb)
> *Solidago patula* (roundleaf goldenrod)
> *Solidago rugosa ssp. aspera* (wrinkleleaf goldenrod)
> *Symphyotrichum lateriflorum* (calico aster)
> *Vernonia noveboracensis* (New York ironweed)

## Hairy-fruit Sedge Wetland

**Formal name:** *Carex trichocarpa Herbaceous Vegetation*

### Environmental summary

**Where it is found:** small, narrow linear patches on floodplain edges, deposition bars and islands with no tree canopy, usually on medium- to large-sized rivers in the mid-Atlantic region and on third- or fourth-order streams above 2,500 feet in elevation in the Central Appalachians.

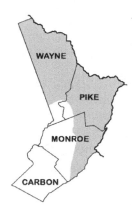

Locally it is found on the upper Delaware River, on low flats associated with the active floodplain, either directly adjacent to the channel or in association with backwater depressions and sloughs.

**Soil information:** typically coarse loamy to sandy, somewhat poorly to very poorly drained glacio-fluvial deposits.

**Characteristics:** reported to be routinely flooded during most high-water events, this community is dominated by dense rhizomatous stands of *Carex trichocarpa* (hairy-fruit sedge), tolerates annual sediment deposition and occasional high-energy ice-scour. Ice-scour during high winter flows maintains an open appearance.

### Vegetation

*Carex trichocarpa* dominates the association. Shrubs are sometimes present, but at less than 25 percent cover, including *Cornus amomum* (silky dogwood), and *Rubus alleghaniensis* (Allegheny blackberry). The invasive *Rosa multiflora* (multiflora rose) is also reported.

Other common herbaceous species include
*Arisaema triphyllum* (Jack-in-the-pulpit)
*Asclepias syriaca* (common milkweed)
*Boehmeria cylindrica* (smallspike false nettle)
*Carex projecta* (necklace sedge)
*Dichanthelium clandestinum* (deertongue)
*Doellingeria umbellata var. umbellata* (parasol whitetop)
*Elymus riparius* (riverbank rye)
*Euthamia graminifolia var. graminifolia* (flat-top goldenrod)
*Lilium superbum* (turks cap lily)
*Onoclea sensibilis* (sensitive fern)
*Scirpus cyperinus* (woolgrass)
*Solidago gigantea* (giant goldenrod)
*Solidago rugosa* (wrinkleleaf goldenrod)
*Thalictrum pubescens* (king of the meadow)
*Urtica dioica* (stinging nettle)
*Veratrum viride* (green false hellebore)
*Verbena hastata var. hastata* (swamp verbena)

Vines may be present at low cover, including *Polygonum convolvulus* (black bindweed) and *Clematis virginiana* (virgins bower).

## Threeway Sedge Basin Marsh

**Formal name:** *Dulichium arundinaceum - Carex folliculata - Juncus spp. Herbaceous Vegetation*

### Environmental summary

**Where it is found:** flat areas of headwater basins, near beaver ponds, shallow basins, swales, bog mat moats, or in areas where seepage is impounded by natural levees, in the Ridge and Valley and Allegheny Mountains regions of Pennsylvania, Virginia and West Virginia at elevations above 1,800 feet.

**Soil information:** peat, muck or sandy soil over deposits of sand, silt, or clay loam; bedrock is usually acidic sandstone or, less frequently, shale.

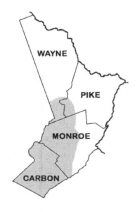

**Characteristics:** Fairly well-developed hummock-and-hollow microtopography occurs on temporarily, semi-permanently or generally saturated peat, where water levels decline enough during dry years to permit at least temporary opportunities for woody species. Hummocks are generally 30 to 60 inches high.

### Vegetation

A few stunted trees and shrubs may occur on hummock tops, including:
*Alnus incana* (gray alder)
*Ilex verticillata* (winterberry)
*Kalmia latifolia* (mountain laurel)
*Picea rubens* (red spruce)
*Rhododendron maximum* (great laurel)
*Rubus hispidus* (bristly dewberry)

However, vegetation is dominated by a combination of low grasses, sedges and rushes. Commonly reported are:
*Carex folliculata* (northern long sedge)
*Dulichium arundinaceum* (threeway sedge)
*Juncus brevicaudatus* (narrow panicle sedge)
*Juncus canadensis* (Canadian rush)
*Juncus subcaudatus* (woodland rush)

Other associates may include:
*Agrostis hyemalis* (winter bentgrass)
*Carex atlantica* (prickly bog sedge)
*Carex canescens* (silvery sedge)
*Drosera spp.* (sundew)
*Eriophorum virginicum* (tawny cottongrass)
*Juncus effusus* (common rush)
*Leersia oryzoides* (rice cutgrass)
*Lycopodiella inundata* (inundated clubmoss)
*Osmunda cinnamomea var. cinnamomea* (cinnamon fern)
*Rhynchospora alba* (white beaksedge)

*Scirpus cyperinus* (woolgrass)

*Sparganium spp.* (bur-reed)

*Triadenum fraseri* (Fraser's marsh St. John-swort)

Bryophytes often include *Sphagnum spp.* (*Sphagnum fallax, Sphagnum recurvum, Sphagnum magellanicum, Sphagnum cuspidatum,* and *Sphagnum papillosum*) and *Polytrichum* spp. (*Polytrichum commune, Polytrichum pallidisetum*).

## Calcareous Bulrush Marsh

**Formal name:** *Hardstem Bulrush - Woolly-fruit Sedge Herbaceous Vegetation*

### Environmental summary, vegetation

Found in standing water on lakeshores in limestone region, this association is scattered throughout primarily Connecticut, New Jersey, Massachusetts, New York and Pennsylvania. Sites are generally less than one acre to smaller than 10 acres; it is considered critically imperiled as a result.

A characteristic of these sites is the dominance of the tall *Schoenoplectus acutus* (hardstem bulrush). Associates generally include:

*Carex lasiocarpa* (woollyfruit sedge)

*Lysimachia thyrsiflora* (tufted loosestrife)

*Schoenoplectus tabernaemontani* (softstem bulrush)

*Typha angustifolia* (narrowleaf cattail)

An understory of sorts may form below bulrushes and cattails, including aquatic plants such as *Utricularia minor* (lesser bladderwort), *Utricularia intermedia* (flatleaf bladderwort), *Lemna* spp. (duckweed), and *Menyanthes trifoliata* (buckbean).

## Medium Fen

**Formal name:** *Myrica gale - Chamaedaphne calyculata / Carex (lasiocarpa, utriculata) - Utricularia spp. Shrub Herbaceous Vegetation*

### Environmental summary

**Where it is found:** peatlands and peaty lakeshores in acidic waters that get fed by weakly-nutritious surface water or seepage from surrounding uplands. While the substrate may be flooded at high water, it stays saturated during the growing season.

**Soil information:** shallow peat, acidic to circumneutral (pH 4.8 to 6.8).

**Characteristics:** Reported as "poor fens," these sites tend to occur in flat basins with peat surface, often as part of a bigger bog complex. These fens are characterized by the dominance of *Carex lasiocarpa* and the absence of richness indicators such as *Dasiphora fruticosa ssp. floribunda*.

### Vegetation

Scattered taller shrubs may protrude over a cover of tall, rhizomatous sedges, including *Alnus incana* (gray alder) and *Spiraea alba* (white meadowsweet), but shorter shrubs like *Myrica gale* (sweetgale), *Andromeda polifolia* (bog rosemary), *Vaccinium macrocarpon* (cranberry) and *Chamaedaphne calyculata* (leatherleaf) are found among the sedges.

*Carex lasiocarpa* (woolyfruit sedge) or *Carex utriculata* (Northwest Territory sedge) are typically the dominant sedges; associates include:

*Calamagrostis canadensis* (bluejoint)

*Carex canescens* (silvery sedge)

*Carex exilis* (coastal sedge)

*Carex lacustris* (hairy sedge)

*Carex limosa* (mud sedge)

*Carex oligosperma* (fewseed sedge)

*Carex stricta* (upright sedge)

*Carex vesicaria* (blister sedge)

*Cladium mariscoides* (smooth sawgrass)

*Dulichium arundinaceum* (threeway sedge)

*Eriophorum angustifolium* (tall cottongrass)

*Eriophorum virginicum* (tawny cottongrass)

*Rhynchospora alba* (white beaksedge)

Forbs found on local sites may include:
   *Comarum palustre* (purple marshlocks)
   *Drosera intermedia* (spoonleaf sundew)
   *Lysimachia terrestris* (earth loosestrife)
   *Osmunda regalis* (royal fern)
   *Pogonia ophioglossoides* (snakemouth orchid)
   *Triadenum virginicum* (Virginia marsh St. Johnswort)
   *Utricularia intermedia* (flatleaf bladderwort)

Sphagnum species dominate the bryophyte layer, including *Sphagnum fallax, Sphagnum papillosum, Sphagnum cuspidatum, Sphagnum fimbriatum, Sphagnum centrale, Sphagnum lescurii,* and others.

## Riverside Prairie Grassland

**Formal name:** *Prunus pumila / Andropogon gerardii - Sorghastrum nutans Herbaceous Vegetation*

### Environmental summary

**Where it is found:** sandy point bars and linear sand and gravel deposits along semi-stable river shores subject to periodic flooding, especially the Delaware River.

**Soil information:** substrate is cobble, gravel or coarse sediment with segments of alluvial sand and silt. Bare cobble is exposed in some areas.

**Characteristics:** Flooding and ice scour strips woody vegetation to maintain a graminoid and herbaceous dominated system, similar to a tall prairie-like grassland.

Ice scour forms the actual shape of the association as floes are pressed toward shorelines. It is described as a meadow community found on cobble shores or outcrops, and often with two or three distinct vegetation zones. Typical are a wet meadow along the shore, a dry grassland just upland from the river, and a shrubby zone farthest from river.

### Vegetation

*Andropogon gerardii* (Big bluestem), *Sorghastrum nutans* (Indiangrass), *Panicum virgatum* (switchgrass), and *Schizachyrium scoparium* (little bluestem) are the dominants in the Poconos.

Other herbaceous species include:
   *Achillea millefolium* (common yarrow)
   *Anemone virginiana* (Virginia anemone)
   *Apocynum cannabinum* (Indian-hemp)
   *Asclepias tuberosa* (butterfly weed)
   *Erigeron strigosus* (prairie fleabane)
   *Helianthus divaricatus* (woodland sunflower)
   *Lespedesa hirta* (hairy lespedeza)
   *Phalaris aruninacea* (reed canarygrass)
   *Solidago rugosa* (wrinkleleaf goldenrod)
   *Spirea alba* (meadowsweet)
   *Thlaspi avense* (field pennycress)

In the absence of ice scour, some woody species may become established. These include *Salix spp.* (willows), *Platanus occidentalis* (sycamore), *Fraxinus spp.* (ashes) *Acer negundo* (boxelder), and *Betula nigra* (river birch).

Farthest inland, a shrubby zone may have species such as *Corylus americana* (hazelnut), *Diervilla lonicera* (bush honeysuckle), *Osmunda claytoniana* (interupted fern), and *Rubus idaeus* (red raspberry).

Vines may also be present, including *Parthenocissus quinquefolia* (Virginia creeper), *Toxicodendron radicans* (eastern poison ivy), *Vitis labrusca* (fox grape), and *Vitis riparia* (riverbank grape).

Bryophytes are absent or at most sparse.

## Little Bluestem Outcrop Opening

**Formal name:** *Schizachyrium scoparium - Danthonia spicata - Carex pensylvanica / Cladonia spp. Herbaceous Vegetation*

### Environmental summary

**Where it is found:** rock outcrops, flat summits, plateaus and southwest facing upper slopes, above 1200 feet.

**Soil information:** thin, rocky, acidic sandy to gravelly soils with bare acidic sandstone and conglomerate rock comprising a major portion of the cover.

**Characteristics:** The association is likely to be

fire initiated and there are few, if any trees or shrubs; grasses and sedges dominate.

### Vegetation

Graminoids dominated by *Danthonia spicata* (poverty oatgrass), *Schizachyrium scoparium* (little bluestem), and *Deschampsia flexuosa* (wavy hairgrass) are typical and create 25 to 50 percent cover. Other associates include:

> *Carex pensylvanica* (Pennsylvania sedge)
> *Cladonia spp.* (reindeer lichen)
> *Piptatherum pungens* (mountain ricegrass)
> *Piptatherum racemosum* (blackseed ricegrass)
> *Prunus pumila* (sandcherry)
> *Rubus spp.* (blackberry)
> *Sibbaldiopsis tridentata* (shrubby fivefingers)
> *Umbilicaria spp.* (navel lichen)

Small patches of shrubs are scattered within the herbaceous matrix, including *Vaccinium spp.* (blueberry), *Gaylussacia baccata* (black huckleberry), and *Photinia melanocarpa* (black chokeberry).

## Bulrush Deepwater Marsh

**Formal name:** *Schoenoplectus (tabernaemontani, acutus) Eastern Herbaceous Vegetation*

### Environmental summary

**Where it is found:** quiet water areas near the shores of ponds, lakes, rivers and larger streams, but also in ditches and flooded basins, primarily in standing water between 15 and 40 inches deep, throughout the northeastern United States and adjacent Canadian provinces.

**Soil information:** deep muck overlying mineral soil, which may be exposed if wave action is prevalent.

**Characteristics:** deep water is present in all but the driest conditions with seasonal flooding and spring rain providing nutrient materials. No trees or shrubs are present, and graminoids

dominate along with scattered emergent forbs. The strong dominance of tall bulrush species distinguishes this association from other standing-water marsh communities.

### Vegetation

Dominant species are usually *Schoenoplectus acutus* (hardstem bullrush), *Schoenoplectus tabernaemontani* (softstem bullrush), and/or *Schoenoplectus americanus* (chairmaker's bullrush).

Local associated herbs usually include;

> *Asclepias incarnata* (swamp milkweed)
> *Carex pellita* (wooly sedge)
> *Carex utriculata* (Northwest Territory sedge)
> *Impatiens capensis* (jewelweed)
> *Leersia oryzoides* (rice cutgrass)
> *Ludwigia palustris* (marsh seedbox)
> *Pontederia cordata* (pickerel weed)
> *Sagittaria latifolia* (broadleaf arrowhead)
> *Scirpus cyperinus* (woolgrass)
> *Scutellaria lateriflora* (blue skullcap)
> *Thelypteris palustris* (eastern marsh fern)
> *Typha latifolia* (common catttail)
> *Verbena hastata* (swamp verbena)

Scattered among the emergent plants may be such floating-leaved and submerged plants, as *Potamogeton* spp. (pondweed), *Sparganium* spp. (bur-reed), *Elodea canadensis* (Canadian waterweed) and *Ceratophyllum* spp. (hornwort)

## Woolgrass Marsh

**Formal name:** *Scirpus cyperinus Seasonally Flooded Herbaceous Vegetation*

### Environmental summary

**Where it is found:** seasonally flooded marshes or the emergent zones of upland depression ponds.

**Soil information:** mucky peat, saturated to ponded in winter months and drying completely in summer.

**Characteristics:** *Scirpus cyperinus* dominance with a pronounced seasonal fluctuation in water level. Monospecific clumps may be either scattered in the marsh or around the pond margin.

### Vegetation

Dominated by *Scirpus cyperinus* (woolgrass), composition can be variable. Associates gnerally include *Glyceria* spp. (mannagrass), *Thelypteris palustris* (marshfern), as well as other species of *Scirpus* (bulrush), including *Scirpus microcarpus* (panicled bulrush) and *Scirpus atrovirens* (green bulrush).

Mats of Sphagnum mosses may be prominent in some sites, including *Sphagnum lescurii, Sphagnum pylaesii, Sphagnum cuspidatum, Sphagnum palustre,* and *Sphagnum recurvum*

Some sites may include scattered woody plants, such as:
*Acer rubrum* (red maple)
*Alnus serrulata* (hazel alder)
*Cephalanthus occidentalis* (buttonbush)
*Nyssa sylvatica* (black gum)
*Rosa palustris* (swamp rose)
*Vaccinium corymbosum* (highbush blueberry)

## Eastern Cattail Marsh

**Formal name:** *Typha (angustifolia, latifolia) — (Schoenoplectus spp.) Eastern Herbaceous Vegetation*

### Environmental summary

**Where it is found:** permanently flooded basins, usually as a segment of a larger wetland group and typically with lakes, ponds or slow streams, throughout the northeastern United States and adjacent Canadian provinces.

**Soil information:** muck over mineral soils, along with a floating peaty mat roots suspended in it.

**Characteristics:** tall graminoids dominate a muck-bottom zone near the shoreline, with a variety of herbaceous species and some low shrubs in the floating mat.

Bryophytes are usually confined to hummocks. Strong dominance of *Typha spp.* distinguishes this association from other freshwater marshes in the northeast.

### Vegetation

Dominant graminoids include Typha angustifolia (narrowleaf cattail), Typha latifolia (common cattail) alone or combined with other tall emergent marsh species. Varied associates include
*Calamagrostis canadensis* (bluejoint)
*Carex aquatilis* (water sedge)
*Carex lurida* (shallow sedge)
*Carex pellita* (wooly sedge)
*Carex rostrata* (beaked sedge)
*Carex stricta* (upright sedge)
*Schoenoplectus acutus* (hardstem bullrush)
*Schoenoplectus americanus* (chairmaker's bullrush)
*Scirpus cyperinus* (woolgrass)

Broad-leaved herbs may include:
*Asclepias incarnata* (swamp milkeweed)
*Calla palustris* (water arum)
*Impatiens capensis* (jewelweed)
*Onoclea sensibilis* (sensitive fern)
*Sagittaria latifolia* (broadleaf arrowhead)
*Scutellaria lateriflora* (blue skullcap)
*Sparganium eurycarpum* (broadfruit bur-reed)
*Symplocarpus foetidus* (skunk cabbage)
*Thelypteris palustris* (marsh fern)
*Verbena hastata* (swamp verbena)

Floating aquatics, such as *Lemna minor* (common duckweed), may be common in deeper zones.

Shrub species may include:
*Myrica gale* (sweetgale)
*Ilex verticillata* (winterberry)
*Spiraea alba* (white meadowsweet)

## Intermediate Graminoid Fen

**Formal name:** *Sweetgale - Shrubby-cinquefoil / Woolly-fruit Sedge - Smooth Sawgrass Shrub Herbaceous Vegetation*

### Environmental summary

**Where it is found:** lakes and other depressions from the Great Lakes to the northeastern United States.

**Soil information:** deep peat

**Characteristics:** small (generally less than an acre) fen constructed from rhizomatous sedges that form a mat over deep peat, with variable shrub cover; critically imperiled due to commercial and residential development and altered hydrology.

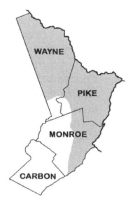

### Vegetation

Larix laricina (tamarack) may occur as scattered individuals atop hummocks. Shrubs, generally limited to hummocks and can exceed 25 percent cover, may locally include:

*Alnus spp.* (alder)
*Cornus sericea* (red osier dogwood)
*Myrica gale* (sweetgale)
*Rhamnus alnifolia* (alderleaf buckthorn)
*Salix candida* (sageleaf willow)
*Vaccinium macrocarpon* (cranberry)
*Vaccinium oxycoccos* (small cranberry)

Typical sedges include:
*Carex aquatilis* (water sedge)
*Carex buxbaumii* (Buxbaum's sedge)
*Carex cryptolepis* (northeastern sedge)
*Carex flava* (yellow sedge)
*Carex lacustris* (hairy sedge)
*Carex lasiocarpa* (woollyfruit sedge)
*Carex leptalea* (bristlystalked sedge)
*Carex prairea* (prairie sedge)
*Carex stricta* (upright sedge)
*Cladium mariscoides* (smooth sawgrass)

Other herbaceous associates include:
*Carex trisperma* (threeseeded sedge)
*Doellingeria umbellata* (parasol whitetop)
*Drosera rotundifolia* (roundleaf sundew)
*Iris versicolor* (harlequin blueflag)
*Muhlenbergia glomerata* (spiked muhly)
*Osmunda regalis* (royal fern)
*Parnassia glauca* (fen grass of parnassis)
*Pogonia ophioglossoides* (snakemouth orchid)
*Rhynchospora alba* (white beaksedge)
*Thelypteris palustris* (marshfern)
*Typha latifolia* (common cattail)

Hollows and channels often support *Utricularia intermedia* (flatleaf bladderwort), *Utricularia gibba* (humped bladderwort), *Menyanthes trifoliata* (buckbean), and *Lobelia kalmii* (Ontario lobelia).

Other herbs include *Symphyotrichum boreale* (northern bog aster) and *Sarracenia purpurea* (purple pitcher plant).

Characteristic mosses include *Campylium stellatum* (star campylium moss), *Limprichtia revolvens* (limprichtia moss), *Scorpidium scorpioides* (scorpidium moss), and *Tomentypnum nitens* (tomentypnum moss). *Sphagnum* spp. is likely absent or only a minor component. When present, species include the more minerotrophic *Sphagnum contortum, Sphagnum warnstorfii, and Sphagnum teres.*

# *Perennial forb vegetation*

## Golden Saxifrage Forested Seep

**Formal name:** *Chrysosplenium americanum Herbaceous Vegetation*

### *Environmental Summary*

Small herbaceous seepage areas with scattered cover of forbs are found throughout the eastern United States. Herbs are strongly dominant and tend to be relatively diverse, especially in richer soils. Soils vary widely and the community is usually over-topped by trees and shrubs from the surrounding forest.

### *Vegetation*

In addition to *Chrysosplenium americanum* (American golden saxifrage), some common species can include:

*Arisaema triphyllum* (jack-in-the-pulpit)
*Cardamine bulbosa* (bulbous bittercress)
*Carex gynandra* (nodding sedge)
*Carex scabrata* (eastern rough sedge)
*Chelone glabra* (white turtlehead)
*Cinna arundinacea* (sweet woodreed)
*Circaea alpina* (small enchanter's night-shade)
*Galium triflorum* (fragrant bedstraw)
*Geum rivale* (purple avens)
*Glyceria melicaria* (mellic mannagrass)
*Glyceria striata* (fowl mannagrass)
*Hydrocotyle americana* (American marsh-pennywort)
*Impatiens capensis* (jewelweed)
*Laportea canadensis* (Canadian woodnettle)
*Mimulus ringens* (monkey-flower)

*Onoclea sensibilis* (sensitive fern)
*Pilea pumila* (Canadian clearweed)
*Poa paludigena* (bog bluegrass)
*Saxifraga pensylvanica* (eastern swamp saxifrage)
*Symplocarpus foetidus* (skunk cabbage)
*Thelypteris noveboracensis* (New York fern)
*Tiarella cordifolia* (foamflower)
*Veratrum viride* (false green hellebore)
*Viola cucullata* (marsh blue violet)

## Water-willow Rocky Bar and Shore

**Formal name:** *Justicia americana Herbaceous Vegetation*

### *Environmental summary*

**Where it is found:** bars and shoals of rocky streams and riverbeds subjected to frequent high-energy flooding, primarily in the Central Appalachians and Piedmont, as well as nearby provinces.

**Soil information:** a generally circumneutral, varied mix of sand, gravel and cobbles, frequently with muck and silt deposits.

**Characteristics:** Usually at the river edges and heads and tails of islands, but also sometimes on deposition bars.

### *Vegetation*

A sparse canopy layer sometimes includes:
*Acer saccharinum* (silver maple)
*Betula nigra* (river birch)
*Carpinus caroliniana ssp. caroliniana* (American hornbeam)

*Fagus grandifolia* (American beech)
*Fraxinus pennsylvanica* (green ash)
*Platanus occidentalis* (American sycamore)
*Salix interior* (sandbar willow)

Scattered shrub seedlings of *Salix nigra* (black willow), *Betula nigra, Acer saccharinum* or *Platanus occidentalis* are also reported..

However, the characteristic dominant is *Justicia americana* (American water willow). Other herbaceous species that may be present include:

*Bidens* spp. (beggarticks)
*Cyperus* spp. (flatsedge)
*Diodia teres* (poorjoe)
*Eleocharis* spp. (spikerush)
*Leersia oryzoides* (rice cutgrass)
*Leersia virginica* (whitegrass)
*Lemna minor* (common duckweed)
*Orontium aquaticum* (goldenclub)
*Podostemum ceratophyllum* (hornleaf river-weed)
*Schoenoplectus pungens* (common three-square)
*Schoenoplectus tabernaemontani* (softstem bulrush)
*Scirpus sp.* (bulrush)
*Xyris difformis var. difformis* (bog yellow-eyed grass)

# Northeastern Leafy Forb Marsh

**Formal name:** *Pontederia cordata - Peltandra virginica - Sagittaria latifolia Herbaceous Vegetation*

### Environmental summary

**Where it is found:** along pond and lake shores, impoundments and quiet riverbanks in the northeastern United States.

**Soil information:** muck soils in shallow to deep standing water.

**Characteristics:** an emergent marsh dominated by broad-leaf plants with large air channels to submerged tissues, creating buoyancy and the exchange of gasses between

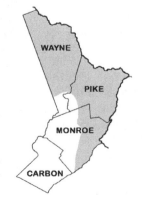

shoots and roots.

### Vegetation

Common species include:
*Peltandra virginica* (green arrow arum)
*Pontederia cordata* (pickerel weed)
*Sagittaria latifolia* (broadleaf arrowhead)
*Sparganium spp.* (bur-reed)

Less frequent emergent species include:
*Acorus calamus* (calamus)
*Eleocharis palustris* (common spikerush)
*Nuphar variegata* (varigated yellow pond lily)
*Nymphaea odorata* (American white water lily)
*Schoenoplectus tabernaemontani* (softstem bulrush)
*Sium suave* (hemlock water parsnip)

Less common submerged species include *Ceratophyllum demersum* (coon's tail) and *Utricularia macrorhiza* (common bladderwort).

# Skunk cabbage - Jewelweed Seep

Formal name: *Symplocarpus foetidus - Impatiens capensis Herbaceous Vegetation*

### Environmental summary

**Where it is found:** low-lying streamheads, borders of small streams where groundwater emerges and the drainages of lower slopes.

**Soil information:** muck, with frequent rocks and boulders protruding above the surface.

**Characteristics:** vegetation is generally shaded by a variety trees on edges and higher ground adjacent to, but not part of, the community.

### Vegetation

*Lindera benzoin* (northern spicebush) is sometimes found, especially along the edges. Typical herbaceous species include *Symplocarpus foetidus* (skunk cabbage), *Impatiens capensis* (jewelweed), and *Arisaema triphyllum* (Jack-in-the-pulpit). Associates vary but may include:

*Caltha palustris* (yellow marsh marigold)
*Cardamine pensylvanica* (Pennsylvania bittercress)
*Carex canescens* (silvery sedge)
*Pilea pumila* (Canadian clearweed)
*Saxifraga pensylvanica* (eastern swamp saxifrage)
*Veratrum viride* (false green hellebore)
*Viola sororia* (common blue violet)

## Ironweed - Marsh Fern Seep

**Formal name:** *Vernonia noveboracensis - Thelypteris palustris - Symplocarpus foetidus Herbaceous Vegetation*

### Environmental summary

**Where it is found:** as patches of one to six acres within forests where calcareous groundwater discharge is found throughout the growing season.

**Soil information:** ranges from mineral soils to peat (sapric muck); if present, peat deposits are usually less than 20 inches.

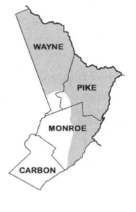

**Characteristics:** small wetlands with a variable composition. While open sites with little woody plant cover tend to be graminoid-dominated, the more shaded sites trend toward forb species. Herbaceous vegetation is usually more than 90 percent and can reach up to 6 feet.

### Vegetation

*Juniperus virginiana* (eastern red cedar) is occasionally present. Tall and short shrubs are sparse — less than 10 percent cover — and may include *Salix spp.* (willow), *Lindera benzoin* (northern spicebush) and *Toxicodendron vernix* (poison sumac).

Common forbs may include:
*Amphicarpaea bracteata* (American hogpeanut)
*Arisaema triphyllum* (Jack-in-the-pulpit)
*Chelone glabra* (white turtlehead)

*Drosera rotundifolia* (roundleaf sundew)
*Eupatorium spp.* (thoroughwort)
*Hydrocotyle americana* (American marsh pennywort)
*Impatiens spp.* (touch-me-not)
*Mitella diphylla* (bishop's cap)
*Packera aurea* (golden ragwort)
*Parnassia glauca* (fen grass of parnassis)
*Pycnanthemum verticillatum* (whorled mountainmint)
*Solidago uliginosa* (bog goldenrod)
*Symplocarpus foetidus* (skunk cabbage)
*Thelypteris palustris* (marsh fern)
*Vernonia noveboracensis* (New York ironweed)
*Viola spp.* (violets)

Common graminoids may include:
*Carex atlantica* (prickly bog sedge)
*Carex debilis* (white edge sedge)
*Carex granularis* (limestone meadow sedge)
*Carex leptalea* (bristlystalked sedge)
*Leersia oryzoides* (rice cutgrass)
*Muhlenbergia glomerata* (spiked muhly)
*Poa palustris* (fowl bluegrass)
*Rhynchospora alba* (white beaksedge)

Mosses, comprising less than 5 percent of total cover, are typically present.

## Pasture Fen

**Formal name:** *Juniperus virginiana / Dasiphora fruticosa ssp. floribunda / Carex flava - Carex tetanica Shrub Herbaceous Vegetation*

### Environmental summary

**Where it is found:** in rare, small patches of often less than an acre, where calcareous groundwater discharges to the surface, generally along the toeslope of ridges and in association with limestone or calcareous siltstone. Identified in New Jersey and Pennsylvania.

**Soil information:** silt loams to shallow mucky peat

**Characteristics:** a saturated wetland of turf-like mineral soil over calcarous bedrock; called a pasture fen because vegetation has been impacted by past grazing, which sometimes continues to the present. Appearance may range from open shrubland to open herbaceous vegetation.

### Vegetation

If present, tall shrubs may range from six to 15 feet with less than 20 percent cover. These may include *Cornus amomum* (silky dogwood), *Juniperous virginiana* (eastern red cedar) and *Toxicodendron vernix* (poison sumac).

Typical short shrubs include:
> *Dasiphora fruticosa ssp. floribunda* (shrubby cinquefoil)
> *Lyonia ligustrina* (maleberry)
> *Salix candida* (sageleaf willow)
> *Salix discolor* (pussy willow)
> *Spiraea alba var. latifolia* (white meadowsweet)
> *Spiraea tomentosa* (steeplebush)

A varied herbaceous layer ranges from a minimum of 75 percent to more typically near 100 percent coverage. Dominant species often include:
> *Carex stricta* (upright sedge)
> *Dryopteris cristata* (crested woodfern)
> *Juncus dudleyi* (Dudley's rush)
> *Juncus subcaudatus* (woodland rush)
> *Onoclea sensibilis* (sensitive fern)
> *Packera aurea* (golden ragwort)
> *Parnassia glauca* (fen grass of parnassis)
> *Pycnanthemum tenuifolium* (narrowleaf mountainmint)
> *Solidago rugosa* (wrinkleleaf goldenrod)
> *Thelypteris palustris* (marsh fern)

Associates generally include:
> *Equisetum fluviatile* (water horsetail)
> *Eupatorium maculatum* (spotted joe pye weed)
> *Juncus nodosus* (knotted rush)
> *Liatris spicata* (dense blazing star)
> *Pedicularis canadensis* (Canadian lousewort)
> *Pedicularis lanceolata* (swamp lousewort)
> *Rudbeckia fulgida* (orange coneflower)
> *Sisyrinchium angustifolium* (narrowleaf blue-eyed grass)
> *Solidago uliginosa* (showy goldenrod)
> *Spiranthes lucida* (shining lady's tresses)

Less frequent are:
> *Bromus kalmii* (artic brome)
> *Carex flava* (yellow sedge)
> *Carex tetanica* (rigid sedge)
> *Castilleja coccinea* (scarlet Indian paintbrush)
> *Cypripedium parviflorum* (lesser yellow lady's slipper)
> *Geum rivale* (purple avens)
> *Juncus brachycephalus* (smallhead rush)
> *Lobelia kalmii* (Ontario lobelia)

## Northern Bayberry Fen

**Formal name:** *Morella pensylvanica - Dasiphora fruticosa ssp. floribunda / Carex sterilis - Carex flava Shrub Herbaceous Vegetation*

### Environmental summary

**Where it is found:** on spring-fed calcareous sites in Pennsylvania, New Jersey and New York.

**Soil information:** minimal peat accumulation over mineral soil or marl actively deposited as a result of groundwater supersaturated with calcium carbonate upslope.

**Characteristics:** Flowing rivulets are typical; substrate is usually marl and stones and woody debris coated with calcium carbonate. Presence of *Morella pensylvanica* is a commonly cited diagnostic. Because of small size and the impact of grazing and invasive species penetration, these sites are considered critically imperiled.

### Vegetation

Woody vegetation is absent to sparse, but serve as a characteristic diagnostic. *Morella pensylvanica* (northern bayberry) and *Dasiphora fruticosa ssp. floribunda* (shrubby cinquefoil) are the key indicators. *Toxicodendron vernix* (poison sumac), *Acer rubrum* (red maple), and *Juniperus virginiana* (eastern red cedar) are often reported as associates.

About 40 percent of cover is herbaceous cover, described as rich and diverse and including:
*Carex cryptolepis* (northeastern sedge)
*Carex flava* (yellow sedge)
*Carex sterilis* (dioecious sedge)
*Carex tetanica* (rigid sedge)
*Deschampsia caespitosa* (tufted hairgrass)
*Drosera rotundifolia* (roundleaf sundew)
*Eleocharis tenuis* (slender spikerush)
*Juncus nodosus* (knotted rush)
*Lobelia kalmii* (Ontario lobelia)
*Muhlenbergia glomerata* (spiked muhly)
*Packera aurea* (golden ragwort)
*Parnassia glauca* (fen grass of parnassis)
*Rhynchospora alba* (white beaksedge)
*Rhynchospora capillacea* (needle beaksedge)
*Sanguisorba canadensis* (Canadian burnet)
*Sarracenia purpurea* (purple pitcher plant)
*Spiranthes cernua* (nodding lady's tresses)

## Prairies, meadows and other open spaces

For as much as the expressions are used to describe habitats, the words "prairie" and "meadow" don't appear in any formal glossary of landforms. Casual descriptions not only abound, but, when compared to each other, form a murky composite.

We most often think of *prairies* on the context of the American *tall grass prairie*, which evolved in glacial till deposits in the rain shadow of the Rocky Mountains and thrive because root systems go very deep — a valuable asset during drought, wildfires and continual grazing by large herbivores such as bison.

Prairies are described as temperate grasslands, savannahs or shrublands by ecologists; the primary characteristic is the absence of trees. They come in three types:

- wet, which has poor drainage, is moist for much of the growing season and is considered prime farmland;

- mesic, with good drainage but also good soil and so popular with farmers that it is one of the most endangered forms of prairies;

- dry, often found on uplands and slopes with good drainage a major characteristic.

With their roots reaching back to *hay meadows* in England, where annual grasses were harvested for hay, and *pasture meadows* used primarily for agricultural grazing, *meadows* tend to conjure a different image than prairies. Most typically picture fewer tall grasses and more forbs on generally rich, moist soils.

The reality of meadows are types called *transitional* and *permanent*. The first is an open grassland created by agricultural clearing, or originally by Native Americans for hunting; unless kept clear, it will eventually revert to woodland. The second will remain open because of unique circumstances, such as arctic or desert climates, but *also as prairies* that are kept clear of woody species by drought and wildfire, and as near wetlands due to the presence of too much water for trees to tolerate.

That water can result in *fens* where the substrate is calcareous, *marshes* where water is shallow and fairly constant, *transitional* or *shrub swamps* where water is deeper and woody vegetation is absent, or *bogs* where water is highly acidic and peat is common.

A wetland with some flooding of large areas of low-relief land by shallow bodies of water, a swamp features dry-land protrusions called *hammocks*, which are covered by aquatic vegetation or vegetation that tolerates occasional inundation. *True swamps* are most typically forested by woody species adapted to that specific type of habitat.

# *Hydromorphic vegetation*

## Duckweed Pond

**Formal name:** *Lemna spp. Permanently Flooded Herbaceous Vegetation*

### *Environmental summary:*

**Where it is found:** permanently, periodically or seasonally flooded wetlands in as little as shallow standing water. Often found in ponds, lakes, ditches, stock ponds, and backwater sloughs, most often less than 7 to 12 feet of water.

**Soil information:** standing water of any depth; they grow where ever the wind pushes them and under eutrophic conditions (where water is rich in mineral and organic materials, especially nitrogen), the biomass may be abundant. The small plants usually float on the water surface and may become stranded and possibly rooted during drawdown periods.

**Characteristics:** composition of the community can change from hour to hour, but the environment may be only a few inches of surface water yet remains homogeneous. Lemna spp. generally dominate but may combine with other plant taxa floating on the water surface. They have little influence on the accumulation of organic matter on the pond bottom.

### *Vegetation*

Lemna taxa that may be present include:
*Lemna minor* (common duckweed)
*Lemna trisulca* (star duckweed)
*Lemna valdiviana* (valdivia duckweed)

Lemna spp. reproduces asexually by budding from a pouch base of the plant, and can also overwinter as rootless, dense starch-filled daughter plants. When water persists long enough, Lemna spp. produce seeds that can survive water drawdown and substrate drying.

Other species present in the community may include:
*Spirodela* spp. (duckmeat)
*Wolffiella* spp. (bogmat)
*Wolffia* spp. (watermeal)
*Riccia* spp. (aquatic liverworts)

*Potamogeton* spp. (pondweed), *Sagittaria* spp. (arrowhead) and *Polygonum* (knotweed) spp. may be present as well. These species are rooted submerged plants and technically not part of the strictly floating community, bit do intermingle.

## Water-lily Aquatic Wetland

**Formal name:** *Nuphar advena - Nymphaea odorata Herbaceous Vegetation*

### *Environmental summary*

**Where it is found:** shallow water depressions, oxbow ponds, backwater sloughs of river floodplains, ponds, small lakes and slow-moving streams of the central and eastern United States.

**Soil information:** sandy substrate of standing water.

**Characteristics:** a rooted or open marsh community dominated by floating-leaved aquatics, with both submergent and emergent species present.

## Vegetation

*Nuphar lutea* (yellow pond lily) and *Nymphaea odorata* (American white water lily) dominate individually or in combination.

Other commonly reported species include:
> *Brasenia schreberi* (watershield)
> *Eleocharis spp.* (spikerush)
> *Lemna spp.* (duckweed)
> *Polygonum amphibium* (water knotweed)
> *Polygonum amphibium var. emersum* (long-root smartweed)
> *Potamogeton spp.* (pondweed)
> *Saururus cernuus* (lizard's tail)
> *Sparganium americanum* (American bur-reed)
> *Spirodela polyrrhiza* (common duckmeat)
> *Stuckenia spp.* (pondweed)
> *Typha latifolia* (common cattail)

Submerged aquatics found locally include *Ceratophyllum demersum* (coon's tail), and *Heteranthera dubia* (grassleaf mudplantain)

## Riverweed Rocky Bar and Shore

**Formal Name:** *Podostemum ceratophyllum Herbaceous Vegetation*

### Environmental summary

**Where it is found:** rocky surfaces of stream and river beds in mature drainage systems, especially where the streams have cut down to rock and the floodplain is somewhat narrow. Found throughout the Central Appalachians and related areas.

**Soil information:** alluvial rock in moderately fast to fast-flowing water.

**Characteristics:** tends to be associated with higher pH streams that have cut through calcareous shales, limestone or diabase.

### Vegetation

Usually pure beds of *Podostemum ceratophyllum* (hornleaf riverweed) as a low mat or crust attached to rocks. Some algae may also be present.

Presence of riverweed is often considered an indicator of good water quality; the species is ranked variously as endangered to of special concern in a number of states where habitats have been damaged by sedimentation and nutrient enrichment, such as runoff from fertilizers, that promote algae growth.

## Open Water Marsh

**Formal name:** *Vallisneria americana — Potamogeton perfoliatus Herbaceous Vegetation*

### Environmental summary

**Where it is found:** sheltered bays of lakes and streams relatively undisturbed by wave action, throughout the northeastern United States.

**Soil information:** stands may be expected on sandy soil bottoms in shallow quiet waters, including lakes, streams, and ponds.

**Characteristics:** aquatic vegetation dominated by submergent or emergent plants with only minor floating-leaved species, generally in alluvial rivers and springs dominated by *Vallisneria americana*.

### Vegetation

In addition to *Vallisneria americana* (American eelgrass) and *Potamogeton perfoliatus* (claspingleaf pondweed) characteristic species may include:
> *Elodea canadensis* (Canadian waterweed)
> *Eriocaulon aquaticum* (seven angle pipewort)
> *Heteranthera dubia* (grassleaf mudplantain)
> *Heteranthera reniformis* (kidneyleaf mudplaintain)
> *Myriophyllum* spp. (watermilfoil)
> *Potamogeton epihydrus* (ribbonleaf pondweed)
> *Potamogeton nodosus* (longleaf pondweed)
> *Utricularia* spp. (bladderwort)

# *Rocky sparse vegetation*

## Calcareous Montane Cliff

**Formal name:** *Asplenium ruta-muraria - Pellaea atropurpurea Sparse Vegetation*

### Environmental summary

**Where it is found:** calcareous cliffs typically associated with dolomite or limestone features throughout the central and southern Appalachians, from Pennsylvania to Alabama, Kentucky, Tennessee, North and South Carolina, Virginia and West Virginia.

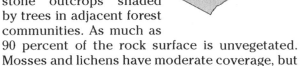

**Soil information:** thin calcareous soils on ledges and in crevices, often somewhat moist.

**Characteristics:** Dry to somewhat moist limestone outcrops shaded by trees in adjacent forest communities. As much as 90 percent of the rock surface is unvegetated. Mosses and lichens have moderate coverage, but vascular plants are found on ledges in cracks.

### Vegetation

Woody species may be scattered throughout or found at margins, including:

*Carya spp.* (hickories)
*Cercis canadensis* (eastern redbud)
*Cornus florida* (flowering dogwood)
*Fraxinus americana* (white ash)
*Hydrangea arborescens* (wild hydrangea)
*Juniperus virginiana* (eastern red cedar)
*Ostrya virginiana* (hop hornbeam)
*Parthenocissus quinquefolia* (Virginia creeper)
*Quercus muehlenbergii* (chinkapin oak)
*Rhus aromatica* (fragrant sumac)
*Tilia americana* (American basswood)
*Toxicodendron radicans* (poison ivy)

Herbs preferring calcareous habitats may locally include:

*Allium cernuum* (nodding onion)
*Aquilegia canadensis* (red columbine)
*Arabis lyrata* (lyrate rockcress)
*Asplenium trichomanes* (maidenhair spleenwort)
*Cystopteris bulbifera* (bulblet bladderfern)
*Dodecatheon meadia* (shooting-star)
*Dryopteris marginalis* (marginal woodfern)
*Heuchera americana* (American alumroot)
*Pellaea atropurpurea* (purple cliffbrake)
*Phlox subulata* (moss phlox)
*Saxifraga virginiensis* (early saxifrage)
*Symphyotrichum ericoides* (white heath aster)
*Symphyotrichum oblongifolium* (aromatic aster)

## Loosestrife - Dogbane Rivershore

**Formal name:** *Lysimachia ciliata — Apocynum cannabinum Sparse Vegetation*

### Environmental summary

**Where it is found:** riverbanks, low terraces, island heads, bars and spits in New Jersey and Pennsylvania.

**Soil information:** varies, but generally cobbles and sand with thin deposits of silt, muck or organic matter.

**Characteristics:** Although highly variable and broadly defined, the common characteristic is frequent scour in the active channel that removes established vegetation and maintains or creates exposed bedrock, cobbles or sediments. New seeds and plant propagules are continually being dispersed to these areas by water, air and animals to create a continual flux in species composition. The association is continually subjected to high-water velocities, floods and ice scour. This community is defined mainly by its setting and disturbance regime.

### Vegetation

Typical species are a mix of annuals and perennials, including:

*Apocynum cannabinum* (Indian hemp)
*Betula nigra* (river birch)
*Boehmeria cylindrica* (smallspike false nettle)
*Convolvulus spp.* (bindweeds)
*Eupatorium spp.* (snakeroots)
*Lysimachia ciliata* (fringed loosestrife)
*Platanus occidentalis* (American sycamore)
*Polygonum spp.,* (smartweed)
*Senecio spp.* (ragworts)

## Acidic Boulderfield

**Formal name:** *Lasallia (papulosa, pensylvanica) - Dimelaena oreina - (Melanelia culbersonii) Nonvascular Vegetation*

### Environmental summary

**Where it is found:** completely exposed and only minimally weathered sandstone and quartzite boulder fields, throughout the low and middle elevations of the Ridge and Valley, northern Blue Ridge and foothills of the Piedmont provinces in the central Appalachians.

**Soil information:** Little to none other than occasional small deposits of organic matter in crevices.

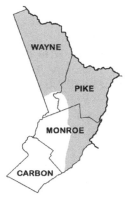

**Characteristics:** Elevation ranges are reported from 1, 000 to 3,300 feet, on slopes exceeding 30 de-

grees, with block sizes ranging from small, loose stones to large boulders in excess of 6 feet in diameter. These areas sometimes also occur on outcrops associated with the boulder fields and large, exposed cliffs.

### Vegetation

Rock surfaces endure constantly fluctuating and daily extremes of weather, humidity and moisture saturation during the growing season, then high winds, low temperatures and ice coverage during winter. Because of localized phenomena, they remain; most other types of boulder fields have been sufficiently weathered to support woodland to forest vegetation.

Smaller, more marginal sites do have some sparse vascular plant cover, primarily stunted trees of *Betula lenta* (sweet birch), *Sassafras albidum* (sassafras) and *Quercus prinus* (chestnut oak), a few ericaceous shrubs, and occasional *Parthenocissus quinquefolia* (Virginia creeper).

However, the larger occurrences have no vascular plants and lichens dominate. *Lasallia papulosa* (blistered naval lichen) and *Lasallia pensylvanica* (Pennsylvania blistered navel lichen), either the individually or together are often common. *Dimelaena oreina* (mountain lichen) covers dry, exposed rock surfaces not covered with *Lasallia* spp. and larger foliose lichens. Although it is more scattered, *Melanelia culbersonii* is reported and considered a helpful diagnostic species because it is limited to primarily siliciclastic rocks and sometimes coarse-grained, quartz-rich granites that are nearly devoid of dark minerals. A variety of other foliose, crustose and fruticose lichen species have been observed in various sites.

## Shale Cliffs and Talus

**Formal name:** *Penstemon hirsutus Sparse Vegetation*

### Environmental Summary

**Where it is found:** harsh, steep, unstable shale talus and cliffs.

**Soil information:** shallow, very well-drained soils usually from shale and siltstone.

**Characteristics:** because the scree is very well-drained, variable and patch vegetation endures droughty soil conditions for much of the growing season.

## Vegetation

Heat, drought and lack of soil development prevent the establishment of many species and limit the community to crevice-rooting herbaceous plants and widely scattered small trees and shrubs.

Typical trees include *Quercus prinus* (chestnut oak), *Pinus strobus* (eastern white pine), and *Juniperus virginiana* (eastern red cedar).

Scattered shrubs are *Vaccinium pallidum* (Blue Ridge blueberry), *Rhus typhina* (staghorn sumac), *Gaylussacia baccata* (black huckleberry), and *Amelanchier arborea* (serviceberry).

The herbaceous layer ranges from absent to nearly 30 percent cover in patches, and consists of drought-tolerant herbs and grasses such as:

*Baptisia tinctoria* (wild indigo)
*Carex pensylvanica* (Pennsylvania sedge)
*Comandra umbellata* (bastard toadflax)
*Deschampsia flexuosa* (wavy hairgrass)
*Dichanthelium linearifolium* (slimleaf panicgrass)
*Geranium robertianum* (Robert geranium)
*Penstemon hirsutus* (hairy beardtongue)
*Schizachyrium scoparium* (little bluestem)
*Solidago arguta* (Atlantic goldenrod)
*Woodsia ilvensis* (rusty woodsia)
*Woodsia obtusa* (bluntlobe cliff fern)

# Eastern Temperate Acidic Cliff

**Formal name:** *Juniperus virginiana - Corydalis sempervirens Cliff Sparse Vegetation*

### Environmental summary

**Where it is found:** in the oak-pine-hemlock forest regions of the northeastern United States on dry vertical exposures of such resistant acidic bedrock as granite, quartzite, sandstone, shale or schist.

**Soil information:** little or no soil development outside of cracks and crevices

**Characteristics:** mostly dry cliffs but may

have small seep areas and the resulting floristic variation; patchy vegetation ranges from barren to well-vegetated across the cliff face, but overall cover is less than 25 percent.

### Vegetation

A mixture of scrubby trees and shrubs, herbaceous plants and bryoids but mostly open rock, the association includes stunted *Juniperus virginiana* (eastern red cedar), *Fraxinus americana* (white ash), *Acer rubrum* (red maple), and *Betula papyrifera* (paper birch). Individuals of other species from surrounding forest may also be present, including *Tsuga canadensis* (eastern hemlock), *Quercus spp.* (oaks), and *Carya spp.* (hickories).

*Rubus odoratus* (purple-flowering raspberry), *Rubus allegheniensis* (Allegheny blackberry), and *Rhus copallinum* (winged sumac) are common shrubs. Woody vines include *Vitis aestivalis* (summer grape) and *Parthenocissus quinquefolia* (Virginia creeper)

A variable herbaceous layer can include:

*Adlumia fungosa* (Allegheny vine)
*Aquilegia canadensis* (red columbine)
*Campanula rotundifolia* (bluebell bellflower)
*Corydalis sempervirens* (rock harlequin)
*Danthonia spicata* (poverty oatgrass)
*Deschampsia flexuosa* (wavy hairgrass)
*Opuntia humifusa* (eastern prickly pear cactus)
*Saxifraga virginiensis* (early saxifrage)
*Woodsia ilvensis* (rusty woodsia)

# Sandstone Cliff Sparse Vegetation

**Formal name:** *Appalachian - Alleghenian Sandstone Dry Cliff Sparse Vegetation*

### Environmental summary

**Where it is found:** steep to vertical exposures of sandstone bedrock, usually on south and west-facing slopes, in the central Appalachians and Western Allegheny Plateau.

**Soil information:** coarse sands and sparse organic matter on shelves and in cracks and crevices.

**Characteristics:** a dry sandstone cliff community, with lichens and mosses common and vegetation generally less than 20 percent coverage.

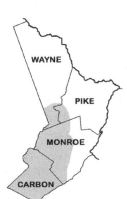

### Vegetation

Woody species reported may include:

*Betula alleghaniensis* (yellow birch)
*Hydrangea arborescens*
*Kalmia latifolia* (mountain laurel)
*Pinus virginiana* (Virginia pine)
*Rhododendron periclymenoides* (pink azalea)
*Toxicodendron radicans* (poison ivy)
*Tsuga canadensis* (eastern hemlock)

A sparse herbaceous layer can include:

*Agrostis perennans* (upland bentgrass)
*Aquilegia canadensis* (red columbine)
*Asplenium montanum* (mountain spleenwort)
*Asplenium rhizophyllum* (walking fern)
*Asplenium trichomanes* (maidenhair spleenwort)
*Cystopteris tenuis* (upland brittle bladderfern)
*Dennstaedtia punctilobula* (hayscented fern)
*Dryopteris intermedia* (intermediate woodfern)
*Dryopteris marginalis* (marginal woodfern)
*Mitchella repens* (partridgeberry)
*Polypodium appalachianum* (Appalachian polypody)
*Polypodium virginianum* (rock polypody)
*Sedum ternatum* (woodland stonecrop)
*Viola blanda* (sweet white violet)
*Woodsia obtusa* (bluntlobe cliff fern)

## Northern Riverside Rock Outcrop

**Formal name:** *Andropogon gerardii — Campanula rotundifolia — Solidago simplex* Sparse

### Vegetation

### *Environmental summary*

**Where it is found:** open flood-scoured exposures of bedrock of major rivers, usually along river narrows, throughout the northeastern United States.

**Soil information:** none to pockets of alluvial silt from flooding

**Characteristics:** a rock outcrop at riverside, usually a gradient from dry acidic conditions higher on the bank to moist and somewhat enriched habitats further down all on an individual site.

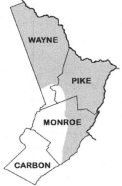

Sites are subjected to both flooding and severe droughts, both of which stress or kill some vegetation.

### Vegetation

Vegetation is sparse and occurs in the cracks and crevices of the bedrock, including a mix of riparian species, xeric-loving crevice plants, and calcareous site species. Often reported are:

*Andropogon gerardii* (big bluestem)
*Anemone virginiana var. alba* (tall thimbleweed)
*Aquilegia canadensis* (red columbine)
*Arabis lyrata* (lyrate rockcress)
*Campanula rotundifolia* (bluebell bellflower)
*Carex crawfordii* (Crawford's sedge)
*Cornus amomum* (silky dogwood)
*Eupatorium perfoliatum* (spotted joe pye weed)
*Euthamia graminifolia* (flattop goldentop)
*Ionactis linariifolius* (flaxleaf whitetop aster)
*Juncus debilis* (weak rush)
*Packera paupercula* (balsam groundsel)
*Potentilla arguta* (tall cinquefoil)
*Prunus pumila* (sandcherry)
*Schizachyrium scoparium* (little bluestem)
*Sisyrinchium montanum* (blue-eyed grass)
*Symphyotrichum lateriflorum* (calico aster)
*Toxicodendron radicans* (poison ivy)

# Successional woodlands: when nature returns

Although not considered ecological communities in the strictest sense, several successional forests studied in the Delaware Water Gap National Recreation area provide interesting clues about what happens when formerly used lands are left to their own devices.

Two major land uses were in play when the area consisted of privately owned plots: agriculture and logging. Almost all such sites feature stone row borders suggesting land clearing for agriculture.

### Agricultural sites

On mid to low-elevation, moderately well drained to well drained soils (typically sandy loams), young forests have returned and within 30 years have nearly completely closed the canopy. Some of the most bottomland areas are subject to temporary flooding.

Recovering forests are dominated by species found in adjacent forests and woodlands:

  *Acer rubrum* (red maple)
  *Acer saccharum* (sugar maple)
  *Betula lenta* (sweet birch)
  *Carya spp.* (hickories)
  *Fagus grandifolia* (American beech)
  *Fraxinus americana* (white ash)
  *Juglans nigra* (black walnut)
  *Liriodendron tulipfera* (tuliptree)
  *Pinus strobus* (eastern white pine)
  *Populus grandidentata* (bigtooth aspen)
  *Prunus serotina* (black cherry)
  *Quercus spp.* (oaks)
  *Robinia pseudoacacia* (black locust)
  *Sassafras albidum* (sassafras)

*Juniperus virginiana* (eastern red-cedar) is a frequent pioneer, but soon declines as the successions evolve.

On higher and usually flat to gently sloping ground, often bounded by stone walls or fence rows, soils are moderately well drained to well drained and early succession is dominated by *Pinus strobus*, which colonizes from the outer edges of fields into the center and will eventually evolve into Eastern White Pine Forest or an Oak-Pine Successional Forest (*see page 153*) if left unchecked.

Scattered trees cover 25 to 60 percent of the field, depending on how long management has been discontinued. *Pinus strobus* (Eastern white pine) is the characteristic tree, which typically extends from 15 to 30 feet in height. Occasionally, *Picea abies* (Norway spruce) or *Picea glauca* (white spruce) may occur with or in place of the eastern white pine trees. *Juniperus virginiana* (Eastern red-cedar) may be present but is not dominant or codominant.

In regions where northern hardwoods are more prevalent, canopy associates include *Fraxinus americana* and *Acer saccharum*. The understory is poorly developed or characterized by scattered individuals found in the canopy.

### Shrub layers

In temporarily flooded bottomlands and low terraces, a tall shrub layer develops and ranges from 5 to 60 percent cover. It may include *Lindera benzoin* (northern spicebush), *Viburnum prunifolium* (black haw), *Viburnum acerifolium* (mapleleaf viburnum) and *Ilex verticillata* (common winterberry).

On pine-dominated fields, the tall shrubs typically consist of *Cornus racemosa* (gray dogwood), *Juniperus virginiana* (Eastern red cedar), *Cornus florida* (flowering dogwood), *Rhus glabra* (smooth sumac) and *Viburnum prunifolium* (black haw).

Berries, notably *Rubus occidentalis* (black raspberry), *Rubus flagellaris* (northern dewberry) and

*Rubus allegheniensis* (Allegheny blackberry) are common to both.

Herbaceous layers vary substantially between the two sites, primarily because of moisture.

Some of the commonly reported species in lower sites include:

*Ageratina altissima var. altissima* (white snakeroot)

*Allium vineale* (wild garlic)

*Arisaema triphyllum* (jack in the pulpit)

*Circaea lutetiana ssp. canadenis* (broadleaf enchanter's nightshade)

*Dennstaedtia punctilobula* (eastern hay-scented fern)

*Galium aparine* (cleavers)

*Impatiens spp* (touch-me-not)

*Oxalis stricta* (common yellow oxalis)

*Podophyllum peltatum* (mayapple)

*Polygonum virginianum* (jumpseed)

*Polystichum acrostichoides* (Christmas fern)

Vines in moist lowland habitats can be absent or so abundant that vegetation structure can be damaged by the weight of vines pulling down trees and shrubs, typically including:

*Parthenocissus quinquefolia* (Virginia creeper)

*Toxicodendron radicans* (eastern poison ivy)

*Vitis labrusca* (fox grape)

In the dry sites, we find species associated with old fields, little bluestem grasslands, and agricultural sites, such as include:

*Solidago rugosa* (wrinkleleaf goldenrod)

*Monarda fistulosa* (wild bergamot)

*Toxicodendron radicans* (eastern poison ivy)

*Oxalis stricta common* (yellow oxalis)

*Euthamia graminifolia* (flat-top goldentop)

*Solidago gigantea* (giant goldenrod)

*Schizachyrium scoparium* (little bluestem)

*Pycnanthemum virginianum* (Virginia mountainmint)

*Potentilla simplex* (common cinquefoil)

In stands that are more heavily forested where the substrate is covered by a thick layer of pine needle duff, typical herbs can include:

*Aralia nudicaulis* (wild sarsaparilla)

*Maianthemum canadense* (Canada mayflower)

*Trientalis borealis* (starflower)

*Mitchella repens* (partridgeberry)

*Lycopodium species* (ground pines)

### Sites involving logging

Sites from which oaks were selectively lumbered are characterized by acidic, generally infertile soils, sometimes covered with a deep surface duff that might include charred wood as evidence of logging and fires.

There are no particular geographic characteristics other than these sites are not found on dry ridgetops, wet bottomlands, active floodplains and only rarely bouldery or rocky sites.

Dominants are usually *Acer rubrum* (red maple) and/or *Betula lenta* (sweet birch) — often more than 50 percent of the cover — with canopy height in the 65 to 100 foot range.

Numerous associate species have been recorded, generally depending on exact site conditions and land use history. Commonly found are:

*Acer saccarum* (sugar maple)

*Carya alba* (mockernut hickory)

*Carya glabra* (pignut hickory)

*Carya ovata* (shagbark hickory)

*Fagus grandifolia* (American beech)

*Fraxinus americana* (white ash)

*Populus tremuloides* (quaking aspen)

*Prunus serotina* (black cherry)

*Quercus rubra* (northern red oak)

*Quercus velutina* (black oak)

*Sassafras albidum* (sassafras)

*Tsuga canadensis* (eastern hemlock)

Subcanopy elements include red maple and/or sweet birch, with black cherry, sugar maple, *Cornus florida* (flowering dogwood), oaks and *Carpinus caroliniana* (American hornbeam) as common associates. This layer varies from 30 to 65 feet with a total cover of 20 to 40 percent.

The tall-shrub layer is usually 5 to 15 feet in height and varies from absent to about 30% total cover. *Lindera benzoin* (northern spicebush) is the most common and locally abundant species in the tall-shrub/sapling layer, although in the southern portion of the range the dominant may be Ilex montana (mountain holly). Several other species may be occasional to locally abundant, including:

*Amelanchier arborea* (serviceberry)

*Hamamelis virginiana* (witch hazel)
*Kalmia latifolia* (mountain laurel)
*Rhododendron maximum* (great rhododen-dron)
*Rhododendron periclymenoides* (pinxter-flower or pink azalea)
*Viburnum prunifolium* (black haw)

The short shrub layer, if present, may include:
*Rubus flagellaris* (northern dewberry)
*Vaccinium angustifolium* (lowbush blue-berry)
*Vaccinium pallidum* (Blue Ridge blueberry)
seedlings of canopy and subcanopy trees

Herbaceous layers may be dominated by dense and extensive colonies of *Lycopodium annotinum* (stiff clubmoss), *Lycopodium dendroideum* (tree ground pine), *Lycopodium clavatum* (running clubmoss) and/or *Lycopodium digitatum* (fan clubmoss).  Also present may be:
*Ageratina altissima* (white snakeroot, or *Eupatorium rugosum*)
*Arisaema triphyllum* (Jack in the pulpit)
*Carex swanii* (Swann's sedge)
*Dennstaedtia punctilobula* (hayscented fern)
*Dryopteris intermedia* (Intermediate wood-fern)
*Galium circaezans* (licorice bedstraw)
*Maianthemum canadense* (Canada may-flower)
*Medeola virginiana* (Indian cucumber)
*Monotropa uniflora* (Indian pipe)
*Osmunda cinnamomea* (Cinnamon fern)
*Polystichum acrostichoides* (Christmas fern)
*Potentilla simplex* (common cinquefoil)
*Smilax rotundifolia* (roundleaf greenbrier)
*Thelypteris noveboracensis* (New York fern)

The most common vines include *Parthenocissus quinquefolia* (Virginia creeper); *Smilax rotundifolia* (roundleaf greenbrier), *Toxicodendron radicans* (poison ivy) and grapes (*Vitis* spp.).

# *Native plants: shrubs and trees*

## Introduction

This section discusses woody perennials, i.e., trees and shrubs (vines are listed separately) subdivided in the following manner.

- Native species whose range includes Pennsylvania and whose observed distribution includes Carbon, Monroe, Pike and/or Wayne counties, all of which are commercially available

- Native species whose range includes Pennsylvania but have not been reported in Carbon, Monroe, Pike or Wayne counties but are commonly available in the marketplace; a secondary list identifies additional species that may be difficult to find in the retail marketplace.

- A listing of native species that do not appear to be commercially available

The 181 entries with distribution including the northeastern counties and the 16 species that are commonly available but have not been reported in the Poconos are organized in the following manner:

    Latin (or scientific) name*
    Common name(s)
    A brief description of natural habitat — i.e., where it is found in nature
    US Fish and Wildlife Service wetland indicators when available
    Height range and, when relevant, flower color and bloom season
    Suggestions for home cultivation, including light requirements, moisture, soil description, and if available soil pH range and preference
    How relatively easy it is to find in the commercial marketplace, in the context of na-

tionwide mail order nurseries
    *Sometimes scientific names have recently changed and not all literature has yet caught up. Where it seems helpful, we have also include "AKA" — also known as.*

### *Abies balsamea*

**Balsam fir** — boreal and northern forests on mountain slopes, glaciated uplands and alluvial flats, peatlands, and swamps in pure, mixed coniferous, and mixed coniferous-deciduous stands; FAC. Mostly northeastern and north central counties in Pennsylvania. Grows to 65 feet; all soil textures from heavy clay to rocky; tolerates a wide range of soil acidity. Prefers cool, acidic wet-mesic sites, pH 5.1 to 6.0. Commonly available.

### *Acer negundo*

**Box-elder** — moist sites along lakes and streams, on floodplains and in low-lying wet places; FAC+. Throughout Pennsylvania, but scattered northwest. Grows 30 to 50 feet; wide variety of soils from gravel to clay but prefers well-drained deep, sandy loam, loam, or clay loam soils with a medium to rocky texture and a pH of 6.5 to 7.5. Commonly available.

### *Acer pensylvanicum*

**Moosewood** — moist, acid soils in deep valleys and on cool, moist, shaded, north-facing slopes; FACU. Throughout Pennsylvania except extreme southeastern and southwestern counties. Grows to 45 feet; small forest openings and under thinned overstories in part shade; prefers cool, moist well-drained loam. Several sources.

### *Acer rubrum*

**Red maple** (var. *rubrum*) and **Trident red maple** (var. *trilobum*) — wet to dry sites in dense woods and in openings in low, rich woods, along the margins of lakes, marshes, and swamps, in hammocks, wet thickets, and on floodplains and stream terraces; also occurs in drier upland woodlands, low-elevation cove forests, dry sandy plains, and on stable dunes. FAC (var rubrum) and FACW+ (var. trilobum). Throughout Pennsylvania. Grows 40 to 70 feet; wide variety of soils; develops best on moist, fertile, loamy soils but also dry, rocky, upland soils. Commonly available.

## Acer saccharinum

**Silver maple** — streamside communities and lake fringes, and occasionally in swamps, gullies, and small depressions of slow drainage; FACW. Throughout Pennsylvania. Grows 50-80 feet; average, medium to wet soils in full sun to part shade. Prefers moist soils, but tolerant of poor dry soils; pH range 4.5 to 7.0. Commonly available.

## Acer saccharum

**Sugar maple** — rich, mesic woods and drier upland woods, on level areas or in coves, ravines and other sheltered locations on adjacent lower especially north-facing slopes. Often associated with stream terraces, stream banks, valleys, canyons, ravines, and wooded natural levees; occasionally found on dry rocky hillsides; FACU. Throughout Pennsylvania. Grows to 80 feet; wide variety of soils derived from shale, limestone and sandstone, but prefers deep, moist, fertile, well-drained sandy to silty loam; also associated with alluvial or calcareous soils. Intolerant of flooded soils and grows poorly on dry, shallow soils; pH 3.7 to 7.3 but prefers pH ranges 5.5 to 7.3. Commonly available.

## Acer spicatum

**Mountain maple** — cool woods where the climate is humid and precipitation is year-round; FACU-. Throughout Pennsylvania. Grows to 35 feet; sun to part shade in moist cool acidic soil. Very few sources.

## Alnus incana ssp. rugosa

**Speckled alder** — moist lowlands, frequently along streams and lakes; common in swamps and the older zones of bogs. Throughout Pennsylvania except for far southeastern and southwestern

counties. Shrub to 20 feet; sun to shade in moist rich loam. Very few sources.

## Alnus serrulata

**Smooth alder** or **Hazel alder** — stream banks, ditches, edges of sloughs, swampy fields and bogs, and lakeshores; OBL. Throughout Pennsylvania except for northern tier counties. Shrub to 20 feet; sun to shade in moist to wet circumneutral fine sandy loams, peats and mucks. Very flood tolerant. Alders fix nitrogen and thus serve as nutrient-giving pioneers in reclamation projects. Very few sources.

## Amelanchier arborea

**Shadbush** — swampy lowlands, dry open woodlands and sandy bluffs, rocky ridges, forest edges and fields; FAC-. Throughout Pennsylvania. Shrub or small tree to 48 feet; well-drained silty clay loam and poorly drained silt loams. White flowers in early spring. Very few sources.

## Amelanchier canadensis

**Shadbush** — moist upland woods and edges, bogs, and swamps; FAC. Extreme southeastern counties in Pennsylvania. Shrub or small tree to 20 feet; average, medium, well-drained soil in full sun to part shade. Tolerant of a somewhat wide range of soils. Often confused in the nursery trade with *A. arborea*. White flowers in spring. Commonly available.

## Amelanchier humilis

**Low juneberry** is found on dry open ground, rocky bluffs and lakeshores; FACU. Widely scattered counties on the Allegheny Plateau and northeast. Shrub to 20 feet; sun to part shade in dry acidic sandy loam. White flowers in spring. Very few sources.

## Amelanchier laevis

**Allegheny serviceberry**, or **smooth serviceberry** — thickets, open woods, sheltered slopes, roadside banks and wood margins. Throughout Pennsylvania. Shrub to 45 feet; full sun to part shade in average, mesic sandy loams. Tolerant of a wide range of soils, but prefers moist, well-drained loams. White flowers in spring. Commonly available.

### Amelanchier sanguinea

**Roundleaf serviceberry** is found on hillsides; upland woods; rocky slopes, barrens. Widely scattered counties, mostly central Pennsylvania. Shrub or small tree to 20 feet; sun to part shade in dry to moist, rocky, well-drained soil. White flowers in spring. Very few sources.

### Amelanchier stolonifera

**Low juneberry** — woods, old fields, fence rows and barrens; FACU. Throughout Pennsylvania. Colonizing shrub to 6 feet; full sun to part shade in mesic to moist, well-drained soil in full sun to part shade. Tolerant of a wide range of soils. White flowers in spring. Several sources.

### Andromeda polifolia var. glaucophylla

**Bog rosemary** — moist to wet acidic peaty ground; OBL. Northeastern counties in Pennsylvania; also reported in Erie, Warren and Clinton counties. To 18 inches; part sun to part shade in acidic moist organic peats, sands and mucks. Pinkish-white flowers in spring. Very few sources.

### Aralia spinosa

**Devil's walking stick** — upland and low woods, thickets, stream edges, palustrine wetlands and savannahs; prefers sites with deep, acidic, sandy peat soils. Scattered counties throughout Pennsylvania, especially west-central counties. Shrub or tree to 32 feet; part shade in well-drained fertile to poor soils. Aggressive spreader via suckers. Several sources.

### Arctostaphylos uva-ursi ssp. coactilis

**Bearberry** or **kinnikinnick** — dry nutrient-poor soils, often in open pine forests during intermediate succession. Reported only in Monroe, Erie and Crawford counties in Pennsylvania. Prostrate stems; sun to shade in dry to mesic uncompacted or loose rocky or sandy acidic soil. Intolerant of fertilizer. Pinkish white flowers in early spring. Commonly available.

### Aronia arbutifolia

**Red chokeberry** — pine bottomlands; swamps and moist woods; open bogs; FACW. Throughout Pennsylvania. Shrub from 18 inches to 10 feet, depending on habitat.; sun to part sun in moist sandy loam. White flowers in late spring. Commonly available. AKA *Photinia pyrifolia*

### Aronia melanocarpa

**Black chokeberry** — swamps, bogs, wet and dry woods, barrens. FAC. Throughout Pennsylvania. Shrub to 10 feet; sun to part shade in average, medium, well-drained soil. Tolerant of wide range of soils, including both dry and boggy soils. Best fruit production occurs in full sun. White flowers in late spring. Commonly available. AKA *Photinia melanocarpa*.

### Aronia prunifolia

**Purple chokeberry** — low woodlands, lake shores, stream banks, or at interface of marshes or bogs with adjacent uplands on sandy soils. Throughout Pennsylvania except north-central counties. A natural hybrid between *Aronia melanocarpa* and *Aronia arbutifolia*; shrub, 8 to 12 feet; average, medium, well-drained soils in full sun to part shade. Wide range of soil tolerance including boggy soils. Best fruit production usually occurs in full sun. White flowers in late spring. Very few sources. AKA *Photinia floribunda*

### Betula alleghaniensis

**Yellow birch** — stream banks, swampy woods, and rich, moist, forested slopes; FAC. Throughout Pennsylvania. Grows to 100 feet; well-drained fertile loams and moderately well-drained sandy loams. Several sources.

### Betula lenta

**Sweet birch** — rich, moist, cool forests, especially on protected slopes, to rockier, more exposed sites; FACU. Throughout Pennsylvania. Grows to 80 feet; part shade to shade in dry to moist slightly acidic rich, moist, well drained soil. Several sources.

### Betula nigra

**River birch** — alluvial, often clay, soils on lowlands, floodplains, stream banks, and lake margins. Typically on sandbars and new land near streams, inside natural levees or fronts. Sometimes found on scattered upland sites, FACW. Eastern counties except northern tier in Pennsylvania. Grows to 100 feet; alluvial, clay soils in full sun to part sun with high soil moisture. Soil can be well or poorly drained as long as it is at or near field capacity year round. Can grow in highly acidic (pH less than 4) soils. Commonly available.

### Betula papyrifera

**Paper birch** — moist open upland forests, especially on rocky slopes, and sometimes in swampy woods; FACU. Mostly northeastern and north-central counties in Pennsylvania; scattered elsewhere. Grows to 100 feet; sun to part sun in moist mineral-organic soil, pH above 5.0; prefers cooler north to northeast facing slopes with slow drainage and little competition. Commonly available.

### Betula populifolia

**Gray birch** — rocky or sandy open woods, moist to somewhat dry slopes, old fields, and waste places; FAC. Mostly eastern counties in Pennsylvania; scattered elsewhere. Grows to 32 feet; sun to shade in dry to moist, poor soils, wide range of pH. Very few sources.

### Carpinus caroliniana

**Hornbeam** — rich, deciduous forests along stream banks, on flood plains, and on moist hillsides; FAC. Throughout Pennsylvania. Tree to 30 feet; average, medium moisture soil in part shade to full shade. Prefers moist, organically rich soils. Commonly available.

### Carya cordiformis

**Bitternut hickory** — river flood plains, well-drained hillsides and limestone glades; FACU+. Throughout Pennsylvania. Grows to 100 feet; dry to moist rich, loamy or gravelly soil. Very few sources.

### Carya glabra

**Pignut hickory** — deep flood plains, well-drained sandy soils, rolling hills and slopes, dry rocky soils, or thin soils on edge of granite outcrops; FACU-. Mostly southern counties in Pennsylvania as well as extreme eastern and western counties. Grows to 100 feet; light, well-drained, loamy soils derived from a variety of sedimentary or metamorphic parent material in full sun to part shade. Very few sources.

### Carya ovata

**Shagbark hickory** — wet bottomlands, rocky hillsides, and limestone outcrops; FACU. Throughout Pennsylvania. Grows to 100 feet; humusy, rich, moist, well-drained loams in full sun to part shade. Commonly available.

### Carya tomentosa

**Mockernut hickory** — moist rocky open woods and slopes; less common on alluvial bottomlands. Throughout Pennsylvania except for counties along New York line. Grows to 100 feet; wide variety of moist soils; prefers finely textured, organic sandy loams. Very few sources.

### Castanea dentata

**American chestnut** — rich deciduous and mixed forests, particularly with oak. Throughout Pennsylvania. Tree to 20 feet; moist, well-drained loams in full sun. Formerly very common and a forest dominant before dieback due to chestnut blight, imported from the far east with Chinese chestnut species. Rarely lives longer than 15 to 20 years. Blight-resistant hybrid may be available from the American Chestnut Foundation. Several sources.

### Ceanothus americanus

**New Jersey tea** — dry open plains and prairie-like areas, on sandy or rocky soils in woodland clearings, edges and slopes, on riverbanks or lakeshores. Throughout Pennsylvania. Shrub to 3 feet; sun to part shade in dry to mesic sandy rocky loam. White flowers in late spring. Commonly available.

### Celtis occidentalis

**Dogberry** — rich moist soil along streams, on flood plains and rocky wooded hillsides and woodlands; FACU. Mostly northeastern and southern counties in Pennsylvania; scattered elsewhere. Grows to 110 feet; prefers moist, organically rich, well-drained soils in full sun. Tolerates part shade, wind, many urban pollutants and a wide range of soil conditions, including both wet, dry and poor soils. Commonly available.

### Celtis tenuifolia

**Dwarf hackberry** — shale banks and slopes along streams in open woods, dry wooded hillsides and limestone bluffs. Mostly southern and northeastern counties in Pennsylvania. Shrub or small tree grows to 15 feet; sun to part shade in mesic to moist humusy, sandy loam. Very few sources.

### Cephalanthus occidentalis

**Buttonbush** — swamps, bogs, lake margins and low wet ground; OBL. Throughout Pennsylvania. Shrub to 10 feet; sun to part shade in moist, humusy soils in full sun to part shade. Grows well in wet soils, including flood conditions and shallow standing water. Adapts to a wide range of soils except dry ones. Commonly available.

### Chamaedaphne calyculata var. angustifolia

**Leatherleaf** — bogs and acidic wetlands, especially at higher elevations; OBL. Mostly northeastern and extreme northwestern counties in Pennsylvania; widely scattered elsewhere. Shrub to 5 feet; sun to part shade in acidic, peaty, moist to wet soils. White flowers in spring. Very few sources.

### Chimaphila maculata

**Striped prince's pine** — moist woodlands in undisturbed organic litter of leaves and especially conifer needles. Southern, northwestern and northeastern counties in Pennsylvania. Subshrub, 4 to 12 inches; part shade to shade in dry, acidic sandy loam with leaf or needle litter, pH 4 to 5. White flowers in late summer. Very few sources.

### Chimaphila umbellata ssp. cisatlantica

**Pipsissewa**, or **prince's pine** — upland woods and barrens. Throughout Pennsylvania. Subshrub 4 to 12 inches; part shade to shade in dry, acidic sandy loam. White or pink flowers in late summer. Very few sources.

### Clethra alnifolia

**Sweet pepperbush** — low wet woods, bogs and acidic swamps in moderately to poorly drained sites; FAC+. Extreme eastern counties in Pennsylvania from Monroe to Chester; also reported in Erie and Warren counties. Shrub, 6 to 12 feet; average, medium to wet, well-drained soil in full sun to part shade. Adaptive to a wide range of

soil, moisture and light conditions. Prefers part shade and consistently moist to wet, acidic soils. Tolerates full shade. pH 4.6 to 6.5. White flowers in summer. Commonly available.

### Comptonia peregrina

**Sweet-fern** — dry, sterile, sandy to rocky soils in pinelands or pine barrens, clearings, or woodlot edges. Throughout Pennsylvania except extreme western counties. Shrub to 5 feet; sun to part shade in average, medium, well-drained soil in full sun to part shade. Prefers sandy, acidic loams, but tolerates poor soils. Spreads to form colonies. Tolerates wet conditions and wind, drought and a wide range of soils. Does not transplant well. Commonly available.

### Cornus alternifolia

**Alternate-leaved dogwood** — moist woodlands, forest margins, stream and swamp borders, and near deep canyon bottoms. Throughout Pennsylvania. Shrub or small tree to 20 feet; sun to part shade in sandy, well-drained deep soils. White flowers in late spring. Commonly available.

### Cornus amomum ssp. amomum

**Red willow** or **Kinnikinik** — swamps, stream banks, moist woods, fields and thickets; FACW. Throughout Pennsylvania. Shrub to 10 feet. Two local subspecies: *amomum* and *obliqua.*; part shade to shade in moist to wet acidic sandy loam. White flowers in late spring. Commonly available.

### Cornus florida

**Flowering dogwood** — mesic deciduous woods, on floodplains, slopes, bluffs, and in ravines; FACU. Throughout Pennsylvania. Tree to 30 feet; varied soils from moist, deep soils to light-textured, well-drained upland soils; prefers coarse to medium-textured acidic soils. White flowers in spring. Commonly available and found at most better garden centers.

### Cornus racemosa

**Silky dogwood** — swampy meadows, moist old fields, thickets; FAC-. Throughout Pennsylvania. Shrub 3 to 16 feet; sun to part shade in dry to mesic sandy loam. Tolerates wide range of soil conditions, including both moist and somewhat dry soils, and of city air pollution. White flowers in spring. Commonly available.

### Cornus rugosa

**Round-leaved dogwood** — well-drained rocky woods and cliffs. Mostly eastern counties in Pennsylvania; scattered elsewhere. Shrub or small tree, 3 to 12 feet; part shade to shade in dry to mesic sandy acidic loam. White flowers in spring. Very few sources.

### Cornus sericea

**Red-osier dogwood** — stream banks, swamps, moist fields, thickets; FACW+. Widely scattered in Pennsylvania, especially eastern and northwestern counties. Shrub to 10 feet; part shade in moist, circumneutral well-drained soil. Adaptable to a wide range of soil and climatic conditions. White flowers in spring. Also known as *Cornus stolonifera*. Commonly available.

### Corylus americana

**American filbert** — moist to dry open woods, thickets, hillsides, roadsides, fencerows, and waste places; FACU-. Throughout Pennsylvania. Grows to 15 feet; average, medium, well-drained soil in full sun to part shade; forms thickets if suckers are not removed. White flowers in early spring. Commonly available.

### Corylus cornuta

**Beaked hazelnut** — moist to dry roadsides, woodland edges, thickets, fencerows, sometimes as an understory in open woodlands; FACU-. Eastern and central counties in Pennsylvania; scattered elsewhere. Shrub to 20 feet; full sun to part shade in organically rich, medium moisture, well-drained circumneutral soils. Tolerates average garden soils, but not unamended heavy clays. Several sources.

### Crataegus chrysocarpa var. chrysocarpa

**Red-fruited hawthorn** — open woods, fields, roadsides and stream banks. Scattered distribution in Pennsylvania, mostly central counties. Shrub or small tree to 32 feet; sun to part sun in mesic to moist well drained sandy loam. Tolerates a wide range of soils as long as drainage is good, light shade and some drought, and many ur-

ban pollutants. White flowers in late spring. Also known as *Crataegus coccinea*. Very few sources.

### Crataegus punctata

**Dotted hawthorn** — open hardwood and conifer-hardwood forests. Mostly western and southeastern counties in Pennsylvania; scattered elsewhere. Large shrub or small tree to 40 feet; sun to shade in dry to moist circumneutral ordinary loams. White, pink, yellow flowers in late spring. Very few sources.

### Crataegus rotundifolia

**Fireberry hawthorn** — rocky pastures, open woodlands and edges. Scattered counties throughout Pennsylvania except extreme northern and western counties. Large shrub or small tree to 25 feet; sun to part sun in mesic to moist sandy loam; drought tolerant. White flowers in early summer. Very few sources.

### Diervilla lonicera

**Bush honeysuckle** — typically on exposed rocky sites with dry to mesic well-drained soil. Throughout Pennsylvania. Shrub to 4 feet; part shade to shade in dry, rocky slightly acidic loam. Red, orange, yellow and purple flowers in summer. Commonly available.

### Diospyros virginiana

**Persimmon** — open woods, floodplains and old fields, seasonally flooded bottomlands, dry ridgetops and abandoned agricultural land; FAC. Pennsylvania distribution includes mostly southern counties; scattered elsewhere. Grows to 50 feet; dry to medium, well-drained soils in full sun to part shade. Wide range of soil tolerance, but prefers moist, sandy soils. Drought tolerant. Blooms late spring, edible fruit in the fall. Commonly available.

### Dirca palustris

**Leatherwood** — rich deciduous woods and thickets; FAC. Mostly southern counties in Pennsylvania; scattered north. Shrub to 5 feet; full sun in moist, deep soils; prefers wet sites; pale yellow flowers in early spring. Very few sources.

### Epigaea repens

**Trailing arbutus** — moist to xeric pine or deciduous forests, clearings and edges, in sandy, rocky, or peaty soil; borders and banks. Throughout Pennsylvania. Creeping subshrub, about 6 inches, with white-pink flowers in early spring; part sun to part shade in dry sandy rocky acid loam. Can be difficult to transplant. Very few sources.

### Fagus grandifolia

**American beech** — rich deciduous and mixed-conifer forest; FACU. Throughout Pennsylvania. Grows to 80 feet; deep, rich, moist but well-drained soils in full sun to part shade. Intolerant of wet, poorly drained soils. Often forms thickets or colonies by suckering from the shallow roots. Commonly available.

### Fraxinus americana

**White ash** — middle, moderately-moist slopes and dry, cold ridges and mountaintops; FACU. Throughout Pennsylvania. Grows to 80 feet; deep, well-drained, moist soils with other hardwoods. Commonly available.

### Fraxinus nigra

**Black ash** — deciduous, coniferous, and mixed lowland forests, poorly drained swamps, bogs, gullies, depressions, valley flats, and stream and lake shores; FACW. Throughout Pennsylvania. Grows to 80 feet; moist to wet, deep, fertile, mineral or organic soils. Several sources.

### Fraxinus pennsylvanica

**Green ash** — riparian areas such as floodplains and swamps, but is also in sites that periodically experience drought; FACW. Throughout Pennsylvania, mostly eastern counties, scattered west. Grows to 80 feet; fertile, clay, silt, and/or loam soils that range from poorly to well drained; prefers constantly moist, humusy, well-drained soils in full sun. Commonly available.

### Gaultheria hispidula

**Creeping snowberry** — wet woods and bogs; FACW. Northern counties in Pennsylvania. Creeping shrub to 6 inches.; part shade to shade in moist to wet cold humusy to peaty acidic soils, pH 4.0 to 5.0. White flowers in spring. Very few sources.

### Gaultheria procumbens

**Teaberry, wintergreen** — oak woods or under evergreens; moist sites but tolerates moisture conditions ranging from dry to poorly drained; FACU. Throughout Pennsylvania. Creeping subshrub spreads from rhizomes; 4-8 inches with white flowers in spring; part shade to shade in mesic to moist sandy, well-drained organic loam. Prefers pH 4.5 to 6.0. Commonly available.

### Gaylussacia baccata

**Black huckleberry** — dry to wet acidic woods and thickets, often among oaks; FACU. Throughout Pennsylvania. Shrub to 3 feet with white to pink flowers in early summer and fruit in late summer; part shade to shade in mesic to moist sandy organic loam. pH 4.0 to 6.0. Very few sources.

### Gaylussacia frondosa

**Dangleberry** — dry to wet acidic oak woods and thickets; FAC. Mostly eastern counties in Pennsylvania, scattered west. Grows to 6 feet, with white to pink flowers in early summer and fruit in late summer; part shade to shade in mesic to moist sandy organic loam, pH 4.0 to 6.5. Very few sources.

### Gleditsia triacanthos

**Honey locust** — well-drained upland woodlands and borders, rocky hillsides, old fields, fencerows and rich moist stream banks, bottomlands and floodplains, FAC-. Mostly southern counties in Pennsylvania; scattered north. Grows to 65 feet; organically rich, moist, well-drained soils in full sun. Tolerant of a wide range of soils, wind, high summer heat, drought and saline conditions. Several sources.

### Hamamelis virginiana

**Witch hazel** — dry to moist woodlands, slopes, bluffs, and high hammocks; FAC-. Throughout Pennsylvania. Grows to 15 feet with yellow flowers in late fall to early winter; part shade to shade in mesic to moist sandy organic loam; prefers rich, deep soils. The familiar astringent is distilled from the bark of young shoots. Among the most widespread shrubs in the region. Commonly available.

### *Hydrangea arborescens*

**Wild hydrangea** or **sevenbark** — rich woods; rocky wooded slopes; stream banks and ravines; FACU. Throughout Pennsylvania. Shrub to 6 feet with white flowers in summer; average, medium moisture, well-drained soil in part shade. Intolerant of drought. Several sources.

### *Hypericum prolificum*

**Shrubby St. John's-wort** — rocky ground, dry wooded slopes, uncultivated fields, gravel bars along streams and in low, moist valleys; FACU. Throughout Pennsylvania except for extreme northeastern counties. Shrub to 6 feet with yellow flowers in early summer; average, medium moisture, well-drained soil in full sun to part shade. Tolerates wide range of soils, including dry rocky or sandy soils. Also tolerates some drought. Several sources.

### *Ilex montana*

**Mountain holly** — cool moist rocky woods, usually at higher elevations along the Allegheny front. Throughout Pennsylvania except for extreme southeastern counties. Shrub or small tree, grows to 30 feet with white flowers in spring and fruit in early fall; sun to partial shade; well drained soil. Very few sources.

### *Ilex mucronata*

**Catberry** or **mountain holly** — swamps, bogs, moist woods, fens; OBL. Northern counties in Pennsylvania, including the Lehigh Valley; scattered elsewhere. Shrub to 10 feet with white-yellow flowers in spring and fruit in late summer; sun to part shade in moist to wet silty organic loam. Very few sources.

### *Ilex verticillata*

**Winterberry** — wet woods, swamps, bogs and moist shores; FACW+. Throughout Pennsylvania. Shrub to 15 feet; sun to part shade in moist acidic organic loam. Tolerates poorly drained soils, including swamps and bogs. Dioecious; only fertilized female flowers will produce the attractive red berries that are the signature of the species. Commonly available.

### *Juglans cinerea*

**Butternut** — rich woods of river terraces and valleys, especially in coves, on stream benches and terraces and on slopes, in the talus of rock ledges, and on other sites with good drainage; FACU+. Throughout Pennsylvania. Grows to 100 feet; moist, organically rich, well-drained soils in full sun. Intolerant of shade. Commonly available.

### *Juglans nigra*

**Black walnut** — rich woods on wet bottomlands, dry ridges and slopes. Common on limestone soils; FACU. Throughout Pennsylvania, mainly south, scattered north. Grows to 130 feet; deep, well-drained neutral soils that are moist and fertile. Commonly available.

### *Juniperus communis*

**Common juniper** — dry open woods, slopes, pastures. Mainly eastern counties in Pennsylvania; widely scattered west. Low growing, spreading shrub, with yellow flowers in early spring; part sun to part shade in dry to mesic sandy loam. Declining due to deer browsing. Fruits used to flavor gin. Several sources.

### *Juniperus virginiana*

**Eastern red-cedar** — upland to low — especially early successional — woodlands, old fields and fence rows, glades and river swamps; FACU. Mostly eastern and southwestern counties in Pennsylvania; scattered northwest. Grows to 65 feet; average, dry to moist, well-drained soils in full sun. Tolerates a wide range of soils and growing conditions. Prefers moist soils, but has the best drought resistance of any conifer native to the eastern U. S. Commonly available.

### *Kalmia angustifolia*

**Sheep laurel** — sandy or infertile soil, bogs, old fields, dry woods, barrens. FAC. Eastern counties in Pennsylvania; somewhat scattered south-central. Grows to 3 feet with rose-pink to crimson flowers in early summer; part sun to part shade in mesic to moist sandy organic loam. pH 4.5 to 6. Very few sources.

### *Kalmia latifolia*

**Mountain laurel** — dry upland sandy, acidic, rocky woods. FACU. Throughout Pennsylvania. Grows to 15 feet with white to pink flowers in early summer; part sun to part shade in dry to mesic humusy sandy loam, pH 4.5 to 6. Very slow growing. The state flower of Pennsylvania. Commonly available; resist the temptation to transplant from the wild, because root systems are long and thin in all but the smallest plants.

### Kalmia polifolia

**Bog laurel** — peaty wetlands and bogs; OBL. Extreme northeastern counties in Pennsylvania. Grows 6 to 36 inches with lavender flowers in summer; part sun to part shade in wet organic soils and peat; flood tolerant. Very few sources.

### Larix laricina

**American larch** or **tamarack** — cold, wet to moist, poorly drained swamps, bogs, and muskegs; also along streams, lakes, swamp borders, and occasionally on upland sites; FACW. Mostly northern counties in Pennsylvania; scattered southwestern counties. Grows to 65 feet; sun to part sun in moist to wet acid soils; intolerant of shade, heat, polluted areas and of dry, shallow chalky soils, but adapts to sites slightly drier than natural habitat. Commonly available.

### Ledum groenlandicum

**Labrador tea** — wetter sites with low subsurface water flow and low nutrients; poorly drained habitats such as boreal forests, open conifer bogs, treeless bogs, wooded swamps, wet barrens, and peatlands; OBL. Northeastern counties in Pennsylvania; also reported in Warren County. Shrub to 3 feet with white flowers in early summer; sun to part shade in moist to wet acidic organic soils, peat and muck. Flood tolerant. Also known as *Rhododendron groenlandicum*. Several sources.

### Leucothoe racemosa

**Fetter-bush, Swamp doghobble** — swamps and moist thickets, shrub-free bogs, along marshy stream banks and forest edges. An important shrub species in palustrine wetlands with deep, acidic, sandy, peat soils; FACW. Eastern counties in Pennsylvania, from Monroe County southward and then west along the Maryland border to Franklin County. Grows to10 feet with white to pink flowers in late spring to early summer; part shade on moist, sandy acidic loam. Also known

as *Eubotrys racemosa*. Very few sources.

### Lindera benzoin

**Spicebush** — moist sites in wooded bottomlands, ravines, valleys and along streams; found in many regional ecosystems; FACW-. Throughout Pennsylvania. Grows to 10 feet with yellow flowers in early spring; average, medium, well-drained soils in full sun to part shade, pH 4.5 to 6.5. Fall color is best in sunny areas. Tolerates full shade. Leaves used to make a mildly spicy herbal tea, hence the name. Commonly available.

### Linnaea borealis var. americana

**Twinflower** — cool, dry to moist forests and woodlands, especially coniferous, in sandy acidic loam, and humus-rich swamps and barrens; FAC. Widely scattered counties in Pennsylvania, mostly north and south central. Trailing subshrub with pinkish-white flowers in spring; part shade to shade in moist to wet cool acidic humus. Low drought tolerance. pH 4-6. Very few sources.

### Liriodendron tulipifera

**Tuliptree** — rich woodlands on hills, bluffs and low mountains; FACU. Throughout Pennsylvania. Grows to 150 feet with creamy-white flowers in spring; moist, organically rich, well-drained loams in full sun. Tolerates part shade. Commonly available.

### Lonicera canadensis

**Fly honeysuckle** — cool, dry to moist woods upland woods, thickets, swamps, fens and sometimes along streams; FACU. Mostly northern and southwestern counties in Pennsylvania; scattered elsewhere. Grows to 5 feet with pale yellow flowers in late spring to early summer. Part sun to part shade in moist sandy organic loam. Very few sources.

### Lonicera villosa

**Water-berry** — bogs, swamps, wet thickets, swamps, treed fens and stream banks. Shrub to 3 feet with pale yellow flowers in late spring to early summer; sun to part sun in moist to wet organic loam. Reported only in Monroe, Warren and Centre Counties in Pennsylvania. Very few sources.

### Lyonia ligustrina

**Maleberry** — low, alluvial woods and thickets, wet meadows, bogs, and lakeshores; FACW. Mostly southern counties in Pennsylvania; scattered north. Shrub to 10 feet with white flowers in late spring; part sun to part shade in mesic to moist sandy clay organic loam. Very few sources.

### Magnolia tripetala

**Umbrella-tree** — rich woods and ravines, mainly in uplands, rarely on the coastal plain; FACU. Far eastern counties in Pennsylvania; widely scattered south. Grows to 30 feet with large white flowers in late spring; part shade in most, rich acidic, well drained sandy loam. Very few sources.

### Malus coronaria var. coronaria

**Sweet crabapple** — open woods, woodland edges and stream banks. Throughout Pennsylvania. Grows to 35 feet with pinkish-white flowers in spring; part shade in moist, well drained humusy soil. Fruit very tart and acidic. Very few sources.

### Myrica gale

**Sweet-gale** — bogs, shallow water of lake and stream edges; OBL. Northeastern counties in Pennsylvania. Shrub to 5 feet with yellowish-green flowers in late spring; sun to part sun in wet to moist sandy loam. Very few sources.

### Myrica pensylvanica

**Bayberry** — old fields, sand dunes, open woods in dry to moist sterile, sandy soils; FAC. Mostly southeastern counties in Pennsylvania; widely scattered elsewhere. Grows to 6 feet with yellowish-green flowers in late spring; sun to part sun in dry to moist sandy clay loam. Prefers moist, peaty or sandy, acidic soils, but tolerates a wide range of soils and growing conditions. Groups of plants need at least one male plant to pollinate female plants for fruit. Fruits have waxy coating used to make traditional bayberry candles. AKA *Morella pensylvanica.* Commonly available.

### Nyssa sylvatica

**Sourgum** or **Black gum** — dry to middle and upper slopes and ridgetops, FAC. Throughout Pennsylvania. Grows to 100 feet; average, medium to wet soils in full sun to part shade. Prefers moist, acidic soils. Tolerates poorly-drained soils and can grow in standing water; tolerates some drought and adapts to some dryish soils. Can spread by sucker growth. Commonly available.

### Ostrya virginiana

**Hop-hornbeam** — moist, open to forested hillsides to dry upland slopes and ridges, occasionally on moist, well-drained flood plains; FACU. Throughout Pennsylvania. Grows to 65 feet; average, medium, well-drained soil in full sun to part shade. Commonly available.

### Physocarpus opulifolius

**Ninebark** — wet woods, moist cliffs, sandy or rocky stream banks, gravel bars and moist thickets; FACW- . Throughout Pennsylvania. Shrub to 10 feet with white to pink flowers in late spring; sun to part shade in mesic to moist, well-drained soil. Tolerates wide range of soil conditions. pH 5.1 to 6.5. Commonly available.

### Picea mariana

**Black spruce** — bottomlands, peat bogs and dry peatlands, swamps, muskegs and transitional sites between peatlands and uplands; FACU-. Mostly northeastern counties in Pennsylvania; scattered south-central. To 65 feet; sun to shade in mesic to wet acidic humusy soils. Shallow root system makes this tree susceptible to wind throw. Commonly available.

### Picea rubens

**Red spruce** — cool upland to sub alpine forests in climates with cool, moist summers and cold winters; on thin soils of steep, rocky slopes and wet bottomlands; often on sites unfavorable for other species such as organic soils overlying rocks in mountainous locales; FACU. Mostly northeastern counties in Pennsylvania; scattered north central. Grows to 100 feet on soils developed from glacial deposits especially from parent materials of unsorted glacial drift and till deposited on the midslopes of hills and mountains with thick mor humus. Very few sources.

### Pinus resinosa

**Red pine** or **Norway pine** — dry slopes and mountaintops and sandy soils in boreal forests; FACU. Scattered throughout Pennsylvania, mainly north. Grows to 120 feet; well-drained, dry to moist acidic to neutral soils in full to part sun. Tolerates poor soils. Commonly available.

### Pinus rigida

**Pitch pine** — upland or lowland, sterile, dry to boggy acidic forests and barrens; FACU. Throughout Pennsylvania. Grows to 100 feet; dry, thin, infertile, and sandy or gravelly soils, ranging from rapidly draining to swampy limestone and sandstone. Very few sources.

### Pinus strobus

**Eastern white pine** — mesic to dry sites ranging from wet bogs and moist stream bottoms to xeric sand plains and rocky ridges, especially on northerly aspects and in coves; FACU. Throughout Pennsylvania. Grows to 130 feet; average, medium moisture, well-drained soil in full sun. Prefers full sun, fairly infertile sandy soils, such as well-drained outwash soils, in cool, humid climates with little hardwood competition. Tolerant of a wide range of soil conditions. Intolerant of many air pollutants such as sulfur dioxide and ozone. Commonly available.

### Pinus virginiana

**Virginia pine** — dry uplands, sterile sandy or shaly barrens, old fields, and lower mountains; barrens slopes and ridgetops. Southern counties in Pennsylvania, scattered north. Grows to 48 feet; full sun in sandy loam; will grow in poor, dry soils including clay. Several sources.

### Platanus occidentalis

**Sycamore** — alluvial soils near streams and lakes and in moist ravines, sometimes on uplands and sometimes on limestone soils; cultivated in parks and gardens and as a street tree; FACW-. Throughout Pennsylvania. Grows to 160 feet; average, medium to wet, well-drained soils in full sun. Tolerates light shade. Prefers rich, humusy, consistently moist soils. Generally tolerant of most urban pollutants. Commonly available.

### Populus balsamifera

**Balsam poplar** — river floodplains, stream and lake shores, moist depressions, and swamps, but will also grow on drier sites; FACW. Widely scattered counties throughout Pennsylvania. Grows

to 100 feet; alluvial gravel, deep sand, clay loam, silt, and silty loam with abundant soil moisture is needed. Several sources.

### Populus grandidentata

**Bigtooth aspen** — floodplains, gently rolling terrain, and lower slopes of uplands; FACU. Throughout Pennsylvania. Grows to 80 feet; light sandy loams, sands, and loamy sands above pH 4.0. Very few sources.

### Populus tremuloides

**Quaking aspen** — moist upland woods, dry mountainsides, high plateaus, talus slopes, gentle slopes near valley bottoms, alluvial terraces, and along watercourses. Throughout Pennsylvania. Grows to 65 feet; soils ranging from shallow and rocky to deep loamy sands and heavy clays. Prefers sites that are well drained, loamy, and high in organic matter and nutrients. Commonly available.

### Prunus americana

**Wild plum** — riparian areas, but also moist to dry open to wooded prairie ravines, pastures, roadsides, fencerows, ditch banks, and natural drainage areas; FACU. Throughout Pennsylvania except extreme northeastern counties. Shrub or small tree to 20 feet with white flowers in spring; average, dry to medium, well-drained soils in full sun to part shade. Control spreading with sucker removal. Fruit used to make jams and jellies. Commonly available.

### Prunus pensylvanica

**Pin cherry** — areas characterized as water-shedding (rocky ridges, cliffs, dry woods, clearings) or water-receiving (sandy and gravelly banks, shores of rivers and lakes); FACU-. Throughout Pennsylvania. Shrub or tree to 40 feet with white flowers in spring; somewhat dry sites and shallow organic layers relatively low in nutrients. Soils very low in moisture may result in a shrub form of pin cherry. Several sources.

### Prunus pumila

**Sand cherry** — open habitats with little shade from trees or other shrubs, typically along edges of openings or in stands where canopy closure has not occurred. Mostly eastern counties in

Pennsylvania; scattered west. Sites are typically dry and excessively drained. Shrub to 5 feet with white flowers in spring; sandy, gravelly, and rocky soils, dunes, beaches, and outwash plains. Very few sources.

### Prunus serotina

**Wild black cherry** — mesic woods and second-growth hardwood forests and old fields, especially on the Allegheny Plateau, on nearly all soil types. Throughout Pennsylvania. Prefers middle and lower slopes of eastern and northern exposures than the dry soils associated with south- or west-facing slopes; FACU. Grows to 100 feet with white flowers in spring; average, medium-moisture, well-drained soils in full sun to part shade. Best in moist, fertile loams in full sun. Fruits used to make wines, jelly. Commonly available.

### Prunus virginiana

**Chokecherry** — very acid to moderately alkaline, well-drained limestone residuum soil with pH ranging from 3.5 to 7.6, often in oak-pine forests; FACU. Throughout Pennsylvania. Grows 3 to 20 feet with white flowers in spring; sun to shade in dry to moist circumneutral limestone-based sandy loam; intolerant of poor drainage and prolonged flooding. Commonly available.

### Quercus alba

**White oak** — moist to fairly dry deciduous forests, usually on deeper, well-drained loams but sometimes on thin soils of dry upland slopes and sometimes on barrens; FACU. Throughout Pennsylvania. Grows to 100 feet.; rich, moist, acidic, well-drained loams in full sun. Adapts to a wide variety of soil conditions with good drought tolerance. Natural hybrid with *Q. prinus* is Saul oak. Commonly available.

### Quercus bicolor

**Swamp white oak** — low swamp forests, moist slopes, poorly drained uplands; FACW+. Mostly western and southeastern counties in Pennsylvania; scattered northeast. Grows to 100 feet; average, medium to wet, acidic soil in full sun. Commonly available.

### Quercus coccinea

**Scarlet oak** — poor soils of well-drained up-

lands, dry slopes and ridges, but sometimes on poorly drained sites. Throughout Pennsylvania. Grows to 100 feet; average, dry to medium, well-drained soil in full sun. Prefers dry, acidic, sandy soils. Commonly available.

### Quercus ilicifolia

**Scrub oak** — dry thickets and barrens in sandy, rocky, well-drained, nutrient-poor soils. Throughout Pennsylvania except northern tier and extreme western counties. Shrub to 15 feet; sun to part sun in dry to mesic, acidic sandy or gravelly soils. Very few sources.

### Quercus palustris

**Pin oak** — poorly drained clay soils in bottomlands intermittently flooded during dormancy but not during the growing season, including clay ridges of first bottoms, flats and other depressions where water accumulates in winter. Mostly southern counties in Pennsylvania, scattered north. Prefers level or near level moist uplands, especially glacial till plains; FACW; average, medium to wet, acidic soils in full sun. Prefers moist loams. Tolerates poorly drained soils and some flooding. Commonly available.

### Quercus prinoides

**Dwarf chestnut oak** — dry rocky soils, such as sandstone or shale outcrops associated with oak pine types. Mostly southeastern and south central counties in Pennsylvania, scattered elsewhere. Shrub to 12 feet; part shade to shade in dry sandy loam. Very few sources.

### Quercus prinus

**Chestnut oak** — rocky, xeric upland forest, dry ridges, mixed deciduous forests on shallow soils usually on south and west-facing upper slopes; FACW. Throughout Pennsylvania. Grows to 80 feet; dry, rocky, infertile soil with a low moisture-holding capacity, although can grow best in rich, well-drained soils along streams; ridge dominance is suggested by its ability to withstand drought. Several sources.

### Quercus rubra

**Northern red oak** — well-drained uplands, rich mesic slopes, sometimes on dry slopes or poorly drained uplands, sandy plains, rock outcrops, and the edges of floodplains, usually on north and east facing slopes. Common in lower and middle slopes, coves, ravines and on valley floors; FACU-. Throughout Pennsylvania. Grows to 100 feet; average, dry to medium moisture, acidic soil in full sun. Prefers deep fertile, sandy, finely-textured soils, well drained with good drainage and a relatively high water table. Soils are derived from a variety of parent materials including glacial outwash, sandstone, shale, limestone, gneiss, schist, or granite. Commonly available.

### Quercus stellata

**Post oak** — dry uplands with southerly or westerly exposure, terraces of smaller streams in well-drained soil, dry sandy or gravelly ridges, dry clays, prairies and limestone hills, woodlands and deciduous forests; UPL. Mostly southeastern counties in Pennsylvania, widely scattered elsewhere, including Monroe. Grows to 100 feet; rich, moist, acidic, well-drained coarse-textured loams in full sun. Adapts to a wide variety of soil conditions from poor dry sandy soils to moist heavy loams, especially where a heavy clay subsurface layer is within a foot of the surface or bedrock is within two or three feet. Also grows in deep sands and dry clay hills. Prefers acidic soils. Good drought tolerance. Very few sources.

### Quercus velutina

**Black oak** — xeric slopes and upland areas, especially with southerly or westerly facing slopes, occasionally on sandy lowlands and poorly drained uplands and terraces. Throughout Pennsylvania. Grows to 100 feet; while it is sensitive to competition in preferred moist, rich, well-drained sites, it is more often found on dry, nutrient-poor, coarse-textured soils, especially sandy or gravelly sites or heavy glacial clay hillsides. Several sources.

### Rhamnus alnifolia

**Alder-leaved buckthorn** — fens, calcareous marshes and wet thickets; OBL. Scattered counties throughout Pennsylvania, mainly west. Shrub to 3 feet with greenish flowers in late spring; moist to wet rich organic loam, full to part sun. Very few sources.

### Rhododendron canadense

**Rhodora** — bogs, wet places with infertile, acidic soil, FACW. Northeastern counties in Pennsylvania. Grows to 3 feet, with rose to purple flowers in spring; sun to part shade in mesic to wet cold acidic peaty soil. Very few sources.

### Rhododendron maximum

**Rosebay** — dry to moist woods, swamps, stream banks. FAC. Throughout Pennsylvania. Grows to 16 feet with creamy white flowers in early summer; part sun to part shade in mesic to moist acid sandy loam, pH 4.5 to 6. Forms vast woodland and woods edge colonies; manage as with any hybrid rhododendron. Several sources.

### Rhododendron periclymenoides

**Pinxter-flower** — mixed deciduous forests along stream bottoms, bogs, shaded mountainsides and ravines, FAC. Throughout Pennsylvania. Grows to 10 feet with white to pink flowers in spring; part sun to part shade in mesic to moist, well-drained acid soils in cool, moist locations. Prefers acidic, humusy, organically rich, medium moisture, moisture-retentive but well-drained soils in part shade; pH 4.5 to 5.5. Very few sources.

### Rhododendron periclymenoides x prinophyllum

**Azalea** — woods, thickets, swamp margins. Throughout Pennsylvania. Grows to 10 feet with white or pink flowers in spring; part sun to part shade in mesic to moist acid sandy loam, pH 4.5 to 5.5. White or pink flowers in spring. A natural hybrid. Very few sources.

### Rhododendron prinophyllum

**Mountain azalea** — dry to moist woods thickets, rocky slopes; FAC. Throughout Pennsylvania except extreme southeastern and southwestern counties. Grows to 10 feet with white to pink flowers in spring; part shade in rich humusy, acidic, medium moisture, well-drained soil in part shade. Several sources.

### Rhododendron viscosum

**Swamp azalea** — swamps, bogs, stream margins and thickets; FACW+. Mostly eastern counties in Pennsylvania; widely scattered elsewhere.

Grows to 10 feet; part shade in moist to wet acidic silty loam. Flood tolerant. White flowers in spring. Commonly available.

### Rhus copallina

**Shining sumac, winged sumac** — hillsides, open woods, glades, fields and along the margins of roadsides. Throughout Pennsylvania except northern tier counties. Grows to 20 feet; full sun to part shade in dry to medium, well-drained soils. Intolerant of poorly drained soils. Several sources. AKA *Rhus copallinum*.

### Rhus glabra

**Smooth sumac** — open woodlands, prairies, dry rocky hillsides and protected ravines. Throughout Pennsylvania. Grows to 15 feet; full sun to part shade in dry to medium, well-drained soils. Intolerant of poorly drained soils. Commonly available.

### Rhus typhina

**Staghorn sumac** — old fields, roadsides, woods edges. Throughout Pennsylvania. Shrub or small tree to 30 feet; full sun to part shade in dry to medium, well-drained soils. Intolerant of poorly drained soils. Commonly available.

### Ribes americanum

**Wild black currant** — moist woods, marshes and thickets; FACW. Throughout Pennsylvania. Grows to 6 feet with yellow flowers in spring; sun to shade in moist circumneutral soil. *Caution: it carries a disease that kills white pine.* Very few sources.

### Ribes cynosbati

**Prickly gooseberry** — thin, moist rocky woods. Throughout Pennsylvania except southeastern counties. Grows to 6 feet; part sun to part shade in moist rich loam. Yellow flowers; fruit: dull red to purple. Very few sources.

### Ribes hirtellum

**Northern wild gooseberry** — moist, rocky woods; cliffs; bogs and fens, calcareous marshes, swamps; FAC. Scattered throughout Pennsylvania, mostly southeastern and northwestern counties. Shrub grows 2 to 4 feet with yellow flowers and dull red fruit; sun to shade in mesic to moist

rocky circumneutral soils. *Carries disease that kills white pine.* Very few sources.

### Ribes lacustre

**Bristly black currant** — mountain streamsides, wet meadows, forests and cool wet woodlands, swamps; FACW. Northeastern counties in Pennsylvania; widely scattered west. Grows 3 to 4 feet with green flowers and black fruit; sun to shade in mesic to moist rocky circumneutral soils. Carries disease which kills white pine. Very few sources.

### Robinia pseudoacacia

**Black locust** — open woods on moist slopes and floodplains with a high probability of flooding in any given year, with pH minimum of 4.0; FACU-. Throughout Pennsylvania. Grows to 80 feet; rich, moist, limestone-derived soils; intolerant of heavy or poorly drained soils, although tolerant of periodic flooding. pH 4.0 to 8.2. Commonly available.

### Rosa blanda

**Meadow rose** — dry, open woods, hillsides, prairies, roadsides. Scattered counties in Pennsylvania, mainly west and northeast. Shrub to 6 feet with pink flowers in early summer; full sun in dry rocky soils. Several sources.

### Rosa carolina

**Pasture rose** — dry, rocky or sandy fields and meadows; UPL. Throughout Pennsylvania. Shrub to 3 feet with pink flowers in early summer; sun to part sun in moist to wet well-drained sandy soil; best flowering and disease resistance in full sun with good air circulation and mulch. Use as a native alternative to the invasive muliflora rose. Commonly available.

### Rosa palustris

**Swamp rose** — swamps; wet thickets; marshy shores of streams, ponds and lakes; OBL. Throughout Pennsylvania. Shrub, to 6 feet with pink flowers in summer; sun to part shade in moist to wet rich soil. Commonly available.

### Rosa virginiana

**Wild rose** — thickets, meadows, pastures, open woods, usually in a moist soil; FAC. Scattered counties in Pennsylvania, mainly south. Shrub to 6 feet with pink flowers in summer; sun to part sun in dry to mesic rich loam. Use as a native alternative to the invasive multiflora rose. Commonly available.

### Rubus allegheniensis

**Allegheny blackberry** — old fields, open woods, clearings; FACU. Stems to 6 feet with white flowers followed by black fruit; sun to part shade in mesic sandy loam, pH 4.5 to 7.5. Very few sources.

### Rubus canadensis

**Smooth blackberry** — cool moist woods, rocky slopes, thickets. Stems 3 to 10 feet with white flowers followed by black fruit; part sun to part shade in moist sandy loam. Very few sources.

### Rubus flagellaris

**Prickly dewberry** — rocky to shaly slopes and cliffs and in fields; FACU. Throughout Pennsylvania. Stems prostrate and rooting at tips, with white flowers becoming black fruits; part sun to part shade in dry to moist sandy loam. Very few sources.

### Rubus hispidus

**Swamp dewberry** — bogs, swamps, moist woods, thickets and barrens; FACW. Throughout Pennsylvania. Trailing stems that root at tips with white flowers becoming black fruits; part sun to part shade in dry to moist sandy loam. Very few sources.

### Rubus idaeus var. strigosus

**Grayleaf red raspberry** — rocky woods, clearings and thickets; FAC-. Throughout Pennsylvania except scattered southeast. Stems to 6 feet with white flowers becoming red fruit; part sun to part shade in dry to moist sandy loam. Very few sources.

### Rubus occidentalis

**Black-cap raspberry** — open woods; bluffs; thickets; stream banks; wet meadows, roadsides and pastures. Throughout Pennsylvania. Stems 3 to 6 feet with white flowers becoming black fruits; part sun to part shade in dry to moist san-dy loam. Very few sources.

### Rubus odoratus

**Purple-flowering raspberry** — moist, shaded cliffs, ledges and rocky wooded slopes. Throughout Pennsylvania. Stems 3 to 6 feet with purple to maroon flowers becoming black fruit; full sun to part shade in mesic sandy loam. Several sources.

### Salix bebbiana

**Long-beaked willow** — Upland deciduous woods, moist to dry thickets and edges; ideally in recent deposits of alluvial silts and gravels along waterways or in silted-in, abandoned beaver ponds; FACW-. Northern, southeastern and scattered southwestern counties in Pennsylvania. Shrub or tree to 32 feet; sun to shade in mesic to moist silty loam. Short-lived and fast-growing. Susceptible to insect, disease, and wind damage. Several sources.

### Salix discolor

**Pussy willow** — Swamps and moist or wet woods; FACW. Mostly northern and southeastern counties in Pennsylvania; scattered elsewhere. Shrub to 15 feet; sun to part sun in moist silty circumneutral loams. Short-lived and fast-growing; cut back heavily every few years to encourage vigorous new growth. Commonly available.

### Salix eriocephala

**Diamond willow** — banks of large streams, flood plains, wet meadows, shores and bottomlands; FACW+. Throughout Pennsylvania. Shrub to 20 feet; sun to part sun in moist to wet sandy loam. Short-lived and fast-growing. Very few sources.

### Salix interior

**Sandbar willow** — open to dense riparian communities along streams, gravel bars, lakeshores, and ditches; OBL. Mostly western counties in Pennsylvania; scattered east. Shrub or small tree to 30 feet; sun to part shade in moist to wet sandy gravelly loam. Favorable for stream stabilization because of profuse suckering. Commonly available. AKA *Salix exigua.*

### Salix humilis

**Upland willow, prairie willow** — moist barrens and dry thickets; FACU. Throughout Pennsylvania. Shrub to 10 feet; two local varieties: *humilis* and *tristis*; sun to part sun in mesic to moist loamy or sandy soil. Insert stems in the ground where they take root to form new stands. More drought tolerant than other willows. Very few sources.

### Salix lucida ssp. lucida

**Shining willow** — wet soils, especially in and near swamps, marshes, peat bogs and on sand banks along creeks; FACW. Mostly eastern and west-central counties in Pennsylvania; scattered elsewhere. Shrub or small tree to 20 feet; sun to part sun in moist to wet circumneutral clayey or silty loam. Prefers poor drainage. Very few sources.

### Salix nigra

**Black willow** — less sandy and wetter river margins, swamps, sloughs, swales, gullies, and drainage ditches; FACW+. Throughout Pennsylvania. Grows to 65 feet; fine moist to wet silt or clay, especially in saturated or poorly drained soil from which other hardwoods are excluded, with pH above 4.5. Not drought tolerant. Commonly available.

### Salix sericea

**Silky willow** — swamps, bogs, stream banks and low woods; OBL. Throughout Pennsylvania. Shrub to 15 feet; sun to part shade in moist to wet acidic sandy or clayey loam. Very few sources.

### Sambucus canadensis

**American elder** — woods, fields, stream banks, moist fields and swamps; FACW. Throughout Pennsylvania. Shrub to 10 feet with white flowers in early summer and purple fruit in late summer; average, medium to wet well-drained soil in full sun to part shade. Prefers moist, humusy soils. Spreads by root suckers to form colonies. Commonly available.

### Sambucus racemosa var. racemosa

**Red-berried elder** — stream banks, ravines, swamps, moist forest clearings and higher ground near wetlands; FACU. Throughout Pennsylvania. Shrub to 10 feet with white flowers in late spring becoming red fruit; sun to part sun in moist, well drained humusy soils. Commonly available.

### Sassafras albidum

**Sassafras** — open woods on moist, well-drained, sandy loam soils, dry ridges and upper slopes, fencerows and old fields; FACU-. Throughout Pennsylvania. Grows to 65 feet; average, medium, well-drained soil in full sun to part shade. Prefers moist, acidic, sandy-loamy soils, pH 6.0 to 7.0. Tolerates dry, sandy soils. Can be aggressive, especially following disturbance such as fire. Familiar for sassafras tea and root beer flavoring, as well as the primary ingredient in the gumbo thickening agent *filé*; considered mildly carcinogenic, sassafras oils are banned by USDA for food use. Commonly available.

### Sorbus americana

**American mountain-ash** — Swamp borders, rocky hillsides, woodland edges, and roadsides; FACU. Mostly northern counties in Pennsylvania; scattered west central. Grows to 32 feet in newly-formed mineral-rich soils to shallow and infertile soils in cool, windy, and humid conditions. Commonly available.

### Sorbus decora

**Showy mountain-ash** — wet to mesic woods, cool moist rocky slopes, lake shores; FAC. Pennsylvania distribution reported only as Wayne, Susquehanna, Erie and Crawford counties. Grows to 35 feet; part shade to shade in moist, circumneutral, poor to well-drained mesic to wet soil. Commonly available.

### Spiraea alba

**Meadow-sweet** — wet prairies, especially open ground along streams, lakes and bogs, and moist meadows; FACW+. Throughout Pennsylvania. Grows to 6 feet with white to pink flowers in late summer; sun to part shade in mesic to wet, well-drained soil. Prefers full sun; soil should not be allowed to dry out. Commonly available.

### Spiraea tomentosa

**Hardhack** or **Steeplebush** — meadows, old fields, pastures, bogs and swamps; FACU-. Mostly northern counties in Pennsylvania; scattered south, especially southeast. Grows to 3 feet with white to pink flowers in summer; sun to part sun in mesic to moist moderately acid soil. Commonly available.

### Staphylea trifolia

**Bladdernut** — bottomlands, woodland thickets and moist soils along streams, FAC. Mostly southern counties in Pennsylvania; scattered northwest and northeast. Grows to 15 feet with white flowers in late spring; part shade to shade in dry to mesic sandy loam, but prefers a moist soil. pH 6.1 to 8. Several sources.

### Taxus canadensis

**Canadian yew** — cool moist rocky slopes or ravines under mixed coniferous (rarely deciduous) forest canopy. Declining because of deer browsing; FAC. Throughout Pennsylvania. Shrub to 5 feet; sun to part shade in mesic to moist sandy circumneutral loam. Needs protection from winter sun and wind. Very few sources.

### Tilia americana var. americana

**Basswood** — rich uplands on mid-slopes in mixed deciduous forests and occasionally swamps, FACU. Throughout Pennsylvania. Grows to 130 feet in sandy loams to silt loams; prefers moist to mesic, finer textured, well-drained loams. Generally intolerant of air pollution and urban conditions. Commonly available.

### Toxicodendron vernix

**Poison sumac** — wet soil of swamps, bogs, seepage slopes, and frequently flooded areas; in shady hardwood forests; OBL. Mostly eastern counties in Pennsylvania, scattered west. Grows to 16 feet. *Not a suitable landscape plant. All parts, in all seasons, will cause severe skin irritation if plant sap contacted.* Very few sources.

### Tsuga canadensis

**Canada hemlock**- moist rocky ridges and hillsides, cool moist valleys, flats and ravines, especially on northern and eastern facing slopes, and swamp borders if peat and muck soils are shallow, usually above 1,200 feet; FACU. Throughout Pennsylvania. Grows to 100 feet; average, medium, well-drained soil in part shade to full shade. Prefers acidic cool, moist, humid condi-

tions with good drainage; textures include sandy loams, loamy sands, and silty loams with gravel of glacial origin in the upper profile. Intolerant of drought and should be watered regularly in prolonged dry spells, particularly when young. Best sited in a location protected from strong winds. Currently under attack by *Adelges tsugae* (wooly adelgid), a pest from Japan; once infected, a tree is usually dead within a few years. Commonly available.

### Ulmus americana

**American elm** — alluvial woods, swamp forests, deciduous woodlands, fencerows, pastures, old fields, waste areas; FACW-. Throughout Pennsylvania. Grows to 130 feet; average, medium moisture, well-drained soils in full sun. Tolerant of light shade. Prefers rich, moist loams. Adapts to both wet and dry sites. Generally tolerant of urban conditions and often planted as a street tree. Once a very common species, it fell victim to a fungus imported from Europe. Commonly available.

### Ulmus rubra

**Red elm** or **slippery elm** — moist rich soils on lower slopes, alluvial flood plains, stream banks, riverbanks and river terraces, and wooded bottom lands, sometimes on drier, limestone-origin sites; FAC-. Throughout Pennsylvania. Grows to 65 feet; average, medium moisture, well-drained soils in full sun. Tolerant of light shade. Prefers rich, moist loams. Adapts to both wet and dry sites. Generally tolerant of urban conditions. Very few sources.

### Vaccinium angustifolium

**Low sweet blueberry** — dry woods and barrens, acidic soils; FACU. Throughout Pennsylvania. Grows to 30 inches with white flowers in spring and dark blue fruit in late summer; part sun to part shade in dry to mesic sandy loam. Several sources.

### Vaccinium corymbosum

**Highbush blueberry** — dry to wet woods, thickets, stream banks, bogs in acidic soil; FACW-. Throughout Pennsylvania. Grows to 10 feet with white flowers in spring and dark blue fruit in late summer; sun to part shade in dry to mesic sandy organic loam. Parent plant of almost all hybrid blueberries. Several sources.

### Vaccinium macrocarpon

**American cranberry** — peaty woodlands, seepy areas and sphagnum bogs; OBL. Throughout Pennsylvania except south-central counties. Trailing shrub with white flowers in spring and the familiar red cranberry in late summer; sun to part shade in damp, acidic (pH 4.0-5.2), organically rich, well-drained soil in full sun. Several sources.

### Vaccinium myrtilloides

**Sour-top blueberry** — wet thickets and barrens; FAC. Scattered counties throughout Pennsylvania, mostly north. Shrub to 30 inches with greenish-white flowers in spring and dark blue fruit in late summer; sun to part shade in moist acidic sandy loam. Very few sources.

### Vaccinium oxycoccos

**Small cranberry** — bogs, especially in cool areas; OBL. Northeastern counties in Pennsylvania, scattered elsewhere. Trailing shrub with white flowers in spring followed by red fruit; sun to part shade in moist to wet acidic sandy loam. Very few sources.

### Vaccinium pallidum

**Lowbush blueberry** — dry, rocky hillsides, upland ridges, rocky outcrops and ledges, sandy knolls, shale barrens and upland swamps. Throughout Pennsylvania. Shrub to 3 feet with white flowers in spring and dark blue-purple fruit in late summer; part sun to part shade in dry to mesic sandy loam. Very few sources.

### Vaccinium stamineum

**Deerberry** — dry woods, openings, barrens and clearings. FACU. Throughout Pennsylvania. Shrub to 6 feet with white flowers and spring and green fruit when ripe in late summer; part sun to part shade in mesic sandy clay loam. Very few sources.

### Viburnum acerifolium

**Maple-leaved viburnum** — upland forests, woodlands, ravine slopes and hillsides in well-drained, moist soils; particularly tolerant of acid soils; UPL. Throughout Pennsylvania. Shrub to 6 feet with white flowers in spring; part sun to part shade in mesic to moist rich sandy loam; pH 5.1 to 6. Several sources.

### Viburnum lantanoides

**Hobblebush** — rich, moist acidic woods, stream banks, ravines and swamps; FAC. Northern Counties in Pennsylvania; scattered southwest. Shrub to 6 feet with white to pink flowers in late spring; part sun to part shade in moist sandy loam. Trailing stems take root where they touch the ground, creating hazards for walkers, hence the name. Nectar host for spring azure butterflies. Very few sources.

### Viburnum lentago

**Nannyberry** — woods, swamps and thickets with rich, moist soil; FAC. Western and extreme eastern counties in Pennsylvania. Shrub to 15 feet with white flowers in spring; part sun to part shade in average, medium, well-drained soil; prefers mostly gravelly sandy loam. Commonly available.

### Viburnum nudum var. cassinoides

**Withe-rod** — swamps, moist upland woods and clearings and exposed rock crevices; FACW. Throughout Pennsylvania. Shrub to 15 feet with white flowers in spring; full sun to part shade in well-drained moist loams, but tolerates a wide range of soils including boggy ones. Commonly available. AKA *Viburnum cassinoides*

### Viburnum prunifolium

**Black-haw** — successional woods, thickets, old fields, roadsides; FACU. Southern two-thirds of Pennsylvania counties, including Monroe and Carbon counties. Shrub or small tree to 25 feet with white flowers in spring; sun to part shade in dry to mesic sandy loam. Tolerates drought. Commonly available.

### Viburnum rafinesqueanum

**Downy arrow-wood** — rocky woods, old fields, dry slopes and banks. Scattered Pennsylvania counties, mostly east and central. Shrub to 5 feet with white flowers in spring; part sun to part shade in dry to mesic rocky sandy loam. White flowers in spring. Very few sources.

## Additional trees and shrubs

The following native species include Pennsylvania in their continental range, but have not been reported in the northeastern counties (Carbon, Monroe, Pike and Wayne). They are commonly available in the commercial marketplace.

### *Viburnum recognitum*

**Northern arrow-wood** — swamps, boggy woods, wet pastures, stream banks; FACW-. Throughout Pennsylvania. Shrub to 15 feet with white flowers in spring; part shade to shade in moist, humusy well-drained acidic loam. Very few sources.

*Aesculus glabra* (Ohio buckeye) — Bottomlands and moist stream banks, 60-80 feet, FACU+, primarily in southwestern counties and from the Lehigh Valley south toward Philadelphia. Grows in average, well-drained soils in full sun to part shade; prefers fertile and moist soil.

*Asimina triloba* (Pawpaw) — Ravine slopes, stream banks and floodplains with deep, rich, moist soils ranging from sandy to clayey, 10-40 feet, FACU+. Native across the southern tier of Pennsylvania and the extreme northwestern counties. Grows in average medium to wet soils but prefers acidic, fertile, moist soil. Sun to part shade, but becomes leggy in shade.

*Cercis canadensis* (Redbud) — Woodlands and stream banks that are neither excessively wet or dry or strongly acidic, 20-30 feet. Has a natural preference for, and can be used as an indicator, of alkaline soils. FACU-. Native across the southern half of Pennsylvania. Grow in well-drained, moist deep soil in full sun to light shade. Popular for its dramatic display of pink flowers in spring.

*Chionanthus virginicus* (Fringe-tree) — Bluffs, thickets, damp woods, 10-35 feet, FAC+. Mostly southeastern counties of Pennsylvania. Grow in well-drained, average moisture soil in full sun to part shade; prefers moist fertile soils and rarely requires pruning. Tolerant of urban pollution, but not prolonged dry conditions.

*Crataegus crus-galli* (Cockspur hawthorn) — woods, meadows, roadsides, thickets, especially in dry or rocky places, and slopes of low hills in rich soils; FACU. Mostly southern and far western counties in Pennsylvania; scattered elsewhere. Large shrub or small tree grows to 32 feet; sun to part sun in mesic to moist well drained san-dy loam. Tolerates a wide range of well drained soils, light shade, some drought and many urban pollutants. White to pink flowers in late spring. Commonly available.

*Diospyros virginiana* — (Persimmon) — open woods, floodplains and old fields, seasonally flooded bottomlands, dry ridgetops and abandoned agricultural land; FAC. Pennsylvania distribution includes mostly southern counties. Grows to 50 feet; dry to medium, well-drained soils in full sun to part shade. Wide range of soil tolerance, but prefers moist, sandy soils. Drought tolerant. Blooms late spring, edible fruit in the fall. Commonly available.

*Gymnocladus dioicus* (Kentucky coffee-tree) — Moist woods, especially lower slopes, and floodplains, 60 to 80 feet. Suckers to form colonies in native habitats. Native to southeastern and southwestern counties in Pennsylvania. Grow in organically rich, moist soils in full sun; avoid heavy clay. Tolerates drought, poorer soils and urban environments.

*Liquidambar styraciflua* (Sweetgum) — Very tolerant of different soils and sites but grows best on the rich, moist, alluvial clay and loamy soils of river bottoms, especially on the Piedmont Plateau, 75-130 feet; FAC+. Luzerne County, southeastern counties and scattered southwestern counties in Pennsylvania. Grow in deep, moist, alluvial loams; can be aggressive in sandy, moist soils. Rapid growth.

*Magnolia acuminata* (Cucumber-tree) — Scattered in cool moist oak-hickory forests, with a preference for bottomlands and north to east-facing, typically gentle slopes that are well-drained and deep; on steeper slopes it prefers coarser loams. Height ranges from 40 to 70 feet. Native range extends across the western three-quarters of Pennsylvania except for extreme south-central counties. The hardiest of the tree-sized magnolias, but intolerant of urban pollutants. Greenish-yellow flowers after 12 years. Grow in full sun to part shade in organically rich, well-drained moist loams.

*Magnolia virginiana* (Sweet-bay magnolia) — Wet woods, swamps, swamp margins, savannas, hammocks, bogs, and floodplains, especially in acidic soils with poor to very poor drainage that are frequently flooded during winter or wet seasons, rarely in major river bottoms. Height: 10-35 feet; FACW+. Native range in Pennsylvania is southeastern counties. Fragrant white flowers in spring. Grow in acidic, medium to wet, rich organic soil in full sun to part shade; can tolerate wet, boggy soils.

*Oxydendrum arboreum* (Sourwood) — sub-xeric open slopes and ridges occupied by oaks and Virginia pine; less common in mesic sites like coves and sheltered slopes. Also along well-drained lowland areas along Piedmont streams not subject to flooding, in gently rolling areas. FACU. Height: 20-50 feet. Native Pennsylvania range is mostly far southwestern counties. Grow in full sun to part shade in well-drained, organically rich, moist soils. Part shade is tolerated, but flowering is diminished. Intolerant of urban pollution.

*Quercus imbricaria* (Shingle oak) — mesic to somewhat dry uplands and slopes, sometimes in bottoms and ravines, FAC. Height: 40-60 feet. Primarily in southwestern Pennsylvania, but also very southeast counties. Grow in full sun in well-drained, humusy, rich, medium moist soils; tolerant of dry soils. Formerly a source of shingles, hence the common name.

*Quercus macrocarpa* (Bur oak) — Prairies, poorly drained areas, riparian slopes and bottomlands, typically on limestone and sometimes calcareous clays. Prominent in oak-basswood, upland oak-hickory and mix-oak communities, more often in coarsely-textured soil and less often on clays, 60-80 feet. FAC-. Pennsylvania range includes western and central Appalachian counties, and the Lehigh Valley southward. Grow in medium to dry, average, well-drained soils in full sun; prefers well-drained moist loams, but adapts. Has good drought tolerance, but may take up to 35 years to bear initial acorn crop.

*Quercus phellos* (Willow oak) — Usually in bottomland flood plains, but also on stream banks, terraces and sometimes poorly drained uplands. Does best on clay loam ridges of new alluvium and diminishes from bottomland to higher terraces. Grows 40 to 75 feet. FAC+. Pennsylvania range is far southeastern counties. Grow in full sun in well-drained, wet to medium average soils; tolerates light shade and urban pollution.

*Quercus shumardii* (Shumard oak) — Mesic slopes and bottoms, stream banks and poorly drained uplands. Prefers rich sites with moist, well-drained loamy soils found on terraces, colluvial sites and bluffs adjacent to large and small streams. Sometimes found in Coastal Plain hammocks, but rarely on first-bottom sites; 40-60 feet. FAC+ Pennsylvania range is limited to extreme south-central counties. Grow in full sun in well-drained, acidic (will tolerate higher pH) dry to medium average soils. Tolerates wide soil range, including wet.

*Salix caroliniana* (Carolina willow) — Wet soils along stream banks and in swamps. To 20 feet; OBL. Pennsylvania range is primarily far southwestern and south-central counties. Grow in continually moist to wet, organically rich silty-clay loams in full sun.

## Possibly challenging to find

The 14 species that may be challenging to find, but are reportedly available:

> *Carya laciniosa* (Shellbark hickory)
> *Castanea pumila* (Chinquapin)
> *Chamaecyparis thyoides* (Atlantic white-cedar)
> *Crataegus dilatata* (Broadleaf hawthorn)
> *Crataegus mollis* (Downy hawthorn)
> *Crataegus succulenta* (Long-spined hawthorn)
> *Morus rubra* (Red mulberry)
> *Pinus echinata* (Short-leaf pine)
> *Pinus pungens* (Table-mountain pine)
> *Populus deltoides* (Eastern cottonwood)
> *Prunus angustifolia* (Chickasaw plum)
> *Quercus falcata* (Southern red oak)
> *Quercus marilandica* (Blackjack oak)
> *Salix amygdaloides* (Peach-leaved willow)

## Apparently unavailable

The 27 species of native trees and shrubs that do not appear to be commercially available on a national basis:

*Acer nigrum* (Black maple)
*Amelanchier bartramiana* (Mountain june-berry )
*Amelanchier intermedia* (Shadbush )
*Amelanchier obovalis* (Coastal juneberry )
*Carya laneyi* (Bitternut)
*Crataegus flabellata* (Fanleaf hawthorn )
*Crataegus intricata* (Biltmore hawthorn )
*Crataegus pensylvanica* (Pennsylvania haw-thorn)
*Crataegus pruinosa* (Frosted hawthorn )
*Fraxinus profunda* (Pumpkin ash)
*Ilex beadlei* (Mountain holly )
*Ilex laevigata* (Smooth winterberry )
*Populus heterophylla* (Swamp-cottonwood)

*Prunus alleghaniensis* (Allegheny plum)
*Quercus muhlenbergii* (Yellow oak)
*Quercus prinoides* (Dwarf chestnut oak )
*Rhamnus alnifolia* (Alder-leaved buck-thorn)
*Ribes americanum* (Wild black currant )
*Ribes glandulosum* (Skunk currant )
*Ribes rotundifolium* (Wild gooseberry )
*Rubus enslenii* (Southern dewberry )
*Rubus pensilvanicus* (Blackberry )
*Rubus pubescens* (Dwarf blackberry )
*Rubus recurvicaulis* (Dewberry )
*Rubus setosus* (Bristly blackberry )
*Salix candida* (Hoary willow )
*Spiraea alba x latifolia* (Meadow-sweet )

# *Native plants: perennial forbs*

## Introduction

This section includes *forbs* — that is, vascular herbaceous species other than ferns, grasses, sedges and rushes — subdivided in the following manner.

- Native species whose range includes Pennsylvania and whose observed distribution includes Carbon, Monroe, Pike and/or Wayne counties, all of which are commercially available

- Native species whose range includes Pennsylvania but have not been reported in Carbon, Monroe, Pike or Wayne counties but are commonly available in the marketplace; a secondary list identifies additional species that may be difficult to find in the retail marketplace.

- A listing of native species that do not appear to be commercially available

This list *does not include* herbaceous vines or annuals/biennials (listed separately). It *does not include* such non-vascular plants as mosses and lichens.

The 336 entries "Pocono" plants and the 38 commonly available other Pennsylvania species are organized in the following manner:

Latin (or scientific) name*
Common name(s)
A brief description of natural habitat — i.e., where it is found in nature
US Fish and Wildlife Service wetland indicators when available
Brief description of distribution in Pennsylvania
Indication of height, flower color and bloom season
Suggestions for home cultivation, including light requirements, moisture, soil description, and if available soil pH range and preference
How relatively easy it is to find in the commercial marketplace, in the context of nationwide mail-order nurseries
*Sometimes scientific names have recently changed and not all literature has yet caught up. Where it seems helpful, we have also include "AKA" — also known as.

## *Actaea pachypoda*

**Dolls-eyes** — rich, open upland woods and thickets, throughout Pennsylvania. Grows 12-30 inches, with white flowers in late spring; part shade to shade in moist sandy humusy loam, pH 5-6; commonly available.

## *Actaea racemosa*

**Black snakeroot** — rich moist woods, wooded slopes, ravines, along riverbanks and thickets, throughout Pennsylvania. Grows 3-8 feet with white flowers on tall racemes in early summer; part shade to shade in moist rich humus, pH 5-7; commonly available.

## *Actaea rubra*

**Red baneberry** — usually upland hardwood and mixed-wood forest habitats on fresh or moist, fine-textured mineral soils. Mostly northeastern Pennsylvania counties; scattered elsewhere. Grows 12-30 inches with white flowers in late spring; part sun to open shade in moist humus rich loam, pH 5-6; commonly available.

## *Agastache nepetoides*

**Yellow giant hyssop** — generally upland moist, rich, open woodland areas, thickets and woodland borders, FACU. From the Poconos south to Philadelphia, then west across the southern counties. Grows 3-5 feet with greenish-yellow flowers in late summer; full sun in moist rich loam; commonly available.

### Agastache scrophulariifolia

**Purple giant hyssop** — moist woods and thickets. Pennsylvania distribution includes most eastern counties, then scattered westward. Grows 3-5 feet with purple flowers in late summer; sun to part shade in moist rich humus, pH 6-7. Shade tolerant, but prefers sun; commonly available.

### Agrimonia parviflora

**Southern agrimony** — moist to wet woods and thickets, FAC. Pennsylvania distribution is the Poconos south, then across the southern tier and up the Ohio line. Grows up to 45 inches with yellow flowers in late summer; part shade to shade in moist sandy loam; very few sources.

### Agrimonia striata

**Roadside agrimony** — moist upland woods and thickets, FACU-. Pennsylvania distribution includes eastern and northern counties. Grows up to 36 inches with yellow flowers in late summer; part shade to shade in moist sandy loam, pH 5-6; very few sources.

### Alisma subcordatum

**Broad-leaved water-plantain** — aquatic; shallow ponds, stream margins, marshes, and ditches, OBL. Throughout Pennsylvania. Grows 12-36 inches with pink to white flowers in summer; sun to part sun in silty loam in ponds and pond edges; several sources.

### Allium canadense

**Wild onion** — upland glades, bluffs, open woods, prairies and disturbed sites, FACU. Throughout Pennsylvania except for the highest elevations on the Allegheny Plateau. Grows 8-12 inches with pink to white flowers in early summer; full sun to part shade in moist rich loam, pH 6.5 to 7; several sources.

### Allium tricoccum

**Ramp** — moist ground in rich upland woods, depressions, streamside bluffs, and colluvial slopes, FACU+. Throughout Pennsylvania except for the central Appalachians. Grows up to 20 inches with white flowers in spring; deciduous shade (needs sun in early spring) in rich moist mesic loam. pH 6.8 to 7.2; commonly available.

### Anaphalis margaritacea

**Pearly everlasting** — dry , sandy or gravelly soil of fields, woods, edges and roadsides. Throughout Pennsylvania except for several extreme southern counties. Grows 1 to 3 feet with white flowers in late summer; average, medium, well-drained soil in full sun to part shade. Prefers full sun and somewhat dry, sandy conditions; commonly available.

### Anemone quinquefolia

**Wood anemone** — moist upland open woods and thickets, banks and shady roadsides, FACU. Throughout Pennsylvania. Grows 4-8 inches with white flowers in spring; part shade to shade in damp to moist rich loam, pH 5 to 6; very few sources.

### Anemone virginiana

**Virginia anemone** — upland rocky and dry open woods, slopes, thickets and prairies. Throughout Pennsylvania. Grows up to 12 inches with greenish-white flowers in early summer, followed by attractive seed pods that persist into fall; sun to part shade in dry to moist sandy loam; commonly available.

### Angelica atropurpurea

**Purple-stemmed angelica** — swamps, moist meadows, stream banks and wet woods, OBL. Throughout Pennsylvania except for higher elevations on the Allegheny Plateau and the central Appalachian ridges and valleys. Grows 3-10 feet with white flowers in summer; full sun to dappled shade in medium to wet soils; commonly available.

### Angelica venenosa

**Hairy angelica** — dry open woods, roadsides, banks, serpentine barrens and old fields. Throughout Pennsylvania except for northern tier counties. Grows up to 6 feet with white flowers in mid-summer; full sun to part shade in dry, sandy to gravelly soil; very few sources.

### Antennaria neglecta

**Overlooked pussytoe** — mesic to dry prairies, slopes of upland open woodlands, dry meadows in woodland areas, savannahs, shale glades, eroded clay banks, pastures, abandoned fields, and roadsides. Pennsylvania distribution includes most eastern counties, scattered elsewhere. Grows up to 6 inches with brown/gray flowers in spring; sun to part sun in dry to moist clay loam, pH 5.5 to 7.5; very few sources.

### Antennaria parlinii

**Parlins pussytoe** — open woods and fields. Throughout Pennsylvania except for highest elevations in the Allegheny Plateau and central Appalachians. Grows up to 8 inches with white flowers in spring; sun to part sun in dry, sandy, well drained loam; very few sources.

### Antennaria plantaginifolia

**Plantain-leaved pussytoe** — dry open woods, pastures, fields, rocky barrens. Throughout Pennsylvania except for northern tier counties. Grows up to about 10 inches with white flowers in spring; sun to part sun in dry, sandy, well drained loam, pH 4 to 7; several sources.

### Aplectrum hyemale

**Puttyroot** — rich moist woods and bottomlands, FAC. Scattered, mostly southern counties, including Monroe County. Grows 12-24 inches with purple flowers in early summer; part shade to shade in moist rich humus. Listed as rare in Pennsylvania; several sources.

### Apocynum androsaemifolium

**Pink dogbane** — well-drained upland forest sites, open hillsides and ridges, especially on dry, fresh, sandy and coarse loamy soils. Throughout Pennsylvania. Also found in clearings and fields, along forest margins, on roadsides and disturbed ground. Grows 8 to 32 inches with pink flowers in early summer; sun to part shade in dry, sandy loam, pH 5-6; very few sources.

### Apocynum cannabinum

**Indian hemp** — upland open woods, pastures, waste ground, disturbed sites, wooded slopes, on roadsides and along railroads, FACU. Throughout Pennsylvania. Grows up to 5 feet, with pink flowers in early summer; sun to part sun in dry to moist sandy loam; several sources.

### Aquilegia canadensis

**Wild columbine** or **American columbine** — open, steep, rocky wooded bluffs of streams, stream banks, wooded slopes of deep ravines, limestone bluffs and ledges, borders and clearings in deciduous or mixed woods or thickets, FAC. Throughout Pennsylvania. Grows up to 32 inches with yellow and red flowers in late spring; sun to part shade in average well-drained soil, pH 5 to 7. Prefers rich, moist soils in light to moderate shade, with pH of 6 to 7; commonly available.

### Arabis glabra

**Towercress** — fields, open woods, ledges, usually in dry soil. Pennsylvania distribution includes most eastern, northern and southwestern counties. Grows 16-40 inches with greenish-white flowers in late spring; part sun to shade in dry to moist rocky clay loam; very few sources.

### Aralia nudicaulis

**Wild sarsaparilla** — dry, upland open woods and thickets with thin soil, FACU. Throughout Pennsylvania. Grows 12-36 inches with greenish flowers in spring; part sun to shade in dry to moist rich humus, pH 5-7; several sources.

### Aralia racemosa

**Spikenard** — rich wooded slopes, ravines, moist ledges and bluffs. Throughout Pennsylvania. Grows up to 6 feet with greenish flowers in early summer; part sun to part shade in moist rich humus; commonly available.

### Arisaema triphyllum

**Jack-in-the-pulpit** — moist low woods, swamps, bogs and floodplains, FACW-. Throughout Pennsylvania. Grows up to 36 inches, with the familiar greenish flowers in spring; part shade to full shade in constantly moist soil rich in organic matter, pH 5-6; commonly available.

### Aristolochia serpentaria

**Virginia snakeroot** — rich, rocky upland woods, thickets, ravines and slopes, UPL. Mostly southern counties of Pennsylvania, but includes

Monroe. Grows up to 20 inches with greenish-white flowers in spring; part shade to shade in dry to moist sandy loam; very few sources.

### Asarum canadense

**Wild ginger** — the understory of upland deciduous forests (rarely coniferous). Throughout Pennsylvania. Grows 6-12 inches with brownish-purple flowers in early spring; part shade to full shade in moist humus, pH 4 to 7. Not related to the culinary spice, but has been used as a substitute, hence the name; commonly available. Slowly spreads by rhizomes to form large colonies.

### Asclepias amplexicaulis

**Blunt-leaved milkweed** — dry fields and upland open woods, usually in sandy soil. Mostly eastern counties, as well as those in the central Appalachians. Grows 12-36 inches with greenish-pink flowers in summer; sun to part sun in dry, sandy loam; very few sources.

### Asclepias exaltata

**Poke milkweed** — rich upland woods and woods edges, FACU. Throughout Pennsylvania. Grows 12 to 32 inches with greenish-purple flowers in early summer; part shade to shade in dry to moist sandy loam, pH 5.5 to 7; very few sources.

### Asclepias incarnata

**Swamp milkweed** — floodplains and wet meadows, OBL. Throughout Pennsylvania. Grows up to 5 feet with pink-rose flowers in early summer; full to part sun in constantly moist rich loam; commonly available.

### Asclepias syriaca

**Common milkweed** — dry, upland woods edges fields and prairies. Throughout Pennsylvania. Grows 3 to 6 feet with very fragrant purple-whitish flowers in early summer; sun to part sun in dry sandy loam, pH 4 to 7; commonly available. Host species for monarch butterflies.

### Asclepias tuberosa

**Butterfly weed** — dry fields, roadsides and shale barrens. Throughout Pennsylvania except for northern tier counties. Grows 12-30 inches with orange-yellow flowers in early summer; sun to part shade in dry to medium wet, well drained sandy loam, pH 4.5 to 6.8; commonly available and a magnet for butterflies.

### Asclepias variegata

**White milkweed** — upland dry or rocky woods, sandy open ground, ravine bottoms, low woods, slopes, ridges and along roadsides, FACU. Pennsylvania distribution ranges from Luzerne and Monroe Counties southward toward Philadelphia. Grows up to 36 inches with white to pinkish flowers in early summer; sun to part shade in dry sandy loam. Listed as endangered in Pennsylvania; very few sources.

### Asclepias verticillata

**Whorled milkweed** — open woods, dry slopes, barrens on dry rocky sandy soil. Pennsylvania distribution includes eastern and central Appalachian counties. Grows 8 to 20 inches with white-greenish flowers in summer; sun to part sun in sandy loam, pH 4.8 to 6.8; commonly available.

### Asclepias viridiflora

**Green milkweed** — dry rocky slopes, serpentine barrens, rocky prairies, glades. Pennsylvania distribution is primarily eastern and central Appalachian counties. Grows 12 to 32 inches with greenish flowers in summer; sun to part sun in dry sandy loam; very few sources.

### Astragalus canadensis

**Milk-vetch** — rocky roadsides, shale barrens, limestone ledges and banks, FAC. Pennsylvania distribution includes Wayne and southwestern counties. Grows up to 5 feet with white flowers in early summer; sun to part shade in mesic to moist sandy loam; commonly available.

### Aureolaria virginica

**Downy false-foxglove** — dry open deciduous woods. Throughout Pennsylvania except for northern-most counties. Grows 20 to 60 inches with yellow flowers in late summer; part shade to shade in dry sandy loam, pH 4 to 6; very few sources.

### Baptisia tinctoria

**Wild indigo** — dry, open woods and clearings in sandy soil. Throughout Pennsylvania except northern-most counties. Grows up to 36 inches with yellow flowers in summer; sun to part shade in dry to moist sandy loam. pH 5 to 7, but prefers acidic soils; several sources.

### Brasenia schreberi

**Purple wendock** — aquatic; ponds, lakes, and sluggish streams, with pink to yellow flowers in summer; ponds with intermediate to low nutrient values, OBL. Eastern-most Pennsylvania counties; scattered elsewhere. Grow in full sun to part shade in still to slow moving standing water; very few sources.

### Cacalia atriplicifolia

**Pale Indian plantain** — open woods, fields and on moist banks. Throughout Pennsylvania except for northern-most counties. Grows up to 9 feet, with yellow flowers in late summer and early fall; sun to part shade in dry to moist sandy loam, pH 4 to 5.5; several sources.

### Calopogon tuberosus

**Grass-pink** — bogs, fens and wet meadows, pine and oak savannahs, grasslands and swales, FACW+. Eastern Pennsylvania counties; scattered elsewhere. Grows 12 to 30 inches with pink-purple and yellow flowers in summer; sun to part sun in wet, rich sandy acidic loam; very few sources.

### Caltha palustris

**Marsh marigold** — soaking wet woods, stream banks, muddy meadows, OBL. Throughout Pennsylvania. Grows up to about 15 inches with yellow to white flowers in spring and early summer; sun to part shade in wet, muddy humus rich loam; commonly available.

### Campanula americana

**Tall bellflower** — moist upland woods, on rocky wooded slopes and stream banks, FAC. Throughout Pennsylvania, except for northern tier counties. Grows up to 6 feet with blue to white flowers in summer; part shade to shade in moist silty loam; several sources.

### Campanula rotundifolia

**Harebell** — dry, rocky upland slopes, bluffs and cliffs, FACU. Eastern Pennsylvania counties; scattered throughout the Ridge and Valley province. Grows up to 6 feet, with blue flowers in sum-mer; sun to shade in dry rocky sandy loam, pH 5-7; several sources.

### Cardamine diphylla

**Crinkleroot toothwort** — rich woods and floodplains, FACU. Northern and western counties in Pennsylvania; scattered in southeast. Grows up to 12 inches with white flowers in spring; sun to part shade in moist to wet humus-rich loam; very few sources.

### Cardamine pratensis

**Cuckoo-flower** — swamps, wet meadows and alluvial woods, OBL. Scattered northern and eastern counties in Pennsylvania. Grows 8 to 20 inches with white to pink flowers in spring; full sun to part shade in cool, moist soils; very few sources.

### Caulophyllum thalictroides

**Blue cohosh** — moist rich deciduous and mixed forests. Throughout Pennsylvania except limestone substrates in the Ridge and Valley province. Grows 12 to 30 inches with greenish yellow/purple flowers in early spring; shady woodland areas in rich, moist, soils that do not dry out; pH 4 to 7; commonly available.

### Ceratophyllum demersum

**Coontail** — aquatic; quiet waters of lakes and ponds, rivers, streams, swamps, generally submerged, sometimes free floating, OBL. Mostly south central and southeastern counties in Pennsylvania; scattered elsewhere. Flowers early summer, fruit in late summer; silty garden ponds ranging from fresh to slightly brackish; several sources.

### Chamaelirium luteum

**Devil's bit** or **Fairywand** — dry-wet open woods, clearings, barrens in humus-rich soil; FAC. Eastern, western and south central counties in Pennsylvania. Grows to 40 inches with white to yellow flowers in late spring; sun to part shade in dry, rich sandy loam, pH 5 to 7; several sources.

### Chamerion angustifolium ssp. circumvagum

**Fireweed** — mesic woods edges and recent clearings in open sandy ground; usually a pioneer species after forest fires, FAC. Throughout Pennsylvania. Grows 3-12 feet with purple-pink flowers in summer; disturbed sandy loam in full sun to part shade; forms dense clumps and spreads aggressively; commonly available.

### Chelone glabra

**White turtlehead** — wet open woods, swamps and stream banks, OBL. Throughout Pennsylvania. Grows 20-30 inches with white to pinkish flowers in summer; sun to part shade in moist rich loam, but prefers full sun, pH 5.5 to 7; commonly available.

### Cicuta maculata var. maculata

**Beaver-poison** or **water hemlock** — swamps, marshes, wet meadows, stream banks and ditches, OBL. Throughout Pennsylvania. Grows up to 8 inches with white flowers in summer; moist to wet silty organic loam in sun to part sun. *All parts highly toxic and may be fatal if eaten;* very few sources.

### Cirsium muticum

**Swamp thistle** — swamps, bogs, stream banks and wet meadows, OBL. Throughout Pennsylvania. Grows 3 to 6 feet with purple flowers in summer; sun to part sun in moist to wet rich loam; very few sources.

### Claytonia caroliniana

**Carolina spring beauty** — moist, rocky upland wooded slopes, open woods and thickets, FACU. Northern and western counties in Pennsylvania. Grows 6 to 12 inches with white to pinkish flowers in spring; part sun to part shade in moist to wet rich loams, pH 5 to 6; very few sources.

### Claytonia virginica

**Spring beauty** — moist woods and meadows, often on alluvial soils, FACU. Throughout Pennsylvania. Grows 6 to 12 inches with white to pinkish flowers in spring; sun to part shade in moist loam, pH 5 to 7; commonly available.

### Clintonia borealis

**Blue bead lily** — shady, cool moist woods and thickets, mostly in the mountains, FAC. Grows up to 16 inches. Northern and south central counties in Pennsylvania. Yellow flowers in late spring, fruit a blue berry in summer; part shade to shade in moist humusy loam, pH 4 to 6; very few sources.

### Collinsonia canadensis

**Horse balm** — moist rich woods and on wooded floodplains and ravines, often on limestone substrates, FAC+. Throughout Pennsylvania. Grows to 48 inches, yellow flowers in summer; part shade to shade in dry to moist organic loam, pH 6 to 7; very few sources.

### Comarum palustre

**Marsh cinquefoil** — emergent aquatic; swamps, bogs and peaty lake margins, OBL. Northeastern and northwestern counties in Pennsylvania. Grows 8 to 24 inches with red-purple flowers in summer; full sun in mucky, peaty soil along pond edges; very few sources.

### Conopholis americana

**Squaw-root** — rich oak or beech woods, where it is parasitic on oaks. Western and southern counties in Pennsylvania; scattered in Wayne and Lackawanna County. Grows up to 6 inches with pale brown to yellowish flowers in late spring; part shade to shade in dry to moist sandy loam, pH 4 to 6; very few sources.

### Coptis trifolia ssp groelandica

**Goldthread** — rich, damp, mossy woods bogs and swamps, often associated with hemlock and mosses, FACW. Northern counties in Pennsylvania; scattered south. Grows 6 to 8 inches with white flowers in early spring; shade in moist, acidic, humusy loam, pH 4 to 5; very few sources.

### Cornus canadensis

**Bunchberry** — cool, damp woods, bogs and swamp edges, FAC-. Northern counties in Pennsylvania; scattered south. Grows 4 to 8 inches with white flowers late spring and fruit in late summer; part shade to shade in moist, rich humus, pH 4 to 5; commonly available.

### Corydalis sempervirens

**Rock harlequin** — dry rocky woods, woodland outcrops and open areas on poor gravelly soil. Throughout Pennsylvania. Grows 12 to 30 inches with pinkish-white to purple flowers in late spring to early fall; sun to part shade in dry sandy loam, pH 5 to 6; several sources.

### Cryptotaenia canadensis

**Honewort** — moist woods, wooded stream banks, seeps; FAC. Throughout Pennsylvania. Grows 10 to 30 inches, white flowers late spring to early summer; part shade in moist, sandy loam; several sources.

### Cunila origanoides

**Common dittany** — dry open woods, shaly slopes, and serpentine barrens. Eastern and southern counties in Pennsylvania. Grows 8 to 16 inches with purple to white flowers in late summer; part sun to part shade in dry, sandy rocky loam; very few sources.

### Cypripedium acaule

**Pink lady's slipper** — well mulched, dry to wet acidic upland forests, bogs, and brushy barrens; FACU. Throughout Pennsylvania. Grows 6 to 16 inches with pink flowers late spring; part shade to shade in dry to moist sandy acidic loam, pH 4 to 5. Very difficult to transplant because of long, thin root system and soil preferences; several sources.

### Cypripedium parviflorum var. pubescens

**Large yellow lady's slipper** — moist, rich, rocky woods and slopes, bogs and swamps, FAC+. Throughout Pennsylvania. Grows 8 to 30 inches with yellow flowers, spring; sun to part shade in moist to wet silty loam, pH 5 to 7, but prefers 6.5 to 7. Listed as endangered in Pennsylvania; several sources.

### Cypripedium parviflorum var. parviflorum

**Lesser yellow lady's slipper** — dry deciduous and deciduous-hemlock forests, usually on slopes, FAC+. Scattered throughout Pennsylvania. Grows 8 to 30 inches, yellow flowers in spring; part shade to shade in rich dry to moist acidic sandy loam. Listed as endangered in Pennsylvania; very few sources.

### Desmodium canadense

**Showy tick-trefoil** — dry open woods and fields, FAC. Eastern and western Pennsylvania counties and scattered central counties. Grows 20-40 inches with blue to violet flowers late summer; sun to part shade in dry to moist sandy loam; commonly available.

### Desmodium glutinosum

**Sticky tick-clover** — dry to moist rich woods. Throughout Pennsylvania except for limestone substrates counties in the Central Appalachians. Grows 12 to 36 inches, with pink to purple flowers in summer; part shade to shade in moist, rich loam; very few sources.

### Desmodium paniculatum

**Tick-trefoil** — clearings and edges of moist or dry upland woods, UPL. Throughout Pennsylvania except for northern-most central counties. Grows 12 to 36 inches with violet to purple flowers, late summer; sun to part shade in dry to moist sandy loam. pH 6 to 7; very few sources.

### Dicentra canadensis

**Squirrel corn** — deciduous woods, often among rock outcrops, in rich loam soils. Western, northern and far southeastern counties in Pennsylvania; absent in limestone-substrate Central Appalachians. Grows up to 10 inches with white flowers in early spring; part shade to shade in moist, rich sandy loam, pH 6 to 7; several sources.

### Dicentra cucullaria

**Dutchman's breeches** — deciduous woods and clearings, in rich loam soils. Throughout Pennsylvania. Grows to 10 inches with white flowers in early spring; part shade to shade in dry to moist, rich sandy loam, pH 6 to 7; commonly available.

### Dicentra eximia

**Wild bleeding heart, fringed bleeding heart** — rich woods and on cliffs; prefers damp woods with oak mulch. Reported only in Luzerne, Northampton, Lawrence, Beaver and Bedford counties. Grows 10 to 15 inches with pink to purple flowers in early spring; part shade to shade in dry to moist rich loam. pH 4 to 7 but prefers 4.5 to 5.5. Listed as endangered in Pennsylvania; commonly available.

## Doellingeria umbellata

**Flat topped white aster** — moist woods, fields and floodplains, FACW. Throughout Pennsylvania. Grows 3 to 6 feet with white flowers in late summer to early fall; sun to part shade in moist to wet sandy loam, pH 5 to 6; commonly available.

## Drosera intermedia

**Spatulate-leaved sundew** — aquatic; open peat and along edges of bogs and glacial lakes, OBL. Northeastern and far southeastern counties of Pennsylvania. Grows 1 to 10 inches, with white flowers; full sun in pond margins in moist to wet rich peaty loam; very few sources.

## Drosera rotundifolia

**Round-leaved sundew** — sphagnum bogs and peaty edges of bogs, OBL. Most eastern, northern tier and south-central counties of Pennsylvania. Grows 3 to 10 inches with white to pink flowers. Aquatic; grow in full sun in pond margins in moist to wet rich peaty loam; very few sources.

## Elodea canadensis

**Ditch-moss** — Aquatic, free floating in shallow, mostly calcareous waters of ponds, lakes, creeks and rivers, OBL. Northeastern and northwestern counties of Pennsylvania and the Appalachians east of the Allegheny front. Flowers in summer; grow in neutral soil at the base of shallow ponds; several sources.

## Epilobium coloratum

**Purple-leaved willow-herb** — moist fields, shores and floodplains, OBL. Throughout Pennsylvania. Grows up to 3 feet with pink to white flowers in late summer; sun to part sun in rich, moist sandy loam; very few sources.

## Erigeron philadelphicus

**Daisy fleabane** — openings and margins of upland woods, marsh and stream edges, fields, roadsides, lawns, and other open, disturbed sites, FACU. Throughout Pennsylvania. Grows 8 to 40 inches, with white-pale lavender flowers in early summer; part sun in mesic to dry sandy loam; very few sources.

## Erigeron pulchellus

**Robin's plantain** — bottomland, especially along creeks; ravines, swamp edges, dry to moist woods, slopes and woodland edges, prairies and meadows, FACU. Throughout Pennsylvania. Grows to 8 feet with blue to pink-white flowers from late spring through summer; part shade in moist, rich, sandy loams; very few sources.

## Erythronium americanum

**Yellow trout lily** — open deciduous moist woods and rich slopes with deep humus-rich loam. Throughout Pennsylvania. Grows up to 8 inches with yellow flowers in spring; part shade in dry to moist sandy loam, pH 5 to 7; commonly available.

## Eupatorium fistulosum

**Trumpet weed** — mesic to moist fields, meadows and thickets, FACW. Throughout Pennsylvania. Grows up to 10 feet with pink-purple flowers in late summer and fall; sun to part sun in moist, rich sandy loam, pH 5.5 to 7; commonly available.

## Eupatorium maculatum

**Spotted Joe-pye-weed, spotted trumpetweed**-floodplains, thickets and swamps, FACW. Northern counties of Pennsylvania; southeast and scattered southern counties. Grows up to 6 feet with purple flowers late summer; sun to part sun in moist silty clay loam, pH 5.5 to 7; commonly available.

## Eupatorium perfoliatum

**Boneset** — flood plains, bogs, swamps and wet meadows, FACW+. Throughout Pennsylvania. Grows up to 5 feet with white flowers in late summer and fall; sun to part sun in moist to wet rich loam; commonly available.

## Eupatorium purpureum

**Joe-pye-weed** — mesic to moist open woods and fields, FAC. Throughout Pennsylvania. Grows up to 6 feet with pink to purple flowers in late summer and fall; sun to part shade in moist to wet rich sandy loam; commonly available.

## Eupatorium rugosum

**White snakeroot** — rich rocky woods, at the base of cliffs and rock outcrops, and in thickets and fields, FACU-. Throughout Pennsylvania. Grows 12 to 60 inches with white flowers in summer and fall; average, medium to wet, well-drained soils in full sun to part shade. Prefers part shade in moist, humusy soils, pH 6-7. AKA *Ageratina altissima*; commonly available.

### Eupatorium sessilifolium

**Upland eupatorium** — dry wooded slopes and roadsides. Eastern and southern counties in Pennsylvania; scattered elsewhere. Grows 24 to 60 inches with white flowers in summer and fall; sun to part shade in dry, rocky sandy loam; very few sources.

### Euphorbia corollata

**Flowering spurge** — dry open woods and shale barrens, fields and sandy waste ground. Southern and western counties in Pennsylvania; scattered elsewhere. Grows up to 3 feet with white flowers in late summer; full sun in dry to mesic sandy loam; several sources.

### Eurybia divaricata

**White wood aster** — dry to mesic, deciduous and mixed deciduous woods, edges and clearings. Throughout Pennsylvania. Grows 10 to 35 inches, with white flowers in autumn; part shade to shade in dry to moist, sandy loam, pH 5 to 7; commonly available.

### Eurybia macrophylla

**Bigleaf aster** — moist, often rocky upland woodlands. Throughout Pennsylvania. Grows 10 to 35 inches with white flowers in autumn; sun to part shade in dry to moist sandy loam, pH 6 to 7; commonly available.

### Euthamia graminifolia

**Grass-leaved goldenrod** — moist fields, roadsides, ditches and shores, FACU+. Throughout Pennsylvania. Two varieties are found locally — *graminifolia* and *nuttalli*. Grows up to 5 feet with yellow flowers in late summer and fall; sun to part sun in dry to moist sandy loam; several sources.

### Filipendula rubra

**Queen-of-the-prairie** — moist meadows, thickets and roadsides, FACW. Scattered throughout Pennsylvania. Grows 3 to 6 feet with pink flowers in early summer; average, medium to wet, well-drained soil in full sun to part shade. Prefers consistently moist, fertile, humusy soils; commonly available.

### Fragaria vesca spp. americana

**Woodland strawberry** — deciduous woods and wooded slopes. Mostly eastern Pennsylvania counties; scattered west. Grows 6 to 8 inches with white flowers in spring and fruit in early summer; part shade to shade in moist sandy loam; commonly available.

### Fragaria virginiana spp. virginiana

**Wild strawberry** — dry to moist open woodlands and clearings, typically in disturbed areas, FACU. Throughout Pennsylvania. Grows 6 to 8 inches with white flowers in spring and fruit in early summer; part sun to part shade in dry to moist sandy loam; commonly available.

### Galearis spectabilis

**Showy orchis** — moist, calcareous woodlands, thickets, and old fields. Throughout Pennsylvania except for north-central counties. Grows 4 to 8 inches with pink to purple flowers in spring; part shade to shade in moist rich loam. pH 5-6; very few sources.

### Galium boreale

**Northern bedstraw** — upland rocky woods, slopes, wet fields, fens, roadside banks, FACU. Mostly eastern and south central counties in Pennsylvania, scattered elsewhere. Grows 1 to 3 feet with white flowers in late summer; average, medium, well-drained soils in part shade. Prefers moist soils where it will often spread by creeping roots and self-seeding; several sources.

### Gentiana andrewsii var. andrewsii

**Bottle gentian** — wet fields and moist, open woods, FACW. Throughout Pennsylvania except for northern tier. Grows up to 3 feet with blue flowers in late summer; sun to part shade in moist to wet sandy humusy loam; commonly available.

### Gentiana clausa

**Meadow closed gentian** — moist meadows, stream banks, and open woods in moist acidic soil, FACW. Throughout Pennsylvania. Grows up to 3 feet with blue flowers in late summer; sun to part shade in moist to wet rich acidic loam, pH 4 to 5; very few sources.

### Geranium maculatum

**Wood geranium** — rich open upland woods, shaded roadsides and areas of fields, FACU. Throughout Pennsylvania. Grows 18 to 24 inches, with pink-purple flowers in spring; part sun to part shade in moist humusy loam, pH 5 to 7; commonly available.

### Geum canadense

**White avens** — upland dry to mesic open woodlands, woodland edges and openings and thickets, FACU. Throughout Pennsylvania. Grows 16-40 inches with white flowers in early summer; sun to part shade in dry to moist sandy loam; very few sources.

### Geum laciniatum

**Herb-bennet** — mesic savannahs, thickets and woodland borders and moist meadows, FAC+. Throughout Pennsylvania. Grows 16-40 inches, with white flowers in summer; sun to part shade in moist, rich loam, pH 4 to 6; very few sources.

### Geum rivale

**Water avens** — bogs, peaty meadows and calcareous marshes, OBL. Northeastern and northwestern counties in Pennsylvania; scattered southwest counties. Grows 6 to 24 inches, flowers are yellowish with purple veins in early summer; full sun in wet, silty, rich circumneutral loam; very few sources.

### Gillenia trifoliata

**Bowman's-root** — dry to moist, upland woods and rocky banks. Throughout Pennsylvania except for several northern tier counties. Grows 24 to 36 inches with white flowers in late spring and early summer; part shade to shade in moist, slightly acidic rich, rocky soil. AKA *Porteranthus trifoliatus;* commonly available.

### Goodyera pubescens

**Downy rattlesnake plantain** — dry to moist warm, deciduous or coniferous forests, FACU-. Eastern and western counties in Pennsylvania; scattered central counties. Grows 8 to 16 inch-

es, with white flowers in summer; part shade to shade in dry to moist silty-sandy loam, pH 5 to 6; commonly available.

### Helenium autumnale

**Common sneezeweed** — meadows, moist riverbanks, wet fields, alluvial thickets and swamps, FACW+. Throughout Pennsylvania. Grows 3 to 5 feet with yellow flowers in late summer to fall; sun to part sun in moist to wet rich loam, pH 5.5 to 7; commonly available.

### Helianthemum bicknellii

**Bicknell's hoary rose** is found on sandy, dry rocky slopes, open woods and prairies. Most eastern counties in Pennsylvania; scattered elsewhere. Grows 8 to 24 inches, with yellow flowers in summer; sun to part shade in dry, sandy soil loam. Listed as endangered in Pennsylvania; very few sources.

### Helianthemum canadense

**Frostweed** — dry sandy or rocky ground, open woods and barrens. Southeastern counties in Pennsylvania; scattered elsewhere. Grows 6 to 12 inches with yellow flowers in early summer; sun to part shade in dry, gravelly loam; very few sources.

### Helianthus decapetalus

**Thin leaved sunflower** — open woodlands, woodland edges, savannahs, meadows, thickets and lightly shaded areas along rivers, FACU. Throughout Pennsylvania. Grows 2 to 5 feet with yellow flowers in late summer; part sun to part, especially dappled, shade in moist sandy loam. Can be aggressive; very few sources.

### Helianthus divaricatus

**Woodland sunflower** — dry open woods and wooded slopes, thickets, shale barrens and roadsides. Throughout Pennsylvania. Grows up to 5 feet with yellow flowers in late summer; part sun to part shade in dry to mesic sandy loam, pH 5-7. Aggressive spreader; several sources.

### Helianthus giganteus

**Swamp sunflower** — wet fields, swamps and ditches, FACW. Throughout Pennsylvania except northern tier counties. Grows 6 to 10 feet with yellow flowers in late summer and fall; sun to part sun in moist, rich silty loam; very few sources.

### Helianthus strumosus

**Rough-leaved sunflower** — fields, dry, open, upland woods and woodland edges. Throughout Pennsylvania. Grows up to 7 feet with yellow flowers in summer. Possibly hybridizing with *Helianthus divaricatus*; sun to part shade in dry, sandy loam, pH 5.5 to 7; several sources.

### Heliopsis helianthoides

**Ox-eye** — open and sometimes rocky woods, thickets, prairies, stream banks. Throughout Pennsylvania. Grows up to 5 feet, with yellow flowers in late summer; full sun to part shade (may require support) in dry to moist sandy loam, pH 5.6 to 6.8; commonly available.

### Hepatica nobilis

**Liverleaf** — rich woods and dry rocky upland slopes. Throughout Pennsylvania. Two varieties — *obtusa* and *acuta* (sharp and round lobed leaves, respectively). Grows 6 to 8 inches with lavender to purple flowers in early spring; part shade to shade in dry sandy loam. pH 4 to 7, but prefers pH 4.5 to 6. Also known as *Hepatica americana;* very few sources.

### Heuchera americana

**Alum-root** — rich woods, rocky slopes, shaly cliffs on rich, well-drained humus, FACU-. Throughout Pennsylvania except for northern tier counties. Grows 12 to 30 inches with greenish-white to pink flowers in spring; part sun to part shade in dry, sandy well-drained humusy loam. pH 5 to 7; commonly available.

### Hieracium kalmii

**Canada hawkweed** — clearings, roadsides and in prairies. Scattered throughout Pennsylvania, mostly eastern counties. Grows 6 to 48 inches with yellow-orange flowers in late summer; sun to part sun in dry to moist sandy loam; very few sources.

### Hieracium scabrum

**Rough hawkweed** — open fields, clearings, woods edges. Throughout Pennsylvania. Grows 8 to 48 inches with yellow-orange flowers, late summer and fall; sun to part sun in dry sandy loam;

very few sources.

### Hieracium venosum

**Rattlesnake weed** — dry upland woods including slopes and edges. Throughout Pennsylvania except northern-most central counties. Grows up to 32 inches with orange-yellow flowers, summer; part shade to shade in dry to moist organic clay sandy loam; very few sources.

### Houstonia caerulea

**Bluets** or **Quaker ladies** — dry to mesic meadows, fields, upland open woods, and woods edges, FACU. Throughout Pennsylvania. Grows up to 16 inches with blue flowers with yellow centers in spring; sun to part shade in moist rich sandy loam, pH 5.5 to 7; very few sources.

### Hydrocotyle americana

**Marsh pennywort** — swampy thickets, boggy fields, wet woods and lake margins, OBL. Throughout Pennsylvania. Low creeping habit with white flowers in summer; sun to part shade in moist to wet marshy soils; very few sources.

### Hydrophyllum canadense

**Canadian waterleaf** — rocky upland wooded slopes, ravines and moist woods, FACU. Scattered throughout Pennsylvania, mostly southwestern counties. Grows 12 to 20 inches with white-pink to purple flowers in summer; part shade to shade in moist humusy soil; very few sources.

### Hydrophyllum virginianum

**Virginia waterleaf** — mesic wooded slopes and stream banks and in thickets, FAC. Throughout Pennsylvania. Grows 12 to 30 inches with white flowers in spring; part shade to shade in moist humusy loam, pH 6 to 7; very few sources.

### Hypericum punctatum

**Spotted St. John's-wort** — floodplains, thickets, moist fields and along roadsides, FAC-. Throughout Pennsylvania. Grows 20 to 40 inches with yellow flowers in summer; sun to part sun in dry to moist sandy loam; very few sources.

### Hypericum pyramidatum

**Great St. John's-wort** — alluvial shores and in moist to mesic fields, rocky banks, and swamps, FAC. Scattered in Pennsylvania, mostly eastern and northwestern counties. Grows 30-60 inches with yellow flowers in summer; sun to part sun in dry to moist rich sandy loam, pH 5 to 6. AKA *Hypericum ascyron.*; commonly available.

### Hypoxis hirsuta

**Yellow star grass** — dry to mesic meadows, fields, clearings, barrens and dry woods, FAC. Throughout Pennsylvania, except central northern tier counties. Grows up to 15 inches with yellow flowers in spring to summer; sun to part shade in dry to wet sandy loam; pH 4.5 to 7; several sources.

### Ionactis linariifolius

**Stiff-leaved aster** — dry rocky woods and edges; typically in acidic soils in pine-oak or pine-hickory woods, ridgetops, upland slopes and glades. Eastern counties in Pennsylvania. Grows 12 to 24 inches with violet flowers in late summer to fall; average, dry to medium, well-drained soil in full sun to part shade. Prefers acidic, sandy soils; pH 4-7; very few sources.

### Iris versicolor

**Northern blue flag iris** — marshes, bogs and wet meadows, OBL. Throughout Pennsylvania except south central counties. Grows 24 to 60 inches with blue-violet flowers in late spring or early summer; sun to part sun in moist to wet rich silty loam, especially in pond margins; commonly available.

### Krigia biflora

**Dwarf dandelion** — moist fields and meadows, FACU. Eastern and western counties in Pennsylvania; scattered in south central areas. Grows 4 to 24 inches, yellow flowers from late spring into fall; sun to part sun in dry to moist sandy loam; very few sources.

### Laportea canadensis

**Wood-nettle** — rich moist deciduous forests, often along seepages and streams, FACW. Throughout Pennsylvania. Grows 20 to 40 inches with tiny white flowers in spring; part shade to shade in moist, humusy loam. Stinging hairs on all parts causes brief burning or itching; very few sources.

### Lathyrus palustris

**Marsh pea** — moist meadows, sand plains, swamps and thickets, FACW+. Scattered Pennsylvania counties, mostly east and south central. Grows up to 3 feet with red-purple flowers in early summer; moist to wet rich loam in full to part sun. Endangered in Pennsylvania; very few sources.

### Lemna minor

**Duckweed** — aquatic; still water of nutrient-average to nutrient-rich lakes and ponds, and in streams, swamps and ditches, OBL. Eastern and northwestern counties in Pennsylvania; scattered elsewhere. Grow in shallow ponds and water features with slow-moving to still water; several sources.

### Lemna trisulca

**Star duckweed** — cool-temperate aquatic; nutrient-average, quiet waters rich in calcium, forms tangled colonies in lakes, ponds, bogs, marshes, streams, OBL. Scattered in eastern and northwestern counties of Pennsylvania. Grow in shallow ponds and water features with slow-moving to still water; very few sources.

### Lespedeza capitata

**Round-headed bush-clover** — upland woods, thickets, prairies, glades and along streams, FACU-. Mostly eastern counties of Pennsylvania; scattered west. Grows 20 to 60 inches with yellow-white flowers, late summer; sun to part sun in dry to moist sandy loam; commonly available.

### Lespedeza hirta

**Bush-clover** — dry prairies, savannahs, fields, meadows. Throughout Pennsylvania, except most northern tier counties. Grows 24 to 48 inches with yellow flowers in summer; sun to part shade in dry sandy loams; very few sources.

### Lespedeza violacea

**Slender bush-clover** — dry upland woods, thickets and openings. Mostly southern tier counties in Pennsylvania; scattered north. Grows 12 to 30 inches with violet-purple flowers in late summer; part sun to part shade in dry sandy loam; very few sources.

### *Lespedeza virginica*

**Slender bush-clover** — dry fields, stony banks, rocky woods. Mostly eastern counties in Pennsylvania; scattered southwest. Grows 12 to 40 inches with violet-purple flowers in summer; sun to part shade in dry sandy loam; very few sources.

### *Liatris spicata*

**Blazing-star** — moist fields, meadows and swamps, usually over limestone, FAC+. Southeastern counties of Pennsylvania on a line east of Monroe to York Counties; scattered southwest. Grows up to 6 feet with blue-purple flowers in late summer; sun to part sun in moist rich sandy loam. pH 5.5 to 7; commonly available.

### *Lilium canadense*

**Canada lily** — wet meadows, moist rich woods especially edges, stream sides and river alluvia, bogs, marshes and swamps, FAC+. Throughout Pennsylvania. Grows up to 6 feet with yellow or red flowers in early summer; sun to part sun in moist to wet organic loam. pH 4 to 7; several sources; several sources.

### *Lilium philadelphicum*

**Wood lily** — open dry woods, borders and clearings on well-drained soil, FACU+. Throughout Pennsylvania except far western counties. Grows up to 3 feet with orange-red flowers in early summer; part sun to part shade in dry to moist sandy loam. pH 5 to 7; several sources.

### *Linum striatum*

**Ridged yellow flax** — moist meadows, wet open ground and wet open woods, FACW. Mostly southern counties in Pennsylvania; scattered north. Grows 12 to 36 inches with yellow flowers in summer; sun to part shade in moist rich loam; very few sources.

### *Lobelia cardinalis*

**Cardinal flower** — wet meadows, swamps, riverbanks and lake shores, FACW+. Throughout Pennsylvania. Grows 20 to 36 inches, with red flowers in late summer; sun to part sun in moist to wet, humus rich, sandy loam, pH 5.5 to 7; commonly available.

### *Lobelia inflata*

**Indian-tobacco** — upland dry to mesic woods, old fields, meadows and along roadsides, FACU. Throughout Pennsylvania. Grows up to 36 inches with blue to white flowers in late summer; sun to part sun in dry to moist sandy loam; commonly available.

### *Lobelia siphilitica*

**Great blue lobelia** — swamps, moist meadows, stream banks and ditches, FACW+. Throughout Pennsylvania. Grows up to 5 feet with blue flowers in summer; sun to part sun in moist to wet silty loam; commonly available.

### *Lobelia spicata var. spicata*

**Spiked lobelia** — dry to mesic fields and open woodlands, FAC-. Throughout Pennsylvania except north central counties. Grows up to 36 inches, with pale blue to white flowers in summer; sun to part shade in dry to moist sandy loam; several sources.

### *Ludwigia alternifolia*

**Seedbox** — swampy fields, wet woods, and the borders of streams and pond and lake shores, FACW+. Throughout Pennsylvania, except northern tier counties. Grows 16 to 48 inches, yellow flowers in early summer; sun to part shade in moist sandy loam. Common name comes from box-like seed pods; several sources.

### *Ludwigia palustris*

**Marsh-purslane** — swamps, wet meadows, muddy shores, stream banks, ditches, OBL. Throughout Pennsylvania. Prostrate, creeping, floating stems; full sun in moist to wet mucky soils, including shallow water; very few sources.

### *Lupinus perennis*

**Blue lupine** — dry fields, woods edges and along roadsides in sandy acidic soil. Mostly central and eastern counties, scattered elsewhere. Grows 8 to 24 inches with blue flowers in spring and early summer; sun to part sun in dry to moist acidic sandy loam, pH 5.5 to 7. Listed as rare in Pennsylvania; commonly available.

### *Lycopus americanus*

**Water-horehound** — mesic to moist hillsides and fields, moist thickets, wet ditches and swamps, OBL. Throughout Pennsylvania. Grows 6 to 24 inches with small white flowers in summer; sun to part shade in moist to wet rich, mucky soils; several sources.

### Lysimachia ciliata

**Fringed loosestrife** — low moist ground and old fields, in floodplains and on stream banks, FACW. Throughout Pennsylvania. Grows 16 to 48 inches with yellow flowers in early summer; sun to part sun in moist sandy rich loam; very few sources.

### Lysimachia hybrida

**Lance-leaved loosestrife** — swamps, wet meadows, fens and pond margins, OBL. Extreme eastern counties in Pennsylvania from Monroe south; also Cumberland and Franklin counties. Grows up to 5 feet with yellow flowers in early summer; full to part sun in mesic to moist organic, clay to sandy/rocky loam. Listed as threatened in Pennsylvania; very few sources.

### Lysimachia quadrifolia

**Whorled loosestrife** — dry to mesic hardwood forests, lowlands, fens, moist clearings, roadsides, and fields, rocky thickets and slopes, FACU-. Throughout Pennsylvania. Grows up to 3 feet with yellow flowers in early summer; full sun to part shade in a wide range of moist soils; very few sources.

### Lysimachia terrestris

**Swamp-candles** — swamps, flood plains, fens, bogs, stream banks, pond and lake margins and wet ditches, OBL. Throughout Pennsylvania. Grows 16 to 30 inches with yellow flowers in early summer; sun to part sun in moist rich loam; very few sources.

### Lysimachia thyrsiflora

**Tufted loosestrife** — bogs, swamps, marshes and wet woods, OBL. Northeastern and northwestern counties in Pennsylvania, also Northampton County. Grows 12 to 30 inches with yellow flowers in early summer; sun to part shade in moist to wet rich loam; very few sources.

### Maianthemum canadense

**Canada mayflower** — dry to moist woods, rich and often sandy clearings, FAC-. Throughout Pennsylvania. Grows 6-8 inches with white flowers in late spring; part shade to shade in dry to moist sandy acidic loam, pH 4-5; several sources.

### Maianthemum racemosum

**False Solomon's-seal, feathery false lily-of-the-valley** — dry to moist deciduous woodlands, FACU-. Throughout Pennsylvania. Grows up to 3 feet, with white flowers in late spring; part shade to shade in dry to moist humusy loam, pH 4 to 6; commonly available.

### Maianthemum stellatum

**Starry false lily-of-the-valley** — moist to wet woods, marginal woodlands, oak openings and on stream banks, FACW. Mostly eastern counties in Pennsylvania on a line from Monroe to York counties; scattered elsewhere. Grows up to 24 inches with white flowers in spring; part shade to shade in moist to wet rich loam. pH 4 to 5; several sources.

### Maianthemum trifolium

**Threeleaf false lily-of-the-valley** — often dense clonal patches in sphagnum bogs, and wet forests, OBL. Northeastern counties in Pennsylvania, as well as Somerset and extreme northwestern counties. Grows up to 8 inches with white flowers in spring; part shade to shade in moist to wet rich loam; very few sources.

### Medeola virginiana

**Indian cucumber root** — mesic woods and moist slopes. Throughout Pennsylvania. Grows 12 to 24 inches with greenish-yellow flowers in late spring; moist to wet soils in part shade to full shade, pH 4-6; several sources.

### Melanthium virginicum

**Bunchflower** — bogs, marshes, wet woods, savannahs, meadows and damp clearings, FACW+. Mostly southeastern counties in Pennsylvania; scattered elsewhere. Grows up to 7 feet with white flowers in early summer; full sun to part shade in moist to wet sandy to clayey loam; very few sources. AKA *Veratrum virginicum*.

## Mentha arvensis

**Field mint** — swamps, wet meadows and moist banks, FACW. Throughout Pennsylvania. Grows 12 to 24 inches with blue-lavender flowers in fall; part shade in mesic to moist rich loam; very few sources.

## Menyanthes trifoliata

**Bogbean or Buckbean** — aquatic; bogs, sphagnum swamps and shallow water of ponds and lakes, OBL. Scattered counties in Pennsylvania, mostly east. White flowers in late spring; grow in water gardens in mud or containers submerged in shallow water (3 inches over rhizome) in full sun to part shade. Best in acidic, peaty soils; several sources.

## Mimulus moschatus

**Muskflower** — wet shores, seeps and spring-fed swales, OBL. Mostly eastern and north central counties in Pennsylvania; scattered elsewhere. Creeping habit, with yellow flowers in summer; muddy moist to wet margins of garden water features in full sun to part shade; very few sources.

## Mimulus ringens

**Allegheny monkey flower** — sunny pond edges, swamps and wet meadows, OBL. Throughout Pennsylvania. Grows up to 6 inches with blue flowers in summer; sun to part sun in moist to wet rich loam; commonly available.

## Mitchella repens

**Partridgeberry** — dry to moist upland woods and sandy bogs, FACU. Throughout Pennsylvania. Trailing stems to 12 inches. White flowers in late spring, with long-lasting red fruits following; part shade to shade in moist rich humus. pH 4 to 5; commonly available. Technically a subshrub.

## Mitella diphylla

**Bishops cap** — rich, cool shaded sites in moist open woods and along stream banks, FACU. Throughout Pennsylvania. Grows 4 to 16 inches with white flowers in early spring; part shade to shade in moist rich sandy loam. pH 5 to 7, but prefers 6.0; commonly available.

## Mitella nuda

**Naked mitrewort** — cool, mossy, mixed woods and cedar swamps, FACW-. Pennsylvania distribution recorded only as Monroe and Warren counties. Grows 2 to 4 inches with greenish-yellow flowers in late spring; part shade to shade in moist rich organic loam. Listed as endangered in Pennsylvania; very few sources.

## Moehringia lateriflora

**Blunt-leaved sandwort** — moist to dry woodlands and moist to mesic meadows, gravelly shores, swales, and low woods, FAC. Mostly eastern and western counties in Pennsylvania, except extreme western counties. Grows up to 24 inches with white flowers in late spring; mesic to moist sandy loams in full sun to part shade; very few sources.

## Monarda clinopodia

**White bergamot** — moist woods, fields and floodplains. Throughout Pennsylvania. Grows up to 36 inches with white-yellow flowers in summer; sun to part shade in dry, rocky, sandy loam; very few sources.

## Monarda didyma

**Bee balm** — rich moist fields, meadows; bottomlands, thickets, woods and especially stream banks, FAC+. Throughout Pennsylvania except south central counties along the Allegheny Front. Grows 2 to 4 feet with red flowers in late summer; sun to part sun in, medium to wet, moisture-retentive soils in full sun to part shade. Prefers rich, humusy soils in full sun, pH 5.5 to 7; commonly available.

## Monarda fistulosa var. mollis

**Horsemint** — moist to wet prairies and upland open woods. Eastern counties in Pennsylvania; scattered elsewhere. Grows 20 to 48 inches with lavender flowers in late summer; sun to part sun in dry to moist sandy loam, pH 5.5 to 7. UPL; commonly available.

## Monarda media

**Bee balm** — rich moist acidic soil on stream banks, thickets, low woods and ditches. Mostly western counties in Pennsylvania; scattered east. Grows up to 36 inches with purple flowers in summer; part shade in moist rich loam; very few sources.

## Nuphar lutea

**Spatterdock**, or **yellow pond lily** — aquatic; lake margins, ponds, slow moving streams, swamps and tidal marshes, OBL. Throughout Pennsylvania except for far southwestern counties. Grows in 1 to 3 feet of water in full sun to part shade. Can be grown in containers for water gardens; for natural ponds, plant rhizomes directly in the muddy bottom of poor sandy soil; very few sources.

## Nymphaea odorata

**Fragrant water-lily** — aquatic; quiet waters of acidic or alkaline ponds, lakes, sluggish streams and rivers, pools in marshes, ditches, canals, or sloughs, OBL. Mostly eastern counties in Pennsylvania; scattered elsewhere. White flowers from late spring to early fall; shallow ponds in silty to sandy soil; several sources.

## Oenothera biennis

**Evening primrose** — dry fields, waste ground, and along roadsides, FACU-. Throughout Pennsylvania. Grows 20 to 60 inches with yellow flowers in late summer to fall; sun to part sun in dry to moist sandy loam; commonly available.

## Oenothera fruticosa

**Sundrops** — mesic meadows, fields and along roadsides, FAC. Throughout Pennsylvania except for extreme northeastern counties. Grows 8 to 30 inches with yellow flowers, early summer. Two local subspecies, *fruticosa* and *glauca*; sun to part shade in dry to moist sandy loam, pH 5.5 to 7; several sources.

## Oenothera perennis

**Sundrops** — mesic pastures, shale slopes and along roadsides, FAC. Throughout Pennsylvania. Grows 4 to 24 inches with yellow flowers in early summer; sun to part sun in dry to moist sandy loam; very few sources.

## Opuntia humifusa

**Eastern prickly-pear cactus** — sandy habitats, especially openings on dry sometimes wooded hillsides. Scattered counties, mostly southeast, in Pennsylvania. Spreading, prostrate habit with yellow flowers in summer; sun to part sun in dry sandy loam, pH 5.5 to 7. Listed as rare in Pennsyl-

vania; commonly available.

## Orontium aquaticum

**Goldenclub** — aquatic; shallow water of bogs, marshes, swamps, and streams, OBL. Eastern half of Pennsylvania from a diagonal line northeast to southwest. Grow in water gardens in containers submerged in 6 to 18 inches of water in full sun. Leaves tend to emerge in water 6 to 9 inches deep, but mostly float in water 12 to 18 inches deep. Listed as rare in Pennsylvania; several sources.

## Osmorhiza claytonii

**Sweet-cicely** — rich upland woods and wooded slopes, FACU. Throughout Pennsylvania except for east central counties along the Allegheny front. Grows 15 to 30 inches with white flowers in early summer; part shade to shade in moist rich loam; several sources.

## Osmorhiza longistylis

**Anise-root** — upland dry to mesic wooded areas, shaded slopes and ravines, FACU. Throughout Pennsylvania. Grows 15 to 30 inches with white flowers in early summer; part sun to part shade in moist rich loam; very few sources.

## Oxalis stricta

**Common yellow wood-sorrel** — dry to mesic fields, lawns, gardens in shallow sandy loams to loamy tills, UPL. Throughout Pennsylvania. Prostrate to 20 inches with yellow flowers in summer; sun to part sun in dry to moist sandy loamy till, pH 4-6; very few sources.

## Oxalis violacea

**Violet wood-sorrel** — dryish, acidic soils in glades, rocky open woods, fields and prairies, stream banks. Southern counties in Pennsylvania, scattered north. Grows 6 to 9 inches with violet flowers in spring; part sun to part shade in dry to moist sandy loam; pH 4 to 7 but prefers 6 to 6.5; very few sources.

## Oxypolis rigidior

**Cowbane** — swamps, bogs, meadows, and moist sandy shores, OBL. Mostly southeastern and southwestern counties in Pennsylvania; also Monroe County. Grows 4 to 5 feet with white flowers in late summer; sun to part shade in wet, sandy or clay loam; very few sources.

### Panax quinquefolius

**Ginseng** — cool, moist, rich mesic woods, often on north-facing slopes. Throughout Pennsylvania. Grows up to 24 inches with greenish flowers in spring, red fruit in fall; moist, fertile, organically rich, medium moisture soils in part shade to full shade; pH 4 to 7 but prefers 4.5 to 6. Listed as vulnerable in Pennsylvania because of harvesting for herbal use; commonly available.

### Parnassia glauca

**Grass-of-parnassus** — boggy meadows or seeps on calcareous soils, OBL. Scattered far eastern and northwestern counties in Pennsylvania. Grows 10 to 20 inches with white flowers in late summer; moist to wet organic loams in full sun to part shade. Listed as endangered in Pennsylvania; very few sources.

### Pedicularis canadensis

**Forest lousewort** — open dry upland woods, old fields, woods edges and mesic grasslands, FACU. Throughout Pennsylvania. Grows 6 to 16 inches with yellow to purple flowers in spring; sun to part shade in dry sandy loam; very few sources.

### Peltandra virginica

**Green arrow-arum** — emergent aquatic; bogs, swamps and ditches, and edges of ponds, lakes, and rivers, OBL. Extreme eastern and western counties of Pennsylvania. Grows 2 to 3 feet with green flowers in spring; water garden, bog, or pond areas in part shade, muddy soil in shallow water; very few sources.

### Penstemon digitalis

**Beards tongue, Talus slope penstemon** — old fields, meadows, prairies and mesic open woods and margins, FAC. Throughout Pennsylvania. Grows up to 60 inches with white flowers in summer; average, dry to medium moisture, well-drained soil in full sun to part sun; commonly available.

### Penstemon hirsutus

**Northern beard-tongue** — dry to mesic, open

rocky slopes, fields, and roadside banks. Scattered throughout Pennsylvania, mostly eastern and southern counties. Grows 15 to 32 inches with violet to purple flowers in early summer; sun to part sun in dry rocky sandy loam; pH 5.5 to 6.5; several sources.

### Phlox divaricata

**Woodland phlox** — humus-rich soil in open upland deciduous woods, FACU. Mostly southern, central and western counties in Pennsylvania; scattered east. Grows up to 12 inches with pale blue to white flowers in spring; humusy, medium moisture, well-drained soil in part shade to full shade. Prefers rich, moist, organic soils, pH 5-7; commonly available.

### Phlox maculata ssp. maculata

**Wild sweet-William** — wet meadows, abandoned fields and thickets, low moist woods and riverbanks, FACW. Throughout Pennsylvania. Grows 12 to 32 inches. Pink-rose to purple flowers in early summer; moderately fertile, medium moisture, well-drained soil in full sun to light shade. Prefers moist, organically rich soils in full sun; several sources.

### Phlox paniculata

**Summer phlox, Fall phlox** — meadows, thickets and along stream banks, often on calcareous substrate, FACU. Throughout Pennsylvania. Grows up to 6 feet with pink flowers in early summer; sun to part sun in moist to wet sandy rich loam, pH 5 to 7; commonly available.

### Phlox stolonifera

**Creeping phlox** — rich open woods and stream banks. Mostly southwestern counties on the Allegheny Plateau in Pennsylvania, as well as Wayne and Crawford County. Grows 4 to 6 inches with violet to rose purple flowers in spring; part shade to shade in dry to moist rich loam, pH 6 to 7; commonly available.

### Phlox subulata

**Moss pink** — dry rocky ledges, slopes, clearings and fields. Mostly eastern and southwestern counties in Pennsylvania. Grows to about 6 inches with pink, purple or white flowers in spring; sun to part sun in dry sandy loam, pH 5.7 to 7.5.

Listed as endangered in Pennsylvania; several sources.

### Phryma leptostachya

**Lopseed** — rich woods, rocky limestone slopes and swamps, UPL. Throughout Pennsylvania except north central counties. Grows 1 to 3 feet with purple flowers in summer; part sun to part shade in moist, rich circumneutral loam; very few sources.

### Physalis heterophylla

**Ground cherry** — fields, sandy or cindery open ground and cultivated areas. Western and southeastern counties in Pennsylvania; scattered elsewhere. Grows 8 to 36 inches with yellow flowers in late summer; sun to part sun in dry, sandy loam; very few sources.

### Physostegia virginiana

**False dragonhead** is found on stream banks and along moist shorelines. Scattered throughout Pennsylvania except for extreme northeastern counties. Grows up to 36 inches with pinkish-purple flowers in late summer; part sun to part shade in moist rich loam, pH 5 to 6.5; commonly available.

### Phytolacca americana

**Pokeweed** — moist to mesic thickets, clearings and forest openings, open ground and along roadsides. FACU+. Throughout Pennsylvania. Grows up to 10 feet, with greenish-white flowers in summer to fall; part sun to part shade in dry to moist sandy loam, pH 5 to 6; several sources.

### Platanthera ciliaris

**Yellow fringed orchid** — bogs, moist meadows, and moist to wet woods, FACW. Monroe and Lackawanna Counties southward in Pennsylvania, then west along the southern tier Grows 15 to 40 inches with orange-yellow flowers in summer; sun to part shade in moist, rich loam. Listed as threatened in Pennsylvania; very few sources.

### Platanthera clavellata

**Clubspur orchid** — bogs, shores, moist woods, thickets, sunny openings, in damp deep humus; FACW+. Throughout Pennsylvania, except for west-central counties. Grows 5 to 15 inches with white flowers in late summer; sun to part sun in moist to wet sandy rich loam, pH 5-6; very few sources.

### Podophyllum peltatum

**Mayapple** — medium wet, well-drained soil in mesic woods, especially maple woods and clearings, FACU. Throughout Pennsylvania. Grows 12 to 18 inches with white flowers in spring followed by green fruits that yellow when ripe. Spreads by rhizomes to form huge colonies and appears to be ignored by deer; part shade to shade in dry to moist humusy loam, pH 4 to 7; commonly available.

### Pogonia ophioglossoides

**Rose pogonia** — sphagnum bogs, fens, moist acidic sandy meadows and prairies, open wet woods, pine savannahs, sandy-peaty stream banks, and seepage slopes, OBL. Mostly eastern counties in Pennsylvania; scattered central and west. Grows 4 to 16 inches with pink flowers in summer; full to part sun in moist to wet acidic humusy loam; very few sources.

### Polemonium reptans

**Spreading Jacob's ladder, Greek valerian** — low moist woods, wooded floodplains, thickets at the base of cliffs and moist ground near streams, FACU. Throughout Pennsylvania. Grows 6 to 20 inches with light blue flowers in spring; part shade to shade in moist, rich sandy loam, pH 5 to 7. Spreads by free-seeding, not rhizomes; commonly available.

### Polemonium vanbruntiae

**Jacob's ladder** — sphagnum glades, swamps, and marshes, FACW. Pennsylvania distribution reported only in Wayne, Sullivan, Berks and Somerset counties. Grows up to 36 inches with blue flowers in summer; moist rich humusy soils in sun to part shade. Listed as endangered in Pennsylvania. AKA *Polemonium caeruleum ssp. vanbruntiae*; very few sources.

### Polygala paucifolia

**Bird-on-the-wing** — rich dry to mesic rocky upland woods and wooded slopes, FACU. Throughout Pennsylvania except for extreme western counties. Grows 3 to 6 inches with rose-purple flowers in spring; part shade to shade in moist rich loam, pH 4 to 6; very few sources.

### Polygonatum biflorum

**Smooth Solomon's seal** — dry to moist woods in fertile, loamy soil; robust plants are known as *var. commutatum*, FACU. Throughout Pennsylvania. Grows up to 6 feet, but more typically around 3 feet, with white-greenish flowers in spring and dark purple fruits following; part shade to shade in dry to moist rich loam. pH 4 to 6 but prefers 5 to 6.5; commonly available.

### Polygonatum pubescens

**Hairy Solomon's seal** — fertile, humus-rich moisture retentive well-drained soil in cool, shaded, dry to moist woods, wooded slopes and coves. Throughout Pennsylvania. Grows up to 36 inches with white-greenish flowers in spring; part shade to shade in dry to moist humusy sandy loam; pH 4 to 6 but prefers 5 to 6.5; commonly available.

### Polygonum amphibium

**Water smartweed** or **Water knotweed** — aquatic, found in very wet prairies and along shorelines, in swamps, ponds, and quiet streams, in mud or floating on still fresh water, OBL. Throughout Pennsylvania, except for the Allegheny Plateau. Two varieties; *emersum* (leaves don't float) and *stipulaceum* (leaves float); full sun to part sun in wet mucky soil or in water gardens. Not to be confused with the invasive *Polygonum cuspidatum* (Japanese knotweed); very few sources.

### Polygonum hydropiperoides var. hydropiperoides

**Mild water-pepper** — wet banks and clearings, shallow water, marshes, moist prairies, ditches, OBL. Southeastern and western counties in Pennsylvania; scattered elsewhere. Grow in full sun in mucky soil, standing water; very few sources.

### Polygonum virginianum

**Jumpseed** — rich deciduous forests, floodplain forests, dry to moist woodlands and thickets, FAC. Throughout Pennsylvania. Grows 15 to 40 inches with white flowers in spring; sun to part shade in rich sandy loam. Also known as *Persicaria virginiana*; several sources.

### Pontederia cordata

**Pickerel-weed** — emergent aquatic; pond and lake margins and swampy edges of lakes and streams, OBL. Eastern and northwestern counties in Pennsylvania. Grows 2 to 4 feet above water with light blue flowers in late summer to fall; full sun in mud at the margins of a pond or in containers of rich organic loams in a water garden under 3 to 5 inches of water; commonly available.

### Potamogeton amplifolius

**Bigleaf pondweed** — aquatic; waters of lakes, ponds, streams, and rivers, OBL. Eastern, south central and northwestern counties in Pennsylvania. Green flowers in summer; full sun in shallow ponds in silty loam; very few sources.

### Potamogeton natans

**Floating pondweed** — aquatic; quiet or slow-flowing waters of ponds, lakes, and streams, OBL. Northeastern and northwestern counties in Pennsylvania; scattered elsewhere. Stems to 6 feet and green flowers in summer; full sun in ponds in silty loam; very few sources.

### Potamogeton nodosus

**Longleaf pondweed** — aquatic; clear to turbid waters of lakes, streams, rivers, and sloughs, OBL. Mostly eastern counties in Pennsylvania; scattered elsewhere. Greenish-white flowers in summer. Serves as an oxygenator in water gardens; grow in aquatic containers of sandy loam or rooted in muddy pool bottoms at depth of 6 to 24 inches, full sun to part shade; very few sources.

### Potamogeton perfoliatus

**Perfoliate pondweed** — aquatic; lakes, streams, rivers, and bays. Scattered counties throughout Pennsylvania, mostly east. Green flowers in summer; full sun in water features and ponds in silty loam; very few sources.

### Potentilla arguta

**Tall cinquefoil** — dry upland rocky ledges, fields and woods, UPL. Scattered counties in Pennsylvania, mostly east and extreme west. Grows 15 to 40 inches with white flowers in early summer; sun to part shade in dry sandy loam; commonly available.

## Potentilla simplex

**Old-field cinquefoil** — dry upland woods, fields, meadows and along roadsides, FACU-. Throughout Pennsylvania. Prostrate stems to 20 inches with yellow flowers in late spring; sun to shade in dry, sandy loam. pH 5.5 to 7; very few sources.

## Potentilla tridentata

**Three-toothed cinquefoil, shrubby fivefingers** — dry ridge tops and in open woods. Pennsylvania distribution listed only as Monroe, Lackawanna and Luzerne Counties. Grows 1 to 10 inches with white flowers in summer; sun to part shade in dry to moist sandy loam, pH 5.5 to 7. AKA *Sibbaldiopsis tridentata*. Listed as endangered in Pennsylvania; very few sources.

## Prenanthes alba

**White rattlesnake root** — moist open woods, along shady roadsides and in thickets, FACU. Mostly eastern, south central and western counties in Pennsylvania. Grows up to 8 inches with white and pinkish-lavender flowers in late summer into fall; part shade to shade in moist, well-drained soils. AKA *Nabalus albus*; very few sources.

## Prunella vulgaris ssp. lanceolata

**Heal-all** — mesic fields, upland woods, floodplains, and along roadsides, FACU+. Throughout Pennsylvania. Grows up to 24 inches with violet-blue to pink or white flowers in summer and fall; sun to part sun in moist rich loam; several sources.

## Pycnanthemum incanum

**Mountain mint** — moist old fields, thickets, and barrens. Eastern, southwestern and extreme northwestern counties in Pennsylvania. Grows up to 36 inches, with purple to white flowers in late summer; sun to part sun in dry moist sandy loam; very few sources.

## Pycnanthemum muticum

**Mountain mint** — moist woods, thickets, meadows and swales, FACW. Mostly southeastern counties in Pennsylvania; scattered south and west. Grows 15 to 30 inches with purple to white flowers in late summer; sun to part shade in moist rich loam, pH 5.5 to 7.5; several sources.

## Pycnanthemum tenuifolium

**Mountain mint** — moist fields, stream banks and floodplains, FACW. Eastern, south central and southwestern counties in Pennsylvania; scattered elsewhere. Grows 20 to 30 inches with purple to white flowers in late summer; sun to part sun in moist rich loam; very few sources.

## Pycnanthemum virginianum

**Mountain mint** — boggy fields, moist woods and floodplains, FAC. Throughout Pennsylvania except northern tier and extreme southwestern counties. Grows up to 36 inches with purple to white flowers in late summer; sun to part shade in moist, sandy loam, pH 5.5 to 7; commonly available.

## Pyrola elliptica

**Shinleaf** — bogs, fens, swamps and moist to wet coniferous woods. Throughout Pennsylvania. Grows 6 to 12 inches with white flowers in early summer; part shade to shade in dry to moist acidic loam, pH 4 to 6; very few sources.

## Ranunculus fascicularis

**Early buttercup** — dry upland woods, grasslands and thickets, FACU. Scattered counties in Pennsylvania, mostly southeast. Grows 4 to 10 inches with yellow flowers in spring; sun to shade in dry sandy loam. Listed as endangered in Pennsylvania; very few sources.

## Ranunculus flammula var. ovalis

**Creeping spearwort** — muddy, wet ground, including shores to shallow water. Pennsylvania distribution limited to Pike, Northampton, Montour, Dauphin, Lancaster and Philadelphia counties. Prostrate stems to 20 inches with yellow flowers in summer; sun to part sun in moist to wet rich loam. Listed as extirpated in Pennsylvania; very few sources.

## Ranunculus hispidus var. hispidus

**Hairy buttercup** — rich dry to mesic woods, usually oak-hickory, and meadows, FAC. Throughout Pennsylvania. Grows 5 to 20 inches with yellow flowers in spring; sun to part shade in dry to moist rich loam, pH 5 to 6; very few sources.

## Ranunculus recurvatus

**Hooked crowfoot** — rich, low moist woods, FAC+. Throughout Pennsylvania. Grows 6 to 20 inches with yellow flowers in early summer; part shade to shade in moist rich loam; very few sources.

## Rhexia virginica

**Meadow beauty** or **Handsome Harry** — rich, acidic sandy soil in moist open areas, OBL. Mostly southeastern counties in Pennsylvania; scattered elsewhere along eastern Allegheny plateau. Grows 10 to 40 inches with dark pink flowers in late summer; sun to part shade in wet rich sandy loam; very few sources.

## Rudbeckia hirta

**Black-eyed Susan** — mesic prairies, plains, meadows, pastures, savannahs, woodland edges and openings, FACU-. Throughout Pennsylvania. Grows up to 36 inches with orange-yellow flowers in late summer. Two local varieties — *hirta* and *pulcherrima*; full sun in average, dry to medium, well-drained soils. Prefers moist, organically rich soils; commonly available.

## Rudbeckia laciniata

**Cutleaf coneflower** — moist, rich soils in fields, floodplains, open woods and thickets, FACW. Throughout Pennsylvania. Grows 2 to 9 feet with yellow flowers in late summer; sun to part shade in moist sandy loam, pH 5 to 7; commonly available.

## Rudbeckia triloba

**Three-lobed coneflower** — mesic to wet woodlands, thickets, pastures, roadsides, and meadows, frequently on limestone, FACU. Throughout Pennsylvania. Grows 18 to 60 inches with yellow to orange flowers in late summer; sun to part sun in dry to moist sandy loam; commonly available.

## Rumex altissimus

**Tall dock** — river bottomlands and wet woods margins in rich alluvial soils, FACW-. Scattered throughout Pennsylvania, mostly southeastern and northwestern counties. Grows up to 50 inches with reddish-green flowers in early summer; sun to part sun in moist, rich sandy loam; very few sources.

## Sagittaria graminea var. graminea

**Grass-leaved sagittaria** — aquatic; streams, lakes and mudflats, erect or immersed or submerged in shallow water. OBL. Eastern counties in Pennsylvania, especially northeast; scattered elsewhere. Blooms in summer; full sun in shallow water in silty soil; very few sources.

## Sagittaria latifolia var. latifolia

**Wapato,** or **duck potato** — aquatic; wet ditches, pools, and margins of streams, lakes and ponds, OBL. Throughout Pennsylvania. Grows 12 to 48 inches with white flowers in summer; plant in mud at the margins of a pond or in containers in a water garden, either along the shore or in up to 6 to 12 inches of water; commonly available.

## Sagittaria rigida

**Arrowhead** — aquatic; calcareous shallow water and shores of ponds, swamps, and rivers, occasionally in deep water, OBL. Scattered throughout Pennsylvania, especially eastern counties. Grows up to 3 feet with white flowers in late summer; plant in mud at pond edges or in containers in a water garden, either along the shore or in up to 6 to 12 inches of water; very few sources.

## Sanguinaria canadensis

**Bloodroot** — moist to dry upland woods and thickets, especially on flood plains and shores or near streams on slopes, FACU. Throughout Pennsylvania. Grows 2 to 6 inches with white flowers early spring; part shade to shade in dry to moist rich sandy loam, pH 5 to 7, and spreads to form small colonies; commonly available.

## Sanguisorba canadensis

**American burnet** — swamps, bogs, meadows and floodplains, FACW+. Mostly eastern, northwestern and south central counties in Pennsylvania; scattered elsewhere. Grows up to 50 inches with white flowers in summer; sun to part sun in moist to wet rich loam, pH 5.5 to 7; very few sources.

## Sarracenia purpurea

**Pitcher plant** — sphagnum bogs and peatlands, fens, swamps, wet conifer woodlands, lake and pond margins, OBL. Northern counties in Pennsylvania, especially northeast and northwest; scattered elsewhere. Grows 4 to 8 inches with maroon to red flowers in early summer; full sun in acidic, humusy muck that is constantly damp but not watery, pH 4.5 to 5.5; a carnivore requiring insects for nutrition, several sources.

### Saxifraga pensylvanica

**Swamp saxifrage** — wet woods, bogs and swamps, OBL. Throughout Pennsylvania. Grows 8 to 30 inches with greenish-white flowers in late spring; part shade in moist to wet circumneutral soils.; very few sources.

### Saxifraga virginiensis

**Early saxifrage** — rock crevices on dry to mesic rocky slopes, FAC-. Throughout Pennsylvania except extreme north central counties. Grows 4 to 12 inches with white flowers in spring; sun to part sun in dry to moist sandy loam, pH 5.5 to 7; very few sources.

### Scrophularia lanceolata

**Lanceleaf figwort** — low woods, thickets, stream banks, and along moist roadsides, FACU+. Throughout Pennsylvania except south central counties. Grows up to 6 feet, with yellowish-green flowers in summer; part shade to shade in moist, rich sandy loam; very few sources.

### Scrophularia marilandica

**Eastern figwort** — alluvial woods, river banks, moist shores and along roadsides, FACU-. Throughout Pennsylvania. Grows up to 10 feet with purple-brownish flowers in summer; part shade to shade in moist, rocky, rich loam; very few sources.

### Scutellaria integrifolia

**Hyssop skullcap** — swamps, bogs and moist fields, FACW. Southeastern and south central counties in Pennsylvania, including Monroe and Carbon counties. Grows 12 to 30 inches, blue flowers in late summer; sun to part sun in moist, silty loam; very few sources.

### Scutellaria lateriflora

**Mad-dog skullcap** — wet woods, stream banks and moist pastures, FACW+. Throughout Pennsylvania. Grows 12 to 30 inches, with blue flowers in late summer; sun to part sun in moist silty loam;

commonly available.

### Sedum ternatum

**Woodland stonecrop** — rocky banks, cliffs and woodlands, as well as damp sites along stream banks, bluff bases and stony ledges. Southeastern (including Monroe and Carbon), south central and western counties in Pennsylvania. Grows 3 to 6 inches with white flowers in early spring; average, medium, well-drained soils in full sun to part shade, pH 5 to 7; commonly available.

### Senecio aureus

**Golden ragwort** — floodplains and in moist fields and woods, FACW. Throughout Pennsylvania. Grows 12 to 32 inches with yellow flowers in early summer; sun to part shade in moist to wet rich loam. AKA *Packera aurea;* commonly available.

### Senecio obovatus

**Ragwort, squaw weed** — moist fields, meadows, upland woods and calcareous slopes. Western, south central and southeastern counties (including Carbon and Monroe) in Pennsylvania; scattered elsewhere Grows up to 30 inches with yellow flowers in early summer; sun to part shade in circumneutral humusy loam. AKA *Packera obvata;* very few sources.

### Senecio pauperculus

**Balsam ragwort** — moist meadows, peaty thickets, stream banks, prairies, meadows; in rocky, loamy soil; FAC. Eastern, south central and extreme southwestern counties in Pennsylvania. Grows up to 30 inches, with yellow flowers in early summer; sun to part sun in moist sandy rich loam. FAC. AKA *Packera paupercula*; very few sources.

### Senna hebecarpa

**Northern wild senna** — moist open woods, wetland edges, floodplains, and along roadsides, FAC. Throughout Pennsylvania except northern tier counties. Grows 3 to 6 feet with yellow flowers in summer; part sun to part shade in moist, rich sandy loam, pH 5.5 to 7; commonly available.

### Silene caroliniana

**Fire pink** — open, typically gravelly to rocky, usually deciduous woodlands. Throughout Pennsylvania except northern tier counties. Grows 9 to 12 inches with pink flowers in spring; average, dry to medium moisture, well-drained soils in full sun to part shade. Prefers sunny sites in dryish sandy or gravelly soils with some part afternoon shade; very few sources.

### Silene nivea

**Snowy campion** — mesic to moist alluvial woodlands and thickets, FAC. Widely scattered throughout Pennsylvania, mostly southern counties but including extreme northeast and northwest. Grows up to 8 to 12 inches, with white flowers in summer; sun to part sun in sandy, well-drained loam; very few sources.

### Silene stellata

**Starry campion** — wooded slopes, barrens and roadside banks. Throughout Pennsylvania except northern tier counties. Grows 12 to 36 inches with white flowers in summer; part sun to part shade in dry to moist sandy loam. pH 5 to 7; several sources.

### Sisyrinchium angustifolium

**Blue-eyed grass** — meadows, flood plains, moist fields, and mesic open woods. Throughout Pennsylvania. Grows up to 15 inches, with pale blue flowers in early summer; sun to part shade in moist sandy loam, pH 5 to 7; commonly available.

### Sisyrinchium montanum

**Blue-eyed grass** — dry to mesic open woods, roadsides and fields, FACW-. Northeastern counties in Pennsylvania; scattered elsewhere. Grows up to 20 inches, with violet flowers in early summer; sun to part shade in dry to moist sandy loam; several sources.

### Sium suave

**Water-parsnip** — swamps, bogs, wet meadows, pond margins, OBL. Scattered throughout Pennsylvania, mostly northern counties. Grows up to 6 feet with white flowers in late summer; full to part sun in moist to wet rich loams; very few sources.

### Solanum carolinense

**Horse-nettle** — dry to mesic fields, roadsides, sandy stream banks, UPL. Grows up to 3 feet with pale violet to white flowers in summer; full to part sun in average sandy loam. Considered a noxious weed in many western states; very few sources.

### Solidago altissima

**Canada goldenrod** — dry to moist soils in fields and river banks as well as disturbed areas such as roadsides, FACU-. Throughout Pennsylvania. Grows up to 6 feet, yellow flowers in late summer and fall; sun to part sun in dry, sandy loam; very few sources.

### Solidago bicolor

**Silver rod** — dry open woods. Throughout Pennsylvania. Grows up to 40 inches; white flowers in late summer to fall; part shade in dry sandy loam, pH 5 to 6; several sources.

### Solidago caesia

**Bluestem goldenrod** — dry upland open woods, thickets and clearings, FACU. Throughout Pennsylvania. Grows 18 to 36 inches with yellow flowers late summer to fall; part sun to shade in dry to moist rich loam, pH 5 to 7; commonly available.

### Solidago canadensis var. hargeri

**Canada goldenrod** — dry to mesic fields and along roadsides, FACU. Throughout Pennsylvania. Grows up to 6 feet with yellow flowers in late summer into fall; sun to part sun in dry to moist sandy loam; several sources.

### Solidago flexicaulis

**Zigzag goldenrod** — moist upland woods and rocky wooded slopes, FACU. Throughout Pennsylvania; scattered in central counties. Grows 18 to 36 inches with yellow flowers in late summer through fall; part shade to shade in moist rich loam, pH 5.5 to 7; commonly available.

### Solidago gigantea var. gigantea

**Smooth goldenrod** — moist fields, woods, and floodplains, FACW. Throughout Pennsylvania. Grows up to 6 feet with yellow flowers in late summer through fall; sun to part sun in dry to moist sandy loam; very few sources.

### Solidago juncea

**Early goldenrod** — fields, meadows, rocky banks and along roadsides. Throughout Pennsylvania. Grows up to 4 feet with yellow flowers in late summer to fall; sun to part sun in dry to moist sandy loam, pH 5 to 6; several sources.

### Solidago nemoralis

**Gray goldenrod** — fields, woods and roadsides in dry sterile soils. Throughout Pennsylvania. Grows up to 3 feet with yellow flowers late summer to fall; sun to part shade in dry sandy loam; commonly available.

### Solidago odora

**Sweet goldenrod, anise-scented goldenrod** — dry open woods and barrens. Eastern counties in Pennsylvania; also reported in Mercer County. Grows up to 4 feet with yellow flowers in late summer to fall; sun to part shade in dry to moist sandy loam, pH 4 to 6; several sources.

### Solidago patula

**Spreading goldenrod** — moist soils in swamp margins, boggy ground, wet meadows, roadside ditches, seeps, and the edges of wet woods, OBL. Mostly western and southeastern counties in Pennsylvania; scattered elsewhere. Grows up to 6 feet, with yellow flowers in late summer to fall; moist sandy loam in sun to part shade; very few sources.

### Solidago rugosa

**Wrinkle-leaf goldenrod** — woods, fields, floodplains and waste ground, FAC; two local varieties — *rugosa* and *villosa*. Throughout Pennsylvania. Grows up to 4 feet, with yellow flowers in late summer into fall; sun to part shade in moist sandy loam; pH 5.5 to 7; several sources.

### Solidago speciosa var. speciosa

**Showy goldenrod** — moist meadows and rocky woods and thickets. Scattered counties in Pennsylvania, mostly southeast. Grows up to 6 feet, with yellow flowers from late summer into fall; sun to part shade in dry to moist sandy loam, pH 6 to 7; commonly available.

### Solidago uliginosa var. uliginosa

**Bog goldenrod** — bogs and wet areas, fens, marshes, and sometimes in wet woods, OBL. Extreme eastern and northwestern counties in Pennsylvania; scattered elsewhere. Grows up to 5 feet with yellow flowers from late summer into fall; sun to part sun in moist, well drained soil; very few sources.

### Solidago ulmifolia var ulmifolia

**Elm-leaved goldenrod** — wooded slopes, roadside banks and shale barrens. Grows up to 4 feet, with yellow flowers in late summer to fall; sun to part shade in dry rocky sandy loam; very few sources.

### Spiranthes cernua

**Nodding ladies tresses** — wet to dry open sites in fens, marshes, meadows, swales, prairies, open woodlands, riverbanks, shores, ditches, roadsides, and moist old fields, FACW. Throughout Pennsylvania. Grows 5 to 15 inches with white flowers in late summer and early fall; sun to part sun in moist silty loam, pH 4.5 to 6.5; very few sources.

### Streptopus amplexifolius var. americanus

**Twisted stalk** — rich, moist, coniferous and deciduous woods, seepy outcrops, often near waterfalls, FAC+. Northeastern counties in Pennsylvania. Grows up to 36 inches with greenish-white flowers in summer; part shade to shade in rich loam, pH 5 to 6. Listed as endangered in Pennsylvania; very few sources.

### Streptopus roseus var. perspectus

**Rose mandaria** — cool to cold, moist woods and stream banks. Northern counties in Pennsylvania as well as southern counties on the Allegheny Plateau. Grows up to 24 inches, with pink-rose flowers in early summer; part shade to shade in moist rich loam, pH 5 to 6. AKA *Streptopus lanceolatus var lanceolatus*; very few sources.

### Symphyotrichum cordifolium

**Blue wood aster** — rich, dry or moist woodlands, bluff bases, stream banks and moist ledges. Throughout Pennsylvania. Grows up to 5 feet with pale blue flowers in late fall; part shade to shade in dry to moist sandy loam, pH 5.6 to 7.5; commonly available.

### Symphyotrichum ericoides

**White heath aster** — dry to mesic meadows and fields, FACU. Scattered counties in Pennsylvania, mostly south central and southeast. Grows 10 to 50 inches with white flowers in fall; sun to part sun in dry sandy loam; commonly available.

### Symphyotrichum laeve

**Smooth blue aster** — dry woods, rocky ledges. Mostly south central and eastern counties in Pennsylvania; scattered elsewhere. Grows 10 to 40 inches with pale to dark blue flowers in fall; sun to part shade in dry sandy loam, pH 4 to 7; commonly available.

### Symphyotrichum lateriflorum

**Calico aster** — mesic to moist old fields, edges of woods, rocky woods, and waste ground, FACW-. Throughout Pennsylvania. Grows 10 to 45 inches with white flowers in autumn; sun to part shade in moist sandy loam; pH 4 to 7, prefers 6.6 to 7; very few sources.

### Symphyotrichum novae-angliae

**New England aster** — moist prairies, meadows, thickets, low valleys and stream banks, FACW-. Throughout Pennsylvania. Grows 3 to 6 feet with purple flowers in fall; average, medium, well-drained soil in full sun. Prefers moist, rich soils, pH 5.5 to 7; commonly available.

### Symphyotrichum patens

**Late purple aster** — dry, sandy, moist, open woods and old fields. Eastern counties in Pennsylvania except northern tier; scattered elsewhere. Grows 15 to 45 inches with blue flowers in fall; part shade to shade in dry to moist sandy loam, pH 5 to 6; very few sources.

### Symphyotrichum prenanthoides

**Zig-zag aster** — swamps, stream banks and low woods, FAC. Throughout Pennsylvania. Grows 10 to 40 inches with blue to pale purple flowers in early fall; sun to part shade in moist, well-drained soil; very few sources.

### Symphyotrichum puniceum var. puniceum

**Purple-stemmed aster** — swampy ground of spring-fed meadows, stream banks and moist ditches, FACW. Throughout Pennsylvania. Grows up to 6 feet with blue flowers in early autumn; average, wet, well-drained soil in full sun. Listed as threatened in Pennsylvania; commonly available.

### Symphyotrichum undulatum

**Heart-leaved aster** — dry woods, sandy slopes and old fields. Throughout Pennsylvania. Grows 15 to 45 inches, with blue-violet flowers in autumn; sun to part shade in dry sandy loam; very few sources.

### Symplocarpus foetidus

**Skunk cabbage** — swamps, wet woods, along streams, and other wet low areas, OBL. Throughout Pennsylvania. Grows 1 to 3 feet with yellow-brown flowers in early spring; part sun to part shade in moist to wet humusy loam; pH 5 to 7; several sources.

### Taenidia integerrima

**Yellow pimpernel** — rocky upland woods, bluffs, thickets and slopes, as well as prairies and savannahs. Throughout Pennsylvania, mostly south and scattered elsewhere. Grows 16 to 32 inches with yellow flowers in early summer; part sun in poor, clay, rocky or sandy soils; very few sources.

### Tephrosia virginiana

**Goat's rue** — dry, sandy acidic woods. Eastern, south-central and southwestern counties in Pennsylvania. Grows 10 to 30 inches with yellow-white/pinkish purple flowers in summer; part sun to part shade in dry acidic sandy loam; several sources.

### Teucrium canadense var. virginicum

**Wild germander** — flood plains, lake margins, moist fields and meadows, FACW-. Throughout Pennsylvania. Grows 18 to 36 inches with purple to pink or cream color flowers in summer; sun to part sun in moist silty loam; very few sources.

### Thalictrum dioicum

**Early meadow-rue** — rich, mesic to moist rocky woods, ravines, alluvial terraces, especially on north-facing slopes, FAC. Throughout Pennsylvania. Grows 10 to 30 inches; greenish to purple flowers in spring; part sun to part shade in moist rich loam, pH 5 to 7; several sources.

### Thalictrum pubescens

**Tall meadow-rue** — rich mesic upland woods and wet meadows, thickets and stream banks, FACW+. Throughout Pennsylvania. Grows 2-10 feet with white to purplish flowers in summer; part sun to part shade in moist rich loam, pH 5.5 to 7; very few sources.

### Thalictrum revolutum

**Purple meadow-rue** — dry open woods, brushy banks, thickets and barrens, UPL. Mostly eastern, south-central and western counties in Pennsylvania. Grows 2 to 6 feet with white flowers in early summer; sun to part shade in dry sandy loam; very few sources.

### Thalictrum thalictroides

**Rue anemone** — rich, moist deciduous upland woods, wooded banks and thickets. Throughout Pennsylvania except for parts of northern tier counties. Grows 4 to 12 inches with white flowers, early spring; part shade to shade in rich humus, pH 4 to 7; goes dormant if the soil becomes too dry; commonly available.

### Tiarella cordifolia

**Foamflower** — moist, rocky deciduous woods and wooded slopes, FAC-. Northern, western and scattered southeastern counties in Pennsylvania. Grows 4 to 14 inches, white flowers in spring; part sun to part shade in moist rich loam. pH 5 to 7; commonly available.

### Tradescantia virginiana

**Spider lily** or **widows tears** — dry to mesic upland wooded slopes, shale outcrops and moist fields, FACU. Mostly southeastern counties in Pennsylvania; scattered elsewhere. Grows 12 to 36 inches with blue to purple flowers in spring; sun to part shade in moist, well-drained sandy loam. Prefers moist acidic soils, but tolerates poor soils; commonly available.

### Triadenum virginicum

**Marsh St. Johns Wort** — marshes, bogs, swampy woods, stream banks; OBL. Throughout Pennsylvania; mostly eastern counties, scattered

elsewhere. Grows 12 to 24 inches with pink to purple flowers in summer; mesic to moist rich loams in sun to part sun; very few sources.

### Trillium cernuum var cernuum

**Nodding trillium** — rich, moist, mixed deciduous-coniferous forests and swamps, FACW. Mostly southeastern counties on a line from Monroe to Franklin County; scattered elsewhere. Grows up to 15 inches with white flowers in spring; part shade to shade in moist rich humus, pH 5 to 6; very few sources.

### Trillium erectum var erectum

**Purple trillium** — cool, rich, moist neutral to acidic soils of upland deciduous forests, mixed deciduous-coniferous forests, and coniferous swamp borders, FACU-. Throughout Pennsylvania except for south central counties. Grows up to 15 inches with maroon flowers, spring; part shade to shade in moist rich loam; pH 4 to 7 but prefers 4.5 to 6; commonly available.

### Trillium grandiflorum

**Large flowered trillium** — rich deciduous or mixed coniferous-deciduous upland woods, floodplains, and along roadsides. Western counties in Pennsylvania; scattered in northeast, southeast. Grows up to 15 inches with white flowers becoming pink in spring; part shade to shade in moist rich loam. pH 6 to 7 but prefers 6.0; commonly available.

### Trillium sessile

**Toadshade trillium** — rich woodlands, calcareous, clayey alluvium on floodplains and riverbanks and less fertile soils in high, dry limestone woods, FACU-. Mostly southwestern counties in Pennsylvania; scattered elsewhere, including Monroe County. Grows up to 12 inches with maroon flowers in spring; part shade to shade in moist rich loam; commonly available.

### Trillium undulatum

**Painted trillium** — deep acidic humus in mixed deciduous-coniferous woods; prefers deep shade except at higher elevations, FACU. Northern counties in Pennsylvania; scattered elsewhere, including southwestern counties and along the eastern Appalachians in the southeast. Grows up to 15 inches with white flowers with rose-purple triangle in late spring; part shade to shade in moist rich loam, pH 4 to 6; several sources.

### Trollius laxus

**Spreading globe-flower** — rich, moist calcareous meadows, swamps and moist, open woods, OBL. Monroe, Lehigh, Northampton and Bucks County in eastern Pennsylvania; widely scattered elsewhere. Grows 4 to 20 inches with yellow flowers in spring; part sun to part shade in moist, rich loam. Listed as endangered in Pennsylvania; very few sources.

### Typha latifolia

**Common cat-tail** — swamps, marshes, wet shores, ditches, or wet soil, OBL. Throughout Pennsylvania. Grows 3 to 9 feet and blooms in early summer; rich loams in full sun to part shade in water to 12 inches deep. Because it is an aggressive colonizer, many plant them in underwater containers; commonly available.

### Urtica dioica ssp. gracilis

**Great nettle** — dry to mesic alluvial upland woods, margins of deciduous woodlands, along fencerows and in waste places, FACU. Eastern counties in Pennsylvania, extreme western counties and scattered elsewhere. Grows 3 to 6 feet with greenish flowers in late spring; part sun to part shade in moist, rich sandy loam; commonly available.

### Utricularia gibba

**Humped bladderwort** — aquatic; shallow water or exposed peat sand or mud flats, OBL. Scattered, mostly eastern counties, in Pennsylvania; widely scattered elsewhere. Yellow flowers in summer. An insectivore, water must be rich in microorganisms for it to survive; grow in full sun. Listed as extirpated in Pennsylvania; very few sources.

### Utricularia purpurea

**Purple bladderwort** — aquatic; suspended in lakes and ponds, OBL. Northeastern counties in Pennsylvania. Pink to purple flowers in late summer; full sun in soft, quiet water from shallow to more than 10 feet deep; very few sources.

### Uvularia perfoliata

**Bellwort** — dry to mesic upland deciduous woods and thickets in acid to neutral soils, FACU. Throughout Pennsylvania. Grows 6 to 18 inches with yellow flowers in spring; part sun to part shade in moist rich loam, pH 5 to 6; several sources.

### Uvularia sessilifolia

**Bellwort** — dry woods, moist hardwood coves, thickets and alluvial bottomlands, FACU-. Throughout Pennsylvania. Grows 6 to 18 inches with yellow flowers in spring; part sun to part shade in dry to moist sandy loam, pH 5 to 6; commonly available.

### Vallisneria americana var. americana

**Tape-grass** — aquatic; streams, lakes, rivers, OBL. Scattered throughout Pennsylvania, especially eastern and southern counties. Grows up to 12 inches, produces green flowers; full sun, rich silty loam covered with sand in water 12 inches deep. An important food source for turtles; several sources.

### Veratrum viride

**False hellebore** — moist to wet woods, stream banks and seeps, FACW+. Throughout Pennsylvania. Grows up to 4 feet, with green flowers in spring; part sun to part shade in moist, rich loam; very few sources.

### Verbena hastata

**Blue vervain** — moist to wet meadows, flood plains and wet river bottomlands, stream banks and the edges of sloughs, FACW+. Throughout Pennsylvania. Grows up to 4 feet, with blue flowers in summer; sun to part sun in moist rich loam; commonly available.

### Verbena urticifolia

**White vervain** — moist meadows, fields, woodland borders, gravelly seeps, abandoned fields and waste ground, especially after site disturbance, FACU. Throughout Pennsylvania. Grows up to 4 feet, white flowers in summer; part sun in moist to mesic fertile loam; very few sources.

### Vernonia noveboracensis

**New York ironweed** — stream banks and in

wet fields and pastures, FACW+. Throughout Pennsylvania except northern tier counties. Grows up to 6 feet, with brownish-purple flowers in summer; sun to part sun in moist rich loam, pH 5.5 to 7. Prefers rich, moist, slightly acidic soils; commonly available.

### Veronica americana

**American speedwell** — moist riverbanks and stream edges and in ditches, OBL. Throughout Pennsylvania. Grows 4 to 10 inches with light blue to violet flowers in summer and fall; part shade in moist, humusy loam; very few sources.

### Veronicastrum virginicum

**Culver's-root** — moist meadows, thickets and swamps, FACU. Northeastern, northwestern and southern counties in Pennsylvania. Grows up to 6 feet with white or pink flowers in summer; sun to part sun in moist rich loam, pH 5.5 to 7. Commonly available.

### Vicia americana

**Purple vetch** — dry to moist, gravelly shores, thickets, meadows, and roadside banks, FAC. Mostly eastern and south central counties just east of the Alleghenty Front. Grows up to 3 feet with blue to violet flowers in early summer; sun to part sun in moist rich loam; very few sources.

### Viola affinis

**LeConte's violet** — rich moist, especially alluvial, woods, FACW. Throughout Pennsylvania. except north-central counties. Grows up to 16 inches with blue-violet flowers in spring; sun to part shade in moist, sandy loam; very few sources.

### Viola bicolor

**Field pansy** — fields, dry open woods and floodplain terraces, FACU. Southern Pennsylvania counties including Luzerne and Monroe; scattered northwest. Grows up to 10 inches with pale blue flowers with yellow centers in spring; sun to part shade in dry to moist rich loam; very few sources.

### Viola blanda

**Sweet white violet** — moist woods and swamps, FACW. Throughout Pennsylvania. Grows up to 16 inches with white flowers in spring; sun

to part shade in moist rich sandy loam. Prefers humusy, moisture-retentive soils and forms large carpets in the wild by spreading through runners; very few sources.

### Viola canadensis

**Canada violet** — moist woods and swamps. Throughout Pennsylvania, except scattered in southeastern Pennsylvania. Grows up to 16 inches with white flowers with yellow centers in spring; part shade to shade in sandy humusy loam, pH 5 to 6.5. Naturalizes by vigorous seeding, not runners; very few sources.

### Viola cucullata

**Blue marsh violet** — bogs, meadows and swamps, FACW+. Throughout Pennsylvania. Grows up to 16 inches with pale purple flowers in spring; sun to part shade in moist to wet loam; very few sources.

### Viola cucullata x saggitata

**Blue marsh violet** — bogs, meadows and swamps. Throughout Pennsylvania. Grows up to 16 inches with blue to violet flowers in spring; part shade to shade in moist rich loam. AKA *Viola obiqua;* very few sources.

### Viola hirsutula

**Southern woodland violet** — open forests and forest clearings. Mostly southern counties in Pennsylvania; scattered north. Grows up to 16 inches with blue to violet flowers in spring; part shade in moist rich humusy loam; very few sources.

### Viola labradorica

**American dog violet** — moist woods and swamps, FAC. Throughout Pennsylvania. Grows up to 16 inches with pale blue flowers in spring; part sun to part shade in moist sandy humusy loam, pH 5 to 6.5. Aggressive spreader by runners and seeds; commonly available.

### Viola lanceolata var. lanceolata

**Lance-leaved violet** — moist, sandy shores, flats and bogs, OBL. Mostly a line of counties across central Pennsylvania from east to near west; scattered counties south. Grows up to 10 inches with white flowers in spring; sun to part shade in moist sandy loam; very few sources.

### Viola macloskeyi ssp. pallens

**Sweet white violet** — bogs, swamps and wet woods, OBL. Throughout Pennsylvania. Grows up to 10 inches with white flowers in spring; sun to part shade in moist, humusy loam; very few sources.

### Viola pedata

**Birdfoot violet** — sandy or rocky barrens and dry forested slopes, UPL. Eastern counties from Monroe County south, as well as south central counties, in Pennsylvania. Grows up to 16 inches with blue to violet flowers in spring; sun to part shade in dry to moist sandy loam, pH 4 to 7; commonly available.

### Viola pubescens var. pubescens

**Downy yellow violet** — dry to moist open woods and swamps, FACU. Throughout Pennsylvania. Grows up to 12 inches with yellow flowers in spring; part shade to shade in moist rich loam, pH 5 to 6; several sources.

### Viola rotundifolia

**Round-leaved violet** — cool moist woods and banks, FAC+. Throughout Pennsylvania except south central and far southwestern counties. Grows up to 10 inches with yellow flowers in spring; part shade to shade in moist humusy loam; soil should not dry out and prefers cooler climates. Freely self-seeds and can become weedy; very few sources.

### Viola sagittata var. ovata

**Ovate-leaved violet** — dry woods, fields and edges, FACW. Throughout Pennsylvania. Grows up to 12 inches with blue-violet flowers in spring; sun to part shade in dry to moist sandy loam; very few sources.

### Viola sagittata var. sagittata

**Arrow-leaved violet** — dry woods, fields and edges, FACW. Throughout Pennsylvania except scattered in southeastern counties. Grows up to 12 inches with blue-violet flowers in spring; sun to part shade in dry to moist rich sandy loam; very few sources.

### Viola sororia

**Common blue violet** — moist woods, swamps, thickets, FAC. Throughout Pennsylvania. Grows up to 12 inches with blue flowers in spring; part sun to part shade in moist rich loam, pH 7 to 8. No runners, but aggressively spreads by seed; commonly available.

### Viola striata

**Striped violet** — alluvial woods and alkaline swamps, FACW. Throughout Pennsylvania. Grows up to 12 inches with white flowers in spring; part sun to part shade in moist, rocky silty loam. No runners; spreads by seed; several sources.

### Waldsteinia fragarioides

**Barren strawberry** — moist rich woods and pastures. Throughout Pennsylvania, except scattered in southeastern counties. Forms a mat to 6 inches in height with yellow flowers in spring; average, medium, well-drained soil in full sun to part shade. Tolerates a wide range of soils, but prefers slightly acidic humusy soil; very few sources.

### Wolffia columbiana

**Water-meal** — aquatic; quiet waters of lakes, ponds, marshes, ditches and bogs. OBL. Mostly northwestern counties in Pennsylvania; scattered elsewhere throughout the state. Grow in full sun in moderate to fertile shallow water; plant in silty loam; very few sources.

### Zizia aptera

**Golden-alexander** — woodlands, wooded slopes, thickets, glades, prairies, clearings and roadsides, FAC. Throughout Pennsylvania except along the northern and western boundaries. Grows 12 to 30 inches with yellow flowers in late spring; part sun to part shade in dry to moist rich loam, pH 5.5 to 7; commonly available.

### Zizia aurea

**Golden-alexander** — moist woods and meadows, thickets, glades and prairies; wooded bottomland, stream banks, floodplains; FAC-. Throughout Pennsylvania. Grows 12 to 32 inches with yellow flowers in late spring; average, medium moisture, well-drained soils in full sun to part shade; pH 5.5 to 7; commonly available.

## Other commonly available species

The following species are commonly available native herbaceous perennials whose range includes Pennsylvania, but have not been reported as observed in the northeastern counties. They are generally quite adaptable to regional climate and reasonable to include in the native plant landscape.

***Allium cernuum*** (Nodding onion) — Wide distribution on moist soils in cool mountainous regions. Pennsylvania range is along a line extending from the Wyoming Valley south along the central Appalachians and into southwestern counties. White flowers in spring. Grow in well-drained soil, especially sandy loams in full sun to light shade; does best in full sun with light afternoon shade and will naturalize by self-seeding and bulb offsets.

***Anemone canadensis*** (Canada anemone) — Moist thickets and open woodlands, meadows and wet prairies, clearings and the shores of lakes and streams; occasionally in swampy areas. FACW. Range in Pennsylvania includes Wyoming and Lehigh Valleys, south central and far western counties. White flowers in early summer. Best in moist, humusy but well-drained soils in part shade; tolerates full sun. A very aggressive spreader (rhizomes and seed), ideal for naturalizing large areas, but a favorite browse of deer.

***Anemone cylindrica*** (Thimbleweed) — Dry open woods, prairies, pastures, roadsides. Pennsylvania native range identified only as Erie and Centre counties. Listed as endangered in Pennsylvania. Grow in sun to part shade in dry, rocky soils.

***Aruncus dioicus*** (Goat's-beard, bride's feathers) — Most, rich woods in mountainous areas, FACU. Pennsylvania native range includes most of the southwestern and western counties. White flowers in late spring; grows to 4 to 6 feet, open habit. Grow in part shade in rich, medium to wet well-drained soils; tolerates flooding. Often found in better garden centers.

***Baptisia australis*** (Blue false-indigo) — Edges of woods, prairies and limestone glades in circumneutral soils. Native range includes Luzerne and Montgomery counties, as well as higher elevation counties in western Pennsylvania. Purple flowers in late spring. Grow in well drained, dry to medium circumneutral soils in full sun (best) to part shade. Drought and poor-soil tolerant.

***Boltonia asteroides*** (Aster-like boltonia) — Moist to wet, gravelly to sandy sites in full sun. FACW. Pennsylvania native range identified as Dauphin, York and Lancaster counties; listed as endangered in Pennsylvania. Grow in well-drained, medium soils, toward dryer and less fertile soils. Rich moist soils will result in plants that tend to flop and need support; poor dry soils will result in shorter plants with smaller flowers.

***Cacalia muhlenbergii*** (Great Indian-plantain) — Wet to mesic prairies and savannahs. Pennsylvania range listed ass Northampton, York, Lancaster, Perry and southwestern counties (except Greene). White flowers in summer; grows to 8 feet. Grow in full sun in moist, rich well-drained loam. AKA *Arnoglossum reniforme*.

***Cypripedium reginae*** (Large white lady's slipper) — Hardwood and coniferous fen forests and meadows, hillside seeps, fen and moist meadows, wet prairies and seeping cliffs. FACW. Listed as threatened in Pennsylvania and threatened to endangered in most other states. Pennsylvania range includes Northampton County, central Appalachian counties, and the far northwest. The largest and most showy of the native orchids, with white and pink flowers in late spring to early summer. Grow in full sun to part shade in moist to wet rich, circumneutral soils.

***Dodecatheon meadia*** (Shooting-star) — wet to dry prairies and moist open rocky woods and rocky slopes. FACU. Pennsylvania range is identified as Columbia, Butler, Allegheny, Bedford, Fulton, Franklin and Perry Counties; listed as endangered. White, pink and rarely purple flowers. Grow in medium, well-drained (especially sandy) soils in sun to full shade; prefers moist, humusy soils in part shade. Intolerant of poor wet soils, especially in winter and reputed to be slow and difficult to grow from seed.

***Eupatorium coelestinum*** (Mistflower) — Along streams, in low woods and woods margins, wet meadows, ditches. FAC. In Pennsylvania, native range extends from the Lehigh Valley south and then westward along the southern tier, except for higher elevations. Pale blue flowers in late summer. Grow in well-drained, medium moist soils in full sun to part shade; prefers full sun. Aggressive spreader through rhizomes and will form large colonies. Cut back in summer for denser habit.

***Helianthus occidentalis*** (Sunflower) — Prairies, dry meadows, fields, glades and occasionally rocky open woods. UPL. Yellow flowers in summer, 2 to 4 feet. Pennsylvania native range identified only as Warren County. Grow in dry to medium, well drained soils in full sun. Tolerates a wide range of dry to moist soils, but intolerant of heavy clays. Spreads by rhizomes to form large colonies.

***Hibiscus moscheutos*** (Rose-mallow) — Marshes, wet meadows, swampy open forests. OBL. Pennsylvania range extends from the Lehigh Valley into southeastern counties, and scattered in western counties. Large white flowers with crimson center in summer, 3 to 8 feet. Very late to appear in spring, then grows rapidly. Best in moist soils rich in organic matter; soil should not dry out and regular watering with fertilization helps. Tolerates light shade, but does best in full sun with good air circulation.

***Hydrastis canadensis*** (Goldenseal) — Mesic deciduous forests, often on clay soils. Native Pennsylvania range extends across the southern half of the state except for highest elevations and along the Ohio border. Endangered in many states, threatened in Pennsylvania, mostly because of harvesting as an herbal medicine. Tiny white flowers in spring, followed by dramatic red fruit. Grow in well drained, medium soil in part shade; prefers soils well composted with much leaf mold.

***Iris cristata*** (Dwarf crested iris) — Typically on calcareous soils in rich woods, ravines and bluffs. Endangered in Pennsylvania, with native range limited to scattered southern counties. Pale blue to purple flowers in spring, rarely white. Grow in well drained soil rich in organic matter and with medium moisture, full sun to part shade; prefers part shade and will tolerate close to full shade; if grown in full sun, keep soil constantly moist. Does well on well-drained slopes.

***Jeffersonia diphylla*** (Twinleaf) — Open rocky slopes and outcrops as well as rich moist woods, typically over limestone or other calcareous rock. Pennsylvania range includes far southwest-

ern, central southern and southeastern counties (including Northampton, Bucks and Montgomery). Very brief bloom with a single white flower in early spring; generally grown for its unique foliage. Grow in well-drained, circumneutral humusy soils in part shade; tolerates full shade. Soil should not dry out, and a summer mulch helps keep roots cool. Ideal sites are under canopies of large deciduous trees.

***Lilium superbum*** (Turk's-cap lily) — Moist meadows and thickets, pine barrens, swamp edges and bottoms, gaps and openings in rich forests. FACW+. The largest native lily in the eastern U.S., typically yellow-orange with maroon spots. Pennsylvania range includes most of the state except for northeastern counties and the Lehigh Valley. Grow in well-drained average soils that are medium to wet in full sun to filtered sun; best in moist, humusy soils that do not dry out. Mulch to keep roots cool. Stoloniferous, and plants can spread to form colonies if growing conditions are optimal.

***Mertensia virginica*** (Virginia bluebells) — River bottoms and floodplains, moist woodlands and forest clearings. FACW. Pennsylvania range includes much of the state, including counties west and south of the Poconos, except for the highest elevations in the Alleghenies. Grow in well-drained, average moist soil in part shade to full shade; prefers rich, moist soils. Blue flowers in very early spring before leaves are out; foliage dies back to the ground when the plant goes dormant in early summer. Slowly spreads by rhizomes, but freely from seed.

***Monarda punctata*** (Spotted bee-balm) — Savannahs, prairies, meadows and pastures; UPL; endangered in Pennsylvania. Identified in Pennsylvania only in Allegheny, Northumberland, Delaware and Philadelphia counties. Greenish pink flowers in spring to summer. Grow in full sun in dry, sandy circumneutral soils. Drought tolerant and like all Monarda, susceptible to powdery mildew.

***Nelumbo lutea*** (American lotus) — Ponds, lakes, marsh pools and swamps, as well as backwaters of reservoirs and lingering ponds in floodplains of major rivers. OBL. Creamy-white flowers in late spring to early summer. Pennsylvania range identified only as Westmoreland, Dauphin,

Delaware and Philadelphia counties. Grow in any still-water pond or submerged pot; saucer-shaped leaves are up to 12 inches in diameter and plant requires room to spread/reproduce.

***Parthenium integrifolium*** (American fever-few, wild quinine) — Dry to mesic woodlands and prairies. Pennsylvania native range has been identified only as McKean, Cambria, Fulton, Adams and Bucks counties; considered extirpated in Pennsylvania. White flowers in early summer. Grow in well-drained, dry to medium average soils in full sun.

***Phlox divaricata ssp. divaricata*** (Wild blue phlox, Sweet William) — Rich, moist deciduous forests and bluffs, FACU. Pennsylvania native range includes most of the state except for the eastern northern tier and northeastern counties. Flowers range from white to light blue to purple in spring. Grow in a well-drained, medium moisture humusy soil in part shade to full shade; prefers richly organic moist soils and light summer mulch to cool roots and retain moisture.

***Phlox pilosa*** (Downy phlox) — Dry open woodlands, prairies, roadsides and thickets. FACU. Native range includes the Lehigh Valley and southeastern counties in Pennsylvania, where it is listed as endangered. Lavender flowers in spring. Grow in sun to part shade in sandy to rocky slightly acidic, well-drained soils.

***Ratibida pinnata*** (Prairie coneflower) — Prairies and thickets, as well as woodland edges. Native range in Pennsylvania identified as Bucks County and several bordering Ohio; listed as extirpated. Yellow flowers in summer; grow in well-drained medium moisture average soils in full sun. Prefers sandy and clay soils, but tolerates poor, dry soils. Grow in average, medium moisture, well-drained soil in full sun. Prefers clay or sandy soils. Tolerates poor, dry soils.

***Rudbeckia fulgida var. fulgida*** (Eastern cone-flower, black-eyed Susan) — Prairies, pastures, open woods; FAC. Native range in Pennsylvania is primarily from the Lehigh Valley southeast to Philadelphia and along the eastern southern tier. Yellow to orange flowers in summer. Tolerant of hot, humid summers and some light shade; grow in well-drained, dry to medium average soil in full sun. Deadhead to prolong bloom and divide when clumps become overcrowded.

***Ruellia humilis*** (Fringed-leaved petunia) — Woodland openings and edges, thickets; UPL. Only Pennsylvania listing as native is in Franklin County; endangered in Pennsylvania and several nearby states. Pale lavender flowers throughout summer, especially if kept moist. Grow in well-drained, dry to medium moisture average soils in full sun to part shade.

***Salvia lyrata*** (Lyre-leaved sage) — rock, rich open woods, wet to dry meadows and alluvial areas, in well-drained sand or loam. UPL. Pennsylvania distribution ranges across the southern tier of counties. Purple flowers in late spring. Medium to wet average soils in full sun; prefers moist sandy soils, and tolerates very light shade. Tolerates heat and humidity and self seeds to naturalize in optimal circumstances.

***Saururus cernuus*** (Lizard's-tail) — Wet soils and mud in lowlands and stream and lake edges, including still standing fresh or slightly brackish water to a depth of 6 inches; OBL. Pennsylvania range includes southern tier counties from Bedford eastward and the extreme northwestern counties. White flowers in late summer. In water gardens, plant in containers in shallow water, about 6 inches deep. In natural ponds, plan in sandy to muddy pond margins under shallow water or in boggy, moist soil. Prefers full sun to part shade, but will flower in full shade. Rhizomes spread to create colonies.

***Senna marilandica*** (Southern wild senna) — Dry open woods, openings and thickets; FAC+. Pennsylvania range is scattered counties along the southern tier, especially in the far west and east. Grow in well-drained sandy to clay medium moisture loams in full sun.

***Silene virginica*** (Fire pink) — Moist deciduous woodland slopes and bluffs. Pennsylvania distribution includes far western counties, as well as Centre County. Red flowers in late spring. Grow in well drained, dry to medium moisture average soil in full sun to part shade; prefers moist, sandy to clay soils in part shade and excellent drainage.

***Solidago rigida*** (Stiff goldenrod) — Dry fields and prairies; UPL. Pennsylvania range includes scattered counties to the west and south of the Poconos; listed as endangered in Pennsylvania and nearby states. Yellow flowers in late summer to fall. Grow in full sun in well-drained, medium to dry moisture average soil.

***Solidago erecta*** (Slender goldenrod) — Dry woods, disturbed open soils, road embankments. Pennsylvania distribution includes several extreme southern tier counties; listed as endangered in Pennsylvania. AKA *Solidago speciosa var. erecta*. Grow in well-drained sandy to rocky soils in full sun.

***Spiranthes vernalis*** (Spring ladies tresses) — Old fields, dry to moist meadows and dune hollows, along roadsides; FAC. Pennsylvania range includes Lancaster, Chester, Montgomery, Delaware and Philadelphia counties; listed as endangered in Pennsylvania. Grow in full sun to part shade in medium moist, rich well-drained soil

***Symphyotrichum novi-belgii var. novi-belgii*** (New York aster) — Meadows, damp thickets, shorelines; FACW+. Pennsylvania native distribution includes Lackawanna County, Northampton County and southeastern counties; listed as threatened in the state. Flowers range from white to blue and bloom in late summer. Grow in well-drained, moist, average soils in full sun.

***Symphyotrichum oblongifolium*** (Aromatic aster) — Fields, prairies and openings, typically over limestone substrates. Pennsylvania native range includes the central Appalachians in the southern half of the state as well as far southwestern counties. Grow in well drained, dry to medium average soils in full sun; prefers sandy soils and tolerates poor soils and drought.

***Thalictrum dasycarpum*** (Purple meadow-rue) — Deciduous woodlands along streams, damp thickets, swamps, and wet meadows and prairies; FACW. Pennsylvania range listed as Warren and Forest counties. Purple-white flowers in late spring. Grow in well-drained, medium moisture average soils in full sun to part shade; prefers rich humusy and moist soil in dappled light. Intolerant of hot and humid conditions.

***Tradescantia ohiensis*** (Spiderwort, Blue-jacket) — fields, thickets, rarely in woodlands, sometimes along streams; FAC. Pennsylvania range includes southeastern counties and central western counties; listed as endangered in the state. Blue flowers in early summer. Grow in well-drained dry to medium average soil in full sun to

part shade; prefers acidic moist sandy soil in full sun. Can be divided to correct overcrowding and cut back to 6-12 inches in summer to encourage new growth and possible fall bloom.

***Typha angustifolia*** (Narrow-leaved cat-tail) — wet meadows, fens, estuaries, marshes, bogs, ditches, and along lake shores; OBL. Pennsylvania range is primarily in counties to the south and west of the Poconos, as well as in western counties. Grow in moist to wet rich organic soils, including shallow standing water, in full sun.

***Uvularia grandiflora*** (Bellwort) — Rich, moist, deciduous forests and thickets, and forested floodplains. Distribution in Pennsylvania is generally along the northern tier west from Bradford County to the Ohio line and then south. Yellow flowers in spring. Grow in well-drained medium moisture average soils in part shade to full shade; prefers humusy, moist soil in part shade.

### Possibly challenging to find

The following 104 species, whose range includes Pennsylvania but observed distribution does not include Carbon, Monroe, Pike or Wayne counties, are reported as commercially available but from very few retail sources:

*Achillea ptarmica* (Sneezeweed)
*Aconitum uncinatum* (Blue monkshood)
*Acorus americanus* (Sweet flag)
*Actaea podocarpa* (American bugbane)
*Aletris farinosa* (Colic-root)
*Alisma triviale* (Broad-leaved water-plantain)
*Antennaria virginica* (Shale-barren pussy-toe)
*Arisaema dracontium* (Green-dragon)
*Aristida purpurascens* (Arrow-feather)
*Blephilia ciliata* (Wood-mint)
*Cacalia suaveolens* (Sweet-scented Indian-plantain)
*Calamintha arkansana* (Calamint)
*Camassia scilloides* (Wild hyacinth)
*Cardamine maxima* (Large toothwort)
*Chrysogonum virginianum* (Green-and-gold)
*Chrysopsis mariana* (Golden aster)
*Clintonia umbellulata* (Speckled wood-lily)
*Commelina erecta* (Erect dayflower)
*Cypripedium candidum* (Small white lady's-slipper)
*Delphinium exaltatum* (Tall Larkspur)

*Delphinium tricorne* (Dwarf larkspur)
*Desmodium sessilifolium* (Sessile-leaved tick-trefoil)
*Diarrhena americana* (American beakgrain)
*Diarrhena obovata* (American beakgrain)
*Disporum lanuginosum* (Yellow mandarin)
*Echinacea laevigata* (Appalachian cone-flower)
*Elephantopus carolinianus* (Elephant's foot)
*Eryngium aquaticum* (Marsh eryngo)
*Erythronium albidum* (White trout-lily)
*Eupatorium altissimum* (Tall eupatorium)
*Eupatorium aromaticum* (Small-leaved white-snakeroot)
*Euphorbia purpurea* (Glade spurge)
*Euthamia tenuifolia* (Grass-leaved golden-rod)
*Gentiana alba* (Yellowish gentian)
*Gentiana villosa* (Striped gentian)
*Helianthus angustifolius* (Swamp sunflower)
*Helianthus hirsutus* (Sunflower)
*Helianthus microcephalus* (Small wood sun-flower)
*Hibiscus laevis* (Halberd-leaved rose-mallow)
*Houstonia longifolia* (Long-leaved bluets)
*Houstonia purpurea var. purpurea* (Purple bluets)
*Houstonia serpyllifolia* (Creeping bluets)
*Hydrocotyle umbellata* (Water pennywort)
*Iris virginica* (Southern blue flag)
*Justicia americana* (Water-willow)
*Lathyrus japonicus var. glaber* (Beach pea)
*Lathyrus venosus* (Veiny pea)
*Lespedeza hirta x intermedia* (Nuttall's bush-clover)
*Lespedeza hirta x procumbens* (Bush-clover)
*Lespedeza hirta x virginica* (Bush-clover)
*Liatris scariosa* (Northern blazing-star)
*Lithospermum caroliniense* (Golden puccoon)
*Lobelia puberula* (Downy lobelia)
*Lobelia spicata* (Spiked lobelia)
*Ludwigia peploides ssp. glabrescens* (Primrose-willow)
*Lythrum alatum* (Winged loosestrife)
*Meehania cordata* (Heart-leafed meehania)
*Mimulus alatus* (Winged monkey-flower)
*Onosmodium molle var. hispidissimum* (False gromwell)
*Pedicularis lanceolata* (Swamp lousewort)
*Penstemon canescens* (Beard-tongue)
*Penstemon laevigatus* (Eastern beard-tongue)
*Phlox maculata ssp. pyramidalis* (Meadow phlox)
*Phyla lanceolata* (Fog-fruit)
*Platanthera dilatata* (Tall white bog-orchid)
*Polygonum punctatum var. punctatum* (Dotted smartweed)
*Potamogeton pectinatus* (Sago pondweed)
*Potamogeton praelongus* (White-stem pond-weed)
*Potentilla anserina* (Silverweed)
*Potentilla fruticosa* (Shrubby cinquefoil)
*Prenanthes racemosa* (Glaucous rattle-snake-root)
*Ranunculus hispidus var. nitidus* (Hairy buttercup)
*Rhexia mariana* (Maryland meadow-beauty)
*Rudbeckia fulgida var. speciosa* (Coneflower)
*Ruellia caroliniensis* (Carolina petunia)
*Ruellia strepens* (Limestone petunia)
*Rumex verticillatus* (Swamp dock)
*Sagittaria subulata* (Subulate arrowhead)
*Saxifraga micranthidifolia* (Lettuce saxifrage)
*Scutellaria incana* (Downy skullcap)
*Scutellaria leonardii* (Small skullcap)
*Scutellaria serrata* (Showy skullcap)
*Silphium trifoliatum var. trifoliatum* (Whorled rosinweed)
*Sisyrinchium albidum* (Blue-eyed-grass)
*Sisyrinchium atlanticum* (Eastern blue-eyed-grass)
*Solidago curtisii* (Curtis's goldenrod)
*Solidago roanensis* (Mountain goldenrod)
*Spiranthes casei* (Case's ladies'-tresses)
*Stachys palustris ssp. pilosa* (Hedge-nettle)
*Swertia caroliniensis* (American columbo)
*Symphyotrichum drummondii var. drummondii* (Hairy heart-leaved aster)
*Symphyotrichum praealtum* (Veiny-lined aster)
*Symphyotrichum shortii* (Short's aster)
*Thaspium trifoliatum var. trifoliatum* (Meadow-parsnip)

*Tipularia discolor* (Cranefly orchid)
*Trautvetteria caroliniensis* (Carolina tassel-rue)
*Trillium cuneatum* (Huger's trillium)
*Trillium flexipes* (Declined trillium)
*Triosteum perfoliatum* (Horse-gentian)
*Utricularia resupinata* (Northeastern bladderwort)
*Verbesina alternifolia* (Wingstem)
*Vernonia gigantea var. gigantea* (Ironweed)
*Vernonia glauca* (Appalachian ironweed)
*Veronica officinalis* (Common speedwell)

## Apparently unavailable

The following 366 species of native plants whose range includes Pennsylvania are apparently unavailable in the commercial marketplace on a national scale:

*Aconitum reclinatum* (White monkshood)
*Agrimonia gryposepala* (Agrimony)
*Agrimonia microcarpa* (Small-fruited agrimony)
*Agrimonia pubescens* (Downy agrimony)
*Agrimonia rostellata* (Woodland agrimony)
*Alopecurus aequalis* (Short-awned foxtail)
*Ambrosia psilostachya* (Western ragweed)
*Amianthium muscaetoxicum* (Fly-poison)
*Angelica triquinata* (Angelica)
*Angelica venenosa* (Deadly angelica)
*Antennaria howellii ssp. canadensis* (Howell's pussytoe)
*Antennaria solitaria* (Solitary pussytoe)
*Apocynum florabundum* (Dogbane)
*Aralia hispida* (Bristly sarsaparilla)
*Arethusa bulbosa ssp. leptoclados* (Dragon's-mouth)
*Arnica acaulis* (Leopard's-bane)
*Asclepias quadrifolia* (Four-leaved milkweed)
*Asclepias rubra* (Red milkweed)
*Aureolaria flava var. macrantha* (Yellow false-foxglove)
*Aureolaria laevigata* (False-foxglove)
*Boehmeria cylindrica var. cylindrica* (False nettle)
*Boehmeria cylindrica var. drummondiana* (False nettle)
*Brickellia eupatorioides* (False boneset)
*Callitriche heterophylla* (Water-starwort)

*Callitriche palustris* (Water-starwort)
*Calystegia sepium* (Hedge bindweed)
*Calystegia spithamaea ssp. spithamaea* (Low bindweed)
*Campanula aparinoides* (Marsh bellflower)
*Cardamine angustata* (Toothwort)
*Cardamine bulbosa* (Bittercress)
*Cardamine concatenata* (Toothwort)
*Cardamine douglassii* (Purplecress)
*Cardamine rotundifolia* (Mountain watercress)
*Cerastium arvense var. villosissimum* (Serpentine barrens chickweed)
*Ceratophyllum muricatum* (Hornwort)
*Chrysosplenium americanum* (Golden saxifrage)
*Cicuta bulbifera* (Water-hemlock)
*Circaea alpina x lutetiana* (Enchanter's-nightshade)
*Circaea lutetiana ssp. canadensis* (Enchanter's-nightshade)
*Circaea x laneyi* (Enchanter's-nightshade)
*Cirsium discolor* (Field thistle)
*Cirsium pumilum* (Pasture thistle)
*Coeloglossum viride var. virescens* (Frog orchid)
*Comandra umbellata* (Bastard toadflax)
*Commelina virginica* (Virginia dayflower)
*Conioselinum chinense* (Hemlock-parsley)
*Corallorhiza maculata* (Spotted coralroot)
*Corallorhiza odontorhiza* (Autumn coralroot)
*Corallorhiza trifida* (Early coralroot)
*Corallorhiza wisteriana* (Wister's coralroot)
*Cryptogramma stelleri* (Slender rockbrake)
*Cynoglossum virginianum* (Wild comfrey)
*Dalibarda repens* (Dewdrop)
*Decodon verticillatus* (Water-willow)
*Desmodium canescens* (Hoary tick-trefoil)
*Desmodium ciliare* (Tick-clover)
*Desmodium cuspidatum* (Tick-clover)
*Desmodium laevigatum* (Smooth tick-clover)
*Desmodium marilandicum* (Maryland tick-clover)
*Desmodium nudiflorum* (Naked-flowered tick-trefoil)
*Desmodium nuttallii* (Nuttall's tick-trefoil)
*Desmodium obtusum* (Tick-trefoil)
*Desmodium perplexum* (Tick-trefoil)

*Desmodium rotundifolium* (Round-leaved tick-trefoil)

*Desmodium viridiflorum* (Velvety tick-trefoil)

*Doellingeria infirma* (Flat-topped white aster)

*Elodea nuttallii* (Waterweed)

*Elodea schweinitzii* (Schweinitz's waterweed)

*Epifagus virginiana* (Beechdrops)

*Epilobium ciliatum* (Willow-herb)

*Epilobium leptophyllum* (Willow-herb)

*Epilobium palustre* (Marsh willow-herb)

*Erigenia bulbosa* (Harbinger-of-spring)

*Eriocaulon aquaticum* (Seven-angle pipewort)

*Eriocaulon decangulare* (Ten-angle pipewort)

*Eriocaulon parkeri* (Parkers's pipewort)

*Eupatorium album* (White-bracted eupatorium)

*Eupatorium pilosum* (Ragged eupatorium)

*Euphorbia ipecacuanhae* (Wild ipecac)

*Eurybia radula* (Rough aster)

*Eurybia schreberi* (Schreber's aster)

*Eurybia spectabilis* (Showy aster)

*Fimbristylis puberula* (Hairy fimbry)

*Galium asprellum* (Rough bedstraw)

*Galium circaezans var. circaezans* (Wild licorice)

*Galium circaezans var. hypomalacum* (Wild licorice)

*Galium concinnum* (Shining bedstraw)

*Galium labradoricum* (Bog bedstraw)

*Galium lanceolatum* (Wild licorice)

*Galium latifolium* (Purple bedstraw)

*Galium obtusum* (Cleavers)

*Galium palustre* (Ditch bedstraw)

*Galium pilosum* (Bedstraw)

*Galium tinctorium* (Bedstraw)

*Galium trifidum* (Cleavers)

*Galium triflorum* (Sweet-scented bedstraw)

*Gentiana catesbaei* (Coastal plain gentian)

*Gentiana linearis* (Narrow-leaved gentian)

*Gentiana saponaria* (Soapwort gentian)

*Geranium bicknellii* (Cranesbill)

*Geranium carolinianum* (Wild geranium)

*Geum canadense var. canadense* (White avens)

*Geum virginianum* (Cream-colored avens)

*Gnaphalium sylvaticum* (Woodland cudweed)

*Goodyera repens* (Lesser rattlesnake-plantain)

*Goodyera tesselata* (Checkered rattlesnake-plantain)

*Gratiola aurea* (Goldenpert)

*Helianthemum propinquum* (Frostweed)

*Heteranthera reniformis* (Mud-plantain)

*Heuchera pubescens* (Alum-root)

*Hieracium gronovii* (Hawkweed)

*Hieracium gronovii x venosum* (Hawkweed)

*Hieracium paniculatum* (Hawkweed)

*Hieracium scabrum* (Hawkweed)

*Hieracium traillii* (Green's hawkweed)

*Hieracium venosum* (Rattlesnake-weed)

*Hottonia inflata* (American featherfoil)

*Houstonia canadensis* (Fringed bluets)

*Hybanthus concolor* (Green-violet)

*Hydrocotyle ranunculoides* (Floating pennywort)

*Hydrophyllum macrophyllum* (Large-leaved waterleaf)

*Hypericum adpressum* (Creeping St.John's-wort)

*Hypericum boreale* (Dwarf St.John's-wort)

*Hypericum denticulatum* (Coppery St.Johns-wort)

*Hypericum dissimulatum* (St.John's-wort)

*Hypericum ellipticum* (Pale St. John's-wort)

*Hypericum ellipticum* (Pale St. John's-wort)

*Hypericum mutilum* (Dwarf St. John's-wort)

*Hypericum sphaerocarpum* (St. John's-wort)

*Iodanthus pinnatifidus* (Purple-rocket)

*Ipomoea pandurata* (Man-of-the-earth)

*Isoetes appalachiana* (Appalachian quillwort)

*Isoetes valida* (Carolina quillwort)

*Isotria medeoloides* (Small whorled-pogonia)

*Isotria verticillata* (Whorled-pogonia)

*Lathyrus ochroleucus* (Wild pea)

*Lechea intermedia* (Pinweed)

*Lechea minor* (Thyme-leaved pinweed)

*Lechea pulchella* (Pinweed)

*Lechea racemulosa* (Pinweed)

*Lechea villosa* (Pinweed)

*Lemna obscura* (Little water duckweed)

*Lemna perpusilla* (Duckweed)

*Lemna turionifera* (Winter duckweed)

*Lespedeza angustifolia* (Narrow-leaved bush-clover)
*Lespedeza intermedia* (Bush-clover)
*Lespedeza procumbens* (Trailing bush-clover)
*Lespedeza repens* (Creeping bush-clover)
*Lespedeza stuevei* (Tall bush-clover)
*Ligusticum canadense* (Lovage)
*Linum intercursum* (Sandplain wild flax)
*Linum medium var. medium* (Yellow flax)
*Linum medium var. texanum* (Yellow flax)
*Linum virginianum* (Slender yellow flax)
*Liparis liliifolia* (Lily-leaved twayblade)
*Liparis loeselii* (Yellow twayblade)
*Listera australis* (Southern twayblade)
*Listera cordata* (Heartleaf twayblade)
*Listera smallii* (Kidney-leaved twayblade)
*Lithospermum canescens* (Hoary puccoon)
*Lithospermum latifolium* (American gromwell)
*Lobelia dortmanna* (Water lobelia)
*Lobelia kalmii* (Brook lobelia)
*Lobelia nuttallii* (Nuttall's lobelia)
*Ludwigia decurrens* (Upright primrose-willow)
*Ludwigia polycarpa* (False loosestrife)
*Ludwigia sphaerocarpa* (Spherical-fruited seedbox)
*Lycopus rubellus* (Gypsy-wort)
*Lycopus uniflorus* (Bugleweed)
*Lycopus uniflorus x virginicus* (Water-horehound)
*Lycopus virginicus* (Bugleweed)
*Lysimachia lanceolata* (Loosestrife)
*Lysimachia producta* (Loosestrife)
*Malaxis bayardii* (Adder's-mouth)
*Malaxis monophyllos var. brachypoda* (White adder's-mouth)
*Malaxis unifolia* (Green adder's-mouth)
*Megalodonta beckii* (Beck's water-marigold)
*Melanthium latifolium* (Bunchflower)
*Melica nitens* (Tall melicgrass)
*Monotropa hypopithys* (Pinesap)
*Monotropa uniflora* (Indian-pipe)
*Montia chamissoi* (Chamisso's miner's-lettuce)
*Montia chamissoi* (Chamisso's miner's-lettuce)
*Myriophyllum farwellii* (Farwell's water-milfoil)

*Myriophyllum heterophyllum* (Broad-leaved water-milfoil)
*Myriophyllum humile* (Water-milfoil)
*Myriophyllum sibiricum* (Northern water-milfoil)
*Myriophyllum tenellum* (Slender water-milfoil)
*Myriophyllum verticillatum* (Whorled water-milfoil)
*Nuphar microphylla* (Yellow pond-lily)
*Nuphar x rubrodisca* (Spatterdock)
*Nymphoides cordata* (Floating-heart)
*Obolaria virginica* (Pennywort)
*Oclemena acuminata* (Wood aster)
*Oclemena nemoralis* (Leafy bog aster)
*Oenothera nutans* (Evening-primrose)
*Oenothera parviflora var. parviflora* (Evening-primrose)
*Oenothera pilosella* (Sundrops)
*Onosmodium virginianum* (Virginia false gromwell)
*Ophioglossum engelmannii* (Limestone adder's-tongue)
*Orobanche uniflora* (Broom-rape)
*Orthilia secunda* (One-sided shinleaf)
*Oxalis acetosella* (Northern wood-sorrel)
*Oxalis dillenii ssp. filipes* (Southern yellow wood-sorrel)
*Oxypolis rigidior* (Cowbane)
*Panax trifolius* (Dwarf ginseng)
*Paspalum floridanum var. glabratum* (Florida beadgrass)
*Penthorum sedoides* (Ditch stonecrop)
*Phemeranthus teretifolius* (Round-leaved fameflower)
*Phlox ovata* (Mountain phlox)
*Physalis subglabrata* (Ground-cherry)
*Physalis virginiana* (Virginia ground-cherry)
*Plantago rugelii* (Rugel's plantain)
*Platanthera blephariglottis* (White fringed-orchid)
*Platanthera cristata* (Crested fringed-orchid)
*Platanthera flava var. herbiola* (Tubercled rein-orchid)
*Platanthera grandiflora* (Large purple fringed-orchid)
*Platanthera hookeri* (Hooker's orchid)
*Platanthera hyperborea var. huronensis* (Tall green bog-orchid)
*Platanthera lacera* (Ragged fringed-orchid)

*Platanthera leucophaea* (Eastern prairie fringed-orchid)
*Platanthera orbiculata var. macrophylla* (Large round-leaved orchid)
*Platanthera orbiculata var. orbiculata* (Large round-leaved orchid)
*Platanthera peramoena* (Purple fringeless orchid)
*Platanthera psycodes* (Purple fringed-orchid)
*Podostemum ceratophyllum* (Riverweed)
*Polygala paucifolia* (Bird-on-the-wing)
*Polygonum densiflorum* (Smartweed)
*Polygonum robustius* (Large water-smartweed)
*Polygonum scandens var. scandens* (Climbing false-buckwheat)
*Polygonum setaceum* (Swamp smartweed)
*Polymnia canadensis* (Leaf-cup)
*Polymnia uvedalia* (Bear's-foot)
*Potamogeton alpinus* (Northern pondweed)
*Potamogeton bicupulatus* (Pondweed)
*Potamogeton confervoides* (Tuckerman's pondweed)
*Potamogeton diversifolius* (Snailseed pondweed)
*Potamogeton epihydrus* (Ribbonleaf pondweed)
*Potamogeton filiformis var. borealis* (Threadleaf pondweed)
*Potamogeton foliosus* (Leafy pondweed)
*Potamogeton friesii* (Fries' pondweed)
*Potamogeton gramineus* (Grassy pondweed)
*Potamogeton hillii* (Hill's pondweed)
*Potamogeton illinoensis* (Illinois pondweed)
*Potamogeton oakesianus* (Oakes' pondweed)
*Potamogeton obtusifolius* (Blunt-leaved pondweed)
*Potamogeton pulcher* (Heartleaf pondweed)
*Potamogeton pusillus* (Pondweed)
*Potamogeton spirillus* (Snailseed pondweed)
*Potamogeton strictifolius* (Narrow-leaved pondweed)
*Potamogeton tennesseensis* (Tennessee pondweed)
*Potamogeton vaseyi* (Vasey's pondweed)
*Potamogeton zosteriformis* (Flat-stemmed pondweed)
*Potentilla canadensis* (Cinquefoil)
*Potentilla norvegica ssp. monspeliensis* (Strawberry-weed)

*Prenanthes altissima* (Rattlesnake-root)
*Prenanthes crepidinea* (Rattlesnake-root)
*Prenanthes serpentaria* (Lion's-foot)
*Prenanthes trifoliolata* (Gall-of-the-earth)
*Proserpinaca palustris var. crebra* (Common mermaid-weed)
*Proserpinaca pectinata* (Comb-leaved mermaid-weed)
*Ptilimnium capillaceum* (Mock bishop's weed)
*Pycnanthemum clinopodioides* (Mountain-mint)
*Pycnanthemum torrei* (Torrey's mountain-mint)
*Pycnanthemum verticillatum var. pilosum* (Mountain-mint)
*Pycnanthemum verticillatum var. verticillatum* (Mountain-mint)
*Pyrola americana* (Wild lily-of-the-valley)
*Pyrola chlorantha* (Wintergreen)
*Ranunculus ambigens* (Water-plantain spearwort)
*Ranunculus aquatilis var. diffusus* (White water-crowfoot)
*Ranunculus caricetorum* (Marsh buttercup)
*Ranunculus flabellaris* (Yellow water-crowfoot)
*Ranunculus hederaceus* (Long-stalked crowfoot)
*Ranunculus micranthus* (Small-flowered crowfoot)
*Rhynchospora alba* (White beak-rush)
*Rhynchospora capitellata* (Beak-rush)
*Rumex hastatulus* (Heart sorrel)
*Sabatia campanulata* (Slender marsh-pink)
*Sagina procumbens* (Bird's-eye)
*Sagittaria australis* (Appalachian arrowhead)
*Sagittaria filiformis* (Arrowhead)
*Samolus parviflorus* (Water pimpernel)
*Sanicula marilandica* (Black snake root)
*Sanicula odorata* (Yellow-flowered sanicle)
*Sanicula trifoliata* (Large-fruited sanicle)
*Schizachyrium scoparium var. littorale* (Seaside bluestem)
*Scutellaria churchilliana* (Skullcap)
*Scutellaria elliptica var. elliptica* (Hairy skullcap)
*Scutellaria galericulata* (Common skullcap)
*Scutellaria nervosa* (Skullcap)
*Scutellaria saxatilis* (Rock skullcap)

*Sedum rosea* (Roseroot stonecrop)
*Sedum telephioides* (Allegheny stonecrop)
*Senecio anonymus* (Appalachian groundsel)
*Senecio antennariifolius* (Shale-barren rag-wort)
*Sericocarpus asteroides* (White-topped aster)
*Sericocarpus linifolius* (Narrow-leaved white-topped aster)
*Setaria geniculata* (Perennial foxtail)
*Sida hermaphrodita* (Virginia mallow)
*Sisyrinchium fuscatum* (Sand blue-eyed-grass)
*Sisyrinchium mucronatum* (Blue-eyed-grass)
*Solidago arguta var. arguta* (Forest golden-rod)
*Solidago hispida* (Hairy goldenrod)
*Solidago puberula* (Downy goldenrod)
*Solidago simplex ssp. randii var. racemosa* (Sticky goldenrod)
*Solidago squarrosa* (Ragged goldenrod)
*Spiranthes lacera var. gracilis* (Southern slender ladies'-tresses)
*Spiranthes lacera var. lacera* (Northern slender ladies'-tresses)
*Spiranthes lucida* (Shining ladies'-tresses)
*Spiranthes magnicamporum* (Great Plains ladies'-tresses)
*Spiranthes ochroleuca* (Yellow nodding ladies'-tresses)
*Spiranthes ovalis var. erostellata* (October ladies'-tresses)
*Spiranthes romanzoffiana* (Hooded ladies'-tresses)
*Spiranthes tuberosa* (Slender ladies'-tresses)
*Spirodela polyrhiza* (Greater duckweed)
*Stachys hyssopifolia var. ambigua* (Hedge-nettle)
*Stachys hyssopifolia var. hyssopifolia* (Hedge-nettle)
*Stachys nuttallii* (Nuttall's hedge-nettle)
*Stellaria borealis* (Northern stitchwort)
*Stellaria corei* (Chickweed)
*Stellaria longifolia* (Long-leaved stitchwort)
*Stellaria pubera* (Great chickweed)
*Stenanthium gramineum* (Featherbells)
*Stylosanthes biflora* (Pencil-flower)
*Symphyotrichum boreale* (Northern bog aster)
*Symphyotrichum depauperatum* (Serpentine aster)

*Symphyotrichum dumosum* (Bushy aster)
*Symphyotrichum laeve var. laeve* (Smooth blue aster)
*Symphyotrichum racemosum* (Small white aster)
*Symphyotrichum urophyllum* (Aster)
*Taenidia montana* (Mountain pimpernel)
*Thalictrum coriaceum* (Thick-leaved meadow-rue)
*Thaspium barbinode* (Meadow-parsnip)
*Thaspium trifoliatum var. flavum* (Meadow-parsnip)
*Triadenum fraseri* (Marsh St. Johns-wort)
*Trichostema brachiatum* (False pennyroyal)
*Trientalis borealis* (Star-flower)
*Trifolium virginicum* (Kate's-mountain clo-ver)
*Triosteum angustifolium* (Horse-gentian)
*Triosteum aurantiacum var. aurantiacum* (Wild-coffee)
*Triosteum aurantiacum var. glaucescens* (Wild-coffee)
*Triphora trianthophora* (Nodding pogonia)
*Typha x glauca* (Cat-tail)
*Utricularia cornuta* (Horned bladderwort)
*Utricularia geminiscapa* (Bladderwort)
*Utricularia inflata* (Inflated bladderwort)
*Utricularia intermedia* (Flat-leaved bladder-wort)
*Utricularia macrorhiza* (Common bladder-wort)
*Utricularia minor* (Lesser bladderwort)
*Verbena simplex* (Narrow-leaved vervain)
*Veronica scutellata* (Marsh speedwell)
*Veronica scutellata* (Marsh speedwell)
*Viola palmata* (Early blue violet)
*Viola primulifolia* (Primrose violet)
*Viola renifolia* (Kidney-leaved violet)
*Viola rostrata* (Long-spurred violet)
*Viola selkirkii* (Great-spurred violet)
*Viola striata* (Striped violet)
*Wolffia brasiliensis* (Pointed water-meal)
*Xyris difformis* (Yellow-eyed-grass)
*Xyris montana* (Yellow-eyed-grass)
*Xyris torta* (Yellow-eyed-grass)
*Zannichellia palustris* (Horned pondweed)
*Zigadenus glaucus* (Camass)
*Zosterella dubia* (Water star-grass)

# *Native plants: grasses, rushes, sedges*

This section includes *graminoids* — that is, grasses, sedges and rushes — subdivided in the following manner.

- Native species whose range includes Pennsylvania and whose observed distribution includes Carbon, Monroe, Pike and/or Wayne counties, all of which are commercially available

- Native species whose range includes Pennsylvania but have not been reported in Carbon, Monroe, Pike or Wayne counties but are commonly available in the marketplace; a secondary list identifies additional species that may be difficult to find in the retail marketplace.

- A listing of native species that do not appear to be commercially available

The 154 local species and seven commonly available elsewhere in Pennsylvania are organized in the following manner:

Latin (or scientific) name*
Common name(s)
A brief description of natural habitat — i.e., where it is found in nature
US Fish and Wildlife Service wetland indicators when available
Height range (blades and culms to panicles)
Suggestions for home cultivation, including light requirements, moisture, soil description
How relatively easy it is to find in the commercial marketplace, in the context of nationwide mail-order nurseries
*Sometimes scientific names have recently changed and not all literature has yet caught up. Where it seems helpful, we have also include "AKA" — also known as.

## *Agrostis hyemalis*

**Hairgrass** or **Winter bentgrass** — dry or moist soil in woods and fields, bogs, meadows, and along roadsides; FAC. Mostly southeastern and far western counties in Pennsylvania; scattered elsewhere. Grows 12 to 32 inches; sun to part shade in dry to moist sandy loam.; very few sources.

## *Agrostis perennans*

**Autumn bentgrass** — woods, thickets, open areas, and on stream banks; FACU. Throughout Pennsylvania. Grows 20 to 40 inches; part sun to part shade in moist silty loam.; very few sources.

## *Agrostis scabra*

**Fly-away grass** — meadows, shrublands, woodlands, marshes, and stream and lake margins; FAC. Western, north-central and eastern counties in Pennsylvania; scattered elsewhere. Grows 12 to 32 inches; sun to part sun in dry to moist sandy loam.; very few sources.

## *Andropogon gerardii*

**Big bluestem** — stream banks, roadsides, moist meadows, and prairies; FAC-. Throughout Pennsylvania. Grows 3 to 10 feet; sun to part sun in average, dry to medium, well to drained soils in full sun, prefers dry, infertile soil; commonly available.

## *Andropogon virginicus*

**Broom sedge** or **bluestem** — old fields, hillsides, and waste grounds; FACU. Mostly eastern, south-central and western counties in Pennsylvania. Grows 20 to 60 inches; sun to part sun in dry to moist sandy to medium loams; commonly available.

### *Brachyelytrum erectum*

**Bearded shorthusk** — moist to dry deciduous woods and thickets, occasionally over limestone bedrock. Throughout Pennsylvania. Grows 20 to 40 inches; part shade, in mesic soil containing loam, sandy loam, or some rocky material; very few sources.

### *Bromus altissimus*

**Bromegrass** — shaded or open woods, along stream banks, and on alluvial plains and slopes; FACW. Throughout Pennsylvania. Also known as *Bromus latigumus;* part sun to part shade in moist, sandy loam; very few sources.

### *Bromus ciliatus*

**Fringed brome** — damp meadows, thickets, woods and stream banks; FACW. Northeastern counties in Pennsylvania; scattered western counties, mostly north. Grows 24 to 60 inches; sun to part shade in rich sandy loam; very few sources.

### *Bromus kalmii*

**Bromegrass** — sandy, gravelly, or limestone soils in open woods and calcareous fens; FACU. Scattered counties in Pennsylvania, mostly east. Grows 20 to 40 inches; part sun to part shade in dry to moist rocky sandy loam; several sources.

### *Bromus pubescens*

**Canada brome** — shaded, moist, often upland deciduous woods. Throughout Pennsylvania. Grows 24 to 60 inches; part shade to shade in dry to moist sandy loam; very few sources.

### *Calamagrostis canadensis*

**Canada bluejoint** — wet meadows, bogs, and swamps; two varieties, *canadensis* and *macouniana;* FACW. Northern and southeastern counties in Pennsylvania; scattered elsewhere. Grows 24 to 60 inches; sun to part sun in rich moist loam.; commonly available.

### *Carex annectens*

**Yellowfruit sedge** — dry to moist, often calcareous soils in open habitats and wet meadows; FACW. Throughout Pennsylvania. Grows 16 to 40 inches; sun to part sun in dry to moist sandy loam; very few sources.

### *Carex appalachica*

**Appalachian sedge** — dry to mesic deciduous or mixed forests, usually on sandy or rocky soils. Northern and extreme eastern counties; scattered elsewhere. Grows 8 to 24 inches; part sun to part shade in dry to moist rocky sandy loam; very few sources.

### *Carex argyrantha*

**Hay sedge** — dry and rocky (especially sandstone) woods and clearings. Throughout Pennsylvania. Grows 12 to 40 inches; part shade to shade in dry rocky sandy loam; very few sources.

### *Carex atlantica ssp. capillacea*

**Prickly bog sedge** — swamps, bogs, and along shores; OBL. Eastern, south-central and northwestern counties in Pennsylvania; scattered elsewhere. Grows 4 to 40 inches; part sun to part shade in moist silty loam; very few sources.

### *Carex baileyi*

**Bailey's sedge** — sandy, peaty, or gravelly pond, lake, and stream shores, meadows, swamps, seeps, ditches, usually in acidic soils; OBL. Throughout Pennsylvania, except southeast and south central counties. Grows 8 to 28 inches; part sun to part shade in moist to wet rich silty loam; very few sources.

### *Carex bebbii*

**Bebb's sedge** — wet places with calcareous or neutral soils, gravelly lakeshores, stream banks, meadows and forest seeps; OBL. Pennsylvania distribution limited to extreme northwestern counties, as well as Monroe, Centre and Huntingdon. Grows 8 to 32 inches; sun to part shade in moist rich loam; commonly available.

### *Carex bicknellii*

**Bicknell's sedge** — dry woods, thickets, fields and barrens. Extreme eastern counties in Pennsylvania, from Monroe southward. Grows 12 to 48 inches; sun to part shade in dry to mesic sandy loam; very few sources.

### *Carex blanda*

**Eastern woodland sedge** — swamps, bottomlands and mesic to dry woods, including lawns, roadsides and stream banks; FAC. Southeastern, south-central, far western counties in Pennsylvania; scattered elsewhere. Grows 6 to 24 inches; sun to part shade in dry to mesic rich sandy loam; very few sources.

### Carex brevior

**Sedge** — prairies, meadows, open woods, dry road banks, often in calcareous or neutral soils. Grows 12 to 40 inches; sun to part shade in dry to mesic rich sandy loam; several sources.

### Carex bromoides

**Brome-like sedge** — wet hardwood forests, wooded floodplains and swamps, occasionally wet meadows and marsh edges; FACW. Throughout Pennsylvania. Grows 10 to 32 inches; part sun to part shade in moist, rich humusy loam; very few sources.

### Carex bushii

**Sedge** — dry to moist upland woods, thickets, and fields; FACW. Mostly southeastern and south central counties in Pennsylvania; scattered elsewhere. Grows 10 to 36 inches; medium to moist soils in full sun to part shade; very few sources.

### Carex buxbaumii

**Bauxbaum's sedge** — calcareous swamps, swales, wet meadows, marshes, and fens; OBL. Southeastern and extreme south-central counties in Pennsylvania; widely scattered elsewhere. Grows 10 to 40 inches; sun to part sun in moist to wet silty loam, circumneutral soils; very few sources.

### Carex cephalophora

**Oval-leaf sedge** — dry to wet to mesic deciduous or mixed forests, thickets, but rarely open grassy habitats; FACU. Throughout Pennsylvania. Grows 12 to 32 inches; part sun to part shade in dry, mesic to wet rich sandy loam; very few sources.

### Carex comosa

**Longhair sedge** — swamps and wet thickets, stream, pond and lakeshores, depressions in wet meadows, marshes, often in shallow water or on emergent stumps, floating logs, and floating mats of vegetation; OBL. Grows 20 to 48 inches; sun to part sun in wet, silty, loam and sometimes standing water; commonly available.

### Carex conoidea

**Open field sedge** — moist meadows and prairies, shores of lakes, ponds, and rivers, usually in acidic sands or loams; FACU. Eastern counties in Pennsylvania except in areas of limestone substrate; extreme northwestern counties and scattered elsewhere. Grows 5 to 30 inches; sun to part sun in moist, rich organic loam; very few sources.

### Carex crinita var. crinita

**Fringed sedge** or **Short-hair sedge** — swamps, floodplain forests, wet meadows, marshes, bogs, stream edges, margins of lakes and ponds and roadside ditches; OBL. Throughout Pennsylvania. Grows 28 to 60 inches; sun to pat shade in moist to wet silty organic loam; commonly available.

### Carex cristatella

**Crested sedge** — moist to wet meadows, marshes, thickets, stream banks, and ditches; FACW. Scattered counties throughout Pennsylvania, mostly south and west. Grows 12 to 40 inches; sun to part sun in moist to wet silty organic loam; very few sources.

### Carex davisii

**Davis' sedge** — rich deciduous floodplain forests and forest margins, usually along streams, meadows, fields and thickets; often on calcareous soils; FAC-. Mostly southeastern counties in Pennsylvania; scattered elsewhere. Grows 12 to 36 inches; sun to part shade in rich humus; very few sources.

### Carex deweyana var. deweyana

**Dewey sedge** — wet to mesic to dry to mesic forests, and forest edges; FACU. Northeastern counties in Pennsylvania; scattered northwest. Grows 8 to 40 inches; part sun to part shade in rich rocky loam; very few sources.

### Carex diandra

**Lesser panicled sedge** — bog hummocks and pond margins; OBL. Extreme northeastern and northwestern counties in Pennsylvania. Grows 12 to 30 inches; sun to part sun on pond edges in wet, organic loam; very few sources.

### Carex echinata

**Prickly sedge** — bogs, swamps, peaty or sandy shores of streams or lakes, wet meadows, usually in acidic soils; OBL. Northern, southeastern and south-central counties in Pennsylvania; scattered elsewhere. Grows 4 to 36 inches; sun to part sun in moist to wet silty loam; very few sources.

### Carex emoryi

**Sedge** — stream banks, swales, marshes, seepy areas and fens; OBL. Mostly eastern counties in Pennsylvania; scattered throughout. Grows 12 to 40 inches; sun to part shade in moist to wet rich sandy loam; very few sources.

### Carex flava

**Yellow sedge** — moist to wet habitats, such as open meadows, fens, partially shaded shrub peaty wetlands and swamps, on lime to rich soils; OBL. Extreme northeastern and northwestern counties in Pennsylvania. Grows 4 to 32 inches; sun to part sun in moist to wet rich loam; very few sources.

### Carex folliculata

**Northern long sedge** — wet forests, bogs, seeps, wet meadows, marsh edges, stream banks, lakeshores, in acidic, sandy, or peaty soils; OBL. Throughout Pennsylvania except for extreme southwestern counties. Grows 12 to 48 inches; part sun to shade in moist to wet rich humusy soils; very few sources.

### Carex glaucodea

**Blue sedge** — mesic to wet to mesic deciduous forests or seasonally moist prairies, usually in clays or loams. Eastern counties except for northern tier in Pennsylvania; scattered southwestern counties. Grows 4 to 20 inches; part sun to part shade in clayey to sandy loams; very few sources.

### Carex gracillima

**Graceful sedge** — mesic to dry deciduous forests, including edges and openings, mixed conifer to hardwood forests, coniferous swamps, thickets, meadows, and along roadsides; FACU. Throughout Pennsylvania. Grows 8 to 40 inches; part shade in dry to mesic sandy loam; very few sources.

### Carex granularis

**Limestone meadow sedge** — meadows, fens, glades, or shores, moist woods, and bottomland swamps, especially along streams usually in clayey or sandy to clay soils; FACW+. Throughout Pennsylvania, except northern tier counties. Grows 8 to 36 inches; part sun to part shade in moist to wet rich silty loam; very few sources.

### Carex grisea

**Wood Gray sedge** — dry to moist rich deciduous woodlands, meadows, swales and ditches; FAC. Scattered counties throughout Pennsylvania, especially southeast. Grows 8 to 30 inches; part shade in rich moist organic loam; very few sources.

### Carex gynandra

**Nodding sedge** — swamps, floodplain forests, wet meadows, marshes, bogs, stream edges, margins of lakes and ponds and roadside ditches; OBL. Throughout Pennsylvania. Grows 30 to 60 inches; part sun to part shade in moist to wet silty loam; very few sources.

### Carex hirsutella

**Fuzzy wuzzy sedge** — meadows and dry to mesic woods in neutral to basic soils. Throughout Pennsylvania. Grows 10 to 30 inches; sun to part shade in dry to mesic sandy loam; very few sources.

### Carex hirtifolia

**Hairy sedge** — mesic to dry thickets, lowland forests and forested slopes. Scattered throughout Pennsylvania, mostly southeast and southwest. Grows 12 to 32 inches; part sun to part shade in mesic to dry soil containing loam, clay to loam, or some rocky material. Above average tolerance of dry conditions; very few sources.

### Carex hystericina

**Bottlebrush sedge** — swamps, moist meadows and fens, seeps and edges of lakes, ponds and streams, mostly in calcareous soils; OBL. Mostly central Appalachian, southeastern and far western counties in Pennsylvania. Grows 8 to 40 inches; sun to part sun in moist to wet rich silty loam; commonly available.

### Carex interior

**Inland sedge** — wet meadows and prairies, fens, swamps, river and lakeshores, seeps; usually in calcareous soils; OBL. Scattered counties throughout Pennsylvania, especially southeast. Grows 8 to 40 inches; sun to part sun in moist to wet, rich silty circumneutral loam; very few sources.

### Carex intumescens

**Great bladder sedge** — dry to wet forests and openings, thickets, and wet meadows; FACW+. Throughout Pennsylvania. Grows 6 to 32 inches; part shade to shade in dry to mesic acidic humus; very few sources.

### Carex lacustris

**Hairy sedge** — swamps, wet thickets, marsh edges, meadows, fens and shores of lakes, ponds and streams; OBL. Northeastern, northwestern, southeastern counties in Pennsylvania except for limestone substrate areas along the Allegheny Front. Grows 10 to 50 inches; sun to part sun in moist to wet silty loam; several sources.

### Carex lasiocarpa

**Wooly fruit sedge** — wet meadows, stream banks, fens and bogs, lakeshores, especially in very wet sites and sometimes forming floating mats; OBL. Scattered eastern and northwestern counties in Pennsylvania. Grows 10 to 50 inches; sun to part sun in moist to wet silty or peaty loam; very few sources.

### Carex laxiculmis var. laxiculmis

**Spreading sedge** — wet, low, deciduous or mixed deciduous and evergreen forests; stream edges and springs, and seeps, especially on clay soils. Throughout Pennsylvania. Grows 4 to 40 inches; part shade to shade in mesic to moist humusy sandy loam; very few sources.

### Carex laxiflora

**Broad looseflower sedge** — higher elevations of dry to moist deciduous or mixed deciduous to evergreen forests; FACU. Throughout Pennsylvania. Grows 5 to 25 inches; part shade to shade in mesic to moist humusy sandy loam; very few sources.

### Carex lupuliformis

**False hop sedge** — calcareous marshes, wet woods, sometimes in shallow water; FACW. Scattered counties in Pennsylvania, mostly northwest and southeast. Grows 20 to 48 inches; full sun to part shade in silty rich soils continually moist to wet; very few sources.

### Carex lupulina

**Hop sedge** — wet mixed to deciduous swampy forests and openings and wet meadows; OBL. Throughout Pennsylvania. Grows 10 to 50 inches; part sun to part shade in moist to wet rich silty loam; very few sources.

### Carex lurida

**Shallow sedge** — pond, lake and stream shores, marshes and wet meadows, seeps and swampy forests, usually in sandy acidic soils; OBL. Throughout Pennsylvania. Grows 10 to 50 inches; sun to part sun in moist to wet rich silty loam; several sources.

### Carex molesta

**Troublesome sedge** — dry to wet, frequently heavy, calcareous soils in fields, bottomlands and along roadsides. Mostly southeastern counties in Pennsylvania; scattered south and elsewhere. Grows 15 to 45 inches; sun to part shade in dry to wet, clayey to silty loam; very few sources.

### Carex muehlenbergii

**Muehlenberg's sedge** — sandy, dry savannahs and open forests. Mostly eastern counties in Pennsylvania; scattered south and northwest. Grows 10 to 40 inches; sun to part shade in dry sandy loam; very few sources.

### Carex normalis

**Greater straw sedge** — generally wet woods, thickets, meadows and along roadsides; FACU. Throughout Pennsylvania. Grows 10 to 50 inches; sun to part shade in moist to mesic sandy clay loam; very few sources.

### Carex pedunculata

**Sedge** — rich, rocky, wooded slopes or swampy woods. Scattered counties throughout Pennsylvania, mostly north. Grows 2 to 12 inches; part shade to shade in moist to dry sandy loams; very few sources.

### Carex pellita

**Sedge** — swamps, moist meadows, and along shores of lakes and ponds; OBL. Mostly eastern and south central counties in Pennsylvania; scattered elsewhere. Grows 12 to 40 inches; full sun to part in moist to wet rich loams; very few sources.

### Carex pensylvanica

**Pennsylvania sedge** — well to drained, acidic but mineral-rich sandy, rocky, and loamy soils in deciduous forests, edges and openings. Throughout Pennsylvania. Grows 4 to 16 inches; part shade to shade in dry to mesic sandy rocky loam. Colonizes by rhizomes; commonly available.

### Carex plantaginea

**Plantain sedge** — rich, moist, deciduous or mixed deciduous to evergreen forests, on slopes along streams or along edges of moist depressions. Mostly northern and southwestern counties in Pennsylvania; scattered elsewhere. Grows 8 to 24 inches; part shade in consistently moist organic loams; commonly available.

### Carex platyphylla

**Broad-leaf sedge** — rocky or gravelly slopes in rich, moist deciduous forests, usually on limestone, shale, or calcareous metamorphic rocks, often on clay soils. Throughout Pennsylvania. Grows 6 to 16 inches; part sun to shade in moist, rich sandy humus; very few sources.

### Carex prairea

**Prairie sedge** — calcareous fens and marshes; FACW. Monroe County southward on a line to Lancaster County in Pennsylvania; scattered central counties along the eastern edge of the Allegheny Front; extreme northwestern counties. Grows 20 to 40 inches; sun to part sun in moist rich silty loam. Very few sources.

### Carex projecta

**Necklace sedge** — moist to wet meadows, low spots in deciduous and mixed forests, thickets, stream banks and lake shores; FACW. Throughout Pennsylvania. Grows 20 to 30 inches; part sun to part shade in moist to wet rich loam; very few sources.

### Carex radiata

**Eastern star sedge** — wet to mesic mixed and deciduous forests in usually seasonally wet areas. Throughout Pennsylvania. Grows 10 to 30 inches; part sun to part shade in mesic to wet to mesic loam; very few sources.

### Carex retrorsa

**Backward sedge** — lake and pond shores, stream banks, marshes, swamps, wet meadows and thickets; FACW. Scattered mostly northern counties in Pennsylvania. Grows 12 to 36 inches; shade to part shade in moist to wet organic loam; very few sources.

### Carex rosea

**Rosy sedge** — dry and mesic deciduous and mixed forests. Throughout Pennsylvania. Grows 10 to 35 inches; part sun to part shade in dry to mesic sandy loam; very few sources.

### Carex scoparia

**Broom sedge** — dry to wet open habitats, often on sandy, acidic soils; FACW. Throughout Pennsylvania. Grows 10 to 40 inches; sun to part sun in dry to wet acidic, sandy loam; several sources.

### Carex sparganioides

**Bur reed sedge** — dry and mesic deciduous and mixed forests on neutral or basic soils; FACU. Throughout Pennsylvania except scattered in north-central counties. Grows 15 to 40 inches; part sun to part shade in dry to moist humusy loam; very few sources.

### Carex sprengelii

**Sprengli's sedge** — dry to mesic hardwood and mixed conifer forests and openings, floodplain forests and riverbanks, lakeshores, limestone river bluffs, frequent on calcareous soils; FACU. Scattered eastern counties in Pennsylvania, mostly north. Grows 10 to 40 inches; sun to part shade in dry to mesic rich sandy and alluvial loam; several sources.

### Carex sterilis

**Atlantic sedge** — white to cedar swamps, wet calcareous prairies, fens and meadows, calcareous seeps, lake and river shores, and wet sunny limestone outcrops; OBL. Eastern counties in Pennsylvania, especially southeast; reported in Lawrence and Bedford Counties. Grows 1 to 3 inches; full sun to part sun in wet to moist circumneutral sandy loams

### Carex stipata var. stipata

**Owl fruit sedge** — soils that are periodically saturated or inundated in wet meadows, swamps, marshes, and alluvial bottomlands. Throughout Pennsylvania. Grows 15 to 40 inches; sun to part sun in moist to wet rich silty and alluvial loam; very few sources.

### Carex stricta

**Tussock sedge** or **Upright sedge** — lake shores, bogs, marshes and wet meadows; OBL. Eastern and northwestern counties in Pennsylvania, scattered south. Grows 6 to 44 inches; sun to part sun in moist to wet rich silty or alluvial loam; commonly available.

### Carex swanii

**Swann's sedge** — mesic to dry forests and scrublands; FACU. Throughout Pennsylvania. Grows 10 to 20 inches; part sun to part shade in mesic to dry sandy loam; very few sources.

### Carex tenera

**Quill sedge** — moist to dry meadows and open forests; FAC. Scattered throughout Pennsylvania, mostly eastern counties and on the eastern edge of the Allegheny Front in central Pennsylvania. Grows 10 to 35 inches; part sun to part shade in mesic to wet sandy loam; very few sources.

### Carex tribuloides

**Sedge** — open floodplain forests, moist to wet grasslands, ditches, stream banks and wet thickets; FACW+. Throughout Pennsylvania. Grows 20 to 40 inches; sun to part shade in wet to moist gravelly, sandy, peaty or loamy soils; very few sources.

### Carex trichocarpa

**Hairy fruit sedge** — wet thickets and meadows, near streams and rivers, and in openings in bottomlands; OBL. Throughout Pennsylvania except southwestern counties. Grows 20 to 50 inches; sun to part sun in moist rich loam; very few sources.

### Carex tuckermanii

**Sedge** — deciduous swamp forests, thickets, often along streams or pond shores and wet meadows; OBL. Scattered counties in Pennsylvania, mostly northwest and extreme northeast. Grows 16 to 40 inches; sun to part shade in moist to wet silty loam; very few sources.

### Carex utriculata

**Northwest territory sedge** — pond and lake shorelines, swamps, marshes, meadows, fens, bogs and wet thickets; OBL. Northwestern and northeastern counties in Pennsylvania; also along the eastern Allegheny Plateau south toward the Maryland line. Grows 16 to 40 inches; sun to part sun in moist rich loam; very few sources.

### Carex vesicaria

**Blister sedge** — stream, pond and lake shores; marshes, bogs, wet meadows, low wet areas in forests, wet thickets and swamps, frequently on sites inundated in spring and dry during summer; OBL. Scattered counties in Pennsylvania, mostly northeast, northwest and south central. Grows 5 to 40 inches; sun to part sun in mesic to moist rich sandy loam; very few sources.

### Carex virescens

**Ribbed sedge** — deciduous forests and banks ranging from mesic to dry. Throughout Pennsylvania except scattered in western counties. Grows 15 to 40 inches; part sun to part shade in mesic to dry sandy loam; very few sources.

### Carex vulpinoidea var. vulpinoidea

**Fox sedge** — marshes, ditches and wet meadows periodically inundated or saturated; OBL. Throughout Pennsylvania. Grows 16 to 40 inches; sun to part sun in moist to wet silty loam; commonly available.

### Chasmanthium latifolium

**Northern sea-oats** or **Indian wood oats** — rich alluvial woods or rocky slopes along streams and on moist bluffs and stream banks; FACU. Widely scattered counties in Pennsylvania, including Monroe, Lancaster, York, Bedford and Allegheny. Grows 20 to 40 inches; part sun to part shade in dry to moist rich sandy loam, pH 5 to 7; commonly available.

### Cinna arundinacea

**Wood reedgrass** — moist woodlands and swamps, depressions, along streams, and in floodplain and upland woods; less frequent in wet meadows, marshes, and disturbed sites; FACU. Throughout Pennsylvania. Grows 40 to 60 inches; part sun to part shade in moist to wet humusy loam; very few sources.

### Cyperus esculentus

**Yellow nutsedge** — low areas of upland prairies and fields, stream edges and pond margins; FACU. Throughout Pennsylvania. Grows 12 to 40 inches; sun to part sun in moist, rich sandy loams; very few sources.

### Danthonia spicata

**Poverty grass** — dry rocky, sandy, or mineral soils, usually in open sunny places. Throughout Pennsylvania. Grows 8 to 24 inches; sun to part shade in dry to mesic sandy loam; very few sources.

### Deschampsia flexuosa

**Common hairgrass** — dry and generally rocky slopes and in woods and thickets, often on disturbed sites. Mostly eastern and south central counties in Pennsylvania. Grows 12 to 40 inches; part sun to part shade in dry to mesic sandy loam; very few sources.

### Dulichium arundinaceum

**Three-way sedge** — open wet places, lake and pond margins, marshes, swamps, bogs and stream shores; OBL. Throughout Pennsylvania. Can reach 48 inches; part shade in moist to wet sandy to clay loam; several sources.

### Echinochloa muricata

**Barnyard grass** — moist ground, alluvial shores and often on disturbed sites; FACW+. Throughout Pennsylvania. Grows 4 to 24 inches; sun to part sun in rich silty loam; very few sources.

### Eleocharis acicularis

**Needle spike-rush** — bare, wet soil or in lakes, ponds, vernal pools, meadows, springs and disturbed places; OBL. Throughout Pennsylvania, except scattered in northwestern counties. Can reach 3 feet; sun to part sun in shallow ponds and pools; several sources.

### Eleocharis erythropoda

**Bald spike-rush** — non-calcareous or calcareous fresh or brackish shores, marshes, wet meadows, fens, stream banks and swales; OBL. Throughout Pennsylvania; scattered northwest. Can reach 3 feet; full sun in wet to mesic sandy loam, prefers pH of 7 to 8; very few sources.

### Eleocharis palustris

**Creeping spike-rush** — large colonies at lake and stream margins, bogs, swamps and marshy swales. Can reach 50 inches; sun to part sun in ponds, rain gardens and retention basins up to 40 inches deep; can be inundated for up to 4 months; very few sources.

### Elymus canadensis var. canadensis

**Canada wild-rye** — alluvial shores and thickets, especially near larger rivers and tributaries; FACU+. Eastern counties in Pennsylvania; scattered west. Can reach 36 inches; sun to part sun in silty alluvial loam; commonly available.

### Elymus hystrix

**Bottlebrush grass** — dry to moist soils in open woods and thickets, especially on base to rich slopes and small stream terraces. Throughout Pennsylvania. Grows 24 to 36 inches; part sun to part shade in moist loam; several sources.

### Elymus riparius

**Riverbank wild-rye** — moist, generally alluvial and often sandy soils in woods and thickets, usually along larger streams and occasionally along upland ditches; FACW. Throughout Pennsylvania. Grows 40 to 60 inches; part sun to part shade in mesic to moist alluvial sandy loam; several sources.

### Elymus trachycaulus

**Slender wheatgrass** — generally open or moderately open areas, but sometimes in forests; FACU. Northeastern counties in Pennsylvania; widely scattered southwest. Grows 15 to 40 inches; sun to part shade in dry to moist sandy loam; very few sources.

### Elymus villosus

**Wild rye** — moist to moderately dry, generally rocky soils in woods and thickets, especially in calcareous or other base to rich soils; also frequent on drier, sandy soils or damper, alluvial soils in glaciated regions; FACU-. Throughout Pennsylvania except on the high Allegheny Plateau. Grows 20 to 40 inches; part sun to part shade in dry to moist sandy or alluvial loam; several sources.

### Elymus virginicus

**Virginia wild rye** — moist-damp or rather dry soil, mostly on bottomland or fertile uplands, in open woods, thickets, tall forbs, or weedy sites; FACW-. Throughout Pennsylvania. Grows 20 to 50 inches; part sun to part shade in sandy, organic loam, pH 5 to 7; commonly available.

### Eragrostis spectabilis

**Purple lovegrass** — dry sandy fields, woods margins, roadsides, usually in sandy to clay loam soils; UPL. Mostly eastern counties in Pennsylvania; widely scattered west. Grows 12 to 24 inches; sun to part sun in dry to moist sandy to clay loams; commonly available.

### Eriophorum virginicum

**Tawny cotton-grass** — bogs and peaty meadows and swamps; OBL. Throughout Pennsylvania, somewhat scattered in southwest. Grows 1 to 3 feet; full sun in wet, rich silty soil; very few sources.

### Festuca subverticillata

**Nodding fescue** — moist to dry deciduous or mixed forests with organic rocky soils; FACU. Throughout Pennsylvania. Grows 24 to 48 inches; part sun to part shade in moist, organic, rocky, sandy loam; very few sources.

### Glyceria borealis

**Northern mannagrass** — edges and muddy shores of freshwater streams, lakes, and ponds; OBL. Northeastern counties in Pennsylvania; also reported in Clinton, Centre, Juniata and Bedford counties. Can reach 40 inches; sun to part sun in moist to wet silty loam; very few sources.

### Glyceria canadensis

**Rattlesnake mannagrass** — bogs, swamps, wet woods and marshes near lakes; OBL. Throughout Pennsylvania. Can reach 36 inches; sun to part sun in moist to wet silty loam; several sources.

### Glyceria grandis

**American mannagrass** — wet woods and meadows, stream banks, swamps, and in the water of streams, ditches and ponds. Northern counties in Pennsylvania; scattered south. Can reach 48 inches; sun to part sun in moist to wet silty loam; several sources.

### Glyceria melicaria

**Slender mannagrass** — swamps, bogs and wet soils; OBL. Throughout Pennsylvania. Grows 20 to 40 inches; sun to part sun in moist to wet silty loam; very few sources.

### Glyceria striata

**Fowl mannagrass** — bogs, along lakes and streams, and in other wet places; OBL. Throughout Pennsylvania. Grows 20 to 40 inches; sun to part sun in moist to wet silty loam; commonly available.

### Hierochloe odorata

**Vanilla sweetgrass** — moist meadows or river shores. Grows 18 to 36 inches; FACW; reported only in Wayne, Butler, Erie and Allegheny counties in Pennsylvania. Grows 12 to 20 inches sun to part sun in moist, organic sandy loam; commonly available. Listed as endangered in Pennsylvania.

### Juncus acuminatus

**Sharp-fruited rush** — wet meadows, swamps, marshes, stream banks, shores, ditches, and near springs on rock outcrops; OBL. Throughout Pennsylvania. Grows 8 to 30 inches; full sun in rich loam, wet to shallow water; very few sources.

### Juncus articulatus

**Jointed rush** — swamps and mud flats; wet ground in ditches, lake and stream margins, generally in calcareous soils. Widely scattered counties in Pennsylvania, mostly west. Grows 4 to 20 inches; full sun in rich loam, wet to shallow water; very few sources.

### Juncus bufonius

**Toad rush** — moist soils in meadows, along lakeshores or stream banks, ditches, or roadsides, frequent in drawdown areas; usually in open sites and often becoming weedy; FACW. Throughout Pennsylvania. Grows 6 to 20 inches, sun to part sun in moist to wet rich loam; very few sources.

### Juncus canadensis

**Canada rush** — swamps, marshes, bogs, swales, fens, lake and pond shores; prefers calcareous soils; OBL. Scattered counties throughout Pennsylvania, mostly east and north. Grows 12 to 48 inches; full sun in moist to wet rich loams; very few sources.

### Juncus dudleyi

**Dudley's rush** — exposed or shaded sites, usually moist areas such as along stream banks, ditches, around springs. Scattered counties in Pennsylvania, mostly southeast. Grows 12 to 32 inches; sun to part shade in sandy to clayey loam; very few sources.

### Juncus effusus var. pylaei

**Soft rush** — swamps and marshes, and moist to saturated meadows; FACW+. Throughout Pennsylvania. Can reach 36 inches; sun to part sun in mesic to moist sandy, rich loam; commonly available.

### Juncus filiformis

**Thread rush** — moist to wet soil along stream banks, pools, lakes or in meadow depressions; rarely in bogs. Northeastern counties in Pennsylvania; also reported in Warren and McKean counties. Grows 6 to 12 inches; sun to part sun in moist to wet sandy rich loam; very few sources.

### Juncus greenei

**Greene's rush** — dry sandy well-drained sites near lake shores, in sand dunes or pinelands; very rare and endangered; FAC. Reported only in Monroe and Pike Counties in Pennsylvania. Grows 10 to 30 inches; sun to part sun in dry sandy loam; very few sources.

### Juncus marginatus var. marginatus

**Grass-leaved rush** — bogs, shores, marshes and ditches in moist to wet clayey, peaty or sandy soils; FACW. Throughout Pennsylvania. Grows 10 to 20 inches; sun to part sun in rich, moist to wet sandy, peaty or clay loam; very few sources.

### Juncus nodosus

**Knotted rush** — moist to wet fields, swamps, fens, marshes, swales, bogs in sandy often calcareous soils; OBL. Widely scattered counties in Pennsylvania, mostly east. Grows 6 to 18 inches; sun to part sun in moist to wet sandy circumneutral soils; very few sources.

### Juncus tenuis

**Path rush** — moist to dry and sometimes heavily compacted soil of woods, fields, waste ground and paths; FAC-. Throughout Pennsylvania. Grows 4 to 32 inches; sun to part shade in dry to moist loam; commonly available.

### Leersia oryzoides

**Rice cutgrass** — clayey to sandy heavy wet soils in meadows and bogs, frequently in standing water; OBL. Throughout Pennsylvania. Grows 30 to 80 inches; full sun in moist to wet mucky to sandy loams; commonly available.

### Leersia virginica

**Cutgrass** — damp to wet woods, often along streams; FACW. Throughout Pennsylvania. Grows 20 to 50 inches; part sun to part shade in moist, rich sandy loam; very few sources.

### Luzula acuminata var. acuminata

**Hairy woodrush** — meadows, hillsides and open woods; FAC. Throughout Pennsylvania except widely scattered southeast. Grows 5 to 15 inches; sun to part sun in rich, sandy loam; very few sources.

### Luzula multiflora

**Field woodrush** — fields and meadows, clearings, open woods and roadside ditches; FACU. Throughout Pennsylvania. Can reach 30 inches; sun to part sun in dry to mesic sandy loam, pH 5 to 7; very few sources.

### Milium effusum var. cisatlanticum

**Milletgrass** — cool rich woods. Northern counties in Pennsylvania; scattered south-central. Grows 4 to 8 inches; part shade to shade in mesic to moist humusy loam; very few sources.

### Muhlenbergia frondosa

**Wirestem muhly** — thickets, clearings and forest edges and alluvial plains; FAC. Throughout Pennsylvania. Grows 20 to 40 inches; sun to part shade in moist sandy loam; very few sources.

## Muhlenbergia glomerata

**Spike muhly** — marshes, bogs, fens, meadows, lake shores and stream banks, prefers calcareous soils; FACW. Mostly eastern counties in Pennsylvania; scattered elsewhere. Grows 12 to 36 inches; sun to part sun in moist, rich sandy loam; very few sources.

## Muhlenbergia mexicana

**Muhly** — bogs, swamps, lake margins, moist prairies and woodlands; FACW. Mostly eastern counties in Pennsylvania; also far northwestern and south-central counties. Grows 20 to 40 inches; sun to part sun in mesic to moist sandy loams; very few sources.

## Muhlenbergia schreberi

**Dropseed** or **Nimblewill** — dry to mesic woodlands and prairies, river banks and ravines, often in sandy to rocky soil; FAC. Throughout Pennsylvania. Can reach 36 inches; sun to part shade in dry to moist sandy loam; can be invasive; very few sources.

## Panicum capillare

**Witchgrass** — fields, pastures, roadsides, waste places and ditches; FAC-. Throughout Pennsylvania. Grows 20 to 40 inches; sun to part sun in dry to moist sandy to clayey loam; very few sources.

## Panicum clandestinum

**Deer-tongue grass** — clearings and edges in damp, sandy woodlands and thickets; FAC+. Throughout Pennsylvania. Grows 30 to 50 inches; part sun to part shade in moist sandy loam; very few sources.

## Panicum dichotomiflorum

**Smooth panic grass** — dry to moist open woods, meadows, bogs, swamps, edges of lakes and ponds; FACW-. Throughout Pennsylvania. Grows 12 to 24 inches; part sun to part shade in dry to moist sandy loam; very few sources.

## Panicum oligosanthes var. oligosanthes

**Hellers rosette grass** — loamy, clayey soil of thickets, especially along the Delaware River; FACU. Eastern counties in Pennsylvania; also reported in Centre and Erie counties. Grows 10 to 30 inches; part sun in dry to moist clay loam; very few sources.

## Panicum rigidulum

**Panic grass** — marshy shorelines of rivers, lakes and ponds, swamps, wet pine savannahs, floodplain forests and wet low woods; rarely in dry sites; FACW+. Eastern, western and south-central counties in Pennsylvania; scattered elsewhere. Grows 20 to 40 inches; sun to part sun in moist to wet silty loam; very few sources.

## Panicum virgatum

**Switchgrass** — dry slopes of open oak or pine woodlands, river banks, marshes, but especially mesic to wet tall grass prairies; FAC. Scattered throughout Pennsylvania, mostly eastern counties. Can reach 6 feet; full sun to part shade in average, medium to wet soils. Prefers moist, sandy or clay soils in full sun. Tends to lose columnar form and flop in rich soils and too much shade; commonly available.

## Phalaris arundinacea

**Reed canary-grass** — dry to wet, well to drained soil, especially in marshes, swamps; FACW. Throughout Pennsylvania. Grows 10 to 30 inches; full sun to part shade in dry to wet sandy rich loam; several sources.

## Phragmites australis var. americana

**Common reed** — marshes, lake shores, swales and ditches in wet, muddy ground; FACW. Eastern counties in Pennsylvania from Monroe south; northwestern counties; scattered elsewhere. Grows 3 to 12 feet; full sun in moist to wet muddy loams. A very aggressive spreader and considered invasive; very few sources.

## Poa palustris

**Fowl bluegrass** — wet meadows, shores, thickets, riparian and upland areas; FACW. Eastern, north-central and northwestern counties in Pennsylvania; scattered elsewhere. Grows 20 to 50 inches; sun to part sun in moist to wet silty loam; several sources.

## Poa saltuensis

**Old-pasture bluegrass** — dry to mesic rich open woodlands and thickets in thin soils over limestone. Mostly northern counties in Pennsylvania; scattered south-central. Grows 20 to 50 inches; part sun to part shade in circumneutral dry to mesic loam; very few sources.

### Schizachyrium scoparium var. scoparium

**Little bluestem** — old fields, roadsides and open woods; FACU. Throughout Pennsylvania except northern tier counties. Grows 20 to 45 inches; sun to part shade in dry to moist sandy loam; commonly available.

### Schoenoplectus purshianus

**Bulrush** — lake shores, ponds and ditches, often emergent with relatively little water to level fluctuations; OBL. Southeastern counties in Pennsylvania; scattered elsewhere. Can reach 36 inches; sun to part sun in sandy soils, shallow standing water; very few sources.

### Schoenoplectus tabernaemontani

**Great bulrush** — fens, marshes, bogs, lakes, stream banks and sandbars, often emergent in water to 3 feet deep; OBL. Throughout Pennsylvania. Grows 18 to 30 inches; sun to part sun in sandy to silty soils, shallow standing water; very few sources.

### Scirpus atrocinctus

**Blackish wool-grass** — moist to wet meadows, marshes, ditches and swales; FACW+. Northeastern counties in Pennsylvania; scattered elsewhere. Grows 10 to 25 inches; sun to part sun in moist to wet rich silty loam; very few sources.

### Scirpus atrovirens

**Black bulrush** — marshes, moist meadows, swales, shores and ditches; FACW+. Throughout Pennsylvania. Grows 20 to 30 inches; sun to part sun in moist to wet rich silty loam; commonly available.

### Scirpus cyperinus

**Wool-grass** — marshes, wet meadows and swales; FACW+. Throughout Pennsylvania. Grows 30 to 60 inches; sun to part sun in moist to wet rich loam, including shallow water; commonly available.

### Scirpus expansus

**Wood bulrush** — marshes, wet meadows and swales; OBL. Far eastern counties in Pennsylvania; widely scattered elsewhere. Grows 12 to 30 inches; full sun in wet silty loam, including standing water; very few sources.

### Scirpus microcarpus

**Bulrush** — marshes, moist meadows, swales and ditches; OBL. Scattered counties in Pennsylvania, mostly north and east. Grows 12 to 30 inches; full sun in wet silty loam, including standing water; very few sources.

### Scirpus pendulus

**Bulrush** — marshes, moist meadows and ditches, often associated with calcareous substrates. Southeastern, south central and northwestern counties in Pennsylvania; scattered elsewhere. Grows 12 to 30 inches; full sun in wet silty circumneutral loam, including standing water; very few sources.

### Scirpus polyphyllus

**Bulrush** — swampy places and along streams, usually shaded by trees; OBL. Throughout Pennsylvania. Grows 12 to 30 inches; part shade in wet rich sandy loam, including standing water; very few sources.

### Sorghastrum nutans

**Indian-grass** — prairies, woodlands and savannahs, including scrublands; FACU. Throughout Pennsylvania, except for northern tier counties. Grows 3 to 6 feet; sun to part sun in dry to mesic sandy loam; commonly available.

### Sparganium americanum

**Bur-reed** — lake and pond shores and shallow, neutral to alkaline waters, sometimes forming large stands; OBL. Throughout Pennsylvania. Grows 20 to 50 inches; sun to part sun in sandy to silty moist to wet loams, including standing water; very few sources.

### Sparganium eurycarpum

**Bur-reed** — shores, ditches, low marshes, neutral to alkaline water on gravel, sand or mud, occasionally among boulders on wave to washed shorelines; OBL. Throughout Pennsylvania, especially northwestern and northeastern counties. Grows 20 to 50 inches; full sun in silty to sandy loam on pond edges or in standing water; commonly available.

### Sparganium fluctuans

**Bur-reed** — cold, still, acidic to neutral low-nutrient waters up to 6 feet deep; sometimes covers the surface with strap to shaped leaves; OBL. Extreme northeastern counties in Pennsylvania. Can reach 6 feet; full sun in standing water on silty to sandy loam; very few sources.

### Spartina pectinata

**Freshwater cordgrass** — marshes, sloughs and floodplains, especially those that are ice-scoured; OBL. Scattered throughout Pennsylvania, mostly northwest and southeast. Grows 3 to 6 feet; sun to part sun in moist to wet silty and alluvial loam; commonly available.

### Sphenopholis obtusata var. major

**Slender wedgegrass** — forests, marsh edges and prairies on dry open sites; FAC-. Southeastern counties in Pennsylvania; scattered elsewhere. Grows 10 to 25 inches; sun to part sun in dry to mesic sandy loam; very few sources.

### Tridens flavus

**Purpletop** — meadows, fields, roadsides and open woods; FACU. Throughout Pennsylvania except for northern tier and northwestern counties. Grows 40 to 50 inches; sun to part sun in dry sandy to clay loam; very few sources.

### Trisetum spicatum

**Oatgrass** — forests, moist meadows, rock ledges and scree fields; FACU. Reported only in Mercer and Lehigh Counties in Pennsylvania. Grows 4 to 20 inches; sun to part sun in dry sandy and rocky soils. AKA *Aira spicata*; very few sources.

### Vulpia octoflora var. glauca

**Six-weeks fescue** — open woodlands and clearings, savannahs, meadows, roadsides in dry and sterile soil; UPL. Southeastern and south-central counties in Pennsylvania; widely scattered elsewhere. Grows 4 to 16 inches; sun to part sun in dry to mesic infertile sandy loams; very few sources.

## Additional Pennsylvania species

The following seven species are commonly available natives whose range includes Pennsylvania, but have not been reported in Carbon, Monroe, Pike or Wayne counties.

***Bouteloua curtipendula*** (Side-oats grama) — Prairies, fields, forest openings, open rocky slopes. Pennsylvania distribution is in scattered counties generally west and south of the Poconos; listed as threatened in Pennsylvania. Clump-forming; grow in dry to medium moisture average soils in full sun; tolerates many soils from well-drained sandy loams to heavy clays. Clumps can be cut to the ground in late winter.

***Carex crinita var. brevicrinis*** (Sedge) — Wet meadows, marshes, bogs, floodplain forests, swamps and edges of streams, lakes and ponds; OBL. Pennsylvania natural distribution is limited to Northampton and Bucks counties. Grow in moist to wet, well-drained rich soils in sun to part shade; prefers part shade.

***Carex grayi*** (Sedge) — Wet to mesic deciduous forests and openings, typically on fine alluvial or lacustrine deposits, and river bottoms; FACW+. Pennsylvania natural range includes southeastern counties from the Lehigh Valley to the Maryland line and scattered counties to the west. Grow in fertile, moist soil in full sun, especially at or near water; tolerates light shade.

***Juncus trey*** (Torrez's rush) — Calcareous wet meadows and swamps, sometimes on clay soils, and on wet sandy shores and the edges of sloughs and slightly alkaline watercourses; FACW. Pennsylvania range includes scattered western and central counties plus the Lehigh Valley; listed as endangered in Pennsylvania and several other states. Grow in full sun in calcareous, moist to wet silty to clay loams.

***Celeriac macrantha*** (June grass) — Generally sandy upland or high prairie sites, woods openings and open rocky slopes that are cool, semi-arid and somewhat infertile; a cool-season grass that goes dormant in late summer. Pennsylvania native range reported only as Bradford County; listed as extirpated. Grow in rocky or sandy soils in full sun.

***Muhlenbergia capillaries*** (Hairgrass, Hair awn muhly) — Dry, exposed ledges, sandy prairies; FACW+. Only in Lancaster County; listed as extirpated in the state. Grow in sandy moist soils in full sun; prized for its stunning pink to lavender floral display in autumn.

***Spurious heterolysis*** (Prairie dropseed) — Mesic prairies, well-drained moraines, rock outcrops, glades, pine savannahs and barrens, lightly grazed pastures; UPL. Pennsylvania native range is reported as Lancaster and Chester counties; listed as endangered in Pennsylvania and adjacent states. Grow in well-drained, dry to medium average soils in full sun; prefers rocky, dry soils. Tolerant of drought, but slow to establish.

### *Possibly challenging to find*

The following 41 native graminoids, whose range includes Pennsylvania but distribution does not include northeastern counties, are available in the commercial marketplace, but may be challenging to find:

*Ammophila breviligulata* (American beachgrass)
*Andropogon glomeratus* (Broom-sedge)
*Carex alata* (Broad-winged sedge)
*Carex albursina* (Sedge)
*Carex aquatilis* (Water sedge)
*Carex atherodes* (Awned sedge)
*Carex aurea* (Golden-fruited sedge)
*Carex conjuncta* (Sedge)
*Carex crawfordii* (Crawford's sedge)
*Carex eburnea* (Ebony sedge)
*Carex frankii* (Sedge)
*Carex geyeri* (Geyer's sedge)
*Carex hyalinolepis* (Shoreline sedge)
*Carex jamesii* (Sedge)
*Carex pseudocyperus* (Cyperus-like sedge)
*Carex shortiana* (Sedge)
*Carex squarrosa* (Sedge)
*Carex typhina* (Cat-tail sedge)
*Carex viridula var. viridula* (Green sedge)
*Carex woodii* (Sedge)
*Chasmanthium laxum* (Slender sea-oats)
*Cyperus schweinitzii* (Schweinitz's flatsedge)
*Distichlis spicata* (Seashore saltgrass)
*Eleocharis parvula* (Dwarf spike-rush)
*Eleocharis quadrangulata* (Four-angled spike-rush)
*Eleocharis rostellata* (Beaked spike-rush)
*Festuca paradoxa* (Cluster fescue)
*Glyceria septentrionalis* (Floating mannagrass)

*Juncus arcticus var. littoralis* (Baltic rush)
*Juncus biflorus* (Grass rush)
*Juncus gerardii* (Blackfoot rush)
*Milium effusum var. cisatlanticum* (Milletgrass)
*Panicum anceps* (Panic grass)
*Panicum leibergii* (Leiberg's panic grass)
*Panicum longifolium* (Long-leaved panic grass)
*Rhynchospora globularis* (Beak-rush)
*Schoenoplectus acutus* (Great bulrush)
*Sparganium androcladum* (Branching bur-reed)
*Spartina patens* (Salt-meadow grass)
*Stipa spartea* (Needlegrass)
*Tripsacum dactyloides* (Gammagrass)

## Apparently unavailable

The following 212 species of native graminoids include Pennsylvania in their range, but do not appear to be commercially available:
*Agrostis altissima* (Tall bentgrass)
*Andropogon gyrans* (Elliott's beardgrass)
*Aristida dichotoma var. dichotoma* (Poverty-grass)
*Bulbostylis capillaris* (Sandrush)
*Calamagrostis cinnoides* (Reedgrass)
*Calamagrostis porteri* (Porter's reedgrass)
*Carex adusta* (Crowded sedge)
*Carex aestivalis* (Sedge)
*Carex aestivalis x gracillima* (Sedge)
*Carex aggregata* (Sedge)
*Carex albicans* (Sedge)
*Carex albolutescens* (Sedge)
*Carex amphibola var. rigida* (Sedge)
*Carex backii* (Back's sedge)
*Carex barrattii* (Barratt's sedge)
*Carex brunnescens* (Sedge)
*Carex bullata* (Bull Sedge)
*Carex canescens var. canescens* (Sedge)
*Carex canescens var. disjuncta* (Sedge)
*Carex careyana* (Carey's sedge)
*Carex caroliniana* (Sedge)
*Carex cephaloidea* (Sedge)
*Carex chordorrhiza* (Creeping sedge)
*Carex collinsii* (Collin's sedge)
*Carex communis* (Sedge)
*Carex cryptolepis* (Northeastern sedge)
*Carex cumulata* (Sedge)
*Carex davisii* (Sedge)
*Carex debilis var. debilis* (Sedge)
*Carex debilis var. pubera* (Sedge)

*Carex debilis var. rudgei* (Sedge)
*Carex digitalis* (Sedge)
*Carex disperma* (Soft-leaved sedge)
*Carex emmonsii* (Sedge)
*Carex festucacea* (Sedge)
*Carex foenea* (Fernald's hay sedge)
*Carex formosa* (Handsome sedge)
*Carex garberi* (Elk sedge)
*Carex gracilescens* (Sedge)
*Carex grisea* (Sedge)
*Carex haydenii* (Cloud sedge)
*Carex hirtifolia* (Sedge)
*Carex hitchcockiana* (Sedge)
*Carex laevivaginata* (Sedge)
*Carex leavenworthii* (Sedge)
*Carex leptalea* (Sedge)
*Carex leptonervia* (Sedge)
*Carex limosa* (Mud sedge)
*Carex longii* (Long's sedge)
*Carex lucorum* (Sedge)
*Carex meadii* (Mead's sedge)
*Carex mesochorea* (Midland sedge)
*Carex mitchelliana* (Mitchell's sedge)
*Carex nigromarginata* (Sedge)
*Carex novae-angliae* (Sedge)
*Carex oligocarpa* (Sedge)
*Carex oligosperma* (Few-seeded sedge)
*Carex ormostachya* (Spike sedge)
*Carex pallescens* (Sedge)
*Carex pauciflora* (Few-flowered sedge)
*Carex paupercula* (Bog sedge)
*Carex planispicata* (Sedge)
*Carex polymorpha* (Variable sedge)
*Carex prasina* (Sedge)
*Carex retroflexa* (Sedge)
*Carex retrorsa* (Backward sedge)
*Carex richardsonii* (sedge)
*Carex sartwellii* (Sartwell's sedge)
*Carex scabrata* (Sedge)
*Carex schweinitzii* (Schweinitz' sedge)
*Carex seorsa* (Sedge)
*Carex siccata* (Sedge)
*Carex straminea* (Sedge)
*Carex striatula* (Sedge)
*Carex styloflexa* (Sedge)
*Carex tonsa var. rugosperma* (Sedge)
*Carex torta* (Sedge)
*Carex trisperma* (Sedge)
*Carex umbellata* (Sedge)
*Carex vestita* (Sedge)

*Carex wiegandii* (Wiegand's sedge)
*Carex willdenovii* (Sedge)
*Carex x florabundum* (Wood's sedge)
*Cinna latifolia* (Drooping woodreed)
*Cladium mariscoides* (Twig-rush)
*Critesion jubatum* (Foxtail-barley)
*Cymophyllus fraserianus* (Fraser's sedge)
*Cyperus bipartitus* (Umbrella sedge)
*Cyperus dentatus* (Umbrella sedge)
*Cyperus diandrus* (Umbrella sedge)
*Cyperus flavescens* (Umbrella sedge)
*Cyperus houghtonii* (Houghton's flatsedge)
*Cyperus lancastriensis* (Umbrella sedge)
*Cyperus lupulinus* (Umbrella sedge)
*Cyperus plukenetii* (Plukenet's flatsedge)
*Cyperus refractus* (Reflexed flatsedge)
*Cyperus retrofractus* (Rough flatsedge)
*Cyperus retrorsus* (Retrorse flatsedge)
*Cyperus squarrosus* (Umbrella sedge)
*Cyperus strigosus* (False nutsedge)
*Deschampsia cespitosa* (Tufted hairgrass)
*Eleocharis compressa var. compressa* (Flat-stemmed spike-rush)
*Eleocharis elliptica* (Slender spike-rush)
*Eleocharis intermedia* (Matted spike-rush)
*Eleocharis obtusa var. obtusa* (Wright's spike-rush)
*Eleocharis olivacea* (Capitate spike-rush)
*Eleocharis pauciflora var. fernaldii* (Spike-rush)
*Eleocharis robbinsii* (Robbins' spike-rush)
*Eleocharis tenuis var. pseudoptera* (Slender spike-rush)
*Eleocharis tenuis var. tenuis* (Spike-rush)
*Eleocharis tenuis var. verrucosa* (Slender spike-rush)
*Eleocharis tricostata* (Three-ribbed spike-rush)
*Eleocharis tuberculosa* (Long-tubercled spike-rush)
*Elytrigia pungens* (Saltmarsh wheatgrass)
*Eragrostis capillaris* (Lacegrass)
*Eragrostis frankii* (Lovegrass)
*Eragrostis hypnoides* (Creeping lovegrass)
*Eragrostis pectinacea* (Carolina lovegrass)
*Erianthus giganteus* (Giant beardgrass)
*Eriophorum gracile* (Slender cotton-grass)
*Eriophorum tenellum* (Rough cotton-grass)
*Eriophorum vaginatum ssp. spissum* (Cotton-grass)
*Eriophorum viridicarinatum* (Thin-leaved cotton-grass)

*Glyceria acutiflora* (Mannagrass)
*Glyceria borealis* (Northern mannagrass)
*Glyceria canadensis x grandis* (Rattlesnake grass)
*Glyceria obtusa* (Coastal mannagrass)
*Juncus brachycephalus* (Small-headed rush)
*Juncus brevicaudatus* (Narrow-panicled rush)
*Juncus debilis* (Weak rush)
*Juncus dichotomus* (Forked rush)
*Juncus gymnocarpus* (Coville's rush)
*Juncus militaris* (Bayonet rush)
*Juncus pelocarpus* (Brown-fruited rush)
*Juncus scirpoides* (Sedge rush)
*Juncus secundus* (Rush)
*Juncus subcaudatus* (Rush)
*Leptoloma cognatum* (Fall witchgrass)
*Luzula bulbosa* (Woodrush)
*Luzula echinata* (Common woodrush)
*Muhlenbergia sobolifera* (Creeping muhly)
*Muhlenbergia sylvatica* (Muhly)
*Muhlenbergia tenuiflora* (Muhly)
*Muhlenbergia uniflora* (Fall dropseed muhly)
*Oryzopsis asperifolia* (Spreading ricegrass)
*Oryzopsis pungens* (Slender mountain ricegrass)
*Oryzopsis racemosa* (Ricegrass)
*Panicum acuminatum* (Panic grass)
*Panicum annulum* (Annulus panic grass)
*Panicum bicknellii* (Bicknell's panicgrass)
*Panicum boreale* (Northern panic grass)
*Panicum boscii* (Panic grass)
*Panicum clandestinum* (Deer-tongue grass)
*Panicum columbianum* (Panic grass)
*Panicum commutatum* (Panic grass)
*Panicum depauperatum* (Poverty panic grass)
*Panicum dichotomum* (Panic grass)
*Panicum gattingeri* (Witchgrass)
*Panicum latifolium* (Panic grass)
*Panicum linearifolium* (Panic grass)
*Panicum lucidum* (Shining panic grass)
*Panicum meridionale* (Panic grass)
*Panicum microcarpon* (Panic grass)
*Panicum philadelphicum* (Panic grass)
*Panicum polyanthes* (Panic grass)
*Panicum recognitum* (Fernald's panic grass)
*Panicum scoparium* (Velvety panic grass)
*Panicum sphaerocarpon* (Panic grass)
*Panicum spretum* (Panic grass)
*Panicum stipitatum* (Panic grass)
*Panicum verrucosum* (Panic grass)
*Panicum villosissimum* (Long-haired panic grass)
*Panicum xanthophysum* (Slender panic grass)

*Panicum yadkinense* (Yadkin River panic grass)
*Paspalum laeve var. circulare* (Field beadgrass)
*Paspalum laeve var. laeve* (Field beadgrass)
*Paspalum laeve var. pilosum* (Field beadgrass)
*Paspalum setaceum var. muhlenbergii* (Slender beadgrass)
*Paspalum setaceum* (Slender beadgrass)
*Piptochaetium avenaceum* (Black oatgrass)
*Poa alsodes* (Woodland bluegrass)
*Poa autumnalis* (Autumn bluegrass)
*Poa cuspidata* (Bluegrass)
*Poa languida* (Woodland bluegrass)
*Poa paludigena* (Bog bluegrass)
*Rhynchospora fusca* (Brown beak-rush)
*Rhynchospora gracilenta* (Beak-rush)
*Scheuchzeria palustris* (Pod-grass)
*Schizachne purpurascens* (Grass)
*Schoenoplectus fluviatilis* (River bulrush)
*Schoenoplectus heterochaetus* (Slender bulrush)
*Schoenoplectus pungens* (Chairmaker's rush)
*Schoenoplectus smithii* (Smith's bulrush)
*Schoenoplectus subterminalis* (Water bulrush)
*Schoenoplectus torreyi* (Torrey's bulrush)
*Scirpus ancistrochaetus* (Northeastern bulrush)
*Scirpus hattorianus* (Bulrush)
*Scirpus pedicellatus* (Wool-grass)
*Scleria minor* (Small nut-rush)
*Scleria pauciflora* (Few-flowered nut-rush)
*Scleria triglomerata* (Whip-grass)
*Sparganium angustifolium* (Bur-reed)
*Sparganium chlorocarpum* (Bur-reed)
*Sparganium minimum* (Small bur-reed)
*Sphenopholis pensylvanica* (Swamp-oats)
*Sporobolus asper* (Dropseed)
*Sporobolus clandestinus* (Rough dropseed)
*Sporobolus vaginiflorus* (Poverty grass)
*Torreyochloa pallida var. fernaldii* (Pale meadow-grass)
*Torreyochloa pallida var. pallida* (Pale meadow-grass)
*Trichophorum planifolium* (Club-rush)
*Triglochin palustre* (Marsh arrow-grass)

# Native plants: ferns and fern allies

This section includes *pteridophytes* — that is, herbaceous species that reproduce from spores rather than flowers, including ferns and fern allies, subdivided in the following manner:

- Native species whose range includes Pennsylvania and whose observed distribution includes Carbon, Monroe, Pike and/or Wayne counties, all of which are commercially available

- Several native species whose range includes Pennsylvania but have not been reported in Carbon, Monroe, Pike or Wayne counties that may be difficult to find in the retail marketplace.

- A list of 49 species that appear to be commercially unavailable

The 50 entries on this list are all represented in the northeastern counties and are organized in the following manner:

Latin (or scientific) name

Common name(s)

A brief description of natural habitat

US Fish and Wildlife Service wetland indicators when available

Observed Pennsylvania distribution

Length of fronds in varied habitats

Rhizome characteristics, an indication of spreading traits

Suggestions for home cultivation, including light requirements, moisture, soil description, and if available soil pH range and preference

How relatively easy it is to find in the commercial marketplace, in the context of nationwide mail order nurseries.

### .Adiantum pedatum

**Northern maidenhair** — rich, deciduous woodlands, often on humus-covered talus slopes and moist lime soils; FAC-. Grows throughout Pennsylvania. Fronds 12 to 30 inches; rhizome: short creeping. Grow in part shade to shade in moist sandy organic loam, pH 5-7; commonly available, including many garden centers.

### Asplenium platyneuron

**Ebony spleenwort** — forest floor or on rocks, often invading masonry and disturbed soils; FACU. Grows throughout Pennsylvania. Fronds 8 to 18 inches; rhizome: short creeping to ascending. Grow in part shade to shade in dry to moist sandy clay loam, pH 5-7.5; several sources.

### Asplenium trichomanes

**Maidenhair spleenwort** — acidic rocks such as sandstone, basalt, and granite, very rarely on calcareous rocks. All but northwestern Pennsylvania counties. Fronds 4 to 7 inches; rhizome: short creeping to ascending. Grow in part shade to shade in dry to moist rocky, humusy loam, pH 4-7.5; very few sources

### Athyrium filix-femina

**Lady fern** — wooded valleys along streams, on rich wooded slopes and on floors of ravines, swamps, moist meadows and thickets; FAC. Throughout Pennsylvania. Fronds 12 to 24 inches; rhizome: erect or ascending in clumps. Grow in sun to part shade in moist rich sandy loam, pH 4-7; commonly available, including many garden centers.

### Botrychium virginianum

**Rattlesnake fern** — moist shaded forests, wooded slopes and shrubby second growth, rare or absent in arid regions; FACU. Throughout

Pennsylvania. Fronds 6 to 20 inches, rhizome: erect, subterranean. Grow in part shade to shade in moist rich sandy loam, pH 4-6; very few sources.

### Camptosorus rhizophyllus

**Walking fern** — shaded, usually moss-covered boulders and ledges, usually on limestone or other basic rocks, but occasionally on sandstone or other acidic rocks, rarely on fallen tree trunks. All but northwestern counties of Pennsylvania. Fronds 4 to 10 inches; rhizome: ascending. Grow in part shade to shade in dry to moist calcareous loam, pH 6.5-7.5; very few sources.

### Cheilanthes lanosa

**Hairy lip fern** — rocky slopes and ledges, on a variety of substrates including limestone and granite, mostly eastern Poconos and into southeastern Pennsylvania. Fronds 6 to 16 inches; rhizome: short creeping. Grow in part sun to shade in dry sandy loam, pH 5-6; very few sources.

### Cystopteris bulbifera

**Bublet bladder fern** — typically moist calcareous cliffs, but also grows on rock in dense woods and occasionally occurs terrestrially in northern swamps; FAC. All but west central counties of Pennsylvania. Fronds 18 to 36 inches; rhizome: short creeping. Grow in part shade to shade in moist calcareous loam, pH 6.5 to 7.5; very few sources.

### Cystopteris fragilis

**Fragile fern** — commonly on cliff faces, also in thin alkaline soil over rock; FACU. Scattered distribution, mostly in central Appalachians and northeastern counties. Fronds 5 to 16 inches; rhizome: compact. Grow in part shade to shade in moist to wet garden soil; very few sources.

### Dennstaedtia punctilobula

**Hay scented fern** — rocky slopes, meadows, woods, stream banks, and roadsides, in acid soils. Throughout Pennsylvania. Fronds 15 to 30 inches, rhizome: very long-creeping. Grow in sun to part shade in dry, well drained sandy and acidic loam, pH 4-6. Aggressive spreader; forms vast colonies, especially where deer pressure is high because deer ignore it; commonly available.

### Deparia acrostichoides

**Silvery glade fern** — along stream edges, river banks and damp woods, often on shaly slopes; FAC. Throughout Pennsylvania. Fronds to 40 inches; rhizome: short creeping. Grow in part sun to shade in moist acidic sandy loam, pH 5-7 but prefers 5 to 5.7; very few sources.

### Diphasiastrum tristachyum

**Deep-rooted running-pine** — sterile, acidic soils in open coniferous forests and oak forests, sandy barrens and clearings. Throughout Pennsylvania except for central counties just east of the Allegheny Front. Stems 6 to 12 inches; rhizome: short creeping. Grow in part shade to shade in moist acidic humusy loam; very few sources.

### Diplazium pycnocarpon

**Narrow-leaved glade fern** — wooded glades and alluvial thickets, neutral soil, but not in ridge and valley provinces; FAC. Northeast, southeast, southwest and northwest counties of Pennsylvania. Fronds 18 to 40 inches; rhizome: short creeping. Grow in part shade in moist organic circumneutral garden loam; very few sources.

### Dryopteris carthusiana

**Spinose wood fern** — swampy woods, moist wooded slopes, stream banks, and conifer plantations; FAC+. Throughout Pennsylvania. Fronds 12 to 36 inches; rhizome: ascending crown. Grow in part sun to shade in moist organic loam; commonly available.

### Dryopteris clintoniana

**Clinton's wood fern** — deep humus in swampy woods, especially maple swamps. Prefers wet mucky woods, thickets; FACW+. Northeastern counties of Pennsylvania, scattered elsewhere. Fronds 24 to 48 inches; rhizome: short creeping. Grow in part shade to shade in moist to wet rich silty loam, pH 4-6; very few sources.

### Dryopteris cristata

**Crested shield fern** — swamps, swampy woods, or open shrubby wetlands; prefers wet mucky woods, thickets; FACW+. Throughout Pennsylvania. Fronds 12 to 36 inches, rhizome: short creeping. Grow in part shade to shade in moist rich silty loam, pH 4-6; very few sources.

### Dryopteris goldiana

**Goldie's wood fern** — dense, moist woods, especially ravines, limey seeps, or at the edge of swamps, in deep humus; FAC+. Northeastern, southeastern and western counties. Fronds 36 to 48 inches, rhizome: short creeping. Grow in part shade to shade in moist rich humusy loam, pH 4-7; commonly available.

### Dryopteris intermedia

**Evergreen wood fern** — moist rocky woods, especially hemlock hardwoods, ravines, and edges of swamps; FACU. Throughout Pennsylvania. Fronds 18 to 36 inches. Rhizome: erect crown Grow in part shade to shade in moist organic loam, pH 4.5 to 7.5; very few sources.

### Dryopteris marginalis

**Marginal wood fern** — rocky, wooded slopes and ravines, edges of woods, stream banks and road banks, and rock walls; FACU-. Throughout Pennsylvania. Fronds 18 to 30 inches, rhizome: erect crown. Grow in part sun to shade in moist rich sandy loam, pH 5-6; commonly available, including many garden centers.

### Equisetum arvense

**Field horsetail** — moist roadsides, riverbanks, fields, marshes, pastures, and tundra; FAC. Throughout Pennsylvania. Stems 8 to 18 inches, rhizome: long creeping. Grow in sun to part sun in moist rich sandy loam; very few sources.

### Equisetum fluviatile

**Water horsetail** — standing water; in ponds, ditches, marshes, swales, edges of rivers and lakes; OBL. Eastern, south central and northwestern counties in Pennsylvania. Stems 24 to 26 inches; rhizome: short creeping. Grow in sun to part sun in ponds and pond edges or frequently inundated or poorly drained low area with a base of silty loam; very few sources.

### Equisetum hyemale var. affine

**Scouring-rush** — riverbanks, lakeshores and woodlands; moist sandy and gravelly slopes; stream banks, embankments and roadsides; FACW. Eastern and western counties of Pennsyl-

vania, scattered elsewhere. Stems 14 to 48 inches; rhizome: creeping. Grow in sun to part shade in rich moist sandy loam. Can be difficult to control because of deep rhizomes; commonly available.

### Equisetum sylvaticum

**Woodland horsetail** — moist open woods and wet meadows; FACW. All but southwestern counties of Pennsylvania. Stems 10 to 30 inches. Rhizome: creeping. Grow in sun to part shade in moist sandy clay loam; very few sources.

### Gymnocarpium dryopteris

**Common oak fern** — cool, coniferous and mixed woods and at base of shale talus slopes often in pockets of humus; UPL. Northern counties in Pennsylvania, scattered elsewhere. Fronds 9 to 12 inches; rhizome: wide or long creeping. Grow in part shade to shade in moist rocky humus; very few sources.

### Lycopodium annotinum

**Bristly clubmoss** — swampy or cool shaded often moist coniferous forests, mountain forests, and exposed grassy or rocky sites; FAC. Mostly northern tier counties in Pennsylvania, as well as Fayette, Somerset, Westmoreland, Cambria and Indiana counties. Stems 2 to 10 inches; rhizome: long creeping. Grow in part sun to shade in mesic to moist rich acidic humus; very few sources.

### Lycopodium clavatum

**Common clubmoss** — bogs, open woods and rocky barrens; FAC. Stems 2 to 10 inches; rhizome: long creeping. Throughout Pennsylvania. Grow in part sun to part shade in mesic rich acidic humus; very few sources.

### Lycopodium obscurum

**Flat branched ground-pine** — rich hardwood forests and successional shrubby areas; FACU. Throughout Pennsylvania. Stems 8 to 10 inches; rhizome: long-creeping. Grow in part shade to shade in mesic to moist rich acidic humus; very few sources.

### Lygodium palmatum

**Climbing fern** or **Hartford fern** — moist thickets, barrens, swamp edges, open woods, acidic, poorly drained and peaty soil; FACW. Scattered, mostly northeastern counties. Twining, climbing to 15 feet; rhizome: short creeping. Grow in full shade in acidic, peaty sandy loam, pH 4-7. Can be difficult to grow; very few sources.

### Matteuccia struthiopteris

**Ostrich fern** — rich humus on rocky stream banks, moist alluvial flats, floodplains, mucky swamps and rich woods; FACW. Northern tier counties of Pennsylvania, scattered elsewhere. Fronds 24 to 72 inches; rhizome: erect, but with wide-reaching stolons. Grow in part sun to shade in moist organic loams. pH 5 to 7.5. Dramatic vase-like habit; forms extensive colonies via multiple stolons; commonly available.

### Onoclea sensibilis

**Sensitive fern** — open swamps, thickets, marshes, or low woods, in muddy soil in sunny wet meadows or shaded stream bank locations, often forming thick stands; FACW. Throughout Pennsylvania. Fronds 12 to 36 inches; rhizome: short creeping. Grow in part sun to shade in moist silty humusy loams, pH 4.5 to 7.5 but prefers acidic soil; commonly available, including better garden centers.

### Osmunda cinnamomea

**Cinnamon fern** — swamps, stream banks, roadsides, Moist areas, acidic soils, frequently in vernal seeps, ponds and swamps; FACW. Throughout Pennsylvania. Fronds 30 to 60 inches; rhizome: erect with occasional offshoots. Grow in part sun to part shade in moist acidic organic humusy to silty soils, pH 5.5 to 7; commonly available.

### Osmunda claytoniana

**Interrupted fern** — oozy mud swamps, bogs, and stream banks; also, rich, mesic woods and open woods and shaded roadsides; FAC. Throughout Pennsylvania. Fronds 24 to 48 inches; rhizome: erect with occasional offshoots. Grow in part sun to part shade in rich mesic to moist silty loam, pH 4-6; commonly available.

### Osmunda regalis

**Royal fern** — swamps, bogs, bluffs, stream banks in moist acidic soils; OBL. Throughout Pennsylvania. Fronds 24 to 60 inches; rhizome: erect with occasional offshoots. Grow in part sun

to part shade in moist to wet silty organic loam, pH 4-6; commonly available.

### Pellaea atropurpurea

**Purple cliffbrake** — dry soils adjacent to dolomite glades and crevices of limestone and dolomite outcrops, bluffs, boulders and sink holes. Mostly eastern and central counties of Pennsylvania, scattered elsewhere. Fronds 8 to 20 inches; rhizome: short creeping. Grow in part sun to part shade in dry to mesic sandy loam, pH 5.5 to 7.5 but prefers 6.5 to 7.5; very few sources.

### Phegopteris connectilis

**Long beech fern** or **narrow beech fern** — cool shade, woods in moist loose humus, strongly to moderately acid soil, or on rocks in shaded rock crevices. Mostly northern and eastern counties of Pennsylvania, scattered elsewhere. Fronds 8 to 18 inches; rhizome: medium creeping. Grow in part shade to shade in mesic to moist rocky sandy humusy loam, pH 4 to 6; very few sources.

### Phegopteris hexagonoptera

**Broad beech fern** — moist woods, usually in full shade, often in moderately acid soils; FAC. Throughout Pennsylvania. Fronds 12 to 24 inches, rhizome: long creeping. Grow in part shade to shade in moist acidic garden loam; very few sources.

### Polypodium virginianum

**Common polypody** — rocks, boulders, cliffs, ledges, rocky woods; on a variety of substrates. Throughout Pennsylvania. Fronds 4 to 14 inches; rhizome: sort to medium creeping. Grow in part shade to shade in moist rich loam, pH 4 to 6; very few sources.

### Polystichum acrostichoides

**Christmas fern** — forest floors and shady, rocky slopes in organically rich, dry to medium wet, well-drained soil; FACU-. Throughout Pennsylvania. Fronds 12 to 24 inches; rhizome: multiple crown. Grow in part shade to shade in dry to moist sandy rich loam, pH 4 to 7; commonly available, including most garden centers.

### Polystichum braunii

**Braun's holly fern** — moist places in boreal

forests; interior moist forests; cool rocky shaded ravines. Distribution limited to Wayne, Luzerne, Sullivan and Columbia counties I Pennsylvania. Fronds 8 to 36 inches; rhizome: clump-forming. Grow in part shade to shade on cool sites in peaty, humusy moist loam; very few sources.

### Pteridium aquilinum

**Northern bracken fern** — sunny to partly shaded dry areas with infertile soil in barrens, pastures, and open woodlands in moderately to strong acid soil, abundant, forming large colonies; FACU. Throughout Pennsylvania. Fronds 18 to 50 inches; rhizome: very long creeping. Grow in sun to part shade in dry to mesic sterile sandy loam, pH 4 to 5. Unpalatable to deer; aggressive spreader and forms large colonies; very few sources.

### Selaginella apoda

**Meadow spikemoss** — swamps, meadows, marshes, pastures, damp lawns, open woods, and stream banks, in basic to acidic soil; FACW. Northeastern, southeastern, south central and northwestern counties of Pennsylvania. Mat forming, low creeping multi-branched rhizome. Grow in part sun to part shade in moist to wet rich loam; very few sources.

### Thelypteris noveboracensis

**New York fern** — terrestrial in moist woods, especially near swamps, streams, and in vernal seeps of ravines, often in slightly disturbed secondary forests, frequently forming large colonies; prefers dry oak, beech, maple and birch woods; FAC. Throughout Pennsylvania. Fronds 12 to 24 inches; rhizome: long creeping. Grow in high shade in mesic to moist humus rich sandy loam, pH 4 to 6. Aggressive spreader and can become invasive, forming huge woodland colonies. Reported to be ignored by deer, hence the carpeting; very few sources. AKA *Parathelypteris noveboracensis*; several sources.

### Thelypteris palustris var. pubescens

**Marsh fern** — swamps, bogs, and marshes in soft rich muddy soil, also along riverbanks and roadside ditches, and in wet woods; FACW. Throughout Pennsylvania. Fronds 18 to 30 inches; rhizome: long creeping. Grow in part sun to part shade in moist to wet rich silty loam, pH 4 to

7 but prefers 4.5 to 6.5; several sources.

### Woodsia ilvensis

**Rusty woodsia** — sunny cliffs and rocky slopes, usually in contact with rock; found on variety of substrates. South central and northeastern counties of Pennsylvania, including the Lehigh Valley and Bucks County. Fronds 3-8 inches; rhizome: erect to ascending. Grow in part sun to part shade in moist to wet acidic garden soil, pH 5 to 6; very few sources.

### Woodsia obtusa

**Blunt lobed woodsia** — cliffs and rocky slopes (rarely terrestrial); found on a variety of substrates including both granite and limestone. Southern, central and northeastern counties of Pennsylvania. Fronds 5 to 15 inches; rhizome: short creeping or ascending. Grow in part sun to part shade in dry to mesic sandy humusy loam, pH 5 to 7.5; very few sources.

### Woodwardia areolata

**Netted chain fern** — acidic bogs, seeps, and wet woods; FACW. Eastern counties of Pennsylvania, scattered western counties. Fronds 12 to 24 inches, rhizome: long-creeping. Grow in part sun to part shade in moist to wet rich loam; very few sources.

### Woodwardia virginica

**Virginia chain fern** — acidic swamps, marshes, bogs, and roadside ditches over noncalcareous substrates; OBL. Eastern and northwestern counties of Pennsylvania, scattered elsewhere. Fronds 18 to 24 inches; rhizome: long creeping. Grow in high shade to dappled shade in acidic moist to wet garden soil; very few sources.

## Other ferns, possibly hard to find

Three species of ferns native to Pennsylvania but not reported in the northeastern counties may be challenging to find in the commercial marketplace

*Adiantum aleuticum* (Aleutian maidenhair) — shaded banks, serpentine barrens, talus slopes, wooded ravines; primarily in the western areas of the continent, but scattered in the northeast. Fronds 12 to 24 inches; rhizome: clump-forming. Pennsylvania distribution limited to serpentine barrens in Lancaster County. Grow in part shade to shade in a moist humusy loam; prefers growing on serpentine rock. Very few sources.

***Asplenium resiliens*** (Black-stemmed spleenwort) — Limestone cliffs and in sinkholes on calcareous rock. Pennsylvania distribution limited to Fulton and Franklin Counties and listed as endangered in Pennsylvania (and several other states). Fronds: several inches; rhizomes: erect. Grow in moist humusy soil over limestone rocks in part shade. Very few sources.

***Dryopteris celsa*** (Log fern) — Range primarily on the Piedmont and Coastal Plain in seepage slopes, hammocks and on logs in swamps; OBL. Pennsylvania distribution in southeastern counties. Fronds to 50 inches; rhizomes: medium to short creeping. Grow in average, mesic to wet soils in part shade to full shade. Prefers acidic, humusy, moist soils in high shade, sheltered from wind. Very few sources.

## Unavailable species

A total of 49 fern and fern ally species do not appear to be commercially available:

*Asplenium montanum* (Mountain spleenwort)
*Asplenium ruta-muraria* (Wall rue spleenwort)
*Asplenium trichomanes* (Maidenhair spleenwort)
*Asplenium x ebenoides* (Scott's spleenwort)
*Botrychium dissectum* (Cut-leaved grape-fern)
*Botrychium lanceolatum* (Triangle moonwort)
*Botrychium matricariifolium* (Daisy-leaved moonwort)
*Botrychium multifidum* (Leathery grape fern)
*Botrychium oneidense* (Blunt-lobed grape fern)
*Botrychium simplex* (Least moonwort)
*Cystopteris protrusa* (Protruding bladder fern)
*Cystopteris tenuis* (Fragile fern)
*Cystopteris x laurentiana* (Laurentian bladder fern)
*Diphasiastrum digitatum* (Deep-rooted running-pine)
*Diphasiastrum digitatum x tristachyum* (Ground-pine)
*Dryopteris intermedia x marginalis* (Hybrid wood-fern)

*Dryopteris x boottii* (Boott's hybrid wood fern)
*Dryopteris x dowellii* (Dowell's wood-fern)
*Dryopteris x pittsfordensis* (Pittsford wood-fern)
*Dryopteris x slossonae* (Boot's hybrid wood fern)
*Dryopteris x triploidea* (Triploid hybrid wood fern)
*Dryopteris x uliginosa* (Braun's wood fern)
*Equisetum variegatum* (Variegated horsetail)
*Equisetum variegatum* (Variegated horsetail)
*Equisetum x ferrissi* (Intermediate scouring-rush)
*Equisetum x litorale* (Shore horsetail)
*Gymnocarpium appalachianum* (Appalachian oak-fern)
*Gymnocarpium appalachianum* (Appalachian oak-fern)
*Huperzia lucidula* (Shining firmoss)
*Huperzia porophila* (Sandstone-loving firmoss)
*Isoetes echinospora* (Spiny-spored quillwort)
*Isoetes engelmannii* (Engelmann's quillwort)
*Isoetes riparia* (Shore quillwort)
*Isoetes x dodgei* (Dodge's quillwort)
*Lycopodiella alopecuroides* (Foxtail bog clubmoss)
*Lycopodiella alopecuroides* (Foxtail bog clubmoss)
*Lycopodiella appressa* (Appressed bog clubmoss)
*Lycopodiella appressa* (Appressed bog clubmoss)
*Lycopodiella inundata* (Northern bog clubmoss)
*Lycopodiella margueritae* (Marguerite's clubmoss)
*Lycopodiella margueritae* (Marguerite's clubmoss)
*Lycopodium dendroideum* (Round-branch ground-pine)
*Ophioglossum pusillum* (Northern adder's-tongue)
*Pellaea glabella var. glabella* (Smooth cliffbrake)
*Pellaea glabella var. glabella* (Smooth cliffbrake)
*Polypodium appalachianum* (Appalachian polypody)
*Polystichum x potteri* (Shield-fern)
*Thelypteris simulata* (Massachusetts fern)
*Trichomanes intricatum* (Filmy fern)

# *Native plants: woody and herbaceous vines*

This section includes woody and herbaceous vines, subdivided in the following manner.

- Native species whose range includes Pennsylvania and whose observed distribution includes Carbon, Monroe, Pike and/or Wayne counties, all of which are commercially available

- One species whose range includes Pennsylvania but have not been reported in Carbon, Monroe, Pike or Wayne counties but are commonly available in the marketplace; a secondary list identifies additional species that may be difficult to find in the retail marketplace.

- A listing of native species that do not appear to be commercially available

The 18 regional entries on this list include both perennial herbaceous and woody vines native to northeastern Pennsylvania and are organized in the following manner:

Latin (or scientific) name*
Common name(s)
A brief description of natural habitat — i.e., where it is found in nature
US Fish and Wildlife Service wetland indicators when available
Characteristics including bloom color and period
Suggestions for home cultivation, including light requirements, moisture, soil description, and if available soil pH range and preference
How relatively easy it is to find in the commercial marketplace, in the context of nationwide mail order nurseries

Not listed is *Toxicodendron radicans* (eastern poison ivy), considered by most to be unsuitable for landscape planting. Those involved in accurate site restoration will find poison ivy is commercially available from a few sources.

### *Adlumia fungosa*

**Allegheny-vine** — moist coves, rocky woods, ledges, alluvial slopes, and thickets. Climbing, to 10 feet. White flowers, summer to fall. Grow in part shade to shade in moist humusy loam. Very few sources.

### *Apios americana*

**Ground-nut** — moist to wet woods and floodplains; FACW. Twining, to 10 feet; pink flowers in summer. Sun to part shade in moist sandy loam. Very few sources.

### *Celastrus scandens*

**American bittersweet** — dry fields, rocky ledges, woods, hedgerows; FACU-. Dioecious, twining, to 12-16 feet, greenish-white flowers in early summer. Grow in lean to average soils with regular moisture in full sun; suckers at the roots to form large colonies and can strangle trees and shrubs. Commonly available.

### *Clematis occidentalis*

**Purple clematis** — open woods, banks, gravelly embankments, rocky woods, slopes and cliffs. Climbing or trailing woody vine to 10 feet; violet flowers in late spring. Grow in part shade to shade in circumneutral mesic sandy to rocky soils. Very few sources.

### *Clematis virginiana*

**Virgin's-bower** — stream edges, wet roadsides, fencerows, and other moist, disturbed, wooded or open sites; FAC. Climbing or trailing woody vine to 15 feet. White flowers in summer. Grow in sun to shade; prefers moist soils in part shade. Commonly available.

### Dioscorea villosa

**Wild yam** — woods, thickets, rocky slopes; FAC+. Twining vine to 15 feet; greenish-yellow flowers, early summer. Grow in part shade to shade in dry to moist rocky loam. Several sources.

### Echinocystis lobata

**Prickly cucumber** — moist alluvial soil on stream banks and woods edges; FAC. Annual vine with 16-20 foot stems; white flowers in summer. Grow in sun to part sun in moist sandy loam. Inedible fruit. Very few sources.

### Humulus lupulus

**Brewer's hops** — moist alluvial soil, woods edges, thickets and waste ground; FACU. Twining vine to 30 feet. Greenish flowers in summer. Grow in sun to part sun in moist sandy loam. Used to flavor beer. Several sources.

### Lonicera dioica var. dioica

**Mountain honeysuckle** — rocky moist woods and thickets; FACU. Climbing woody vine or shrub, 3 to 6 feet; red to purple flowers in late spring. Grow in part sun to part shade in dry to moist circumneutral sandy loam. Very few sources.

### Lonicera hirsuta

**Hairy honeysuckle** — moist woods, swamps and rocky thickets; FAC. Climbing woody vine, to 10 feet; orange-yellow flowers in spring. Grow in part sun to part shade in dry to moist sandy loam. Very few sources.

### Lonicera sempervirens

**Trumpet honeysuckle** — roadsides, woods, thickets; FACU. Woody vine, 10 to 20 feet; red-orange flowers in summer, red fruit in fall. Grow in sun to part sun in moist loamy well drained soil. Tolerates shade, but will flower less; very popular with hummingbirds. Several sources.

### Menispermum canadense

**Moonseed** — deciduous woods and thickets, along streams, bluffs and rocky hillsides, fencerows; FACU. Shade tolerant woody twining vine, 5 to 30 feet; whitish flowers in early fall. Grow in part sun to part shade in moist sandy loam. Very few sources.

### Parthenocissus quinquefolia

**Virginia-creeper** — open woods, fields, clearings, stream banks; FACU. Woody tendril vine, 30 to 50 feet. White flowers in spring, with fruit in late fall. Grow in average, medium, well-drained soil in full sun to part shade. Tolerates full shade and a wide range of soil and environmental conditions. Often mistaken for poison ivy, but harmless. Commonly available.

### Polygonum arifolium

**Halberd-leaf tearthumb** — shaded swamps, ponds, tidal marshes along rivers, wet ravines in forests; OBL. Annual vine; white to pink flowers in summer. Grow in moist to wet rich loams in sun to part shade. Very few sources.

### Smilax herbacea

**Carrion-flower** — higher elevations in rich woods and floodplains, alluvial thickets, and meadows, often in calcareous soils; FAC. Climbing vine, 3 to 10 feet greenish-yellow flowers in early summer. Grow in part shade to shade in moist average soil. Very few sources.

### Smilax hispida

**Bristly greenbrier** — swamps, moist woods thickets and roadsides. Climbing vine, 20 to 40 feet. Greenish yellow flowers late spring. Grow in moist loams in full sun to part shade. Tolerates wet soils. Very few sources.

### Vitis aestivalis

**Summer grape** — open forests, woodlands, woodland borders and thickets; climbs nearly all hardwood and conifer tree species that grow in its range; FACU. Climbing vine, 15 to 30 feet; yellowish green flowers in spring, fruit in fall. Grow in deep, loamy, medium moisture, well-drained soils in full sun. Very few sources.

### Vitis riparia

**Frost grape** is found on riverbanks and in alluvial thickets; FACW. Climbing vine, 30 to 70 feet; yellow-green flowers in May, fruit in late fall. Grow in sun to shade in moist, rich soil. Several sources.

## Additional Pennsylvania vines

Listed as a native of Pennsylvania, commonly available, but without reported distribution in the northeastern counties is:

***Campsis radicans*** (Trumpet-vine) — Trees of moist woodlands and along fence rows in old fields; FAC. Pennsylvania native range includes southeastern and southwestern counties. Grow in most soils, but prefers average soils in full sun with regular moisture. Orange to scarlet flowers in summer. Tolerant of shade, but flowers best in full sun. Extremely aggressive grower suckering from underground runners and free self-seeding; can form impenetrable colonies in the wild. Because of weight, vines should be grown on sturdy structures; prune heavily in spring.

### Other vine species

Seven other species of native vines, which are not reported in the northeastern counties may be difficult to find in the commercial marketplace:

*Aristolochia macrophylla* (Dutchman's pipe)
*Clematis viorna* (Leather-flower)
*Clitoria mariana* (Butterfly pea)
*Dioscorea quaternata* (Wild yam)
*Parthenocissus inserta* (Grape woodbine)
*Passiflora lutea* (Passion-flower)
*Wisteria frutescens* (American wisteria)

## Apparently unavailable

A total of 23 herbaceous and woody vines do not appear to be commercially available:

*Calystegia sepium* (Hedge bindweed)
*Calystegia silvatica ssp. fraterniflora* (Bindweed)
*Calystegia spithamaea ssp. purshiana* (Low bindweed)
*Calystegia spithamaea ssp. stans* (Low bindweed)
*Cynanchum laeve* (Smooth sallow-wort)
*Desmodium humifusum* (Tick-trefoil)
*Galactia regularis* (Eastern milk-pea)
*Galactia volubilis* (Downy milk-pea)
*Matelea obliqua* (Anglepod)
*Mikania scandens* (Climbing hempweed )
*Phaseolus polystachios* (Wild bean)
*Polygonum cilinode* (Fringed bindweed )
*Polygonum scandens var. cristatum* (Climbing false-buckwheat )
*Smilax glauca* (Catbrier )
*Smilax pseudochina* (False chinaroot)
*Smilax pulverulenta* (Carrion-flower )
*Strophostyles umbellata* (Wild bean)
*Toxicodendron radicans* (Poison-ivy )
*Toxicodendron rydbergii* (Giant poison-ivy )
*Vitis cinerea var. baileyana* (Possum grape)
*Vitis labrusca* (Fox grape )
*Vitis novae-angliae* (New England grape )
*Vitis vulpina* (Frost grape)

# *Native plants: annuals and biennials*

A total of 28 species of native annuals with observed distribution in northeastern Pennsylvania are typically sold as seed from a variety of mail-order sources. Many more are not on the market, but seed can often be harvested from wild populations without causing much disturbance.

***Ambrosia artemisiifolia*** (Common ragweed) — fields, roadsides, floodplains; FAC. To 3 feet, yellow flowers in late summer and fall.

***Ambrosia trifida*** (Giant ragweed) — fields, roadsides, floodplains; FAC. To 6 feet; greenish-brown flowers in late summer and fall.

***Amphicarpaea bracteata*** (Hog peanut) — moist woods and floodplains, to 5 feet, twining. White flowers in fall.

***Aureolaria pedicularia*** (Cut-leaf false-foxglove) — dry open woods and edges. To 3 feet, yellow flowers in late summer.

***Bidens cernua*** (Bur-marigold) — swamps, wet shores, ditches; OBL. To 36 inches, yellow flowers in late summer and fall.

***Bidens frondosa*** (Beggar-ticks) — fields, roadsides and moist open ground; FACW. To 36 inches; orange flowers in late summer and fall.

***Blephilia hirsuta*** (Wood-mint) — moist woods and swamps; FACW-. To 30 inches; blue-purple flowers in early summer.

***Castillea coccinea*** (Indian paintbrush) — moist meadows on limestone; FAC. 8-28 inches, red/yellow flowers

***Chenopodium capitatum*** (Indian-paint) — moist to dry soil, sandy or grassy meadows, thickets, open woods, old fields of clearings in forests. 18-24 inches, red flowers in late summer and early fall.

***Conyza canadensis var. canadensis*** (Horseweed) — fields, roadsides, railroad tracks and waste ground; UPL. To 5 feet; white flowers in late summer.

***Crotalaria sagittalis*** (Rattlebox) — dry sandy or gravelly soil of woods and old fields, roadsides. to 15 inches; yellow flowers in late summer.

***Galium aparine*** (Bedstraw) — woods, stream banks and roadsides; FACU. To 36 inches; greenish-white flowers in spring and early summer.

***Gaura biennis*** (Gaura) — moist meadows, floodplains, stream banks, thickets, roadsides; FACU. To 6 feet, white to pink flowers in late summer and fall.

***Gentianella quinquefolia*** (Stiff gentian) — moist open woods, springy slopes, stream banks, at higher elevations along the Allegheny front; FAC. 10-30 inches, violet flowers in late summer and fall.

***Gentianopsis crinita*** (Eastern fringed gentian) — wet meadows, swamps, fens, stream banks, other moist open sites on calcareous soils; OBL. 24 inches, blue to white flowers in late summer and fall.

***Geranium robertianum*** (Herb-robert) — moist wooded rocky slopes and ravines. To 24 inches; pink to purple flowers from spring to fall.

***Gnaphalium obtusifolium*** (Fragrant cudweed) — dry pastures, old fields, shale barrens, roadsides. 12-36 inches; gray-white flowers in fall., 12-36 in. Aug-Nov

***Hedeoma pulegioides*** (American pennyroyal) — dry fields, pastures, woods and roadsides. 4 to 16 inches; blue flowers in fall.

***Impatiens capensis*** (Jewelweed) — moist ground of meadows, swamps, stream banks, open woods. To five feet, yellow-white flowers from spring to fall.

*Impatiens pallida* (Pale jewelweed) — swamps, moist woods and stream banks. To 5 feet; pale yellow flowers from late spring to fall.

*Lactuca canadensis var. canadensis* (Wild lettuce) — meadows, fields, rocky hillsides, roadside banks; FACU. To 7 feet; yellow flowers in fall.

*Myosotis laxa* (Wild forget-me-not) — wet open ground and swamps; OBL. To 15 inches; blue flowers with a yellow center, from spring to fall.

*Polanisia dodecandra ssp. dodecandra* (Clammyweed) — dry, sandy or gravelly alluvial soils; FACU. To 20 inches; purple and white flowers, late summer.

*Polygonum sagittatum* (Tearthumb) — bogs, marshes, wet meadows; OBL. Vine like, 3 to 6 feet tall; pink to whitish flowers in fall.

*Ranunculus abortivus var. abortivus* (Small-flowered crowfoot) — rich low woods, low fields, moist waste places, meadows, fallow fields, and clearings; FACW-. To 30 inches; yellow flowers in summer.

*Ranunculus pensylvanicus* (Bristly crowfoot) — stream banks, bogs, moist clearings, depressions in woodlands; OBL. 8-20 inches, yellow flowers in summer.

*Sicyos angulatus* (Bur cucumber) — moist open soil, stream banks, roadsides, waste ground; FACU. Stem to 25 feet, white flowers in summer.

*Triodanis perfoliata var. perfoliata* (Venus's looking-glass) — roadsides, woods edges, fields, dry waste ground. 6-12 inches; purple flowers in summer.

## Additional Pennsylvania annuals

An additional six species of annuals and biennials include Pennsylvania in native range, but have not been observed in Carbon, Monroe, Pike or Wayne Counties, and are somewhat available in the commercial marketplace:

> *Campanula americana* (Tall bellflower)
> *Chamaecrista fasciculata* (Partridge-pea)
> *Lobelia inflata* (Indian-tobacco)
> *Polygonum pensylvanicum* (Smartweed)
> *Portulaca oleracea* (Purslane)
> *Zizania aquatica* (Wild-rice)

Another 32 species are reportedly available, but may be difficult to find:

> *Agalinis purpurea* (False-foxglove)
> *Agalinis tenuifolia* (Slender false-foxglove)
> *Amaranthus albus* (Tumbleweed)
> *Atriplex patula* (Spreading orach)
> *Cakile edentula* (American sea-rocket)
> *Crotalaria sagittalis* (Rattlebox)
> *Cuscuta pentagona* (Field dodder)
> *Cyperus erythrorhizos* (Redroot flatsedge)
> *Dracocephalum parviflorum* (Dragonhead)
> *Echinochloa muricata* (Barnyard-grass)
> *Echinocystis lobata* (Prickly cucumber)
> *Juncus bufonius* (Toad rush)
> *Lactuca floridana* (Woodland lettuce)
> *Linum sulcatum* (Grooved yellow flax)
> *Oenothera laciniata* (Cut-leaved evening-primrose)
> *Panicum capillare* (Witchgrass)
> *Panicum dichotomiflorum* (Smooth panic grass)
> *Phacelia purshii* (Miami-mist)
> *Polygonum arifolium* (Halberd-leaf tear-thumb)
> *Polygonum punctatum var. confertiflorum* (Dotted smartweed)
> *Ranunculus abortivus var. eucyclus* (Small-flowered crowfoot)
> *Sabatia angularis* (Common marsh-pink)
> *Salvia reflexa* (Lance-leaved sage)
> *Strophostyles helvola* (Wild bean)
> *Trichostema dichotomum* (Blue-curls)
> *Utricularia gibba* (Humped bladderwort)
> *Utricularia subulata* (Slender bladderwort)
> *Verbena urticifolia* (White vervain)
> *Viola bicolor* (Field pansy)
> *Vulpia octoflora var. glauca* (Six-weeks fescue)
> *Xanthium strumarium* (Common cocklebur)

## Apparently unavailable

Species that appear to be unavailable in the commercial marketplace include:

*Acalypha deamii* (Three-seeded mercury)
*Acalypha gracilens* (Slender mercury)
*Acalypha rhomboidea* (Three-seeded mercury)
*Acalypha virginica* (Three-seeded mercury)
*Adlumia fungosa* (Allegheny vine)
*Aeschynomene virginica* (Sensitive joint-

vetch)
*Agalinis auriculata* (Eared false-foxglove)
*Agalinis decemloba* (Blue Ridge false-fox-glove)
*Agalinis paupercula* (Small-flowered false-foxglove)
*Alopecurus carolinianus* (Carolina foxtail)
*Amaranthus cannabinus* (Salt-marsh water-hemp)
*Amaranthus pumilus* (Seabeach amaranth)
*Ammannia coccinea* (Tooth cup)
*Arabis canadensis* (Sicklepod)
*Arabis laevigata var. burkii* (Smooth rock-cress)
*Arabis lyrata* (Lyre-leaved rockcress)
*Arabis missouriensis* (Missouri rockcress)
*Aristida dichotoma var. curtissii* (Poverty-grass)
*Aristida dichotoma var. dichotoma* (Pover-tygrass)
*Aristida longispica var. geniculata* (Slender threeawn)
*Aristida longispica var. longispica* (Slender threeawn)
*Aristida oligantha* (Prairie threeawn)
*Atriplex littoralis* (Seashore orach)
*Atriplex prostrata* (Halberd-leaved orach)
*Atriplex prostrata* (Halberd-leaved orach)
*Bartonia paniculata* (Screwstem)
*Bartonia paniculata* (Screwstem)
*Bartonia virginica* (Bartonia)
*Bidens bidentoides* (Swamp beggar-ticks)
*Bidens bipinnata* (Spanish needles)
*Bidens comosa* (Beggar-ticks)
*Bidens connata* (Beggar-ticks)
*Bidens discoidea* (Small beggar-ticks)
*Bidens laevis* (Showy bur-marigold)
*Bidens vulgata* (Beggar-ticks)
*Bulbostylis capillaris* (Sandrush)
*Callitriche terrestris* (Water-starwort)
*Cardamine parviflora var. arenicola* (Small-flowered bittercress)
*Cardamine pensylvanica* (Pennsylvania bit-tercress)
*Cenchrus longispinus* (Sandbur)
*Cerastium nutans* (Nodding chickweed)
*Chaerophyllum procumbens* (Slender cher-vil)
*Chamaecrista nictitans* (Wild sensitive-plant)

*Chamaecrista nictitans* (Wild sensitive-plant)
*Chamaesyce maculata* (Spotted spurge)
*Chamaesyce nutans* (Eyebane)
*Chamaesyce polygonifolia* (Seaside spurge)
*Chamaesyce vermiculata* (Hairy spurge)
*Chenopodium album var. missouriense* (Lamb's quarters)
*Chenopodium bushianum* (Pigweed)
*Chenopodium foggii* (Goosefoot)
*Chenopodium simplex* (Maple-leaved goose-foot)
*Chenopodium standleyanum* (Woodland goosefoot)
*Collinsia verna* (Blue-eyed-Mary)
*Crassula aquatica* (Water-pigmyweed)
*Critesion pusillum* (Little-barley)
*Croton capitatus* (Hogwort)
*Crotonopsis elliptica* (Elliptical rushfoil)
*Cuphea viscosissima* (Blue waxweed)
*Cuphea viscosissima* (Blue waxweed)
*Cuscuta campestris* (Dodder)
*Cuscuta cephalanthii* (Buttonbush dodder)
*Cuscuta cephalanthii* (Buttonbush dodder)
*Cuscuta compacta* (Dodder)
*Cuscuta corylii* (Hazel dodder)
*Cuscuta corylii* (Hazel dodder)
*Cuscuta gronovii var. gronovii* (Common dodder)
*Cuscuta gronovii var. gronovii* (Common dodder)
*Cuscuta gronovii var. latiflora* (Dodder)
*Cuscuta polygonorum* (Smartweed dodder)
*Cynoglossum boreale* (Northern hound's-tongue)
*Cyperus acuminatus* (Short-pointed flat-sedge)
*Cyperus bipartitus* (Umbrella sedge)
*Cyperus compressus* (Umbrella sedge)
*Cyperus diandrus* (Umbrella sedge)
*Cyperus engelmannii* (Engelmann's flat-sedge)
*Cyperus filicinus* (Umbrella sedge)
*Cyperus flavescens* (Umbrella sedge)
*Cyperus odoratus* (Umbrella sedge)
*Cyperus polystachyos var. texensis* (Many-spiked flatsedge)
*Cyperus squarrosus* (Umbrella sedge)
*Cyperus tenuifolius* (Thin-leaved flatsedge)
*Digitaria filiformis* (Slender crabgrass)

*Digitaria serotina* (Dwarf crabgrass)
*Diodia teres* (Rough buttonweed)
*Draba reptans* (Whitlow-grass)
*Echinochloa walteri* (Walter's barnyard-grass)
*Eclipta prostrata* (Yerba-de-tajo)
*Elatine americana* (American waterwort)
*Elatine minima* (Small waterwort)
*Eleocharis caribaea* (Spike-rush)
*Eleocharis engelmannii* (Spike-rush)
*Eleocharis intermedia* (Matted spike-rush)
*Eleocharis microcarpa* (Spike-rush)
*Eleocharis obtusa var. obtusa* (Wright's spike-rush)
*Eleocharis obtusa var. peasei* (Spike-rush)
*Ellisia nyctelea* (Waterpod)
*Epifagus virginiana* (Beechdrops)
*Eragrostis capillaris* (Lacegrass)
*Eragrostis frankii* (Lovegrass)
*Eragrostis hypnoides* (Creeping lovegrass)
*Eragrostis pectinacea* (Carolina lovegrass)
*Erechtites hieraciifolia* (Fireweed)
*Erechtites hieraciifolia* (Fireweed)
*Erigeron annuus* (Daisy fleabane)
*Erigeron strigosus var. beyrichii* (Daisy fleabane)
*Erigeron strigosus var. strigosus* (Daisy fleabane)
*Euphorbia commutata* (Wood spurge)
*Euphorbia obtusata* (Blunt-leaved spurge)
*Fimbristylis annua* (Annual fimbry)
*Fimbristylis autumnalis* (Slender fimbry)
*Floerkea proserpinacoides* (False-mermaid)
*Gentianopsis virgata* (Narrow-leaved fringed gentian)
*Geranium bicknellii* (Cranesbill)
*Geranium carolinianum* (Wild geranium)
*Gnaphalium macounii* (Fragrant cudweed)
*Gnaphalium purpureum var. purpureum* (Purple cudweed)
*Gnaphalium uliginosum* (Low cudweed)
*Gratiola neglecta* (Hedge hyssop)
*Hackelia virginiana* (Beggar's-lice)
*Hedeoma pulegioides* (American penny-royal)
*Hypericum canadense* (Canadian St.John's-wort)
*Hypericum dissimulatum* (St.John's-wort)
*Hypericum drummondii* (Nits-and-lice)
*Hypericum gentianoides* (Orange-grass)

*Hypericum gymnanthum* (Clasping-leaved St. John's-wort)
*Hypericum majus* (Canadian St. John's-wort)
*Ipomoea lacunosa* (White morning-glory
*Krigia virginica* (Dwarf dandelion)
*Lactuca biennis* (Blue lettuce)
*Lactuca biennis* (Blue lettuce)
*Lactuca canadensis var. latifolia* (Wild lettuce)
*Lactuca canadensis var. longifolia* (Wild lettuce)
*Lactuca canadensis var. obovata* (Wild lettuce)
*Lactuca floridana var. villosa* (Woodland lettuce)
*Lactuca hirsuta var. hirsuta* (Downy lettuce)
*Lactuca hirsuta var. sanguinea* (Downy lettuce)
*Lemna valdiviana* (Pale duckweed)
*Lepidium virginicum* (Poor-man's-pepper)
*Leptochloa fascicularis var. maritima* (Sprangletop)
*Limosella australis* (Awl-shaped mudwort)
*Linaria canadensis* (Old-field toadflax)
*Lindernia dubia var. anagallidea* (False pimpernel)
*Lindernia dubia var. dubia* (False pimpernel)
*Lindernia dubia var. inundata* (False pimpernel)
*Lipocarpha micrantha* (Common hemi-carpa)
*Melampyrum lineare var. pectinatum* (Cow-wheat)
*Micranthemum micranthemoides* (Nuttall's mud-flower)
*Minuartia glabra* (Appalachian sandwort)
*Minuartia michauxii* (Rock sandwort)
*Minuartia patula* (Sandwort)
*Myosotis macrosperma* (Big-seed scorpion-grass)
*Myosotis verna* (Spring forget-me-not)
*Najas flexilis* (Northern waternymph)
*Najas gracillima* (Slender waternymph)
*Najas guadalupensis* (Southern water-nymph)
*Najas marina* (Holly-leaved naiad)
*Panicum flexile* (Old witchgrass)
*Panicum gattingeri* (Witchgrass)

*Panicum philadelphicum* (Panic grass)
*Panicum tuckermanii* (Tuckerman's panic grass)
*Panicum verrucosum* (Panic grass)
*Parietaria pensylvanica* (Pellitory)
*Paronychia canadensis* (Forked chickweed)
*Paronychia fastigiata var. fastigiata* (Whitlow-wort)
*Paronychia fastigiata var. nuttallii* (Whitlow-wort)
*Paronychia montana* (Forked chickweed)
*Phacelia dubia* (Scorpion-weed)
*Phyllanthus caroliniensis ssp. caroliniensis* (Carolina leaf-flower)
*Physalis pubescens var. integrifolia* (Hairy ground-cherry)
*Pilea fontana* (Lesser clearweed)
*Pilea pumila* (Clearweed)
*Plantago pusilla* (Dwarf plantain)
*Plantago virginica* (Dwarf plantain)
*Pluchea odorata* (Marsh fleabane)
*Poinsettia dentata* (Spurge)
*Polygala cruciata* (Cross-leaved milkwort)
*Polygala curtissii* (Curtis's milkwort)
*Polygala incarnata* (Pink milkwort)
*Polygala nuttallii* (Nuttall's milkwort)
*Polygala polygama* (Bitter milkwort)
*Polygala sanguinea* (Field milkwort)
*Polygala verticillata var. ambigua* (Whorled milkwort)
*Polygala verticillata var. isocycla* (Whorled milkwort)
*Polygala verticillata var. verticillata* (Whorled milkwort)
*Polygonella articulata* (Jointweed)
*Polygonum achoreum* (Homeless knotweed)
*Polygonum buxiforme* (Knotweed)
*Polygonum careyi* (Pinkweed)
*Polygonum erectum* (Erect knotweed)
*Polygonum ramosissimum* (Knotweed)
*Polygonum tenue* (Slender knotweed)

*Potentilla norvegica ssp. monspeliensis* (Strawberry-weed)
*Potentilla paradoxa* (Bushy cinquefoil)
*Ranunculus allegheniensis* (Allegheny crowfoot)
*Ranunculus pusillus* (Low spearwort)
*Rorippa palustris ssp. fernaldiana* (Marsh watercress)
*Rorippa palustris ssp. hispida* (Marsh watercress)
*Rorippa palustris ssp. palustris* (Marsh watercress)
*Rotala ramosior* (Tooth cup)
*Sagina decumbens* (Pearlwort)
*Sagittaria calycina* (Long-lobed arrowhead)
*Sanicula canadensis* (Canadian sanicle)
*Schoenoplectus purshianus* (Bulrush)
*Scleria muhlenbergii* (Reticulated nut-rush)
*Scleria verticillata* (Whorled nut-rush)
*Silene antirrhina* (Sleepy catchfly)
*Solanum americanum* (Black nightshade)
*Sporobolus neglectus* (Small rushgrass)
*Sporobolus vaginiflorus* (Poverty grass)
*Stachys tenuifolia* (Creeping hedge-nettle)
*Symphyotrichum subulatum* (Salt-marsh aster)
*Trichophorum planifolium Trichophorum planifolium* (Blue-curls)
*Trichostema setaceum* (Narrow-leaved blue-curls)
*Trifolium reflexum* (Buffalo clover)
*Triplasis purpurea* (Purple sandgrass)
*Utricularia inflata* (Inflated bladderwort)
*Utricularia radiata* (Floating bladderwort)
*Valerianella umbilicata* (Corn-salad)
*Veronica peregrina ssp. peregrina* (Neckweed)
*Veronica peregrina ssp. xalapensis* (Neckweed)

# *Appendix I — Protected species*

A total of 540 species of native plants are considered protected in Pennsylvania because they are rare, threatened, endangered or extirpated (i.e., gone in the state). As with any native species, they should never be collected from the wild. However, many are propagated by legitimate nurseries and are to varying degrees commercially available. Including them in the home landscape is a positive environmental step. These include:

## *Pennsylvania's protected species*

| *Scientific Name* | *Common Name* | *Pa. Status* |
| --- | --- | --- |
| *Acalypha deamii* | Two-seeded copperleaf | Extirpated |
| *Aconitum reclinatum* | White monkshood | Endangered |
| *Aconitum uncinatum* | Blue monkshood | Threatened |
| *Acorus americanus* | Sweet flag | Endangered |
| *Actaea podocarpa* | Mountain bugbane | Rare |
| *Aeschynomene virginica* | Sensitive joint-vetch | Extirpated |
| *Agalinis auriculata* | Eared false-foxglove | Endangered |
| *Agalinis obtusifolia* | Blue-ridge false-foxglove | Extirpated |
| *Agalinis paupercula* | Small-flowered false foxglove | Endangered |
| *Agrostis perennans* | Tall bentgrass | Extirpated |
| *Aletris farinosa* | Colic-root | Endangered |
| *Alisma triviale* | Broad-leaved water plantain | Endangered |
| *Alnus viridis* | Mountain alder | Endangered |
| *Amaranthus cannabinus* | Waterhemp ragweed | Rare |
| *Amelanchier bartramiana* | Oblong-fruited serviceberry | Endangered |
| *Amelanchier humilis* | Low serviceberry | Endangered |
| *Amelanchier obovalis* | Coastal Plain serviceberry | Endangered |
| *Amelanchier sanguinea* | Roundleaf serviceberry | Endangered |
| *Ammannia coccinea* | Scarlet ammannia | Threatened |
| *Ammophila breviligulata* | America beachgrass | Threatened |

## Pennsylvania's protected species

| Scientific Name | Common Name | Pa. Status |
| --- | --- | --- |
| Andromeda polifolia | Bog-rosemary | Rare |
| Anemone cylindrica | Long-fruited anemone | Endangered |
| Antennaria solitaria | Single-head pussytoes | Endangered |
| Antennaria virginica | Shale-barren pussytoes | Rare |
| Aplectrum hyemale | Puttyroot | Rare |
| Arabis hirsuta | Hairy rock-cress | Endangered |
| Arabis missouriensis | Missouri rock-cress | Endangered |
| Arceuthobium pusillum | Dwarf mistletoe | Threatened |
| Arctostaphylos uva-ursi | Bearberry manzanita | Extirpated |
| Arethusa bulbosa | Swamp-pink | Endangered |
| Argentina anserina | Silverweed | Threatened |
| Aristida purpurascens | Arrow feather | Threatened |
| Arnica acaulis | Leopard's-bane | Endangered |
| Artemisia campestris | Beach wormwood | Endangered |
| Asclepias rubra | Red milkweed | Extirpated |
| Asclepias variegata | White milkweed | Endangered |
| Asplenium bradleyi | Bradley's spleenwort | Endangered |
| Asplenium pinnatifidum | Lobed spleenwort | Rare |
| Asplenium resiliens | Black-stalked spleenwort | Endangered |
| Astragalus neglectus | Cooper's milk-vetch | Endangered |
| Baccharis halimifolia | Eastern baccharis | Rare |
| Berberis canadensis | American barberry | Extirpated |
| Bidens beckii | Beck's water-marigold | Endangered |
| Bidens bidentoides | Swamp beggar-ticks | Endangered |
| Boltonia asteroides | Aster-like boltonia | Endangered |
| Bouteloua curtipendula | Tall gramma | Threatened |
| Buchnera americana | Bluehearts | Extirpated |
| Cakile edentula | American sea-rocket | Rare |
| Camassia scilloides | Wild hyacinth | Endangered |
| Carex adusta | Crowded sedge | Extirpated |
| Carex alata | Broadwinged sedge | Threatened |
| Carex aquatilis | Water sedge | Threatened |
| Carex atherodes | Awned sedge | Endangered |

## Pennsylvania's protected species

| Scientific Name | Common Name | Pa. Status |
| --- | --- | --- |
| *Carex aurea* | Golden-fruited sedge | Endangered |
| *Carex backii* | Rocky Mountain sedge | Extirpated |
| *Carex barrattii* | Barratt's sedge | Extirpated |
| *Carex bebbii* | Bebb's sedge | Endangered |
| *Carex bicknellii* | Bicknell's sedge | Endangered |
| *Carex bullata* | Bull sedge | Endangered |
| *Carex buxbaumii* | Brown sedge | Rare |
| *Carex careyana* | Carey's sedge | Endangered |
| *Carex chordorrhiza* | Creeping sedge | Extirpated |
| *Carex collinsii* | Collin's sedge | Threatened |
| *Carex crawfordii* | Crawford's sedge | Endangered |
| *Carex crinita* | Short hair sedge | Endangered |
| *Carex cryptolepis* | Northeastern sedge | Endangered |
| *Carex diandra* | Lesser pinacled sedge | Threatened |
| *Carex disperma* | Soft-leaved sedge | Rare |
| *Carex eburnea* | Ebony sedge | Endangered |
| *Carex flava* | Yellow sedge | Threatened |
| *Carex formosa* | Handsome sedge | Endangered |
| *Carex garberi* | Elk sedge | Endangered |
| *Carex geyeri* | Geyer's sedge | Endangered |
| *Carex hyalinolepis* | Shore-line sedge | Extirpated |
| *Carex lasiocarpa* | Slender sedge | Rare |
| *Carex limosa* | Mud sedge | Threatened |
| *Carex magellanica* | Bog sedge | Rare |
| *Carex meadii* | Mead's sedge | Endangered |
| *Carex mitchelliana* | Mitchell's sedge | Endangered |
| *Carex oligosperma* | Few seeded sedge | Threatened |
| *Carex pauciflora* | Few-flowered sedge | Endangered |
| *Carex polymorpha* | Variable sedge | Threatened |
| *Carex prairea* | Prairie sedge | Threatened |
| *Carex pseudocyperus* | Cyperus-like sedge | Endangered |
| *Carex retrorsa* | Backward sedge | Endangered |
| *Carex richardsonii* | Richardson's sedge | Endangered |

## Pennsylvania's protected species

| Scientific Name | Common Name | Pa. Status |
|---|---|---|
| *Carex sartwellii* | Sartwell's sedge | Extirpated |
| *Carex schweinitzii* | Schweinitz's sedge | Endangered |
| *Carex siccata* | Fernald's hay sedge | Extirpated |
| *Carex sterilis* | Atlantic sedge | Endangered |
| *Carex tetanica* | Wood's sedge | Threatened |
| *Carex typhina* | Cattail sedge | Endangered |
| *Carex viridula* | Green sedge | Endangered |
| *Carex wiegandii* | Wiegand's sedge | Threatened |
| *Cerastium arvense ssp. velutinum* | Mouse-ear chickweed | Endangered |
| *Chamaecyparis thyoides* | Atlantic white cedar | Extirpated |
| *Chamaesyce polygonifolia* | Small sea-side spurge | Threatened |
| *Chasmanthium laxum* | Slender sea-oats | Endangered |
| *Chenopodium foggii* | Fogg's goosefoot | Endangered |
| *Chrysogonum virginianum* | Green-and-gold | Endangered |
| *Chrysopsis mariana* | Maryland golden aster | Endangered |
| *Cirsium horridulum* | Horrible thistle | Endangered |
| *Cladium mariscoides* | Twig rush | Endangered |
| *Clematis viorna* | Vase-vine leather-flower | Endangered |
| *Clethra acuminata* | Mountain pepper-bush | Endangered |
| *Clitoria mariana* | Butterfly-pea | Endangered |
| *Commelina erecta* | Slender day-flower | Extirpated |
| *Commelina virginica* | Virginia day-flower | Extirpated |
| *Conioselinum chinense* | Hemlock-parsley | Endangered |
| *Corallorhiza wisteriana* | Wister's coral-root | Endangered |
| *Coreopsis rosea* | Pink tickseed | Extirpated |
| *Corydalis aurea* | Golden corydalis | Endangered |
| *Crassula aquatica* | Water pigmy-weed | Extirpated |
| *Croton willldenowii* | Elliptical rushfoil | Extirpated |
| *Cryptogramma stelleri* | Slender rock-brake | Endangered |
| *Cymophyllus fraserianus* | Fraser's sedge | Endangered |
| *Cynanchum laeve* | Smooth swallow-wort | Endangered |
| *Cynoglossum virginianum var. boreale* | Northern hound's-tongue | Extirpated |
| *Cyperus diandrus* | Umbrella flatsedge | Endangered |

## *Pennsylvania's protected species*

| *Scientific Name* | *Common Name* | *Pa. Status* |
| --- | --- | --- |
| *Cyperus houghtonii* | Houghton's flatsedge | Endangered |
| *Cyperus odoratus* | Engelmann's flatsedge | Rare |
| *Cyperus polystachyos* | Many-spiked flatsedge | Extirpated |
| *Cyperus refractus* | Reflexed flatsedge | Endangered |
| *Cyperus retrorsus* | Retrorse flatsedge | Extirpated |
| *Cyperus schweinitzii* | Schweinitz's flatsedge | Rare |
| *Cypripedium candidum* | Small white lady's-slipper | Extirpated |
| *Cypripedium parviflorum* | Small yellow lady's-slipper | Endangered |
| *Cypripedium parviflorumvar. pubescens* | Large yellow lady's slipper | Vulnerable |
| *Cypripedium reginae* | Showy lady's-slipper | Threatened |
| *Cystopteris laurentiana* | Laurentian bladder fern | Endangered |
| *Dasiphora fruticosa ssp. floribunda* | Shrubby cinquefoil | Endangered |
| *Delphinium exaltatum* | Tall larkspur | Endangered |
| *Desmodium sessilifolium* | Sessile-leaved tick-trefoil | Extirpated |
| *Diarrhena obovata* | American beakgrain | Endangered |
| *Dicentra eximia* | Wild bleeding-hearts | Endangered |
| *Dichanthelium dichotomum var. dichotomum* | Annulus panic-grass | Endangered |
| *Panicum lucidum* | Shining panic-grass | Endangered |
| *Dichanthelium laxiflorum* | Panic-grass | Endangered |
| *Dichanthelium leibergii* | Leiberg's panic-grass | Extirpated |
| *Dichanthelium oligosanthes var. scribnerianum* | Velvety panic-grass | Endangered |
| *Dichanthelium ovale var. addisonii* | Cloaked panic-grass | Extirpated |
| *Dichanthelium sabulorum var. patulum* | Panic-grass | Endangered |
| *Dichanthelium spretum* | Acuminate dichanthelium) | Endangered |
| *Dichanthelium xanthophysum* | Slender panic-grass | Endangered |
| *Digitaria cognata* | Fall witchgrass | Threatened |
| *Distichlis spicata* | Sea-shore salt-grass | Extirpated |
| *Dodecatheon amethystinum* | Jeweled shooting-star | Threatened |
| *Dodecatheon meadia* | Common shooting-star | Endangered |
| *Draba reptans* | Carolina whitlow-grass | Extirpated |
| *Dryopteris campyloptera* | Mountain wood fern | Endangered |
| *Dryopteris celsa* | Log fern | Endangered |
| *Dryopteris clintoniana* | Clinton's shield fern | Threatened |

## Pennsylvania's protected species

| Scientific Name | Common Name | Pa. Status |
|---|---|---|
| Echinacea laevigata | Smooth coneflower | Extirpated |
| Echinochloa walteri | Walter's barnyard-grass | Endangered |
| Elatine americana | Long-stemmed water-wort | Endangered |
| Elatine minima | Small waterwort | Rare |
| Eleocharis compressa | Flat-stemmed spike-rush | Endangered |
| Eleocharis elliptica | Slender spike-rush | Endangered |
| Eleocharis geniculata | Capitate spike-rush | Endangered |
| Eleocharis intermedia | Matted spike-rush | Threatened |
| Eleocharis obtusa | Spike-rush | Endangered |
| Eleocharis olivacea | Capitate spike-rush | Rare |
| Eleocharis parvula | Dwarf spike-rush | Endangered |
| Eleocharis quadrangulata | Four-angled spike-rush | Endangered |
| Eleocharis quinqueflora | Few-flowered spike-rush | Endangered |
| Eleocharis robbinsii | Robin's spike-rush | Threatened |
| Eleocharis rostellata | Beaked spike-rush | Endangered |
| Eleocharis tenuis var. verrucosa | Slender spike-rush | Endangered |
| Eleocharis tricostata | Three-ribbed spike-rush | Extirpated |
| Eleocharis tuberculosa | Long-tubercled spike-rush | Extirpated |
| Elephantopus carolinianus | Elephant's foot | Endangered |
| Ellisia nyctelea | Ellisia | Threatened |
| Elodea schweinitzii | Schweinitz's waterweed | Extirpated |
| Epilobium strictum | Downey willow-herb | Endangered |
| Equisetum × ferrissii | Scouring rush | Endangered |
| Equisetum variegatum | Variegated horsetail | Endangered |
| Erigenia bulbosa | Harbinger-of-spring | Threatened |
| Eriocaulon decangulare | Ten-angle pipewort | Extirpated |
| Eriocaulon parkeri | Parker's pipewort | Extirpated |
| Eriophorum gracile | Slender cotton-grass | Endangered |
| Eriophorum tenellum | Rough cotton-grass | Endangered |
| Eriophorum viridicarinatum | Thin-leaved cotton-grass | Threatened |
| Eryngium aquaticum | Marsh eryngo | Extirpated |
| Eubotrys racemosa | Swamp dog-hobble | Threatened |
| Eupatorium album | White thoroughwort | Extirpated |

## *Pennsylvania's protected species*

| *Scientific Name* | *Common Name* | *Pa. Status* |
|---|---|---|
| *Eupatorium leucolepis* | White-bracted thoroughwort | Extirpated |
| *Euphorbia ipecacuanhae* | Wild ipecac | Endangered |
| *Euphorbia purpurea* | Glade spurge | Endangered |
| *Euphorbia spathulata* | Blunt-leaved spurge | Endangered |
| *Eurybia spectabilis* | Low showy aster | Endangered |
| *Euthamia caroliniana* | Grass-leaved goldenrod | Threatened |
| *Festuca paradoxa* | Cluster fescue | Endangered |
| *Fimbristylis annua* | Annual fimbry | Threatened |
| *Fimbristylis puberula* | Hairy fimbry | Extirpated |
| *Frasera caroliniensis* | American columbo | Endangered |
| *Fraxinus profunda* | Pumpkin ash | Endangered |
| *Galactia regularis* | Eastern milk-pea | Extirpated |
| *Galactia volubilis* | Downy milk-pea | Extirpated |
| *Galium labradoricum* | Labrador marsh bedstraw | Endangered |
| *Gaultheria hispidula* | Creeping snowberry | Rare |
| *Gaylussacia brachycera* | Box huckleberry | Endangered |
| *Gaylussacia dumosa* | Dwarf huckleberry | Endangered |
| *Gentiana alba* | Yellow gentian | Extirpated |
| *Gentiana catesbaei* | Elliott's gentian | Extirpated |
| *Gentiana saponaria* | Soapwort gentian | Endangered |
| *Gentiana villosa* | Striped gentian | Endangered |
| *Gentianopsis virgata* | Lesser fringed gentian | Extirpated |
| *Geranium bicknellii* | Cranesbill | Endangered |
| *Glyceria borealis* | Small-floating manna-grass | Threatened |
| *Glyceria obtusa* | Blunt manna-grass | Endangered |
| *Goodyera tesselata* | Checkered rattlesname-plantain | Threatened |
| *Gratiola aurea* | Golden-pert | Endangered |
| *Gymnocarpium appalachianum* | Appalachian oak fern | Endangered |
| *Gymnocarpium × heterosporum* | Oak fern | Extirpated |
| *Gymnopogon ambiguus* | Broad-leaved beardgrass | Extirpated |
| *Helianthemum bicknellii* | Bicknell's hoary rockrose | Endangered |
| *Helianthus angustifolius* | Swamp sunflower | Extirpated |
| *Heteranthera multiflora* | Multiflowered mud-plantain | Endangered |

## Pennsylvania's protected species

| Scientific Name | Common Name | Pa. Status |
|---|---|---|
| *Hieracium greenii* | Maryland hawkweed | Endangered |
| *Hierochloe odorata* | Vanilla sweet-grass | Endangered |
| *Hordeum pusillum* | Little barley | Extirpated |
| *Hottonia inflata* | American featherfoil | Extirpated |
| *Houstonia serpyllifolia* | Creeping bluets | Extirpated |
| *Huperzia porophila* | Rock clubmoss | Endangered |
| *Huperzia selago* | Mountain clubmoss | Extirpated |
| *Hydrastis canadensis* | Goldenseal | Vulnerable |
| *Hydrocotyle umbellata* | Many-flowered pennywort | Extirpated |
| *Hydrophyllum macrophyllum* | Large-leafed water-leaf | Endangered |
| *Hylotelephium telephioides* | Allegheny stonecrop | Rare |
| *Hypericum adpressum* | Creeping St. John's-wort | Extirpated |
| *Hypericum crux-andreae* | St. Peter's-wort | Extirpated |
| *Hypericum densiflorum* | Bushy St. John's-wort | Threatened |
| *Hypericum denticulatum* | Coppery St. John's-wort | Extirpated |
| *Hypericum drummondii* | Nits-and-lice | Extirpated |
| *Hypericum gymnanthum* | Clasping-leaved St. John's-wort | Extirpated |
| *Hypericum majus* | Larger Canadian St. John's-wort | Threatened |
| *Ilex glabra* | Ink-berry | Extirpated |
| *Ilex opaca* | American holly | Threatened |
| *Iodanthus pinnatifidus* | Purple rocket | Endangered |
| *Iris cristata* | Crested dwarf iris | Endangered |
| *Iris prismatica* | Slender blue iris | Endangered |
| *Iris verna* | Dwarf iris | Endangered |
| *Iris virginica* | Virginia blue flag | Endangered |
| *Isotria medeoloides* | Small-whorled pogonia | Endangered |
| *Itea virginica* | Virginia willow | Extirpated |
| *Juncus alpinoarticulatus ssp. nodulosus* | Richardson's rush | Threatened |
| *Juncus arcticus ssp. littoralis* | Baltic rush | Threatened |
| *Juncus biflorus* | Grass-leaved rush | Threatened |
| *Juncus brachycarpus* | Short-fruited rush | Endangered |
| *Juncus brachycephalus* | Small-headed rush | Threatened |
| *Juncus dichotomus* | Forked rush | Endangered |

## *Pennsylvania's protected species*

| *Scientific Name* | *Common Name* | *Pa. Status* |
| --- | --- | --- |
| *Juncus filiformis* | Thread rush | Rare |
| *Juncus greenei* | Greene's rush | Extirpated |
| *Juncus gymnocarpus* | Coville's rush | Rare |
| *Juncus militaris* | Bayonet rush | Endangered |
| *Juncus scirpoides* | Scirpus-like rush | Endangered |
| *Juncus torreyi* | Torrey's rush | Endangered |
| *Koeleria macrantha* | Junegrass | Extirpated |
| *Lathyrus japonicus* | Beach peavine | Threatened |
| *Lathyrus ochroleucus* | Wild-pea | Threatened |
| *Lathyrus palustris* | Marsh pea | Endangered |
| *Ledum groenlandicum* | Common labrador-tea | Rare |
| *Leiophyllum buxifolium* | Sand-myrtle | Extirpated |
| *Lemna obscura* | Little water duckweed | Extirpated |
| *Lemna valdiviana* | Pale duckweed | Extirpated |
| *Lespedeza angustifolia* | Narrowleaf bush clover | Endangered |
| *Lespedeza stuevei* | Tall bushclover | Extirpated |
| *Ligusticum canadense* | Lovage | Endangered |
| *Limosella australis* | Awl-shaped mudwort | Extirpated |
| *Linnaea borealis* | Twinflower | Threatened |
| *Linum intercursum* | Sandplain wild flax | Endangered |
| *Linum sulcatum* | Grooved yellow flax | Endangered |
| *Lipocarpha micrantha* | Common hemicarpa | Endangered |
| *Listera australis* | Southern twayblade | Endangered |
| *Listera cordata* | Heart-leaved twayblade | Endangered |
| *Listera smallii* | Kidney-leaved twayblade | Endangered |
| *Lithospermum caroliniense* | Hispid gromwell | Endangered |
| *Lithospermum latifolium* | American gromwell | Endangered |
| *Lobelia dortmanna* | Water lobelia | Threatened |
| *Lobelia kalmii* | Brook lobelia | Endangered |
| *Lobelia nuttallii* | Nuttall's lobelia | Extirpated |
| *Lobelia puberula* | Downy lobelia | Endangered |
| *Lonicera hirsuta* | Hairy honeysuckle | Endangered |
| *Lonicera oblongifolia* | Swamp fly honeysuckle | Endangered |

## Pennsylvania's protected species

| Scientific Name | Common Name | Pa. Status |
| --- | --- | --- |
| Lonicera villosa | Mountain fly honeysuckle | Endangered |
| Ludwigia decurrens | Upright primrose-willow | Endangered |
| Ludwigia polycarpa | False loosestrife seedbox | Endangered |
| Ludwigia sphaerocarpa | Spherical-fruited seedbox | Extirpated |
| Lupinus perennis | Wild blue lupine | Rare |
| Luzula bulbosa | Wood-rush | Endangered |
| Lycopodiella alopecuroides | Foxtail clubmoss | Endangered |
| Lycopodiella appressa | Southern bog clubmoss | Threatened |
| Lycopodium sabinifolium | Fir clubmoss | Extirpated |
| Lycopus rubellus | Taper-leaved bugle-weed | Endangered |
| Lygodium palmatum | Hartford fern | Rare |
| Lyonia mariana | Stagger-bush | Endangered |
| Lysimachia hybrida | Lance-leaved loosestrife | Threatened |
| Lythrum alatum | Winged loosestrife | Endangered |
| Magnolia tripetala | Umbrella magnolia | Rare |
| Magnolia virginiana | Sweet bay magnolia | Threatened |
| Malaxis bayardii | Bayard's malaxis | Rare |
| Malaxis brachypoda | White adder's-mouth | Endangered |
| Marshallia grandiflora | Large-flowered marshallia | Endangered |
| Matelea obliqua | Oblique milkvine | Endangered |
| Meehania cordata | Heart-leafed meehania | Endangered |
| Melica nitens | Three-flowered meltic-grass | Threatened |
| Menziesia pilosa | Minniebush | Rare |
| Micranthemum micranthemoides | Nuttall's mud-flower | Extirpated |
| Minuartia glabra | Applachian sandwort | Threatened |
| Mitella nuda | Naked bishop's-cap | Endangered |
| Monarda punctata | Spotted bee-balm | Endangered |
| Montia chamissoi | Chamisso's miner's-lettuce | Endangered |
| Muhlenbergia capillaris | Short muhly | Extirpated |
| Muhlenbergia uniflora | False dropseed muhly | Endangered |
| Myrica gale | Sweet bayberry | Threatened |
| Myriophyllum farwellii | Farwell's water-milfoil | Endangered |
| Myriophyllum heterophyllum | Broad-leaved water-milfoil | Endangered |

## *Pennsylvania's protected species*

| *Scientific Name* | *Common Name* | *Pa. Status* |
| --- | --- | --- |
| Myriophyllum sibiricum | Northern water-milfoil | Endangered |
| Myriophyllum tenellum | Slender water-milfoil | Threatened |
| Myriophyllum verticillatum | Whorled water-milfoil | Endangered |
| Najas gracillima | Bushy naiad | Threatened |
| Najas marina | Holly-leaved naiad | Endangered |
| Nelumbo lutea | American lotus | Endangered |
| Nymphoides cordata | Floating-heart | Threatened |
| Oclemena nemoralis | Bog aster | Endangered |
| Oenothera argillicola | Shale-barren evening-primrose | Threatened |
| Oligoneuron rigidum var. rigidum | Stiff goldenrod | Endangered |
| Onosmodium bejariense var. hispidissimum | False gromwell | Endangered |
| Onosmodium virginianum | Virginia false-gromwell | Extirpated |
| Ophioglossum engelmannii | Limestone adder's-tongue | Endangered |
| Ophioglossum vulgatum | Southeastern adder's tongue | Extirpated |
| Opuntia humifusa | Prickly-pear cactus | Rare |
| Orontium aquaticum | Golden club | Rare |
| Packera anonyma | Plain ragwort | Rare |
| Packera antennariifolia | Cat's-paw ragwort | Endangered |
| Packera plattensis | Prairie ragwort | Extirpated |
| Panax quinquefolius | Ginseng | Vulnerable |
| Panicum amarum var. amarulum | Southern sea-beach panic-grass | Endangered |
| Panicum philadelphicum | Tuckerman's panicgrass | Threatened |
| Parnassia glauca | Carolina grass-of-parnassus | Endangered |
| Paronychia fastigiata var. nuttallii | Forked chickweed | Endangered |
| Parthenium integrifolium | American fever-few | Extirpated |
| Paspalum floridanum | Florida beadgrass | Extirpated |
| Passiflora lutea | Passion-flower | Endangered |
| Paxistima canbyi | Canby's mountain-lover | Endangered |
| Pedicularis lanceolata | Swamp lousewort | Endangered |
| Phemeranthus teretifolius | Round-leaved fame-flower | Threatened |
| Phlox latifolia | Mountain phlox | Endangered |
| Phlox pilosa | Downy phlox | Endangered |
| Phlox subulata ssp. brittonii | Moss pink | Endangered |

## Pennsylvania's protected species

| Scientific Name | Common Name | Pa. Status |
|---|---|---|
| Phoradendron leucarpum | Christmas mistletoe | Extirpated |
| Phyla lanceolata | Fog-fruit | Rare |
| Phyllanthus caroliniensis | Carolina leaf-flower | Endangered |
| Physalis virginiana | Virginia ground-cherry | Endangered |
| Piptatherum pungens | Slender mountain-ricegrass | Endangered |
| Piptochaetium avenaceum | Black oatgrass | Extirpated |
| Platanthera ciliaris | Yellow fringed-orchid | Threatened |
| Platanthera cristata | Crested yellow orchid | Extirpated |
| Platanthera dilatata | Leafy white orchid | Endangered |
| Platanthera hookeri | Hooker's orchid | Endangered |
| Platanthera hyperborea | Leafy northern green orchid | Endangered |
| Platanthera leucophaea | Prairie white-fringed orchid | Extirpated |
| Platanthera peramoena | Purple fringeless orchid | Threatened |
| Pluchea odorata | Shrubby camphor-weed | Endangered |
| Poa autumnalis | Autumn bluegrass | Endangered |
| Poa paludigena | Bog bluegrass | Threatened |
| Poa saltuensis | Woodland bluegrass | Threatened |
| Polemonium vanbruntiae | Jacob's-ladder | Endangered |
| Polygala cruciata | Cross-leaved milkwort | Endangered |
| Polygala curtissii | Curtis's milkwort | Endangered |
| Polygala incarnata | Pink milkwort | Endangered |
| Polygala lutea | Yellow milkwort | Extirpated |
| Polygala polygama | Bitter milkwort | Endangered |
| Polygonella articulata | Eastern jointweed | Endangered |
| Polygonum careyi | Carey's smartweed | Endangered |
| Polygonum ramosissimum | Bushy knotweed | Extirpated |
| Polygonum setaceum | Swamp smartweed | Endangered |
| Polystichum braunii | Braun's holly fern | Endangered |
| Populus balsamifera | Balsam poplar | Endangered |
| Populus heterophylla | Swamp cottonwood | Extirpated |
| Potamogeton alpinus | Northern pondweed | Extirpated |
| Potamogeton confervoides | Tuckerman's pondweed | Threatened |
| Potamogeton friesii | Fries' pondweed | Endangered |

## *Pennsylvania's protected species*

| *Scientific Name* | *Common Name* | *Pa. Status* |
|---|---|---|
| *Potamogeton gramineus* | Grassy pondweed | Endangered |
| *Potamogeton hillii* | Hill's pondweed | Endangered |
| *Potamogeton illinoensis* | Illinois pondweed | Rare |
| *Potamogeton oakesianus* | Oakes' pondweed | Endangered |
| *Potamogeton obtusifolius* | Blunt-leaved pondweed | Endangered |
| *Potamogeton praelongus* | White-stemmed pondweed | Endangered |
| *Potamogeton pulcher* | Spotted pondweed | Endangered |
| *Potamogeton richardsonii* | Red-head pondweed | Threatened |
| *Potamogeton robbinsii* | Flat-leaved pondweed | Rare |
| *Potamogeton strictifolius* | Narrow-leaved pondweed | Endangered |
| *Potamogeton tennesseensis* | Tennessee pondweed | Endangered |
| *Potamogeton vaseyi* | Vasey's pondweed | Endangered |
| *Potamogeton zosteriformis* | Flat-stem pondweed | Rare |
| *Potentilla paradoxa* | Bushy cinquefoil | Endangered |
| *Prenanthes crepidinea* | Rattlesnake-root | Endangered |
| *Prenanthes racemosa* | Glaucous rattlesnake-root | Extirpated |
| *Proserpinaca pectinata* | Comb-leaved mermaid-weed | Extirpated |
| *Prunus alleghaniensis* | Allegheny plum | Threatened |
| *Prunus maritima* | Beach plum | Endangered |
| *Prunus pumila* | Sand cherry | Rare |
| *Ptelea trifoliata* | Common hop-tree | Threatened |
| *Ptilimnium capillaceum* | Mock bishop-weed | Extirpated |
| *Pycnanthemum pycnanthemoides* | Southern mountain-mint | Endangered |
| *Pycnanthemum torrei* | Torrey's mountain-mint | Endangered |
| *Pycnanthemum verticillatum var. pilosum* | Hairy mountain-mint | Extirpated |
| *Pyrularia pubera* | Buffalo nut | Rare |
| *Quercus falcata* | Southern red oak | Endangered |
| *Quercus phellos* | Willow oak | Endangered |
| *Quercus shumardii* | Shumard's oak | Endangered |
| *Ranunculus fascicularis* | Tufted buttercup | Endangered |
| *Ranunculus flammula* | Creeping spearwort | Extirpated |
| *Ranunculus hederaceus* | Long-stalked crowfoot | Extirpated |
| *Ranunculus longirostris* | Eastern white water-crowfoot | Threatened |

## Pennsylvania's protected species

| Scientific Name | Common Name | Pa. Status |
| --- | --- | --- |
| *Ranunculus pusillus* | Low spearwort | Endangered |
| *Ranunculus trichophyllus* | White water-crowfoot | Rare |
| *Ratibida pinnata* | Prairie coneflower | Extirpated |
| *Rhamnus lanceolata* | Lanceolate buckthorn | Endangered |
| *Rhexia mariana* | Maryland meadow-beauty | Endangered |
| *Rhodiola rosea* | Roseroot stonecrop | Endangered |
| *Rhododendron atlanticum* | Dwarf azalea | Endangered |
| *Rhododendron calendulaceum* | Flame azalea | Extirpated |
| *Rhynchospora capillacea* | Capillary beaked-rush | Endangered |
| *Rhynchospora fusca* | Brown beaked-rush | Extirpated |
| *Rhynchospora gracilenta* | Beaked-rush | Extirpated |
| *Ribes lacustre* | Bristly black currant | Endangered |
| *Ribes missouriense* | Missouri gooseberry | Endangered |
| *Ribes triste* | Red currant | Threatened |
| *Rotala ramosior* | Tooth-cup | Rare |
| *Rubus cuneifolius* | Sand blackberry | Endangered |
| *Ruellia caroliniensis* | Carolina petunia | Extirpated |
| *Ruellia humilis* | Fringed-leaved petunia | Endangered |
| *Ruellia strepens* | Limestone petunia | Threatened |
| *Rumex hastatulus* | Heart sorrel | Extirpated |
| *Sabatia campanulata* | Slender marsh pink | Extirpated |
| *Saccharum giganteum* | Sugarcane plumegrass | Extirpated |
| *Sagittaria calycina var. spongiosa* | Long-lobed arrow-head | Endangered |
| *Sagittaria filiformis* | Arrow-head | Extirpated |
| *Sagittaria subulata* | Subulate arrow-head | Rare |
| *Salix candida* | Hoary willow | Endangered |
| *Salix caroliniana* | Carolina willow | Endangered |
| *Salix pedicellaris* | Bog-willow | Endangered |
| *Salix petiolaris* | Slender willow | Endangered |
| *Salix serissima* | Autumn willow | Threatened |
| *Samolus valerandi ssp. parviflorus* | Pineland pimpernel | Endangered |
| *Saxifraga micranthidifolia* | Lettice saxofrage | Rare |
| *Scheuchzeria palustris* | Pod-grass | Endangered |

## Pennsylvania's protected species

| Scientific Name | Common Name | Pa. Status |
|---|---|---|
| *Schizachyrium littorale var. littorale* | Seaside bluestem | Rare |
| *Schoenoplectus acutus var. acutus* | Hard-stemmed bullrush | Endangered |
| *Schoenoplectus fluviatilis* | River bullrush | Rare |
| *Schoenoplectus heterochaetus* | Slender bullrush | Extirpated |
| *Schoenoplectus smithii* | Smith's bullrush | Endangered |
| *Schoenoplectus torreyi* | Torrey's bullrush | Endangered |
| *Scirpus ancistrochaetus* | Northeastern bullrush | Threatened |
| *Scirpus pedicellatus* | Stalked bullrush | Threatened |
| *Scleria minor* | Minor nutrush | Endangered |
| *Scleria pauciflora* | Few-flowered nutrush | Threatened |
| *Scleria reticularis* | Reticulated nutrush | Endangered |
| *Scleria verticillata* | Whorled nutrush | Endangered |
| *Scutellaria saxatilis* | Rock skullcap | Endangered |
| *Scutellaria serrata* | Showy skullcap | Endangered |
| *Sericocarpus linifolius* | Narrow-leaved white-topped aster | Endangered |
| *Shepherdia canadensis* | Canada buffalo-berry | Endangered |
| *Sibbaldiopsis tridentata* | Three-toothed cinquefoil | Endangered |
| *Sida hermaphrodita* | Sida | Endangered |
| *Sisyrinchium albidum* | Blue-eyed-grass | Extirpated |
| *Sisyrinchium atlanticum* | Eastern blue-eyed grass | Endangered |
| *Sisyrinchium fuscatum* | Sand blue-eyed grass | Extirpated |
| *Smilax pseudochina* | Long-stalked greenbrier | Extirpated |
| *Solidago arguta* | Harris' goldenrod | Endangered |
| *Solidago curtisii* | Curtis' goldenrod | Endangered |
| *Solidago erecta* | Slender goldenrod | Endangered |
| *Solidago roanensis* | Tennessee golden-rod | Rare |
| *Solidago simplex ssp. randii var. racemosa* | Sticky goldenrod | Endangered |
| *Sorbus decora* | Showy mountain-ash | Endangered |
| *Sparganium androcladum* | Branching bur-reed | Endangered |
| *Sparganium natans* | Small bur-reed | Extirpated |
| *Spiraea betulifolia* | Dwarf spiraea | Threatened |
| *Spiraea virginiana* | Virginia spiraea | Extirpated |
| *Spiranthes casei* | Case's ladies'-tresses | Endangered |

## Pennsylvania's protected species

| Scientific Name | Common Name | Pa. Status |
| --- | --- | --- |
| *Spiranthes magnicamporum* | Ladies'-tresses | Extirpated |
| *Spiranthes ovalis* | October ladies'-tresses | Endangered |
| *Spiranthes romanzoffiana* | Hooded ladies'-tresses | Endangered |
| *Spiranthes tuberosa* | Slender ladies'-tresses | Extirpated |
| *Spiranthes vernalis* | Spring ladies'-tresses | Endangered |
| *Sporobolus clandestinus* | Rough dropseed | Endangered |
| *Sporobolus cryptandrus* | Sand dropseed | Rare |
| *Sporobolus heterolepis* | Prairie dropseed | Endangered |
| *Stachys cordata* | Nuttall's hedge-nettle | Endangered |
| *Stachys hyssopifolia* | Hyssop hedge-nettle | Extirpated |
| *Streptopus amplexifolius* | White twisted-stalk | Endangered |
| *Stuckenia filiformis ssp. filiformis* | Threadleaf pondweed | Extirpated |
| *Stylosanthes biflora* | Pencil-flower | Endangered |
| *Symphyotrichum boreale* | Rush aster | Endangered |
| *Symphyotrichum depauperatum* | Serpentine aster | Threatened |
| *Symphyotrichum novi-belgii* | Long-leaved aster | Threatened |
| *Symphyotrichum puniceum* | Shining aster | Threatened |
| *Taenidia montana* | Mountain pimpernel | Endangered |
| *Thalictrum coriaceum* | Thick-leaved meadow-rue | Endangered |
| *Tipularia discolor* | Crainfly orchid | Rare |
| *Tradescantia ohiensis* | Ohio spiderwort | Endangered |
| *Trautvetteria caroliniensis* | Carolina tassel-rue | Rare |
| *Trichostema setaceum* | Blue-curls | Endangered |
| *Trifolium reflexum* | Buffalo clover | Extirpated |
| *Trifolium virginicum* | Kate's mountain clover | Endangered |
| *Triglochin palustris* | Marsh arrowgrass | Extirpated |
| *Trillium nivale* | Snow trillium | Rare |
| *Triosteum angustifolium* | Horse-gentian | Endangered |
| *Triphora trianthophora* | Nodding pogonia | Endangered |
| *Triplasis purpurea* | Purple sandgrass | Endangered |
| *Tripsacum dactyloides* | Gamma grass | Endangered |
| *Trisetum spicatum* | Narrow false oats | Endangered |
| *Trollius laxus* | Spreading globe flower | Endangered |

## Pennsylvania's protected species

| Scientific Name | Common Name | Pa. Status |
| --- | --- | --- |
| Utricularia gibba | Fibrous bladderwort | Extirpated |
| Utricularia intermedia | Flat-leaved bladderwort | Threatened |
| Utricularia minor | Lesser bladderwort | Threatened |
| Utricularia purpurea | Purple bladderwort | Rare |
| Utricularia radiata | Floating bladderwort | Endangered |
| Utricularia resupinata | Northeastern bladderwort | Extirpated |
| Uvularia puberula | Mountain bellwort | Rare |
| Vernonia glauca | Tawny ironweed | Endangered |
| Viburnum nudum | Possum haw viburnum | Endangered |
| Viburnum opulus var. americanum | Highbush cranberry | Rare |
| Viola brittoniana | Coast violet | Endangered |
| Viola pedatifida | Prairie violet | Endangered |
| Viola renifolia | Kidney-leaved white violet | Extirpated |
| Viola tripartita | Three-parted violet | Extirpated |
| Vitis cinerea var. baileyana | Possum grape | Endangered |
| Vitis × novae-angliae | New England grape | Endangered |
| Vitis rupestris | Sand grape | Endangered |
| Vittaria appalachiana | Appalachian gametophyte fern | Threatened |
| Wolffiella gladiata | Bog mat | Rare |
| Woodwardia areolata | Netted chain fern | Threatened |
| Xyris montana | Yellow-eyed grass | Rare |
| Xyris | Yellow-eyed-grass | Threatened |
| Zigadenus elegans ssp. glaucus | Death-camas | Endangered |
| Zizania aquatica | Indian wild rice | Rare |

# *Appendix II — Wetland indicators*

The U.S. Fish and Wildlife Service, the principal federal agency dealing with information on wetlands, has over the years researched species of plants and their probability of being found in wetlands.

A product of this work are wetland indicators, which include five basic designations and options for gradients in between. The implications for landscapers is that the designations can suggest relative moisture requirements for plants. For example, a wetland species will almost certainly require constant moisture, while an upland species can manage with dryer habitats.

Indicator codes have been assigned to many native species. A summary of names and definitions:

- OBL — Obligate Wetland. Probability of 99 percent that it occurs naturally in wetlands.

- FACW — Facultative Wetland. Usually found in wetland, with a probability of 67 to 99 percent, but occasionally is found in non-wetlands.

- FAC — Facultative. Equally likely to be found in wetlands or non-wetlands, with a probability of 34 to 66 percent in wetlands.

- FACU — Facultative Upland. Usually occurs in non-wetlands, with a probability of 1 to 33 percent of being found in wetlands.

- UPL — Obligate Upland. Occurs almost always naturally in non-wetlands, probability of 99 percent.

Frequently attached to indicators are plus and minus (+ and -) symbols, which suggest the likelihood that the species is either on the less likely or more likely side of the range. For example, an indicator of FAC+ would be interpreted as 50 to 66 percent probability of being in wetlands, while FAC- would be interpreted as 34 to 50 percent probability.

Occasionally found is the indicator "NI," which means insufficient information is available to assign an indicator status.

The U.S. Department of Agriculture uses these indicators in its database of plants and will list it for various regions of the United States. The USDA cautions, however, that wetland indicator categories should not be equated to degrees of wetness. While many OBL species are found in wetland that are permanently or semi-permanently flooded, many also are found in wetlands that are only seasonally or temporarily flooded.

At the same time, UPL species can include many that survive in a wide range of difficult circumstances, including ecotypes adapted to both semi-permanently and seasonally flooded wetlands.

# *Appendix III- Invasive species*

From an extensive list of introduced plant species, a number are listed by state and federal agencies as invasive and/or noxious as a consequence to becoming a hazard to ecosystems, agriculture and in some cases, human health.

A number of species are of particular concern because of infestations in northeastern counties of Pennsylvania, and are well documented elsewhere (including effective means of control and eradication). A public service site offers many images to assist in identification.

Invasives that arrived inadvertently or for non-horticultural use, or have escaped from cultivation, commonly share traits of having few natural predators (primarily insects and herbivores). They often have textures and tastes disliked by herbivores or are chemically "invisible" to insects that normally keep plant populations in check; in fact, introduced exotics are sometimes promoted as being "pest resistant."

Although these species are becoming illegal for commercial sale, they often remain traded among friends, especially if they are deer resistant. Species listed as "others" are reported outside of Carbon, Monroe, Pike and Wayne Counties but still may yet arrive through a variety of means — hence, there is no need in compounding the problem by bringing them in.

## Herbaceous Plants

### *Aegopodium podagraria*

**Goutweed, aka bishop's weed, snow-on-the-mountain** — Commonly planted in the past and escaped; spreads aggressively by roots to form dense patches, displace native species, and greatly reduce species diversity in the ground layer. Goutweed patches inhibit the establishment of conifers and other native tree species as well.

### *Alliaria petiolata*

**Garlic mustard** — Invasive in many states; spreading aggressively in woodlands by seed. Once introduced to an area, garlic mustard outcompetes native plants by aggressively monopolizing light, moisture, nutrients, soil and space. Wildlife species that depend on early plants for foliage, pollen, nectar, fruits, seeds and roots are deprived of these essential food sources when garlic mustard replaces them.

### *Cirsium arvense*

**Canada thistle** — Noxious weed in Pennsylvania and 42 other states. Canada thistle grows in barrens, glades, meadows, prairies, fields, pastures, and waste places. As it establishes itself in an area, Canada thistle crowds out and replaces native plants, changes the structure and species composition of natural plant communities and reduces plant and animal diversity. This highly invasive thistle prevents the coexistence of other plant species through shading, competition for soil resources and possibly through the release of chemical toxins poisonous to other plants.

### *Cirsium vulgare*

**Bull thistle** — Pennsylvania noxious weed. Bull thistle can invade almost any type of disturbed area, such as forest clearcuts, riparian areas and pastures. Plants can form dense thickets, displacing other vegetation.

### *Hesperis matronalis*

**Dame's rocket** — Planted in gardens, it has escaped and naturalized along roads; spreads by seed. It is still being used as a landscape plant and has become so common that many, mistakenly, believe that it is a native wildflower. Although it is not a large-scale invasive, dame's rocket can dominate moist areas of meadow, forest edge and alluvial woods to the exclusion of native plants.

### Lythrum salicaria, Lythrum virgatum

**Purple loosestife** — Escaped from gardens and become invasive in many states; Pennsylvania noxious weed. Purple loosestrife adapts readily to natural and disturbed wetlands. As it establishes and expands, it outcompetes and replaces native grasses, sedges, and other flowering plants that provide a higher quality source of nutrition for wildlife. The highly invasive nature of purple loosestrife allows it to form dense, homogeneous stands that restrict native wetland plant species, including some federally endangered orchids, and reduce habitat for waterfowl.

### Myriophyllum spicatum

**Eurasian water-milfoil** — An emergent, herbaceous aquatic plant that forms large, floating mats of vegetation on the surface of lakes, rivers, and other water bodies, preventing light penetration for native aquatic plants and impeding water traffic. Eurasian water-milfoil tends to invade disturbed areas where native plants cannot adapt to the alteration. It does not spread rapidly into undisturbed areas where native plants are well established.

### Ornithogalum umbellatum

**Star-of-Bethlehem** — Common garden plant which has widely escaped. Since this plant is still being used horticulturally, it is likely to continue spreading beyond its current range. *Ornithogalum umbellatum* is poisonous if not lethal to livestock and should be prevented from spreading into agricultural situations. *Ornithogalum umbellatum* produces new bulbs each year that are readily moved downstream to new localities. It has the ability to form locally dense stands along the edges of the rivers and streams, allowing it to crowd out native riparian species.

### Pastinaca sativa

**Wild parsnip** — Found commonly along roadsides where it is widespread; spreads by seed. Well-established prairies are not likely to be invaded by parsnip, but it can become quite abundant on prairie edges and in disturbed patches within otherwise high-quality prairies. Once established at the edges, parsnip can spread.

### Polygonum cuspidatum

**Japanese knotweed** (AKA *Fallopia japonica*) and giant knotweed (*Polygonum sachalinense*) are herbaceous perennials that form large colonies of erect stems that can reach 9 feet in height. They spread by vigorous rhizomes. Japanese knotweed and giant knotweed are very similar in appearance and known to hybridize. It is most commonly found along stream and river banks. where it often forms an impenetrable wall of stems; it also occurs in wetlands, waste ground, and along roads and railroads. Dense stands of knotweed exclude other plant species leading to very limited biological diversity in infested sites.

### Trapa natans

**Water chestnut** — Wetland plant; should not be introduced as it will escape, spread, and naturalize. Plants grow in quiet streams, ponds, freshwater regions of estuaries, and on exposed mud flats. One acre of water chestnut can produce enough seeds to cover 100 acres the following year. Each seed can give rise to 10 to 15 rosettes, and each rosette may produce as many as 20 seeds. Seeds have been known to remain viable for up to 12 years. The fruits may be dispersed when individual plants are uprooted and float downstream.

## Grasses, rushes, sedges

### Bromus tectorum

**Cheatgrass** — Annual grass on the noxious weed lists of at least 35 states. Bromus tectorum draws down soil moisture and nutrients to very low levels, making it difficult for other species to compete. Due to its tendency to mature early and then dry out, it gains a competitive advantage through the promotion of fire. An increased cycle of fires favors annual species at the expense of many perennials.

### Microstegium vimineum

**Japanese stiltgrass** — Annual grass; invasive in many states; spreading through woodlands by seed, especially in Monroe and Pike Counties. Stilt grass occurs in a wide variety of habitats and readily invades areas subject to regular mowing, tilling, foot traffic, and other soil disturbing activities. It threatens native plants and natural habitats in open to shady, and moist to dry locations. Stilt grass spreads to form extensive patches, displacing native species that are not able to compete with it.

### Phalaris arundinacea

**Reed canary-grass** — Aggressive wetland grass with both native and introduced strains; widespread and abundant. Reed canary-grass forms dense stands in open wetlands, wet meadows, riparian areas, and shores and effectively excludes all other plant species, causing greatly decreased biological diversity in wetland communities.

### Phragmites australis

**Common reed** — a tall, perennial grass that can grow to over 15 feet in height found in tidal and nontidal brackish and freshwater marshes, river edges, shores of lakes and ponds, roadsides and disturbed areas. Once introduced Phragmites invades a site it quickly can take over a marsh community, crowding out native plants, changing marsh hydrology, altering wildlife habitat, and increasing fire potential. Its high biomass blocks light to other plants and occupies all the growing space below ground

## Shrubs

### Berberis thunbergii and Berberis vulgaris

**Japanese barberry (B. thunbergii) and European barberry (B. vulgaris)** — Escaped from cultivation and invasive in many states; spread by birds. Shade tolerant, drought resistant, and adaptable, barberry forms dense stands in natural habitats including canopy forests, open woodlands, wetlands, pastures, and meadows and alters soil pH, nitrogen levels, and biological activity in the soil. Once established, barberry displaces native plants and reduces wildlife habitat and forage.

### Euonymus alatus

**Winged Euonymus** or **Burning Bush** — Escaped from plantings; invasive in moist forests. Winged euonymus is a threat to mature forests and successional fields and woodlands because it creates dense thickets that can shade out native herbs and shrubs.

### Lonicera morrowii

**Morrow's honeysuckle** — Escaped from plantings and invasive in many states; seeds spread by birds. Native bush honeysuckles may be confused with these exotic species and cultivars. Unlike the exotics, most of native bush honeysuckles have solid stems. Morrow's honeysuckle is capable of invading bogs, fens, lakeshores, sand plains and other uncommon habitat types, forming a dense shrub layer that crowds and shades out native plant species. They alter habitats by decreasing light availability, by depleting soil moisture and nutrients, and possibly by releasing toxic chemicals that prevent other plant species from growing in the vicinity.

### Rosa multiflora

**Multiflora rose** — Invasive in many states; seeds spread by birds; PA noxious weed. Multiflora rose is extremely prolific and can form impenetrable thickets that exclude native plant species. This exotic rose readily invades open woodlands, forest edges, successional fields, savannas and prairies that have been subjected to land disturbance.

### Spiraea japonica

**Japanese spiraea** — Frequently planted and escaped in some areas, Japanese spiraea can rapidly take over disturbed areas. Growing populations creep into meadows, forest openings, and other sites. Once established, spiraea grows rapidly and forms dense stands that out compete much of the existing native herbs and shrubs. Seeds of Japanese spiraea last for many years in the soil, making its control and the restoration of native vegetation especially difficult.

### Viburnum opulus var. opulus

**Guelder rose** — Guelder rose and native highbush cranberry (*Viburnum opulus var. americanum*) are varieties of the same shrub species, and distinguishing between them can be difficult. Guelder rose usually can be identified by the large saucer — shaped glands on the leafstalk. Guelder rose grows in natural areas and uncommon natural habitats, including fens, where it may displace native plants and its reported ability to interbreed with the native highbush cranberry could produce a truly invasive shrub.

## Trees

### Acer platanoides

**Norway maple** — a frequent invader of urban and suburban forests. Its extreme shade tolerance, especially when young, allows it to penetrate beneath an intact forest canopy. Forests invaded by Norway maple suffer losses in diversity of native forest wildflowers compared with forests in which the canopy is dominated by native species such as sugar maple. This is at least in part due to the dense shade cast by Norway maples, and the shallow roots, which compete with other vegetation.

### Ailanthus altissima

**Tree-of-heaven** — Invasive in many states; wind spreads prolific seeds. Tree-of-heaven is a prolific seed producer, grows rapidly, and can overrun native vegetation. Once established, it can quickly take over a site and form an impenetrable thicket. Ailanthus trees also produces toxins that prevent the establishment of other plant species. The root system is aggressive enough to cause damage to sewers and foundations.

## Vines

### Celastrus orbiculatus

**Oriental bittersweet** — Escaped from cultivation and invasive in many states; spreading rapidly by birds. Oriental bittersweet is a deciduous, woody, perennial vine and an aggressive invader that threatens all vegetation levels of forested and open areas. It grows over other vegetation, completely covering it, and kills other plants by preventing photosynthesis, girdling, and uprooting by force of its massive weight.

### Lonicera japonica

**Japanese honeysuckle** — Invasive in many states, Japanese honeysuckle is a perennial vine that climbs by twisting its stems around vertical structures, including limbs and trunks of shrubs and small trees. The vines cut off the flow of water through the plant and kill it. Dense growths of honeysuckle covering vegetation can also gradually kill plants by blocking sunlight from reaching their leaves. Vigorous root competition also helps Japanese honeysuckle spread and displace

neighboring native vegetation.

### Polygonum perfoliatum

**Mile-a-minute vine** — a Pennsylvania noxious weed, Mile-a-minute weed, also known as Devil's tail tearthumb, is an herbaceous, annual, trailing vine. Mile-a-minute weed grows rapidly, scrambling over shrubs and other vegetation, blocking the foliage of covered plants from available light, and reducing their ability to photosynthesize, which stresses, weakens and kills them. Large infestations of mile-a-minute weed eventually reduce native plant species in natural areas.

### Other species invasive in Pennsylvania

*Carduus nutans* (Musk thistle) — Pennsylvania noxious Weed

*Galega officinalis* (Goatsrue) — Pennsylvania and Federal Noxious Weed

*Heracleum mantegazzianum* (Giant hogweed) — Pennsylvania and Federal Noxious Weed

*Perilla frutescens* (Beefsteak plant) — Garden escape; widespread mostly along roadsides; spread by seed

*Ranunculus ficaria* (Lesser celandine) — Spreads by roots and shoots; can be very aggressive in wetlands

*Miscanthus sinensis* (Maiden grass) — Commonly planted ornamental grass which can escape and spread by seed

*Sorghum bicolor ssp. drummondii* (Shattercane) — Pennsylvania noxious Weed

*Sorghum halepense* (Johnson grass) Pennsylvania noxious Weed; spreads by roots and seeds

*Elaeagnus angustifolia* (Russian olive) — Escaped from plantings and invasive in many states; spread by birds

*Elaeagnus umbellata* (Autumn olive) — Escaped from plantings and invasive in many states; rapidly spread by birds

*Ligustrum obtusifolium* (Border privet) — Escaped from cultivation; seeds spread by birds

*Ligustrum vulgare* (Common privet) — Planted very commonly in the past and escaped; invasive in many states

*Lonicera maackii* (Amur honeysuckle) — Escaped from plantings; seeds spread by birds

*Lonicera morrowii x tatarica* (Bell's honeysuckle) — Escaped from cultivation

*Lonicera standishii* (Standish honeysuckle) — Escaped from plantings; seeds spread by birds

*Lonicera tatarica* (Tartarian honeysuckle) — Escaped from plantings; seeds spread by birds

*Rhamnus cathartica* (Common buckthorn) — Becoming a problem in Pennsylvania

*Rhamnus frangula* (Glossy buckthorn) — Becoming a problem in Pennsylvania

*Rubus phoenicolasius* (Wineberry) — Common bramble; not cultivated; spread by seed

*Acer pseudoplatanus* (Sycamore maple) — Escaped from cultivation; wind spreads prolific seeds

*Pennsylvaniaulownia tomentosa* (Princess tree) — Prolific seeds fall to start new seedlings south

*Pyrus calleryana* (Callery pear) — Commonly planted street tree; becoming a problem as an escape

*Ulmus pumila* (Siberian elm) — Escaped from cultivation

*Akebia quinata* (Fiveleaf akebia) — Escaped from cultivation south

*Ampelopsis brevipedunculata* (Porcelain-berry) — Escaped from cultivation

*Pueraria lobata* (Kudzu) — Invasive in many states; Pennsylvania Noxious Weed

# *Appendix IV — Sources of plants*

## *Major regional nurseries*

Edge of the Woods Nursery, Orefield
 A retail container nursery specializing in regional native plants.  Over 300 species of trees, shrubs, perennials, grasses, ferns and wildflowers; also offers design and landscape services. (www.edgeofthewoodsnursery.com)

Go Native Tree Farms, Lancaster
 A wide variety of native trees. Dedicated to the understanding, preservation, and recovery of the Eastern American forest. (www.gonativetrees.com)

American Native Nursery, Quakertown
 Operates farms dedicated to propagating native flowers, grasses, shrubs and trees for wholesale and retail sale. (www.americannativenursery.com)

Redbud Native Plant Nursery, Glen Mills
 Plants for woodlands, wetlands, riparian buffers, meadows, hedgerows, shrub borders, rain gardens, ponds and home landscapes. (www.redbudnativeplantnursery.com)

Meadowwood Nursery, Hummelstown
 Specializes in native plants for land trusts, environmental groups, educational institutions, government agencies, landscape contractors and home gardeners. (www.meadowoodnursery.com)

Heartwood Nursery Stewartstown
 Specializes in woody propagation and native woody propagation, especially hollies; significant amount of inventory is propagated on site. (www.heartwoodnurseryinc.com)

Northeast Natives and Perennials, Quakertown
 Offers high quality plants at a reasonable price to the home gardener, and helps educate them about the benefits of using native plants in the landscape. (www.nenativesandperennials.com)

## *Local garden centers*

Garden centers that carry some native plants:
 Brickhouse Garden Center, Blooming Grove
 Bunting's Nursery, Honesdale
 Davitt's Nursery, Honesdale
 Flood's Nursery, Paradise Valley
 Pocono Home and Garden, Tobyhanna
 Point Phillip Nursery, Danielsville
 Ross and Ross Nursery, Cresco
 Sensinger's Greenhouses, Lehighton
 Sprig N Twig Nursery, Tyler Hill
 Stonewall Garden Center, Canadensis
 Vogel's Flower Mart, Saylorsburg

## *Area design services and consultants*

Landscape designers who use native plants:
 Fox Hill Farms, Honesdale
 Maciejewski Landscaping, Damascus
 Strauser Nature Helpers, East Stroudsburg

## *Seasonal Plant Sales*

Brodhead Watershed Association, early May, Monroe County.

Pocono Environmental Education Center, early May, Pike County

Bowman's Hill Wildflower Preserve, Bucks County, Mother's Day weekend and in September.

## *National searches*

 A free online service offered by the University of Minnesota Libraries permits anyone to search a national database for retail and wholesale nurseries that ship. Listings specify if seed is available and links directly to vendor directory information and websites. The site is at http://plantinfo.umn.edu/

# *Appendix V — Additional reading*

American Horticultural Society, Alan Toogood, ed. *Plant Propagation.* New York: DK Publishing, 1999.

Art, Henry W. *The Wildflower Gardener's Guide (Northeast, Mid-Atlantic, Great Lakes and Eastern Canada Edition).* Pownal, Vt.: Storey Publications, 1987.

Barker, Joan. *The Encyclopedia of North American Wildflowers.* Bath, U.K.: Parragon Publishing, 2004.

Baskin, Jerry M. and Baskin, Carol C. *Seeds: Ecology, Biogeography, and Evolution of Dormancy and Germination.* New York: Academic Press, 2001.

Bir, Richard E. *Growing and Propagating Showy Native Woody Plants.* Chapel Hill, N.C.: University of North Carolina Press, 1992.

Birdseye, Clarence and Eleanor G. *Growing Woodland Plants.* Oxford: Oxford University Press, 1951; republished New York: Dover Publications, 1972.

Brady, Nyle C. *The Nature and Properties of Soils (Tenth Edition).* New York: MacMillan Publishing Co., 1990.

Braun, E. Lucy. *Deciduous Forests of Eastern North America.* Caldwell, N.J.: The Blackburn Press, 1950.

Cox, Jeff. *Landscaping with Nature: Using Nature's Designs to Plan Your Yard.* Emmaus, Pa.: Rodale Press, 1991.

Cullina, William. *Growing and Propagating Wildflowers of the United States and Canada.* Boston: Houghton Mifflin Company, 2000.

Cullina, William. *Native Ferns, Moss and Grasses.* Boston: Houghton Mifflin Company, 2008.

Darke, Rick. *The American Woodland Garden.* Portland, Ore: Timber Press, 2002.

Deno, Norman C. *Seed Germination Theory and Practice* and *First Supplement to the Second Edition.* State College, Pa., published by the author.

Diekelmann, John and Schuster, Robert. *Natural Landscaping — Designing with Native Plant Communities.* Madison, Wis., The University of Wisconsin Press, 2002.

Dirr, Michael A. *Manual of Woody Landscape Plants.* Champaign, Ill.: Stipes Publishing, 1975, rev. 1998.

Druse, Ken. *The Natural Shade Garden.* New York: Clarkson Potter, 1992.

Fike, Jean. *Terrestrial and Palustrine Plant Communities of Pennsylvania.* Harrisburg, Pa.: Pennsylvania Department of Conservation and Natural Resources, 1999.

Gilliam, Frank. S. and Roberts, Mark R., editors. *The Herbaceous Layer in Forests of Eastern North America.* New York: Oxford University Press, 2003.

Haywood, Mary Joy and Monk, Phyllis Testal. *Wildflowers of Pennsylvania.* Pittsburgh: The Botanical Society of Western Pennsylvania, 2001.

Hitchock, A.S. *Manual of the Grasses of the United States.* Washington: United States Department of Agriculture (Publication 200), 1971.

Hoshizaki, Barbara Joe and Moran, Robbin C. *Fern Grower's Manual.* Portland, Ore: Timber Press, 2001.

Knobel, Edward. *Field Guide to the Grasses, Sedges and Rushes of the United States.* Boston: Bradlee Whidden, 1899, republished New York: Dover Publications, 1977.

Küchler, A.W. *Vegetation Mapping.* New York: The Ronald Press Company, 1967.

Leopold, Donald J. *Native Plants of the Northeast.* Portland, Ore: Timber Press, 2005.

Lord, Thomas R. and Travis, Holly J. *The Ferns and Fern Allies of Pennsylvania.* Pemberton, N.J.: The Pinelands Press, 2006.

Lutz, Harold and Chandler, Robert F. Jr., *Forest Soils.* New York: John Wiley & Sons, 1946.

McPhee, John. *Annals of the Former World.* New York: Farrar, Strauss and Giroux, 1981.

Mickel, John T. *Ferns for American Gardens.* Portland, Ore: Timber Press, 2003.

Moerman, Daniel E. *Native American Ethnobotany.* Portland, Ore: Timber Press, 1998.

Munch, Susan. *Outstanding Mosses and Liverworts of Pennsylvania and Nearby States.* Reading, Pa.: Albright College.

National Resources Conservation Service, *Land Resource Regions and Major Land Resource Areas of the United States, the Caribbean and the Pacific Basin.* Washington: United States Department of Agriculture (Handbook 296), 2006.

Pennsylvania Geological Survey and Pittsburgh Geological Society, ed. Charles H. Schultz. *The Geology of Pennsylvania.* Harrisburg, Pa., The Commonwealth of Pennsylvania, 1999.

Phillips, Harry R. *Growing and Propagating Wildflowers.* Chapel Hill, N.C.: University of North Carolina Press, 1985.

Rhoads, Ann Fowler and Block, Timothy A. *The Plants of Pennsylvania.* Philadelphia: The University of Pennsylvania Press, 2000.

Rickett, Harold William, et al. *Wildflowers of the United States — Northeastern States.* New York: The New York Botanical Garden, 1965.

Roth, Sally. *Natural Landscaping.* Emmaus, Pa.: The Rodale Press, 1997.

Schenk, George. *Moss Gardening.* Portland, Ore: Timber Press, 1997.

Slawson, David A. *Secret Teachings in the Art of Japanese Gardens.* Tokyo: Kodansha International, 1987.

Sperka, Marie. *Growing Wildflowers: A Gardener's Guide.* New York: Harper & Row, 1973.

Sternberg, Guy and Wilson, Jim. *Landscaping with Native Trees.* Shelburne, Vt.: Chapters Publishing, 1995.

Tallamy, Douglas W. *Bringing Nature Home.* Portland, Ore: Timber Press, 2007.

Tenenbaum, Frances. *Taylor's Dictionary for Gardeners.* New York: Houghton Mifflin Company, 1997.

United States Forest Service. *Seeds of Woody Plants in the United States.* Washington: United States Department of Agriculture (Handbook 450), 1974.

United States Forest Service. *Silvics of North America (Vol. 1 — Conifers; Vol. 2 — Hardwoods).* Washington: United States Department of Agriculture (Handbook 654)

Wherry, Edgar T. *Wildflower Guide — Northeastern and Midland United States.* New York: Doubleday & Co., 1948.

Woodward, Carol H. and Rickett, Harold William. *Common Wildflowers of the Northeastern United States.* New York: The New York Botanical Garden, 1979.

Young, James. A and Young, Cheryl G. *Collecting, Processing and Germinating Seeds of Wildland Plants.* Portland, Ore.: Timber Press, 1986.

### *Useful internet resources*

An excellent starting point to research a specific species is the database maintained by the U.S. Department of Agriculture, www.plants.gov.

Search by scientific or common name to find images, range data, occasionally detailed information materials, wetland indicators and synonymous names. At the bottom of the page, USDA provides links to other helpful sites, most notably:

Propagation protocols at the University of Idaho (http://nativeplants.for.uidaho.edu/network/search.aspx)

U.S. Forest Service fire effects service (which discusses associations and habitats) at http://www.fs.fed.us/database/feis/plants/

Kemper Center for Home Gardening at the Missouri Botanical Garden: http://www.mobot.org/gardeninghelp/plantfinder/Alpha.asp

The Lady Bird Johnson Wildflower Center at http://www.wildflower.org/plants/

# *Index*

Chokeberry, Red 200
Chokecherry 209
Christmas fern 277
*Cicuta maculata* 164, 224
*Cinna arundinacea* 90, 97, 99, 120, 184, 265
Cinnamon fern 277
Cinquefoil
    Marsh 224
    Old-field 238
    Tall 237
    Three-toothed 238
*Cirsium arvense* 306
*Cirsium muticum* 174, 224
*Cirsium vulgare* 306
Clammyweed 284
*Claytonia caroliniana* 224
*Claytonia virginica* 104, 106, 107, 112, 116, 129, 224
Clematis, Purple 280
*Clematis occidentalis* 108, 136, 280
*Clematis virginiana* 176, 178, 280
*Clethra alnifolia* 92, 166, 167, 168, 202
Cliffbrake, Purple 277
Climbing fern 277
Clinton's wood fern 275
*Clintonia borealis* 102, 103, 110, 139, 224
Clubmoss, Bristly 276
Clubmoss, Common 276
Clubspur orchid 236
Cockspur hawthorn 216
Coffee-tree, Kentucky 216
Cohosh, Blue 223
*Collinsonia canadensis* 224
Colluvium 18
Columbine, American 221
Columbine, Wild 221
*Comarum palustre* 173, 175, 180, 224
Common cat-tail 245
Common clubmoss 276
Common dittany 225
Common hairgrass 265
Common juniper 205
Common milkweed 222
Common oak fern 276
Common polypody 277
Common ragweed 283
Common reed 268
Common sneezeweed 228
Common blue violet 247
Common yellow wood-sorrel 234

*Comptonia peregrina* 26, 115, 135, 147, 148, 165, 169, 170, 202
Coneflower
    Cutleaf 239
    Eastern 250
    Prairie 250
    Three-lobed 239
*Conopholis americana* 120, 224
Conventional landscapes, natives in 4
*Conyza canadensis* 283
Coontail 223
*Coptis trifolia* 94, 139, 144, 156, 158, 224
Cordgrass, Freshwater 270
*Cornus alternifolia* 100, 104, 105, 202
*Cornus amomum* 90, 92, 96, 97, 98, 111, 114, 116, 120, 133, 155, 163, 164, 165, 166, 167, 172, 173, 176, 177, 178, 187, 194, 202
*Cornus canadensis* 144, 148, 152, 157, 224
*Cornus florida* 101, 108, 110, 112, 117, 119, 125, 126, 127, 129, 134, 136, 149, 152, 191, 202
*Cornus racemosa* 154, 202
*Cornus rugosa* 103, 203
*Cornus sericea* 111, 113, 162, 163, 165, 166, 174, 183, 203
*Corydalis sempervirens* 124, 131, 147, 166, 193, 224
*Corylus americana* 110, 117, 152, 180, 203
*Corylus cornuta* 102, 117, 126, 127, 157, 203
Cowbane 234
Crabapple, Sweet 207
Cranberry, American 214
Cranberry, Small 215
*Crataegus chrysocarpa* 203
*Crataegus crus-galli* 216
*Crataegus punctata* 203
*Crataegus rotundifolia* 203
Creeping phlox 235
Creeping snowberry 204
Creeping spearwort 238
Creeping spike-rush 265
Crested sedge 260
Crested shield fern 275
Crinkleroot toothwort 223
*Crotalaria sagittalis* 283, 284
Crowfoot, Bristly 284

Crowfoot, Hooked 239
Crowfoot, Small-flowered 284
*Cryptotaenia canadensis* 92, 98, 225
Cuckoo-flower 223
Cucumber, Bur 284
Cucumber, Prickly 281
Cucumber-tree 216
Cucumber root, Indian 232
Cudweed, Fragrant 283
Cultivars 12
Culver's-root 246
*Cunila origanoides* 135, 160, 225
Currant, Wild black 211
Currant, Bristly black 211
Cut-leaf false-foxglove 283
Cutgrass 267
Cutgrass, Rice 267
Cutleaf coneflower 239
*Cyperus esculentus* 265
*Cypripedium acaule* 119, 120, 123, 124, 141, 147, 225
*Cypripedium parviflorum* 113, 187, 225
*Cypripedium reginae* 248
*Cystopteris bulbifera* 104, 106, 109, 136, 149, 191, 275
*Cystopteris fragilis* 275

**- D -**
Daisy fleabane 226
Dame's rocket 306
Dandelion, Dwarf 230
Dangleberry 204
*Danthonia spicata* 108, 110, 118, 120, 123, 124, 129, 132, 134, 135, 140, 143, 147, 150, 160, 166, 169, 170, 180, 181, 193, 265
Davis' sedge 260
Deep-rooted running-pine 275
Deer, problems with 26
Deer-tongue grass 268
Deerberry 215
Deer fencing 26
Delaware Water Gap National Recreation Area 6, 87
*Dennstaedtia punctilobula* 275
*Deparia acrostichoides* 104, 106, 107, 275
*Deschampsia flexuosa* 5, 118, 124, 126, 129, 131, 132, 135, 140, 142, 145, 146, 147, 150, 153, 159, 160, 166, 169, 170, 181, 193, 265

Made in United States
Orlando, FL
11 December 2022